Theory of Computation

(With Formal Languages)

Second Edition

Theory of Computation

(With Formal Languages)

Second Edition

Dr. R.B. Patel
Professor, Chandigarh College of Engineering and Technology, Chandigarh (U.T.)

Dr. Prem Nath
Associate Professor,
Computer Engineering Department,
Mizoram University (A Central University),
Aizawl, Mizoram

KHANNA BOOK PUBLISHING CO. (P) LTD.
Publisher, of Science, Technology and Engineering Books
4C/4344, Ansari Road, Darya Ganj, New Delhi-110002
Phone: 011-23244447-48 **Mobile:** +91-99109 09320
E-mail: contact@khannabooks.com
Website: www.khannabooks.com

Dear Readers,

To prevent the piracy, this book is secured with HIGH SECURITY HOLOGRAM on the front title cover. In case you don't find the hologram on the front cover title, please write us to at contact@khannabooks.com or whatsapp us at +91-99109 09320 and avail special gift voucher for yourself.

Specimen of Hologram on front Cover title:

Moreover, there is a SPECIAL DISCOUNT COUPON for you with EVERY HOLOGRAM.

How to avail this SPECIAL DISCOUNT:

Step 1: Scratch the hologram
Step 2: Under the scratch area, your "coupon code" is available
Step 3: Logon to www.khannabooks.com
Step 4: Use your "coupon code" in the shopping cart and get your copy at a special discount
Step 5: Enjoy your reading!

ISBN: 978-93-80016-52-8

Theory of Computation
by R.B. Patel, Prem Nath

First Edition: 2010
Second Edition: 2020
Reprint: 2025, 2026

To view complete list of books, Please scan the QR Code:

Published by:
Khanna Book Publishing Co. (P) Ltd.
CIN: U22110DL1998PTC095547

Visit us at: **www.khannabooks.com**
Write us at: **contact@khannabooks.com**

Printed in Bharat.

Preface

This book covers the syllabus of the various courses like: B.E./B. Tech. (Computer Science and Engineering), MCA, BCA, M. Tech. (Computer Science and Engineering), and other courses related to Computer Science running by various Universities/Institutions. It also covers the almost whole syllabus of Graduate Aptitude Test in Engineering (GATE). This book contains numerous solved problems, objective questions and answer, and supplementary problems that provide good platform to prepare for various competitive exams, and entrance examinations. The content of this book is developed in very easier and readable way. The approach applied for solving the problems in this book is straightforward. Readers shall feel very much comfortable while reading the concepts.

The brief contents of the book chapter-wise are as follows:

Chapter 1 provides the familiarity with the basics basic concepts and terms used throughout the book. Readers familiar with these basics may skip this chapter.

Chapter 2 starts with the introduction of Automata Theory, Deterministic and Nondeterministic Finite Automata (DFA and NFA). This chapter presents the detailed discussion regarding NFA and DFA, the equivalence of NFA and DFA, and comparison of NFA and DFA. Finally, this chapter ends with a look on Two-way Finite Automata.

Chapter 3 begins with discission on Finite State Machines (FSMs). Two types of the FSM; namely Moore and Mealy machines are addressed. The minimization of FSMs, the equivalence of FSMs, and the behaviour of sequential circuit by FSM are also presented.

Chapter 4 contains the discussion on languages, grammars and classification of languages/grammars by Noam Chomsky, and languages and their related automata/machines.

Chapter 5 starts with definition of regular expressions, sets, equivalence of regular expression and finite automata. This chapter addresses the Pumping Lemma which provides the platform to prove the certain languages are not regular languages. The Myhill-Nerode Theorem, minimization of finite automata and properties of regular language are also presented.

Chapter 6 begins with Context-free grammars and Languages (CFGs and CFLs), leftmost derivation, rightmost derivation, and derivation (parse) tree. This chapter also covers the ambiguity, left recursion, left factoring, simplifications of CFGs, normal forms of CFGs, decisions algorithms for CFLs, Pumping Lemma for CFLs, and closure properties of CFLs.

Chapter 7 starts with discussion on Pushdown Automata (PDA), Deterministic PDA, and equivalence of CFLs and PDA. This chapter also contains the discussion over parsing techniques like top-down and bottom-up.

Chapter 8 contains detailed discussion over the Turing machine. The variations of Turing machine, universal Turing machine (UTM) are also addressed. Some other powerful computational models like Random Access machine (RAM), and Post machine are discussed. The Church's Thesis is also presented which supports the Turing machine as a most powerful computing device.

Chapter 9 starts with discussion on computation and how a Turing machine can be used as a computing device. The type of computed functions like partial and total are also discussed.

Chapter 10 contains the discussion on decidability and undecidability. The decidable and undecidable problems about regular languages, finite automata, CFGs, CFLs, and Turing machine are discussed. This chapter also contains with some languages that are not Turing machine computable. The famous problems in Computer Science like Halting problem (HP), Post correspondence problem (PCP) are also presented.

Chapter 11 introduces linear bounded automata (LBA) and context-sensitive languages (CSLs). This chapter contains the closure properties of the context-sensitive languages. There are many theorems and lemmas to discuss about the relation between linear bounded automata and context-sensitive languages.

Chapter 12 is the final chapter and is focussed on computational complexity of Turing machine. This chapter covers some problems of N and NP classes that have polynomial or exponential time complexity. This chapter ends with conclusion about "N = NP?"

The **Appendix–A** provides the basic concepts about sets.

Authors

Acknowledgement

Sitting on the seashore we had thought that it was an easy task to dive but it was only when we dived into one ocean of Computer and brought for you the pearl **"Theory of Computation (With Formal Languages)"**. We realize how much helpful were so many people to us. Without these people this exploration could never have been materialized. We now realize that the acknowledgement is something that really comes from the bottom of the heart of every writer.

Our primary obligation is to son of the soil Shri Tarsem Kumar Garg, Chancellor, Dr. N. P. Mehta, Director, M. M. Engineering College, Mullana, Ambala. For those who knew him, no words are necessary and for those who do not know him, no words will suffice. Inspiration from these persons aided me immensely at all stages in the development and production of this book and without their guidance this book would not have seen the light of the day.

We are deeply indebted to the contributions made by my faculty members and friends especially Professor Vijay Kumar, and other faculty and staff of the Computer Science and Engineering, M. M. Engineering College, Mullana whose moral boosting and support motivated me to work efficiently in the odd hours.

We are also deeply indebted to the contribution offered by Prof. Devendra Prasad, (Computer Science and Engineering), M. M. Engineering College, Mullana, Mr. Rejesh Kumar Yadav, Lecturer, Delhi College of Engineering, Delhi, and Mr. Madhurjya Thakur, Assistant Controller of Patents and Design, Patents Office, Kolkata to us.

Last but not the least, the contribution of our wives and kids cannot be overlooked for their pain staking efforts and finding even the minutes bugs that had creped into the manuscript and deserve sincere appreciation.

Suggestions and queries are most welcome through Publisher.

Authors

A Note to the Readers

This book gives the basic idea about Automata Theory, Formal Languages, and Computations (Theory of Computer Science). Readers are advised to be familiar with the basics about stack, queue, etc. We hope that readers are familiar with the "statement concept" and "if-else statement structure" of language C.

We have observed that the students reading this subject very closely and analysed their problems. This is why this book has been developed to overcome the students' problem. We have tried our best effort to give the best about this subject and to make the readers understood well. The contents of this book are developed in very easier and readable way. Further, diagrams of this book give better understanding of the concept.

Readers are advised to take open-minded approach to this subject. Just read the book, and you shall find finally that this subject is nothing but an easier mathematics.

Authors

Contents

CHAPTER 1

Preliminaries Used in Theory of Computation

We will discuss about the set theory, relations, trees, graphs, and the principle of mathematical induction in this chapter. These are used in discussion throughout. The readers who are familiar with these can skip this chapter.

1.1 DEFINITION OF SET

We have so many objects on the earth and collection of similar objects known as a set. **For example**, Books, Students, Person, Computers, Monitors, etc.

Definition: A well-defined collection of distinct objects is known as a set. **For example,**

1. Students = {All students of second year}
2. $N = \{0, 1, 2, 3, \ldots\}$
3. Person = {Ram, Shyam, Mohan}

The objects in a set are called the **elements** or **members** of that set. The definition of the set suggests that the objects are distinct in a set. In other words, duplicate objects are not allowed in a set. **For example**, the set Person ={Ram, Gita, Mohan, Ram}, has a duplicate member "*Ram*" and precisely represented as {Ram, Gita, Shyam, Mohan}. The order of objects in a set is not restricted unless it is given. The sets {Ram, Shyam, Mohan}, {Shyam, Ram, Mohan}, {Shyam, Mohan, Ram}, {Ram, Mohan, Shyam}, {Mohan, Ram, Shyam}, {Mohan, Shyam, Ram} have the same objects and represent the equivalent set.

1.1.1 Infinite and Finite Sets

The number of objects (or elements) in a set is called the size or length of the set. If the number of elements is finite then set is known as a finite otherwise infinite.

For example:

1. Alphabet = $\{a, b, c, \ldots, z\}$ is a finite set having 26 elements
2. $N = \{0, 1, 2, 3, \ldots\}$ is an infinite set having infinite number of elements

1.1.2 Universal Set

A set that contains all the sets, which are in application, is known as universal set and it is represented by U. **For example,** U_1 = {All the people in India}, $U_2 = \{x : x \text{ is a point in a plane}\}$

1.1.3 Empty Set

A set with no object is called empty or null set and denoted by { } or ϕ. *It is just like an empty box.* **For example,**

1. $P = \{x: x \text{ is positive integer and } x^2 = 5\}$,
2. $B = \{y: y \text{ is an integer divisible by } 0\}$

1.1.4 Subsets

If all elements of a set A are also elements of another set B then A is called a subset of B and represented by $A \subset B$. In other words, *we say that A is contained in B or B contains A*. **For example,** consider the sets $A = \{b, a, c, d, e\}$, $B = \{a, b, c\}$, $C = \{a, b\}$, $D = \{c, d, a, e, b\}$, then

1. $C \subset B \subset A$
2. $A = D$

- For any set A, we have $A \subseteq A$
- For any set A and universal set U, we have $\phi \subset A \subset U$
- If $A \subset B$ and $B \subset C$, then $A \subset C$
- $A = B$ if and only if $A \subseteq B$ and $B \subseteq A$

1.1.5 Ordered Set

We have already discussed that a set is an unordered collection of distinct objects and if the order is given then the set is known as an ordered set. "An ordered set is a collection of ordered pair of objects and in each pair, objects are arranged in a fixed order." **For example,** (x, y) is pair of objects and 'x' is the first object and 'y' is the second object. *In ordered sets, the pairs should be distinct and objects in a pair should be in some fixed order and the order of the pairs does not matter.*

The representation of ordered pair can be extended to have more than two objects. Depending upon the number of objects (n) in an order, the set may be triple ordered or in general n^{th} ordered, where $n >= 2$. Any n^{th} ordered ($n >= 3$) set can be represented by using ordered pairs. *For an nth ($n>=3$) ordered object, we have (n–1) ordered pairs.* **For example,**

1. $X = \{(a, b), (c, d), (a, a)\}$ is a ordered pair set
2. $Y = \{(1, 2, 2), (2, 1, 3), (4, 5, 1)\}$ is triple ordered set

1.1.6 Power Set

The power set of a set A is a set which contains all the subsets of A and denoted by powerset (A) or 2^A. **For example,** let $A = \{0, 1\}$, then

powerset $(A) = \{\phi, \{0\}, \{1\}, \{0,1\}\}$

Number of elements in powerset $(A) = 2^2 = 4$

1.2 RELATIONS

In practical world, we have certain relations between the objects. For example, relation between students and teacher, son and his father, Citizen and Country, etc. "*A relation is a certain connection between (among) objects*" The relations will be defined in terms of ordered pair (a, b) where 'a' is designated as the first object and 'b' is designated as the second object. Let A and B be two sets and we have a relation R from A to B, then this relation defined on product set $A \times B$, also known as **Cartesian product** of A and B, is called *binary relation*. Relation R is a set of ordered pairs, where each first element comes from the set A and second element from the set B.

> **$R: A \rightarrow B$ or $R = \{(a, b): a \in A$ and $b \in B\}$,**
> **where R is a subset of $A \times B$, and $A \times B = \{(a, b)$: For all $a \in A, b \in B\}$**

1. If $(a, b) \in R$; we say "Object ***a*** is R-related to object ***b***" written as ***aRb***.
2. If $(a, b) \notin R$; we say "Object ***a*** is not R-related to object ***b***" written as ***aRb***.

1.2.1 Domain and Range

The domain of a relation R is the set of all first elements of ordered-pairs and **range** of relation R is the set of all second elements of ordered-pairs. **For example,** let $P = \{1, 2, 3\}$, $Q = \{x, y, z\}$ and a relation $R = \{(1, y), (1, x), (1, z)\}$ then R is a subset of $P \times Q$. Domain(R) = $\{1, 1, 1\} \equiv \{1\}$ and Range(R) = $\{x, y, z\}$ as shown in Fig. 1.1.

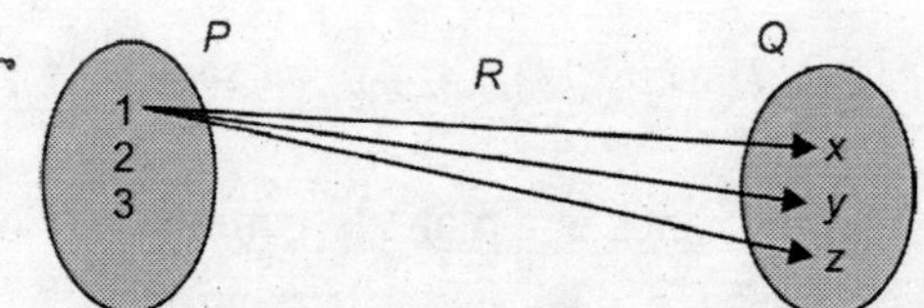

Fig. 1.1: Representation of relation

We represent a relation by matrix or table also. The first column elements are of one set and the elements of first row are of second set, and other entry of matrix is 0 or 1. If relation is there, then 1 and 0 if relation is not there.

Total relation (or function): If a relation R is defined for all the elements of the set A to the set B, then R is said to be total relation (function).

Partial relation (or function): If a relation R is defined for some of the elements of the set A to the set B, then R is said to be partial relation (function).

1.2.2 Composition of Relations

Let A, B, and C are three sets and a relation R is from A to B and another relation S is from B to C, then R is subset of $A \times B$ and S is the subset of $B \times C$. The relations R and S give rise to a relation from A to C denoted by RoS and defined as following:

$$a(RoS)c \quad \text{for some } b \in B, \text{ we have } aRb \text{ and } bRc$$

The relation RoS is called the composite relation of R and S. Sometimes, this composite relation is represented by RS. **For example,** let $A = \{1, 2, 3, 4\}$, $B = \{a, b, c, d\}$, $C = \{x, y, z\}$, $R = \{(1, a), (3, a), (2, d), (3, b), (3, d)\}$, and $S = \{(b, x), (b, z), (c, y), (d, z)\}$, then RoS or simply $RS = \{(2, z), (3, x), (3, z)\}$ as shown in Fig. 1.2

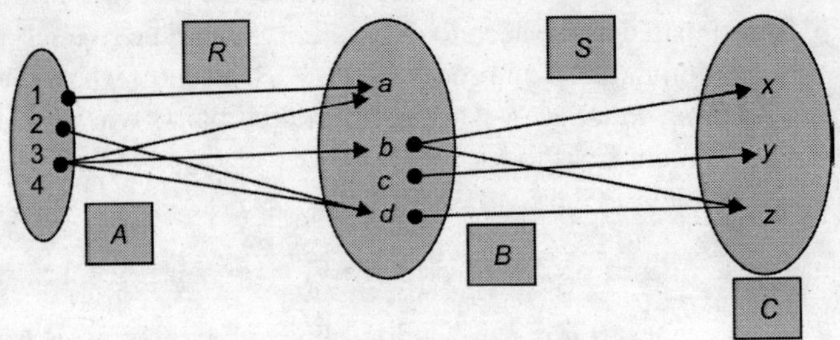

Fig. 1.2: Composite relation *RoS*

1.2.3 Properties of Relation

Let R be a relation on a set A itself, then R is

1. Reflexive, if aRa in R for all a in A, otherwise irreflexive,
2. Symmetric, if aRb in R then bRa in R for a, b are in A, otherwise asymmetric,
3. Transitive, if aRb and bRc in R then aRc is in R for a, b, c are in A.

For example,

1. The relation $R = \{(1, 1), (2, 2), (3, 3), (4, 4)\}$ on the set $A = \{1, 2, 3, 4\}$ is transitive and reflexive.
2. The relation between parallel lines in a plane is symmetric relation.

In general, for a relation R on a set A, the composite relation

$$RoR = R^2 \text{ and } R^n = R^{n-1}\, oR \text{ for } n \geq 2$$

Closure properties: Let R be a relation on a set S, then

(i) Reflexive closure of $R = R \cup \{(a, a): (a, a)$ is diagonal element and not in R, for all $a \in S\}$

(ii) Symmetric closure of $R = R \cup R^{-1}$, where R^{-1} is the inverse relation of R and

(iii) Transitive closure of R is $\boldsymbol{R^+ = R \cup R^2 \cup R^3 \cup \ldots}$

(iv) Reflexive-Transitive Closure of R is denoted by R^* and defined as: $\boldsymbol{R^* = R^+ \cup \{(a, a): a \in R\}}$

Example 1: Consider a set $S = \{1, 2, 3, 4\}$ and a relation shown below:

$R = \{(1, 1), (1,3), (2, 4), (3, 1), (3, 3), (4, 3)\}$

$$\begin{array}{c} \\ \mathbf{1} \\ \mathbf{2} \\ \mathbf{3} \\ \mathbf{4} \end{array} \begin{pmatrix} \mathbf{1} & \mathbf{2} & \mathbf{3} & \mathbf{4} \\ 1 & 0 & 1 & 0 \\ 0 & \underline{0} & 0 & 1 \\ 1 & 0 & 1 & 0 \\ 0 & 0 & 1 & \underline{0} \end{pmatrix}$$

Then Reflexive closure of $R = R \cup \{\text{diagonal elements which are not in } R\}$

$$= R \cup \{(2, 2), (4, 4)\}$$

$$= \{(1, 1), (1, 3), (2, 2), (2, 4), (3, 1), (3, 3), (4, 3), (4, 4)\}$$

Symmetric closure of $R = R \cup R^{-1}$

$$= \{(1, 1), (1, 3), (2, 4), (3, 1), (3, 3), (4, 3)\}$$

$$\cup \{(1, 1), (3, 1), (4, 2), (1, 3), (3, 3), (3, 4)\}$$

$$= \{1, 1), (1, 3), (2, 4), (3, 1), (3, 3), (4, 3), (4, 2), (3, 4)\}$$

Example 2: Let a relation R on a set $A = \{1, 2, 3\}$ is $\{(1, 2), (2, 3), (3, 3)\}$.

Find transitive closure of R.

Solution:

$$RoR = R^2 = \{(1, 2), (2, 3), (3, 3)\} \text{ o } \{(1, 2), (2, 3), (3, 3)\}$$

$$= \{(1, 3), (2, 3), (3, 3)\}$$

$$R^3 = R^2oR = \{(1, 3), (2, 3), (3, 3)\} \text{ o } \{(1, 2), (2, 3), (3, 3)\}$$

$$= \{(1, 3), (2, 3), (3, 3)\} = R^2$$

$$R^4 = R^2 \text{ and so on}$$

$$R^+ = R \cup R^2 \cup R^3 \cup \ldots = \{(1, 2), (1, 3), (2, 3), (3, 3)\}$$

1.2.4 Equivalence Relations

In equivalence relations, *two objects share some common property or satisfy some common requirement and therefore these objects are equivalent with respect to that property or requirement*. A binary relation R on a set A is said to be an equivalent relation if it is

1. Reflexive,
2. Symmetric, and
3. Transitive

So, in other way, if R is an equivalence relation on set A, then it has following:

1. For all $a \in A$, aRa
2. If aRb, then bRa for $a, b \in A$
3. If aRb and bRc, then aRc for $a, b, c \in A$

Example 1: Consider a set Z of positive and negative integers and an integer $m \geq 1$ such that $x \equiv y(\text{mod } m)$ if $(x - y)$ is divisible by m. Show that the relation is an equivalence relation.

Solution: Given set $Z = \{\ldots -3, -2, -1, 1, 2, 3 \ldots\}$ and consider $x, y, z \in Z$.

Reflexive:

For any $x \in Z$, we have $x \equiv x(\text{mod } m)$ because $(x - x) = 0$ is divisible by m. So, the relation is reflexive.

Symmetric:

Suppose, $x \equiv y$ (mod m) so $(x - y)$ is divisible by m,

Then $-(x - y) = (y - x)$ is also divisible by m. Therefore, $y \equiv x$ (mod m) is true. So, the relation is symmetric,

Transitive:

Suppose, $x \equiv y \pmod{m}$ and $y \equiv z \pmod{m}$

So, $(x - y)$ and $(y - z)$ are divisible by m. Then sum of these is also divisible by m. Therefore, $(x - y) + (y - z)$ is divisible by m or $(x - z)$ is divisible by m. Hence, $x \equiv z \pmod{m}$ is true. Thus, the given relation is transitive.

The given relation has Reflexive, symmetric, and transitive properties; hence, it is an equivalence relation.

If a binary relation R is represented by matrix or table, then it is

(i) Reflexive, if and only if all cells on main diagonal are 1's as shown in Fig. 1.3(a).

(ii) Symmetric, if and only if all upper and lower cells of main diagonal are symmetrical. If we put a mirror along main diagonal then upper half is image of lower half and vice-versa as shown in Fig. 1.3(b).

	a	b	c	d
a	1	0	1	0
b	0	1	0	1
c	1	0	1	0
d	0	0	1	1

Fig. 1.3(a): Reflexive relation

	1	2	3	4
1	1	0	1	1
2	0	0	0	1
3	1	0	1	0
4	1	1	0	0

Fig. 1.3(b): Symmetric relation

1.3 GRAPH AND TREE

Before discussing the graph and tree, let us consider one example of route between two cities namely Delhi and Kolkata. This route shows the connectivity between these two cities. It may be, Kolkata has a route to Guwahati and Guwahati has a route to Delhi. These routes show the connectivity of two cities as shown in Fig. 1.4. This type of connectivity is represented by graph. Formally, a graph is a pictorial representation of connectivity (relation) between objects.

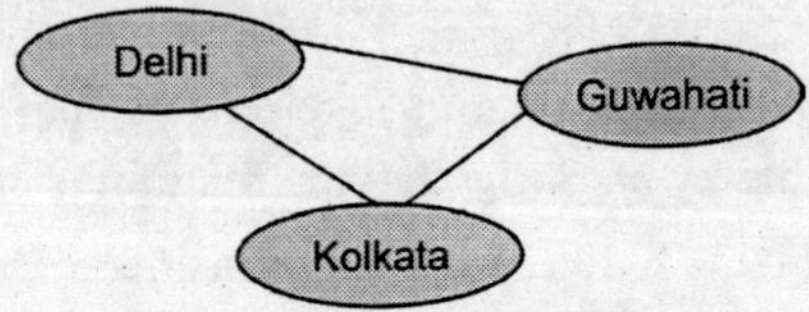

Fig. 1.4: Graph representation

1.3.1 Graph

In graph, we represent a relation between two objects. *A* graph is defined as following:

(a) A set consisting of nodes (objects), denoted by V, and

(b) Another set consisting of edges denoted by E.

So, a graph $G = (V, E)$, where V and E are sets defined above. Suppose, an edge $e \in E$ which connects the nodes v_1 and v_2, then $e = [v_1, v_2]$, and v_1 and v_2 are called neighbors or end points of the edge e. **For example**, A and B be end points of e_1, B and C are end points of e_2, A and C are end points of e_5 as shown in Fig. 1.5.

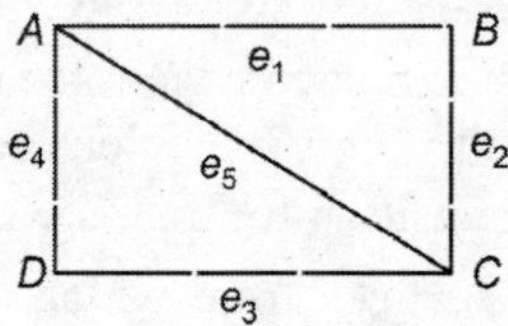

Fig. 1.5: Graph

Degree of a node v_1 is denoted by degree (v_1) and defined as the number of edges merging into v_1. So, considering the graph shown in Fig. 1.5:

Degree (A) = 3, Degree (B) = 2, Degree(C) = 3, and Degree (D) = 2

Here, Degree (A) + Degree (B) + Degree(C) + Degree (D) = 10 = 2* Number of edges

In general,

$$\sum_{1}^{n} Degree\,(Ai) = 2^{*} \text{ Number of edges (where } n \text{ is the number of nodes in graph)}$$

A graph said to be connected, if there is a path between any two of its nodes. One connected graph is shown in Fig. 1.6.

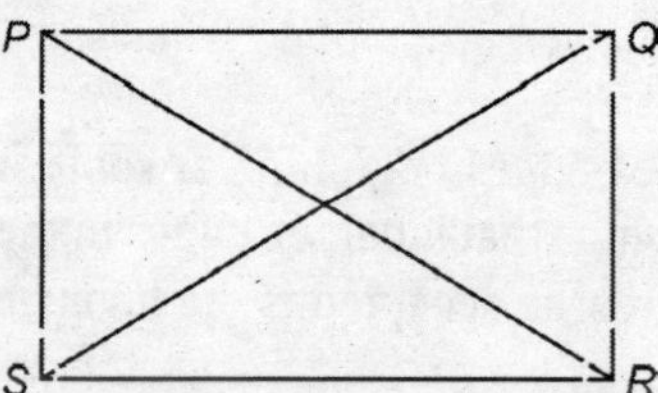

Fig. 1.6: Connected graph

1.3.1.1 Directed graphs

If all the edges of a graph contain a direction then such graphs are called directed graphs or *digraph*. One digraph is shown in Fig. 1.7.

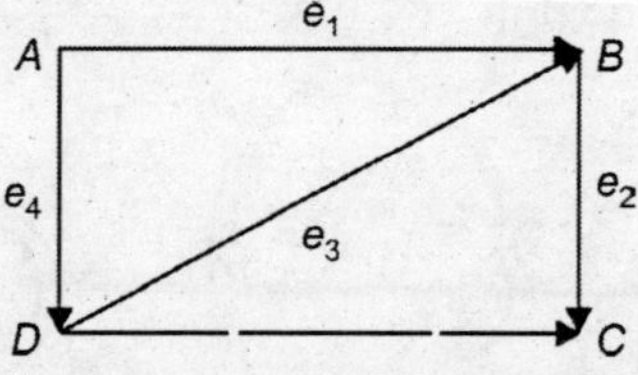

Fig. 1.7: Directed or Digraph

1.3.1.2 Transition graph (TG)

Transition graphs are used to represent the automata. We will discuss in following chapters. A graph T is called a transition graph on some alphabet Σ if and only if T has following three things:

1. The alphabet Σ is called input alphabet from which inputs (also called labels) are formed.
2. T has is a finite directed graph and each edge (also called arc or arrow) of T is labeled by a word $w \in \Sigma^*$. This also shows that how transitions occur from vertex to vertex. There may be zero or one or more possible transition for $w \in \Sigma^*$.
3. There is a non-empty set of vertices from which at least one vertex designated as initial (or starting) vertex and some vertices (possibly none sometimes) designated as final vertices. An initial vertex can also be called as final vertex. A vertex is also known as state.

For example, a transition graph over $\Sigma = \{a, b\}$ is shown in Fig. 1.8.

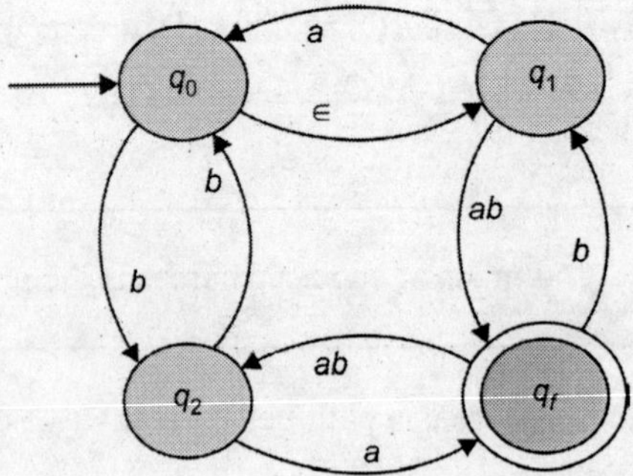

Fig. 1.8: Transition graph of deterministic finite automation

A **successful path** is a series of edges beginning at some initial state and ending at a final state. The concatenation of all the sub-strings that label the edges in the successful path is a word accepted by the transition graph and the set of words accepted is the language of the transition graph.

For example, words "*ababa*", "*ba*", "*bba*" are accepted by the transition graph shown in Fig. 1.8. The set states $V = \{q_0, q_1, q_2, q_f\}$, set of final states is $\{q_f\}$, and initial state is q_0, and the input alphabet $\Sigma = \{a, b\}$.

1.3.1.3 Generalized transition graph (GTG)

Generalized transition graph is a transition graph edge is labeled with a regular expression. **For example,** consider an input alphabet $\Sigma = \{0, 1\}$. The regular expressions $0 + 1$, 011 are the labels of the edges of the generalized transition graph shown in Fig. 1.9.

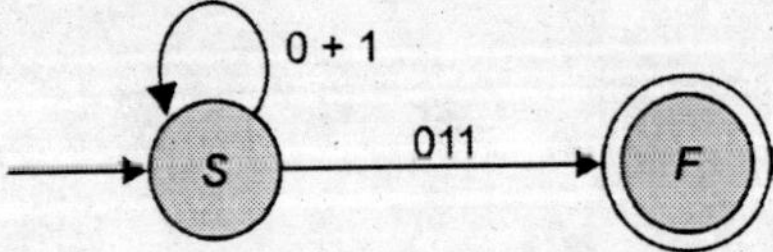

Fig. 1.9: Generalized transition graph

In the above generalized transition graph, set of states is $\{S, F\}$, initial state is S, final state is F and accepted language is $(0 + 1)^*011$.

Generalized transition graphs are used to represent the finite automaton (FA). The language accepted by the generalized transition graph is known as regular language. We will discuss finite automaton (FA) in Chapter 2 and the regular expressions, regular languages in Chapter 5.

1.3.2 Tree

A connected graph without any cycles is called a tree. A tree T is a finite set of nodes such that

1. T contains a special node called root (R), and
2. The remaining nodes $T_1, T_2, T_3, \ldots, T_n$ are called subtrees. If tree T has at most two subtrees for all nodes, then it is known as binary tree as shown in Fig. 1.10. The first node R is the root, T_1 and T_3 are sub trees or children of R, T_2 is only child or sub tree of T_1 and T_4, T_5 are children of T_3. The nodes T_2, T_4, and T_5 have no subtree and these are called terminal nodes or leaves.

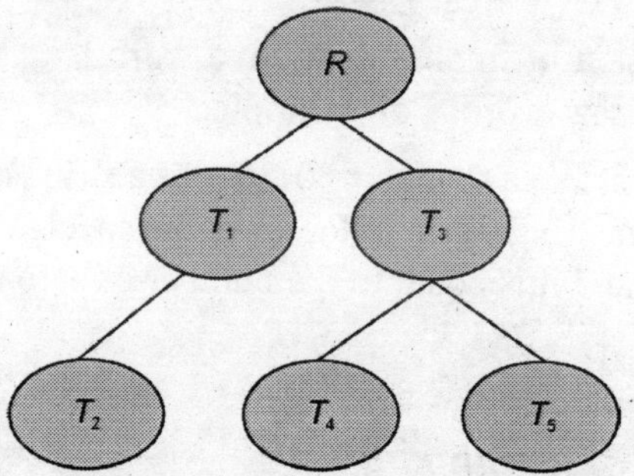

Fig. 1.10: Binary tree

1.4 ALPHABET, STRING, AND LANGUAGE

In this section, we will discuss about the alphabet, string (or word), and language. We are aware of many languages like Hindi, English, French, etc which are used in conversation. We use many languages in computer programming also, for example, C, C^{++}, Java, etc. Let us see many basic definitions before defining language in general.

1.4.1 What is Alphabet?

The term alphabet denotes the finite and non-empty set of symbols (or characters). **For example,**

1. If Σ is an alphabet containing all the 26 characters used in English language, then Σ is finite and non-empty set, and $\Sigma = \{a, b, c, \ldots, z\}$.
2. $B = \{0, 1\}$ is an alphabet.
3. $X = \{1, 2, 3, \ldots\}$ is not an alphabet because it is infinite.
4. $A = \{\ \}$ is not an alphabet because it is empty.

1.4.2 String (or Word)

String and word are synonyms. Sometimes, sentence is also used for string. *A string is a finite sequence of symbols from some fixed alphabet.* **For example,** "*abc*" is a string over an alphabet $\Sigma = \{a, b, c, \ldots, z\}$. The empty string or null string is denoted by *e*. A word (or string) is the smallest unit used in representation of a language; although, a word is formed over some alphabet.

1.4.2.1 Length of a string

The length of a string is the number of occurrences (or appearances) of characters or symbols in that string. If *w* is a string then its length is denoted by $|w|$. There may be situation that, single symbol in a string occurs one or more times. **For example,**

1. $w = abcd$, then length of *w* is $|w| = 4$
2. $n = 124$ is a string, then $|n| = 3$
3. ε is the empty string and has length zero.

Sometimes, we are interested in finding restrictive word length. A restrictive word length is the number of specified symbol in that word. **For example,**

1. $B = \{0, 1\}$ is an alphabet and a string $w = 011010$ is a string over *B*. We are interested in finding the number of zero's in string 011010, then it is the specified length of string with respect to 0 and denoted by $|w|_0$ and it is equal to the number of zero's. $|w|_0 = 3$ (Number of zero's)
2. $s = xyzabcaaa$, then $|s|_a = 4$

1.4.2.2 The set of words of length k (k ≥ 1)

Let Σ be an alphabet and $\Sigma = \{0, 1\}$, then all words of length k ($k \geq 1$) is denoted by Σ^k and

$$\Sigma k = \{x : x \text{ is a string or word of length } k,\ k \geq 1\}$$

For example,

1. Let us consider alphabet $\Sigma = \{0, 1\}$, then $\Sigma^1 = \{0,1\}$, $\Sigma^2 = \{00, 01, 10, 11\}$, $\Sigma^3 = \{000, 001, 010, 011, 100, 101, 110, 111\}$.

   $|\Sigma^1| = 2 = 2^1$ (No. of strings of length one),

   $|\Sigma^2| = 4 = 2^2$ (No. of strings of length two), and

   $|\Sigma^3| = 8 = 2^3$ (No. of strings of length three)
2. $S = \{a, b, c\}$, then $S^2 = \{aa, ab, ac, bb, ba, bc, cc, ca, cb\}$, and $|S^2| = 9 = 3^2$

1.4.2.3 Concatenation of strings

If w_1 and w_2 are two strings then concatenation of string w_2 with string w_1 is a string and it is denoted by $\mathbf{w_1 w_2}$. In other words, we say that w_1 is *followed by* w_2. The length of string $w_1 w_2$ is the sum of lengths of strings w_1 and w_2, i.e.

$$|w_1 w_2| = |w_1| + |w_2|$$

1.4.2.4 Prefix and suffix of a string

A string obtained by removing zero or more trailing symbols from a string w is called prefix. **For example**, if a string $w = xyz$, then x, xy, xyz are prefixes of w.

A string obtained by removing zero or more leading symbols from a string w is called suffix. **For example**, if a string $w = xyz$, then z, yz, xyz are suffixes of w. *A string x is a proper prefix or suffix of a string w if and only if* $x \neq w$.

1.4.2.5 Substrings of a string

A string obtained by removing a prefix and a suffix from a string w is called sub-string. **For example**, if a string $w = xyz$, then y is a sub-string of w. Every prefix and suffix of a string w is a sub-string of w, but not every sub-string of w is a prefix or suffix of w. For every string w, both w and ε are prefixes, suffixes, and sub-strings of w.

Substring of $w = w$ – (One prefix) – (One suffix)

1.4.3 What a Language is?

A language L denotes a set of strings over certain alphabet. The ϕ and $\{e\}$ are languages. The language ϕ is without a string and $\{e\}$ is similar to an empty box inside a box i.e. a language with string e. We will discuss more about languages, grammars and classification in Chapter 4. **For example**, let us see some languages given below:

1. $L_1 = \{ab, aabb, aaabbb\}$ is a language over alphabet $\{a, b\}$
2. $L_2 = \{\varepsilon, a, aa, aaa, \ldots\}$ is a language over alphabet $\{a\}$
3. $L_3 = \{a^n b^n c^n : n \geq 1\}$ is a language over $\{a, b, c\}$.
4. $L_4 = \{a^n b^n c^m : m, n \geq 1\}$ is a language over $\{a, b, c\}$.
5. $L_5 = \{w : w \in (a + b)^*$ and has even number of a's and odd number of b's$\}$
6. $L_6 = \{w : w \in (a + b)^*$ and has either "aaa" or "bb" as sub-string$\}$
7. $L_7 = \{w : w \in (a + b)^*$ and has neither "aa" nor "bb" as sub-string$\}$

1.4.3.1 Kleene closure

Let Σ be some alphabet. Then Kleene closure of Σ is denoted by Σ^*, also known as **reflexive-transitive closure**. *The length of Kleene closure of any alphabet is infinite.* It is defined as follows:

Σ^* = {Set of all words over Σ}
= {Word of length zero, words of length one, words of length two, ...}
= (Σ^K)
= $\Sigma^0 \cup \Sigma^1 \cup \Sigma^2 \cup \Sigma^3 \ldots$ where Σ^i is set of words over Σ of length i

For example,

1. $\Sigma = \{0, 1\}$ and a language L over Σ. Then $\Sigma^* = \Sigma^0 \cup \Sigma^1 \cup \Sigma^2 \cup \ldots$

   $\Sigma^0 = \{e\}$,

$\Sigma^1 = \{0, 1\}$,

$\Sigma^2 = \{00, 01, 10, 11\}$, and so on

So, $\Sigma^* = \{e, 0, 1, 00, 01, 10, 11 \ldots\}$

2. $S = \{a\}$, then $S^* = \{\varepsilon, a, aa, aaa, aaaa, aaaaa, ..\}$
3. Let $A = \varepsilon$, then $A^* = \varepsilon^* = \{\varepsilon\}$

1.4.3.2 Positive closure

If Σ is an alphabet then positive closure of Σ is denoted by Σ^+ and defined as follows:

$$\Sigma^+ = \Sigma^* - \{\varepsilon\}$$
$$= \{\text{Set of all words over } S \text{ excluding empty string } \varepsilon\}$$

For example,

1. If $\Sigma = \{a\}$, then $\Sigma^+ = \{a, aa, aaa, aaaa, aaaaa, \ldots\}$
2. If $A = \{0, 1\}$, then $A^+ = \{0, 1, 00, 11, 01, 10, 000, 111, 001, \ldots\}$

1.4.3.3 Useful operations on languages

Languages are represented by sets, so all the operations applicable on the sets are also applicable on the languages. Most used operations are: Union, Concatenation, Intersection, and Complement. Let us consider two languages L_1 and L_2 over the alphabet Σ and see the operations.

Union: Union of two or more languages is a language, that is, $L = L_1 \cup L_2$

Concatenation: Concatenation of two or more languages is a language, that is, $L = L_1L_2$

Intersection: Intersection of two languages is a language, that is, $L = L_1 \cap L_2$

Complement: Complement of language L_1 is defined as: $\Sigma^* - L_1$

Theorem 1.1: For a language L over Σ, $L^n = L^{n-1} L$ for $n \geq 2$

Theorem 1.2: For a language L over Σ,

$$L^* = \bigcup_{k=0}^{\infty} (\Sigma^k) \text{ for } k \geq 0$$

Theorem 1.3: For a language L over Σ, $L^n \subseteq L^*$

Theorem 1.4: For a language L over Σ, $L^+ = L^*L = LL^*$

Theorem 1.5: For a language L over Σ, $L^* = (L^*)^*$

1.4.3.4 Formal languages

We have several languages in our world. These languages are basically communication means in form of symbols. To define the concept of a *Formal Language*, we need the ideas of an *Alphabet* and a *string*. We have seen the Kleene Closure and positive closure.

A **formal language** L on the alphabet Σ is a subset of Σ^*, i.e.,

$$L \subseteq \Sigma^*$$

Here we are defining a formal language L as a collection of strings (words). Is it appearing practical in our real world? Obviously, the answer is no, because without the grammar we cannot get the desired language. In our real life, a language means a means of communication of our thoughts, desires, facts, etc.

Formal Grammars: Suppose we have a formal language L. That is to say, we have an Alphabet Σ and this language is a certain subset; $L \subset \Sigma^*$. How do we set about *defining* L? There are many approaches to this but one has become very standard in recent years, particularly in Computer Science. This approach is due to the well-known linguistic theorist Noam Chomsky (1959). He developed this approach in studying "natural languages", but it has since been taken over in a big way to describe computer languages. We will discuss this in Chapter 4.

1.5 PRINCIPLE OF MATHEMATICAL INDUCTION

If f is a declarative statement involving a natural number n ($n \geq 0$), then using the principle of mathematical induction, we can show the following:

Step 1: Basis of induction:

The statement f is true for $n = n_0$, where no is a natural number.

Step 2: Induction hypothesis:

The statement f is true for $n = k$, where k is a natural number and $k \geq n_0$.

Step 3: Induction step:

If the statement is true for $n = k + 1$ then we conclude that the statement f is true for all natural number $n \geq n_0$.

Example 1: Let us show the following using mathematical induction.

$1 + 2 + 3 + 4 + \ldots + n = n(n + 1)/2$

Proof:

Step 1: Basis of induction:

Let $f(n) = 1 + 2 + 3 + 4 + \ldots\ldots.. + n = n(n + 1)/2$

Putting $n = 1$, we have LHS = 1 and RHS = $1(1 + 1)/2 = 1$

So, $f(n)$ is true for $n = 1$.

Step 2: Induction hypothesis:

Suppose $f(n)$ is true for $n \geq k$, where $k \geq 1$.

Step 3: Induction step:

Putting $n = k + 1$, we have

RHS = $(k + 1)(k + 2)/2$

LHS = $1 + 2 + 3 + \ldots + k + (k + 1) = k(k + 1)/2+(k + 1) = (k + 1)(k/2 + 1) = (k + 1)(k + 2)/2$

= RHS

Therefore, we conclude that $f(n)$ is true for all $n \geq 1$.

1.6 SOLVED EXAMPLES

Example 1.1: $U = \{0, 1, 2, 3, 4, 5, 6, 7, 8, 9\}$ is universal set and $A = \{1, 2, 3\}$, $B = \{2, 3, 4, 5, 6\}$, $C = \{0, 2, 4, 6, 8\}$, and $D = \{1, 3, 5, 7, 9\}$. Find

(a) $A \cap B$ (b) $A \cup B$ (c) $(A \cap B)^C, C^C, D^C$

(d) $C^C \backslash C$ (e) $(C^C)^C$

Solution:

(a) $A \cap B = \{\text{Common elements between the sets } A \text{ \& } B\}$

$= \{2, 3\}$

(b) $A \cup B = \{x: x \in A \text{ or } x \in B\}$

$= \{1, 2, 3, 4, 5, 6\}$

(c) $(A \cap B)^C = U - (A \cap B) = \{0, 1, 4, 5, 6, 7, 8, 9\}$

$C^C = U - C = \{1, 3, 5, 7, 9\}$

$D^C = U - D = \{0, 2, 4, 6, 8\}$

(d) $C^C \backslash C = C^C - C = \{1, 3, 5, 7, 9\}$

(e) $(C^C)^C = U - (C^C) = U - (U - C) = C$

Example 1.2: Prove that $A = \{1, 2, 3, 4\}$ is proper subset of $B = \{0, 1, 2, 3, 4, 5, 6, 7, 8, 9\}$.

Solution: All elements of set A belong to set B. So, $A \subseteq B$, But, $0 \in B$ and $0 \notin A$, and for A to be proper subset of B, at least one element of B should not be in A. Therefore, A is proper subset of B.

Example 1.3: Determine the, where sets $A = \{a, b, c\}$, and $B = \{0, 1\}$.

(a) $\phi \cup A$ (b) $\phi \cap (A \cap B)$

(c) $\{\phi\} \cup \{A\}$ (d) $\{\phi\} \cap \{A\}$

Solution:

(a) $\phi \cup A = A$ (ϕ is subset of all the sets)

(b) $\phi \cap (A \cap B) = \phi$ (ϕ is subset of the set $A \cap B$)

(c) $\{\phi\} \cup \{A\} = \{\phi, A\}$

(d) $\{\phi\} \cap \{A\} = \phi$

Example 1.4: Determine the following sets:

(a) $\phi \cap \{\phi\}$ (b) $\phi \cup \{\phi\}$

(c) $\{\phi\} \cap \{\phi, a, \{\phi\}\}$ (d) $\{\phi\} \oplus \{\phi, a, \{\phi\}\}$

(e) $\phi \oplus \{\phi, a, \{\phi\}\}$ (ϕ) $\{\phi\} \cup \{\phi, a, \{\phi\}\}$

Solution:

(a) $\phi \cap \{\psi\} = \phi$

(b) $\phi \cup \{\phi\} = \{\phi\}$

(c) $\{\phi\} \cap \{\phi, a, \{\phi\}\} = \{\phi\}$ (Element ϕ is common in both the sets)

(d) $\{\phi\} \oplus \{\phi, a, \{\phi\}\} = \{a, \{\phi\}\}$($\{a, \{\phi\}\}$ is in $\{\phi, a, \{\phi\}\}$ but not in $\{\phi\}$)

(e) $\phi \oplus \{\phi, a, \{\phi\}\} = \{\phi, a, \{\phi\}\}$

(ϕ) $\{\phi\} \cup \{\phi, a, \{\phi\}\} = \{\phi, a, \{\phi\}\}$

Example 1.5: Determine the sets:

(a) 2^X, where $X = \{a, b, \{a, b\}\}$

(b) $2^B - 2^A$, where $A = \{1, 2\}$, and $B = \{1, 2, 3\}$

(c) $\{a\} \times \{a, b\} \times \{a, b, c\}$

(d) $\phi \times \{1, 2\}$

(e) $2^{\{1, 2\}} \times \{1, 2\}$

Solution:

(a) $X = \{a, b, \{a, b\}\}$,

Then $2^X = \{$All subsets of set $X\}$

$= \{\phi, \{a\}, \{b\}, \{a, b\}, \{\{a, b\}\}, \{a, \{a, b\}\}, \{b, \{a, b\}\}, \{a, b, \{a, b\}\}\}$

(b) $A = \{1, 2\}$, and $B = \{1, 2, 3\}$, then

$2^B = \{$All subsets of $B\} = \{\phi, \{1\}, \{2\}, \{3\}, \{1, 2\}, \{1, 3\}, \{2, 3\}, \{1, 2, 3\}\}$

$2^A = \{$All subsets of $A\} = \{\phi, \{1\}, \{2\}, \{1, 2\}\}$

$2^B - 2^A = \{\{3\}, \{1, 3\}, \{2, 3\}, \{1, 2, 3\}\}$

(c) $\{a\} \times \{a, b\} \times \{a, b, c\} = \{$Ordered pairs of $\{a\} \times \{a, b\}\} \times \{a, b, c\}$

$= \{(a, a), (a, b)\} \times \{a, b, c\} = \{(a, a, a), (a, a, b), (a, a, c), (a, b, a), (a, b, b), (a, b, c)\}$

(d) $\phi \times \{1, 2\} = \{\ \} \times \{1, 2\} = \phi$ (Since, ϕ has no element to be paired with $\{1, 2\}$)

(e) $2^{\{1, 2\}} \times \{1, 2\} = \{\phi, \{1\}, \{2\}, \{1, 2\}\} \times \{1, 2\}$

$= \{(\{1\}, 1), (\{1\}, 2), (\{2\}, 1), (\{2\}, 2), (\{1, 2\}, 1), (\{1, 2\}, 2)\}$

Example 1.6: Find string xyz, where

(a) $x = abc, y = \varepsilon$, and $z = 00$,

(b) $x = 010, y = \alpha\beta$, *and* $z = \varepsilon$, and

(c) $x = \varepsilon, y = cba$, *and* $z = 11$

Solution:

(a) $x = abc, y = \varepsilon$, and $z = 00$, then

$xyz = abc\varepsilon00 \equiv abc00$

(Concatenation result of any string with ε is the same string.)

(b) $x = 010, y = \alpha\beta$, *and* $z = \varepsilon$, then

$xyz = 010\alpha\beta\varepsilon \equiv 010\alpha\beta$

(c) $x = \varepsilon, y = cba$, and $z = 11$, then

$xyz = \varepsilon cba11 \equiv cba11$

Example 1.7: Let sets $A = \{a, b\}$, and $B = \{1\}$and find 2^A, 2^B, and $2^{A \cup B}$.

Solution: $2^A = \{\phi, a, b, \{a, b\}\}$

$2^B = \{\phi, \{1\}\}$

$2^{A \cup B} = 2^{\{a, b, 1\}} = \{\phi, \{a\}, \{b\}, \{1\}, \{a, b\}, \{a, 1\}, \{b, 1\}, \{a, \text{b}, 1\}\}$

Example 1.8: Prove that for any set A, having elements n $(n \geq 0)$, the power set of set A has 2^n elements.

Solution: **Proof:** (Using mathematical induction method)

Step 1: Let the set A is empty, that is $n = 0$, then $2^A = \{\phi\}$ and $|2^A| = 1 = 2^0$

Let the set A contains one element and $A = \{a\}$, then

$2^A = \{\phi, a\}$ and $|2^A| = 2 = 2^1$

So, the statement is true for $n = 0$ and $n = 1$.

Step 2: Let the set A has $n = k$ $(k \geq 0)$, and the statement "2^A has 2^k elements" is true.

Step 3: Let A has $n = k + 1$ elements and $A = B \cup \{a\}$, where $|B| = k$

Now $2^{B \cup \{a\}} = 2^B \cup \{x \cup \{a\}\}$ for all $x \in 2^B$ (See the solved problem (7))

Now $|2^{B \cup \{a\}}| = |2^B \cup \{x \cup \{a\}\}| = |2^B| + |\{x \cup \{a\}\}|$ for all $x \in 2^B = 2^k + 2^k = 2^{k+1}$

Step 4: The given statement is true for all $n = k + 1$, therefore the statement "2^A has 2^n elements" is true for all value of $|A| = n$ $(n \geq 0)$.

Example 1.9: Find the number of prefixes and suffixes for string w of length n $(n \geq 0)$.

Solution: Let $w = a_1a_2a_3....a_n$ is the given string.

Number of trailing symbols removed	prefix
Zero	$a_1a_2a_3....a_n$
One	$a_1a_2a_3....a_{n-1}$
Two	$a_1a_2a_3.....a_{n-2}$
...	....
$n - 1$	a_1
All	ε

Total number of prefixes = $n + 1$

We can obtain the same result for number of suffixes.

Example 1.10: Binary tree is shown in Fig. 1.11 Find

(a) The root node,

(b) The interior nodes,

(c) All subtrees of D,

(d) All the leaves.

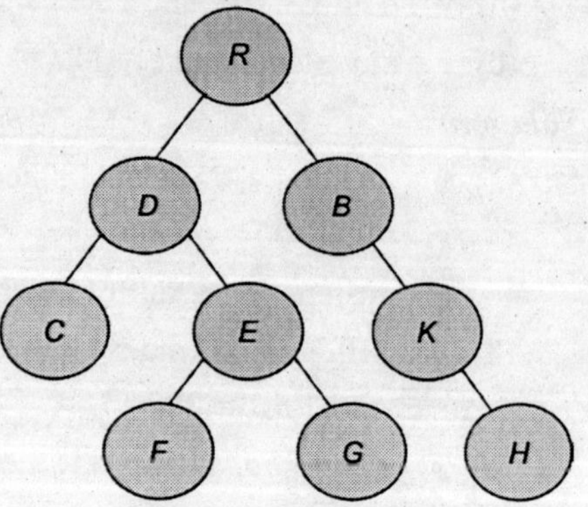

Fig. 1.11: Binary tree

Solution:

(a) The root node is R.

(b) The interior nodes are D, B, E, and K.

(c) Subtrees of D are C and E.

(d) Leaves are C, F, G, and H.

Example 1.11: Prove the following using mathematical induction for $n \geq 1$, where* represents multiplication operator:

(a) $1^3 + 2^3 + 3^3 + \ldots + n^3 = (n(n+1)/2)^2$

(b) $1*2 + 2*3 + 3*4 + \ldots + n*(n+1) = n(n+1)(n+2)/3$

(c) $1*2*3 + 2*3*4 + 3*4*5 + \ldots + n*(n+1)*(n+2) = n(n+1)(n+2)(n+3)/4$

(d) $\frac{1}{1*2} + \frac{1}{2*3} + \frac{1}{3*4} + \ldots + \frac{1}{n*(n+1)} = \frac{n}{n+1}$

Solution:

(a) Let $F(n) = 1^3 + 2^3 + 3^3 + \ldots + n^3 = (n(n+1)/2)^2$

Putting $n = 1$, we have

LHS = RHS = 1

Let $F(n)$ is true for $n = k \geq 1$. Now, putting $n = k + 1$, we have

LHS $= (1^3 + 2^3 + 3^3 + \ldots + k^3) + \mathbf{(k+1)^3} = (k(k+1)/2)^2 + (k+1)^3$

$= (k+1)^2 (k^2 + 4k + 4)/4 = (k+1)^2((k+2)/2)^2$

$= ((k+1)(k+2)/2)^2 =$ RHS

Hence, F(n) is true for all value of $n \geq 1$.

(b) Let $F(n) = 1*2 + 2*3 + 3*4 + \ldots + n*(n+1) = n(n+1)(n+2)/3$

Putting $n = 1$, we have

LHS = RHS = 2

Let $F(n)$ is true for $n = k \geq 1$. Now, putting $n = k + 1$, we have

LHS $= 1*2 + 2*3 + \ldots + k*(k+1) + \mathbf{(k+1)*(k+2)} = k(k+1)(k+2)/3 + (k+1)*(k+2)$

$= (k+1)(k+2)(k+3)/3 =$ RHS

Hence, $F(n)$ is true for all value of $n \geq 1$.

(c) Let $F(n) = 1*2*3 + 2*3*4 + 3*4*5 + \ldots + n*(n+1)*(n+2) = n(n+1)(n+2)(n+3)/4$

Putting $n = 1$, we have

LHS = RHS = 6

Let $F(n)$ is true for $n = k \geq 1$.Now, putting $n = k + 1$, we have

LHS $= 1*2*3 + 2*3*4 + 3*4*5 + \ldots + k*(k+1)*(k+2) + \mathbf{(k+1)*(k+2)*(k+3)}$

$= k(k+1)(k+2)(k+3)/4 + (k+1)*(k+2)*(k+3)$

$= (k+1)(\mathrm{k}+2)(k+3)(k+4)/4 =$ RHS

Hence, $F(n)$ is true for all value of $n \geq 1$.

(d) Let $F(n) = \frac{1}{1*2} + \frac{1}{2*3} + \frac{1}{3*4} + ... + \frac{1}{n*(n+1)} = \frac{n}{n+1}$

Putting $n = 1$, we have

LHS = RHS = $\frac{1}{2}$

Let $F(n)$ is true for $n = k \geq 1$. Now, putting $n = k + 1$, we have

$$\text{LHS} = \frac{1}{1*2} + \frac{1}{2*3} + \frac{1}{3*4} + ... + \frac{1}{k*(k+1)} + \frac{1}{(k+1)*(k+2)}$$

$$= \frac{k}{k+1} + \frac{1}{(k+1)*(k+2)} = \frac{1}{(k+1)} * \frac{(k+1)^2}{(k+2)} = \frac{k+1}{k+2}$$

= RHS

Hence, $F(n)$ is true for all value of $n^3 1$.

Example 1.12: Suppose $X = \{2, 3\}$, $Y = \{a, b, c\}$, and $C = \{0, 1\}$. Find the following:

(a) $A \times B$ (b) $A \times B \times C$

Solution:

(a) $X \times Y = \{2, 3\} \times \{a, b, c\}$
$= \{(2, a), (2, b), (2, c), (3, a), (3, b), (3, c)\}$

(b) $X \times Y \times C = \{2, 3\} \times \{a, b, c\} \times \{0, 1\} = \{(2, a), (2, b), (2, c), (3, a), (3, b), (3, c)\} \times \{0, 1\}$
$= \{(2, a, 0), (2, a, 1), (2, b, 0), (2, b, 1), (2, c, 0), (2, c, 1), (3, a, 0), (3, a, 1), (3, b, 0), (3, b, 1), (3, c, 0), (3, c, 1)\}$

Example 1.13: Let $X = \{a, b, c, d\}$, $B = \{c, d, e\}$, and $C = \{0, 1\}$. Show that

(a) $(X - B) \times C = X \times C - B \times C$ (b) $(X \oplus B) \times C = (X \times C) \oplus (B \times C)$

Solution:

(a) **Proof**:

$(X - B) \times C = \{a, b\} \times \{0, 1\} = \{(a, 0), (a, 1), (b, 0), (b, 1)\}$

$X \times C - B \times C = \{(a, 0), (a, 1), (b, 0), (b, 1), (c, 0), (c, 1)\} - \{(c, 0), (c, 1), (d, 0), (d, 1), (e, 0), (e, 1)\}$
$= \{(a, 0), (a, 1), (b, 0), (b, 1)\}$

Therefore, $(X - B) \times C = X \times C - B \times C$

(b) $(X \oplus B) \times C = \{a, b, e\} \times \{0, 1\} = \{(a, 0), (a, 1), (b, 0), (b, 1), (e, 0), (e, 1)\}$

$(X \times C) \oplus (B \times C) = \{(a, 0), (a, 1), (b, 0), (b, 1), (c, 0), (c, 1), (d, 0), (d, 1)\} \oplus \{(c, 0), (c, 1), (d, 0), (d, 1), (e, 0), (e, 1)\}$
$= \{(a, 0), (a, 1), (b, 0), (b, 1), (e, 0), (e, 1)\}$

Hence, $(X \oplus B) \times C = (X \times C) \oplus (B \times C)$

Example 1.14: Let $R = \{(1, a), (1, b), (2, a), (2, c), (3, a), (3, b)\}$ be a relation from the set $A = \{1, 2, 3\}$ to the set $B = \{a, b, c\}$.

(a) Find the inverse relation of R.

(b) Show the matrix representation of R.

(c) Draw the arrow diagram of R.

(d) Find the universal relation from A to B.

(e) Find the domain and range of R.

Solution:

(a) The inverse relation of R is denoted by R^{-1}, and

$R^{-1} = \{(a, 1), (b, 1), (a, 2), (c, 2), (a, 3), (b, 3)\}$

(b) The matrix representation R is shown in Fig. 1.12.

	a	b	c
1	1	1	0
2	1	0	1
3	1	1	0

Fig. 1.12

(c) The arrow diagram is shown in Fig. 1.13.

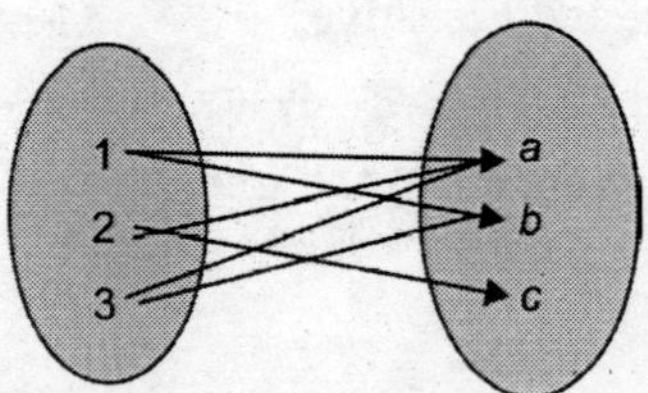

Fig. 1.13

(d) The universal relation

$U = A \times B = \{(1, a), (1, b), (1, c), (2, a), (2, b), (2, c), (3, a), (3, b), (3, c)\}$

(e) Domain $(R) = \{1, 2, 3\}$, Range $(R) = \{a, b, c\}$

Example 1.15: Let $X = \{a, b, c, d\}$ and a relation $R = \{(a, a), (a, b), (a, c), (b, a), (b, b), (b, d), (c, a), (c, c), (d, b), (d, d)\}$.

(a) Is R reflexive?

(b) Is R symmetric?

(c) Is R transitive?

(d) List two chains in R.

(e) How many cycles (nontrivial) are in R?

Solution:

(a) Since, for all $a \in X$, $(a, a) \in R$, so R is reflexive relation.

(b) Since, for all $(a, b) \in R$, $(b, a) \in R$, so R is symmetric relation.

(c) Since, $(a, b), (b, d) \in R$ but $(a, d) \notin R$, so R is not transitive relation.

(d) The arrow diagram of R is shown in Fig. 1.14. Two chains are: (a, b, d), (a, c)

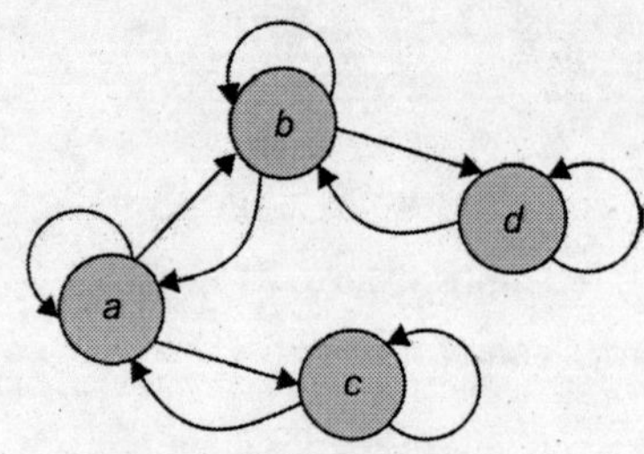

Fig. 1.14

(e) Following cycles are there in R: (a, b, a), (b, d, b), (a, c, a)

Example 1.16: Let $X = \{a, b, c\}$ be a set. Find the following relation on X which is:

(a) Symmetric and antisymmetric

(b) Symmetric and not antisymmetric

(c) Symmetric, antisymmetric, and transitive

(d) A transitive relation R such that $R \cup R^{-1}$ is not transitive

(e) Reflexive, symmetric, antisymmetric, and transitive

Solution:

(a) $R_1 = \{(a, a), (b, b)\}$

(b) $R_2 = \{(a, b), (b, a)\}$

(c) $R_3 = \{(a, a), (c, c)\}$

(d) $R = \{(a, b), (c, b)\}$, so $R \cup R^{-1} = \{(a, b), (b, a), (c, b), (b, c)\}$

Therefore, $R \cup R^{-1}$ is not transitive.

(e) $R_4 = \{(a, a), (b, b), (c, c)\}$

Example 1.17: Let $R = \{(a, b), (c, a), (b, c)\}$ is a relation on $A = \{a, b, c\}$. Find

(a) Reflexive closure of R

(b) Symmetric closure of R

(c) Transitive closure of R

Solution: Reflexive(R) = $R \cup \{(a, a): \forall a \in A\} = \{(a, a), (a, b), (b, b), (b, c), (c, a), (c, c)\}$

(a) Symmetric(R) = $R \cup R^{-1} = \{(a, b), (c, a), (b, c)\} \cup \{(b, a), (a, c), (c, b)\}$

$= \{(a, b), (b, a), (c, a), (a, c), (b, c), (c, b)\}$

(b) Transitive closure of R is denoted by $R+$ and

$R^+ = R \cup R^2 \cup R^3$ (Since, A has only three elements.)

Now, $R^2 = \{(a, b), (c, a), (b, c)\} \text{ o } \{(a, b), (c, a), (b, c)\} = \{(a, c), (c, b), (b, a)\}$

$R^3 = \{(a, c), (c, b), (b, a)\} \text{o} \{(a, b), (c, a), (b, c)\} = \{(a, a), (c, c), (b, b)\}$

So, $R^+ = \{(a, b), (c, a), (b, c), (a, c), (c, b), (b, a), (a, a), (c, c), (b, b)\}$

Example 1.18: Let us consider two relations R and S on the non-empty set A, then prove the following:

(a) If R and S are reflexive then $R \cup S$ is reflexive.

(b) If R and S are reflexive then $R \cap S$ is reflexive.

(c) If R and S are symmetric then $R \cup S$ is symmetric.

(d) If R and S are symmetric then $R \cap S$ is symmetric.

(e) If R is antisymmetric then R^{-1} is also antisymmetric.

(f) If R and S are transitive then $R \cup S$ is not necessarily transitive.

(g) If R and S are antisymmetric then $R \cup S$ is not necessarily antisymmetric.

Proof:

(a) Since, R and S are reflexive relations, it means, for all $a \in A$, (a, a) is in both R and S. So, $\forall a \in A, (a, a) \in R \cup S$.

Hence, $R \cup S$ is reflexive.

(b) Since, R and S are reflexive relations, it means, for all $a \in A$, (a, a) is in both R and S. So, $\forall a \in A, (a, a) \in R \cap S$.

Hence, $R \cap S$ is reflexive.

(c) Since, R and S are symmetric relations on A, it means, if $(a, b) \in R$, then $(b, a) \in R$ and therefore $(a, b), (b, a) \in R \cup S$.

Similarly, we can show the above for the relation S.

Hence, $R \cup S$ is symmetric relation.

(d) Suppose, (a, b) is in both R and S, it means, (b, a) will be in both and thus $(a, b), (b, a) \in R \cap S$. It means if R and S are symmetric then $R \cap S$ is also symmetric.

(e) Since, R is antisymmetric relation on A. Suppose $(a, b) \in R$, then $(b, a) \in R$ for $a = b$. It means $(b, a) \in R^{-1}$ for $a = b$. In other words, if $(a, b) \in R$, then $(b, a) \in R^{-1}$ for $a = b$.

Hence, R^{-1} is also antisymmetric.

(f) We give some examples to show that if R and S are transitive then $R \cup S$ may or may not be transitive.

Let $R = \{(a, b), (b, a), (a, a)\}$, and $S = \{(b, b)\}$ for $a, b \in A$.

So, $R \cup S = \{(a, b), (b, a), (a, a), (b, b)\}$ is a transitive relation.

Now, let $R = \{(a, b)\}$, and $S = \{(b, a)\}$

So, $R \cup S = \{(a, b), (b, a)\}$ is not transitive relation because $(a, a) \notin R \cup S$.

Hence, $R \cup S$ is not necessarily transitive relation.

(g) We give some examples to show that if R and S are antisymmetric then $R \cup S$ may or may not be antisymmetric.

Let $R = \{(a, a)\}$, and $S = \{(b, b)\}$

So, $R \cup S = \{(a, a), (b, b)\}$ is antisymmetric relation.

Now, let $\{(a, b)\}$, and $S = \{(b, a)\}$

So, $R \cup S = \{(a, b), (b, a)\}$ is not transitive relation for $a \neq b$.

Example 1.19: Let A be a set of all triangles in a plane and a relation R on A such that $(a, b) \in R$ if and only if a and b are similar triangles. Show that R is an equivalence relation.

Solution: Given that $(a, b) \in R$ if and only if a and b are similar triangles. Since, each triangle is similar to itself, so $\forall\ a \in A, (a, a) \in R$. So, R is a reflexive relation.

Now, if a and b are similar triangles, then $(a, b), (b, a) \in R$. It means, R is a symmetric relation. Let a and b are similar triangles, so $(a, b) \in R$, and b and c are similar triangles, so $(b, c) \in R$ and therefore a and c are similar triangles and $(a, c) \in R$.

So, R is transitive relation. Hence, R is an equivalence relation.

Example 1.20: Let R be a transitive and symmetric relation on a set X. Show that for every a in X there exists b in X such that $(a, b) \in R$ then R is an equivalence relation.

Solution: Given that R is transitive and symmetric relation on X and for every $a \in X$, there exists some b in X such that $(a, b) \in R$. It means, if $(a, b) \in R$ then $(b, a) \in R$ due to the symmetric property. Now, for every a in X, $(a, b), (b, a) \in R$, so due to transitive property or R, $(a, a) \in R$. So, R is reflexive relation also.

Hence, R is an equivalence relation.

Example 1.21: A relation $R = \{(a, b), (a, a), (b, b), (c, a)\}$ is on $A = \{a, b, c\}$. Find the following:

(a) Reflexive (R)
(b) Symmetric (R)
(c) Transitive (R)

Solution:

(a) Reflexive $(R) = R \cup \{(a, a): \forall\ a \in A\}$

$$= \{(a, b), (a, a), (b, b), (c, a)\} \cup \{(a, a), (b, b), (c, c)\}$$
$$= \{(a, b), (a, a), (b, b), (c, a), (c, c)\}$$

(b) Symmetric $(R) = R \cup R^{-1}$

$$= \{(a, b), (a, a), (b, b), (c, a)\} \cup \{(b, a), (a, a), (b, b), (a, c)\}$$
$$= \{(a, b), (b, a), (b, b), (c, a), (a, c)\}$$

(c) Transitive $(R) = R \cup R^2 \cup R^3$

$$R^2 = RoR = \{(a, b), (a, a), (b, b), (c, a)\} \text{ o } \{(a, b), (a, a), (b, b), (c, a)\}$$
$$= \{(a, b), (a, a), (b, b), (c, b), (c, a)\}$$
$$R^3 = R^2oR = \{(a, b), (a, a), (b, b), (c, b), (c, a)\} \text{ o } \{(a, b), (a, a), (b, b), (c, a)\}$$
$$= \{(a, b), (a, a), (b, b), (c, b), (c, a)\}$$

So, Transitive $(R) = \{(a, b), (a, a), (b, b), (c, b), (c, a)\}$

Example 1.22: Let $R = \{(a, a), (b, a), (a, b), (b, b), (c, c), (d, d)\}$ be an equivalence relation on set $A = \{a, b, c, d\}$. Find

(a) Equivalence classes of A by R, and

(b) The quotient set of A by R

Solution:

(a) We have $[a] = \{a, b\}$, $[b] = \{a, b\}$, $[c] = \{c\}$, $[d] = \{d\}$ and $[a] = [b]$

So, the equivalence class or partition of A by R is $[\{a, b\}, \{c\}, \{d\}]$.

(b) The quotient of A by R

$A/R = \{[a], [c], [d]\} = \{[b], [c], [d]\}$

Example 1.23: Let $R = \{(a, a), (b, b), (a, b), (c, a)\}$, $S = \{(a, a), (a, b), (b, b), (c, a), (c, c)\}$, and $T = \{(a, b), (a, a), (b, b), (c, a), (c, b)\}$ be three relations on $A = \{a, b, c\}$.

(a) Find the composite relation RoS

(b) Find the composite relation RoT

(c) Find the composite relation $RoSoT$

(d) Show that $Ro(SoT) = (RoS)oT$

Solution:

(a) We represent the composition of R and S relations as shown in Fig. 1.15(a).

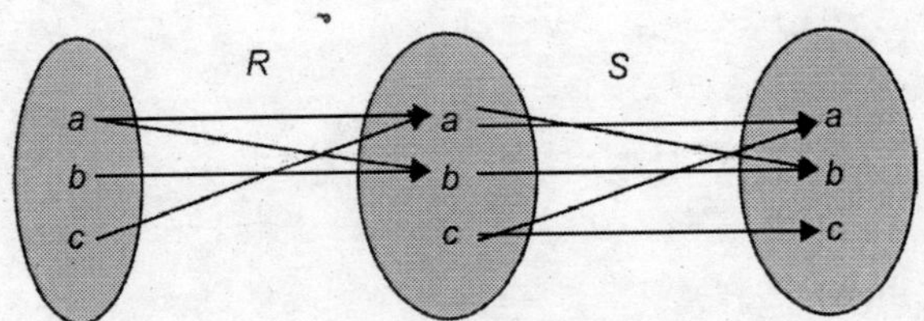

Fig. 1.15(a)

So, $RoS = \{(a, a), (a, b), (b, b), (c, a), (c, b)\}$

(b) The composition of the relations R and T is shown in Fig. 1.15(b).

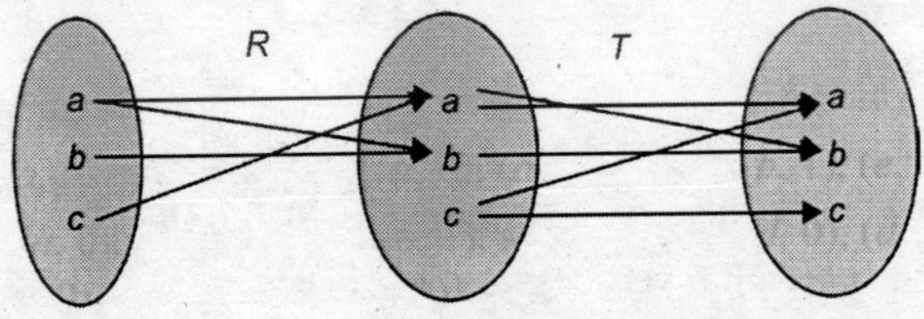

Fig. 1.15(b)

So, $RoT = \{(a, a), (a, b), (b, b), (c, a), (c, b)\}$

(c) The composition of relations R, S, and T is shown in Fig. 1.15(c).

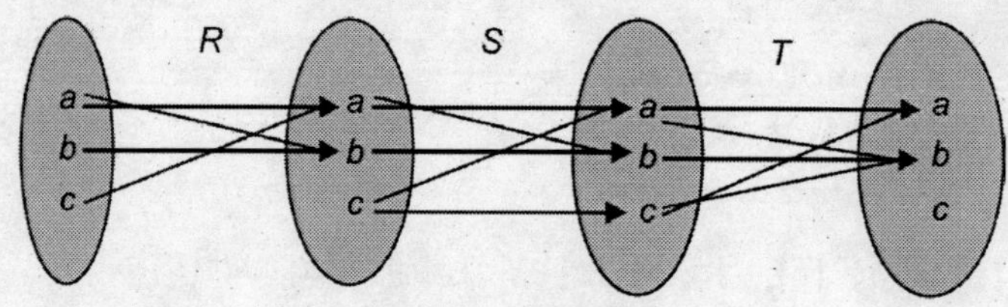

Fig. 1.15(c)

So, $RoSoT = \{(a, a), (a, b), (b, b), (c, a), (c, b)\}$

(d) $Ro(SoT) = Ro\{(a, a), (a, b), (b, b), (c, a), (c, b)\}$

$= \{(a, a), (a, b), (b, b), (c, a)\} \text{ o } \{(a, a), (a, b), (b, b), (c, a), (c, b)\}$

$= \{(a, a), (a, b), (b, b), (c, a), (c, b)\}$

$(RoS)oT = \{(a, a), (a, b), (b, b), (c, a), (c, b)\} \text{ o } \{(a, b), (a, a), (b, b), (c, a), (c, b)\}$

$= \{(a, a), (a, b), (b, b), (c, a), (c, b)\}$

Hence, $Ro(SoT) = (RoS)oT$

Example 1.24: Find the transitive closure R^+ and reflexive and transitive closure R^* of the relation: $R = \{(1, 2), (2, 3), (3, 4), (5, 4)\}$

Solution: Transitive closure of R, that is

$R^+ = R \cup R^2 \cup R^3 \cup \ldots$

So, $R^2 = RoR = \{(1, 3), (2, 4)\}$

$R^3 = R^2 \cup R = \{(1, 4)\}$

$R^4 = \phi$

Similarly, $R^n = \phi$ for $n >= 4$.

So, $R^+ = \{(1, 2), (2, 3), (3, 4), (5, 4), (1, 3), (2, 4), (1, 4)\}$

$R^* = R^+ \cup \{(a, a): a \in R\}$

So, $R^* = \{(1, 2), (2, 3), (3, 4), (5, 4), (1, 3), (2, 4), (1, 4), (1, 1), (2, 2), (3, 3), (4, 4), (5, 5)\}$

TEST YOUR SKILLS

Supplementary Problems

1.1 Show that for two arbitrary sets X and Y, $|2^{X \cup Y}| = |2^X| \times |2^Y|$

1.2 Find the number of sub-strings for a string w of length n ($n \geq 0$).

1.3 Prove that a graph tree with n vertices has $(n - 1)$ edges.

1.4 If $\Sigma = \{a, b\}$, then find:

(a) Σ^* (b) Σ^+

(c) Σ^3 (d) $aa\Sigma^3bb$

1.4 Describe all the words from $(\{a, b\}\{c\}^*\{d\})$.

1.5 If $A = \{q_0, q_1, q_2, q_3\}$, then find 2^A.

1.6 If $A = \{\phi, \{\phi\}, \{\{\phi, \{\phi\}\}\}\}$, then find 2^A and $n(2^A)$.

1.7 Show the following using mathematical induction principle for $n \geq 1$:

(a) $1 + 2 + 2^2 + 2^3 + \ldots + 2^n = 2^{n+1} - 1$

(b) $1 + 3^2 + 5^2 + \ldots + (2n-1)^2 = n(2n-1)(2n+1)/3$

(c) $1*1! + 2*2! + 3*3! + \ldots + n*n! = (n+1)! - 1$

(d) $2 + 4 + 6 + \ldots + 2n = n(n+1)$

(e) $1 + 4 + 7 + \ldots + (3n-2) = 2n(3n-1)$

(f) $\dfrac{1}{1*3} + \dfrac{1}{3*5} + \dfrac{1}{5*7} + \ldots + \dfrac{1}{(2n-1)*(2n+1)} = \dfrac{n}{2n+1}$

(g) $\dfrac{1}{1*3} + \dfrac{2^2}{3*5} + \dfrac{3^2}{5*7} + \ldots + \dfrac{n^2}{(2n-1)*(2n+1)} = \dfrac{n(n+1)}{2(2n+1)}$

1.8 Prove the following for three arbitrary sets X, B, and C:

(a) $X \oplus B = (X - B) \cup (B - X) = (X \cup B) - (X \cap B)$

(b) $(X \cup B) \cap (X \cup B^c) = X$

(c) $(X \cap B) \subseteq B$, $(X \cap B) \subseteq X$, then $(X \cap B) \subseteq (X \cup B)$

(d) $X \subseteq B$ if and only if $X - B = \phi$

(e) $(X \cup B) \times C = X \times C \cup B \times C$

(f) $C \times (X \cup B) = C \times X \cup C \times B = C \times B \cup C \times X$

(g) $(X \cap B) \times C = X \times C \cap B \times C$

(h) $C \times (X \cap B) = C \times X \cap C \times B$

(i) $(X - B) \times C = X \times C - B \times C$

(j) $(X \oplus B) \times C = (X \cup B) \times C - (X \cap B) \times C = (X \times C) \oplus (B \times C)$

(k) $(X^c \cap B^c)^c = X \cup B$

1.9 Suppose R is an equivalence relation on set X. Is it possible that $R^n \cap R = \phi$? Give some examples to satisfy your answer(s).

1.10 Let S be a binary relation on the set A and another relation $R = \{(a, b): (a, c), (b, c) \in S$ for some $c \in A\}$. Show that if S is an equivalence relation then R is also equivalence relation.

1.11 Show that transitive closure of a symmetric binary relation is symmetric.

1.12 Suppose R is a binary relation from A to B and its inverse relation is denoted by R^{-1} and defined from B to A such that

$R^{-1} = \{(b, a): (a, b) \in R\}$

(a) If R_1 and R_2 are two binary relations from A to B then show that

$$(R_1 \cup R_2)^{-1} = R_1^{-1} \cup R_2^{-1}.$$

(b) If R_1 and R_2 are two binary relations from A to B, then show that

$$(R_1 \cap R_2)^{-1} = R_1^{-1} \cap R_2^{-1}.$$

(c) Show that R^{-1} is reflexive relation if R is reflexive.

(d) Show that R^{-1} is symmetric relation if R is symmetric.

(e) Show that R^{-1} may or may not be transitive relation if R is transitive.

1.13 Let N is the set of non-zero integers and a relation R is on N such that $(a, b) R (c, d)$ whenever $ad = bc$. Prove that R is an equivalence relation.

1.14 Let a set $A = \{a, b, c\}$.

(a) List all possible different reflexive relations on A.

(b) List all possible different symmetric relations on A.

(c) List all possible different reflexive and symmetric relations on A.

(d) How many different binary relations are on A?

1.15 Let $R = \{(a, a), (a, c), (a, b), (c, b), (b, c), (c, d), (d, d)\}$ be a relation on $A = \{a, b, c, d\}$.

(a) Show the matrix representation of R.

(b) Show the arrow diagram of R.

(c) Find the domain and range of R.

(d) Find the inverse relation of R.

1.16 Consider a set $X = \{1, 2, 3\}$ and a relation on X $R = \{(1, 1), (1, 2), (2, 3), (3, 3)\}$. Find the following:

(a) Reflexive closure of R

(b) Symmetric closure of R

(c) Transitive closure of R

1.17 Let relation $R = \{(a, a), (a, e), (b, b), (b, c), (b, f), (c, b), (c, c), (c, f), (d, d), (e, a), (e, e), (f, b), (f, c), (f, f)\}$. Find the equivalence classes and quotient of A induced by R.

Give some examples of following relations on $A = \{a, b, c\}$ having the following given property.

(a) Symmetric and reflexive

(b) Reflexive and transitive

(c) Antisymmetric and symmetric

(d) Symmetric and not antisymmetric

(e) Reflexive, symmetric, and transitive

(f) Reflexive, symmetric, transitive, and antisymmetric

1.18 Let $R = \{(a, a), (c, b), (c, d), (d, b)$, $S = \{(b, a), (c, c), (c, d), (d, a), (d, b)\}$ are two relations on $A = \{a, b, c, d\}$. Find the following:

(a) RoR

(b) RoS

(c) SoR and show that $RoS \neq SoR$

Multiple Choice Questions

1.19 Which of the following is true?

(a) $\phi \subseteq \phi$

(b) $\phi \in \phi$

(c) $\{\phi\} \subseteq \phi$

(d) None

1.20 If set $X = \{1, 2, 3\}$, then X^1 has elements

(a) 3

(b) 2

(c) 3^3

(d) None

1.21 Let L be a language over alphabet $\Sigma = \{0, 1\}$. The Kleene closure of L is denoted by

(a) $L^+ = \bigcup_{i=0}^{\infty} L^i$

(b) $L^* = \bigcup_{i=1}^{\infty} L^i$

(c) $L^* = \bigcup_{i=0}^{\infty} L^i$

(d) None

1.22 Let set $A = \{1, 2, 3, 4, 5, 6\}$ then the number of strings in A^* of length 4 such that no symbol is used more than once is

(a) 24

(b) 720

(c) 360

(d) 120

1.23 Let $A = \{abc, a, b, c\}$ be a set. Which of the following is true?

(a) $\phi \subseteq A$

(b) $abc \in A$

(c) $a, b \in A$

(d) All the above

1.24 Let set $A = \{0, 1\}$, then the number of possible strings of length n ($n \geq 0$) is

(a) $n!$

(b) $n \times n$

(c) 2^n

(d) $2*n$

1.25 An alphabet is a

(a) Finite set

(b) Finite or infinite set

(c) Nonempty set

(d) both (a) and (c)

1.26 Which one is true?

(a) $\{a, b\} \in 2^{\{a, b, \{a, b\}\}}$

(b) (a) is false

(c) $\{a, b, \{a, b\}\} - \{a, b\} = \{a, b\}$

(d) None

1.27 For any alphabet S then $(S^*)^*$ is equivalent to

(a) Σ^+

(b) Σ^*

(c) Σ

(d) $\Sigma^* - \{\varepsilon\}$

1.28 Which is true about Palindromes?

(a) Are equivalent in reading either form left to right or right to left

(b) May be of even length or odd length

(c) Both (a) and (b) are true

(d) None

1.29 Which one of the following is false?

(a) $\{a, b\} \in \{a, b, c, ab, \{a, b, c, d\}\}$ (b) $\{a, b\} \subseteq \{a, b, c, ab, \{a, b, c, d\}\}$

(c) $\{a, f\} \in \{a, b, \{a, f\}\}$ (d) None

1.30 If A and B be two disjoint sets and the elements have common properties P_a and P_b respectively then select the true statement

(a) The elements of $A \cup B$ have either property

(b) The elements of $A \cap B$ have both P_a and P_b

(c) The elements of $A \oplus B$ have either property P_a or P_b but not both

(d) All statements

1.31 Which is not countable?

(a) The list of all strings over $A = \{a, b, \mathrm{c}, \ldots, z\}$

(b) The set of square of natural numbers

(c) The set of all floating-point number

(d) The set of all living beings on the earth

1.32 If A is a set which contains one element. If we find the n times successive power set of A i.e. powerset(...powerset(powerset(A))...), then how many elements are in the final power set?

(a) 2^{2n-1} (b) 2^n

(c) 2^{2n+1} (d) None

1.33 Consider the binary relation **(GATE 2004)**

$S = \{(x, y): y = x + 1 \text{ and } x, y \in \{0, 1, 2, \ldots\}\}$

The reflexive transitive closure of S is

(a) $\{(x, y): y > x \text{ and } x, y \in \{0,1, 2, \ldots\}\}$

(b) $\{(x, y): y \geq x \text{ and } x, y \in \{0,1, 2, \ldots\}\}$

(c) $\{(x, y): y < x \text{ and } x, y \in \{0,1, 2, \ldots\}\}$

(d) $\{(x, y): y \leq x \text{ and } x, y \in \{0,1, 2, \ldots\}\}$

1.34 Which one is true?

(a) $\phi \not\in 2^{\phi}$ (b) $\phi \subseteq 2^{\phi}$

(c) $\phi \in \phi$ (d) None

1.35 The power set of the set $\{\phi, \{\phi\}\}$ is

(a) $\{\phi, \{\phi\}, \{\{\phi\}\}, \{\phi, \{\{\phi\}\}\}\}$ (b) $\{\phi, \{\phi\}, \{\phi, \{\{\phi\}\}\}\}$

(c) $\{\phi, \{\phi\}\}$ (d) None

1.36 If $A = \{\phi\}$, then powerset(powerset(A)) is:

(a) $\{\phi, \{\phi\}\}$ (b) $\{\phi, \{\phi\}, \{\{\phi\}\}, \{\phi, \{\phi\}\}\}$

(c) ϕ (d) None

1.37 Which is true for two finite sets A and B?

(a) $|A \cup B| = |A| + |B| - |A \cap B|$ (b) $|A \cup B| = |A \backslash B| + |B \backslash A|$

(c) $|A \cup B| = |A \backslash B| + |B \backslash A| + |A \cap B|$ (d) Both (a) and (c)

1.38 Choose the correct statement for three finite sets X, B, and C

(a) If $X \cup B = X \cup C$, then necessarily $B = C$

(b) If $X - B = B - X$, then conclusion is $X = B$

(c) $X - B = B$, then conclusion is that X and B are multisets

(d) $X - B = B$, then conclusion is that it is not possible for any kind of set

1.39 The set theory is invented by

(a) George Cantor (b) Anna Bohm

(c) Richard Dedekind (d) None

1.40 How many elements are there in the set $\{\phi, \{\phi\}, \{\phi, \{\phi\}\}, \{\phi, \{\{\phi, \{\phi\}, \{\phi\}\}\}\}\}$?

(a) 2 (b) 4

(c) 9 (d) 3

1.41 Let X and Y are sets and let A^c and B^c denote the complements of the sets A and B. the set $(A - B) \cup (B - A) \cup (A \cap B)$ is equal to

(a) $A \cup B$ (b) $A^c \cup B^c$

(c) $A \cap B$ (d) $A^c \cap B^c$ **(GATE 1996)**

1.42 Let A be a finite set of size n. The number of elements in the power set of $A \times A$ is

(a) 2^{2n} (b) 2^{n2}

(c) $(2n)^2$ (d) $(2^2)n$ **(GATE 1993)**

1.43 The number of elements in the power set $P(S)$ of the set $S = \{\{\phi\}, 1, \{2, 3\}\}$ is

(a) 2 (b) 4

(c) 8 (d) None of the above **(GATE 1995)**

1.44 In a room containing 28 people, there are 18 people who speak English, 15 people who speak Hindi, and 22 people who speak Kannada. 9 persons speak both English and Hindi, 11 persons speak both Hind and Kannada, whereas 13 persons speak both Kannada and English. How many people speak all the three languages? **(GATE 1998)**

(a) 6 (b) 8

(c) 9 (d) None

1.45 Which one of the following sets is uncountable set?

(a) The list of all the binary strings over $\{0, 1\}$

(b) $L = \{a^n b^n : n \geq 1\}$

(c) The set of all the human being on the earth

(d) None of the above

1.46 Which one of the following is incorrect for two arbitrary sets X, and Y?

(a) $X \oplus Y = (X - Y) \cup (Y - X) = (X \cup Y) - (X \cap Y)$

(b) $(X \cup Y) \cap (X \cup Y^c) = X$

(c) $(X \cap Y) \subseteq Y$, $(X \cap Y) \subseteq X$, then $(X \cap Y) \subseteq (X \cup Y)$

(d) $X \subseteq Y$ if and only if $X - Y = \phi$

(e) None of the above

1.47 Which one of the following is incorrect?

(a) $\{\phi\} \cap \{\phi, a, \{\phi\}\} = \{\phi\}$
(b) $\{\phi\} \oplus \{\phi, a, \{\phi\}\} = \{a, \{\phi\}\}$
(c) $\phi \oplus \{\phi, a, \{\phi\}\} = \{\phi, a, \{\phi\}\}$
(d) None

1.48 Which one of the following is equal to $2^{\{1, 2\}} \times \{1, 2\}$?

(a) $\{(\{1\}, 1), (\{1\}, 2), (\{2\}, 1), (\{2\}, 2), (\{1, 2\}, 1), (\{1, 2\}, 2)\}$
(b) $\{\phi, (\{1\}, 1), (\{1\}, 2), (\{2\}, 1), (\{2\}, 2), (\{1, 2\}, 1), (\{1, 2\}, 2)\}$
(c) $\{\phi, (\{1\}, 2), (\{2\}, 1), (\{2\}, 2), (\{1, 2\}, 1), (\{1, 2\}, 2)\}$
(d) ϕ

1.49 How many elements are there in the power set $2^{\{\phi, \{\phi\}, \{1, \phi\}\}}$?

(a) 2
(b) 4
(c) 8
(d) 0

1.50 How many ordered pairs are there in representation of nth $(n \geq 3)$ order ordered pairs?

(a) n
(b) $n + 1$
(c) $n - 1$
(d) $n + 2$

1.51 Consider the two multi sets given below

$$M_1 = \{x, y, z, a, b, 1, 2\}, M_2 = \{1, 2, b, c, x\}$$

The union of M_1 and M_2 is

(a) $\{x, y, z, a, b, c, 1, 2\}$
(b) $\{x, y, z, x, a, b, b, c, 1, 1, 2, 2\}$
(c) $\{2x, y, z, a, 2b, c, 21, 22\}$
(d) $\{x, y, z, a, b, c, 1\}$

1.52 Duality of $(U \cap A) \cup (X \cap A) = A$, where U is universal set for the sets A, X, is

(a) $(U \cup A) \cap (X \cup A) \neq A$
(b) $(\phi \cup A) \cap (X \cup A) \neq A$
(c) $(U \cup A) \cap (X \cup A) = A$
(d) $(\phi \cup A) \cap (X \cup A) = A$

1.53 Consider three sets A, X, and Y, when $A \cap Y = A \cap X$?

(a) When $X = Y$
(b) Not necessarily $x = y$
(c) When $X \cap Y = A \cap Y = A \cap X$
(d) Both (b) and (c)

1.54 Let 2^X denotes the power set of the set X, then

(a) $\phi \subseteq 2^X$
(b) $\phi \notin 2^X$
(c) $\phi \not\subset 2^X$
(d) Both (a) and (b)

1.55 Let S be an infinite set and $S_1, S_2, \ldots, S_n$ be sets such that $S_1 \cup S_2 \cup \ldots \cup S_n = S$, then

(a) At least one of the sets S_i is a finite set.
(b) Not more than one of the sets S_i can be finite set.
(c) At least one of the sets S_i is an infinite set.
(d) Not more than one of the sets S_i can be infinite.
(e) None of the above. **(GATE 1993)**

1.56 Let X and B be sets with cardinalities m and n respectively. The number of one-to-one mapping (injections) from X to B, when $m < n$ is

(a) m^n (b) nP_m

(c) mP_n (d) nC_m

(e) mC_n

1.57 Let R be a symmetric and transitive relation on a set A, then **(GATE 1995)**

(a) R is reflexive and hence an equivalence relation

(b) R is reflexive and hence a partial order

(c) R is reflexive and hence not an equivalence relation

(d) None of the above

1.58 Let R be non-empty relation on a collection of sets defined by ARB is and only if $A \cap B = \phi$, then (pick the true statement) **(GATE 1996)**

(a) R is reflexive and transitive

(b) R is symmetric and not transitive

(c) R is an equivalence relation

(d) R is not reflexive and not transitive

1.59 A binary relation is an equivalent relation if and only if

(a) Reflexive (b) Transitive

(c) Symmetric (d) All

1.60 If A and B be two finite sets, then $n(A) + n(B)$ is equal to

(a) $n(A \cup B)$ (b) $n(A \cap B)$

(c) $n(A \cup B) - n(A \cap B)$ (d) $n(A \cup B) + n(A \cap B)$

1.61 A and B are two subsets of an universal set U and $A^c = U - A$, then the set $A - B$ is

(a) $A \cap B^c$ (b) $A \cap B$

(c) $A^c \cap B$ (d) $A^c \cap B^c$

1.62 A and B be two subsets of an universal set U and $A^c = U - A$, then the set $A \cap (A \cup B)^c$ is equal to

(a) B (b) A

(c) ϕ (d) None

1.63 If X, B, C, and D are any four sets, then $(A \times B) \cap (C \times D)$ is equal to

(a) $(X \times C) \cap (B \times D)$ (b) $(X \cap D) \times (B \cap C)$

(c) $(X \cap C) \times (B \cap D)$ (d) $(X \times D) \cap (B \times C)$

1.64 There are 100 students in a class. In the annual examination 20 failed in English, 36 in mathematics, and 40 in Science, 18 failed in two subjects and none failed in all three subjects. 17 failed in English not in Science, and 5 failed in both English and mathematics. The number of students successful in all the three subjects is

(a) 22
(b) 23
(c) 24
(d) 25

1.65 If $A \cup B = A \cap B$, then
(a) $A = B$
(b) $B = \phi$
(c) $A \subset B$
(d) $A = \phi$

1.66 Set $A \cap B$ is: (1) $\subset B$, (2) $\subset A$, (3) $\subset (A \cup B)$, (4) $\subset (\phi \cap A) \cup B$.
Which is correct?
(a) 1, 2, 3
(b) 1, 3, 4
(c) 2, 3, 4
(d) 1, 2, 3, 4

1.67 Which of the following statements are true?
(1) Equivalent sets are equal sets
(2) Equal sets are equivalent sets
(3) {0} is subset of empty set
(4) ϕ is subset of any universal set
(a) 1, 3
(b) 1, 2
(c) 1, 4
(d) 1, 2, 3, 4

1.68 Let set $A = \{a\}$, then the total number of relations on A is
(a) 1
(b) 2
(c) 3
(d) 0

1.69 Consider set $B = \phi$, then the total number of relations on B is
(a) 0
(b) 1
(c) 2
(d) None

1.70 Consider set $A = \{\phi, \{\phi\}\}$, then the total number of relations on A is
(a) 0
(b) 4
(c) 16
(d) None

1.71 If R is a non-empty relation on $A = \{a\}$, then which is true about R?
(a) Reflexive relation
(b) Symmetric relation
(c) Transitive relation
(d) Equivalence relation

1.72 There are two sets A and B are such that $|A| \neq 0$, and $|B| = 0$, then the total number of relations from A to B is
(a) 0
(b) 1
(c) 2
(d) None

1.73 Let R is an equivalence relation on the set $B = \{a, b, c, \ldots, z\}$ and R is represented by matrix M_R, then which is/are true?
(a) $M_R = M^T_R$
(b) $R^{26} \cup R = R$
(c) $M_R \times M_R = M_R$
(d) All

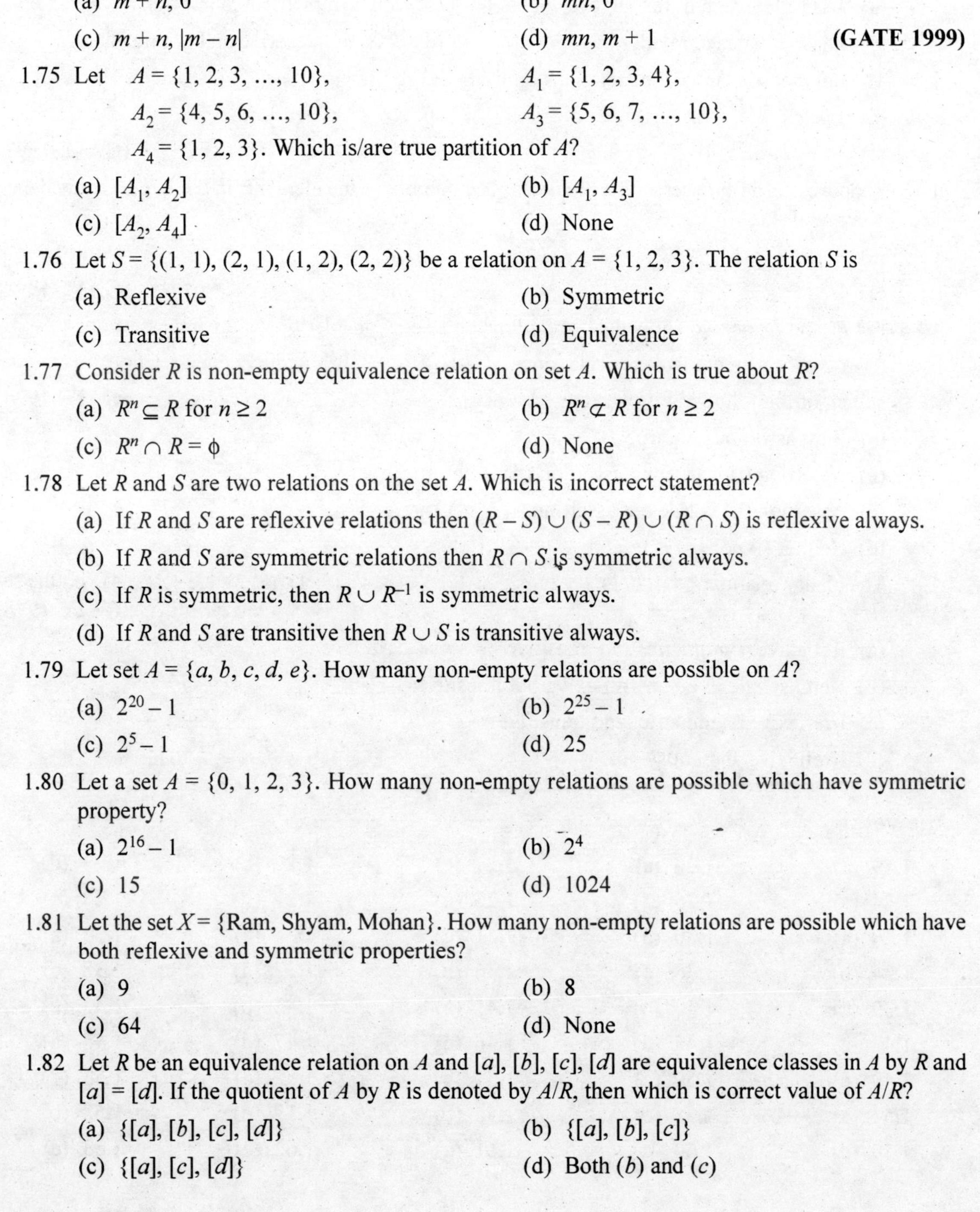

1.74 Consider the join of a relation R with relation S. If R has m tuples and S has n tuples then the maximum and minimum sizes of the join respectively are

(a) $m + n, 0$ (b) $mn, 0$

(c) $m + n, |m - n|$ (d) $mn, m + 1$ **(GATE 1999)**

1.75 Let $A = \{1, 2, 3, \ldots, 10\}$, $A_1 = \{1, 2, 3, 4\}$,

$A_2 = \{4, 5, 6, \ldots, 10\}$, $A_3 = \{5, 6, 7, \ldots, 10\}$,

$A_4 = \{1, 2, 3\}$. Which is/are true partition of A?

(a) $[A_1, A_2]$ (b) $[A_1, A_3]$

(c) $[A_2, A_4]$ (d) None

1.76 Let $S = \{(1, 1), (2, 1), (1, 2), (2, 2)\}$ be a relation on $A = \{1, 2, 3\}$. The relation S is

(a) Reflexive (b) Symmetric

(c) Transitive (d) Equivalence

1.77 Consider R is non-empty equivalence relation on set A. Which is true about R?

(a) $R^n \subseteq R$ for $n \geq 2$ (b) $R^n \not\subset R$ for $n \geq 2$

(c) $R^n \cap R = \phi$ (d) None

1.78 Let R and S are two relations on the set A. Which is incorrect statement?

(a) If R and S are reflexive relations then $(R - S) \cup (S - R) \cup (R \cap S)$ is reflexive always.

(b) If R and S are symmetric relations then $R \cap S$ is symmetric always.

(c) If R is symmetric, then $R \cup R^{-1}$ is symmetric always.

(d) If R and S are transitive then $R \cup S$ is transitive always.

1.79 Let set $A = \{a, b, c, d, e\}$. How many non-empty relations are possible on A?

(a) $2^{20} - 1$ (b) $2^{25} - 1$

(c) $2^5 - 1$ (d) 25

1.80 Let a set $A = \{0, 1, 2, 3\}$. How many non-empty relations are possible which have symmetric property?

(a) $2^{16} - 1$ (b) 2^4

(c) 15 (d) 1024

1.81 Let the set X = {Ram, Shyam, Mohan}. How many non-empty relations are possible which have both reflexive and symmetric properties?

(a) 9 (b) 8

(c) 64 (d) None

1.82 Let R be an equivalence relation on A and $[a]$, $[b]$, $[c]$, $[d]$ are equivalence classes in A by R and $[a] = [d]$. If the quotient of A by R is denoted by A/R, then which is correct value of A/R?

(a) $\{[a], [b], [c], [d]\}$ (b) $\{[a], [b], [c]\}$

(c) $\{[a], [c], [d]\}$ (d) Both (*b*) and (*c*)

1.83 Let R be a non-empty relation on a collection of sets defined by ARB if and only if $A \cap B = \phi$. Then pick the true statement

(a) R is reflexive and transitive
(b) R is symmetric and not transitive
(c) R is equivalence relation
(d) R is not reflexive and not transitive

1.84 The number of equivalence relations on the set {1, 2, 3, 4} is

(a) 15
(b) 16
(c) 24
(d) 4 **(GATE 1997)**

1.85 Suppose A is a finite set with n elements. The number of the elements in the largest equivalence relation of A is

(a) n
(b) n^2
(c) 1
(d) $n + 1$ **(GATE 1998)**

1.86 Let R_1 and R_2 be two equivalence relations on a set. Consider the following assertions

(i) $R_1 \cup R_2$ is an equivalence relation (ii) $R_1 \cap R_2$ is an equivalence relation

Which of the following is correct? **(GATE 1998)**

(a) Both assertions are true
(b) Assertion (i) is true but assertion (ii) is not true
(c) Assertion (ii) is true but assertion (i) is not true
(d) Neither (i) nor (ii) is true

1.87 The binary relation $R = \{(1, 1), (2, 1), (2, 2), (2, 3), (2, 4), (3, 1), (3, 2), (3, 3), (3, 4)\}$ on the set $A = \{1, 2, 3, 4\}$ is **(GATE 1998)**

(a) Reflexive, symmetric, and transitive
(b) Neither reflexive nor irreflexive but transitive
(c) Irreflexive, symmetric, and transitive
(d) Irreflexive and antisymmetric

Answers

1.19 (a)	1.20 (a)	1.21 (c)	1.22 (c)	1.23 (d)
1.24 (c)	1.25 (d)	1.26 (a)	1.27 (b)	1.28 (c)
1.29 (a)	1.30 (d)	1.31 (c)	1.32 (a)	1.33 (a)
1.34 (b)	1.35 (a)	1.36 (b)	1.37 (d)	1.38 (c)
1.39 (a)	1.40 (b)	1.41 (a)	1.42 (b)	1.43 (c)
1.44 (a)	1.45 (d)	1.46 (e)	1.47 (d)	1.48 (a)
1.49 (c)	1.50 (c)	1.51 (b)	1.52 (a)	1.53 (d)
1.54 (a)	1.55 (c)	1.56 (b)	1.57 (d)	1.58 (b)
1.59 (d)	1.60 (d)	1.61 (a)	1.62 (c)	1.63 (c)

1.64 (a)	1.65 (a)	1.66 (d)	1.67 (c)	1.68 (b)
1.69 (b)	1.70 (c)	1.71 (d)	1.72 (b)	1.73 (d)
1.74 (b)	1.75 (b), (c)	1.76 (b), (c)	1.77 (a)	1.78 (d)
1.79 (b)	1.80 (d)	1.81 (b)	1.82 (d)	1.83 (b)
1.84 (a)	1.85 (b)	1.86 (a)	1.87 (b)	

CHAPTER 2

Introduction to Finite Automata

We will discuss about the finite automata and its applications in this chapter. Finite automata are the simplest model of an automatic machine. If we see the history of designing of the automatic machines, the first calculating device was the *abacus* first time used in *China*. *Abacus* was used to perform some arithmetic operations like addition, multiplication etc. on positive integers. This was the first initiation toward the designing of calculating devices. Further, we found several enhancements and presently we have numerous calculating devices.

There are other powerful models like pushdown automaton, linear bounded automaton, and Turing machines which will be discussed in the coming chapters. Today all automatic machines are designed based on some kind of models. One great example of this machine is the computer system and finite automaton (FA) is its abstract model.

2.1 COMPUTER SYSTEM AND FINITE AUTOMATON (FA)

Let us see first what a computer is in brief. A computer is an automatic computing device, which is programmable also. A user of computer can instruct the computer to do whatever he/she wants. In general, a computer has four main parts- input means, output means, finite control, and finite memory as shown in Fig. 2.1.

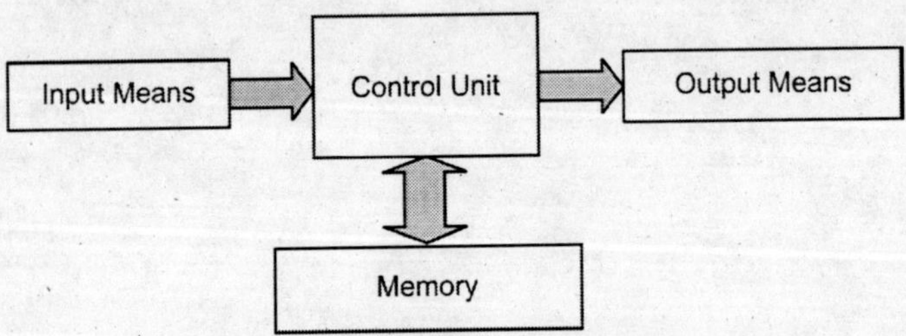

Fig. 2.1: Logical units of a computer

The inputs means are keyboard, floppy, disks, scanner, mouse, etc. The output means are monitor, disks, tape, printers, etc. There are two types of memories used- volatile and non-volatile (permanent).

Random access memories (RAMs) are volatile and Read-only-memory (ROM), disks, tapes are some non-volatile or permanent memories. Computer reads its input from the input means and sends the output to the output means as per the control of the control unit. The control unit is a processor (or central processing unit, CPU), which has finite control. The memory of the computer is expandable but finite and the control unit is programmable.

Computer is a great example of computing device. In the early days of computer, mathematicians had tried to build an abstract model of computing devices. They have given several models like finite automata (FA), pushdown automata (PDA), linear bounded automata (LBA), Turing machine (TM), Post machine, Random Access machine RAM), etc. These models have been mathematically described and used to model computing machines. We will discuss these all models. In this chapter, we will discuss finite automata.

Finite Automaton (FA) is the simplest model. *This is* **abstract model** *of computer system. The meaning of being abstract is that theoretically it is closest to the description of a computer system and it formally describes the behavior of a computer system.* For example, finite automaton model for login process is shown in Fig. 2.2.

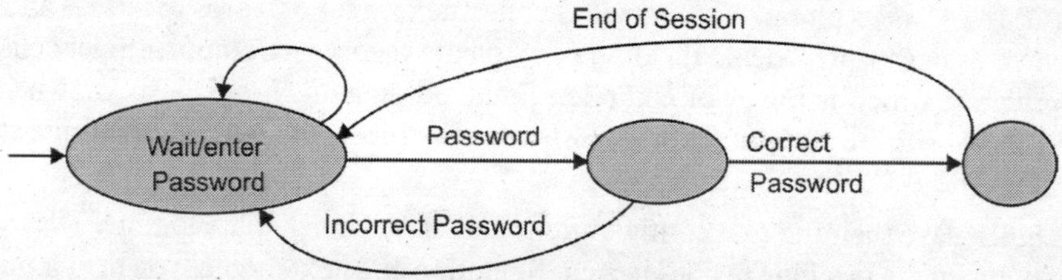

Fig. 2.2: Login process

Finite automaton (FA) is mainly used for modeling the reactive systems. For example, control circuits of computers, computer network communication protocols, lexical analyzers for compilers etc. Many of those systems fall into the class of reactive systems. A **reactive system** is a system that changes its actions, outputs and conditions/status in response to stimuli from within or outside it. A reactive system is an event driven or control driven system continuously having to react to external and/or internal stimuli.

In general, finite automata are useful models to describe dynamic behaviors of reactive systems. When we use a finite automaton to describe a reactive system, we are not bothering about the physical implementation of finite automaton because finite automata are very formal and rigorous to be implemented. But we can simulate the behavior of finite automaton by computer programs.

To model a reactive system with finite automaton, first the states and operations of that system are identified. These states become the states of the finite automaton that models it. Then the transitions between the states triggered by events and conditions (external or internal to the system) are identified and they become arcs in the transition diagram of the finite automaton. In addition to the above, actions that may take place in those states can also be added to the model to make the model clearer. For example, consider the following very simplified version of login process to a computer from the computer point of view. Let us assume that computer accepts a single user at a time as shown in Fig. 2.2.

Initially the computer waits for a user name to be typed in. This is one state of the system. When a name is typed in, it checks whether or not the name is valid. If it is valid, then it asks for and then waits for the password, which is another state. If the user name typed in is not valid, it loops into the initial state. We could make it go to a different state and count the number of login attempts for security purpose. But let us make it simple. When a password is typed in and it is correct, it accepts the user and starts a session. When the session terminates, it goes back to the initial state and waits for another login. Similarly, all the computer interfaces can be modeled using finite automata.

We have several things to be done in designing and implementation of a reactive system. One important and initial thing is: *what is the behavior of a machine*? If we want to describe the behavior, there should be some effective way. An effective way is using some kind of modeling system. Finite automata are basic and simplest model to be used for this purpose.

Automata theory is used to describe the behavior of automatic machines mathematically, in other words, a *computational model or a recognition model can be described by some kind of automata*; it is philosophy of automatic machines mathematically.

In Computer Science field, the word **"AUTOMATON"** is used for *recognizing* or *recognizer* and word "AUTOMATA" is its plural. An automaton understands a set of words or strings and rejects other. It is also known as **acceptor**. One application of automata theory in Computer Science is in designing of *lexical analyzer*, which is a part of compiler. Finite automaton (FA) is also known as **finite state automaton** (FSA) or **finite state machine** (FSM) or **transducer**. We will discuss finite state machines in Chapter 3.

All machines have their internal configurations and these change time to time. The meaning is that at particular moment the machine resides in a configuration and next moment on next input the machine changes its configuration and enters the next configuration. Such types of internal configurations are *known as states*. Let us think about storage of an automatic machine. In practice, it may be in large size but still it is finite. In theory, the storage may be of infinite capacity as we consider the term infinity in mathematics. The number of storage may be more than one. One question arise here that the storage is read-only storage or read-write storage? We consider both the types.

2.2 BASIC MODEL OF FINITE AUTOMATA (FA)

Finite automaton (FA) consists of a finite memory called input tape, a read-only head, and finite control. The input is written on the tape and head reads one symbol at a time on the tape and moves forward into next state and go on until the last symbol of the input string. The movement of head and transition into next state are decided by the finite control. When an input is read, the finite automaton decides the validity (or acceptability) of the input by acceptance (lighting the bulb) or rejection (not lighting the bulb). There is a restart button to reset the finite automaton. It does not write its output on the tape, which is a limitation of this model. Only the input can be written on the tape. The tape contains the input symbols from some set of input symbols, which in known as input alphabet. A basic model of finite automaton is shown in Fig. 2.3.

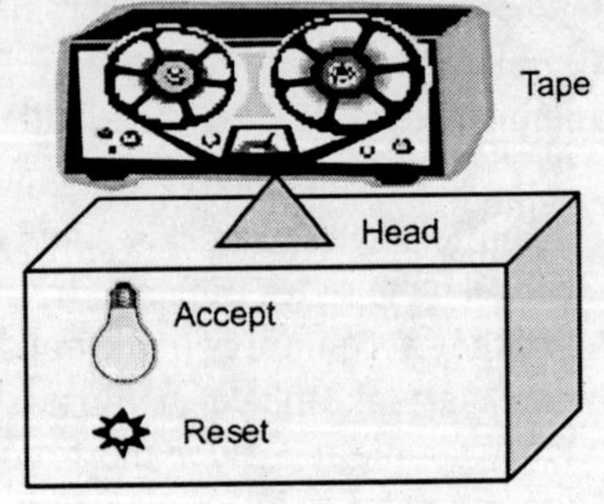

Fig. 2.3: Basic model of finite automata

The input tape is divided into cells and each cell contains one symbol from the input alphabet. The symbol '\$' is used at the leftmost cell and the symbol 'ψ' is used at the rightmost cell to indicate the beginning and end of the input tape. It is similar to read-only file in a computer system, which has both beginning and end. The head reads one symbol on the tape and finite control controls the next configuration. The head can read either form left-to-right or right-to-left one cell at a time. The head cannot write its output and cannot move backward once the input symbol(*s*) has been read. So, finite automaton cannot remember its previous read symbols. This is one of the major limitations of finite automaton (FA), which shows that it cannot be used in such computations where knowledge of previous input is necessary.

Sometimes, FA fall into self transiting state which is not a final state. Such state is called **dead state.** There may be one or group of states that make self transition and create dead feature. This is very much undesirable while considering the application of finite automata.

2.2.1 Deterministic Finite Automaton (DFA)

A deterministic finite automaton *M* is described by 5-tuple (Q, Σ, δ, q_0, F), where

1. Q is finite, nonempty set of states. It contains all the states,
2. Σ is an input alphabet (non-empty and finite),
3. δ is transition function which maps $Q \times \Sigma \rightarrow Q$, i.e. the head reads a symbol in its present state and moves into next state (configuration),
4. $q_0 \in Q$, known as initial state or starting state, and
5. $F \subseteq Q$, known as set of final states.

2.2.2 Nondeterministic Finite Automaton (NDFA or NFA)

A non-deterministic finite automaton *M* is described by 5-tuple (Q, Σ, δ, q_0, F), where

1. Q is finite, nonempty set of states. It contains all the states,
2. Σ is an input alphabet,
3. δ is transition function which maps $Q \times \Sigma \rightarrow 2^Q$ i.e. the head reads a symbol in its present state and moves into **the set of next state**(*s*). 2^Q is power set of Q,
4. $q_0 \in Q$, known as initial state or starting state, and
5. $F \subseteq Q$, known as set of final states.

The difference between a DFA and a NFA is only in transition function. In DFA, transition function maps on *at most one state* and in NFA transition function maps on *at least one state* for a valid input symbol. In general, there are zero or one next state in DFA and zero, one, or more next states in NFA for an input symbol. NFA also uses ε-transition.

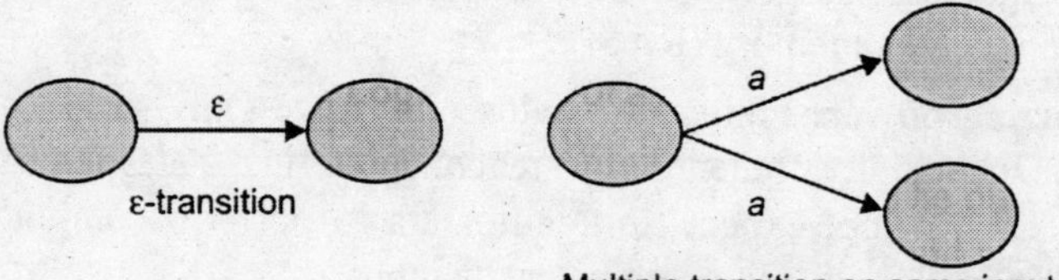

ε-transition

Multiple transition on same input symbol '*a*'

2.2.3 States of the Finite Automaton (FA)

Finite Automata have following possible states:

1. **Initial state or starting state:** The initial or starting state is an unique state; from this state the processing starts.
2. **Final or accepting or terminating states:** These are special states in which if execution of input string is ended then execution is known as successful otherwise unsuccessful. In other words, validity of input is decided after reaching a final state.
3. **Non-final states:** All states except final states are known as non-final states.
4. **Hang-states:** These are the state, which are not included into Q, and after reaching these states, FA sits in dilemma (also known as **trap state**). *These have no outgoing edge*, although there is incoming (reaching) edge. These states are generally denoted by ϕ. **For example**, consider the finite automaton shown in Fig. 2.4.

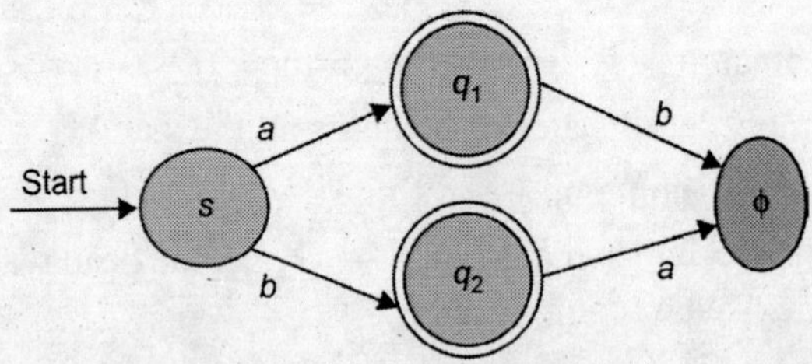

Fig: 2.4: Finite automaton

The transition graph for finite automaton is shown in Fig. 2.4. The initial state is s. Final states are q_1, q_2 and ϕ is the hang state. On input '*a*' in state s, FA reaches to the final state q_1 and if input '*b*' is further apply, FA reaches the hang state. In other words, on for input "*ab*" is invalid input and finite automaton reaches to the hang state. The similar happening is for the input "*ba*". The arch or arrow labeled with some input is used for representing the transition. The initial state is shown with an entering arrow.

2.2.4 Limitations of Finite Automata (FA)

A FA is most restricted and simplest model of automatic machines. *It is an abstract model of a computer system*. FA has following limitations:

1. **Limited memory:** The memory (input tape) is limited. In other words, the storage capacity of finite automaton (FA) is limited.
2. **Sequential read-only memory:** The storage of finite automaton (FA) is read-only and sequential. Finite automaton can read only from the input tape and cannot write or modify the contents on the tape. The reading process of input symbols on the tape is sequential, that is, cell by cell one after another in sequential manner because the input tape is sequential memory; it is not random access like random access memory (RAM).
3. **Limited recognizing power:** Finite Automaton (FA) have Only string (pattern) recognizing power and decide the validity of the input by reaching the final states. FA can recognize regular languages only. One cannot expect finite automata to perform computation like addition, subtraction, multiplication, division, etc. over the input.

4. **Limited movement of reading head:** Generally, the head movement is restricted in one direction, either from **left-to-right** or from **right-to-left**. Although, there are enhanced finite automata that move in both directions, known as two-way finite automata. But this enhancement does not enhance the power of the finite automata. The drawback of this limitation is that finite automata cannot move backward once it read the input on the tape and hence it cannot recall its previous input by moving backward.
5. **No writing:** Finite automata have no writing capability. Finite automaton cannot write its output over the tape. It uses some fixed set of outputs (for example YES, NO) to show its result.
6. **Finite control instructions:** The control instructions for finite automaton (FA) are finite. It is similar to the control of a computer system, which is also finite.
7. **Abstract model:** Finite automaton (FA) is formal description (abstract) of a simple automatic machine and also considered as abstract model of computer system. The application fields for finite automata are limited.

The comparison between a general-purpose computer and finite automata is given in table 2.1.

Table 2.1

S. No.	Index	Finite Automata (FA)	General-purpose Computer
1.	Memory	• Limited • Read-only	• Limited • Read/write
2.	Control	Finite	• Finite • Programmable
3.	Read/write capability	Head can read sequentially, but cannot write	Has both capabilities; reading and writing sequentially, semi-sequentially, and randomly
4.	Use	Used in restricted fields	Used for general purpose
5.	Power	Recognizing of input or recognizing of regular languages	All languages are recognizable and computations

2.2.5 Enhancements of Finite Automata (FA)

We can enhance a FA in following ways:

1. The read-only head is restricted to move in only one direction. Removing this restriction and making the movement in both directions (in one direction at a time), we get a less-restricted model of finite automata and this is known as two-way finite automata.
2. There may be that FA changes its present state to next state without reading the input-symbol from the input tape. In other words, we say that FA changes its state on null string. We will discuss this enhancement in this chapter later on.
3. FA can have two or more input tapes or heads.
4. We can enhance the FA to produce a limited set of outputs. This enhanced FA is known as finite-state machine (FSM) discussed in Chapter 3.

As we have discussed some enhancements of FA above, but these enhancements do not increase the recognizing power of FA. Even after the above enhancements, FA can only recognize the input, which is a regular language.

2.2.6 How to Represent Finite Automata (FA)

We represent a FA by describing all the five-terms (Q, Σ, δ, q_0, F). Transition graph (system) is used for representing FA. We use following notations for representing the FA:

1. The starting state is represented by a state within a circle and an arrow entering into circle as shown below:

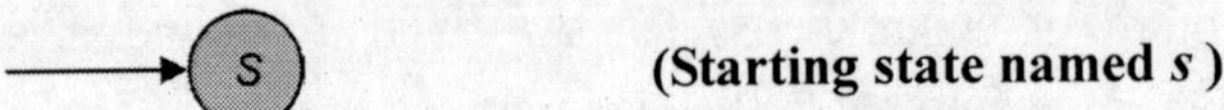

(Starting state named *s*)

Sometimes, initial state is represented by the sign "–" within a circle as below:

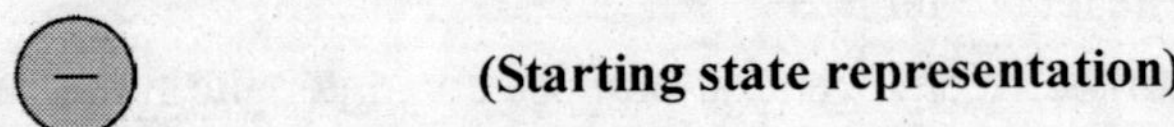

(Starting state representation)

2. Final state is represented by final state within double circles:

(Final state *q*)

Sometimes, final state is represented by the sign "+" within a circle as below:

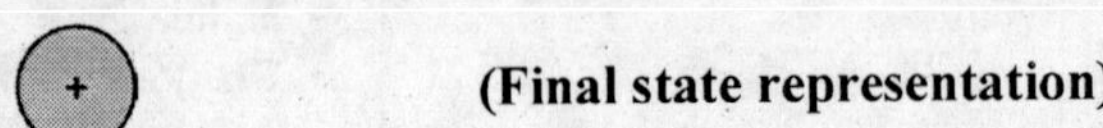

(Final state representation)

3. The hang (or trap) state is represented by the symbol 'ϕ' within a circle as follows:

4. Other states are represented by the state name within a circle.
5. A directed edge or arch with label shows the transition (or move). Suppose p is the present state and q is the next state on input-symbol 'a', then this is represented by:

(Represents $\delta(p, a) = q$)

6. A directed edge with more than one label shows the transitions (or moves). Suppose p is the present state and q is the next state on input-symbols 'a_1' or 'a_2' or ...or 'a_n' then this is represented by

2.2.7 Transition Functions

There are two transitions functions based on the length of the input. If length of the input is zero or one, then direct transition otherwise indirect transition.

- **Direct transition function (δ):** When the input is single symbol, transition function is known as direct transition function. *It is also known as one step transition.* **For example,** $\delta(p, a) = q$ (where p is present state and q is the next state.)
- **Indirect transition function (δ'):** When the input is a string, transition function is known as indirect transition function. *It is also known as one step or more than one steps transition.* **For example,** $\delta'(p, w) = q$, where p is the present state and q is the next state after $|w|$ transitions.

Properties of transition functions

1. If $\delta(p, a) = q$, then $\delta(p, ax) = \delta(q, x)$ and
   if $\delta'(p, x) = q$, then $\delta'(p, xa) = \delta'(q, a)$
2. For two strings x and y; $\delta(p, xy) = \delta[\delta(p, x), y]$,
   and $\delta'(p, xy) = \delta'[\delta'(p, x), y]$

For example,

1. **DFA M** = $(\{p, q, r, s\}, \{a, b\}, \delta', q_0, \{q_f\})$ is shown in Fig. 2.5. The transition graph shown in Fig. 2.5. Where transition function δ is defined as follows:

Transition table		
	Next state/Input	
Present state	a	b
→ p	q	r
q	p	s
r	s	p
(s)	r	q

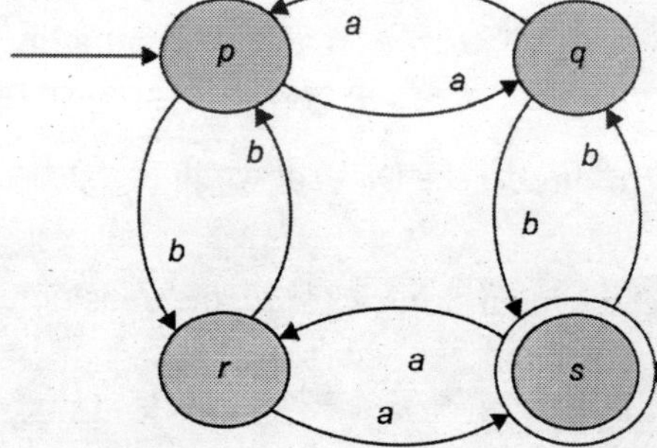

Fig. 2.5: Transition graph of DFA

Now, consider the transition table of DFA shown in Fig. 2.5. Inputs are '*a*' and '*b*' and states are *p*, *q*, *r*, *s*. In the first row of table, inputs are given and other rows represent the transitions. For example, the second row shows that when input '*a*' is given in state *p*, transition is in state *q* and on input '*b*' transition is in state r. Similarly, when input '*a*' is applied in state s, transition is in state r. Transitions from all the states on inputs '*a*' and '*b*' are given in transition table. The initial and final states are indicated by the entering arrow and circle respectively. The order of putting transitions is not fixed. We can put a transition in any row in the transition table.

Transition table		
	Next state/Inputs	
Present state	a	b
→ q_0	$\{q_0, q_1\}$	$\{q_0\}$
q_1	–	$\{q_2\}$
q_2	–	$\{q_f\}$
(q_f)	–	–

2. **NFA M_1** = $(\{q_0, q_1, q_2, q_f\}, \{a, b\}, \delta, q_0, \{q_f\})$ is shown in Fig. 2.6. Transition function δ is defined as follows:

We have following statistics for the NFA:

- Set of states $Q = \{q_0, q_1, q_3, q_f\}$,
- Set of input symbol $\Sigma = \{a, b\}$,
- Set of final state $F = \{q_f\}$, and
- Initial state is q_o

In second row of transition table, when present state is q_0 and input is '*a*', then there are two next states q_0, and q_1. This shows the non-determinism of the NFA. When input '*a*' is applied in states q_1, q_2, and q_f, there is no transition and it has been shown by dash. We can represent the no transition situation by the trap or hang state ϕ.

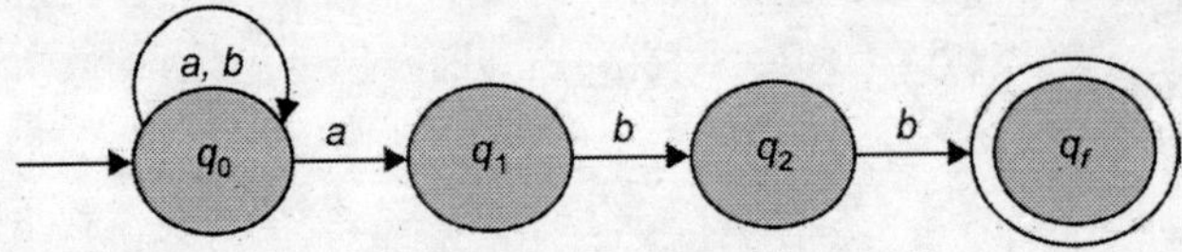

Fig. 2.6: NFA

2.2.8 Acceptability of a String by Deterministic Finite Automata (DFA)

Let DFA M = $(Q, \Sigma, \delta, q_0, F)$ and an input string $w \in \Sigma^*$. The string w is accepted by M if only if $\boldsymbol{\delta(q_0, w) = q_f}$, where $q_f \in F$. In case w is accepted by M, the execution of string w ends in a final state.

Example 1: Consider the DFA shown in Fig. 2.5. Check the acceptability of strings: *ab*, *abb*.

Solution:

1. Let the input string $w_1 = ab$, the transition sequence is as follows:

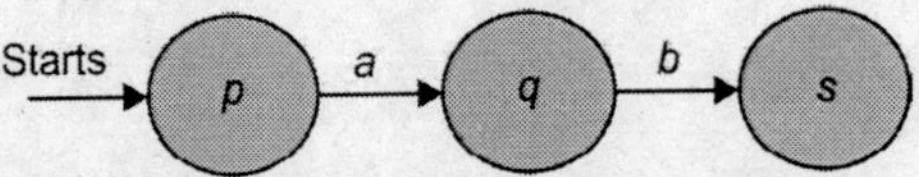

Execution ends in final state *s*, hence string "*ab*" is accepted.

2. Let input string $w_2 = abb$, the transition sequence is as follows:

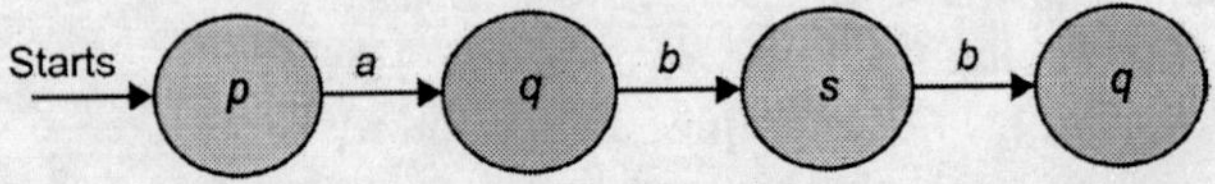

Execution ends in non-final state *q*, hence string "*abb*" is not accepted.

As far as the languages reorganization is concerned, if all the strings of a language are recognized by a DFA then that language is said to be recognizable by the DFA. All regular languages are recognizable by FA and it will be discussed in Chapter 5.

2.2.9 Acceptability of a String by Non-deterministic Finite Automata (NFA)

Let a NFA $M = (Q, \Sigma, \delta, q_0, F)$ and an input string $w \in \Sigma^*$. The string w is accepted by M if only if $\boldsymbol{\delta (q_0, w) = \{q_i : q_i \in F}$, for some $i = 0, 1, \ldots, n\}$. If w is accepted by M, the execution of string w ends in some final state and the execution is known as successful otherwise unsuccessful. All the regular languages are recognized by NFA. We will discuss it in Chapter 5.

Example 2: Consider the NFA shown in Fig. 2.6. Check the acceptability of strings: *abb*, *abbabb*.

Solution:

1. Transition sequence for the input string "*abb*" is as follows:

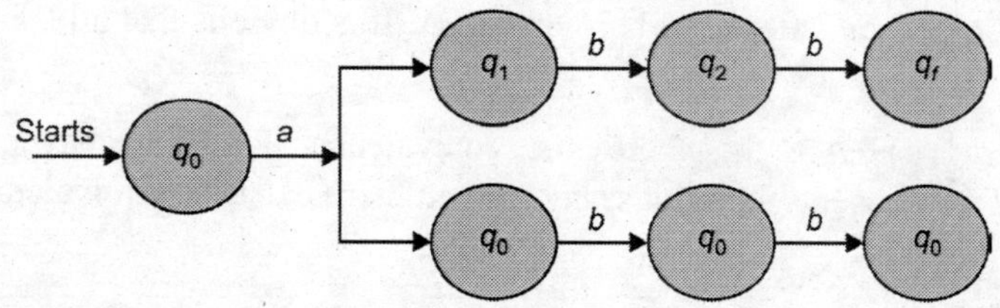

One execution sequence ends in final state q_f, hence string "*abb*" is accepted.

2. Transition sequence for the input string "*abbabb*" is as follows:

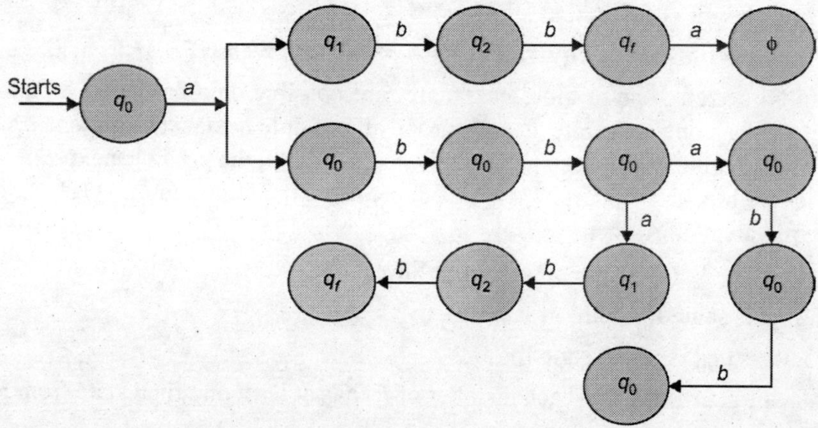

One execution ends in hang state ϕ, second ends in non-final state q_0, and third ends in final state q_f, hence string "*abbabb*" is accepted by third execution.

2.2.10 Comparison of DFA and NFA

Following table shows the summary of the comparison between DFA and NFA.

Table 2.2: Comparison of NFA and DFA

S.No.	Index	NFA	DFA
1.	Power	Same	Same
2.	Transition Function	Maps $Q \times \Sigma \rightarrow 2^Q$, the number of next states is zero or one or more	$Q \times \Sigma \rightarrow Q$, the number of next states is zero or one
3.	Time complexity	The time needed for executing an input string is generally more as compare to DFA due to non-determinism	The time needed for executing an input string is less as compare to NFA
4.	Supremacy	All DFA are NFA, but not all NFA are DFA	All DFA are NFA

2.3 EQUIVALENCE OF NFA AND DFA

As we have discussed in comparison of NFA and DFA that the power of NFA and DFA is equal. It means if NFA M_1 recognizes language L, then some DFA M_2 also recognizes it and vice-versa. In this section, we will discuss about the equivalence of NFA and DFA. It is obvious that all DFA are NFA from NFA definition.

Theorem 2.1: If there is a NFA M, then there exists equivalence DFA M_1 that has equal string recognizing power or if some NFA M accepts an input string w, then there exists an equivalent DFA M_1, which also accepts w.

Proof:

While discussing the proof, we will concentrate on two things:

1. How to construct the equivalent DFA from the given NFA? and
2. The acceptability of NFA and DFA.

Step 1: Construction of the equivalent DFA *M*1 from given NFA *M*:

In NFA, zero, one or more next states are possible on a particular input. When we have more than one next state then we group all possible next states into one such as $[q_1, q_2, q_3]$ and we call it one next state for equivalent DFA. All the possible next states are grouped by square brackets [ ]. Let $M = (Q, \Sigma, \delta, q_0, F)$ be the NFA and $M_1 = (Q_1, \Sigma, \delta_1, s, F_1)$ be the equivalent DFA, then

1. $Q_1 \subseteq 2^Q$ (2^Q is the power set of the set Q.),
2. Σ is same for both,
3. $s = [q_0]$ is initial state for M_1,
4. $F_1 \subseteq 2^Q$ such that each member of F_1 has at least one final state from F.
5. δ_1 is constructed as follows:

Let $w = a \in \Sigma$	
If for given NFA M:	$\delta(q_0, a) = \{q_1, q_2 \ldots q_n\}$, then
For equivalent DFA M_1:	$\delta_1([q_0], a) = [q_1, q_2 \ldots q_n]$
And	
If for NFA M:	$\delta(\{q_1, q_2, \ldots, q_n\}, a) = \{q_1, q_2, \ldots, q_m\}$, then
For equivalent DFA M_1:	$\delta_1([q_1, q_2, \ldots, q_n], a) = [q_1, q_2, \ldots, q_m]$

Step 2: The acceptability of DFA and NFA:

We use the mathematical induction method to prove that $L(M) \subseteq L(M_1)$ and $L(M_1) \subseteq L(M)$ for all input strings $w \in \Sigma^*$.

Case 1

Let $|w| = 0$, it means, $w = \varepsilon$ (Null string)

String w is accepted by NFA M if and only if

$\delta(q_0, \varepsilon) = q_0$, and $q_0 \in F$ (Starting state is final state.)

So, the initial state of DFA will be the final state, hence $w = \varepsilon$ is accepted by DFA also.

Case 2

Let $|w| = 1$ and $w = a \in \Sigma$ is accepted by NFA M, then for NFA M:

$\delta(q_0, a) = \{q_1, q_2, ..., q_n\}$, and set $\{q_1, q_2, ..., q_n\}$ has at least one final state. Then by constructive proof of equivalent DFA M_1, we have

$\delta_1([q_0], a) = [q_1, q_2, ..., q_n]$ and $[q_1, q_2, ..., q_n]$ has at least one final state, so state $[q_1, q_2, ..., q_n]$ is a final state for equivalent DFA M_1. Therefore, the equivalent DFA M_1 also accepts string $w = a$.

Case 3

Suppose $|w| = n$ and $w = a_1 a_2 ... a_n$ is accepted by both M and M_1 and

For NFA M: $\delta'(q_0, a_1 a_2 ... a_n) = \{q_1, q_2, ..., q_m\}$, and

For equivalent DFA M_1: $\delta'_1([q_0], a_1 a_2 ... a_n) = [q_1, q_2, ..., q_m]$

Case 4

Let $|w| = n + 1$ and $w = yb$, where $|y| = n$, $y = a_1 a_2 ... a_n$ and $y, b \in \Sigma^*$ is accepted by NFA M if and only if

For NFA M : $\delta'(q_0, a_1 a_2 ... a_n b) = d(\{q_1, q_2, ..., q_m\}, b) = \{q_1, q_2, ..., q_p\}$,

(Set $\{q_1, q_2, ..., q_p\}$ has at least one final state from the set F.)

By constructive proof of equivalent DFA M_1, we have

$\delta'_1([q_0], a_1 a_2 ... a_n b) = d_1([q_1, q_2, ..., q_m], b) = [q_1, q_2, ..., q_p]$

The state $[q_1, q_2, ..., q_p]$ contains one final state from F and thus it is a final state for equivalent DFA M_1. Therefore, M_1 also accepts the string $w = yb$.

(δ' and δ'_1 are indirect transition functions for NFA M and DFA M_1 respectively)

It has been proved that if NFA M accepts w then DFA M_1 also accepts w for any arbitrary string $w \in \Sigma^*$. Therefore, $L(M_1) \subseteq L(M)$ ...(1)

Similarly, we prove that if equivalent DFA M_1 accepts any string $w \in \Sigma^*$, then NFA also accepts it. Therefore, $M(L) \subseteq L(M_1)$ ...(2)

Hence, from (1) and (2), statement of Theorem 2.1 is true.

Example 3: Consider a NFA shown in Fig. 2.8. Find equivalent DFA.

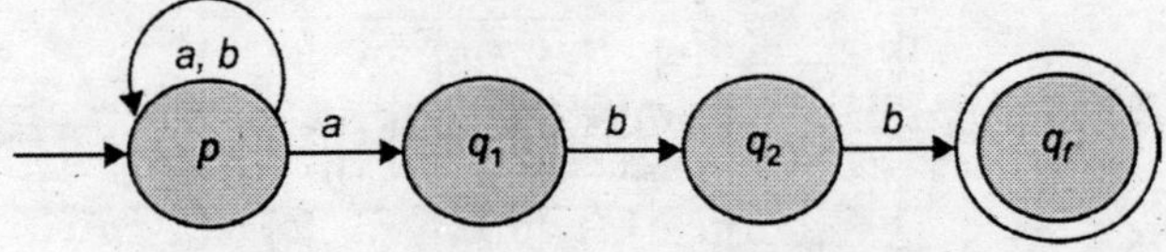

Fig. 2.8: Non-deterministic finite automata

Solution: Let give NFA $M = (Q, \Sigma, \delta, p, F)$ and equivalent DFA $M_1 = (Q_1, \Sigma, \delta_1, [p], F_1)$, where $Q = \{p, q_1, q_2, q_f\}$, $\Sigma = \{a, b\}$, p is starting state, $F = \{q_f\}$, and δ is defined as follows:

Transition table		
	Next state/Inputs	
Present state	*a*	*b*
→ p	$\{p, q_1\}$	$\{p\}$
q_1	–	$\{q_2\}$
q_2	–	$\{q_f\}$
(q_f)	–	–

Transition function δ_1 is defined as follows:

1. Keep the first row of NFA as it is with square bracket as follows:

Transition table		
	Next state/Inputs	
Present state	*a*	*b*
→ $[p]$	$[p, q_1]$	$[p]$

2. Now, we have two states: $[s]$, $[s, q_1]$. We select the one next state that is not a present state till now and define the transition for it. So, we have only one next state $[s, q_1]$, which is not a present state so far.

Transition table		
	Next state/Inputs	
Present state	*a*	*b*
→ $[p]$	$[p, q_1]$	$[p]$
$[p, q_1]$	$[p, q_1]$	$[p, q_2]$

(Since, $\delta_1([s, q_1], a) = [\delta(s, a) \cup \delta(q_1, a)] = [\{s, q_1\} \cup \phi] = [s, q_1]$, and $\delta_1([s, q_1], b) = [\delta(s, b) \cup \delta(q_1, b)] = [\{s\} \cup \{q_2\}] = [s, q_2]$)

3. Now $[s, q_2]$ is the next selected state, because $[s, q_1]$ is defined already.

Transition table		
	Next state/Inputs	
Present state	*a*	*b*
→ $[p]$	$[p, q_1]$	$[p]$
$[p, q_1]$	$[p, q_1]$	$[p, q_2]$
$[p, q_2]$	$[p, q_1]$	$[p, q_f]$

4. Now, the state $[p, q_f]$ is the next selected state.

Transition table		
	Next state/Inputs	
Present state	*a*	*b*
→ $[p]$	$[p, q_1]$	$[p]$
$[p, q_1]$	$[p, q_1]$	$[p, q_2]$
$[p, q_2]$	$[p, q_1]$	$[p, q_f]$
$[p, q_f]$	$[p, q_1]$	$[p]$

5. Now, we have no new choice of the next state to be considered as present state. This is the completion of transition table. We have, $Q_1 = \{[p], [p, q_1], [p, q_2], [p, q_f]\}$ (All selected states in transition), and $F_1 = \{[p, q_f]\}$ (Only one final state)

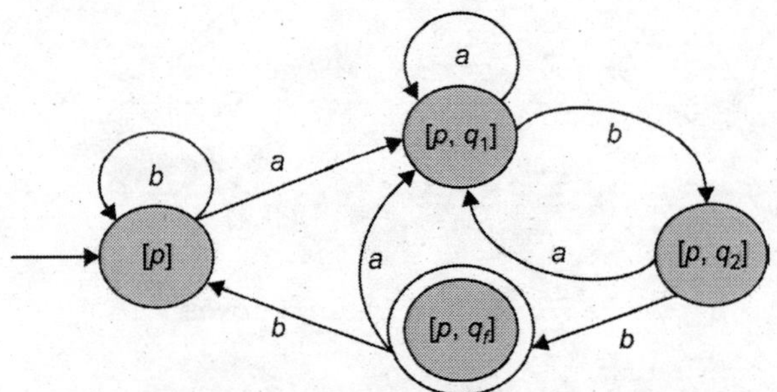

Fig. 2.9 Transition Diagram of equivalent DFA

We see one thing here that not all states of 2^Q are selected for transition. **We have selected those states, which are reachable from the initial state only and other remaining states of 2^Q are neglected.** So, finally *we conclude that only those states of 2^Q are considered in transitions, which are reachable from the initial state.*

2.4 NFA WITH ε-MOVES (NULL MOVES)

A NFA can make transition on ε (null) input string. It means, the transition function of a NFA maps $Q \times \Sigma^* \rightarrow 2^Q$. This enhancement shows that a NFA can make a transition without reading the input string on the input tape. *This enhancement does not increase the power of NFA* as proved in Theorem 2.2.

Example 4: A NFA with ε-moves is shown in Fig. 2.10 show moves on input '*a*'.

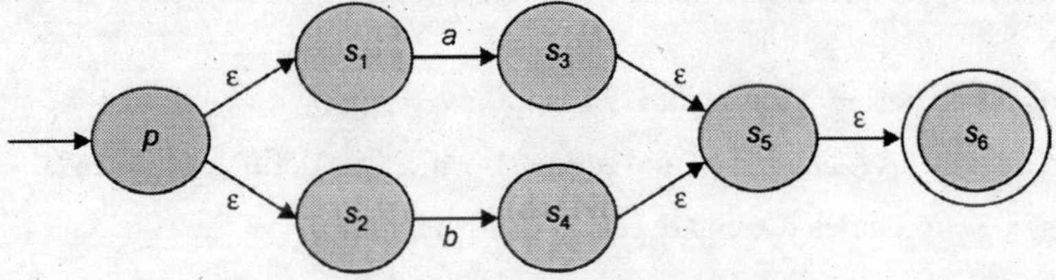

Fig. 2.10: NFA with ε-moves

Solution: NFA moves from the initial state p to either the state s_1 or the state s_2 on ε (null) input and from the state s_3 or the state s_4 to the final state s_6 through the state s_5 on ε-input. If input '*a*' is applied in sate s_1, NFA moves in the state s_3 and if input '*b*' is applied in state s_2 then transition is in state s_4. When input symbol '*a*' is given, following moves are executed:

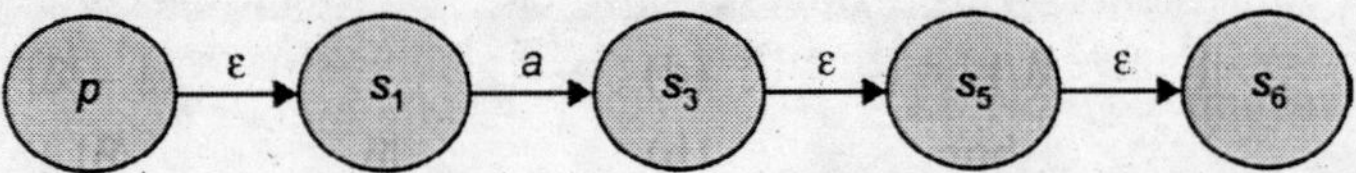

Example 5: Consider the NFA shown in Fig. 2.11.

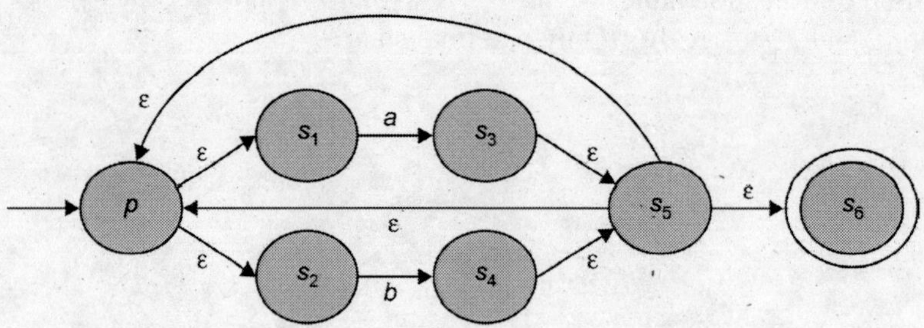

Fig. 2.11: NFA with ε-moves

Consider an input string $w = ab$ and check the acceptability.

Solution: The transition sequence is as follows:

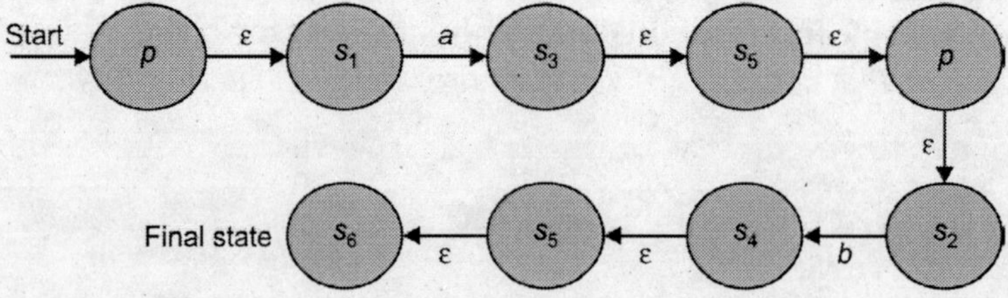

So, the string $w = \varepsilon a \varepsilon\varepsilon\varepsilon b \varepsilon\varepsilon \equiv ab$ is accepted by NFA with with ε-moves

Theorem 2.2: If there is a NFA M with ε-moves, then there exists an equivalence DFA M_1 which has equal string recognizing power or if some NFA M with e-moves accepts an input string w, then there exists an equivalent DFA M_1 which also accepts w.

Proof: We will discuss a construction method for constructing an equivalent DFA for a given NFA with ε-moves.

Method for constructing equivalent DFA from given NFA with ε-moves:

We use two operations **ε-closure( )** and **move( )**, which are defined as follows:

ε-closure(*q*) = Set of states which are reachable from state *q*

on **ε-input** including state *q*

It is equivalent to one state of equivalent DFA.

move(*q*, *a*) = Set of reachable states on input a from state *q*

ε-closure(move(*q*, *a*)) ≡ Next state from state *q* on input *a*

(Note: ε-closure(ϕ) = ϕ)

Starting state of equivalent DFA is **ε-closure(*s*),** where *s* is the starting state of given NFA and final states are those sets, which have at least one final state of given NFA.

Example 6: Consider the NFA with ε-moves shown in Fig. 2.12. Find the equivalent DFA.

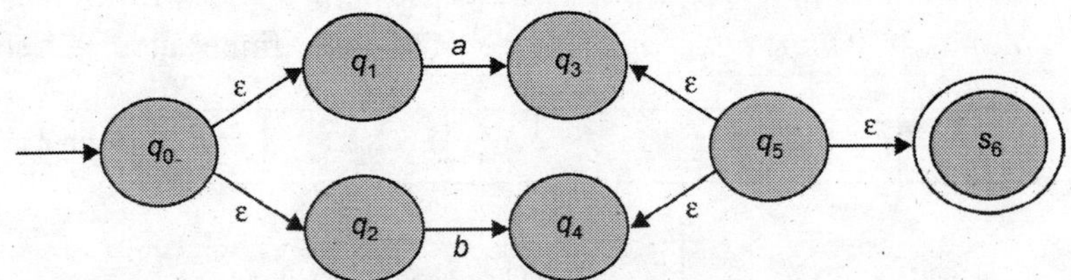

Fig. 2.12: NFA with ε-moves

Solution: Let equivalent DFA $M = (Q, \Sigma, \delta, p, F)$

Now, p = ε-closure (starting state of NFA) = ε-closure (q_0)

= {States reachable from state q_0 on input ε including state q_0}

$= \{q_0, q_1, q_2\}$

$\delta(p, a)$ = ε-closure(move($\{q_0, q_1, q_2\}, a$)) = ε-closure(q_3) = $\{q_3, q_5, s_6\}$ (Next state)

Let $A = \{q_3, q_5, s_6\}$

$\delta(p, b)$ = ε-closure(move($\{q_0, q_1, q_2\}, b$)) = ε-closure(q_4) = $\{q_4, q_5, s_6\}$ (Next state)

Let $B = \{q_4, q_5, s_6\}$

Here, we have two next states A and B, so we have to define the possible transitions from these states and we continue the process until no next states remain to be considered for defining its transition.

$\delta(A, a)$ = ε-closure (move($\{q_3, q_5, s_6\}, a$)) = ε-closure (move(ϕ)) = ϕ

$\delta(A, b)$ = ε-closure (move($\{q_3, q_5, s_6\}, b$)) = ϕ

$\delta(B, a)$ = ε-closure (move($\{q_4, q_5, s_6\}, a$)) = ϕ

$\delta(B, b)$ = ε-closure (move($\{q_4, q_5, s_6\}, b$)) = ϕ

Now, we tabularize the all transitions:

Transition table		
	Next state/Inputs	
Present state	a	b
→ p	A	B
(A)	ϕ	ϕ
(B)	ϕ	ϕ

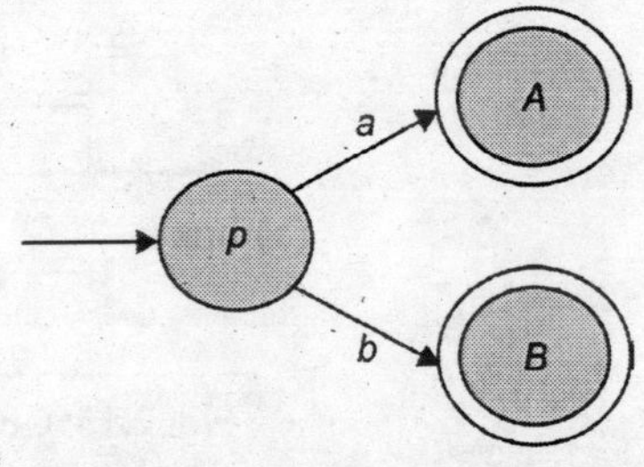

Fig. 2.13: DFA

We have, $Q = \{s, A, B\}$, $\Sigma = \{a, b\}$, and $F = \{A, B\}$

2.5 TWO-WAY FINITE AUTOMATA

As we have discussed in earlier finite automata that the head movement is restricted and it is either from left-to-right or from right-to-left, but not in both direction. We remove this restriction and make the head movement in both directions, but in one direction at a time. This type of enhancement in finite automata results in a new model of finite automata, known as *two-way finite automata. This type of enhancement does not increase the power of finite automata.* A model of two-way finite automaton shown in Fig. 2.14

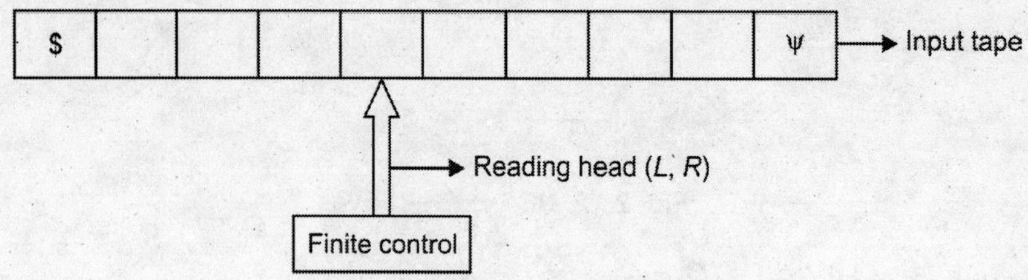

Fig. 2.14: Model of a two-way FA

Let $M = (Q, \Sigma, \delta, s, F)$ be a two-way FA, then terms Q, Σ, s, and F have same meaning as defined for FA and enhanced δ is defined as

$$Q \times \Sigma \rightarrow Q \times \{L, R\} \qquad (L \text{ stands for left and } R \text{ stands for right.})$$

For example, if $\delta(p, a) = (q, R)$, then two-way FA reads symbol 'a' in present state p and moves right one cell and reaches the next state q. In describing the behavior of two-way FA, we have to indicate the following:

1. What is the present state?
2. What is the present input symbol under the reading head?
3. What is the next state?
4. What is the direction of movement?

All these things together give rise to the concept of instantaneous description (ID) of two-way finite automata. Suppose a two-way DFA (2DFA) is following shown in Fig. 2.15.

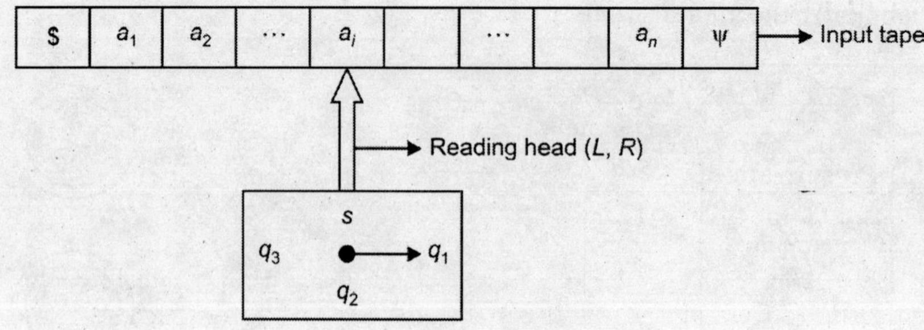

Fig. 2.15: Configuration of a 2DFA

The head is under the input symbol 'a_i' and present state is q_1. Let after reading this symbol, 2DFA moves in state s and head movement is right, then we represent this configuration as shown below:

$$a_1 a_2 \ldots (q_1)\, a_i a_{i+1} \ldots a_n \vdash a_1 a_2 \ldots a_i (s)\, a_{i+1} \ldots a_n$$

This representation of the form $\Sigma^* Q \Sigma^*$ is known as ID (instantaneous description), which indicates read symbols, present state, and remaining symbols of the input string.

Let $ID_1 = a_1a_2 \ldots (q_1)\, a_i a_{i+1} \ldots a_n$ and $ID_2 = a_1\, a_2 \ldots a_i (s)\, a_{i+1} \ldots a_n$

Then, $$ID_1 \vdash ID_2$$

Similarly, if we have $ID_1, ID_2, \ldots, ID_n$ at time instants $t_1, t_2, \ldots, t_n$ then

$$ID_1 \vdash ID_2 \vdash ID_3 \vdash ID_n$$

Acceptability of String by 2DFA

If w is an input string, then w is accepted by 2DFA $M = (Q, \Sigma, \delta, s, F)$ if and only if

$$(s)\, w \vdash w\, (q_f), \text{ for some } q_f F$$

2DFA is an enhanced version of finite automata. The enhancement is the movement in two directions. But power is same as finite automata, i.e. 2DFA recognize the regular language.

Example 7: Consider a 2DFA M given as follows:

Transition table		
	Next state/Inputs	
Present state	*a*	*b*
→ *s*	(*s*, *R*)	(q_1, *R*)
(q_1)	(q_1, *R*)	(q_2, *L*)
(q_2)	(*s*, *R*)	(q_2, *L*)

Check the acceptability of string "101001".

Solution: Initial configuration is $(s)\ 101001 \equiv ID_1$

$(s)101001$	$\vdash 1(q_1)01001$	(Using δ (s, 1) = (q_1, *R*))
	$\vdash 10(q_1)1001$	(Using δ (q_1, 0) = (q_1, *R*))
	$\vdash 1(q_2)01001$	(Using δ (q_1, 1) = (q_2, *L*))
	$\vdash 10(s)1001$	(Using δ (q_2, 0) = (s, *R*))
	$\vdash 101(q_1)001$	(Using δ (s, 1) = (q_1, *R*))
	$\vdash 1010(q_1)01$	(Using δ (q_1, 0) = (q_1, *R*))
	$\vdash 10100(q_1)1$	(Using δ (q_1, 0) = (q_1, *R*))
	$\vdash 1010(q_2)01$	(Using δ (q_1, 1) = (q_2, *L*))
	$\vdash 10100(s)1$	(Using (q_2, 0) = (*s*, *R*))
	$\vdash 101001(q_1)$	(using δ (*s*, 1) = (q_1, *R*))

Since, q_1 is a final state, so the string 101001 is accepted by 2DFA.

2.6 APPLICATIONS OF FINITE AUTOMATA (FA)

We have many applications based on finite automata. Some are given below:

1. **Lexical analyzers:** The main use of finite automaton in Computer Science filed is in compiler design. Lexical analysis is a part of compiler and it is designed using finite automaton, which is known as Lexical Analyzer. Lexical analyzer is used to recognize the validity of input program, whether the input program is grammatically constructed or not. Each programming languages has their own syntactic structure (grammar). For example, consider a statement in 'C' language

   printf("Applications of FA");

   In above statement "printf" is a valid string (a keyword in 'C' language). A FA is used to recognize this string as follows:

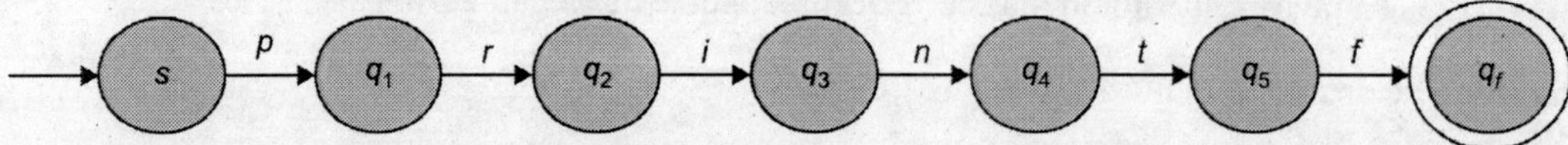

2. **Text editors:** Text editors can be constructed using finite automaton. Smart text editors are implemented today to help in writing the text. One example of such application is in Microsoft Word.
3. **Spell checkers:** Spelling checkers are designed based on finite automata. In general-purpose computer system, there is a word dictionary and finite automata can recognize the correctness of a word and give the appropriate suggestion to the users using data from the dictionary.
4. **Sequential circuits design:** Finite automata are used in sequential circuits design, discussed in Chapter 3 "Finite State Machines". The behavior of synchronous sequential circuits is described by the transition diagram or transition table which is a form of representation of finite automaton. The memory elements used in sequential circuits are served as states in transition diagram.

2.7 SOLVED EXAMPLES

Example 2.1: Let a DFA $M = (Q, \Sigma, \delta, s, F)$ is shown in Fig. 2.16.

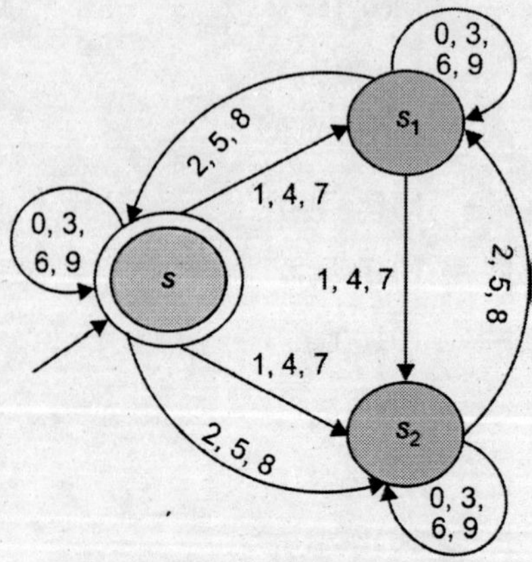

Fig. 2.16: Deterministic finite automata

Check that string 33150 is recognized by above DFA or not?

Solution: For string 33150 the transition sequence is as follows:

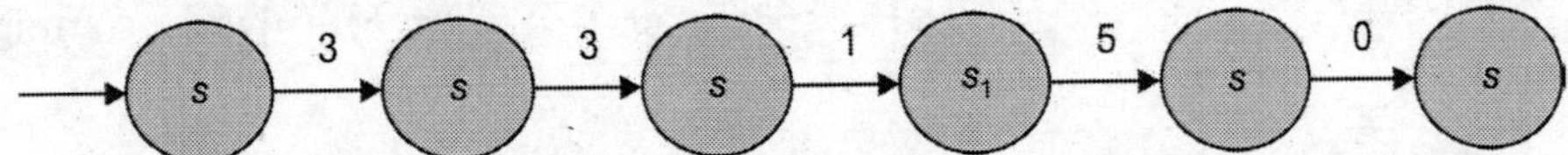

Since, transition ends in final state s, so string 33150 is recognized.

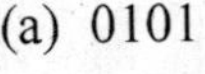

Example 2.2: Consider the finite automaton shown in Fig. 2.17 and check the acceptability of following strings:

(a) 0101 (b) 0111

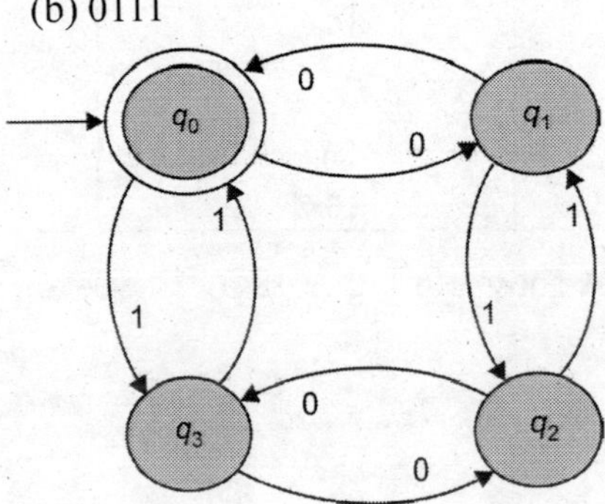

Fig. 2.17: Finite automaton

Solution:

(a) The transition sequence for input string 0101 is as follows:

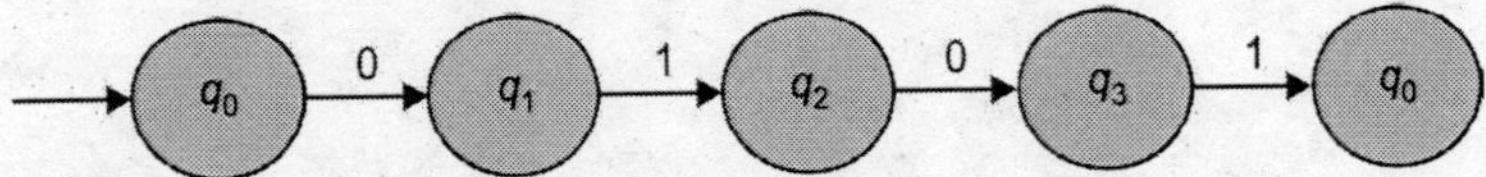

Execution ends in final state q_0, hence string 0101 is accepted.

(b) The transition sequence for input string 0111 is as follows:

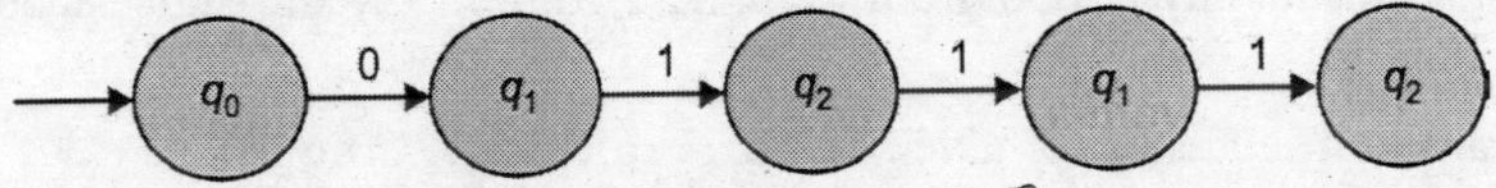

Execution ends in non-final state q_2, hence string 0111 is not accepted.

Example 2.3: Construct equivalent DFA for NFA $M = (\{p, q, r, s\}, \{a, b\}, \delta, p, \{q, s\})$, where δ is given below:

Transition table		
	Next state/Inputs	
Present state	***a***	***b***
p	$\{q, s\}$	$\{q\}$
q	$\{r\}$	$\{q, r\}$
r	$\{s\}$	$\{q, r\}$
s	–	$\{p\}$

Solution: Let equivalent DFA be M_1, and M_1=(Q, Σ, δ, [p], F).

Q = {[p], [q], [r], [s], [q, r], [r, s], [q, s], [p, q, r], [q, r, s]}, Σ = {a, b}, [p] is the starting state, and F = {[q], [s], [q, r], [r, s], [q, s], [p, q, r], [q, r, s].

	a	*b*
→ [p]	[q, s]	[q]
[q]	[r]	[q, r]
[q, s]	[r]	[p, q, r]
[r]	[s]	[q, r]
[q, r]	[r, s]	[q, r]
[p, q, r]	[q, r, s]	[q, r]
[s]	ϕ	[p]
[r, s]	[s]	[p, q, r]
[q, r, s]	[r, s]	[p, q, r]

Example 2.4: Consider the NFA shown in Fig. 2.18(a). Check the acceptability of following string: scanf("%d", &num);

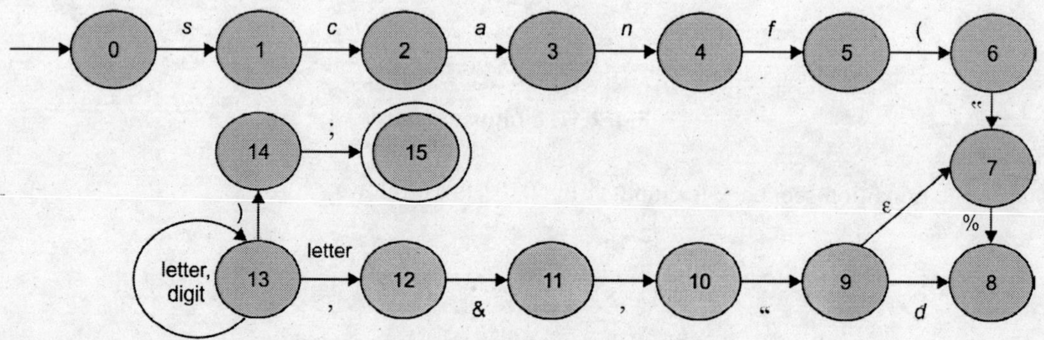

Fig. 2.18(a): NFA

(**Note**: Letter stands for any symbol from {a, b, …, z, A, B, …, Z} and digit stands for any digit from {0, 1, 2, …9})

Solution: The transition sequence for given string: **scanf("%d", &num);**

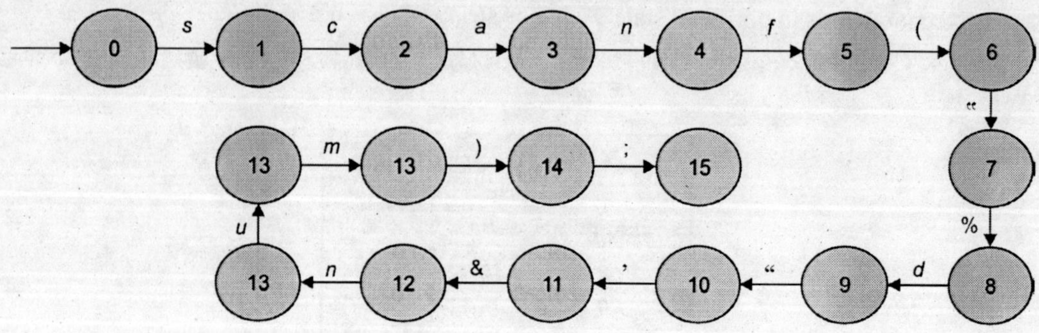

Fig. 2.18(b): Transition sequence

Since, execution of given string ends in final state 15, so the string is recognized as a valid string.

Example 2.5: Consider the NFA with ε-moves given in Fig. 2.19. Construct an equivalent DFA.

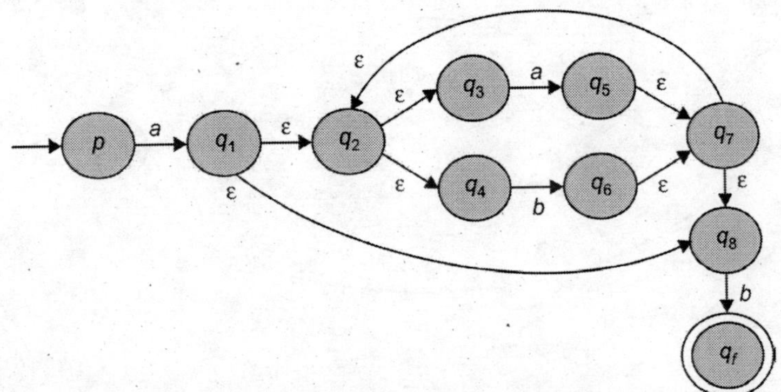

Fig. 2.19: NFA with ε-moves

Solution: Let $M = (Q, \Sigma, \delta, s, F)$ be the equivalent DFA.

Removing the ε-moves from the given NFA:

$s =$ ε-closure (starting state of NFA)= ε-closure $(p) = \{p\}$

$\delta(s, a) =$ ε-closure (move($\{p\}, a$)) = ε-closure $(q_1) = \{q_1, q_2, q_3, q_4, q_8\}$

Let $A = \{q_1, q_2, q_3, q_4, q_8\}$

$\delta(s, b) =$ ε-closure (move($\{p\}, b$)) = ε-closure $(\phi) = \phi$

$\delta(A, a) =$ ε-closure (move($\{q_1, q_2, \mathbf{q_3}, q_4, q_8\}, a$)) = ε-closure$(q_5) = \{q_5, q_7, q_8, q_2, q_3, q_4\}$

Let $B = \{q_5, q_7, q_8, q_2, q_3, q_4\}$

$\varepsilon(A, b) =$ ε-closure (move($\{q_1, q_2, q_3, \mathbf{q_4}, \mathbf{q_8}\}, b$)) = ε-closure$(q_6, q_f)$

$= \{q_6, q_f, q_7, q_8, q_2, q_3, q_4\}$

Let $C = \{q_6, q_f, q_7, q_8, q_2, q_3, q_4\}$

$\delta(B, a) =$ ε-closure (move($\{q_5, q_7, q_8, q_2, \mathbf{q_3}, q_4\}, a$)) = ε-closure$(q_5)$

$= \{q_5, q_7, q_8, q_2, q_3, q_4) = B$

$\delta(B, b) =$ ε-closure (move($\{q_5, q_7, \mathbf{q_8}, q_2, q_3, \mathbf{q_4}\}, b$)) = ε-closure$(q_6, q_f)$

$= \{q_6, q_f, q_7, q_8, q_2, q_3, q_4\} = C$

$\delta(C, a) =$ ε-closure {move($\{q_6, q_f, q_7, q_8, q_2, \mathbf{q_3}, q_4\}$), a) = ε-closure(q_5)

$= \{q_5, q_7, q_8, q_2, q_3, q_4) = B$

$\delta(C, b) =$ ε-closure {move($\{q_6, q_f, q_7, \mathbf{q_8}, q_2, q_3, \mathbf{q_4}\}, b$))

$=$ ε-closure $(q_6, q_f) = \{q_6, q_f, q_7, q_8, q_2, q_3, q_4\} = C$

Collecting all the transitions into table:

Transition table		
	Next state/Inputs	
Present state	**a**	**b**
→ s	A	B
A	B	C
B	B	C
(C)	B	C

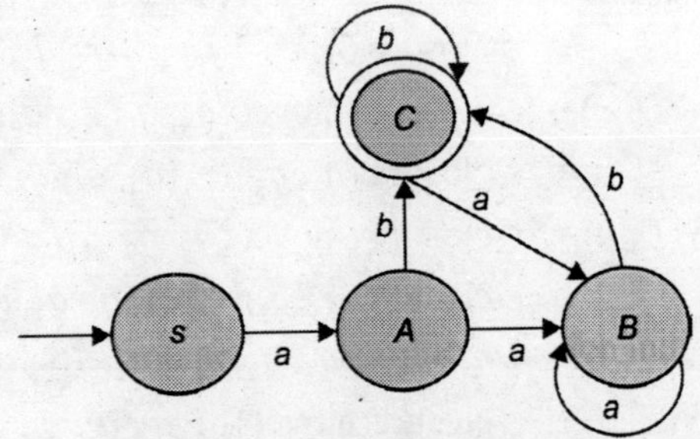

Fig. 2.20: Equivalent DFA

Example 2.6: Consider the NFA shown in Fig. 2.21. Construct equivalent DFA.

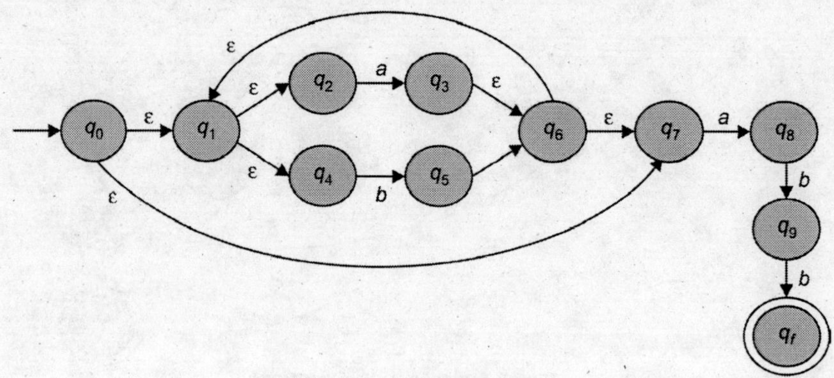

Fig. 2.21: NFA with ε-moves

Solution: Let equivalent DFA $M = (Q, \Sigma, \delta, A, F)$, $\Sigma = \{a, b\}$

$A =$ ε-closure (starting state of NFA) = ε-closure$(q_0) = \{q_0, q_1, q_2, q_4, q_7\}$

$= \{q_0, q_1, q_2, q_4, q_7\}$

$\delta(A, a) =$ ε-closure(move($\{q_0, q_1, q_2, q_4, q_7\}, a$)) = ε-closure$(q_3, q_8\}$

$= \{q_3, q_8, q_6, q_7, q_1, q_2, q_4\}$

Let $\boldsymbol{B} = \{q_3, q_8, q_6, q_7, q_1, q_2, q_4\}$

$\delta(A, b) =$ ε-closure (move($\{q_0, q_1, q_2, q_4, q_7\}, b$))

$=$ ε-closure$(q_5) = \{q_5, q_6, q_7, q_1, q_2, q_4\}$

Let $\mathbf{C} = \{q_5, q_6, q_7, q_1, q_2, q_4\}$

$\delta(B, a) =$ ε-closure (move($\{q_3, q_8, q_6, q_7, q_1, q_2, q_4\}, a$))

$=$ ε-closure $(q_3, q_8\} = \{q_3, q_8, q_6, q_7, q_1, q_2, q_4\} = B$

$\delta(B, b) =$ ε-closure (move($\{q_3, q_8, q_6, q_7, q_1, q_2, q_4\}, b$))

$=$ ε-closure $(q_5, q_9) = \{q_5, q_9, q_6, q_7, q_1, q_2, q_4\}$

Let $\boldsymbol{D} = \{q_5, q_9, q_6, q_7, q_1, q_2, q_4\}$

$\delta(C, a) =$ ε-closure (move($\{q_5, q_6, q_7, q_1, q_2, q_4\}, a$))

$=$ ε-closure $(q_3, q_8\} = \{q_3, q_8, q_6, q_7, q_1, q_2, q_4\} = B$

$\delta(C, b) =$ ε-closure (move($\{q_5, q_6, q_7, q_1, q_2, q_4\}, b$))

$=$ ε-closure $(q_5) = \{q_5, q_6, q_7, q_1, q_2, q_4\} = C$

$\delta(D, a) =$ ε-closure (move($\{q_5, q_9, q_1, q_2, q_4, q_6, q_7\}, a$)

$=$ ε-closure $(q_3, q_8\} = \{q_3, q_8, q_6, q_7, q_1, q_2, q_4\} = B$

$\delta(D, b) =$ ε-closure (move($\{q_5, q_9, q_1, q_2, q_4, q_6, q_7\}, b$)

$=$ ε-closure $(q_5, q_f) = \{q_5, q_f, q_1, q_2, q_4, q_6, q_7\}$

Let $\boldsymbol{E} = \{q_5, q_f, q_1, q_2, q_4, q_6, q_7\}$

$\delta(E, a) =$ ε-closure(move($\{q_5, q_f, q_1, q_2, q_4, q_6, q_7\}, a$))

$=$ ε-closure $(q_3, q_8\} = \{q_3, q_8, q_6, q_7, q_1, q_2, q_4\} = B$

$\delta(E, b) =$ ε-closure (move($\{q_5, q_f, q_1, q_2, q_4, q_6, q_7\}$, b))

$=$ ε-closure $(q_5) = \{q_5, q_6, q_7, q_1, q_2, q_4\} = C$

$Q = \{A, B, C, D, E\}$, $F = \{E\}$

Transition diagram

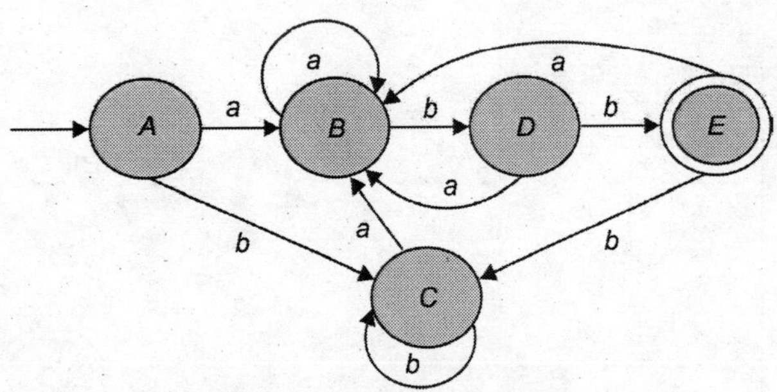

Fig. 2.22: Equivalent DFA

Example 2.7: A NFA for $L = \{ab \cup aba\}^*$ is shown in Fig. 2.23. Construct an equivalent DFA.

(**Note:** *e* stands for empty or null input.)

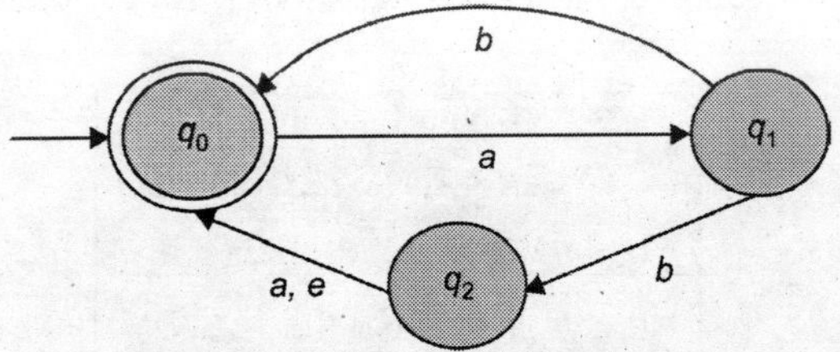

Fig. 2.23: Non-deterministic finite automata

Solution: Let equivalent DFA $M = (Q, \Sigma, \delta, s, F)$

Transition table for given NFA:

Transition table			
	Next state		
Present state	*a*	*b*	*e*
→ q_0	$\{q_1\}$	–	–
q_1	–	$\{q_0, q_2\}$	–
q_2	$\{q_0\}$	–	$\{q_0\}$

Here, ε stands for null input, so we have to use ε-closure( ) and move( ) operations to remove the null transitions to get the equivalent DFA.

s $=$ ε-closure$(q_0) = \{q_0\}$

$\delta(s, a) =$ ε-closure(move($\{q_0\}$, a)) $=$ ε-closure $(q_1) = \{q_1\}$

Let $A = \{q_1\}$

$\delta(s, b) =$ ε-closure (move($\{q_0\}$, b)) $=$ ε-closure$(\phi) = \phi$

$\delta(A, \text{a}) =$ ε-closure (move($\{q_1\}$, a)) $=$ ε-closure$(\phi) = \phi$

$\delta(A, b) =$ ε-closure (move($\{q_1\}$, b)) $=$ ε-closure$(q_0, q_2) = \{q_0, q_2\}$

Let $B = \{q_0, q_2\}$

$\delta(B, a) =$ e-closure (move($\{q_0, q_2\}$, a)) $=$ ε-closure$(q_0, q_1) = \{q_0, q_1\}$

Let $C = \{q_0, q_1\}$

$\delta(B, b) =$ ε-closure (move($\{q_0, q_2\}, b$)) = ε-closure(ϕ) = ϕ

$\delta(C, a) =$ ε-closure (move($\{q_0, q_1\}, a$)) = ε-closure(q_1) = $\{q_1\} = A$

$\delta(C, b) =$ ε-closure (move($\{q_0, q_1\}, b$)) = ε-closure(q_0, q_2) = $\{q_0, q_2\} = B$

Transition table		
	Next state/Inputs	
Present state	*a*	*b*
→ *s*	*A*	ϕ
A	ϕ	*B*
(*B*)	C	ϕ
(*C*)	*A*	*B*

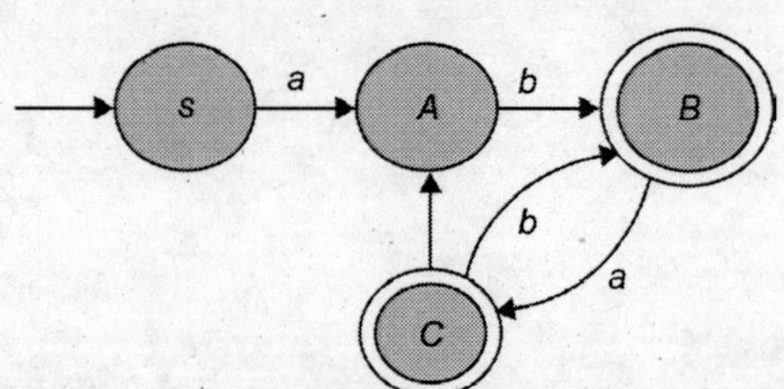

Fig. 2.24: Equivalent DFA

Where $Q = \{s, A, B, C\}$, $\Sigma = \{a, b\}$, $F = \{B, C\}$ and *s* is the starting state.

Example 2.8: Find a DFA equivalent to NFA $M = (\{q_0, q_1, q_2\}, \{a, b\}, \delta, q_0, \{q_2\})$, where δ is defined as follows:

Transition table		
	Next state/Inputs	
Present state	*a*	*b*
→ q_0	$\{q_0, q_1\}$	$\{q_2\}$
q_1	$\{q_0\}$	$\{q_1\}$
(q_2)	–	$\{q_0, q_1\}$

Solution: Let $M' = (Q, \Sigma, \delta, [q_0], F)$ be the equivalent DFA, where $\Sigma = \{a, b\}$, and $[q_0]$ is the initial state. Constructing the transition table:

Transition table		
	Next state/Inputs	
Present state	*a*	*b*
→ $[q_0]$	$[q_0, q_1]$	$[q_2]$
$[q_2]$	ϕ	$[q_0, q_1]$
$[q_0, q_1]$	$[q_0, q_1]$	$[q_1, q_2]$
($[q_1, q_2]$)	$[q_0]$	$[q_0, q_1]$

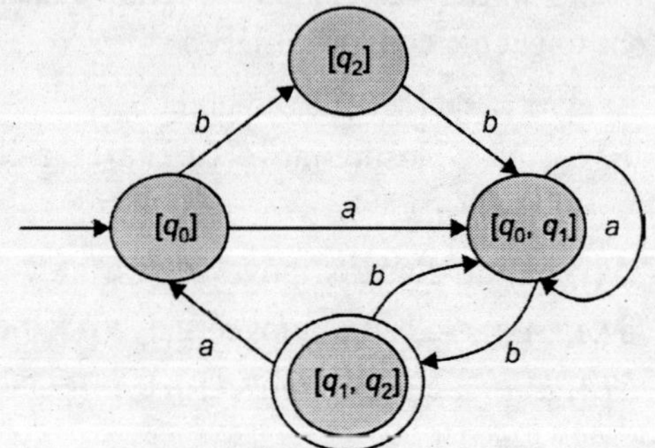

Fig. 2.25: Equivalent DFA

$Q = \{[q_0], [q_2], [q_0, q_1], [q_1, q_2]\}$, and $F = \{[q_1, q_2]\}$

Example 2.9: Construct equivalent DFA for NFA, which is defined below:

Transition table			
	Next state		
Present state	*a*	*b*	*c*
→ q_0	$[q_1, q_4]$	$[q_4]$	$[q_2, q_3]$
q_1	–	$[q_4]$	–
q_2	–	–	$[q_2, q_3]$
(q_3)	$[q_0]$	$[q_4]$	–
$[q_4]$	–	–	–

Solution: Let equivalent DFA $M = (Q, \Sigma, \delta, [q_0], F)$

Construction of equivalent transition table:

Transition table			
	Next state		
Present state	*a*	*b*	*c*
→ $[q_0]$	$[q_1, q_4]$	$[q_4]$	$[q_2, q_3]$
$[q_4]$	ϕ	ϕ	ϕ
$[q_1, q_4]$	ϕ	$[q_4]$	ϕ
$[q_2, q_3]$	ϕ	$[q_4]$	$[q_2, q_3]$

Where, $Q = \{[q_0], [q_4], [q_1, q_4], [q_2, q_3]\}$, $\Sigma = \{a, b, c\}$, $\boldsymbol{F} = \{[q_2, q_3]\}$ and δ is defined in above table.

Example 2.10: A NFA which accepts set of strings over $\{0, 1\}$ such that some two zero's are separated by a string over $\{0, 1\}$ whose length is $4n$ ($n \geq 0$) is shown in Fig. 2.26. Construct equivalent DFA.

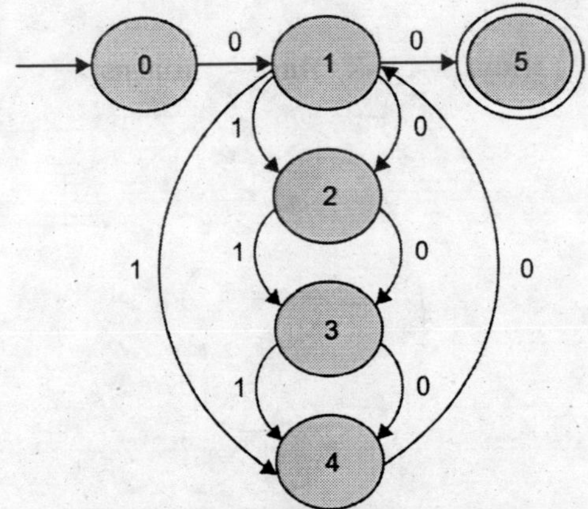

Fig. 2.26: NFA

Solution: Let equivalent DFA $M = (Q, \Sigma, \delta, [0], F)$.

Constructing transition table for given NFA:

Transition table		
	Next state	
Present state	0	1
→ 0	{1}	–
1	{2, 5}	{2}
2	{3}	{3}
3	{4}	{4}
4	{1}	{1}
(5)	–	–

Constructing transition table for equivalent DFA:

Transition table		
	Next state	
Present state	0	1
→ [0]	[1]	ϕ
[1]	[2, 5]	[2]
[2]	[3]	[3]
[3]	[4]	[4]
[4]	[1]	[1]
([2, 5])	[3]	[3]

Where, $Q = \{[0], [1], [2], [3], [4], [2, 5]\}$, $\Sigma = \{0, 1\}$, [0] is starting state, $F = \{[2, 5]\}$, and transition function is defined above.

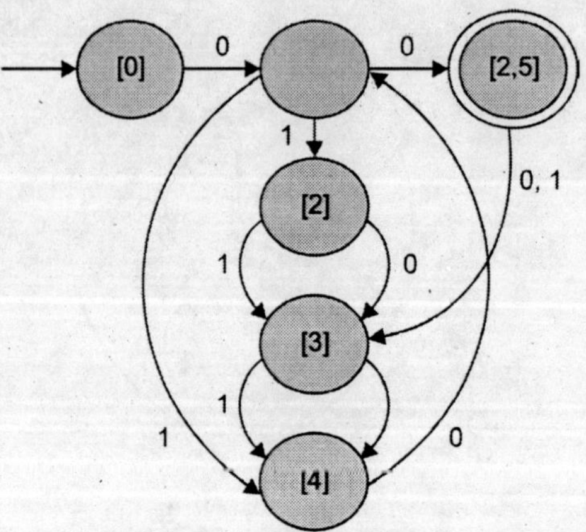

Fig. 2.27: Equivalent DFA

Example 2.11: Consider the following deterministic finite automaton *M*.

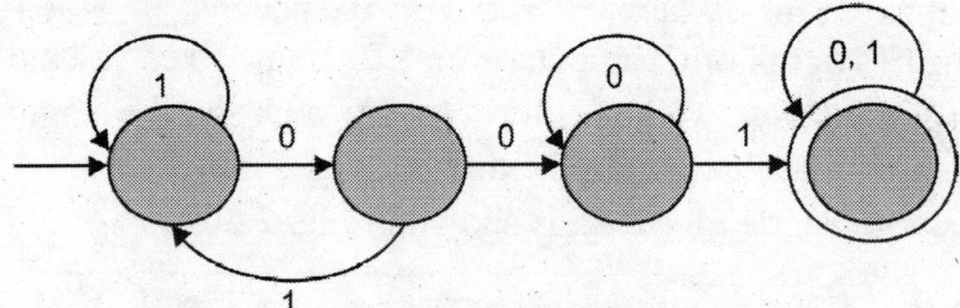

Fig. 2.28: DFA

Let *S* denotes the set of seven bit binary strings in which the first, the fourth, and the last bits are 1. What is the number of strings in *S* that are accepted by *M*? **(GATE 2003)**

Solution: Let *w* be a string in given set of strings *S*. So, w has following format according to the given conditions:

1st bit	2nd bit	3rd bit	4th bit	5th bit	6th bit	7th bit
1	*X*	*X*	1	*X*	*X*	1

(Here, *X* = 0 or 1)

If 2nd bit is 0 and 3rd bit is 0 or 1 and 5th & 6th bits are 0 or 1 then five strings in *S* are accepted by given DFA which are as follows:

1	0	0	1	0	0	1
1	0	0	1	0	1	1
1	0	0	1	1	0	1
1	0	0	1	1	1	1
1	0	1	1	0	0	1

So, the given DFA accepts five strings.

Example 2.12: Consider a DFA with two tapes. It reads two symbols at a time; one symbol from the first tape and second symbol from the second tape as a pair (*a*, *b*), where symbol '*a*' is on first tape and symbol '*b*' is on second tape. Transition function depending upon the string set refers to the first tape or second tape. For example, $w_1 \times w_2$ where $w_1, w_2 \in (a+b)^*$ such that $|w_2| = 2 \times |w_1|$, transition diagram is as follows:

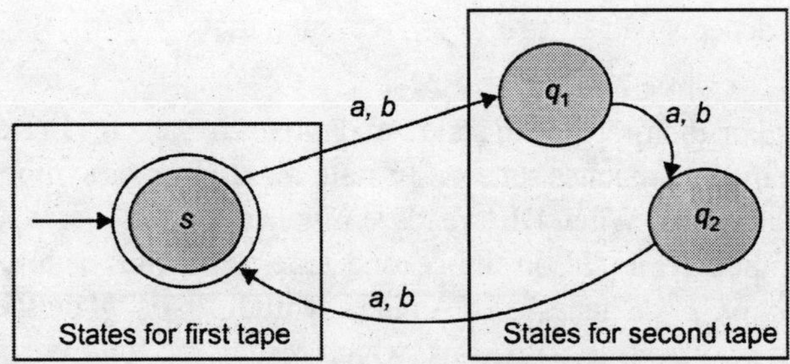

Fig. 2.29: Two-tape DFA

Draw state diagrams for two-tape DFA that accepts each of the following:

(a) All pairs of strings (w_1, w_2), where $w_1, w_2 \in (a+b)^*$ such that $|w_2| = |w_1|$ and $w_1(i) = a$ if and only if $w_2(i) = b$ (the ith symbol of w) and vice-versa for some fixed value of n and $i = 1, 2,.., n$.

(b) All pairs of strings (w_1, w_2), where $w_1, w_2 \in \{a, b\}^*$ such that the length of string w_2 is twice the number of a's in w_1 plus three times the number of b's in w_1.

Solution: (a) The transition diagram for DFA is shown in Fig. 2.30.

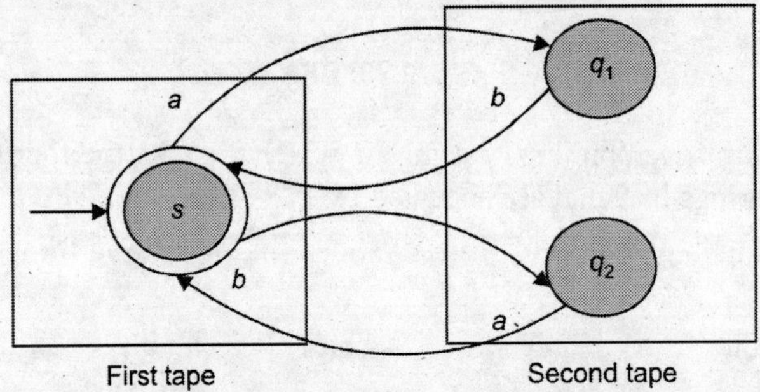

Fig. 2.30: Two-tape DFA

DFA reads symbol 'a' on the first tape in state **s** and moves to state $\boldsymbol{q_1}$ and after reading symbol 'b' on the second tape it reaches the final state $\boldsymbol{s}$. Similarly, when DFA reads symbol 'b' on the first tape, it moves to state $\boldsymbol{q_2}$ and after reading symbol 'a' on the second tape, it reaches final state $\boldsymbol{s}$.

(b) The transition diagram for DFA is shown in Fig. 2.31.

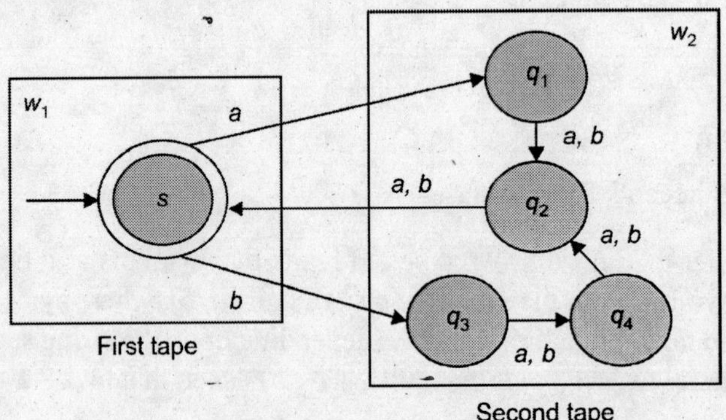

Fig. 2.31: Two-tape DFA

It is given that DFA accepts pair of string (w_1, w_2) such that

$$|w_2| = 2\,|w_2|_a + 3\,|w_2|_b$$

DFA reads symbol 'a' on the first tape in state $\boldsymbol{s}$ and moves to state $\boldsymbol{q_1}$. In state q_1, DFA reads symbol 'a' or 'b' on the second tape and reaches state q_2. In state q_2, DFA reads symbol 'a' or 'b' on the second tape and reaches the final state $\boldsymbol{s}$. When DFA reads symbol 'b' on the first tape in state s, reaches state $\boldsymbol{q_3}$ and after reading symbol 'a' or 'b' on the second tape, it reaches state $\boldsymbol{q_4}$ and then reaches state $\boldsymbol{q_2}$ while reads symbol 'a' or 'b'. Whenever DFA reads symbol 'a' or 'b' on the first tape, it follows the path $\boldsymbol{s} \to q_1 \to q_2 \to \boldsymbol{s}$ or $\boldsymbol{s} \to q_3 \to q_4 \to q_2 \to \boldsymbol{s}$, which results the following:

$$|w_2| = 2\,|w_2|_a + 3\,|w_2|_b$$

Example 2.13: Design a Finite Automaton that converts the input binary numbers into hexadecimal numbers. Assume that input binary digits are multiple of four. The conversion is based on following data:

Binary No.	Hexadecimal No.	Binary No.	Hexadecimal No.
0000	0	1000	8
0001	1	1001	9
0010	2	1010	A
0011	3	1011	B
0100	4	1100	C
0101	5	1101	D
0110	6	1110	E
0111	7	1111	F

For example,

Input	Output
00101000	28
00111100	2B

Solution: Finite Automaton (FA) is shown in Fig. 2.32. We assume that FA reads four symbols at a time on the input tape and produces single digit in hexadecimal number. It is just like pattern matching. FA looks four bits pattern in binary on the tape and outputs single digit in hexadecimal and then reading head is moved forward on the tape. When end of the input is reached then FA stops matching in final state.

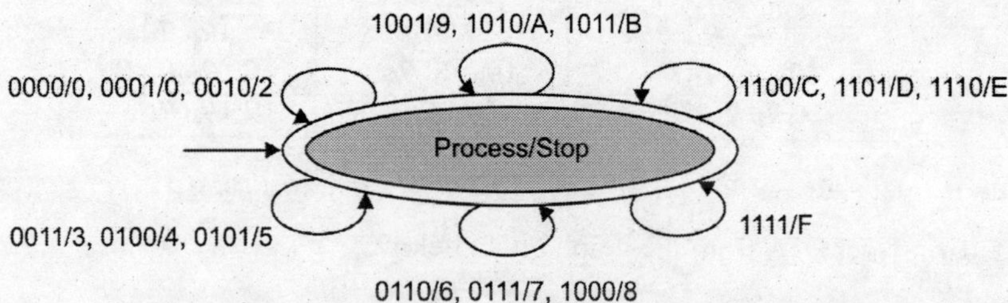

Fig. 2.32: Finite automata for hexadecimal numbers

Example 2.14: Construct a DFA equivalent to the following NDFA:

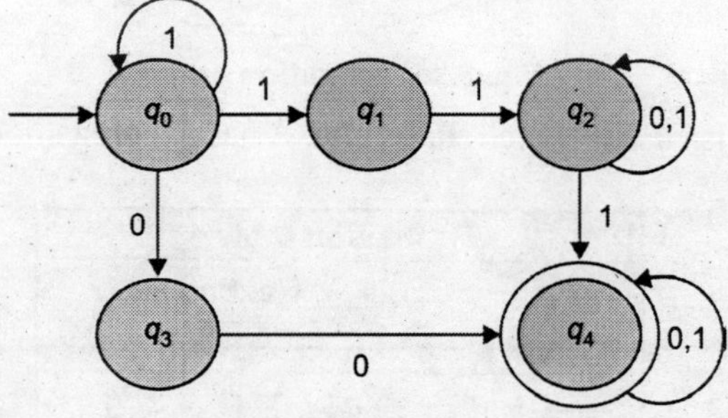

Fig. 2.33: NDFA

Solution: NDFA $M = (Q, \Sigma, \delta, q_0, \{q_4\})$ and transition table is below:

Transition table		
	Next state	
Present state	0	1
$\rightarrow q_0$	$\{q_3\}$	$\{q_1, q_0\}$
q_1	–	$\{q_2\}$
q_2	$\{q_2\}$	$\{q_2, q_4\}$
q_3	$\{q_4\}$	–
q_4 (final)	$\{q_4\}$	$\{q_4\}$

The transition table for the equivalent DFA = $(Q', \{0,1\}, \delta', [q_0], F)$ and transiton function is below:

Transition table		
	Next state	
Present state	0	1
$\rightarrow [q_0]$	$[q_3]$	$[q_1, q_0]$
$[q_3]$	$[q_4]$	ϕ
$[q_4]$	$[q_4]$	$[q_4]$
$[q_1, q_0]$	$[q_3]$	$[q_2, q_1, q_0]$
$[q_2, q_1, q_0]$	$[q_2, q_3]$	$[q_4, q_2, q_1, q_0]$
$[q_2, q_3]$	$[q_2, q_4]$	$[q_2, q_4]$
$[q_2, q_4]$	$[q_2, q_4]$	$[q_2, q_4]$
$[q_4, q_2, q_1, q_0]$	$[q_2, q_3, q_4]$	$[q_4, q_2, q_1, q_0]$
$[q_2, q_3, q_4]$	$[q_2, q_4]$	$[q_2, q_4]$

Where, set of final states $F = \{[q_4], [q_2, q_4], [q_4, q_2, q_1, q_0], [q_2, q_3, q_4]\}$

Example 2.15: Construct DFA from the graph given below:

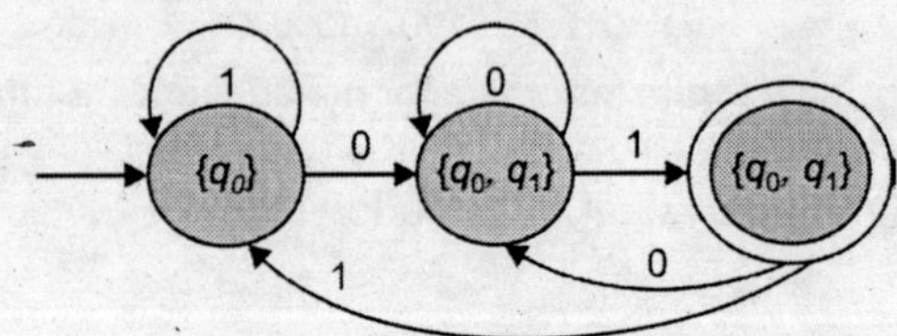

Fig. 2.34: Transition graph

Solution: The given graph is NFA in which state $\{q_0, q_1\}$ has two transitions for input '1'. The transition table is below:

Transition table		
	Next state	
Present state	*a*	*b*
$\rightarrow \{q_0\}$	$\{q_0, q_1\}$	$\{q_0\}$
$\{q_0, q_1)$	$\{q_0, q_1\}$	$\{q_0, q_1\}, \{q_0\}$

Let $A = \{q_0\}$ and $B = \{q_0, q_1\}$. The equivalent transition for DFA is below:

Transition table		
	Next state	
Present state	0	1
→ [A]	[B]	[A]
[B]	[B]	[A, B]
[A, B]	[B]	[A, B]

The transition graph is shown in Fig. 3.35.

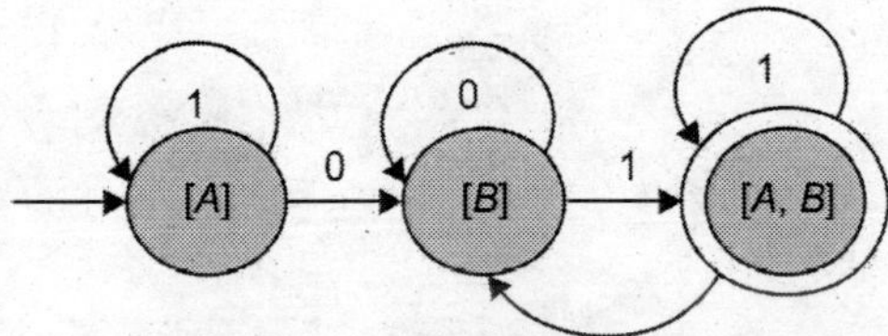

Fig. 2.35: Equivalent DFA

TEST YOUR SKILLS

Supplementary Problems

2.1 Consider the transition diagram shown in Fig. 2.5 and assume p and r as final states and check the acceptability of following strings:

(a) *ababa* (b) *aabb*

(c) *baaa*

2.2 Consider the NFA and the equivalent DFA shown in solved problem (3) and check the acceptability of following strings:

(a) *abbba* (b) *abbb*

(c) *abab*

Also, compare the number of iterations required in transition sequence for all strings.

2.3 Consider the NFA shown in Fig. 2.18(a) and check the acceptability of following strings: scanf ("%d%d",&const, &num);

2.4 Construct equivalent DFA for NFA $M = (\{p, q, r, s\}, \{a, b\}, \delta, p, \{s\})$, where δ is given below:

Transition table		
	Next state	
Present state	*a*	*b*
→ *p*	{*p*, *q*}	{*p*}
q	{*r*}	{*r*}
r	{*s*}	–
s	{*s*}	{*s*}

2.5 Construct equivalent DFA for the following NFA.

(a)

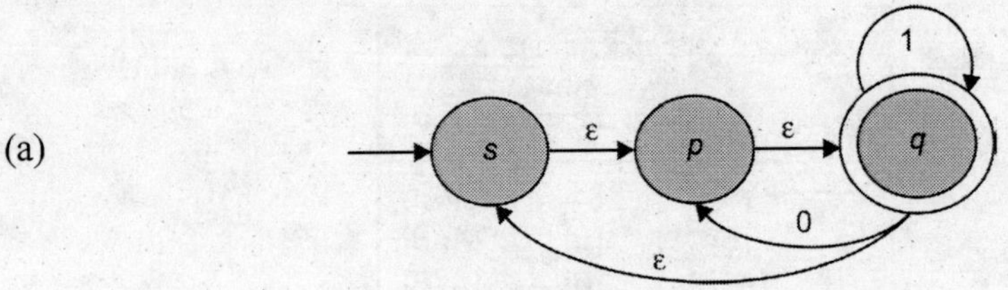

Fig. 2.36: NFA with ε-moves

(b)

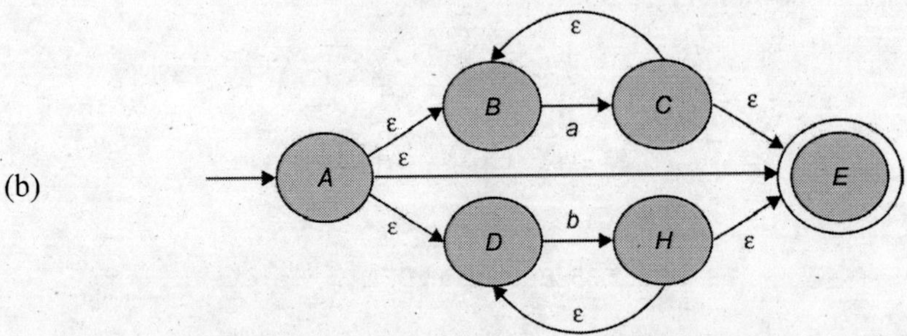

Fig. 2.37: NFA with ε-moves

2.6 **Construct equivalent DFA for NFA** $M = (\{p, q, r, s\}, \{a, b\}, \delta, p, \{p, s\})$, where δ is given below:

Transition table		
	Next state	
Present state	***a***	***b***
→ p	$\{p, q\}$	$\{p\}$
q	$\{r\}$	$\{r\}$
r	$\{s\}$	–
s	$\{s\}$	$\{s\}$

2.7 What is finite automaton? How it is a abstract model of a computer system?

2.8 Describe the deterministic and non-deterministic finite automaton. How deterministic finite automaton differs from non-deterministic finite automaton?

2.9 What is acceptability of a string by finite automaton? Discuss the acceptability of the DFA and NFa.

2.10 What are the limitations of finite automaton? How a finite automaton can be enhanced? Is there any change in power of finite automaton after enhancement?

2.11 Discuss the two-way finite automata. How two-way finite automata differ from DFA or NFA?

2.12 Consider a 2DFA given following:

Check the acceptability of the following strings:

ababa, aaabb, bbbab, babaab

Transition table		
	Next state	
Present state	***a***	***b***
→ p	(p, R)	(q_1, R)
q_1	(q_1, R)	(q_2, L)
q_2	(p, R)	(q_2, L)

2.13 In what respect a general-purpose computer is better than a finite automaton (FA)?

2.14 Consider a DFA as a decoder. It uses two tapes, first tape to read the input and second tape to output the result. The possible symbols in the input and their corresponding output values are given below:

Symbol	Decoded value
A	000
B	001
C	010
D	011
a	100
b	101
c	110
d	111

Draw the transition diagram for DFA.

2.15 Design a DFA that converts the integer number in decimal into binary coded decimal (BCD). Assume that only positive integer numbers are there to be converted and each decimal digit is converted into four bits (binary digits). For example,

Decimal number	BCD
0	0000
1	0001
2	0010
3	0011
...	
11	0001 0001
12	0001 0010
...	
456	0100 0101 0110

2.16 Design finite automaton that converts the input integer numbers into octal numbers.

2.17 Construct a DFA equivalent to the following NFA given in Fig. 2.38.

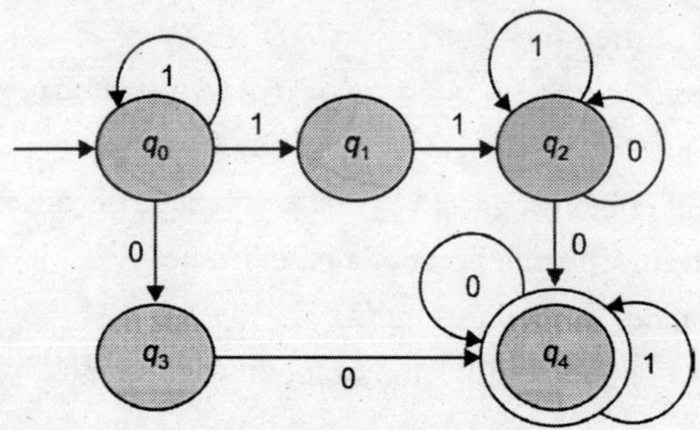

Fig. 2.38

2.18 Consider the following transition diagram shown in Fig. 2.50.Test whether the string 110101 is accepted by the finite automaton represented by above transition diagram. Show the entire sequence of states traversed.

Multiple Choice Questions

2.19 Finite automata have

(a) Finite tape
(b) Finite control
(c) Read-only head
(d) All (a), (b), and (c)

2.20 Compare to NFA, DFA has

(a) Less power
(b) More power
(c) Deterministic transition
(d) None

2.21 Finite automata are used for

(a) Finding a pattern
(b) Sequential circuit design
(c) Lexical design
(d) All (a), (b), and (c)

2.22 A finite automaton is a/an

(a) Acceptor
(b) Computing device
(c) Both (a) and (b)
(d) None

2.23 The class of languages accepted by finite automaton is

(a) Context-free
(b) Regular
(c) Non-regular
(d) None

2.24 Finite automata can be stored in Computer System as

(a) Table
(b) Two-dimensional array
(c) Graph
(d) All (a), (b), and (c)

2.25 Which of the followings is true?

(a) All NFA are DFA
(b) All DFA are NFA
(c) Both (a) and (b)
(d) NFA and DFA have different power

2.26 Finite automata can be used for

(a) String recognition
(b) Arithmetic operations
(c) Both (a) and (b)
(d) None

2.27 The palindromes cannot be recognized by finite automata because

(a) FA cannot determine the mid point of a palindrome
(b) FA cannot remember its previous input
(c) FA head has read-only capability and cannot move in both directions
(d) (a) and (b)

2.28 Suppose DFA M_1 takes T_1 unit time and NFA M_2 takes T_2 unit time in recognizing a regular expression r, then

(a) $T_1 \leq T_2$
(b) $T_1 = T_2$
(c) $T_2 \leq T_1$
(d) $T_1 < T_2$

2.29 Suppose $SPACE_1(r)$ and $SPACE_2(r)$ spaces are required to recognize the regular expression r using DFA M_1 and NFA M_2 respectively, then

(a) $SPACE_1(r) < SPACE_2(r)$
(b) $SPACE_1(r) \geq SPACE_2(r)$
(c) $SPACE_1(r) \leq SPACE_2(r)$
(d) $SPACE_1(r) > SPACE_2(r)$

2.30 Two-way finite automata have

(a) Two tapes
(b) Two heads
(c) Bi-directional head movement
(d) All the above

2.31 The behavior of NFA can be simulated by DFA

(a) Always
(b) Sometime
(c) Never
(d) Depend on NFA

2.32 NFA can be enhanced to move forward without reading the input tape is

(a) True
(b) False
(c) Enhancement is invalid
(d) Depends upon NFA

2.33 Finite automata with null string accepting capability are known as

(a) NFA
(b) DFA
(c) NFA with ε-moves
(d) All (a), (b), and (c)

2.34 Finite automata with atmost one transition capability are known as

(a) NFA
(b) DFA
(c) 2DFA
(d) NFA with ε-moves

2.35 Finite automata with atleast one transition capability are known as

(a) NFA
(b) DFA
(c) 2DFA
(d) NFA with ε-moves

2.36 Finite automata having more than one input tape have

(a) More power than one tape FA
(b) Equal power as one tape FA
(c) More storage than one tape FA
(d) (b) and (c)

2.37 Finite automata having more than one reading head have

(a) More power than one tape FA
(b) Equal power as one tape FA
(c) More storage than one tape FA
(d) (b) and (c)

2.38 Limitation of finite automata is

(a) Writing
(b) Finite memory
(c) Sequential memory (Input tape)
(d) All (a), (b), and (c)

2.39 What is true about finite automata?

(a) Acceptor
(b) Recognizer
(c) Pattern Matcher
(d) All

2.40 Which is false about DFA and NFA?

(a) In DFA, there is only one transition for one input symbol.

(b) In NFA, there is atleast one transition for one input symbol.

(c) All DFA are NFA, but not all NFA are DFA. So, NFA have more power as compare to DFA.

(d) The acceptability of NFA is not equal to the its equivalent DFA.

2.41 Finite automata can

(a) Check the validity of input string

(b) Manipulate the input and calculate the output

(c) Both (a) and (b)

(d) None

2.42 Which is correct?

(a) Two-way FA has equal power as an equivalent FA.

(b) Generally, processing of an input string is more time consuming when NFA is used.

(c) Generally, processing of an input string is less time consuming when DFA is used.

(d) All are correct.

2.43 If NFA $N = (Q, \Sigma, \delta, s, F)$ and the equivalent DFA $D = (Q_1, \Sigma, \delta_1, s, F_1)$, then which is incorrect?

(a) $Q_1 \subseteq 2^Q$

(b) $F_1 \subseteq F$

(c) $|Q_1| \geq |Q|$

(d) None

2.44 If NFA $N = (Q, \Sigma, \delta, s, F)$ and the equivalent DFA $D = (Q_1, \Sigma, \delta_1, s, F_1)$, then which is correct?

(a) $Q_1 \subseteq Q$

(b) $F_1 \subseteq 2^Q$

(c) $|Q_1| \leq |Q|$

(d) None

2.45 The following finite state machine accepts all those binary strings in which the number or 1's and 0's are respectively **(GATE 2004)**

(a) Divisible by 3 and 2

(b) Odd and even

(c) Even and odd

(d) Divisible by 2 and 3

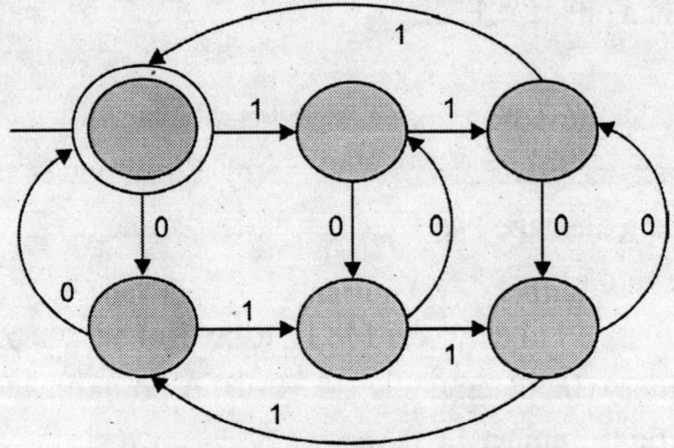

Fig. 2.39: Finite state machine

2.46 Consider the following deterministic finite automaton M.

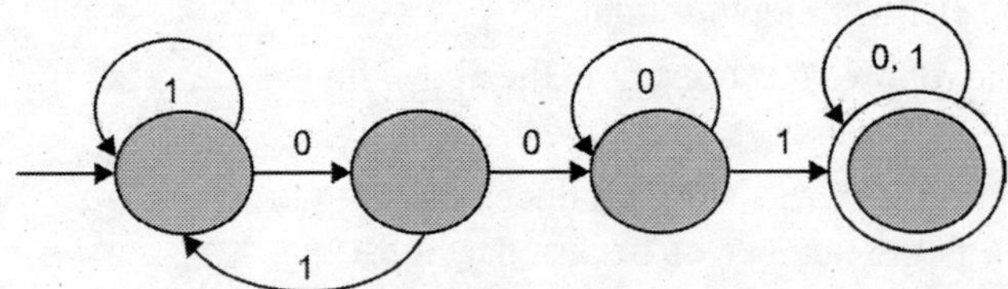

Fig. 2.40

Let S denotes the set of seven bit binary strings in which the first, the fourth, and the last bits are 1. What is the number of strings in S that are accepted by M? **(GATE 2003)**

(a) 1 (b) 5

(c) 7 (d) 8

2.47 Consider the following DFA:

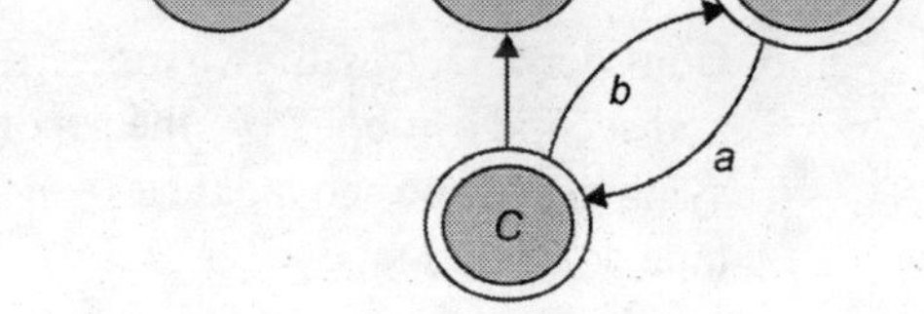

Fig. 2.41

The regular expression accepted by DFA is

(a) $(ab + aba)^*$

(b) $(ab + abab)^*$

(c) $(ab + abaa + abaab)^*$

(d) None

2.48 Consider the following DFA:

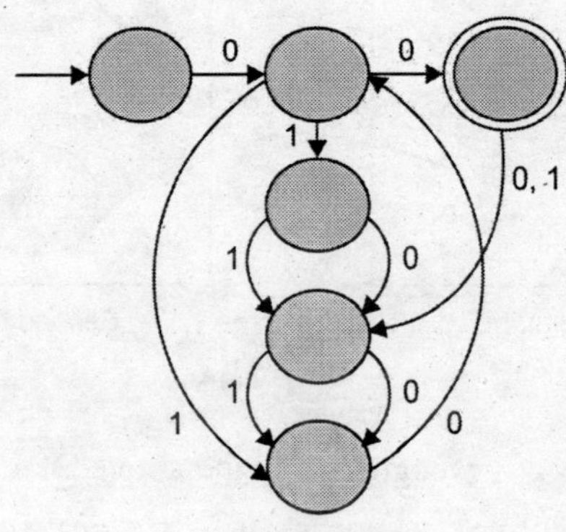

Fig. 2.42

Which one of the following languages is accepted by DFA?

(a) Language over {0, 1} such that some two zero's are separated by a string over {0, 1}, whose length is $4n$ $(n \geq 0)$.

(b) Language which contains all the strings over {0, 1}.

(c) Language which contains all the strings over {0, 1} such that in each string the number of 0's and 1' is equal.

(d) None

2.49 Consider the following finite state machine. The transition arrows/edges labeled with input/output.

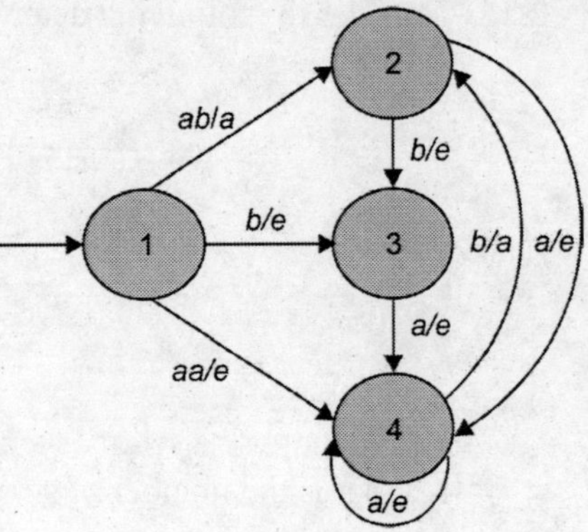

Fig. 2.43

Which one of the following is true about the above finite state machine?

(a) On input string $w \in (a + b)^*$, produces the output a^n, where n is the number of occurrence substring "aa" in w.

(b) On input string $w \in (a + b)^*$, produces the output a^n, where n is the number of occurrence substring "ab" in w.

(c) On input string $w \in (a + b)^*$, produces the output a^n, where n is the number of occurrence substring "ba" in w.

(d) None

2.50 Consider a DFA with two tapes. It reads two symbols at a time; one symbol from the first tape and second symbol from the second tape as a pair (a, b), where symbol 'a' is on first tape and symbol 'b' is on second tape. Transition function depending upon the string set refers to the first tape or second tape. Consider the following DFA with two tapes:

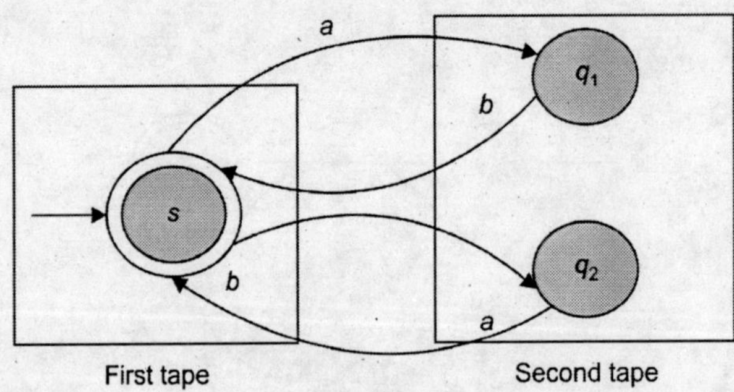

Fig. 2.44

Which one of the following is recognized by the above DFA?

(a) All pairs of strings (w_1, w_2), where $w_1, w_2 \in (a + b)^*$ such that $|w_2| = |w_1|$ and $w_1(i) = a$ if and only if $w_2(i) = b$ (the ith symbol of w) and vice-versa for some fixed value of n and $i = 1, 2,.., n$.

(b) All pairs of strings (w_1, w_2), where $w_1, w_2 \in (a + b)^*$ such that $|w_2| = |w_1| + 1$ and $w_1(i) = a$ if and only if $w_2(i) = b$ (the ith symbol of w) and vice-versa for some fixed value of n and $i = 1, 2,.., n$.

(c) All pairs of strings (w_1, w_2), where $w_1, w_2 \in (a + b)^*$ such that $|w_2| = |w_1| - 1$ and $w_1(i) = a$ if and only if $w_2(i) = b$ (the ith symbol of w) and vice-versa for some fixed value of n and $i = 1, 2,.., n$.

(d) None

2.51 The Consider the following diagram of a non-deterministic finite automaton.

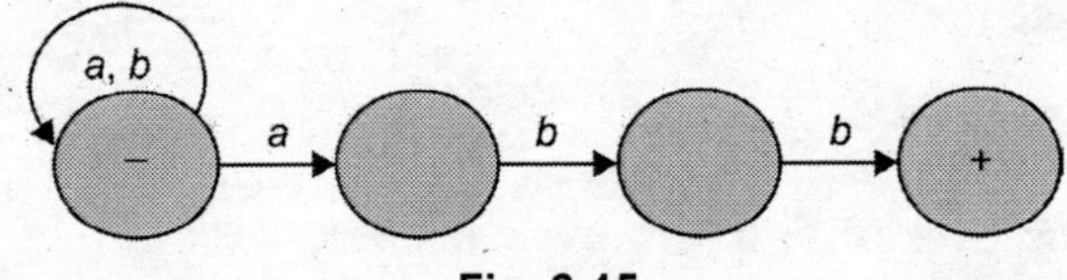

Fig. 2.45

The non-deterministic finite automaton accepts

(a) All the words over $\{a, b\}$ that contain substring "*ab*" and end with "*bb*".

(b) All the words over $\{a, b\}$ that contain substring "*ab*" and end with "*abb*".

(c) All the words over $\{a, b\}$, excluding null string, that end with "*abb*".

(d) None

2.52 The smallest finite automaton which accepts the language $\{x : x$ is a word over $\{a, b\}$ and divisible by 3$\}$ has

(a) 3 states (b) 2 states

(c) 4 states (d) 5 states

2.53 Consider the DFA shown in Fig. 2.46.

The regular language recognized by the DFA is

(a) L = {all strings over $\{a, b\}$ with exactly one 'a'}

(b) L = {all strings over $\{a, b\}$ with at least one 'a'}

(c) L = {all strings over $\{a, b\}$ with more than one 'a'}

(d) None

Fig. 2.46: DFA

2.54 Consider the DFA shown in Fig. 2.47.

The regular language recognized by the DFA is

(a) L = {all strings over $\{a, b\}$ with exactly one 'a'}

(b) L = {all strings over $\{a, b\}$ with at least one 'a'}

(c) L = {all strings over $\{a, b\}$ with more than one 'a'}

(d) None

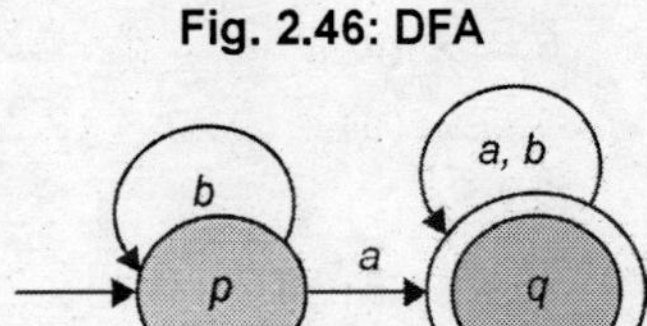

Fig. 2.47: DFA

2.55 Consider the DFA shown in Fig. 2.48.

The regular language recognized by the DFA is

(a) L = {all strings over $\{a, b\}$ with exactly three 'a'}

(b) L = {all strings over $\{a, b\}$ with at least one 'a'}

(c) L = {all strings over $\{a, b\}$ with more than three 'a'}

(d) None

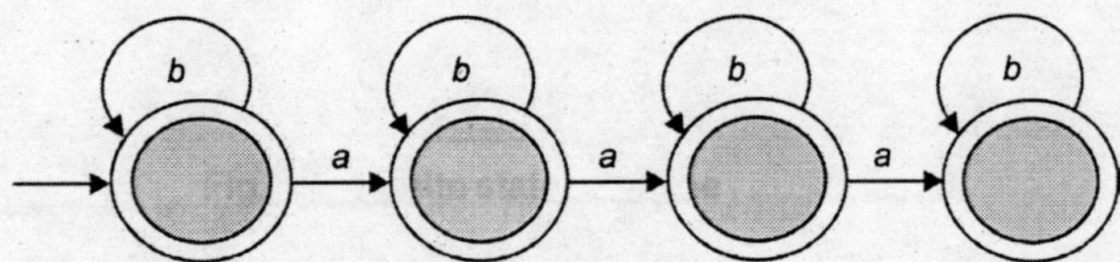

Fig. 2.48: DFA

2.56 Consider the transition diagram given below. What is the language accepted?

(a) Set of all strings over {0,1} having even number of 0's and 1's.

(b) Set of all strings over {0,1} having even number of 0's and odd number of 1's.

(c) Set of all strings over {0,1} having odd number of 0's and odd number of 1's.

(d) Set of all strings over {0,1} having odd number of 0's and even number of 1's.

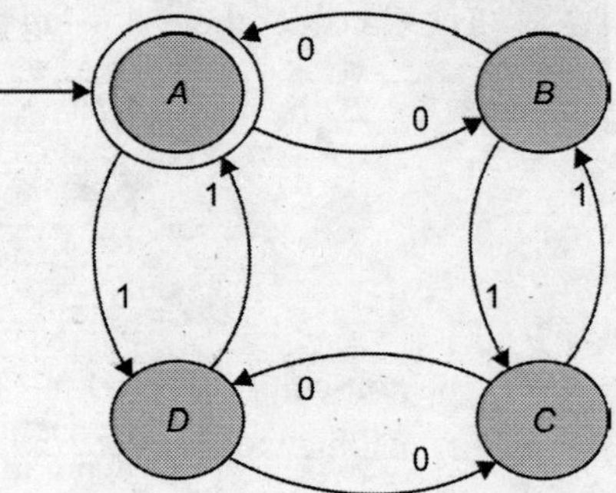

Fig. 2.49: Transition diagram

2.57 Consider the finite automaton shown in Fig. 2.50. Which of the following language is recognized?

(a) Set of all strings over {0, 1} having even number of 0's and 1's.

(b) Set of all strings over {0, 1} having even number of 0's and odd number of 1's.

(c) Set of all strings over {0, 1} having odd number of 0's and odd number of 1's.

(d) Set of all strings over {0, 1}.

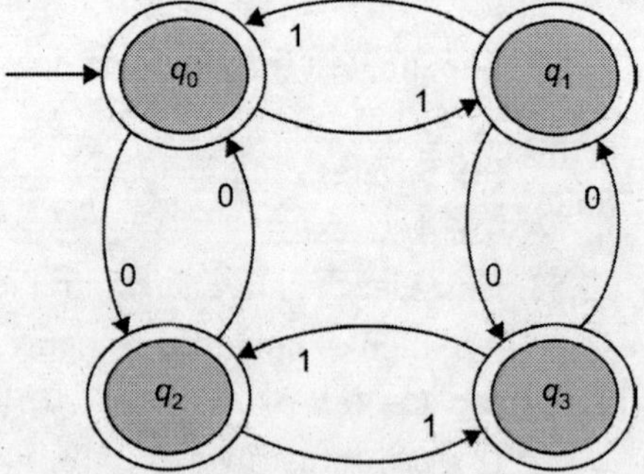

Fig. 2.50

Answers

2.19 (d)	2.20 (c)	2.21 (d)	2.22 (a)	2.23 (b)
2.24 (d)	2.25 (b)	2.26 (a)	2.27 (d)	2.28 (a)
2.29 (c)	2.30 (c)	2.31 (a)	2.32 (a)	2.33 (c)
2.34 (b)	2.35 (a)	2.36 (d)	2.37 (b)	2.38 (d)
2.39 (d)	2.40 (c)	2.41 (a)	2.42 (d)	2.43 (b)
2.44 (b)	2.45 (a)	2.46 (b)	2.47 (a)	2.48 (a)
2.49 (b)	2.50 (a)	2.51 (c)	2.52 (c)	2.53 (a)
2.54 (b)	2.55 (c)	2.56 (a)	2.57 (d)	

CHAPTER 3

Finite State Machines (Transducers)

In this chapter, we will discuss the finite state machines (FSMs). We have discussed in the Chapter 2 that finite automata (FA) are used to produce outputs YES or NO, i.e., recognization of regular languages only. FA can be enhanced to produce output other than "YES" or "NO" known as finite state machine (FSM) or *transducer* which is used in sequential circuit design. A *finite state machine* is used to represent behavior of an event-driven (reactive) system. In an event-driven system, the system makes a transition from one state (mode) to another prescribed state, provided that the condition defining the change is true.

3.1 FINITE STATE MACHINES (FSMs)

A finite state machine is finite automaton (FA) having additional capability of outputs. We have seen in the Chapter-2 that FA has limited outputs and used to recognize the regular languages only. Generally, FA outputs YES or NO based on the validity of the input. We use enhanced finite automaton in integrated circuit design, which are known as finite state machines (FSMs). These machines have same logical structure what finite automata have, but have some more output producing capability.

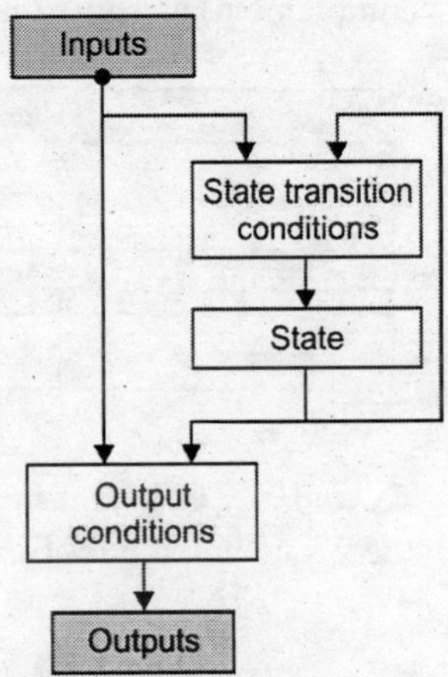

Fig. 3.1: Logic of finite state machine

We use the finite state machines in hardware applications like digital circuit design. In a digital circuit, a FSM may be built using a *programmable logic device*, *a programmable logic controller*, *logic gates*, *counters*, and *flip flops* or *relays*. More specifically, a hardware implementation requires a **register** to store state variables, a combinational logic, which determines the state transition and another block of combinational logic that determines the output of FSM. The logic of the FSM is shown in Fig. 3.1.

3.1.1 Description of Finite State Machine (FSM)

Finite state machines have similar constructional features what finite automata have. FSM reads its input from a set of input symbols, produces output from set of output symbols. The additional feature of FSM is its set of output symbols as compared to finite automata (FA). Finite state machines do not have special state like final state. A finite state machine is described by 6-tuple (Q, Σ, Δ, δ, λ, s), where

1. Q is finite and non-empty set of states,
2. Σ is input alphabet,
3. Δ is output alphabet,
4. δ is transition function which maps present state and input symbol on to the next state or $Q \times \Sigma \rightarrow Q$,
5. λ is the output function, and
6. $s \in Q$, is the initial state or starting state.

3.1.2 Representation of FSMs

We represent a finite state machine (FSM) in the same way as finite automata are represented, that is, transition graph or transition table. In transition graph, *edges or arches are labeled with Input/output* and input/output is represented in transition table also.

Let us consider that in transition table, entries are defined by a function ***F***. For example, for input a_i and state q_i, function F is defined as below:

$$F(q_i, a_i) = (\delta(q_i, a_i), \lambda(q_i, a_i))$$

(where δ is transition function, λ is output function.)

Example 1: Consider a finite state machine (FSM), which changes 1's into 0's and 0's into 1's (1's complement) as shown in Fig. 3.2.

Transition table				
	Inputs			
	0		**1**	
Present state	**Next state**	**Output**	**Next state**	**Output**
→ s	s	1	s	0

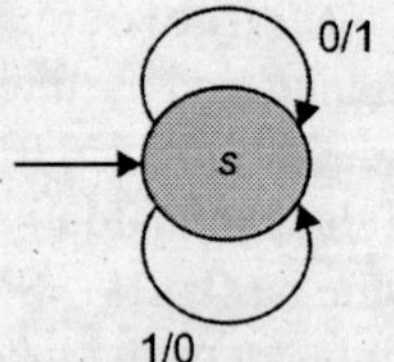

Fig. 3.2: Transition graph of FSM

Example 2: Consider the finite state machine shown in Fig. 3.3, which outputs the 2's complement of input binary number reading from least significant bit (LSB).

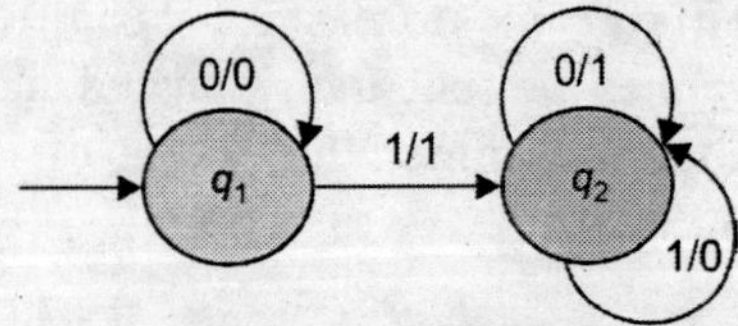

Fig. 3.3: Finite state machine

Suppose inputs are 10100, 1001. What are the outputs?

Solution: The finite state machine reads the input from right side (LSB).

Transition sequence for input 10100:

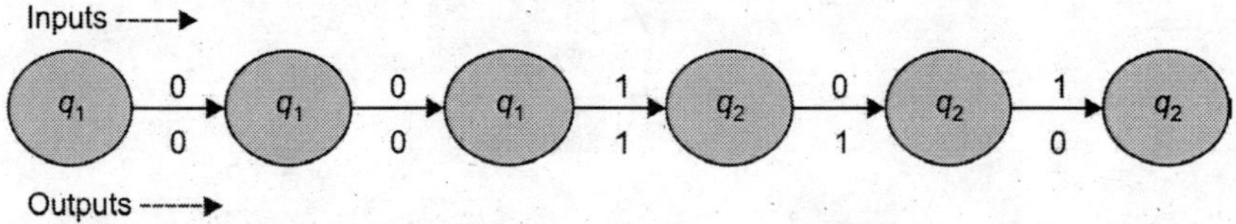

So, output is **01100.**

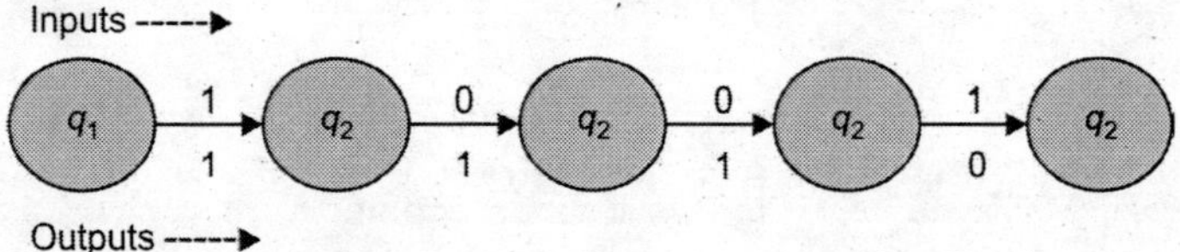

Transition sequence for input 1001:

So, output is **0111.**

3.2 MOORE MACHINE

The name **Moore machine** comes from promoter **Edward F. Moore**, a state machine pioneer. **Edward Forrest Moore** was a professor of mathematics and computer sciences at the University of Wisconsin-Madison from 1966 until he retired in 1985. He was the first person to use the type of Finite State Machine that is most commonly used today, the Moore finite state machine.

Most electronics are designed as clocked sequential systems. Clocked sequential systems are a restricted form of **Moore machine** where the state changes only when the global clock signal changes. The present state is stored in flip-flops, and global clock signal is connected to the flip-flops. The *output of this finite state machine is dependent on present state only*. A Moore machine can be described by 6-tuple (Q, Σ, Δ, δ, λ, s), where

1. Q is finite and non-empty set of states,
2. Σ is input alphabet,
3. Δ is output alphabet,
4. δ is transition function which maps present state and input symbol on to the next state or $Q \times \Sigma \rightarrow Q$,
5. λ is the output function which maps $Q \rightarrow \Delta$, (Present state $\rightarrow$ Output), and
6. $s \in Q$, is the initial state or starting state.

If $Z(t)$, $q(t)$ are output and present state respectively at time t, then

$$Z(t) = \lambda(q(t))$$

For input ε (null string), $Z(t)$ = λ(starting state)

Example 1: Consider the Moore machine shown in Fig. 3.4. Construct the transition table. What is the output for the input 01010?

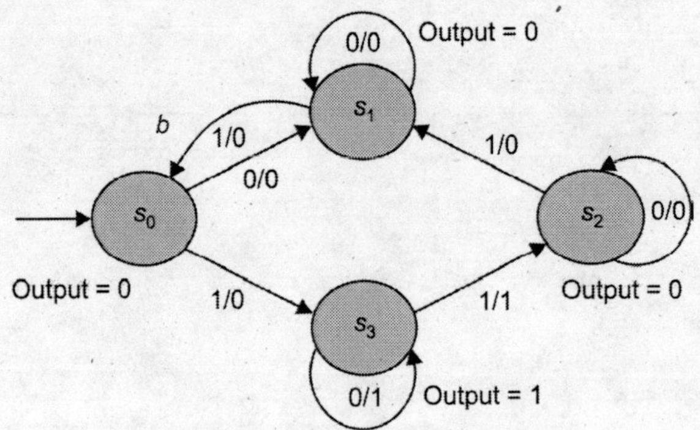

Fig. 3.4: Moore machine

Solution: Transition table for Moore machine shown in Fig. 3.4 is below:

Transition table			
	Inputs		
	0	1	
Present state	**Next state**	**Next state**	**Output**
s_0	s_1	s_3	0
s_1	s_1	s_0	0
s_2	s_2	s_1	0
s_3	s_3	s_2	1

Transition sequence for input string 01010 is shown in Fig. 3.4(a) and output produced is: **000000.**

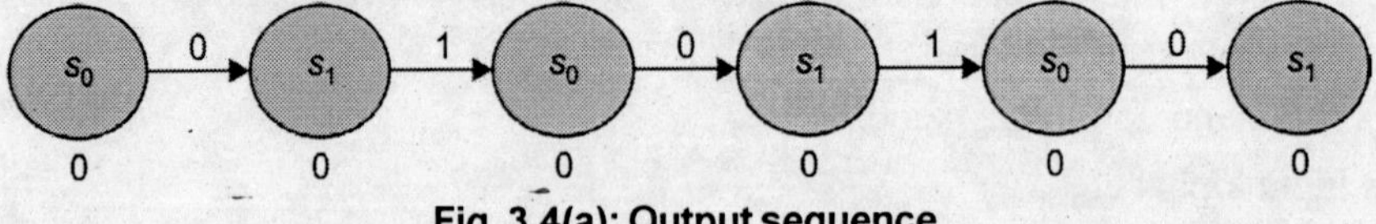

Fig. 3.4(a): Output sequence

Since, the output of Moore machine does not depend on input. So, the first output symbol is additional from the initial state without reading the input i.e. null input and output length is one greater than the input length. The input is important for the transitions and does not afffect the output. Moore machine produces output whenever reaches a state and initial state produces first output before transition to next state.

3.3 MEALY MACHINE

If the *output of finite state machine is dependent on present state and present input*, then this model of finite state machine is known as **Mealy machine.** The name "Mealy machine" comes from the promoter **G. H. Mealy**, a state machine pioneer who wrote "A Method for Synthesizing Sequential Circuits" in 1955. A Mealy machine can be described by 6-tuple $(Q, \Sigma, \Delta, \delta, \lambda, s)$ where

1. Q is finite and non-empty set of states,
2. Σ is input alphabet (finite, non-empty set),
3. Δ is output alphabet(finite, non-empty set),
4. is transition function which maps present state and input symbol on to the next state or $Q \times \Sigma \rightarrow Q$,
5. is the output function which maps $Q \times \Sigma \rightarrow \Delta$, ((Present state, present input symbol) $\rightarrow$ Output), and
6. $s \in Q$, is the initial state or starting state.

If $Z(t)$, $q(t)$, and $x(t)$ are output, present state, and present input respectively at time t, then, $Z(t) = \lambda(q(t), x(t))$ and

For input ε (null string), $Z(t) = \varepsilon$

Example 2: Consider the Mealy machine shown in Fig. 3.5. Construct the transition table and find output for input 01010.

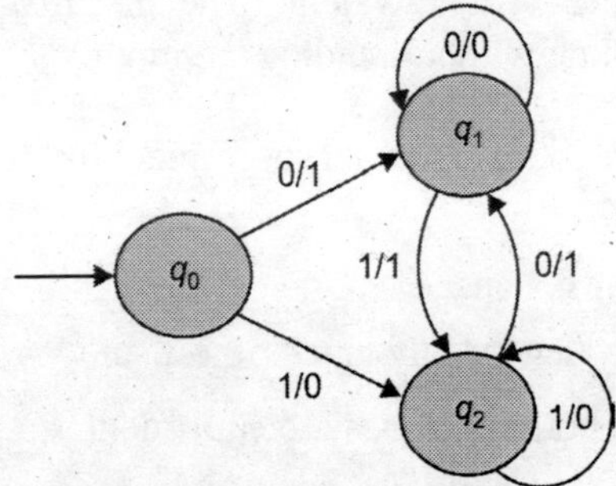

Fig. 3.5: Mealy machine

Solution: Transition table is constructed as follows:

Transition table				
	Inputs			
	0		1	
Present state	**Next state**	**Output**	**Next state**	**Output**
$\rightarrow q_0$	q_1	1	q_2	0
q_1	q_1	0	q_2	1
q_2	q_1	1	q_2	0

Transition sequence for the input 01010:

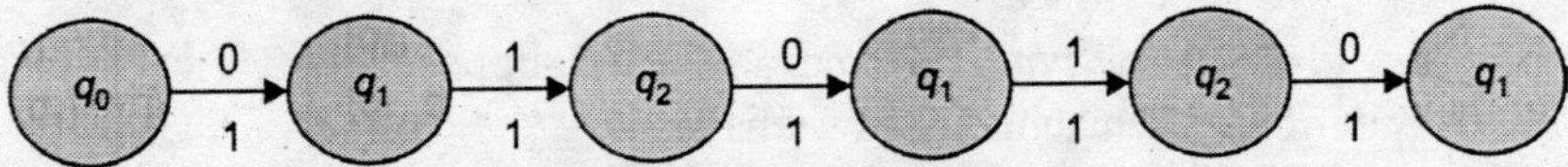

Fig. 3.5(a): Output sequence

So, the output is 11111. The output length is equal to the input length because output is dependent on input also. So, number of transitions for the input decides the length of the output, which is equal to the input length.

3.4 EQUIVALENCE OF MOORE AND MEALY MACHINES

We will see that Moore and Mealy machines are equivalent in their capability although these machines differ in their output function. We will discuss how to construct equivalent Mealy machine for a Moore machine and vice-versa. Let M_1 and M_2 be equivalent Moore and Mealy machines respectively.

The two outputs $T_1(w)$ and $T_2(w)$ are produced by the machines M_1 and M_2 respectively for input string w. We known that the length of $T_1(w)$ (output of Moore machine) is one greater than the length of $T_2(w)$ (output of Mealy machine), i.e.

$$|T_1(w)| = |T_2(w)| + 1$$

The additional length is due to the output produced by initial state of Moore machine. Let output symbol b is the additional output produced by the initial state of Moore machine, then

$$T_1(w) = bT_2(w)$$

It means, if we neglect the one initial output produced by the initial state of Moore machine then outputs produced by both machines are equivalent. (The *additional output is produced by the initial state of* (for input e) Moore machine without reading the input.)

Theorem 3.1: If $M_1 = (Q, \Sigma, \Delta, \delta, \lambda, s)$ is a Moore machine then there exists a Mealy machine M_2 equivalent to M_1.

Proof: We will discuss proof in two steps:

Step 1: Construction of equivalent Mealy machine M_2, and

Step 2: Outputs produced by both machines are equivalent.

Step 1: Construction of equivalent Mealy machine M_2

Let $M_2 = (Q, \Sigma, \Delta, \delta, \lambda', s)$, where all terms $Q, \Sigma, \Delta, \delta, s$ are same as for Moore machine and λ' is defined as following:

$$\lambda'(q, a) = \lambda(\delta(q, a)) \text{ for all } q \in Q \text{ and } a \in \Sigma$$

The first output produced by initial state of Moore machine is neglected and we consider the output produced by the next state. Transition sequences remain unchanged.

Step 2: If b is the output symbol produced by initial state of Moore machine M_1, and $T_1(w)$, $T_2(w)$ are outputs produced by Moore machine M_1 and equivalent Mealy machine M_2 respectively for input string w, then

$$T_1(w) = bT_2(w)$$

If we delete the output symbol b from $T_1(w)$ and suppose it is $T_1'(w)$ which is equivalent to the output of Mealy machine. So, we have,

$$T_1'(w) = T_2(w)$$

Hence, Mealy machine M_2 is equivalent to Moore machine M_1.

Example 3: Construct a Mealy machine equivalent to Moore machine M_1 given in following transition table.

Transition table			
	Inputs		
	0	1	
Present state	Next state	Next state	Output
→ s	q_1	q_2	1
q_1	q_3	q_2	0
q_2	q_2	q_1	1
q_3	s	q_3	1

Solution: Let equivalent Mealy machine $M_2 = (Q, \Sigma, \Delta, \delta, \lambda', s)$, where

$Q = \{s, q_1, q_2, q_3\}$, $\Sigma = \{0, 1\}$, $\Delta = \{0, 1\}$, and λ' is defined as following:

For state s: $\lambda'(s, 0) = \lambda(\delta(s, 0)) = \lambda(q_1) = 0$ $\quad$ $\lambda'(s, 1) = \lambda(\delta(s, 1)) = \lambda(q_2) = 1$

For state q_1: $\lambda'(q_1, 0) = \lambda(\delta(q_1, 0)) = \lambda(q_3) = 1$ $\quad$ $\lambda'(q_1, 1) = \lambda(\delta(q_1, 1)) = \lambda(q_2) = 1$

For state q_2: $\lambda'(q_2, 0) = \lambda(\delta(q_2, 0)) = \lambda(q_2) = 1$ $\quad$ $\lambda'(q_2, 1) = \lambda(\delta(q_2, 1)) = \lambda(q_1) = 0$

For state q_3: $\lambda'(q_3, 0) = \lambda(\delta(q_3, 0)) = \lambda(s) = 1$ $\quad$ $\lambda'(q_3, 1) = \lambda(\delta(q_3, 1)) = \lambda(q_3) = 1$

Transition table				
	Inputs			
	0		1	
Present state	Next state	Output	Next state	Output
→ s	q_1	0	q_2	1
q_1	q_3	1	q_2	0
q_2	q_2	1	q_1	1
q_3	s	1	q_3	1

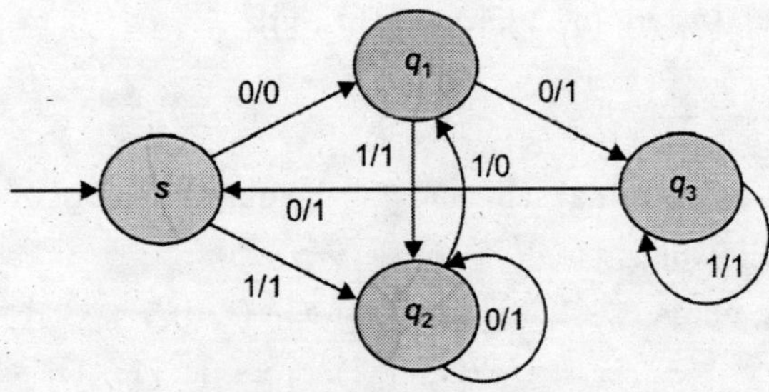

Fig. 3.6: Mealy machine

Theorem 3.2: If $M_1 = (Q, \Sigma, \Delta, \delta, \lambda, s)$ is a Mealy machine then there exists a Moore machine M_2 equivalent to M_1.

Proof: We will discuss proof in two steps:

Step 1: Construction of equivalent Moore machine M_2, and

Step 2: Outputs produced by both machines are equivalent.

Step 1: Construction of equivalent Moore machine M_2:

We define the set of states as order pair over Q and Δ. There is also a change in transition function and output function.

Let equivalent Moore machine $M_2 = (Q', \Sigma, \Delta, \delta', \lambda', s')$, where

1. $Q' \subseteq Q \times \Delta$ is the set of states formed with order pair over Q and Δ,
2. Σ remains unchanged,
3. Δ remains unchanged,
4. λ' is defined as following:

   $\boldsymbol{\delta'([q, b], a) = [\delta(q, a), \lambda(q, a)]}$, where δ and λ are transition function and output function of Mealy machine.
5. λ' is the output function of equivalent Moore machine which is dependent on present state only and defined as follows:

   $$\boldsymbol{\lambda'([q, b]) = b}$$
6. s' is the initial state and defined as $\boldsymbol{[s, b_0]}$, where **s** is the initial state of Mealy machine and b_0 is any arbitrary symbol selected from output alphabet Δ.

Step 2: Outputs of Mealy and Moore machines:

Suppose, Mealy machine M_1 enters states $q_0, q_1, q_2 \ldots q_n$ on input $a_1, a_2, a_3, \ldots, a_n$ and produces outputs $b_1, b_2, b_3, \ldots, b_n$, then M_2 enters the states $[q_0, b_0], [q_1, b_1], [q_2, b_2], \ldots, [q_n, b_n]$ and produces outputs $b_0, b_1, b_2, \ldots, b_n$ as discussed in Step1.

Hence, outputs produced by both machines are equivalent.

Therefore, Moore machine M_2 is equivalent to Mealy machine M_1.

Example 4: Consider the Mealy machine shown in Fig. 3.7. Construct an equivalent Moore machine.

Solution: Let $M_1 = (Q, \Sigma, \Delta, \delta, \lambda, s)$ is a given

Mealy machine and $M_2 = (Q', \Sigma, \Delta', \delta', \lambda', s')$ be the equivalent Moore machine, where

1. $Q' \subseteq \{[s, n], [s, y], [q_1, n], [q_1, y], [q_2, n], [q_2, y]\}$ (Since, $Q' \subseteq Q' \times \Delta$),
2. $\Sigma = \{0, 1\}$,
3. $\Delta' = \{n, y\}$,
4. $s' = [s, y]$, where s is the initial state and y is the output symbol of Mealy machine,
5. δ' is defined as following:

   For initial state $[s, y]$: $\delta'([s, y], 0) - [\delta(s, 0), \lambda(s, 0)] - [q_1, n]$

   $\delta'([s, y], 1) = [\delta(s, 1), \lambda(s, 1)] = [q_2, n]$

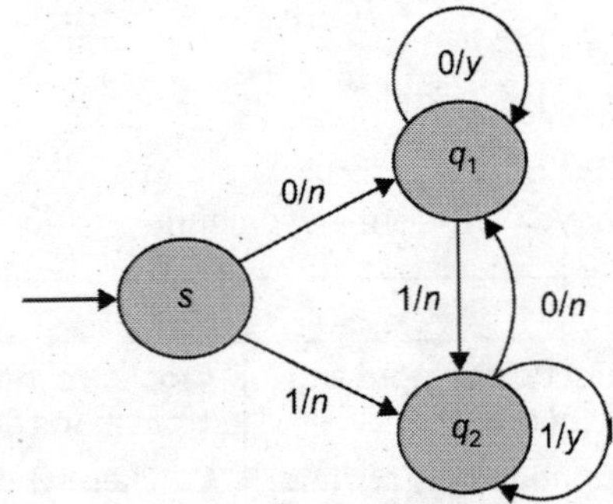

Fig. 3.7: Mealy machine

For state $[q_1, n]$: $\delta'([q_1, n], 0) = [\delta(q_1, 0), \lambda(q_1, 0)] = [q_1, y]$

$\delta'([q_1, n], 1) = [\delta(q_1, 1), \lambda(q_1, 1)] = [q_2, n]$

For state $[q_2, n]$ $\delta'([q_2, n], 0) = [\delta(q_2, 0), \lambda(q_2, 0)] = [q_1, n]$

$\delta'([q_2, n], 1) = [\delta(q_2, 1), \lambda(q_2, 1)] = [q_2, y]$

For state $[q_1, y]$: $\delta'([q_1, y], 0) = [\delta(q_1, 0), \lambda(q_1, 0)] = [q_1; y]$

$\delta'([q_1, y], 1) = [\delta(q_1, 1), \lambda(q_1, 1)] = [q_2, n]$

For state $[q_2, y]$: $\delta'([q_2, y], 0) = [\delta(q_2, 0), \lambda(q_2, 0)] = [q_1, n]$

$\delta'([q_2, y], 1) = [\delta(q_2, 1), \lambda(q_2', 1)] = [q_2, y]$

Let us conclude some important points here. We have considered those states only, which are reachable from initial state $[s, y]$. Although there are six states $\{[s, n], [s, y], [q_1, n], [q_1, y], [q_2, n], [q_2, y]\}$ because $Q' \subseteq Q \times \Delta$. There are two possible initial states $[s, y]$, and $[s, n]$ and we have considered the first one, that is, $[s, y]$. We can choose any one of these two states as initial state.

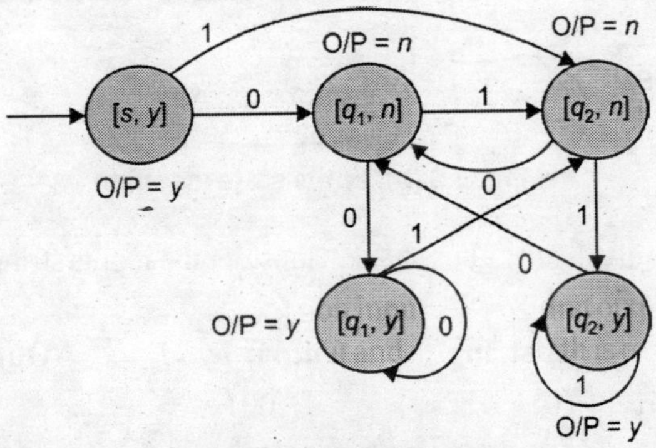

Fig. 3.8: Moore machine

6. λ' is defined as follows:

$$\lambda'[s, y] = y,$$
$$\lambda'[q_1, n] = n,$$

$\lambda' [q_2, n] = n,$
$\lambda' [q_1, y] = y,$ and
$\lambda' [q_2, y] = y$

Mealy and Moore machines have well-defined semantics, which is given in following table:

Type of machine	Semantics	Applications
Mealy	**Output is a function of input and state: $Z(t) = \lambda(q(t), x(t))$**	**Clocked synchronous machines where state transitions occur on clock edges**
Moore	**Output is a function only of state: $Z(t) = \lambda(q(t))$**	**Clocked synchronous machines where outputs are modified at clock edges**

3.5 EQUIVALENCE OF FSMs

Two finite state machines (FSMs) are said to be equivalent if and only if every input sequence yields identical output sequence when process by two machines. For example, consider the FSM M_1 shown in Fig. 3.9 (a) and FSM M_2 Fig. 3.9(b).

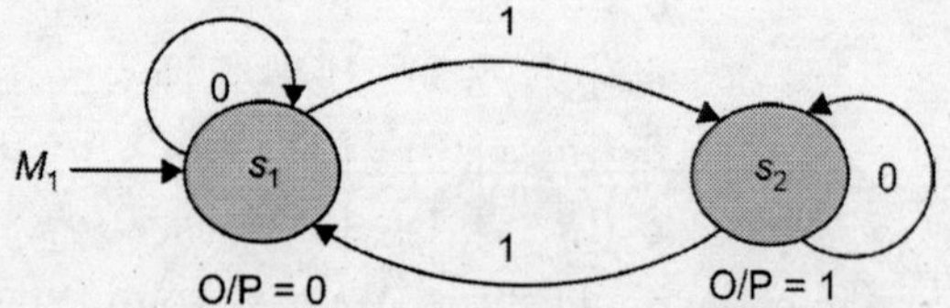

Fig. 3.9(a): Finite state machine

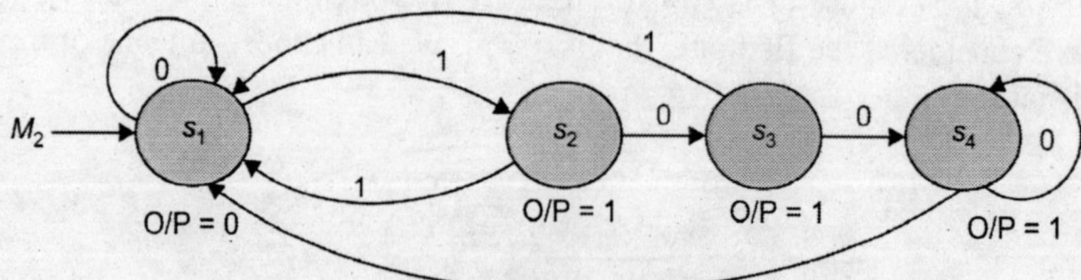

Fig. 3.9 (b): Finite state machine

Are these two FSMs equivalent? Let us check. Consider the inputs strings and corresponding outputs of both the machines as given following:

	Input string	Output by M_1	Output by M_2
1.	01	001	001
2.	010	0011	0011
3.	0101	00110	00110
4.	1000	01111	01111
5.	10001	011110	011110

Now, we come to this conclusion that for each input sequence, outputs produced by both machines are identical. So, these machines are equivalent. In other words, both machines do the same job.

But, M_1 has two states and M_2 has four states. It appears that some states of M_2 are equivalent and doing the same job, producing identical outputs for same input, and have identical transitions. Such states are known as **equivalent states** and require extra resources when implemented. Thus, our goal is to find the simplest and equivalent FSM with minimum number of states. The process of finding the minimum state FSM is known as **optimization**. Optimization is a complex process and has non-linear time complexity.

Optimization (or minimization) of Finite State Machines (FSMs)

We minimize a FSM using the following method, which finds the equivalent states, and merges these into one state and finally construct the equivalent FSM.

Method: (Initially we assume that all pairs (s_1, s_2) over states are non-equivalent states)

Step 1: Construct the transition table.

Step 2: Repeat for each pair of non-equivalent states (s_1, s_2):

(a) Do s_1 and s_2 produce same output?

(b) Do s_1 and s_2 reach the same states for each input $a \in \Sigma$?

(c) If answers of (a) and (b) are YES, then s_1 and s_2 are equivalent states and merge these two states into one state $[s_1, s_2]$ and replace the all occurrences of s_1 and s_2 by $[s_1, s_2]$ and mark these equivalent states.

Step 3: Check the all-present states, if any redundancy is found, remove that.

Step 4: Exit

Example 5: Let us consider the transition table for FSM shown in Fig. 3.9(b).

Transition table			
	Inputs		
	0	1	
Present state	**Next state**	**Next state**	**Output**
s_1	s_1	s_2	0
s_2	s_3	s_1	1
s_3	s_4	s_1	1
s_4	s_4	s_1	1

Solution: Pairs over $\{s_1, s_2, s_3, s_4\}$ are: (s_1, s_2), (s_1, s_3), (s_1, s_4), (s_2, s_3), (s_2, s_4), (s_3, s_4).

Consider the pair (s_1, s_2):

Since, $\lambda(s_1) = 0$, and $\lambda(s_2) = 1$ and hence, s_1 and s_2 are not equivalent.

Consider the pair (s_1, s_3):

Since, $\lambda(s_1) = 0$, and $\lambda(s_3) = 1$ and hence, s_1 and s_3 are not equivalent.

Consider the pair (s_1, s_4):

Since, $\lambda(s_1) = 0$, and $\lambda(s_4) = 1$ and hence s_1 and s_3 are not equivalent.

Consider the pair (s_2, s_3):

Since, $\lambda(s_2) = 1$, and $\lambda(s_3) = 1$, thus outputs are identical.

Now, consider the transitions: $\delta(s_2, 0) = s_3$, $\delta(s_2, 1) = s_1$, $\delta(s_3, 0) = s_4$, $\delta(s_3, 1) = s_1$

So, transitions from s_2 and s_3 are not identical for input 0. Hence, s_2 and s_3 are not equivalent.

Consider the pair (s_2, s_4):

Since, $\lambda(s_2) = 1$, and $\lambda(s_4) = 1$, thus outputs are identical.

Now, consider the transitions: $\delta(s_2, 0) = s_3$, $\delta(s_2, 1) = s_1$, $\delta(s_4, 0) = s_4$, $\delta(s_4, 1) = s_1$

So, transitions from s_2 and s_4 are not on the same state for 0 input. Hence, s_2 and s_4 are not equivalent.

Consider the pair (s_3, s_4):

Since, $\lambda(s_3) = 1$, and $\lambda(s_4) = 1$, thus outputs are identical.

Now, consider the transitions: $\delta(s_3, 0) = s_4$, $\delta(s_3, 1) = s_1$, $\delta(s_4, 0) = s_{4,}$ $\delta(s_4, 1) = s_1$

So, transitions from s_2 and s_3 are identical for inputs 0 and 1. Hence, s_3 and s_4 are equivalent states. So, merging states s_3 and s_4 into one state represented as [s_3, s_4] and replacing states s_3 and s_4 by [s_3, s_4], we have intermediate transition table 1:

Intermediate transition table 1			
	Inputs		
	0	1	
Present state	Next state	Next state	Output
s_1	s_1	s_2	0
s_2	[s_3, s_4]	s_1	1
[s_3, s_4]	[s_3, s_4]	s_1	1
[s_3, s_4]	[s_3, s_4]	s_1	1

Aplying Step 2 further on intermediate transition Table 1 and we see that states s_2, [s_3, s_4] are equivalent. So, replacing states s_2 and [s_3, s_4] by single state [s_2, s_3, s_4], we have intermediate transition Table 2.

Intermediate transition table 2			
	Inputs		
	0	1	
Present state	Next state	Next state	Output
s_1	s_1	[s_2, s_3, s_4]	0
[s_2, s_3, s_4]	[s_2, s_3, s_4]	s_1	1
[s_2, s_3, s_4]	[s_2, s_3, s_4]	s_1	1
[s_2, s_3, s_4]	[s_2, s_3, s_4]	s_1	1

Now, there are no equivalent states in intermediate transition Table 2. So, applying Step 3 and for removing redundancy, we have to delete two rows of present state [s_2, s_3, s_4]. Now, we have the final transition table.

Final transition table 3			
	Inputs		
	0	1	
Present state	Next state	Next state	Output
s_1	s_1	$[s_2, s_3, s_4]$	0
$[s_2, s_3, s_4]$	$[s_2, s_3, s_4]$	s_1	1

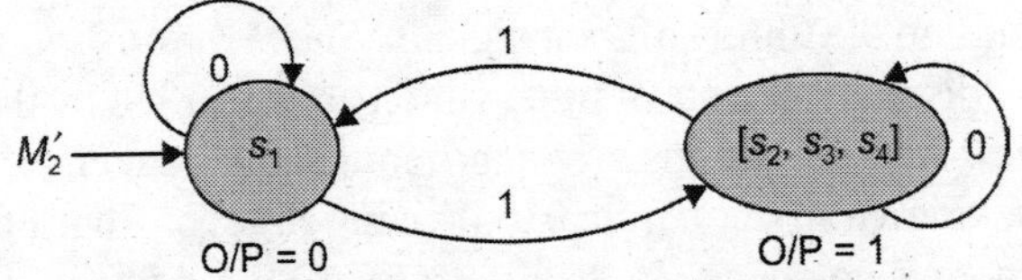

Fig. 3.9(c): Minimum states FSM

Now, we can compare the finite state machines shown in Fig. 3.9(a) and Fig. 3.9(c) and we find that these machines are equivalent.

3.6 DIGITAL CIRCUITS AND FSMs

In digital logic, we have two types of circuits: **combinational circuit** and **sequential circuit**. Combinational circuit is made of gates (AND, OR, NOT, etc.) and characteristic fully specified by the truth table. Sequential circuit is made of gates (combinational circuit) and memory elements like flip-flops. It requires state table (also known as transition table) for specification of its behavior. Combinational logic refers to circuits whose output is strictly depended on the present value of the inputs. As soon as inputs are changed, the information about the previous inputs is lost, that is, combinational logics circuits have no memory. Digital circuits whose outputs depend not only on the present input value but also the past input value are known as **sequential circuits**. Sequential circuits have memory to store the previous inputs. The mathematical model of a sequential circuit is usually referred to as a **sequential machine or transducer** or **finite state machine** (FSM). A general block diagram of a sequential circuit is shown in Fig. 3.10.

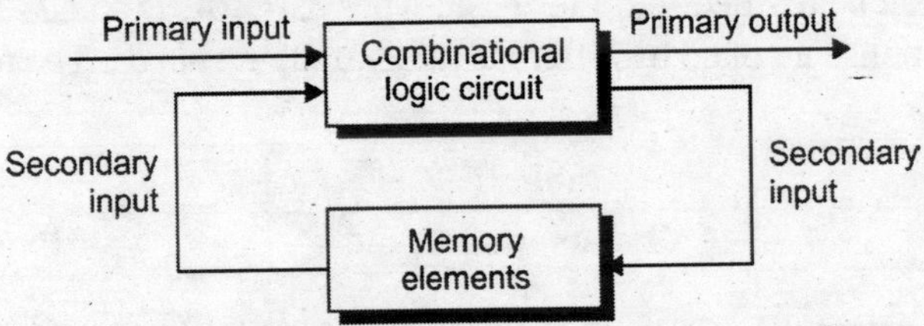

Fig. 3.10: Block diagram of sequential circuit

The diagram consists of combinational circuit to which memory elements are connected to form a feedback path. The memory elements are devices capable of storing binary information within them. The combinational part of the circuit receives two sets of inputs: one is **primary** (coming from the circuit environment or external input) and **secondary** (coming from memory elements). The particular combination of secondary inputs (or variables) at a given time is called the **present state** of the circuit. The secondary input variables are also known as the **state variables**.

The block diagram of sequential circuit shown in Fig. 3.10 shows that the external outputs in a sequential circuit are a function not only of external inputs but also of the present state of the memory elements. The next state of the memory elements is also a function of external inputs and the present state. Thus a sequential circuit is specified by a time sequence of inputs, outputs, and internal states. If the output of the sequential circuit depends on the present state and external inputs then behavior of such circuit is described by mealy machine and if output is dependent on present state only, not on external input, then behavior is described by Moore machine.

Sequential circuits are divided into two main types: **synchronous** and **asynchronous**. Their classification depends on the timing of their signals. ***Synchronous*** sequential circuits change their states and output values at discrete instants of time, which are specified by the rising and falling edge of a free-running **clock signal**. State transitions in synchronous sequential circuits are made to take place at times when the clock is making a transition from 0 to 1 (rising edge) or from 1 to 0 (falling edge). Between successive clock pulses there is no change in the information stored in memory elements. Synchronous sequential circuits are also known as **clocked sequential circuits**. The memory elements used in synchronous sequential circuits are usually flip-flops. A flip-flop is used as binary cell capable of storing one bit of information. A flip-flop circuit has two outputs, one for the normal value and one for the complement value of the bit stored in it. Binary information can enter a flip-flop in a variety of ways, a fact that give rise to the different types of flip-flops. We will see different types of flip-flops in next section.

In **asynchronous** sequential circuits, the transition from one state to another is initiated by the change in the primary inputs; there is no external synchronization. The memories commonly used in asynchronous sequential circuits are time-delayed devices, usually implemented by feedback among logic gates. Thus, asynchronous sequential circuits may be regarded as combinational circuits with feedback. Because of the feedback among logic gates, asynchronous sequential circuits may, at times, become unstable due to transient conditions. The instability problem imposes many difficulties on the designer. Hence, they are not as commonly used as synchronous systems.

3.6.1 Types of Flip-flops and their Behaviors

We will concentrate on synchronous sequential circuits only. Since memory elements in sequential circuits are usually flip-flops, it is worth summarizing the behavior of various flip-flops before proceeding further. All flip-flops can be divided into four basic types: ***SR***, ***JK***, ***D*** and ***T***. They differ in the number of inputs and in the response invoked by different value of input signals. The four types of flip-flops are defined below:

Table 1: *SR* Flip-Flop

Symbol	Characteristic table			Excitation table			
	S	R	Q_{next}	Q	Q_{next}	S	R
S, Q, Clk, R, Q'	0	0	Q	0	0	0	X
	0	1	0	0	1	1	0
	1	0	1	1	0	0	1
	1	1	?	1	1	X	0
	Characteristic equation $Q(\text{next}) = S + R'Q$ $SR = 0$						

Table 2: *JK* Flip-Flop

Symbol	Characteristic table			Excitation table			
J, Q, Clk, K, Q'	*J*	*K*	Q_{next}	*Q*	Q_{next}	*J*	*K*
	0	0	*Q*	0	0	0	*X*
	0	1	0	0	1	1	*X*
	1	0	1	1	0	*X*	1
	1	1	*Q*	1	1	*X*	0
	Characteristic equation $Q(\text{next}) = JQ' + K'Q$						

Table 3: *T* Flip-Flop

Symbol	Characteristic table		Excitation table		
T, Q, Clk, Q'	*T*	Q_{next}	*Q*	Q_{next}	*T*
	0	*Q*	0	0	0
	1	*Q*	0	1	1
			1	0	1
			1	1	0
	Characteristic equation $Q(\text{next}) = TQ' + T'Q$				

Table 4: *D* Flip-Flop

Symbol	Characteristic table		Excitation table		
T, Q, Clk, Q'	*D*	Q_{next}	*Q*	Q_{next}	*D*
	0	0	0	0	0
	1	1	0	1	1
			1	0	0
			1	1	1
	Characteristic equation $Q(\text{next}) = D$				

The graphical symbol, characteristic table, and characteristic equation or excitation table can uniquely describe each of the above flip-flops. All flip-flops have output signals *Q* and *Q*'. Output *Q*' is complement of the output *Q*. The ***characteristic table*** defines the state of each flip-flop as a function of its inputs and previous state. *Q* refers to the present state and $Q_{\textbf{next}}$ refers to the next state after the occurrence of the clock pulse. The characteristic table for the *RS* flip-flop shows that the next state is equal to the present state when both inputs *S* and *R* are equal to 0. When $R = 1$, the next clock pulse clears the flip-flop. When $S = 1$, the flip-flop output *Q* is set to 1. The equation mark (?) for the next state when *S* and *R* are equal to 1 designates an indeterminate next state. The characteristic table for the *JK* flip-flop is the same as that of the *RS* flip-flop when *S* and *R* replace *J* and *K* respectively, except for the indeterminate case. When both *J* and *K* are equal to 1, the next state is equal to the complement of the present state, that is, $Q(\text{next}) = Q'$. The next state for the T flip-flop is the same as the present state Q if $T = 0$ and complemented if $T = 1$. The next state of the D flip-flop is completely dependent on the input D and independent of the present state.

The **characteristic table** is useful during the analysis of sequential circuits when the value of flip-flop inputs are known and we want to find the value of the flip-flop output Q after the rising edge of the clock signal. As with any other truth table, we can use the map method to derive the characteristic equation for each flip-flop. During the design process we usually know the transition from present state to the next state and wish to find the flip-flop input conditions that will cause the required transition. For this reason we will need a table that lists the required inputs for a given change of state. Such a list is called the **excitation table.** There are four possible transitions from present state to the next state. The required input conditions are derived from the information available in the characteristic table. The symbol X in the table represents a "don't care" condition, that is, it does not matter whether the input is 1 or 0.

3.6.2 State Tables and State Diagrams

We have examined a general model for sequential circuits. In this model the effect of all previous inputs on the outputs is represented by a state of the circuit. Thus, the output of the circuit at any time depends upon its current state and the input. These also determine the next state of the circuit. The relationship that exists among the inputs, outputs, present states and next states can be specified by either the **state or transition table** or the **state or transition diagram.**

State (or transition) diagram

In addition to graphical symbols, tables or equations, a state diagram can also represent flip-flops graphically. A transition diagram is a very convenient way to visualize the operation of a flip-flop or even of large sequential components. In this diagram, a state is represented by a circle and the transition between states is indicated by directed lines (or arcs) connecting the circles in similar way what we have seen in finite automaton representation. An example of a state diagram is shown in Fig. 3.11 is given below:

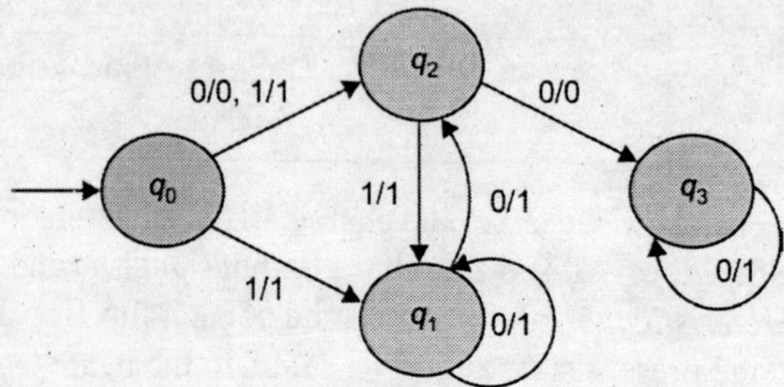

Fig. 3.11: State diagram

Transition or state table

The state table representation of a sequential circuit consists of three sections labeled *present state*, *next state* and *output*. The present state designates the state of flip-flops before the occurrence of a clock pulse. The next state shows the states of flip-flops after the clock pulse, and the output section lists the value of the output variables during the present state. State table for transition diagram as shown in Fig. 3.11.

State or Transition table				
	Inputs			
	0		1	
Present state	Next state	Output	Next state	Output
→ q_0	q_2	0	q_2	1
q_1	q_2	1	q_0	1
q_2	q_3	0	q_1	1
q_3	q_3	1	q_1	1

Example 1: Consider a sequential circuit shown in Fig. 3.12. Draw the transition table.

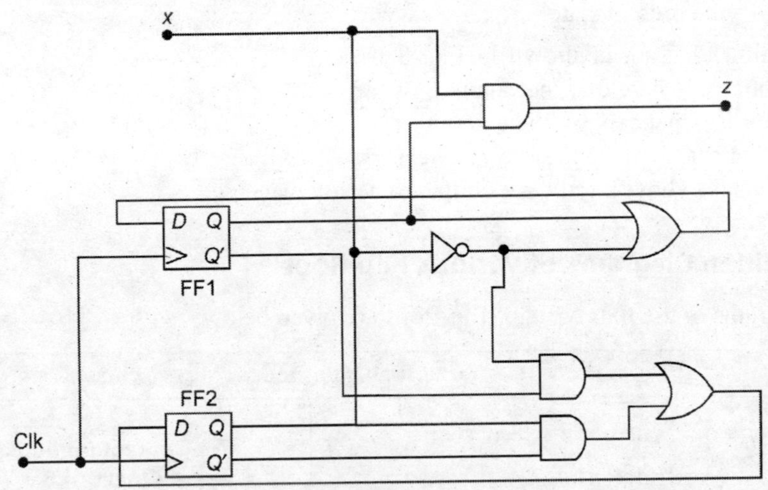

Fig. 3.12: Sequential circuit

Solution: Sequential circuit has one input *x*, one output *Z* and two state variables Q_1 (for first *D*-Flip-flop) and Q_2 (for second *D*-flip-flop) thus having four possible present states 00, 01, 10, 11. The behavior of the circuit is determined by the following Boolean expressions:

$$Z = x \wedge Q_1 \quad \text{(Output equation)}$$

$$Q1_{next} = x' \vee Q_1 \quad \text{(Next State equation for first } D\text{-flip-flop)}$$

$$Q2_{next} = x \wedge Q_2' \vee x' \wedge Q_1' \quad \text{(Next State equation for Second } D\text{-flip-flop)}$$

The above equations are used to form the transition table. Suppose the present state Q_1Q_2 is 00 (i.e. $Q_1 = 0$, $Q_2 = 0$) and input $x = 0$. Using the above equations, we get output $Z = 0$, $Q1_{next} = 1$, and $Q2_{next} = 1$. Thus the next state of the circuit $Q_1Q_2 = 11$ (i.e. $Q1_{next} = 1$ and $Q2_{next} = 1$), and this will be the present state after the clock pulse has been applied. The output of the circuit corresponding to the present state $Q_1Q_2 = 00$ and $x = 1$ is $Z = 0$. All possible transitions are given in following transition table:

State or Transition table				
	Inputs			
	$x = 0$		$x = 1$	
Present state (Q_1 Q_2)	Next state	Output(z)	Next state	Output (z)
00	11	0	01	0
01	11	0	00	0
10	10	0	11	1
11	10	0	10	1

We can number the states 00, 01, 10, 11 as Q_0, Q_1, Q_2, Q_3 respectively as per their binary values in decimal as subscript of the Q. We have not mark any initial state. We assume that when clock is not there and memory elements are clear, i.e. 0 is stored then state $Q_1Q_2 = 00$ is the present state.

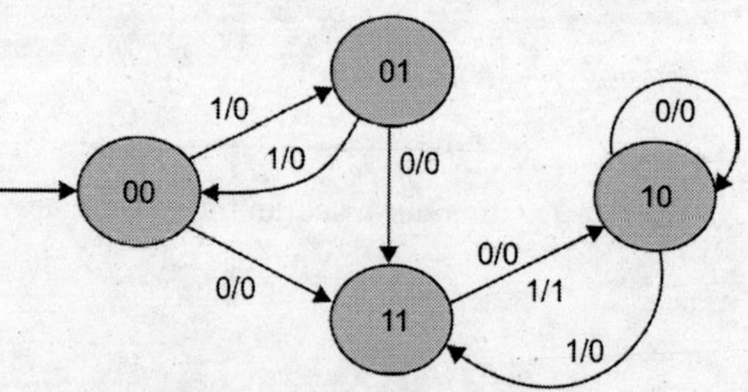

Fig. 3.13: Transition diagram

The transition diagram is shown in Fig. 3.13. One thing is noticeable here that the output z of the sequential circuit is dependent on the external input x and present state Q_1 (present state of the First D-flip-flop). Thus the above circuit is example of Mealy machine.

3.6.3 Transition Diagrams of Various Flip-flops

Transition diagrams of the four types of flip-flops are given below:

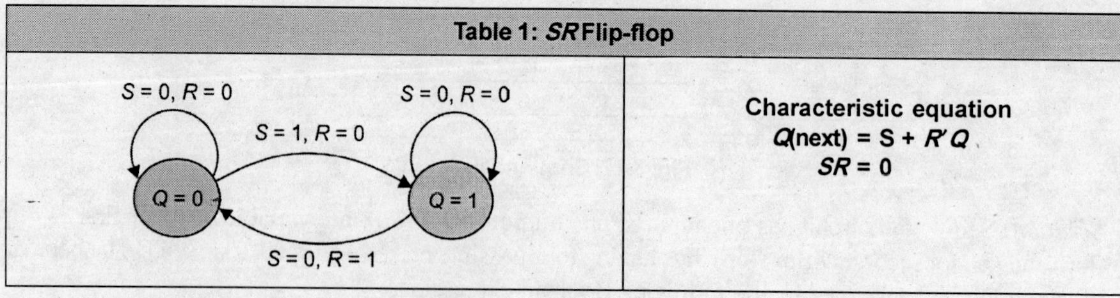

Table 1: *SR* Flip-flop

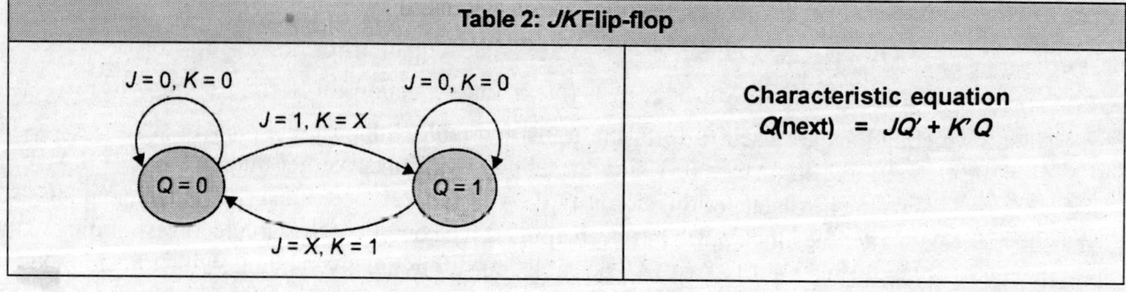

Table 2: *JK* Flip-flop

Table 3: *T* Flip-flop

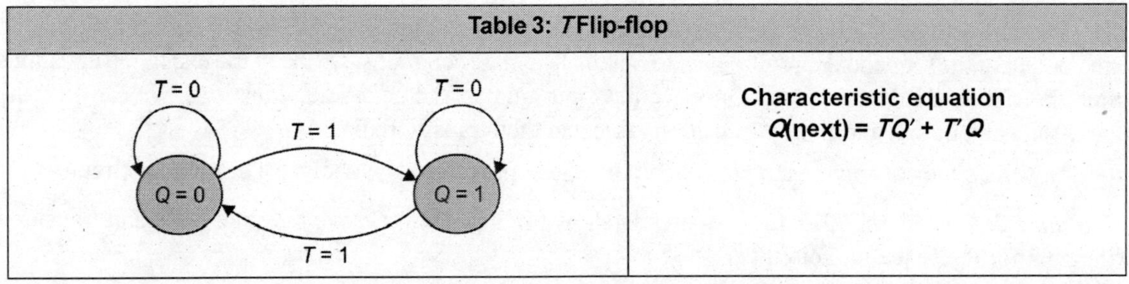

Table 4: *D* Flip-flop

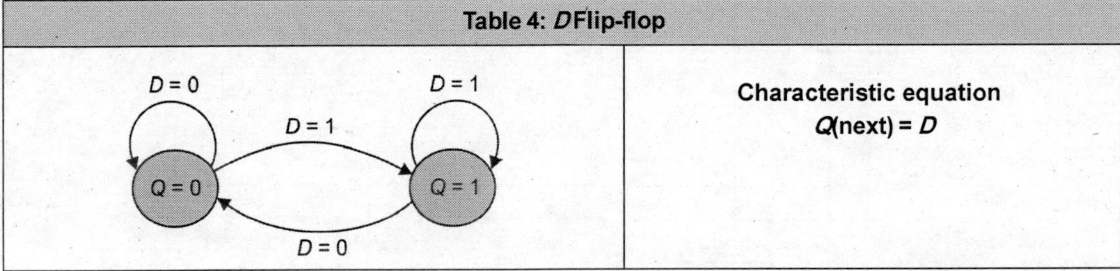

We can see from the above tables that all four flip-flops have the same number of states and transitions. Each flip-flop is in the set state when $Q = 1$ and in the reset state when $Q = 0$. Also, each flip-flop can move from one state to another, or it can re-enter the same state. The only difference between the four types lies in the values of input signals that cause these transitions.

3.7 ANALYSIS OF SEQUENTIAL CIRCUITS

The behavior of a sequential circuit is determined from the inputs, the outputs and the states of its memory elements (flip-flops). Both the output and the next state are a function of the inputs or the present state or both. We can represent the behavior of a sequential circuit by following the steps given in Fig. 3.14.

(Logical operators AND ($\wedge$), OR($\vee$), NOT, EX-OR ($\oplus$) are used along with memory elements. Readers are advised to be familiar with these operators and truth-values of logical equations.)

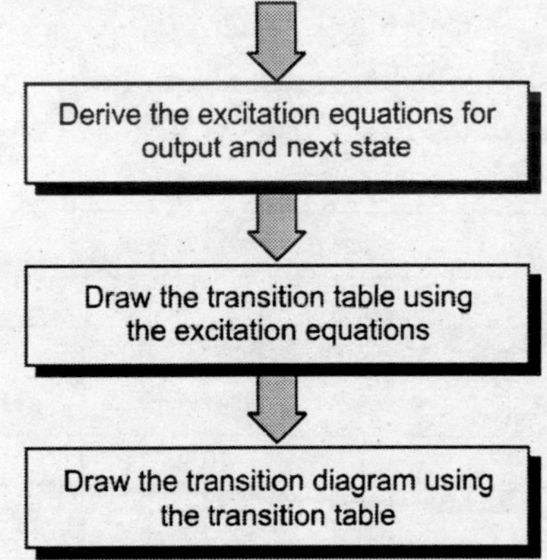

Fig. 3.14: Analysis procedure of sequential circuit

We start with the logic circuit from which we can derive excitation equations for each flip-flop input and output of the sequential circuit. Then, to obtain next-state equations, we insert the excitation equations into the characteristic equations. Once we have our output and next-state equations, we can find the next-state and output and finally transition table and then transition diagram.

Now let's look at some examples, using the above procedures to analyze a sequential circuit.

Example 2: Consider a Modulo-4 counter as shown in Fig. 3.15. Derive the state table and transition diagram for the sequential circuit.

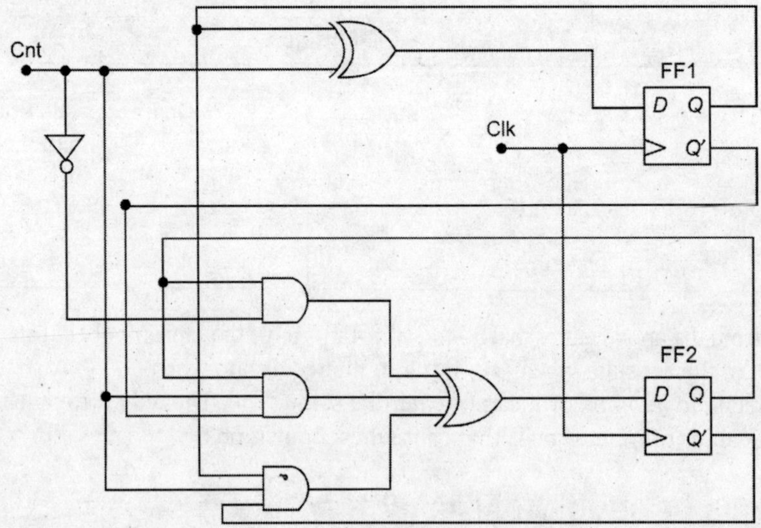

Fig. 3.15: Modulo-4 counter

Solution: First we derive the Boolean expressions for the inputs of each flip-flop in the schematic, in terms of external input **Cnt** and the flip-flop outputs Q_1 and Q_0. Since there are two D flip-flops in this example, we derive two expressions for the next state $D0_{next}$ and $D1_{next}$. There is no primary output.

$$D0_{next} = \text{Cnt} \oplus Q_0 = \text{Cnt}' \wedge Q_0 \vee \text{Cnt} \wedge Q_0'$$

$$D1_{next} = \text{Cnt}' \oplus Q_1 \vee \text{Cnt} \wedge Q_1' \wedge Q_0 \vee \text{Cnt} \wedge Q_1 \wedge Q_0'$$

These Boolean expressions are called **excitation equations** since they represent the inputs to the flip-flops of the sequential circuit in the next clock cycle. Now convert these next-state equations into tabular form as given below:

Transition table		
	Inputs	
	Cnt = 0	Cnt = 1
Present state(Q_0Q_1)	**Next state**	**Next state**
00	00	10
01	01	11
10	10	01
11	11	00

Each row is corresponding to a state of the sequential circuit and each column represents one set of input values. Since we have two flip-flops, the number of possible states is four, i.e. Q_0Q_1 can be equal to 00, 01, 10, or 11. These are present states as shown in the table. For the next state part of the table, each entry defines the value of the sequential circuit in the next clock cycle after the rising edge of the clock (**Clk**). Since this value depends on the present state and the value of the input signals, the next state table will contain one column for each assignment of binary values to the input signals. The transition diagram is shown in Fig. 3.16.

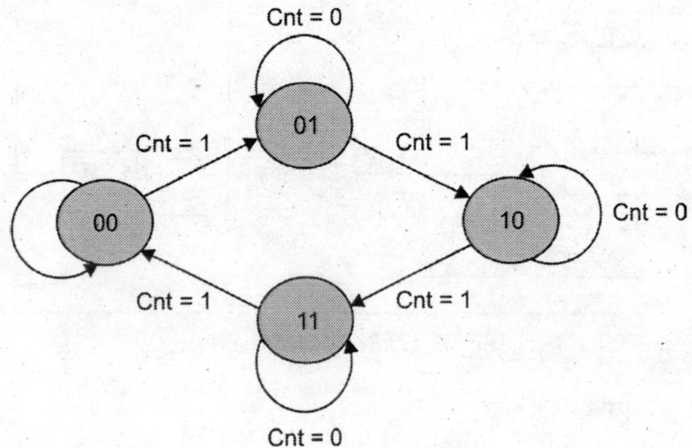

Fig. 3.16: Transition diagram of Modulo-4 counter

Each arc is labeled with the values of the input signals that cause the transition from the present state to the next state. There are four states, which are determined by the number of flip-flops used. Here we have two *D*-flip-flops and thus there are four, that is, 2^2 states.

In general, the number of states in a next-state table or a state diagram will equal 2^m, where ***m*** is the number of flip-flops. Similarly, the number of arcs or arrows will equal $2^m \times 2^k$, where ***k*** is the number of binary input signals. Therefore, in the state diagram, there must be four states and eight transitions. We can see that as long as input Cnt = 1, the sequential circuit goes through the states in the following sequence: **0, 1, 2, 3, 0, 1, 2, 3,** .... On the other hand, when Cnt = 0, the circuit stays in its present state until Cnt changes to 1, at which the counting continues. Since this sequence is characteristic of modulo-4 counting, we can conclude that the sequential circuit shown in Fig. 3.15 is a modulo-4 counter with one control signal, Cnt, which enables counting when Cnt = 1 and disables it when Cnt = 0.

Example 6: Derive the transition table and the state diagram for the sequential circuit shown in Fig. 3.17.

Solution: We have following excitation equations for next state:

$$D0_{next} = \mathbf{Cnt} \oplus Q_0 = \mathbf{Cnt}' \wedge Q_0 \vee \mathbf{Cnt} \wedge Q_0'$$

$$D1_{next} = \mathbf{Cnt}' \wedge Q_1 \vee \mathbf{Cnt} \wedge Q_1' \wedge Q_0 \vee \mathbf{Cnt} \wedge Q_1 \wedge Q_0'$$

We have following output equation:

$$Y = Q_1Q_0$$

The above output equation shows that the output *Y* will be equal to 1 when the state Q_1Q_0 is equal to 11 and it will stay 1 as long as the counter stays in that state. The output *Y* is dependent on the states of flip-flops only, not on the input Cnt. So, the sequential circuit given in Fig. 3.17 is an example of Moore machine.

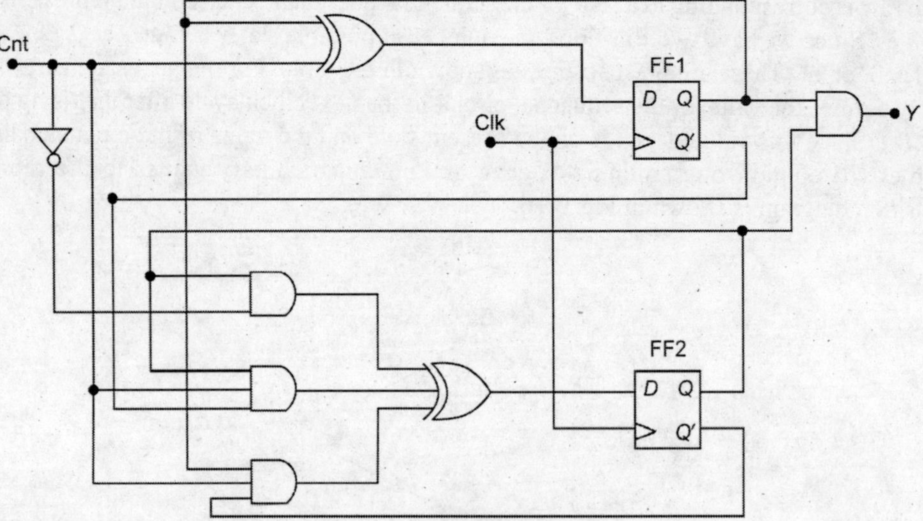

Fig. 3.17: Sequential circuit

The transition table is given below:

Transition table			
	Inputs		
	Cnt = 0	Cnt = 1	
Present state (Q_0Q_1)	Next state	Next state	Output (Q_0Q_1)
00	00	10	0
01	01	11	0
10	10	01	0
11	11	00	1

The transition diagram is shown in Fig. 3.18.

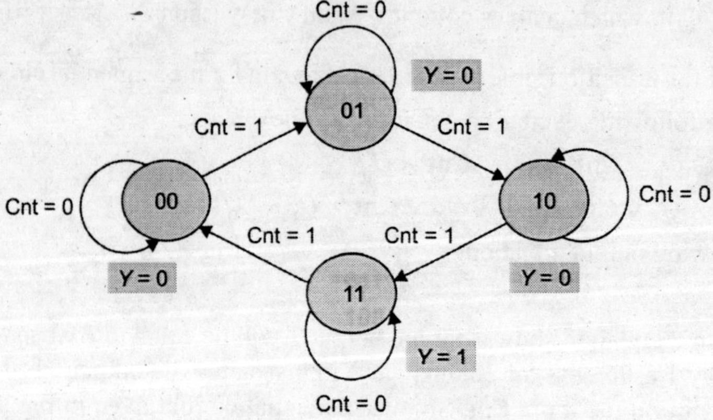

Fig. 3.18: Transition diagram

3.8 DESIGN OF SEQUENTIAL CIRCUITS

In this section, we will see how to draw the synchronous circuit from the given specification. The design of a synchronous sequential circuit starts from a set of specifications and culminates in a logic diagram or a list of Boolean functions from which a logic diagram can be obtained. In contrast to a combinational logic, which is fully specified by a truth table, a sequential circuit requires a state table for its specification. The first step in the design of sequential circuits is to obtain a state table or an equivalence representation, such as a state diagram.

A synchronous sequential circuit is made up of flip-flops and combinational gates. The design of the circuit consists of choosing the flip-flops and then finding the combinational structure which, together with the flip-flops, produces a circuit that fulfils the required specifications. The number of flip-flops is determined from the number of states needed in the description of behavior of circuit. We follow the following steps in designing a sequential circuit as given in Fig. 3.20.

Example 3: Consider the transition diagram shown in Fig. 3.19. Design a synchronous sequential circuit for it using *JK* flip-flops.

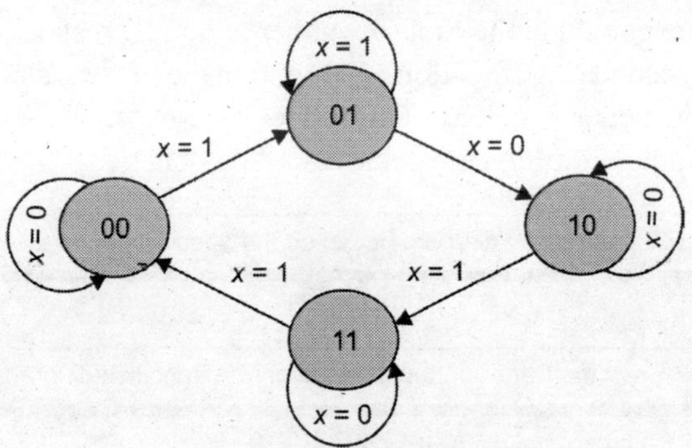

Fig. 3.19: Transition diagram

Solution: From the transition diagram, we can get the transition table, which is given below. Note that there is no output section for this sequential circuit. Since, there are four states, so two flip-flops are needed to represent the four states. The input variable is labeled as *x*.

Transition table		
	Inputs	
	$x = 0$	$x = 1$
Present state(Q_0Q_1)	Next state	Next state
00	00	01
01	10	01
10	10	11
11	11	00

We shall now derive the excitation table and the combinational structure. The table is now arranged in a different form shown below, where the present state and input variables are arranged in the form of a truth table. We use the excitation table for the *JK* flip-flop and decide the combination of the inputs for *J* and *K* as given below:

Present state	Next state	Input	Inputs of *JK* Flip-flops	
(Q_0Q_1)	(Q_0Q_1)	x	$J_0\ K_0$	$J_1\ K_1$
00	00	0	0 *X*	0 *X*
00	01	1	0 *X*	1 *X*
01	10	0	1 *X*	*X*1
01	01	1	0 *X*	*X*0
10	10	0	*X*0	0 *X*
10	11	1	*X*0	1 *X*
11	11	0	*X*0	*X*0
11	00	1	*X*1	*X*1

In the first row of above table, we have a transition for first J_0K_0 flip-flop Q_0 from 0 in the present state to 0 in the next state. We find that a transition of states from 0 to 0 requires that input $J = 0$ and input $K = X$. So, 0 and X are copied in the first row under J_0 and K_0 respectively. Since the first row also shows a transition for the second J_1K_1 flip-flop Q_1 from 0 in the present state to 0 in the next state, 0 and X are copied in the first row under J_1 and K_1. This process is continued for each row of the table and for each flip-flop, with the input conditions as specified in above table.

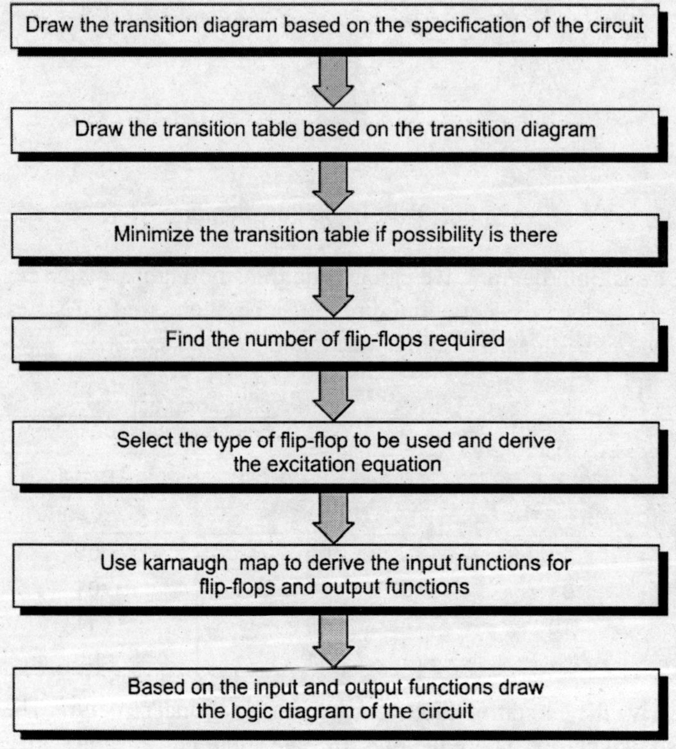

Fig. 3.20: Steps for designing a sequential circuit

The simplified Boolean functions for the combinational circuit can now be derived. The input variables are Q_0, Q_1, and x; the outputs are the variables J_0, K_0, J_1 and K_1. The information from the truth table is plotted on the **Karnaugh** maps shown in Fig. 3.21.

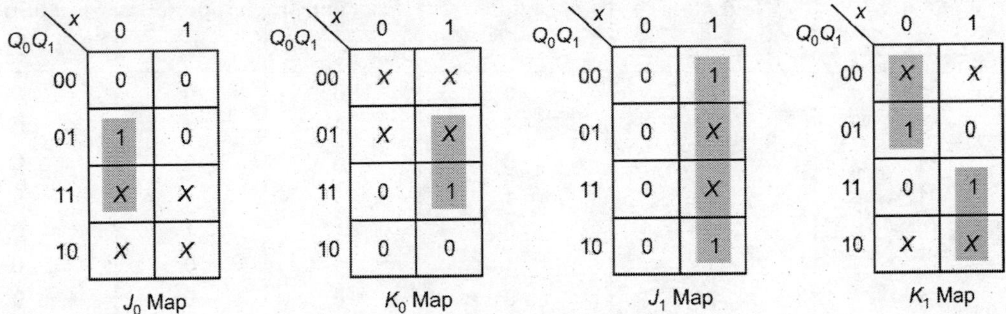

Fig. 3.21: Karnaugh map plotting

The flip-flop input functions are derived as follows:

$$J_0 = Q_1 \wedge x'$$
$$K_0 = Q_1 \wedge x$$
$$J_1 = x$$
$$K_1 = Q_0' \wedge x' \vee Q_0 \wedge x = (Q_0 \oplus x)'$$

The logic diagram is shown in Fig. 3.22.

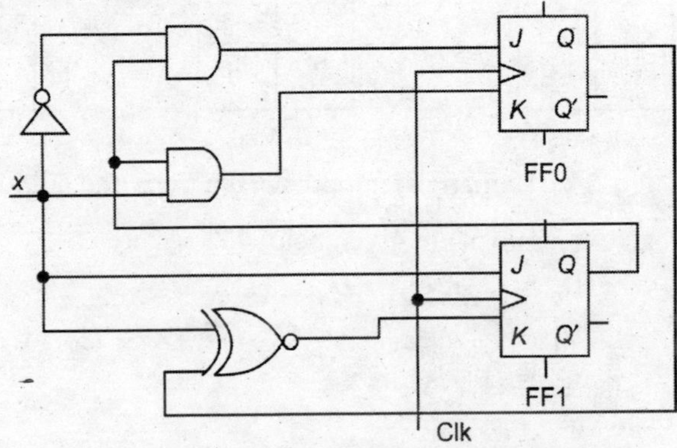

Fig. 3.22: Logic diagram of sequential circuit

Example 4: Design a sequential circuit whose transition table is given below using *D* flip-flops.

Present state	Next state		Output	
Q_0Q_1	x = 0	x = 1	x = 0	x = 1
00	00	01	0	0
01	00	10	0	0
10	11	10	0	0
11	00	01	0	1

(Readers are advised to be familiar about Karnaugh map and its application)

Solution: There are four states, one input, and one output. First we find the combination of input (x), output (z), and states (Q_0Q_1) and possible inputs (D_0 and D_1) for two D-flip-flops as given below:

Present state	Next state	Input	Flip-flops inputs		Output
Q_0 Q_1	Q_0 Q_1	x	D_0	D_0	D_0
00	00	0	0	0	0
00	01	1	0	1	0
01	00	0	0	0	0
01	10	1	1	0	0
10	11	0	1	1	0
10	10	1	1	0	0
11	00	0	0	0	0
11	01	1	0	1	1

Now plot the flip-flop inputs and output functions on the Karnaugh map to derive the Boolean expressions, which is shown in Fig. 3.23.

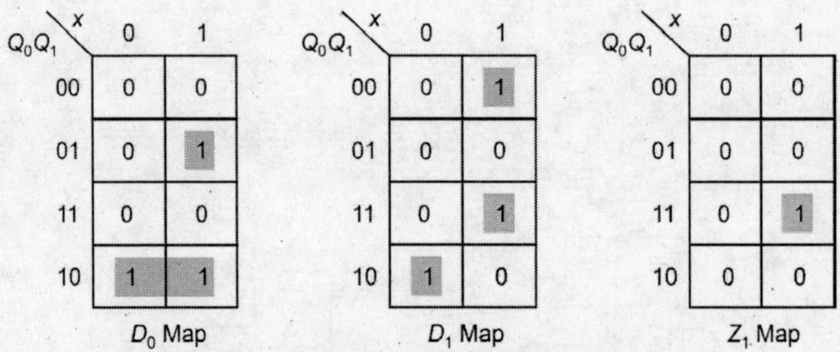

Fig. 3.23: Karnaugh for Inputs of flip-flops and output

The simplified Boolean expressions are given below:

$$D_0 = Q_0 \wedge Q_1' \vee Q_0' \wedge Q_1 \wedge x$$

$$D_1 = Q_0' \wedge Q_1' \wedge x \vee Q_0 \wedge Q_1 \wedge x \vee Q_0 \wedge Q_1' \wedge x'$$

$$Z = Q_0 \wedge Q_1 \wedge x$$

The logic diagram is shown in Fig. 3.24.

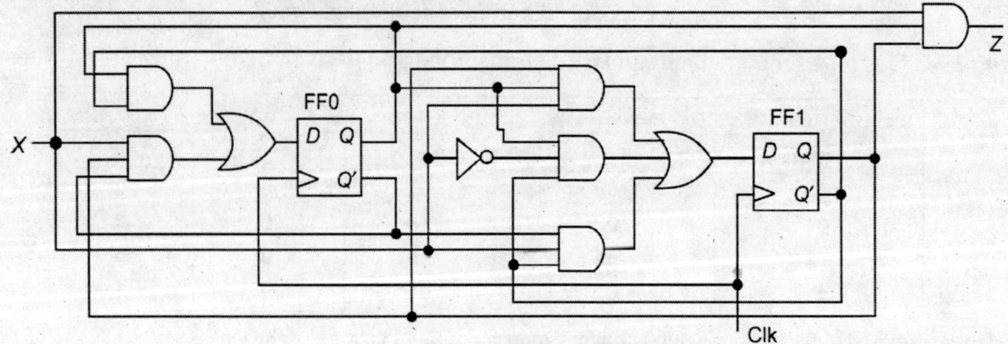

Fig. 3.24: Logic diagram

Example 5: Consider the 3-bit binary counter given in Fig. 3.25. Draw the logic circuit of this counter. The circuit has no inputs other than the clock pulse and no outputs other than its internal state (outputs are taken off each flip-flop in the counter). The next state of the counter depends entirely on its present state, and the state transition occurs every time the clock pulse occurs.

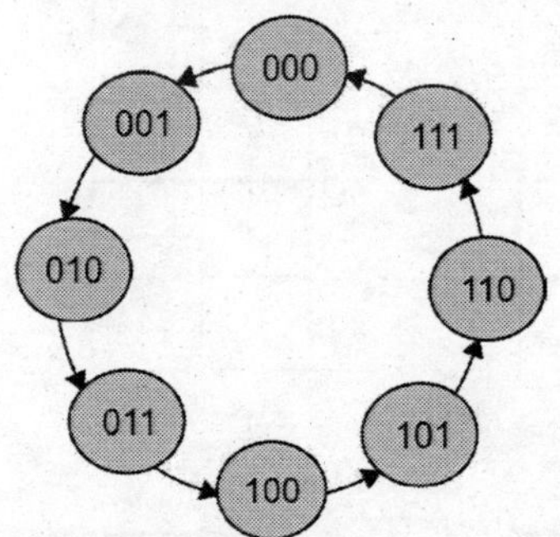

Fig. 3.25: 3-bit Binary Counter

Solution: First we draw the transition table as given below:

Present state $Q_2Q_1Q_0$	Next state $Q_2Q_1Q_0$
000	001
001	010
010	011
011	100
100	101
101	110
110	111
111	000

Since there are eight states, the number of flip-flops required would be three. Now we want to implement the counter design using *JK* flip-flops. The next step is to develop an excitation table from the transition table, which is given below:

Transitions		*JK* Flip-flops Inputs		
Present state $Q_2Q_1Q_0$	Next state $Q_2Q_1Q_0$	J_2K_2	$J_1 K_1$	$J_0 K_0$
000	001	0 *X*	0 *X*	1 *X*
001	010	0 *X*	1 *X*	*X*1
010	011	0 *X*	*X*0	1 *X*
011	100	1 *X*	*X*1	*X*1
100	101	*X*0	0 *X*	1 *X*
101	110	*X*0	1 *X*	*X*1
110	111	*X*0	*X*0	1 *X*
111	000	*X*1	*X*1	*X*1

Now we transfer the states of the flip-flop inputs from the excitation table to Karnaugh maps to derive a simplified Boolean expression for each flip-flop inputs, which is shown in Fig. 3.26.

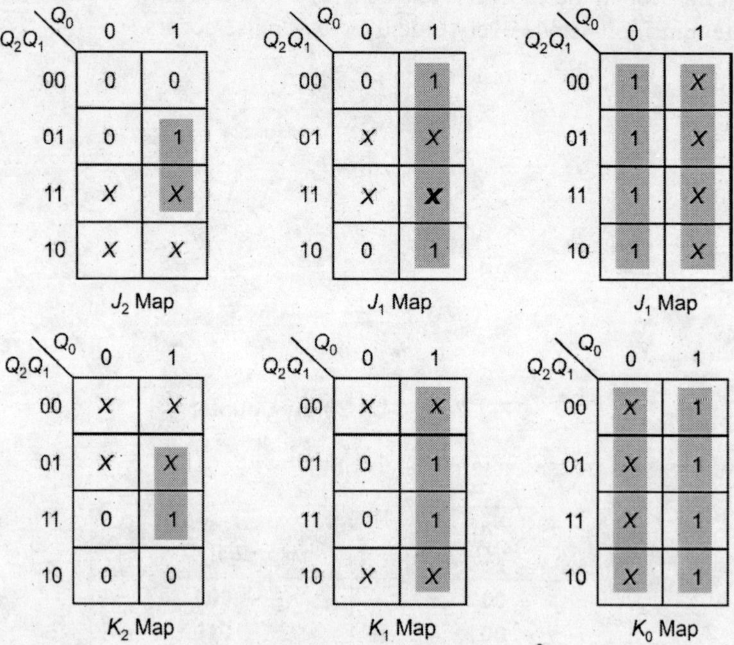

Fig. 3.26: Karnaugh map plotting

We have following equations for the inputs of three *JK* flip-flops:

$$J_0 = K_0 = 1$$
$$J_1 = K_1 = Q_0$$
$$J_2 = K_2 = Q_1 \wedge Q_0$$

The final step is to implement the combinational logic from the equations and connect the flip-flops to form the sequential circuit. The complete logic of a 3-bit binary counter is shown in Fig. 3.27.

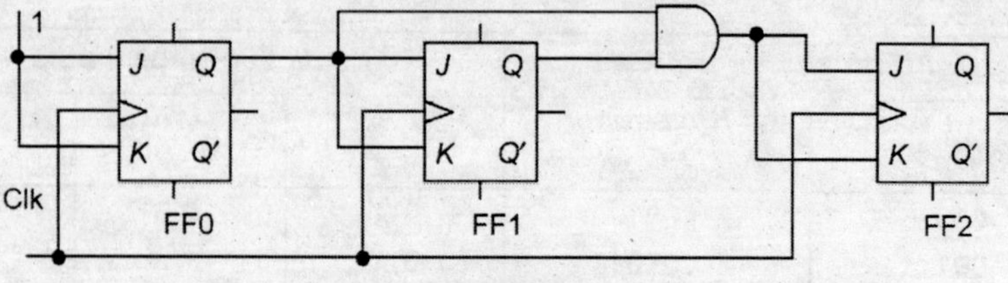

Fig. 3.27: 3-bit binary counter

3.9 SOLVED EXAMPLES

Example 3.1: Construct a Mealy machine equivalent to Moore machine $M_1 = (Q, \Sigma, \Delta, \delta, \lambda, s)$ described in following transition table.

Transition table			
	Inputs		
	0	1	
Present state	Next state	Next state	Output
s	q_3	q_1	0
q_1	q_1	q_2	1
q_2	q_2	q_3	0
q_3	q_3	s	0

Solution: Let equivalent Mealy machine $M_2 = (Q, \Sigma, \Delta, \delta, \lambda', s)$, where

$Q = \{s, q_1, q_2, q_3\}$, $\Sigma = \{0, 1\}$, $D = \{0, 1\}$, and λ' is defined as following:

For state s: $\lambda'(s, 0) = \lambda(\delta(s, 0)) = \lambda(q_3) = 0$

$\lambda'(s, 1) = \lambda(\delta(s, 1)) = \lambda(q_1) = 1$

For state q_1: $\lambda'(q_1, 0) = \lambda(\delta(q_1, 0)) = \lambda(q_1) = 1$

$\lambda'(q_1, 1) = \lambda(\delta(q_1, 1)) = \lambda(q_2) = 0$

For state q_2: $\lambda'(q_2, 0) = \lambda(\delta(q_2, 0)) = \lambda(q_2) = 0$

$\lambda'(q_2, 1) = \lambda(\delta(q_2, 1)) = \lambda(q_3) = 0$

For state q_3: $\lambda'(q_3, 0) = \lambda(\delta(q_3, 0)) = \lambda(q_3) = 0$

$\lambda'(q_3, 1) = \lambda(\delta(q_3, 1)) = \lambda(s) = 0$

Transition is same for both machines, and s is the starting state.

Transition table				
	Inputs			
	0		1	
Present state	Next state	Output	Next state	Output
→ s	q_3	0	q_1	1
q_1	q_1	1	q_2	0
q_2	q_2	0	q_3	0
q_3	q_3	0	s	0

Example 3.2: Construct a Moore machine equivalent to Mealy machine $M_1 = (Q, \Sigma, \Delta, \delta, \lambda, s)$ described in following transition table.

Transition table				
	Inputs			
	0		1	
Present state	Next state	Output	Next state	Output
→ s	s_1	z_1	s_2	z_1
s_1	s_1	z_2	s_2	z_1
s_2	s_1	z_1	s_2	z_2

Solution: Let $M_1 = (Q, \Sigma, D, \delta, \lambda, s)$ is given Mealy machine and $M_2 = (Q', \Sigma, \Delta', \delta', \lambda', s')$ be the equivalent Moore machine, where

1. $Q' \subseteq \{[s, z_1], [s, z_2], [s_1, z_1], [s_1, z_2], [s_2, z_1], [s_2, z_2]\}$ (Since, $Q' \subseteq Q \times \Delta$),
2. $\Sigma = \{0, 1\}$,
3. $\Delta' = \{z_1, z_2\}$,
4. Let starting state $s' = [s, z_1]$, where s is the initial state and z_1 is the output symbol of Mealy machine,
5. δ' is defined as follows:

   For initial state $[s, z_1]$:

   $$\delta'([s, z_1], 0) = [\delta(s, 0), \lambda(s, 0)] = [s_1, z_1]$$
   $$\delta'([s, z_1], 1) = [\delta(s, 1), \lambda(s, 1)] = [s_2, z_1]$$

   (Note: Both states $[s_1, z_1]$ and $[s_2, z_1]$ are reachable from initial state.)

   For state $[s_1, z_1]$:

   $$\delta'([s_1, z_1], 0) = [\delta(s_1, 0), \lambda(s_1, 0)] = [s_1, z_2]$$
   $$\delta'([s_1, z_1], 1) = [\delta(s_1, 1), \lambda(s_1, 1)] = [s_2, z_1]$$

   For state $[s_2, z_1]$:

   $$\delta'([s_2, z_1], 0) = [\delta(s_2, 0), \lambda(s_2, 0)] = [s_1, z_1]$$
   $$\delta'([s_2, z_1], 1) = [\delta(s_2, 1), \lambda(s_2, 1)] = [s_2, z_2]$$

   (Note: Both states $[s_1, z_2]$ and $[s_2, z_2]$ are reachable states.)

   For state $[s_1, z_2]$:

   $$\delta'([s_1, z_2], 0) = [\delta(s_1, 0), \lambda(s_1, 0)] = [s_1, z_2]$$
   $$\delta'([s_1, z_2], 1) = [\delta(s_1, 1), \lambda(s_1, 1)] = [s_2, z_1]$$

   For state $[s_2, z_2]$:

   $$\delta'([s_2, z_2], 0) = [\delta(s_2, 0), \lambda(s_2, 0)] = [s_1, z_1]$$
   $$\delta'([s_2, z_2], 1) = [\delta(s_2, 1), \lambda(s_2, 1)] = [s_2, z_2]$$

   (Note: We have considered those states, which are reachable from initial state.)
6. λ' is defined as follows:

   $$\lambda'[s, z_1] = z_1, \lambda'[s_1, z_1] = z_1, \lambda'[s_2, z_1] = z_1, \lambda'[s_1, z_2] = z_2, \lambda'[s_2, z_2] = z_2$$

Transition table			
	Inputs		
	0	1	
Present state	**Next state**	**Next state**	**Output**
→ $[s, z_1]$	$[s_1, z_1]$	$[s_2, z_1]$	z_1
$[s_1, z_1]$	$[s_1, z_2]$	$[s_2, z_1]$	z_1
$[s_2, z_1]$	$[s_1, z_1]$	$[s_2, z_2]$	z_1
$[s_1, z_2]$	$[s_1, z_2]$	$[s_2, z_1]$	z_2
$[s_2, z_2]$	$[s_1, z_1]$	$[s_2, z_2]$	z_2

Example 3.3: Construct a Mealy machine which reads input from {0, 1} and outputs EVEN or ODD according to total number of 1's even or odd.

Solution: We consider two states p, which outputs EVEN and q, which outputs ODD.

Suppose $x \in (0 + 1)^*$ has even number of 1's, then $X11$ also has even number of 1's.

Suppose $y \in (0 + 1)^*$ has odd number of 1's, then $Y1$ also has odd number of 1's.

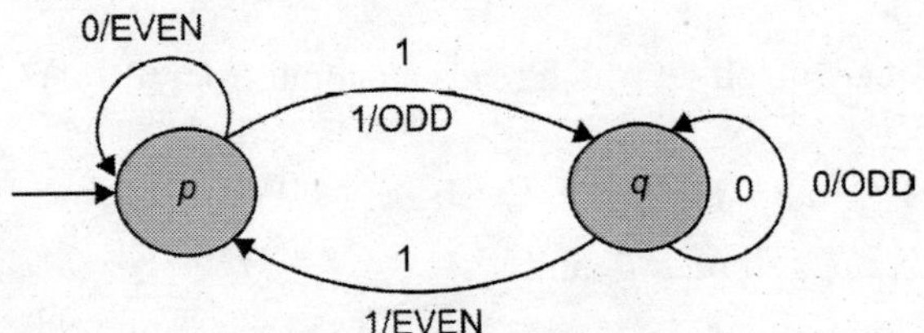

Fig. 3.28: Mealy machine

Example 3.4: Design a Moore machine, which outputs residue mod 3 for each binary input string treated as a binary integer.

Solution: Let Moore machine $M = (Q, \Sigma, \Delta, \delta, \lambda, q_0)$, where

$\Sigma = \{0, 1\}$, $\Delta = \{0, 1, 2\}$(outputs after mod 3),

Let three states $\{q_0, q_1, q_2\}$ are there and

- State q_0 outputs 0,
- State q_1 outputs 1, and
- State q_2 outputs 2.

If input is binary string X, then

> ***X* is followed by a 0 is equivalent to twice of *X*.**
> ***X* is followed by a 1 is equivalent to twice of *X* plus 1**

or

$$X0 \equiv (2*X)_{10} \quad \text{(in decimal system), and}$$
$$X1 \equiv (2*X)_{10} + 1 \quad \text{(in decimal system)}$$

If X mod 3 = p, for p = 0 or 1 or 2, then

$X0$ mod 3 = $2*p$ mod 3 (For input 0 and P = 0, 1, 2)

= 0 or 2 or 1

For transition:

$$q_p \rightarrow q_{2*p \bmod 3} \quad \text{for } p = 0, 1, 2$$

$X1$ mod 3 = $(2*p + 1)$ mod 3 (**For input 1** and P = 0, 1, 2)

= 1, 0, 2

For transition:

$$q_p \rightarrow q_{(2*p + 1) \bmod 3} \quad \text{for } p = 0, 1, 2$$

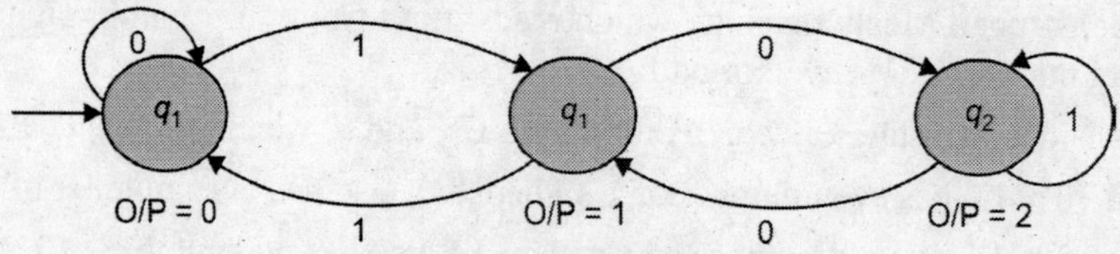

Fig. 3.29: Transition diagram

Example 3.5: Design a Mealy machine which reads the input from (0 + 1)* and produces the following outputs:

(i) If input ends in 101, output is *A*,

(ii) If input ends 110, the output is *B*, and

(iii) For other inputs, output is *C*.

Solution: Suppose, Mealy machine $M = (Q, \Sigma, \Delta, \delta, \lambda, q_0)$ which reads the inputs from (0 + 1)*, starting from the least significant bit (LSB).

Consider three LSBs of Input		Output
...000	(*X*)	*C*
...001	(*X*)	*C*
...010	(*X*)	*C*
...011	(*X*)	*C*
...100	(*X*)	*C*
...101		*A*
...110		*B*
...111	(*X*)	*C*

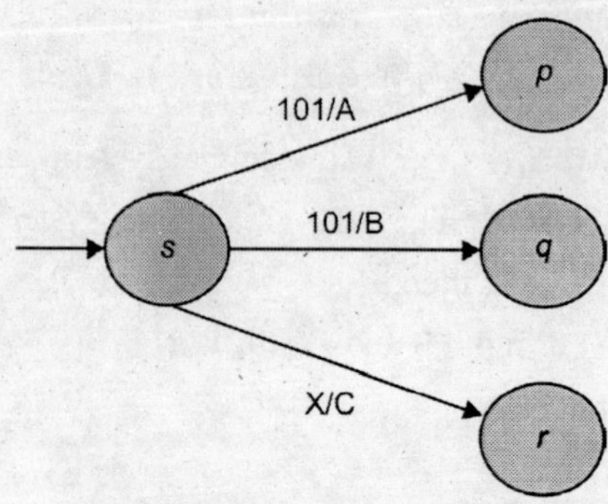

Fig. 3.30: Moore machine

Example 3.6: Design a Moore machine which reads input from (0 + 1 + 2)* and outputs residue mod 5 of the input. Input considered at base 3 and it is treated as ternary integer.

Solution: Let Moore machine $M = (Q, \Sigma, \Delta, \delta, \lambda, q_0)$ produces output residue mod 5 for each input string written in base 3.

$$\Sigma = \{0, 1, 2\}, \Delta = \{0, 1, 2, 3, 4\}$$

Let five states $\{q_0, q_1, q_2, q_3, q_4\}$ are there and

- State q_0 outputs 0,
- State q_1 outputs 1,
- State q_2 outputs 2,
- State q_3 outputs 3, and
- State q_4 outputs 4.

If input is binary string W, then

- W is followed by a 0 is equivalent to thrice of W
- W is followed by a 1 is equivalent to thrice of W plus 1
- W is followed by a 2 is equivalent to thrice of W plus 2

Or $W0 \equiv (3*X)_{10}$ (in decimal system), and

$W1 \equiv (3*X)_{10} + 1$ (in decimal system),

$W2 \equiv (3*X)_{10} + 2$ (in decimal system)

If W mod 5 = p, for p = 0, 1, 2, 3, 4 (in the order of the elements), then

$W0$ mod 5 = $3*p$ mod 5 **(For input 0)**

= 0, 3, 1, 4, 2 (In the order of elements and P = 0, 1, 2, 3, 4)

For transition:

$Q_p \rightarrow Q_{3*p \bmod 5}$ for p = 0, 1, 2, 3, 4 (in the order of the elements)

$W1$ mod 5 =$(3*p + 1)$ mod 5 **(For input 1)**

= 1, 4, 2, 0, 3 (In the order of elements and P = 0, 1, 2, 3, 4)

For transition:

$Q_p \rightarrow Q_{(3*p + 1) \bmod 5}$ for p = {0, 1, 2, 3, 4} (in the order of the elements)

$W2$ mod 5 =$(3*p + 2)$ mod 5 **(For input 2)**

=2, 0, 3, 1, 4 (In the order of elements and P = 0, 1, 2, 3, 4)

For transition:

$Q_p \rightarrow Q_{(3*p + 2) \bmod 5}$ for p = 0, 1, 2, 3, 4 (in the order of the elements)

Transition table				
	Inputs			
	0	1	2	
Present state	Next state	Next state	Next state	Output
q_0	q_0	q_1	q_2	0
q_1	q_3	q_4	q_0	1
q_2	q_1	q_2	q_3	2
q_3	q_4	q_0	q_1	3
q_4	q_2	q_3	q_4	4

Example 3.7 Consider the following transition table of a Mealy machine. Construct minimum state Mealy machine

Transition table				
	Inputs			
	0		1	
Present state	Next state	Output	Next state	Output
→ q_1	q_1	0	q_2	0
q_2	q_1	0	q_3	1
q_3	q_1	0	q_3	1

Solution: Last two rows of transition table show that states q_2 and q_3 are equivalent states. So, replacing these states by $[q_2, q_3]$ we have the following intermediate transition table:

Transition table				
	Inputs			
	0		1	
Present state	Next state	Output	Next state	Output
→ q_1	q_1	0	$[q_2, q_3]$	0
$[q_2, q_3]$	q_1	0	$[q_2, q_3]$	1
$[q_2, q_3]$	q_1	0	$[q_2, q_3]$	1

Deleting the last row, we have the following final transition table:

Transition table				
	Inputs			
	0		1	
Present state	Next state	Output	Next state	Output
→ q_1	q_1	0	$[q_2, q_3]$	0
$[q_2, q_3]$	q_1	0	$[q_2, q_3]$	1

Example 3.8: Consider following Mealy machine described in following transition table. Construct equivalent minimum state Mealy machine.

Transition table				
	Inputs			
	0		1	
Present state	Next state	Output	Next state	Output
→ *a*	*a*	0	*b*	0
b	*c*	0	*d*	0
c	*a*	0	*f*	0
d	*e*	0	*f*	1
e	*a*	0	*f*	1
f	*g*	0	*f*	1
g	*a*	0	*f*	1

Solution: State *e* and *g* (row 7 and row 5) are equivalent states. So replacing *e* and *g* by [*e*, *g*], we have the following intermediate transition table:

Transition table				
	Inputs			
	0		1	
Present state	Next state	Output	Next state	Output
→ *a*	*a*	0	*b*	0
b	*c*	0	*d*	0
c	*a*	0	*f*	0
d	[*e*, *g*]	0	*f*	1
[*e*, *g*]	*a*	0	*f*	1
f	[*e*, *g*]	0	*f*	1
[*e*, *g*]	*a*	0	*f*	1

Now, states *d* and *f* (row 4 and 6) are equivalent states. So, replacing these states by [*d*, *f*], we have the following transition table:

Transition table				
	Inputs			
	0		1	
Present state	Next state	Output	Next state	Output
→ *a*	*a*	0	*b*	0
b	*c*	0	*d*	0
c	*a*	0	[*d*, *f*]	0
[*d*, *f*]	[*e*, *g*]	0	[*d*, *f*]	1
[*e*, *g*]	*a*	0	[*d*, *f*]	1
[*d*, *f*]	[*e*, *g*]	0	[*d*, *f*]	1
[*e*, *g*]	*a*	0	[*d*, *f*]	1

Now, we have no more equivalent states. Removing the redundancy from the above transition table, we have the following **final transition table:**

Transition table				
	Inputs			
	0		1	
Present state	Next state	Output	Next state	Output
→ *a*	*a*	0	*b*	0
b	*c*	0	*d*	0
c	*a*	0	[*d*, *f*]	0
[*d*, *f*]	[*e*, *g*]	0	[*d*, *f*]	1
[*e*, *g*]	*a*	0	[*d*, *f*]	1

Example 3.9: Full adder shown in Fig. 3.31 receives two external inputs x and y; the third input z comes from the output of a D flip-flop. The carry output is transferred to the flip-flop every clock pulse. The external output gives the sum of x, y, and z. Obtain theTransition diagram of the sequential circuit.

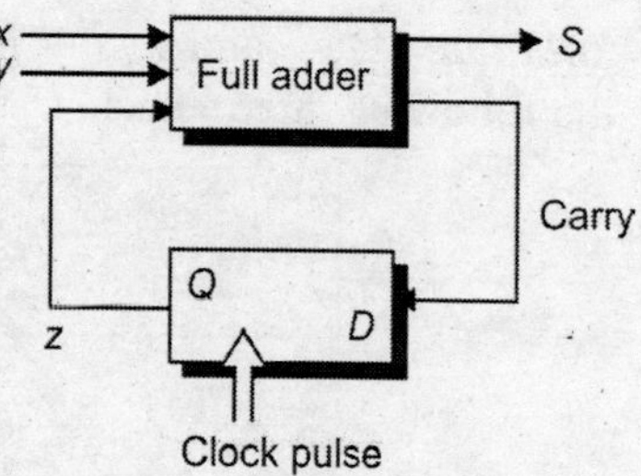

Fig. 3.31: Full adder

Solution: One flip-flop is used, so it may be in state 0 or 1. Inputs are x, y, and z, so eight different possible combinations are there. When carry = 0 (or D = 0), then state 0 is reachable otherwise state 1 is reachable.

State	Input			Output (sum)	Carry	Next state
	x	*y*	*z*		*D*	
0	0	0	0	0	0	0
0	0	1	0	1	0	0
0	1	0	0	1	0	0
0	1	1	0	0	1	1
1	0	0	1	1	0	0
1	0	1	1	0	1	1
1	1	0	1	0	1	1
1	1	1	1	1	1	1

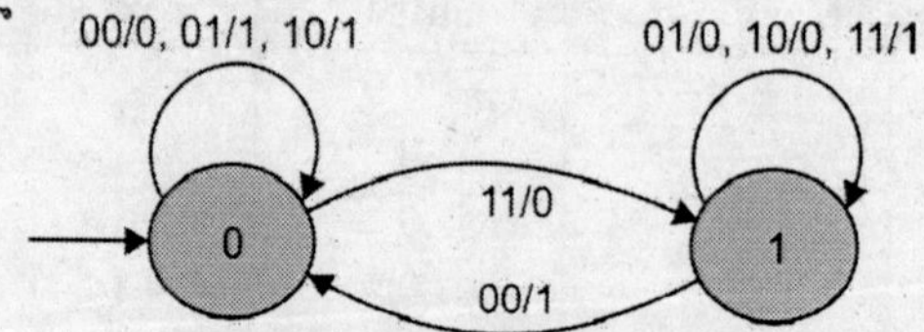

Fig. 3.32: Full adder

Example 3.10: Suppose a deterministic finite automaton has reading and additional output capabilities. The given alphabet is {0, 1} and following input and output are obtained:

	INPUT	OUTPUT (Sum of two binary bits)
(i)	00	0
(ii)	01	1
(iii)	10	1
(iv)	11	0
(v)	Other	*e* (*e* stands for NULL string.)

Draw the transition diagram.

Solution: We have two symbols (bits) in given alphabet. So, from initial state two possible transitions are there, and same for the other states.

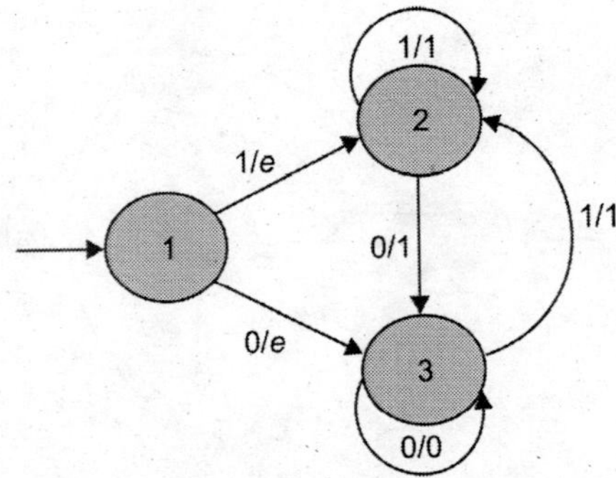

Fig. 3.33: DFA with output capability

We have following inputs and outputs combinations:

(a) When input is 1 in the state 1, then output is e and next state is 2.

(b) When input is 0 in the state 1, then output is e and next state is 3.

(c) When input is 0 in the state 2, then input is 10 (including previous input bit) and output is 1 and next state is 3.

(d) When input is 1 in the state 2, then input is 11 (including previous input bit) and output is 0 and next state is 2.

(e) When input is 0 in the state 3, then input is 00 (including previous input bit) and output is 0 and next state is 3.

(f) When input is 1 in the state 3, then input is 01 (including previous input bit) and output is 1 and next state is 2.

(**Note**: If we consider the previous input 0 in the initial state 1, then outputs are 0 and 1 for inputs 00 and 01 respectively.)

Example 3.11: Consider a DFA with additional output capability over the input-output alphabet $\{a, b\}$. Draw the state diagram for the following:

(a) On input string $w \in (a + b)^*$, produces the output a^n, where n is the number of occurrence substring "*ab*" in *w*.

(b) On input string $w \in (a + b)^*$, produces a string of length $|w|$ as output whose i^{th} symbol is an '*a*' if $i = 1$, or if $i > 1$ and i^{th} symbol $(i - 1)^{th}$ symbols of w are different; otherwise the ith symbol of output is *a* '*b*'.

Examples are as follows:

	INPUT	**OUTPUT**
(i)	*aabba*	*ababa*
(ii)	*aaaab*	*abbba*

Solution:

(a) Let DFA *M* decides the occurrence of substring "*ab*" in input string $w \in (a + b)^*$.

$M = (Q, \Sigma, \delta, s, \phi)$, here set of final state $F = \phi$, because DFA has output capability, so no need of final states. Edges are labeled with *input/output*. *M* is shown in Fig. 3.34.

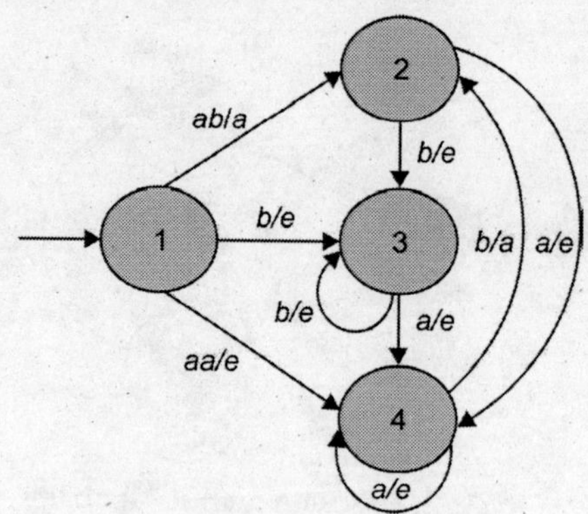

Fig. 3.34: DFA with output.

(b) Suppose desired DFA $M = (Q, \Sigma, \delta, s, \phi)$. Here, set of final state $F = \phi$, because DFA has output capability, so no need of final states. M is shown in Fig. 3.35.

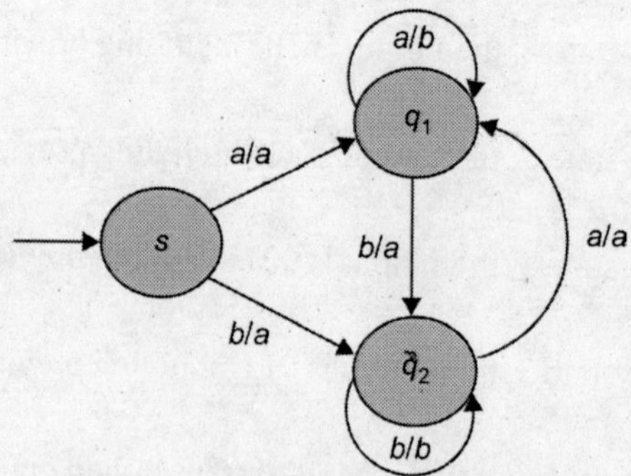

Fig. 3.35: DFA with output capability

Where, $Q = \{s, q_1, q_2\}$, and $\Sigma = \{a, b\}$.

Example 3.12: Convert the following Mealy machine (Fig. 3.36) into equivalent Moore machine.

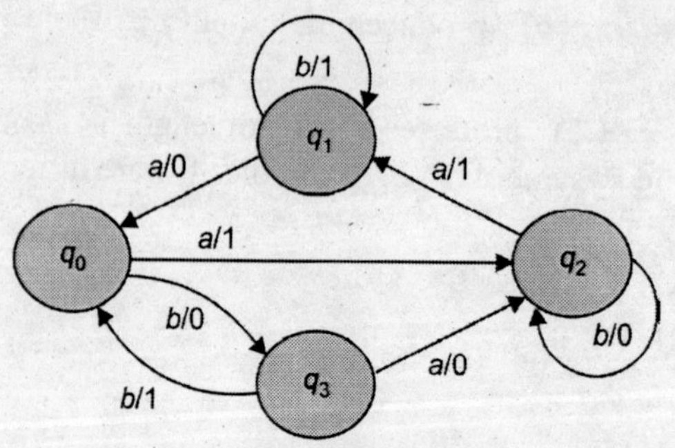

Fig. 3.36

Solution: Let $M_1 = (Q, \Sigma, \Delta, \delta, \lambda, q_0)$ is a given Mealy machine and $M_2 = (Q', \{a, b\}, (0, 1\}, \delta', \lambda', s')$ be the equivalent Moore machine, where $Q' \subseteq \{[q_0, 0], [q_0, 1], [q_1, 0], [q_1, 1], [q_2, 0], [q_2, 1], [q_3, 0], [q_3, 1]\}$ (Since, $Q' \subseteq Q \times \Delta$), $s' = [q_0, 1]$, where q_0 is the initial state and 1 is one the output symbol of Mealy machine.

Transition function δ′ is defined as following:

Transition table			
Present state	Next state		Output
	a	*b*	
→ $[q_0, 0]$	$[q_2, 1]$	$[q_3, 0]$	0
$[q_2, 1]$	$[q_1, 1]$	$[q_2, 0]$	1
$[q_3, 0]$	$[q_2, 0]$	$[q_0, 1]$	0
$[q_1, 1]$	$[q_0, 0]$	$[q_1, 1]$	1
$[q_2, 0]$	$[q_1, 1]$	$[q_2, 0]$	0
$[q_0, 1]$	$[q_2, 1]$	$[q_3, 0]$	1

Equivalent Moore machine is shown in Fig. 3.36(a).

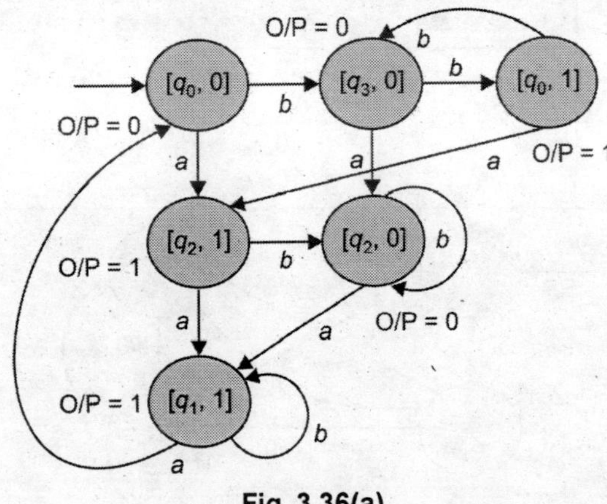

Fig. 3.36(a)

Example 3.13: Change the given Moore machine into Mealy machine:

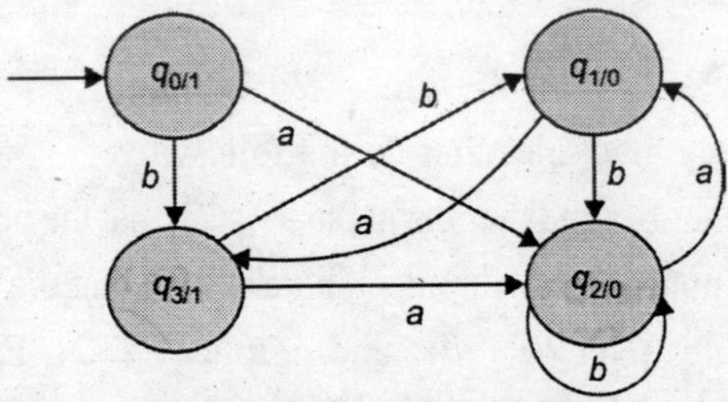

Fig. 3.37: Moore machine

Solution: Let $M_1 = (Q, \Sigma, \Delta, \delta, \lambda, q_0)$ be the given Moore machine, where transitions and output is as follows:

Transition table			
	Inputs		
	a	*b*	
Present state	Next state	Next state	Output
→ q_0	q_2	q_3	1
q_1	q_3	q_2	0
q_2	q_1	q_2	0
q_3	q_2	q_1	1

Let equivalent Mealy machine $M_2 = (Q, \Sigma, \Delta, \delta, \lambda', s)$ as shown in Fig. 3.37(a), where $Q = \{q_0, q_1, q_2, q_3\}$, $\Sigma = \{a, b\}$, $\Delta = \{a, b\}$, λ' is defined as following:

Transition table				
	Inputs			
	a		*b*	
Present state	Next state	Output	Next state	Output
→ q_0	q_2	0	q_3	1
q_1	q_3	1	q_2	0
q_2	q_1	0	q_2	0
q_3	q_2	0	q_1	0

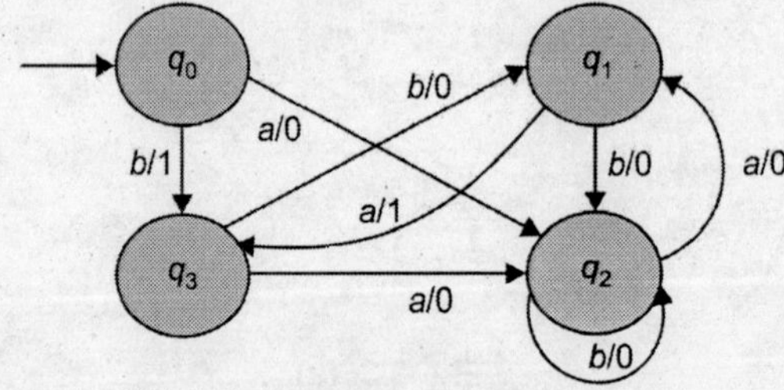

Fig. 3.37(a)

TEST YOUR SKILLS

Supplementary Problems

3.1 Design Moore and Mealy machines that do the following:

(a) Reads input binary number and outputs in binary such that the output is one greater than the input.

(b) Reads input binary number and outputs in binary such that the output is one less than the input.

(c) Recognize the strings over $(a + b)^*$ and output (EVEN, EVEN), (ODD, ODD), (EVEN, ODD), or (ODD, EVEN) according to the number of a's and b's.

3.2 Draw transition diagram of Mealy machine which reads string over $(a + b)^*$ and does the following:

(a) Produces output a^n, where n is the number of occurrence substring *ab*.

(b) Produces output a^n, where n is the number of occurrence substring *aba*.

3.3 Design a FSM which checks input whether it is even or odd. Assume that input is provided in decimal.

3.4 Consider the 3-bit binary counter shown in Fig. 3.25 and draw the logic diagram using: *T* Flip-flops, *D* Flip-flops, *SR* Flip-flops

3.5 Derive excitation equations, transition table, and state diagram for the circuit shown in Fig. 3.38.

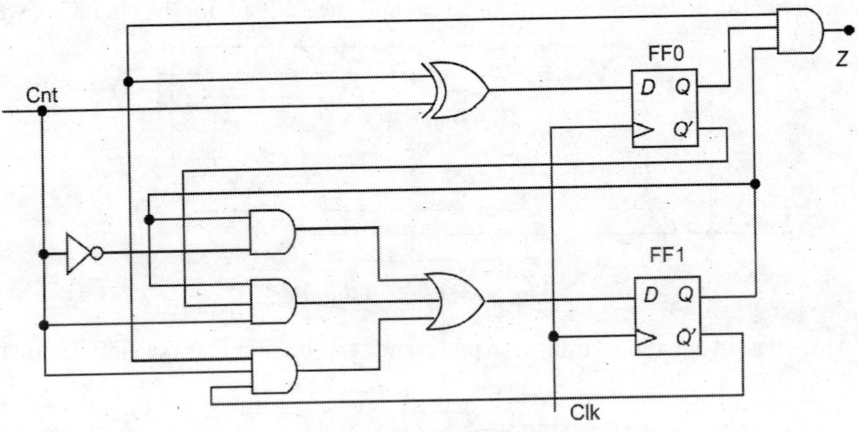

Fig. 3.38: Logic diagram

3.6 Derive excitation equations, transition table, and state diagram for the circuit shown in Fig. 3.39.

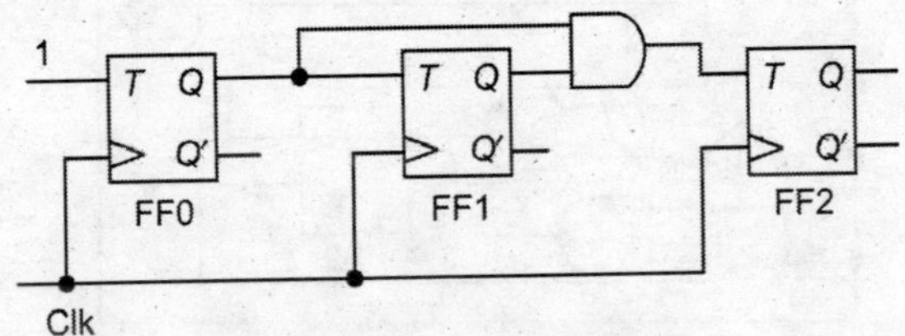

Fig. 3.39: Logic diagram

3.7 Derive excitation equations, transition table, and state diagram for the circuit shown in Fig. 3.40.

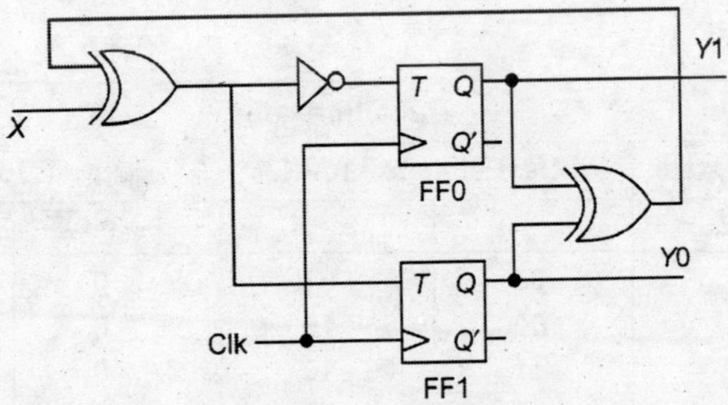

Fig. 3.40: Logic diagram

3.8 A sequential circuit uses two D flip-flops as its memory elements. The behavior of the circuit is described by the following Boolean equations:

$$D_1 = Q_1 + x'*Q_2$$
$$D_2 = x*Q_1' + x'*Q_2$$
$$Z = x'*Q_1*Q_2 + x*Q_1'*Q_2'$$

Derive the transition table and diagram of the circuit.

3.9 Derive excitation equations, transition table, and state diagram for the circuit shown in Fig. 3.41.

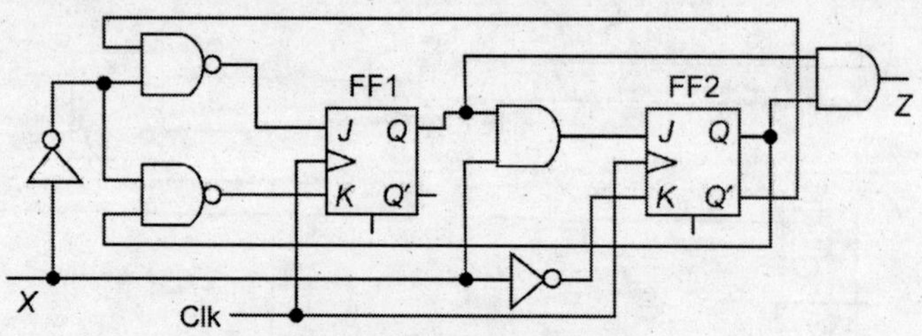

Fig. 3.41: Logic diagram

3.10 Derive excitation equations, transition table, and state diagram for the circuit shown in Fig. 3.42.

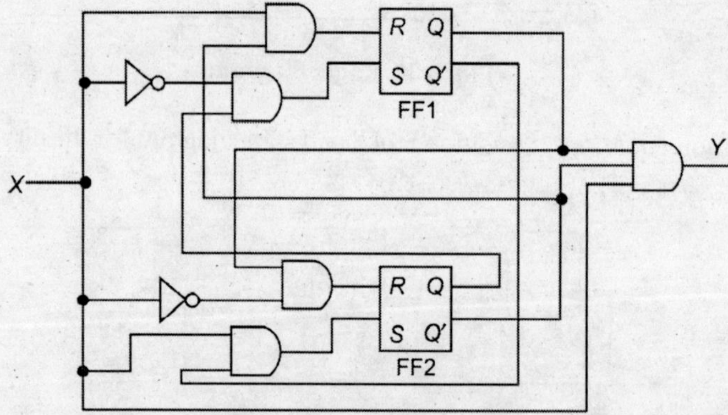

Fig. 3.42: Logic diagram

3.11 Design a sequential circuit specified in the following table using

- *JK* Flip-flops
- *SR* Flips-flops
- *T* Flip-flops
- *D* Flip-flops

Transition table				
Present state	**Next state for input**		**Output for input**	
$Q_0\ Q_1$	$x = 0$	$x = 1$	$x = 0$	$x = 1$
00	00	01	0	0
01	00	10	0	0
10	11	10	0	0
11	00	01	0	1

3.12 Design a sequential circuit specified in the following table using

- *JK* Flip-flops
- *SR* Flips-flops
- *T* Flip-flops
- *D* Flip-flops

Transition table				
Present state	**Next state for input**		**Output for input**	
Q_0Q_1	$x = 0$	$x = 1$	$x = 0$	$x = 1$
00	00	01	0	0
01	01	10	1	0
10	11	10	0	0
11	00	01	1	1

3.13 Design a sequential circuit specified in the following table using

- *JK* Flip-flops
- *SR* Flips-flops
- *T* Flip-flops
- *D* Flip-flops

Transition table			
Present state	**Next state for input**		**Output**
Q_0Q_1	$x = 0$	$x = 1$	
00	00	01	0
01	01	10	1
10	11	10	0
11	00	01	11

3.14 Compare the Moore and Mealy machines and prove that both machines have equivalent power.

3.15 What is difference between finite automaton (FA) and finite state machines?

3.16 Discuss how the finite state machines are used in designing of synchronous sequential circuits.

3.17 What are equivalent finite state machines? How a finite state machine is minimized?

3.18 Consider the transition diagram of the binary subtraction shown in Fig. 3.43. Draw the logic circuit diagram.

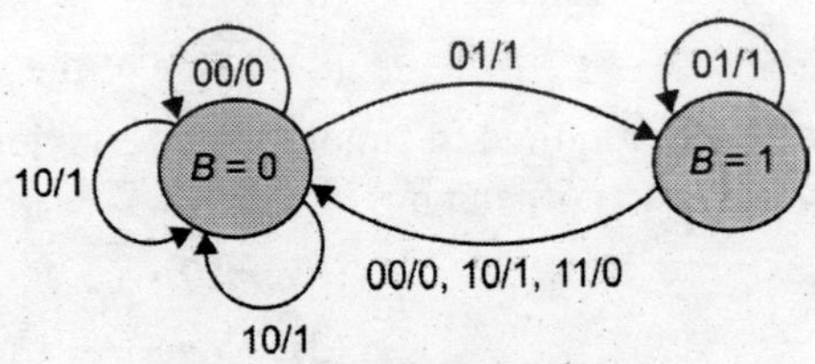

Fig. 3.43: Binary subtraction

3.19 Describe the finite state machine. How Moore and Mealy machines are mathematically described?

Multiple Choice Questions

3.20 Choose the correct statement.

(a) Moore and Mealy machines are FA with output capability

(b) Moore machine is more powerful than FA

(c) Mealy machine is more powerful than FA

(d) Moore and Mealy machines are not FA

3.21 The major difference between a Moore and a Mealy machine is that

(a) The output of Moore machine depends upon present state and input

(b) The output of Moore machine depends upon present state only

(c) The output of Moore machine depends upon present input

(d) None of the above

3.22 Choose the correct statement.

(a) Output length of equivalent Moore machine is one greater than output length of Mealy machine

(b) Output length of equivalent Mealy is equal to output length of Moore machine

(c) Output length of Moore and Mealy machine is equal

(d) Both (a) and (b) are correct

3.23 FSM can recognize

(a) Any language
(b) Only regular language
(c) Only context-free
(d) None

3.24 The basic limitation of FSM is that

(a) It can't remember large amount of information

(b) It sometimes recognizes languages that are not regular

(c) It sometimes fails to recognize regular language

(d) All statements are true

3.25 A FSM can add two given integers. This is

(a) True
(b) False
(c) May be true
(d) None of the above

3.26 The number of states of FSM, required to simulate the behavior of a computer, with a memory capable of storing m words, each of length n bits, is

(a) 2^{mn}
(b) $m*2n$
(c) 2^{m+n}
(d) None

3.27 Choose the correct statement.

(a) A FSM with one stack is more powerful than a FSM without stack

(b) A FSM with three stacks is more powerful than a FSM with two stacks

(c) A FSM with two stack is more powerful than a FSM with one stack

(d) (a) and (c)

3.28 If an input string w has n symbols and can be recognized by a Mealy machine M, then number of output symbols is

(a) $n - 1$ (b) n

(c) $n + 1$ (d) None

3.29 If an input string w has n symbols and can be recognized by a Mealy machine M_1 and equivalent Moore machine M_2 then number of output symbols by M_1 and M_2 are

(a) n, n (b) $n + 1, n$

(c) $n, n + 1$ (d) $n + 1, n + 1$

3.30 For input null the output produced by a Mealy machine is

(a) Null (b) Depends on present state

(c) Depends on given machine (d) Can't decide

3.31 For input null the output produced by a Moore machine is

(a) Null (b) Depends on present state

(c) Depends on given machine (d) Can't decide

3.32 If a Mealy machine has m states and n output symbols, then for equivalent Moore machine the maximum number of states is

(a) $mn + 1$ (b) mn

(c) m (d) 2^m

3.33 The output of Moore machine is not depend on

(a) Present state (b) Present input

(c) Present state and present input (d) None

3.34 The output of Mealy machine depends on

(a) Present state (b) Present input

(c) Present state and present input (d) None

3.35 Suppose three inputs, one output, and four states are used in transition table of a synchronous sequential circuit. How many flip-flops are required to form the logic diagram of this circuit?

(a) 12 (b) 3

(c) 2 (d) None

3.36 Suppose m inputs, z outputs, and n states are used in transition table of a synchronous sequential circuit. If number of flip-flops required to form the logic diagram of this circuit is X then

(a) $X \geq 2^{mn}$ (b) $X \leq 2^n$

(c) $X = 2^{mn}$ (d) None

3.37 Suppose m inputs, z outputs, and n states are used in transition table of a synchronous sequential circuit. How many arch or arrows or both will be required in transition table?

(a) $X \geq 2^{mn}$ (b) $X \leq 2^{mn}$

(c) $X = 2^{mn}$ (d) None

3.38 Moore machine named for

(a) Edward Forrest Moore (b) G.H. Mealy

(c) Allan Turing (d) None

3.39 Melay machine named for

(a) Edward Forrest Moore (b) G.H. Mealy

(c) Allan Turing (d) None

Answers

3.20 (a)	3.21 (b)	3.22 (a)	3.23 (b)	3.24 (a)
3.25 (b)	3.26 (a)	3.27 (d)	3.28 (b)	3.29 (c)
3.30 (a)	3.31 (b)	3.32 (b)	3.33 (b)	3.34 (c)
3.35 (c)	3.36 (b)	3.37 (b)	3.38 (a)	3.39 (b)

CHAPTER 4

Grammars and Languages

We all are familiar with the term "language", whether it is Hindi or English or other. Each language has its own construct (well-defined representation). Construct of a language has well-defined rules over some fixed notations. These rules over fixed notations are known as grammars. We are also familiar with computer languages like C, C++, etc. These languages have fixed and well-defined construct. *A language is a collection of words arranged in some well-defined fashion.*

For example, consider a sentence written in English language:

"Ram is going"

In this sentence, the word "Ram" is followed by the word "is" and "is" is followed by the word "going". Here, "Ram" is a noun, "is" is auxiliary verb, and "going" is the main verb. One question here, can we write, "Going is Ram" and has it some sense or has it the same meaning as the earlier sentence? The answer is no. It means, *we have a well-defined fashion in which we can put the words and we can get some legal sentences.*

Let us take another question here, is there any universal set of rules that govern the construct of all languages (natural or computer)? This question stricken earlier in nineteenth century and mathematicians were trying to give some suitable set of rules for construction of languages. In 1956 **Noam Chomsky** had suggested some mathematical rules, which are in four categories and provided a platform to describe a language mathematically. We will discuss these rules later on in this chapter. One thing is noticeable about these rules that these are not much powerful to describe the constructs of natural languages like English, etc. but still powerful to describe all most all computer languages.

4.1 CONSTRUCT OF A LANGUAGE

Each language has its own construct, its own structure. In other words, we can say that each language has its own type of word organization.

For example,

1. Consider the English language having three tenses: present, past, and future and these three have four subcategories namely indefinite, continuous, perfect, and prefect continuous.

Now, let us describe the construction of sentences mathematically. In present indefinite tense, construction rules look like:

(**Noun**) or (**Pronoun**) | | (**Verb**) | | (**Adverb**).

(Symbol | | represents concatenation of two words.)

For example, Shyam goes slowly.

If we describe the above sentence mathematically, we find that following some rules are useful to construct legal sentences in English language:

Sentence ≡ (Noun) | | (Verb).

Sentence ≡ (Noun) | | (Verb) | | (Adverb).

Sentence ≡ (Pronoun) | | (Verb).

Sentence ≡ (Pronoun) | | (Verb) | | (Adverb).

Shyam, goes, and slowly are called **terminals** or **constants** and SENTENCE, Noun, Pronoun, Verb, and Adverb are called **non-terminals** or **variables.** The rules are given in terms of variables and variables are replaced by terminals to get some legal sentence.

For example,

Sentence ≡ (Noun) | | (Verb) | | (Adverb).
≡ Richard | | (Verb) | | (Adverb).
≡ Richard talks | | (Adverb).
≡ Richard talks loudly.

Here, we have legal sentence, "Richard talks loudly."

2. Consider a statement format in ***C*** language:

```
if (x = 1)
    {
printf("AUTOMATA THEORY");
    }
```

Mathematically this statement can be described as:

If-statement ≡ if ‖(Condition)‖ (Stmt);

Where Condition ≡ $x = 1$ (True or False) and Stmt ≡ printf("AUTOMATA THEORY")

Terminals are **if, (, *x* = 1, {, printf("AUTOMATA THEORY"), ;** , **}** and variables are **If-statement, Condition**, and **Stmt**.

4.2 HOW TO DEFINE GRAMMAR

In this section, we will concentrate on grammar. A grammar is a finite set of rules over some fixed notations and rules are used to construct legal statements for some language. A **phrase-structured** grammar or simply a grammar is defined by four terms (V_n, Σ, P, S), where

1. V_n is the finite, nonempty set of variables or non-terminals,
2. Σ is finite, nonempty set of constants or terminals,

3. P is finite, nonempty set of production rules, and
4. $S \in V_n$ and known as start symbol.

Here, $V_n \cap \Sigma = \phi$ and P includes the production rules like $\alpha \rightarrow \beta$ *read as* "**α derives β**", where $\alpha, \beta \in (V_n \cup \Sigma)^*$ and a must have a symbol from V_n.

We will use following notations:

1. All capital letters like $A, B, C, \ldots$ are used as variables.
2. All small letters like $a, b, c, \ldots$are used as terminals.
3. x, y, z, w denote strings of terminals.
4. α, β, δ denote strings of terminals or variables or both, including null string.
5. Any symbol to the power 0 is equivalent to null i.e. **$X^0 = \varepsilon$, where $X \in (V_n \cup \Sigma)$.**

Derivation: If $\alpha \rightarrow \beta$ is a production in grammar G, then $\delta\alpha\gamma \underset{G}{\Longrightarrow} \delta\beta\gamma$ is called **one-step derivation** (or production). If $\alpha \Rightarrow \alpha_1 \Rightarrow \alpha_2 \ldots \Rightarrow \alpha_n \Rightarrow \beta$, then $\alpha \overset{n}{\underset{G}{\Longrightarrow}} \beta$ is called ***n*-step derivation**. The notation $\underset{G}{\Longrightarrow}$ represents relation for grammar G.

For example, consider a grammar G defined as $G = (\{S\}, \{a, b\}, \{S \rightarrow aSa, S \rightarrow \varepsilon\}, S)$. We have $V_n = \{S\}$, $\Sigma = \{a, b\}$, $P = \{S \rightarrow aSa, S \rightarrow \varepsilon\}$, and starting symbol is S. Now, let us see how terminal string is derived:

$$
\begin{aligned}
S &\underset{G}{\Longrightarrow} aSa && \text{(Using one-step derivation)}\\
&\underset{G}{\Longrightarrow} aaSaa && \text{(Using two-step derivation)}\\
&\underset{G}{\Longrightarrow} aaaSaaa && \text{(Using three-step derivation)}\\
&\ldots\\
&\overset{n}{\underset{G}{\Longrightarrow}} a^nSa^n && \text{(Using } n\text{-step derivation)}\\
&\underset{G}{\Longrightarrow} a^na^n && \text{(Using production } S \rightarrow \varepsilon \text{ and replacing } S \text{ by } \varepsilon)
\end{aligned}
$$

Sometime, we use one-step or more than one-step derivation. This is represented by $\alpha \overset{*}{\underset{G}{\Longrightarrow}} \beta$ $\left(\overset{*}{\underset{G}{\Longrightarrow}} \text{ is known as positive, transitive closure relation}\right)$. A variable may have one or more productions. If any variable has more than one production rule then production rules are represented with **or connectivity** symbol.

For example, consider two S-productions: $S \rightarrow aSa$, $S \rightarrow \varepsilon$ which are represented as:

$$S \rightarrow aSa \mid \varepsilon$$

A production rules like $S \rightarrow aSa$, $S \rightarrow Sa$, $S \rightarrow aS$, $S \rightarrow aSA$ are recursive production rules over the variable S, where A is also a variable and 'a' is a terminal. If a variable appears in right-hand side of in any production rule, whether it is recursive or non-recursive then that variable should derive some terminal(s) in finite number of steps. Otherwise such production rules will be useless. We will discuss it later on.

4.2.1 Language Generated by Grammar *G*

The language generated by grammar G is represented by $\boldsymbol{L(G)}$ and defined as the set of all terminal strings derived by G. It has been discussed that a language is a set of collection of strings. Depending upon the number of strings in $L(G)$, it may be finite, infinite or empty language.

Example 1: A grammar $G = (\{S\}, \{a, b\}, \{S \to aS, S \to \varepsilon\}, S)$. Describe the language generated by G, that is $L(G)$.

Solution: Let $G = (V_n, \Sigma, P, S)$, where

$V_n = \{S\}$, $\Sigma = \{a\}$, $P = \{S \to aS, S \to \varepsilon\}$, and S is the starting symbol.

Let first production rule $\boldsymbol{P_1}$: $S \to aS$,

And second production rule P_2: $S \to \varepsilon$

Using rule P_2, we get: $S \Rightarrow \varepsilon$

It means, null string ε is in $L(G)$.

Using rule P_1, we get

$$
\begin{aligned}
S &\Rightarrow aS && \text{(One step derivation)} \\
&\Rightarrow a^2S && \text{(Second step derivation, replacing variable } S \text{ by } aS) \\
&\;\;\ldots \\
&\Rightarrow a^nS && (n\text{-step derivation, replacing variable } S \text{ by } aS,\ n\text{-times}) \\
&\Rightarrow a^n && \text{(Using } P_2 \text{ and replacing } S \text{ by } \varepsilon)
\end{aligned}
$$

Here, one thing noticeable that we can get terminal string in each step by replacing variable S by null ε. It means following strings are derived:

$$a, aa, aaa, aaa, \ldots$$

We have already seen that null string is in $L(G)$.

Therefore, $L(G) = \{\varepsilon, a, aa, aaa, \ldots\} = a^*$

$= \{a^n : n = 0, 1, 2, 3, \ldots\}$

Example 2: The productions of a grammar are given as follows, find the language generated.

$S \to SS$, $S \to a$

The terminal is '***a***' and starting symbol is S.

Solution: Let grammar $G = (\{S\}, \{a\}, \{P_1, P_2\}, S)$, where production rules

$\boldsymbol{P_1}$: $S \to SS$, and

$\boldsymbol{P_2}$: $S \to a$

Using rule P_2: $S \Rightarrow a$

It means, string "***a***" is in $L(G)$.

Using rule P_1:

$$
\begin{aligned}
S &\Rightarrow SS && \text{(One step derivation)} \\
&\Rightarrow SSS && \text{(Replacing leftmost } S \text{ by } SS) \\
&\;\;\ldots
\end{aligned}
$$

$\Rightarrow$ ***SSSSS***...*n*-times (Replacing leftmost S by SS, $(n-1)$ times)
$\Rightarrow$ *aSSSSS*... (Using P_2 and replacing leftmost variable S by ***a***)
$\Rightarrow$ *aaSSSS*... (Using P_2 and replacing leftmost variable S by ***a***)
...
$\Rightarrow$ *aaaaa*...*S* (Using P_2 and replacing $(n-1)^{th}$ leftmost variable S by ***a***)
$\Rightarrow$ *aaaa*a...*n*-times (Using P_2 *n*-times and replacing S by ***a***)

In another representation, we represent:

$$S \underset{G}{\overset{n-1}{\Longrightarrow}} S^n \underset{G}{\overset{n-1}{\Longrightarrow}} a^n \text{ for } n \geq 2 \quad (\text{Using } S \to SS, n\text{-times and } S \to a, n\text{-times})$$

We find that following words are derived if we replace variable S by terminal '*a*' in each step: *aa*, *aaa*, *aaa*, ...

It means, string a^n for $n = 2, 3, 4, ...$ is in $L(G)$ and '***a***' is also in $L(G)$, therefore,

$$L(G) = \{a, aa, aaa, ...\} = \{a^n: \text{for } n \geq 1\}$$

Example 3: A grammar G has following productions:

$$S \to SS \mid aa \mid \varepsilon$$

Find the language generated $L(G)$.

Solution: Let $G = (V_n, \Sigma, P, S)$, where $V_n = \{S\}$, $\Sigma = \{a\}$,

$P = \{P_1: S \to SS, P_2: S \to aa, P_3: S \to \varepsilon\}$

Using rule P_3: $S \Rightarrow \varepsilon$

It means, null string $\boldsymbol{\varepsilon}$ is in $L(G)$.

Using rule P_2: $S \Rightarrow aa$

It means, string "***aa***" is in $L(G)$.

Using rule P_1: $S \Rightarrow$ ***SS*** (Using one step derivation)
$\Rightarrow$ ***SSS*** (Replacing rightmost S by SS)
...
$\Rightarrow$ **SSSSS** ... *n*-times (Using $(n-1)$ step derivation)
$\Rightarrow$ **(*aa*) ...** *n*-times (Using P_2 and replacing leftmost S by "*aa*" *n*-times)
or $\Rightarrow$ **εεεε ...** *n*-times (Using P_3 and replacing leftmost S by ε *n*-times)

It means, strings $(aa)^n$ for $n \geq 1$and ε are in $L(G)$. So, ε, *aa*, and $(aa)^n$ for $n \geq 1$ are in $L(G)$.

Therefore, $L(G) = \{\varepsilon, aa, aaaa, ...\}$

$$= \{(aa)^n: \text{for } n \geq 0\}$$

4.2.2 How to Construct a Grammar?

We follow three steps in construction of a grammar. In first step, we expand the given language; in second step we introduce possible variables and production rules; and in third step we verify the language generated by the grammar. If possible, we try recursive production rules after defining some terminating production(s). The smallest length word(s) is used as the terminating point for the recursive production. In the first step, we try to conclude the pattern of the strings of the language for which a grammar is to be constructed. There may be case in which we will not be able to get any pattern in strings of a language. In such cases recursive production rules cannot be used. In any case, we find production rules that could produce all strings of the language.

Example 1: Construct a grammar, which generates $L = \{a^n b^n : n \geq 1\}$.

Solution: Let grammar $G = (V_n, S, P, S)$ generates L.

Step 1: We express the strings of the language L.

$$L = \{ab, aabb, \ldots\}$$

In given language L, "***ab***" is the smallest length string. We get a pattern in strings, that is, all strings contains n number of consecutive a's followed by n number of consecutive b's.

Step 2: We introduce the necessary variables and production rules. We introduce recursive production(s) for variable S. We have found the pattern of each string:

"*n* numbers of a's is followed by *n* numbers of b's"

We introduce start symbol S to produce the string "*ab*" and to be used as recursive variable. Production rule P_1:

$$S \rightarrow ab$$

The first production is used as terminating production in case of recursive production(s). Now, we introduce second production rule P_2: $S \rightarrow aSb$, a recursive production over S. This production rule is applicable for production of those strings that have more than two a's and b's. The first production rule is used as terminating point for the second production rule. In other words, whenever variable S in production rule P_2 is replaced by the right hand side of the first production rule (that is "*ab*"), we get terminal strings.

Step 3: Verification of language generated:

$$S \Rightarrow ab \qquad \text{(Using } P_1\text{)}$$

It means, $ab \in L$. Now, let us see higher step derivation using both rules:

Two step derivation	Three step derivation	Four step derivation	Five step derivation	...	*n*-step derivation
$S \Rightarrow aSb$ $\Rightarrow aabb$	$S \Rightarrow aSb$ $\Rightarrow aaSbb$ $\Rightarrow aaabbb$	$S \Rightarrow aSb$ $\Rightarrow aaSbb$ $\Rightarrow aaasbbb$ $\Rightarrow aaaabbbb$	$S \Rightarrow aSb$ $\Rightarrow aaSbb$ $\Rightarrow aaaSbbb$ $\Rightarrow aaaaSbbbb$ $\Rightarrow aaaaabbbbb$	... ...	$S \Rightarrow aSb$ $\Rightarrow aaSbb$ $\Rightarrow aaaSbbb$ $\Rightarrow aaaaSbbbb$ ... $S \Rightarrow a^n b^n$
$a^2b^2 \in L$	$a^3b^3\ L$	$a^4b^4 \in L$	$a^5b^5 \in L$		$a^nb^n \in L$ for $n \geq 2$

We have, $L(G) = \{ab, aabb, aaabbb, \ldots\} = \{a^nb^n : n \geq 1\}$

Therefore, languages $L(G)$ and L are equivalent.

Example 2: Construct a grammar for language $L = \{a^n cb^n : n \geq 0\}$.

Solution: Let grammar $G = (V_n, \Sigma, P, S)$ generates L.

Step 1: We have, $L = \{c, acb, aacbb, aaacbbb, \ldots\}$

In given language L, "c" is the smallest length string. We get a pattern in strings, that is, all strings contains n number of consecutive a's followed by a 'c' and n number of consecutive b's, where $n \geq 0$.

Step 2: We introduce recursive production(s) over variable S. We have found the pattern of each string:

"n numbers of a's is followed by c and n numbers of b's, where $n \geq 0$"

We introduce start symbol S to produce the string "c" and to be used as recursive variable. This production rule is used as terminating production in case of recursive production(s) over S.

Production rule P_1: $\boldsymbol{S \rightarrow c}$

Now, we introduce second production rule P_2: $\boldsymbol{S \rightarrow aSb}$, a recursive production over S. This production rule is applicable for production of those strings that have a's and b's. The first production rule is used as terminating point for the second production rule. In other words, whenever variable S in production rule P_2 is replaced by the right hand side of the first production rule (that is "ab"), we get terminal strings.

Step 3: Verification of language generated:

$$S \Rightarrow c \qquad \text{(Using } P_1\text{)}$$

It means, $c \in L$.

Now, let us see higher step derivation using both production rules:

Two step derivation	Three step derivation	Four step derivation	Five step derivation	...	$(n+1)$step derivation
$S \Rightarrow aSb$ $\Rightarrow acb$	$S \Rightarrow aSb$ $\Rightarrow aaSbb$ $\Rightarrow aacbb$	$S \Rightarrow aSb$ $\Rightarrow aaSb$ $\Rightarrow aaaSbbb$ $\Rightarrow aaacbbb$	$S \Rightarrow aSb$ $\Rightarrow aaSbb$ $\Rightarrow aaaSbbb$ $\Rightarrow aaaaSbbbb$ $\Rightarrow aaaacbbbb$	... ...	$S \Rightarrow aSb$ $\Rightarrow aaSbb$ $\Rightarrow aaaSbbb$ $\Rightarrow aaaaSbbbb$ ... $S \Rightarrow a^n cb^n$
$acb \in L$	$a^2cb^2 \in L$	$a^3cb^3 \in L$	$a^4cb^4 \in L$		$a^n cb^n \in L$ for $n \geq 1$

We have, $L(G) = \{c, acb, aacbb, aaacbbb, \ldots\} = \{a^n cb^n : n \geq 0\}$

Therefore, languages $L(G)$ and L are equivalent.

4.3 CHOMSKY HIERARCHY

Noam Chomsky has classified all grammars in four categories (type 0 to type 3) based on the right hand side forms of the production rules. A grammar may be subset or superset of another grammar as per its type. A higher type grammar is superset of its all-lower types grammars. Firstly let us see the types of grammars in details:

1. **Type 0**: These types of grammars are also known as **phrase-structured grammars**, and right-hand side of rules of these grammars are free from any restriction. *All grammars are type 0 grammar and all languages are type 0.*

   For example, productions of types $AS \to aS$, $SB \to Sb$, $S \to \varepsilon$, $ASB \to aASB$ are type 0 production, where A, B, S are variables and a, b are terminals.

2. **Type 1:** Restricted type 0 grammars are known as type 1 or **context-sensitive grammars** (CSGs). Suppose a type 0 production rule $\gamma\alpha\delta \to \gamma\beta\delta$ and the production rule $\boldsymbol{a} \to \boldsymbol{b}$ is restricted such that $|\alpha| \le |\beta|$ and $\beta \ne \varepsilon$, then this type of productions are known as type 1 production rule. If all productions of a grammar are of type 1 production, then grammar is known as type 1 grammar. The language generated by a context-sensitive grammar is called **context-sensitive language** (CSL). Almost every language can be thought as CSL.

   In CSG, there is left context or right context or both.

   For example, consider the production $\alpha A\beta \to \alpha a\beta$. In this, α is left context and β is right context of variable A, which is replaced by 'a'. If left or right context is missing then we assume that ε is the context. The production of type $S \to \varepsilon$ is allowed in type 1 if ε is in $L(G)$, but S should not appear on right hand side of any production.

   For example, production rules: $S \to AB$, $S \to \varepsilon$, $A \to c$ are type 1 productions, but the production of type $A \to Sc$ is not allowed because we have production rule $S \to \varepsilon$. In these rules, A, B, S are variables and c is terminal.

3. **Type 2:** The restricted form of type 1 production rules are known as type 2 or context-free productions. A production of the form $\alpha \to \beta$, where $\alpha, \beta \in (V_n \cup \Sigma)^*$ is known as type 2 production rule. A grammar whose production rules are type 2 production rules is known as type 2 or **context-free grammar** (CFG) and the languages generated by this grammar is known as **context-free language** (CFL). For **example** $S \to S+S$, $S \to S{*}S$, $S \to id$ are type 2 production rules, where S is variable and +, *, id are terminals.

4. **Type 3:** This is the most restricted type. Productions of types $A \to \alpha$ or $A \to aB \mid Ba$, where $A, B \mid V_n$ (variables) and $a \in \Sigma$ (terminal) are known as type 3 or **regular grammar** production rules. A production of type $S \to$ is also allowed, if ε is in grammar generated language. **For example,** the productions $S \to aS$, $S \to a$ are type 3 production rules, where S is variable and $\boldsymbol{a}$ is terminal.

   - **Left-linear production rule:** A production rule of type $A \to Ba$ is called left-linear production rule, where A and B are variables and a is terminal.
   - **Right-linear production rule:** A production rule of type $A \to aB$ is called right-linear production rule, where A and B are variables and a is terminal.

A left-linear or right-linear grammar is called regular grammar. The language generated by a regular grammar is known as **regular language**. One obvious question is here. Can a right-linear production rule be converted into left-linear production rule and vice-versa? Yes, we can have an equivalent right-linear production rule for left-linear production rule and vice-versa. See the solved example (16) in Chapter 5.

A production rule of type $A \to w$ or $A \to wB$ (right-linear production rule) or $A \to Bw$ (left-linear production rule), where $w \in \Sigma^*$ can be converted into the forms $A \to a$ or $A \to aB$ or $A \to Ba$, where A, $B \in V_n$ and $a \in \Sigma$. **For example,** $A \to 10A$ can be replaced by productions $A \to 1B$, where B is a new variable and $B \to 0A$. In general, if $A \to a_1a_2a_3 \ldots a_na_{n+1}B$, then this production can replaced by the productions:

$$A \to a_1B_1,\ B_1 \to a_2B_2,\ B_2 \to a_3B_3,\ \ldots\ B_n \to a_{n+1}B$$

Where A, B, B_1, B_2, B_3, …, B_n are variables and a_1, a_2, a_3, …, a_{n+1} are terminals.

Similar result can be obtained for left-linear grammars also.

Relation among grammars and languages:

Type 0 is the super set and type 1 is contained in type 0, type 2 is contained in type 1, and type 3 is contained in type 2.

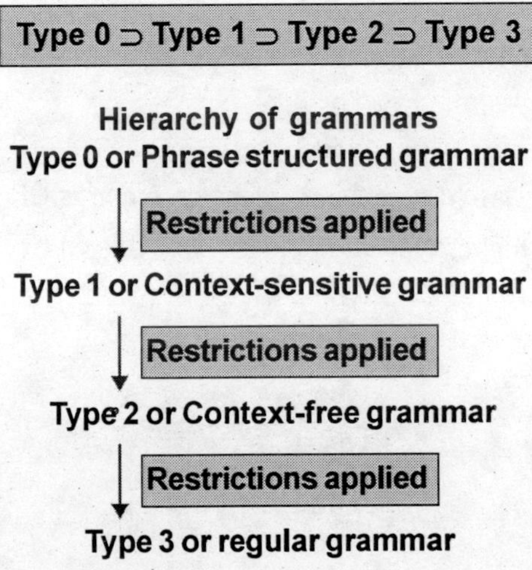

Languages and their related automata:

Each type of language (Type 0 to Type 3) is accepted by some automatic machine that is shown in Fig. 4.1.

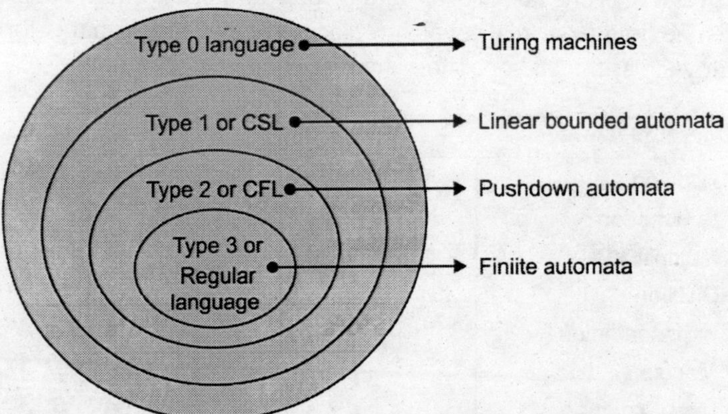

Fig. 4.1: Languages and their related automaton

Example 1: Consider the following grammars find the type of the grammars.

1. $S \to Aa, A \to c \mid Ba, B \to abc$
2. $S \to aSa \mid c$
3. $S \to aAS \mid SBb, AS \to aAS \mid aS, SB \to Sb \mid SBb$

Solution:

1. **Production** — **Type**

Production	Type
$S \to Aa$	type 3
$A \to c$	type 3
$A \to Ba$	type 3
$B \to abc$	type 3

So, given productions are of type 3 and hence grammar is regular.

2.

Production	Type
$S \to aSa$	type 2
$S \to c$	type 3

So, given productions are of type 2 and hence grammar is CFG.

(**Note:** We select the higher type and higher type between type 3 and type 2 is type 2.)

3.

Production	Type
$S \to aAS$	type 2
$S \to SBb$	type 2
$AS \to aAS$	type 1
$AS \to aS$	type 1
$SB \to Sb$	type 1
$SB \to SBb$	type 1

So, given productions are of type 1 and hence grammar is CSG.

4.4 ARITHMETIC EXPRESSIONS

An **arithmetic expression** is one that is evaluated by performing a sequence of arithmetic operations to obtain a numeric value (integer or real), which replaces the expression that is formed on operands and operators. The following arithmetic operators denote arithmetic operations:

Operator Name	Symbol	Example
Addition	+	A + B
Subtraction	–	A – B
Multiplication	*	A * B
Division	/	A/B
Exponentiation	**	A** B or A^B
Modulo	%	A%10
Unary Addition	+ +	A++, B++, ++A
Unary Subtraction	– –	A– – or – – A, B–

An **operand** of an arithmetic expression may be:

- A numeric constant like 24, 10, 0.99, 1.02, etc.
- A numeric variable, which may be preceded or followed by a unary operator + or – like A^{++} or ^{++}A.
- An arithmetic expression in parentheses, i.e., (*arithmetic expression*) like $(A + B)/C$

An arithmetic expression has the form:

operand [operator operand] ...

The square brackets indicate that the items *operator operand* are optional and the ellipsis (...) that they may be repeated indefinitely. Spaces may be used to improve readability. Two operators cannot be written consecutively.

For example, $A*–B$ cannot consider as arithmetic expression but A^{++} is legal arithmetic expression because unary addition has been used with operand A. The operands must be such that the operations are mathematically defined, e.g., dividing by zero, raising zero to a negative or zero power, or raising a negative number to a real power are all illegal. **For examples,** following are legal arithmetic expressions:

- 4.14159
- $A + B$
- $(A + B)*(C + D)$
- $–1.0/X + Y/Z**2$
- 2.0 * 3.14159

4.4.1 Evaluation of Arithmetic Expressions

An arithmetic expression is evaluated by replacing variable operands and parenthesized expressions by their numeric values, and performing the operations indicated in sequence, using the result of each operation as an operand of the next. Clearly, the sequence in which the operations are performed is significant.

For example, arithmetic expression: 5.0 + 6.0*2.0, which evaluates to 22.0 if the addition is performed first or 17.0 if the multiplication is performed first. The sequence of operations is determined by the following precedence order, in which operators on any line have equal precedence and precedence decreases downwards.

Table Precedence of Arithmetic Operators

Precedence	Operator
Highest	++(Unary Increment), —(Unary Decrement) ** (Exponentiation) *(Multiplication), / (Division), % (Modulo)
Lowest	+(Addition), – (Subtraction)

Using this precedence order, the rules for the evaluation of an arithmetic expression may be stated as follows:

- Evaluation begins with the leftmost operand, i.e., evaluation start from left to right.
- Operators having same precedence are evaluated from left to right.

- A variable operand, or a parenthesized expression, is evaluated before the following rules are applied.
  - Exponentiation is performed from right to left.

    For example, 2**2**3 = 2**(2**3) = 2**6 = 64
- All other operations are performed from left to right unless the operator precedence rules stipulate the opposite. **For examples,**
  - 4 + 6*3 = 22
  - (4 + 6)*3 = 30
  - 4 + 6*3/2 = 4 + 18/2 = 13

4.4.2 Arithmetic Expressions and Phrase-structured Grammar

Now, let us see how arithmetic expressions are produced by phrase-structured grammar. We know that a grammar deals with set of terminals, set of variables, and production rules. Any production or derivation using production rules is treated as string. A string may have terminals or variables or both. An arithmetic expression is considered or treated as string in a grammar system. For examples, consider the following expressions and let us see the constituents:

Arithmetic expression	Constituents		Terminal symbols for grammar
	Operands	Operators	
a + *b* + *C***D*	*a*, *b*, *C*, *D*	+, *	*a*, *b*, *C*, *D*, +, *
10.0 + *x* – *y****z*	*x*, *y*, *z*	+, –, **	10.0, *x*, *y*, *z*, +, -, **
++*a*	*a*	+ +	++, *a*
b––	*b*	– –	– –, *b*
(*a* + *b*)**c*	*a*, *b*, *c*	+, *	+, *, *a*, *b*, *c*, (,)

No, let us see how the syntax of arithmetic expressions (AEs) are described mathematically or by grammar. We assume that small letters from English alphabet $\{a, b, c, d\ldots z\}$ represent operands and operands are replaced by numeric value (integer or real). We first see how arithmetic expressions involving operands and operators are derived by grammar. Later on we will see how numbers are formed in decimal number system.

The grammar for arithmetic expressions (**AE**s) is as follows:

Let grammar $G = (V_n, \Sigma, P, \text{expr})$ derives arithmetic expressions, where

- V_n = {expr, var, binary-op, unary-op}
- $\Sigma = \{a, b, c, \ldots, z, +, -, *, /, ++, --, \%\}$
- expr $\in V_n$ is the starting variable

Now, let see what the production rules are. Operators z, +, –, / are binary operators and required two operands. **For examples,** $a + b$, cd, etc.

So, production rule for binary operation is:

P_1: **expr → expr binary-op expr**

We use parenthesis to the precedence of the operation. *P*roduction rule for this is:

P_2: **expr → (expr)**

The unary operations required only one operand. For example, ^{++}a, a^{++}, b^{-}, ^{-}b, etc. are unary operations. Production rules for unary operations are:

P_3: **expr → unary-op expr**

P_4: **expr → expr unary-op**

The starting variable expr should produce operands from $\{a, b, c, \ldots, z\}$. Production rules for this purpose are:

P_5: **expr →** $a \mid b \mid c \mid \ldots \mid z$

The variables binary-op and unary-op replace binary operators and unary operators respectively. Production rules are:

P_6: **binary-op** → + | – |*| / |%

P_7: **unary-op** → ++ |– –

Grammar G = ({expr, var, binary-op, unary-op}, {a, b, c, …, z, +, -, *, /, ++, -}, {expr → expr binary-op expr | (expr) | unary-op expr | expr unary-op | a | b | c | … | z, binary-op → + | – |*| / | %, unary-op → ++ |– –}, expr)

Now, let us verify the grammar G. Using rule P_1, we get binary operations and using P_3, and P_4, we get unary operations. Whenever parenthesis is needed, it can be obtained by using production rule P_2. Using rule P_5, variable *expr* is replaced by an operand and using P_6, P_7, we get the desired operators. So, we conclude that grammar G produces all the arithmetic expressions. Let us check that arithmetic expressions $a + b - c*d$, $^{++}a*b$ are produced by grammar G or not.

Production of First Arithmetic Expression $a + b - c * d$:

expr ⇒ expr binary-op expr	(Using production rule P_1)
⇒ a binary-op expr	(Using production rule P_5)
⇒ a + expr	(Using production rule P_6)
⇒ a + expr binary-op expr	(Using production rule P_1)
⇒ $a + b$ binary-op expr	(Using production rule P_5)
⇒ $a + b -$ expr	(Using production rule P_6)
⇒ $a + b -$ expr binary-op expr	(Using production rule P_1)
⇒ $a + b - c$ binary-op expr	(Using production rule P_5)
⇒ $a + b - c *$ expr	(Using production rule P_6)
⇒ $a + b - c*d$	(Using production rule P_5)

Production of Second Arithmetic Expression $^{++}a*b$:

expr ⇒ unary-op expr	(Using production rule P_3)
⇒ ++ expr	(Using production rule P_7)
⇒ ++ expr binary-op expr	(Using production rule P_1)
⇒ $^{++}$a binary-op expr	(Using production rule P_5)

$\Rightarrow {}^{++}a * \text{expr}$ (Using production rule P_6)

$\Rightarrow {}^{++}a*b$ (Using production rule P_5)

4.4.3 Decimal Numbers and Phrase-structured Grammar

We have ten digits in decimal number system, that is, {0, 1, 2, 3… 9}. We have two types of numbers: **integer** and **real**.

For examples, 1255, 2834, 27, 2, etc. are integer numbers and 21.33, 0.993, 383.001, etc are real numbers. Let us see how decimal numbers are generated by grammar G.

Let grammar $G = (V_n, \Sigma, P, \text{Number})$ derives arithmetic expressions, where

- V_n = {Number, Digit, Sign}
- $\Sigma = \{0, 1, 2, \ldots 9, ., +, -\}$
- Number $\in V_n$ is the starting variable

An unsigned integer number may have one or more decimal digits. Production rules for unsigned integer numbers are:

P_1: Number → Digit

P_2: Number → Number Number

For signed integer numbers, we have following production rules:

P_3: Number → Sign Digit

P_4: Number → Sign Number Number

The variable Digit and Sign are replaced by digit and sign by using following production rules:

P_5: Digit → 0 | 1 | 2 | 3 | 4 | 5 | 6 | 7 | 8 | 9

P_6: Sign → + | –

Now, let us construct production rules for real numbers. Real numbers are integer numbers having decimal point. Similar to the unsigned and signed integer numbers, real numbers may be signed or unsigned. Production rules for real numbers are:

P_7: Number → Digit . Digit

P_8: Number → Number . Number

P_9: Number → Sign Digit . Digit

P_{10}: Number → Sign Number . Number

We can easily verify the production of grammar G. Using P_1, P_2, P_3, and P_4, we get unsigned and signed integer numbers of one or more digit. Using P_7, P_8, P_9, and P_{10}, we get unsigned and signed real numbers. Using P_5, and P_6, variables Digit and Sign are replaced by a digit and sign respectively. **For examples,** let us consider decimal numbers 235 and 23.08 and check the production of grammar G.

Production of First Decimal Number: 235

Number ⇒ Number Number (Using production rule P_2)

⇒ Digit Number (Using production rule P_1)

⇒ 2 Number (Using production rule P_5)

⇒ 2 Number Number (Using production rule P_2)

⇒ 2 Digit Number	(Using production rule P_1)
⇒ 2 3 Number	(Using production rule P_5)
⇒ 23 Digit	(Using production rule P_1)
⇒ 235	(Using production rule P_5)

Production of Second Decimal Number: 23.08

Number ⇒ Number . Number	(Using production rule P_8)
⇒ Number Number . Number	(Using production rule P_1)
⇒ Digit Number. Number	(Using production rule P_1)
⇒ 2 Number . Number	(Using production rule P_5)
⇒ 2 Digit . Number	(Using production rule P_1)
⇒ 2 3. Number	(Using production rule P_5)
⇒ 23. Number Number	(Using production rule P_2)
⇒ 23. Digit Number	(Using production rule P_1)
⇒ 23. 0 Number	(Using production rule P_5)
⇒ 23. 0 Digit	(Using production rule P_1)
⇒ 23. 08	(Using production rule P_5)

4.5 SOLVED EXAMPLES

Example 4.1: Construct grammar for the following languages:

(a) $\{\varepsilon, aa, aaaa, aaaaaa, \ldots\}$

(b) $\{ab, aabb, aaabbb, \ldots\}$

Solution:

(a) Let grammar $G = (V_n, \{a\}, P, S)$ generates the given language. P has following productions:

$$S \to \varepsilon, S \to aaS, S \to Saa, S \to aSa$$

(b) Let grammar $G = (V_n, \{a\}, P, S)$ generates the given language. P has following productions:

$$S \to ab, S \to aSb$$

Example 4.2: Consider language $L = a^*ab$, find a suitable grammar which generates it.

Solution: Let grammar $G = (V_n, \Sigma, P, S)$ generates L.

$$L = a^*ab = \{\varepsilon, a, aa, \ldots\}ab = \{ab, aab, aaab, \ldots\}$$
$$= \{\text{All the words over } \{a\} \text{ ending in } ab\}$$

So, production rule $\boldsymbol{P_1}$: $S \to ab$ is in P

Strings in L are all strings over $\{a\}$ ending in string "*ab*". The smallest length string is "*ab*" and we have production rule: $S \to ab$

We can get all strings over $\{a\}$ by production rule $\boldsymbol{P_2}$: $S \to aS$

So, $P = \{S \to ab, S \to aS\}$ and rule $S \to ab$ is taken as terminating production rule for recursive production rule $\boldsymbol{S \to aS}$. $\Sigma = \{a, b\}$ and S is the starting symbol.

Verification of language generated:

$$S \underset{G}{\Rightarrow} ab$$

It means, string ab is in $L(G)$.

$$S \overset{n}{\underset{G}{\Rightarrow}} a^nS \qquad \text{(Using } S \to aS,\ n\text{-times)}$$

$$\underset{G}{\Rightarrow} a^nab \qquad \text{(Using } S \to ab \text{ and replacing } S \text{ by "}ab\text{")}$$

So, string a^nab for $n \geq 0$ is in $L(G)$.

Therefore, L and $L(G)$ are equivalent languages.

Example 4.3: Find the language generated by the following grammars.

(a) $S \to 0S1 \mid 0A1,\ A \to 1A \mid 1$

(b) $S \to 0A \mid 1S \mid 1 \mid 0,\ A \to 1A \mid 1S \mid 1$

(c) $S \to 0SBA \mid 01A,\ AB \to BA,\ 1B \to 11,\ 1A \to 10,\ 0A \to 00$

Solution:

(a) Let
$$P_1 : S \to 0S1$$
$$P_2 : S \to 0A1$$
$$P_3 : A \to 1A$$
$$P_4 : A \to 1$$

Since S is starting symbol so starting with P_2:

$$S \Rightarrow 0A1$$

$$\Rightarrow 011 \qquad \text{(Using } P_4 \text{ and replacing } A \text{ by 1)}$$

It means, string 011 is in $L(G)$.

$$S \Rightarrow 0A1$$

$$\overset{n-2}{\underset{G}{\Rightarrow}} 01^{n-2}A1 \qquad \text{(Using } P_3\ n-2 \text{ times)}$$

$$\underset{G}{\Rightarrow} 01^n \qquad \text{(Using } P_4 \text{ and replacing } A \text{ by 1)}$$

Starting with P_1:

$$S \overset{m}{\underset{G}{\Rightarrow}} 0^{m-1}S1^{m-1} \qquad \text{(Using } P_1\ m-1 \text{ times)}$$

$$\underset{G}{\Rightarrow} 0^{m-1}0A11^{m-1} \qquad \text{(Using } P_2 \text{ and replacing } S \text{ by } 0A1)$$

$$\overset{n-1}{\underset{G}{\Rightarrow}} 0^mA1^{m+n-1} \qquad \text{(Using } P_3\ n-1 \text{ times)}$$

$$\underset{G}{\Rightarrow} 0^m1^{m+n} \qquad \text{(Using } P_4 \text{ and replacing } A \text{ by 1)}$$

It means, string 0^m1^{m+n} for $m, n \geq 1$ is in $L(G)$.

So, $L(G) = \{0^m1^{m+n} : m, n \geq 1\}$

(b) Let $P_1: S \to 0A$

$P_2: S \to 1S$

$P_3: S \to 1$

$P_4: S \to 0$

$P_5: A \to 1A$

$P_6: A \to 1S$

$P_7: A \to 1$

Starting with S-production P_3 and P_4:

$S \Rightarrow 0$ (Using P_3)

$S \Rightarrow 1$ (Using P_4)

It means, strings 0 and 1 are in $L(G)$.

Starting with S-production P_1:

$S \Rightarrow 0A$

$\Rightarrow 01$ (Using P_7 and replacing A by 1)

It means, string 01 is in $L(G)$, or

$\overset{n-1}{\Longrightarrow}\ 01^{n-1}A$ (Using P_5 $n-1$ times and replacing A by $1A$)

$\Rightarrow\ 0^{1n}$ (Using P_7 and replacing A by 1)

It means, string 01^n for $n \geq 1$ is in $L(G)$, or

$S \Rightarrow 01S$ (Using P_6 and replacing A by $1S$)

$\Rightarrow 010A$ (Using P_1 and replacing S by $0A$)

$\Rightarrow 0101S$ (Using P_6 and replacing A by $1S$)

...

$\Rightarrow 010101\ldots n-1$ times S

(Using P_6 and P_1 $n-1$ times)

$\Rightarrow (01)^{n-1}0A$ (Using P_1 and replacing S by $0A$)

$\Rightarrow (01)^n$ (Using P_7 and replacing A by 1)

It means, string $(01)^n$ for $n \geq 1$ is in $L(G)$.

Starting with S-production P_2:

$S \overset{n}{\Longrightarrow} 1^nS$ (Using P_2 n times)

$\Rightarrow 1^{n+1}$ or 1^n0 (Using P_4 or P_3)

It means, strings 1^n0 and 1^n for $n \geq 1$ are in $L(G)$.

So, combining all the results, we find that $L(G)$ contains all the words over $\{0, 1\}$ Excluding null word and no word has 00 as a substring.

(c) Let $P_1: S \rightarrow 0SBA$ (*S*-production)

$P_2: S \rightarrow 01A$ (*S*-production)

$P_3: AB \rightarrow BA$

$P_4: 1B \rightarrow 11$

$P_5: 1A \rightarrow 10$

$P_6: 0A \rightarrow 00$

Starting with *S*-production P_2:

$S \Rightarrow 01A$

$\Rightarrow 010$ (Using P_5 and replacing $1A$ by 10)

It means, string 010 is in $L(G)$.

Starting with *S*-production P_1:

$S \Rightarrow SBA$

$\overset{n-1}{\Rightarrow} 0^{n-1}S(BA)^{n-1}$ (Using P_1 $n-1$ times)

$(\equiv 0^{n-1}\boldsymbol{S}B^{n-1}A^{n-1})$

$\Rightarrow 0^{n-1}01\boldsymbol{AB}B^{n-2}A^{n-1}$ (Using P_2 and replacing S by $01A$)

$\overset{n-1}{\Rightarrow} 0^{n-1}01B^{n-1}AA^{n-1}$ (Using P_3 $n-1$ times and replacing AB by BA)

$(\equiv 0^{n}\boldsymbol{1B}B^{n-2}A^{n})$

$\overset{n-1}{\Rightarrow} 0^{n}1^{n-1}\boldsymbol{1A}A^{n-1}$ (Using P_4 $n-1$ times)

$\Rightarrow 0^{n}1^{n-1}1\boldsymbol{0A}A^{n-1}$ (Using P_5 and replacing $1A$ by 10)

$\overset{n}{\Rightarrow} 0^{n}1^{n}0^{n}$ (Using P_6 n times)

It means, $L(G) = \{0^{n}1^{n}0^{n} : n \geq 1\}$

Example 4.4: If language $L = \{a^{2*i}: i = 1, 2, \ldots\}$, construct a grammar for L.

Solution: Let grammar $G = (V_n, \Sigma, P, S)$ generates L. All words of L are even length over $\{a\}$ and first word is "*aa*".

So, $P_1: S \rightarrow aa$ is in P and a recursive production rule $P_2: S \rightarrow aSa$ is also in P.

Thus, $G = (\{S\}, \{a\}, \{S \rightarrow aa, S \rightarrow aSa\}, S)$

Verification of language generated:

$S \Rightarrow aa$ (Using $S \rightarrow aa$)

It means, string "*aa*" is in $L(G)$.

$S \overset{n-1}{\rightarrow} a^{n-1}Sa^{n-1}$ (Using $S \rightarrow aSa$, $n-1$ times)

$\Rightarrow a^{n-1}aaa^{n-1}$ ($\equiv a^{2n}$ for $n \geq 1$, using $S \rightarrow aa$)

So, $L(G)$ and L are equivalent languages.

Example 4.5: Construct a suitable grammar for language $L = \{a^n b^{2n} : n \geq 1\}$.

Solution: Let grammar $G = (V_n, \Sigma, P, S)$ generates L.

$$L = \{abb, aabbbb, \ldots\}$$

So, the production rule $P_1: S \rightarrow abb$ is in P.

In all words, number of b's are double of number of a's.

So, recursive production rule $P_2: S \rightarrow aSbb$ is in P.

Thus, $G = (\{S\}, \{a, b\}, \{S \rightarrow abb, S \rightarrow aSbb\}, S)$

Verification of language generated:

$$S \Rightarrow bb \qquad \text{(Using } S \rightarrow abb\text{)}$$

It means, string "*abb*" is in $L(G)$.

$$S \overset{n-1}{\Longrightarrow} a^{n-1}S(bb)^{n-1} \qquad \text{(Using } S \rightarrow aSbb,\ n-1 \text{ times)}$$

$$\Rightarrow a^{n-1}abb(bb)^{n-1} \text{ (Using } S \rightarrow abb\text{)}$$

$$\equiv a^n b^{2n} \text{ for } n \geq 1 \text{ is in } L(G).$$

Therefore, languages $L(G)$ and L are equivalent.

Example 4.6: Consider language $L = \{a^n c^m d^m b^n : m, n \geq 1\}$and construct a suitable grammar.

Solution: Let grammar $G = (V_n, \Sigma, P, S)$ generates L.

All words of L have number of consecutive a's at starting is equal to number of consecutive b's at the end and number of consecutive c's is followed by same number of consecutive d's in the middle.

So, production rule $P_1: S \rightarrow aSb$ is in P for generating equal number of a's and b's,

Production rule $P_2: S \rightarrow aAb$ is in P for generating equal number of c's and d's in the middle, where rule $P_3: A \rightarrow cd$ and rule $P_4: A \rightarrow cAd$ are also in P.

So, $P = \{S \rightarrow aSb, S \rightarrow aAb, A \rightarrow cd, A \rightarrow cAd\}$, $V_n = \{S, A\}$, $\Sigma = \{a, b, c, d\}$

Verification of language generated by *G*:

$$S \Rightarrow aAb$$

$$\Rightarrow acdb$$

It means, string "*acdb*" is in $L(G)$.

$$S \overset{n-1}{\Longrightarrow} a^{n-1}Sb^{n-1} \qquad \text{(Using } S \rightarrow aSb\ n-1 \text{ times)}$$

$$\Rightarrow a^{n-1}aAbb^{n-1} \qquad \text{(Using } S \rightarrow a\,Ab\text{)}$$

$$\overset{m-1}{\Longrightarrow} a^n c^{m-1}Ad^{m-1}b^n \text{ (Using } A \rightarrow cAd\text{)}$$

$$\Rightarrow a^n c^{m-1}cdd^{m-1}b^n \text{(Using } A \rightarrow cd\text{)}$$

$$\equiv a^n c^m d^m b^n \in L(G) \text{ for } m, n \geq 1$$

So, $L(G)$ and L are equivalent languages.

Example 4.7: For language $L = \{a^n c^m d^m b^n \cup a^n b^{2n}: m, n \geq 1\}$, construct a grammar.

Solution: (See the solved examples (5) and (6))

Let $L = L_1 \cup L_2$, where $L_1 = \{a^n c^m d^m b^n : m, n \geq 1\}$, $L_2 = \{a^n b^{2n}: m, n \geq 1\}$

Suppose $G_1 = (V_1, \Sigma, P_1, S_1)$ generates L_1 and $G_2 = (V_2, \Sigma, P_2, S_2)$ generates L_2.

$G_1 = (\{S_1, A_1\}, \{a, b, c, d\}, \{S_1 \to aS_1b \mid aA_1b, A_1 \to cd \mid cA_1d\}, S_1)$

And $G_2 = (\{S_2\}, \{a, b\}, \{S_2 \to abb \mid S_2 \to aS_2bb\}, S_2)$

$$G = G_1 \cup G_2$$

So, $$S \to S_1 \mid S_2$$

$$\begin{aligned} L(G) &= L(G_1) \cup L(G_2) \\ &= \text{Languages generated by } G_1 \text{ or language generated by } G_2 \\ &= \{a^n c^m d^m b^n \cup a^n b^{2n} : m, n \geq 1\} \end{aligned}$$

Hence, languages $L(G)$ and L are equivalent.

Example 4.8: Context-free grammar G for a propositional calculus subsystem is:

$S \to (S) \mid S \wedge S \mid \; \mid S \vee S \mid {}^{\sim}S \mid p \mid q$, where S is only variable. Find terminals and check whether the string $w = (\sim\sim p \vee (p \wedge {}^{\sim\sim}q)) \in L(G)$ or not.

Solution: Let $G = (V_n, \Sigma, P, S)$, where $\Sigma = \{p, q, \wedge, \vee, {}^{\sim}\}$

$$\begin{aligned} S &\Rightarrow (S) && \text{(Using } S \to (S)\text{)} \\ &\Rightarrow (\boldsymbol{S} \vee S) && \text{(Using } S \to S \vee S\text{)} \\ &\Rightarrow ({}^{\sim}\boldsymbol{S} \wedge S) && \text{(Using } S \to {}^{\sim}S\text{)} \\ &\Rightarrow ({}^{\sim\sim}\boldsymbol{S} \vee S) && \text{(Using } S \to {}^{\sim}S\text{)} \\ &\Rightarrow ({}^{\sim\sim}p \vee \boldsymbol{S}) && \text{(Using } S \to p\text{)} \\ &\Rightarrow ({}^{\sim\sim}p \vee (\boldsymbol{S})) && \text{(Using } S \to (S)\text{)} \\ &\Rightarrow ({}^{\sim\sim}p \vee (\boldsymbol{S} \wedge S)) && \text{(Using } S \to S \wedge S\text{)} \\ &\Rightarrow ({}^{\sim\sim}p \vee (p \wedge \mathbf{S})) && \text{(Using } S \to p\text{)} \\ &\Rightarrow ({}^{\sim\sim}p \vee (p \wedge {}^{\sim}\boldsymbol{S})) && \text{(Using } S \to {}^{\sim}S\text{)} \\ &\Rightarrow ({}^{\sim\sim}p \vee (p \wedge {}^{\sim\sim}\boldsymbol{S})) && \text{(Using } S \to {}^{\sim}S\text{)} \\ &\Rightarrow ({}^{\sim\sim}p \vee (p \wedge {}^{\sim\sim}q)) && \text{(Using } S \to q\text{)} \end{aligned}$$

So, $w \in L(G)$.

Example 4.9: Construct suitable grammar for the language $L = \{a^{\alpha} : \alpha \text{ is } 2^i \text{ for } i \geq 1\}$.

Solution: Let $G = (V_n, \Sigma, P, S)$ generates L.

$$L = \{aa, aaaa, \ldots\}$$

The first word is aa and successors are of double length of their predecessors. We use variable A to make the number of a's double and variable B to mark the end of the word.

So, $S \to aa$ is in P and for the other words $S \to ASB$ is used, where $aA \to aaA$ and $AB \to \varepsilon$ are also in P.

So, $P = \{S \to aa, S \to ASB, Aa \to aaA, AB \to \varepsilon\}$

Verification of language generated by *G*:

$$S \Rightarrow aa \qquad \text{(Using } S \to aa\text{)}$$

It means, aa is in $L(G)$.

$S \Rightarrow ASB$	(Using $S \rightarrow ASB$)
$\Rightarrow AASBB$	(Using $S \rightarrow ASB$)
$\Rightarrow AAaaBB$	(Using $S \rightarrow aa$)
$\Rightarrow AaaAaBB$	(Using $Aa \rightarrow aaA$)
$\Rightarrow AaaaaABB$	(Using $Aa \rightarrow aaA$)
$\Rightarrow AaaaaB$	(Using $AB \rightarrow \varepsilon$)
$\Rightarrow aaAaaaB$	(Using $Aa \rightarrow aaA$)
$\Rightarrow aaaaAaaB$	(Using $Aa \rightarrow aaA$)
$\Rightarrow aaaaaaAaB$	(Using $aA \rightarrow aaA$)
$\Rightarrow aaaaaaaaAB$	(Using $Aa \rightarrow aaA$)
$\Rightarrow aaaaaaaa$	(Using $AB \rightarrow \varepsilon$)

It means, string $aaaaaaaa$ is in $L(G)$.

Similarly, we see the general thing that number of A variable decides the number of a's as follows:

$$\text{Total no. of a's} = 2*(2*(\ldots2*(aa)\ldots))$$

It means, all the strings of L are in $L(G)$ and all the words of $L(G)$ are in L. So, these languages are equivalent.

Example 4.10: If language $L = \{xy: x, y \in (a + b)^*$ and y is the mirror image of $x\}$. Construct a grammar for L. Suppose mirror image of a^n is a^n and mirror image of b^m is b^m for $m, n \geq 1$.

Solution: Let $G = (V_n, \Sigma, P, S)$ generates L.

$$L = \{aa, bb, abba, \ldots\}$$

All the words have two constituents x and y and y is mirror image of x. x may be any string on $\{a, b\}$, so,

Case 1: When $x = a$, then $y = a$ So, $S \rightarrow aa$ is in P.

Case 2: When $x = b$, then $y = b$ So, $S \rightarrow bb$ is in P.

Case 3: We use recursive production for the other words.

$S \rightarrow aSa$ and $S \rightarrow bSb$ are recursive production rules in P.

So, $G = (\{S\}, \{a, b\}, \{S \rightarrow aa, S \rightarrow bb, S \rightarrow aSa, S \rightarrow bSb\}, S)$

Verification of language generated by G:

$$S \Rightarrow aa$$

$$S \Rightarrow bb$$

It means, strings "aa" and "bb" are in $L(G)$.

$S \overset{n}{\Rightarrow} a^nSa^n$	(Using $S \rightarrow aSa$, n times)
$S \overset{m}{\Rightarrow} a^nb^mSb^ma^n$	(Using $S \rightarrow bSb$, m times)
$\Rightarrow a^nb^maab^ma^n$	(Using $S \rightarrow aa$)

It means, strings $a^nb^maab^ma^n$ for $m, n \geq 1$ are in $L(G)$. Similarly, we see that strings $a^nb^mbbb^ma^n$, $b^na^maaa^mb^n$, and $b^na^mbba^mb^n$ for $m, n \geq 1$ are also in $L(G)$.

So, $L(G)$ and L are equivalent languages.

Example 4.11: Consider language $L = \{xx: x \in (a + b)^*\}$ and construct grammar.

Solution: Let grammar $G = (V_n, \Sigma, P, S)$ generates L, that is, $L(G) = L$.

$$L = \{\varepsilon, aa, bb, abab, \dots\}$$

Since, null string is in L, so P_1: $S \to \varepsilon$ is in P.

All strings in L are of even length and if we place a marker in the middle of a string, then symbols from the marker at the same distance (left or right) are same.

$$\underbrace{a_{J-1}a_J \dots a_i \dots}\ \Big|\ \underbrace{\dots a_i \dots a_J a_{J-1}}, \text{ where } a_i \text{ and } a_j \text{ are } a \text{ or } b$$

Marker

Suppose, S is just like a marker used in production rules: P_2: $S \to XSX$ and P_3: $S \to YSY$, where P_4: $X \to a$ and P_5: $Y \to b$ are also in P.

So, $G = (\{S, X, Y\}, \{a, b\}, \{S \to \varepsilon, S \to XSX, S \to YSY, X \to a, Y \to b\}, S)$

Verification of language generated by G:

Using production P_1: $S \Rightarrow \varepsilon$

It means, null string ε is in $L(G)$.

Using production rule P_2:

$$S \overset{n}{\Rightarrow} X^nSX^n \qquad \text{(Using } S \to XSX, n \text{ times)}$$
$$\overset{m}{\Rightarrow} X^nY^mSY^mX^n \qquad \text{(Using } S \to YSY, m \text{ times)}$$
$$\Rightarrow a^nb^mb^ma^n \qquad \text{(Using } X \to a, Y \to b \text{ and } S \to \varepsilon)$$

So, string $a^nb^mb^ma^n$ $m, n \geq 1$ is in $L(G)$. Similarly, we see that string $b^na^ma^mb^n$ for $m, n \geq 1$ is in $L(G)$.

So, $L(G)$ and L are equivalent.

Example 4.12: Construct regular grammar for the following:

(a) $L = \{a^{2n}: n \geq 0\}$

(b) $L = \{(ab)^n: n \geq 1\}$

(c) A language over $\{a, b\}$ of which all words have even number of a's and b's.

(d) A language over $\{a, b\}$ in which all words end in *abb*.

Solution:

(a) Let $G = (V_n, \Sigma, P, S)$, generates L.

$$L = \{\varepsilon, aa, aaaa, \dots\}$$

All words are of even length and smallest word is ε has length 0.

So, $S \to \varepsilon$ is in P.

For other words, $S \rightarrow aA$ and $A \rightarrow aS$ are in P.

Thus, $G = (\{S, A\}, \{a\}, \{S \rightarrow \varepsilon, S \rightarrow aA, A \rightarrow aS\}, S)$

Verification of language generated:

$$S \Rightarrow \varepsilon \qquad \text{(Using } S \rightarrow \varepsilon)$$

It means, null string ε is in $L(G)$.

$$S \overset{n}{\Rightarrow} a^n S a^n \qquad \text{(Using } S \rightarrow aA, A \rightarrow aS, n \text{ times)}$$

$$\Rightarrow a^n a^n \qquad \text{(Using } S \rightarrow \varepsilon)$$

It means, string a^{2n} for $n \geq 0$ is in $L(G)$.

So, L and $L(G)$ are equivalent languages.

(b) Let $G = (V_n, \Sigma, P, S)$ generates L.

$$L = \{ab, abab, \ldots\}$$

The first word is "ab" and other words have multiple (ab)'s. So, $S \rightarrow ab, S \rightarrow aA, A \rightarrow bS$ are P. Variable A is used to derive b and return to S. So, $G = (\{S, A\}, \{a, b\}, \{S \rightarrow ab, S \rightarrow aA, A \rightarrow bS\}, S)$

Verification of language generated:

$$S \Rightarrow ab \qquad \text{(Using } S \rightarrow ab)$$

It means, string ab is in $L(G)$.

$$S \overset{n}{\Rightarrow} (ab)^{n-1} S \qquad (S \rightarrow aA, A \rightarrow bS, n-1 \text{ times)}$$

$$\overset{m}{\Rightarrow} (ab)^n \qquad \text{(Using } S \rightarrow ab)$$

It means, string $(ab)^n$ for $n \geq 1$ is in $L(G)$.

Therefore, the languages L and $L(G)$ are equivalent.

(c) Let $G = (V_n, \Sigma, P, S)$ generates L.

$$L = \{\varepsilon, aa, bb, abab, \ldots\}$$

All words are of even length having even number a's and b's. The first word is null, so $S \rightarrow \varepsilon$ is in P. Other words start with either 'a' or 'b'. Using variable A to derive 'a' and variable B to derive 'b', we have $S \rightarrow aA$ and $S \rightarrow bB$ are in P. The symbol 'a' or 'b' follows 'a' or 'b' such that the number of a's or b's or both become even.

So, $A \rightarrow a, A \rightarrow aS, A \rightarrow bD$ are in P and $B \rightarrow b, B \rightarrow bS, B \rightarrow aD$ are also in P.

We see that when S is appeared at RHS (right hand side) any production then number of a's and b's are even; when A is appeared at RHS of any production then number of a's is odd and b's is even; when B is appeared at RHS of any production then number of a's is even and b's is odd; when D is appeared at RHS of any production then number of a's and b's are odd.

So, for variable D, $D \rightarrow bA, D \rightarrow aB$ are in P.

So, $P = \{S \rightarrow \varepsilon \mid aA \mid bB, A \rightarrow a \mid aS \mid bD, B \rightarrow b \mid bS \mid aD, D \rightarrow bA \mid aB\}$

Verification of language generated by G:

$$S \Rightarrow \varepsilon \qquad \text{(Using } S \rightarrow \varepsilon)$$

It means, null word is in $L(G)$.

$S \Rightarrow (aa)^n S$ (Using $S \to aA$ and $A \to aS$, n times)

$\Rightarrow (aa)^n$ (Using $S \to \varepsilon$)

It means, word $(aa)^n$ for $n \geq 1$ is in $L(G)$. Similarly, we can see the other words and find that number of a's and b's are even. So, L and $L(G)$ are equivalent languages.

(d) Let $G = (V_n, \Sigma, P, S)$, generates L.

$$L = \{abb, aabb, babb, \ldots\} \equiv (a+b)^* abb$$

All words end in "abb".

So, $S \to abb$ is in P.

For other words over $\{a, b\}$ that end in "abb", we use recursive production and the terminating production is $S \to abb$.

So, $S \to aS$, $S \to bS$ are in P.

So, $G = (\{S\}, \{a, b\}, \{S \to abb, S \to aS, S \to bS\}, S)$

Verification of language generated by *G*:

$S \overset{n}{\Rightarrow} a^n S$ (Using $S \to aS$, n times)

$\overset{m}{\Rightarrow} a^n b^m S$ (Using $S \to bS$, m times)

$\Rightarrow a^n b^m abb$ (Using $Sabb$)

It means, string $a^n b^m abb$ for $m, n \geq 0$ is in $L(G)$.

So, L and $L(G)$ are equivalent language.

Example 4.13: Construct suitable grammar that generates all palindromes over $\{a, b\}$.

Solution: Let grammar $G = (V_n, \Sigma, P, S)$ generates all the palindromes. We have two types of palindromes based on length:

(i) Even length, and

(ii) Odd length

For even length palindromes:

- ε is a palindrome
- aa or bb are palindromes
- If x is a even length palindrome, then axa and bxb are also even length palindromes

So, productions $S \to \varepsilon$, $S \to aSa$, $S \to bSb$ are in P.

For odd length palindromes:

- a or b are palindromes
- If x is a odd length palindrome, then axa and bxb are also odd length palindromes

So, productions $S \to a$, $S \to b$, $S \to aSa$, $S \to bSb$ are in P.

Therefore, combining all the productions, we have

$$P = \{S \to \varepsilon, S \to a, S \to b, S \to aSa, S \to bSb\}$$

Verification of language generated by G

$$S \Rightarrow \varepsilon \text{ or } a \text{ or } b$$

It means, strings ε, "a" and "b" are in $L(G)$.

$$S \overset{n}{\Rightarrow} a^nSa^n \text{ or } b^nSb^n \quad (\text{Using } S \to aSa \text{ or } S \to bSb, n \text{ times})$$

$$\Rightarrow a^na^n \text{ or } b^nb^n \text{ or } a^naa^n \text{ or } a^nba^n \text{ or } b^nab^n \text{ or } b^nbb^n$$

$$(\text{Using } S \to \varepsilon \text{ or } S \to a \text{ or } S \to b)$$

It means, all palindromes are in $L(G)$.

Thus, L and $L(G)$ are equivalent languages.

Example 4.14: If $L = \{a^nb^nc^n: n \geq 1\}$, construct a grammar for L.

Solution: Let $G = (V_n, \Sigma, P, S)$, generates L.

$$L = \{abc, aabbcc, aaabbbccc, \ldots\}$$

In language L, all words have equal number of consecutive a's, b's and c's and first word is "*abc*". So, production rule: $S \to abc$ is in P.

We use a recursive production over variable S and variable A, which will produce number of b's in the middle of a word.

So, production rule: $S \to aSA$ is in P for making a's and A's equal.

Suppose, we use this production n-1 times, then

$$S \overset{n-1}{\Rightarrow} a^{n-1}S(A)^{n-1}$$

$$\equiv a^{n-1}SA^{n-1}$$

$$\Rightarrow a^{n-1}abcA^{n-1} \quad (\text{Using } S \to abc)$$

$$\equiv a^nbcA^{n-1}$$

It means, we have to use variable A, which shifts the c at the end and makes number of b's and c's equal to number of a's.

So, $cA \to Ac$ is in P. Using this production rule $n - 1$ time in above derivation, we have, $Sa^nbA^{n-1}c$.

Now, number of b's should be equal to a's and c's.

So, $bA \to bbc$ is in P. Using this production rule and production rule $cA \to Ac$, $n - 1$ time, we have, $Sa^nb^nc^n$.

So, in $L(G)$ all words have equal number of a's, b's and c's and G has production rules:

$S \to abc \mid aSA$, $cA \to Ac$, and $bA \to bbc$

Thus, L and $L(G)$ are equivalent languages.

Example 4.15: Consider the following languages and construct grammars.

(a) $L = \{w: |w| \bmod 3 > 0$ and w is string over $\{a\}\}$

(b) $L = \{w: |w| \bmod 3 = 0$ and w is string over $\{b\}\}$

Solution:

(a) Let grammar G generates L. The given language L contains strings over $\{a\}$ such that length of strings modulo 3 is greater than zero. It means, length of strings in L is not multiple of three. Therefore, if $w \in L$, then

$|w| \bmod 3 = 1$, and

$|w| \bmod 3 = 2$

So, $L = \{a^{3m+1} : m \geq 0\} \cup \{a^{3m+2} : m \geq 0\}$

We have following production rules in G:

$$S \to a \mid aa \mid aaaS$$

It is obvious from the production rules that strings "a" and "aa" are in $L(G)$. If we apply the recursive production rule $S \to aaaS$ then we get number of a's multiple of three and finally variable S is replaced by "a" or "aa", which makes the length of generated string modulo three equal to one or two. Therefore, we conclude that L and $L(G)$ are equivalent language.

(b) Let grammar G generates L. The given language L contains strings over $\{b\}$ such that length of strings modulo 3 is equal to zero. It means, length of strings in L is multiple of three. Therefore, if $w \in L$, then $|w| \bmod 3 = 0$

So, $L = \{b^{3m} : m \geq 0\} = \{\varepsilon, aaa, aaaaaa, \ldots\}$

We have following production rules in G:

$$S \to \varepsilon \mid aaaS$$

We can easily show that

$$L(G) = \{\varepsilon, aaa, aaaaaa, \ldots\}$$

Therefore, $L(G)$ and L are equivalent.

Example 4.16: Find the regular grammar for the language $L = \{a^n b^m : n + m \text{ is even}\}$.

Solution: The given language can be expressed as:

$$L = \{ab, ba, aa, bb, ababa, aabb, abaa, baaa, abbb, babb, \ldots.\}$$

$$= (ab + ba + aa + bb)^*$$

Let regular grammar for L is G and $G = (\{A, B, C, D\}, \{a, b\}, P, A)$, where production rules are:

$A \to aB$, $A \to bD$, $B \to aA$, $B \to a$, $B \to bC$, $B \to b$, $C \to aB$, $C \to bD$, $D \to aC$, $D \to bA$, $D \to a$, $D \to b$

Example 4.17: Find the context-free grammar for the following languages with $m, n, k \geq 0$:

(i) $L = \{a^n b^n c^k \mid k \geq 3\}$

(ii) $L = \{a^m b^n c^k \mid m = n \text{ or } m <= k\}$

Solution:

(i) Let the desired grammar $G = (V_n, \{a, b, c\}, P, S)$, where production rules are:

$S \to AB$, $A \to aAb$, $A \to \varepsilon$, $B \to cccD$, $B \to \varepsilon$, $D \to cD$, $D \to c$

(ii) We thing the language L as union of two languages in which first language has equal number of a's and b's and second language has the number of a's equal to or greater than number of c's. Let the desired grammar $G = (V_n, \{a, b, c\}, P, S)$, where production rules are:

$S \to AB$, $A \to aAb$, $A \to \varepsilon$, $B \to cB$, $B \to \varepsilon$,

$S \to aSc$, $S \to aDc$, $S \to \varepsilon$, $D \to bD$, $D \to Dc$, $D \to b$, $D \to c$

Example 4.18: Using Chomsky hierarchy, find the highest type number which can be applied to the following grammars, give reason also.

(i) $A \to Aa, A \to c \mid Ba, B \to abc$

(ii) $S \to ASB \mid d, A \to \text{a}A$

(iii) $S \to aS \mid ab$

(iv) $AAbcD \to abcDbcD$

(v) $A \to abA$

(vi) $AB \to AbBc$

Solution:

(i)

Production Rule	**Type of Grammar**
$A \to Aa$	Type 3
$A \to c$	Type 3
$A \to Ba$	Type 3
$B \to abc$	Type 3

The given production rules are Type 3.

(ii)

$S \to ASB$	Type 2
$S \to d$	Type 3
$A \to aA$	Type 3

Since, Type 3 $\subset$ Type 2, therefore the given production rules are Type 2.

(iii)

$S \to aS$	Type 3
$S \to ab$	Type 3

The production rules are Type 3.

(iv) $AAbcD \to abcDbcD$ Type 1

The right context in the given production rule is "bcD" and hence the given production rule is Type 1.

(v) $A \to abA$ Type 1

In the given production rule "*ab*" is considered as string of terminals and hence the production rule is right linear.

(vi) $AB \to AbBc$ Type 1

The given production rule, the left context is "*A*" and hence the production rule is Type 1.

Example 4.19: Let *G* be the grammar with the following productions:

$\Sigma \to aAA, A \to bB, A \to aB, A \to a, B \to aAA$

Describe informally $L(G)$.

Solution: The given grammar *G* generates two types of strings:

(i) $\Sigma \Rightarrow aAA \Rightarrow aaa, \mid \Rightarrow aAA \Rightarrow aaBA \Rightarrow aaaAAA \ldots \Rightarrow aaaaaa$

That is, $a^{3n} \in L(G)$ for $n = 1, 2, 3, \ldots$

(ii) $\Sigma \Rightarrow aAA \Rightarrow abBA \Rightarrow abaAAA ... \Rightarrow abaaaa$

$\Sigma \Rightarrow aAA \Rightarrow abBA \Rightarrow abaAAA ... \Rightarrow ababaaaaa$

$\Sigma \Rightarrow aAA \Rightarrow abBA \Rightarrow abaAAA ... \Rightarrow abababaaaaaa$

That is, $(ab)^m a^{3+m} \in L(G)$ for $m = 0, 1, 2, ...$

Therefore, $L = \{0^{3n} \cup (ab)^m a^{3+m} : n > 0, m \geq 0\}$

Example 4.20: Construct a grammar generating the language $\{a^i b^j c^k \mid i^1 j \text{ or } j^1 k\}$.

Solution: Let grammar $G = (V_n, \{a, b, c\}, P, S)$ generates the given language. The production rules for the G are:

$$S \to A_1B_1,\ A_1 \to C_1D_1 \mid E_1D_1,\ C_1 \to aC_1 \mid a,\ D_1 \to aD_1b \mid \varepsilon,\ E_1 \to bE_1 \mid b,\ B_1 \to cB_1 \mid \varepsilon$$
$$S \to A_2B_2,\ A_2 \to aA_2 \mid \varepsilon,\ B_2 \to C_2D_2 \mid E_2D_2,\ C_2 \to bC_2 \mid b,\ D_2 \to bD_2c \mid \varepsilon,\ E_2 \to cE_2 \mid c$$

TEST YOUR SKILLS

Supplementary Problems

4.1 For $L = \{0^n 1^n 2^n : n \geq 1\}$, construct a grammar.

4.2 If $L = \{xy : x, y \in (a + b + c)^*$ and y is the mirror image of $x\}$. Construct a grammar for L.

Suppose, the mirror image of a^n is a^n, mirror image of b^p is b^p and mirror image of c^m is c^m for $p, m, n \geq 1$. Construct a grammar

4.3 For $L = \{xx : x \in (a + b + c)^*\}$, construct a grammar.

4.4 Construct regular grammar for

(a) $L = (a + b)^* aa$

(b) language over $\{a, b\}$ in which all words contain number of a's and b's odd.

(c) A language over $\{a, b\}$ in which all words contain number of a's odd and number of b's even.

4.5 Consider a language $L = \{a^n b^n c^n : n \geq 1\} \cup \{a^n b^n : n \geq 1\}$. Construct a grammar G for L. What is the type of grammar G?

4.6 Discuss the phrase-structured grammar.

4.7 Discuss the classification of grammars given by Noam Chomsky.

4.8 What is the importance of the mathematical description of grammars?

4.9 Consider the following languages and find the grammars that generate these languages.

(a) $L_1 = \{a^n b^{2n} c^n : n \geq 1\}$

(b) $L_2 = \{a^n b^{2n} c^{2n} : n \geq 1\}$

(c) $L_3 = \{a^{2n} b^{2n} c^n : n \geq 1\}$

(d) $L_4 = a^m c^n : m, n \geq 1$ and $m > n\}$

(e) $L_5 = \{a^n b^{2n-3} : n \geq 2\}$

(f) $L_6 = L_1^2$, where $L_1 = \{a^n b^n : n \geq 0\}$

(g) $L_7 = L_1L_2$, where $L_1 = \{a^n b^{2n} c^n : n \geq 1\}$ and $L_2 = \{a^n b^{2n} c^{2n} : n \geq 1\}$

(h) $L_8 = \{w : |w| \bmod 4 = 0$ and w is string over $\{a\}\}$

(i) $L_9 = \{w : |w| \bmod 3 = 1$ and w is string over $\{a\}\}$

(j) $L_{10} = \{w : |w|_a \bmod 3 = 1,\ |w|_b \bmod 3 = 0$, and w is string over $\{a, b\}$ such that a's and b's are consecutive}

(k) $L_{11} = \{w : |w|_a \bmod 3 = |w|_b \bmod 3 + 1$, and w is string over $\{a, b\}$ such that a's and b's are consecutive}

4.10 Let us talk about the data types used in the *C* language. The names that are used to reference variables, functions, labels and various user-defined objects, etc. are called *identifiers*. The size of an identifier in C language can vary from 1 to 32 characters. The first character must be a letter or an underscore ('_') character with subsequent characters being letters, numbers or underscores. We can define an identifier in lower case letters or in upper case letters or in combination. Letters from the English language are used to construct identifiers.

For example, following are some identifiers declared in C language:

- Temp1, Temp2
- __date123
- YEAR_2006
- January_2006

Following are **incorrect declarations**:

- 2number (Leading character is numeric)
- float (Keyword)
- .right (Leading character is special character dot)
- father.name (In the middle there is a special character dot)
- num&num (In the middle there is a special character &)
- Tepm; (last character semicolon is special character)
- My_flat_No_street_no_city_name_country_name

(Invalid identifier name, more than 32 characters are used)

Construct grammar for generating identifiers in *C* language.

4.11 Construct grammar for generating postfix expressions.

4.12 Construct grammar for generating arithmetic exponential expressions in *C* language.

4.13 Consider the logical operators given below in *C* language:

Table Logical Operators

Operator	Name	Example (*A*, *B* are operands)
&&	AND	*A* && *B*
||	OR	*A*||*B*
!	NO	!*A*

Construct grammar for logical expressions in C language.

Multiple Choice Questions

4.14 The language $\{a^ib^jc^k: i = j \text{ or } j = k\}$ is

(a) Regular
(b) Context-free but not regular
(c) Context-sensitive but not context-free
(d) Type 0 but not context-sensitive

4.15 Phrase-structured Grammar can be described by

(a) (V_n, Σ, P, S)
(b) (V_n, P, S)
(c) (Σ, V_n, P, S)
(d) Both (a) & (c)

4.16 The word "FORMAL" in formal languages means

(a) No meaning
(b) The symbols used have well-defined meaning
(c) Only strings are significant
(d) None of the above

4.17 If grammar $G = (\{S\}, \{a\}, \{S \to SS\}, S)$, then language $L(G)$ is

(a) ϕ
(b) $aa(a)^*$
(c) $(aa)^*$
(d) None

4.18 The CFG G having production rules: $S \to aS \mid bS \mid a \mid b$, generates

(a) $(a + b)^+$
(b) $(a + b)(a + b)^*$
(c) $(a + b)^*(a + b)$
(d) All the above

4.19 The grammar $S \to aSb \mid \varepsilon$ generates

(a) $\{a^nb^n : n \geq 0\}$
(b) $\{a^nb^n : n \geq 1\}$
(c) $\{a^nb^m : m \geq 1, n \geq 0\}$
(d) $\{a^nb^m : m \geq 0, n \geq 1\}$

4.20 The regular languages are accepted by

(a) Finite automata
(b) Pushdown automata
(c) Turing machines
(d) All

4.21 The language $\{a^ib^jc^k : i = j \text{ and } j = k\}$ is

(a) Regular
(b) Context-free but not regular
(c) Context-sensitive but not context-free
(d) Type 0 but not context-sensitive

4.22 The context-free languages are accepted by

(a) Finite automata
(b) Pushdown automata
(c) Turing machines only
(d) None

4.23 The context-sensitive languages are accepted by

(a) Finite automata
(b) Pushdown automata only
(c) Turing machines only
(d) Linear bounded Automata

4.24 The CFG G having production rules: $S \to aB \mid bA, A \to aS \mid a, B \to bS \mid b$, generates

(a) Odd number of a's and b's
(b) Equal number of a's and b's
(c) Even number of a's and b's
(d) Even number of a's and odd number of b's

4.25 The language $\{a^ib^jc^k : i = \text{MIN}(j, k)\}$, where MIN($j$, k) returns minimum of j and k, is

(a) Regular
(b) Context-free but not regular
(c) Context-sensitive but not context-free
(d) Type 0 but not context-sensitive

4.26 Choose the regular productions

(a) $S \to aS \mid a$
(b) $S \to aaSbb \mid \varepsilon$
(c) $S \to aA \mid bB \mid \varepsilon, A \to a \mid aS, B \to b \mid bS$
(d) Both (a) & (c)

4.27 Consider grammar G and language L, if $L = L(G)$, then

(a) All the words of $L(G)$ are in L
(b) All words of L are in $L(G)$
(c) All words of $L(G)$ are in L and all words of L are in $L(G)$
(d) All words generated by G are in L

4.28 Choose the correct statement

(a) All regular grammars are CFG
(b) All CFGs are CSG
(c) Regular grammars are most restricted grammars
(d) All the above

4.29 The language $\{a^i b^j c^k : i + j \geq k\}$ is

(a) Regular
(b) Context-free but not regular
(c) Context-sensitive but not context-free
(d) Type 0 but not context-sensitive

4.30 Consider the production rules: $S \to abc \mid aSA$, $cA \to Ac$, and $bA \to bbc$. The language generated by this grammar is:

(a) $L = \{a^n b^n c^n : n \geq 1\}$
(b) $L = \{a^n b^n c^m : m, n \geq 1\}$
(c) $L = \{a^n b^n c^n : n \geq 1\}$
(d) None

4.31 Consider the grammar $G = (\{S, A\}, \{a\}, \{S \to \varepsilon, S \to aA, AaS\}, S)$. The language generated by this grammar is:

(a) $L = \{a^{2n} : n \geq 1\}$
(b) $L = \{a^{2n} : n \geq 0\}$
(c) $L = \{a^n : n \geq 0\}$
(d) None

4.32 Consider set of production rules $P = \{S \to aSb, S \to aAb, A \to cd, A \to cAd\}$ for a grammar, where set of variable is $\{S, A\}$ and set of terminals is $\{a, b, c\}$. The language generated by this grammar is

(a) $\{a^n c^m d^m b^n : m, n \geq 1\}$
(b) $\{a^m c^m d^m b^n : m, n \geq 1\}$
(c) $\{a^n c^n d^m b^m : m, n \geq 1\}$
(d) $\{a^n c^m d^n b^m : m, n \geq 1\}$

4.33 Noam Chomsky has classified grammars into

(a) Three categories
(b) Two categories
(c) Five categories
(d) Four categories

4.34 Which one is not correct?

(a) C language is regular language.
(b) C language is type 0 language
(c) C language is type 1 language
(d) None

4.35 Grammar G has set of production rules $\{S \to aAS \mid SBb, AS \to aAS \mid aS, SB \to Sb \geq SBb\}$. What is the type of grammar G?

(a) Type 1
(b) Type 2
(c) Type 3
(d) None

4.36 Grammar G has set of production rules $\{S \to aS \mid Sb, S \to abS \mid aaS, S \to Sba \mid Sbb\}$. What is the type of grammar G?

(a) Context-sensitive (b) Context-free

(c) Regular (d) *A*ll

4.37 Grammar G has set of production rules $\{S \to S + S \mid S^*S, S \to a \mid b\}$. What is the type of grammar G?

(a) Context-sensitive (b) Context-free

(c) Regular (d) Both (a) & (b)

4.38 The language $\{a^i b^j c^k : i \geq j \text{ or } j \geq k\}$ is

(a) Regular (b) Context-free but not regular

(c) Context-sensitive but not context-free (d) Type 0 but not context-sensitive

4.39 The language $\{a^i b^i c^k d^k : i, j \geq 0\}$ is

(a) Regular (b) Context-free

(c) Context-sensitive but not context-free (d) Type 0 but not context-sensitive

4.40 The language $\{a^i b^i : i \geq 0\} \cup \{a^i b^{2i} : i \geq 0\}$ is

(a) Deterministic Context-free (b) Context-free but regular

(c) Context-sensitive but not context-free (d) Type 0 but not context-sensitive

4.41 The Language $L = \{a^{n!} : n \geq 1\}$ is

(a) Regular (b) Context-free

(c) Context-sensitive but not context-free (d) Type 0 but not context-sensitive

4.42 The Language $L = \{a^{n!} : 1 \leq n \leq 10\}$ is

(a) Regular (b) Context-free

(c) Context-sensitive but not context-free (d) Type 0 but not context-sensitive

4.43 The Language $L = \{a^n : n \text{ is prime}\}$ is

(a) Regular (b) Context-free

(c) Context-sensitive but not context-free (d) Type 0 but not context-sensitive

Answers

4.14 (b)	4.15 (d)	4.16 (c)	4.17 (a)	4.18 (d)
4.19 (a)	4.20 (d)	4.21 (c)	4.22 (b)	4.23 (d)
4.24 (b)	4.25 (c)	4.26 (d)	4.27 (c)	4.28 (d)
4.29 (b)	4.30 (a)	4.31 (b)	4.32 (a)	4.33 (d)
4.34 (a)	4.35 (a)	4.36 (d)	4.37 (d)	4.38 (b)
4.39 (b)	4.40 (a)	4.41 (c)	4.42 (a)	4.43 (c)

CHAPTER 5

Regular Expressions, Regular Languages and Finite Automata

We will discuss the regular expressions, regular sets, regular languages and relationship with finite automata in this chapter. We will discuss application of finite automata in pattern matching. It is important to understand the behavior of finite automata which accept the regular languages only. We will see Pumping Lemma exclusively used to prove certain language as non-regular and Myhill-Nerode's Theorem which is used to prove the certain language as regular or non-regular. We will also see the minimization method of finite automata and application of Myhill-Nerode Theorem in minimization of finite automata. Closure properties of regular sets (or languages) and equivalence of regular expressions and DFA are also discussed.

5.1 REGULAR EXPRESSION

The languages recognized by finite automata (FA) are regular languages and these languages are described by simple expressions called regular expressions. We use some algebraic notations to represent the regular expressions. Regular expressions are condensed representation for regular languages or regular set.

"Regular expressions are means to represent certain sets of strings in some algebraic manner and describe the language accepted by finite automata."

If Σ is an alphabet then the regular expression(s) over this alphabet are described by following rules:

What are Regular Expression

1. Any symbol from Σ, ε, and ϕ are regular expressions.
2. If r_1 and r_2 are two regular expressions then *union* of these represented as $\boldsymbol{r_1 \cup r_2}$ or $\boldsymbol{r_1 + r_2}$ is also a regular expression.
3. If r_1 and r_2 are two regular expressions then *concatenation* of these represented as $\boldsymbol{r_1 r_2}$ is also a regular expression.
4. The Kleene closure (or *iteration* or *reflexive-transitive closure*) of a regular expression r is denoted by $\boldsymbol{r^*}$ is also a regular expression.
5. If r is a regular expression then $\boldsymbol{(r)}$ is also a regular expression.
6. The regular expressions obtained by applying rules 1 to 5 once or more than once are also regular expressions.

Let us see some **examples,**

Example 1: If alphabet $\Sigma = \{a, b\}$, then

(a) a is a regular expression. (Using rule 1)

(b) b is a regular expression. (Using rule 1)

(c) $a + b$ is a regular expression (Using rule 2)

(d) a^* is a regular expression. (Using rule 4)

(e) ab is a regular expression. (Using rule 3)

(f) $ab + a^*$ is a regular expression. (Using rule 6)

Example 2: Find regular expression for the following languages over $\{a, b\}$:

(a) A language consists of all the words over $\{a, b\}$ ending in 'a'.

(b) A language consists of all the words over $\{a, b\}$ ending in "aa".

(c) A language consists of all the words over $\{a, b\}$ starting with 'a' and ending in 'b'.

(d) A language consists of all the words over $\{a, b\}$ having "aa" as a substring.

(e) A language consists of all the words over $\{a, b\}$ ending in "abb".

Solution: Let $\Sigma = \{a, b\}$, and

All the words over $\Sigma = \{\varepsilon, a, b, aa, bb, ab, ba, aaa, \ldots\}$

$= \Sigma^*$ or $(a + b)^*$ or $(a \cup b)^*$

(a) Regular expression for the given language is $(a + b)^*a$

(b) Regular expression for the given language is $(a + b)^*aa$

(c) Regular expression for the given language is $a\,(a + b)^*b$

(d) Regular expression for the given language is $(a + b)^*aa$ or $aa(a + b)^*$ or $(a + b)^*aa(a + b)^*$

(e) Regular expression for the given language is $(a + b)^*abb$

Regular sets: A set represented for a regular expression is called a regular set. Regular languages are also represented in set notation. We use the curly brackets ({ }) while representing a set. **For example,**

1. If $\Sigma = \{a, b\}$ be an alphabet, then

Regular set	Regular expression
$\{\}$	ϕ
$\{a\}$	a
$\{a, b\}$	$a + b$
$\{\varepsilon, a, aa, aaa, \ldots\}$	a^*
$\{a, aa, aaa, \ldots\}$	$aa^* \equiv a^+$
{All the words over $\{a, b\}$}	$(a + b)^*$
$\{\varepsilon\}$	ε
$\{01, 00, 10, 11\}$	$00 + 01 + 10 + 11$
$\{aabb, aaabb, aaaabb, aaaaabb, \ldots\}$	a^*abb

We say that a regular expression is a **condensed representation** of certain sets of strings using some algebraic representations like union, concatenation, Kleene closure, etc. We will see all these notations one by one. It should be noted that there may be one or more regular expression for certain regular language. Let us see how union, concatenation, Kleene's closure, etc. are used in representation of regular expressions.

Regular set	Formal description	Regular expression
$\{a\}$	Single string "*a*"	a
$\{a, b\}$	String "*a*" or "*b*"	$a + b$ (a Union b)
$\{ab\}$	String "*ab*"	ab (a concatenation b)
$(aa, ab, ba, bb\}$	String "*aa*" or "*ab*" or "*ba*" or "*bb*"	$aa + ab + ba + bb$ (aa Union ab Union ba Union bb)
$\{\varepsilon, a, aa, aaa, \ldots\}$	All strings over $\{a\}$	a^* (ε Union a Union aa Union …)
$\{abb, aabb, babb, aaabb, bbabb, \ldots\}$	All strings over $\{a, b\}$ ending in abb	$(a + b)^* abb$ (a Union b)* a concatenation (abb)

Hierarchy of evaluation of regular expressions: We follow the following order when we evaluate or simplify a regular expression:

1. Parenthesis
2. Iteration or Kleene closure
3. Concatenation
4. Union

Example 1: Consider the regular expression $(a + b)^* abb$ and describe all words represented by this expression. Also describe the corresponding regular set.

Solution: We follow the evaluation order of regular expression as discussed above.

$$(a + b)^* abb = \{\text{All words over } \{a, b\}\}abb \qquad (\text{Evaluating } (a + b)^* \text{ first})$$
$$= \{\varepsilon, a, b, aa, bb, ab, ba, aaa, \ldots\}abb$$
$$= \{abb, aabb, babb, aaabb, \ldots\}$$
$$\equiv \text{All strings over } \{a, b\} \text{ ending in "}abb\text{"}$$

Example 2: Consider the regular expression $(a^* + b^*)^*$ and describe the regular set.

Solution: We first evaluate a^* and b^* and then $(a^* + b^*)^*$.

$$(a^* + b^*)^* = (\text{All the words over } \{a\} + \text{all the words over } \{b\})^*$$
$$= (\{\varepsilon, \text{a}, aa, \ldots\} \text{ or } \{\varepsilon, \text{b}, bb, \ldots\})^* = (\{\varepsilon, a, b, aa, bb, \ldots\})^*$$
$$= \{\varepsilon, a, b, aa, bb, ab, ba, aaa, bbb, abb, baa, aabb, \ldots\}$$
$$\equiv \text{All the words over } \{a, b\} \equiv (a + b)^*$$

So, $(a^* + b^*)^* \equiv (a + b)^*$

Example 3: Consider the regular expression $abb + a + b + aa$. What is the regular set for the given regular expression?

Solution: The regular set is $\{abb, a, b, aa\}$.

Example 4: Consider the following regular set and find the equivalent regular expression:

{00, 0000, 000000, ...}

Solution: The given set contains the string over {0} having even length greater than equal to two. So, the equivalent regular expression is: $\mathbf{(00)^+}$.

5.1.1 Useful Identities for Regular Expressions

In this section, we will see some identities for regular expressions. Regular expressions are looked similar to strings. The additional notations are union, parenthesis, and Closures (positive and Kleene). Regular expression ε represents null string and regular expression ϕ represents empty box very much similar to the zero in decimal number system. It should be noted here that when ϕ is concatenated (similar to multiply) with any regular expression results in ϕ (similar to zero) and when union operation is performed with any regular expression results the regular expression along with which ϕ has been considered (similar to addition with zero). Following are some useful identities for regular expressions. We assume that R is a regular expression over some alphabet Σ.

1. $\phi + R = R + \phi = R$

   Proof: LHS $= \phi + R = \{\ \} + R = R + \{\ \} \equiv$ {Element of { } or R}
   $= R =$ RHS (Since, $\phi = \{\ \}$ has no element.)

2. $\phi R = R\phi = \phi$

   Proof: LHS $= \phi R = \{\ \}R =$ {Element of { } followed by element(s) of R}
   $= \{\ \} = \phi$ (Since, ϕ has no element.)
   $= R$HS

3. $\varepsilon R = R\varepsilon = R$

   Proof: LHS $= \varepsilon R \equiv$ {ε followed by R}
   $= R =$ RHS (Since, concatenation of ε with any string/symbol results in the same string.)

4. $\varepsilon^* = \varepsilon$ and $\phi^* = \varepsilon$

   Proof: LHS $= \varepsilon^*$
   $= \{\varepsilon, \varepsilon, \varepsilon, \ldots\}$
   $= \{\varepsilon\}$
   $= \varepsilon$
   $= R$HS

   LHS $= \phi^*$
   $= \{\varepsilon, \phi, \phi\phi, \ldots\}$
   $= \{\varepsilon\}$ ($\phi\phi = \phi$, and $\phi + \varepsilon = \varepsilon$)
   $= \varepsilon$
   $=$ RHS

5. $R + R = R$

   Proof: LHS $= R + R = R =$ RHS (Union of R and R is R.)

6. $RR^* = R^*R = R^+$

   Proof: LHS $= RR^* = R\{\varepsilon, R, RR, RRR, \ldots\}$
   $= \{R, RR, RRR, RRRR, \ldots\} = R^+$
   $= \{\varepsilon, R, RR, RRR, \ldots\}R = R^*R$

   So, $R^*R = RR^* = R^+$

7. $(R^*)^* = R^*$

Proof: $\text{LHS} = (R^*)^* = (\{\varepsilon, R, RR, RRR, \ldots\})^*$
$= (\varepsilon + R + RR + RRR + \ldots)^* = \{\varepsilon, R, RR, RRR, \ldots\}$
$= R^*$

8. $R^*R^* = R^*$

Proof: $\text{LHS} = R^*R^* = \{\varepsilon, R, RR, RRR, \ldots\}\{\varepsilon, R, RR, RRR, \ldots\}$
$= \{\varepsilon, \varepsilon R, \varepsilon RR, \ldots, R\varepsilon, RR, \ldots\} = \{\varepsilon, R, RR, RRR, \ldots\} = R^*$

9. $(P + Q)^* = (P^*Q^*)^* = (P^* + Q^*)^*$, where P and Q are regular expressions.

Proof: $\text{LHS} = (P + Q)^* = \{\varepsilon, P, Q, PP, QQ, PQ, QP, \ldots\}$
= All possible words over $\{P, Q\}$

$(P^*Q^*)^* = (\{\varepsilon, P, PP, PPP, \ldots\}\{\varepsilon, Q, QQ, QQQ, \ldots\})^*$
$= (\{\{\varepsilon, P, PP, PPP, \ldots, Q, QQ, QQQ, \ldots, PQ, PQQ, \ldots\})^*$
= All possible words over $\{P, Q\}$

$(P^* + Q^*)^* = (\{\varepsilon, P, PP, PPP, \ldots\} + \{\varepsilon, Q, QQ, QQQ, \ldots\})^*$
$= (\{\varepsilon, P, Q, PP, QQ, PQ, QP, \ldots\})^*$
= {All possible words over $\{P, Q\}$}

Therefore, $(P + Q)^* = (P^*Q^*)^* = (P^* + Q^*)^*$

10. $R(P + Q) = RP + RQ$ and $(P + Q)R = PR + QR$

Proof:

LHS = $R(P + Q)$	LHS = $(P + Q)R$
= R followed by P or Q	= P or Q followed by R
= RP or RQ	= PR or QR
= $RP + RQ$	= $PR + QR$
= RHS	= RHS

5.2 Equivalence of Regular Expressions and Finite Automata (FA)

In this section, we will discuss the equivalence of regular expressions and finite automata. Let us see how to convert a regular expression into NFA with ε-transitions and NFA with ε-transitions is converted into equivalent DFA as we have discussed in Chapter 2. Finally, we find the regular expression for DFA. The equivalence of finite automata and regular expressions is known as **Kleene's theorem.** Fig. 5.1 shows how regular expressions are used to draw finite automata and acceptance of finite automata are converted into regular expressions.

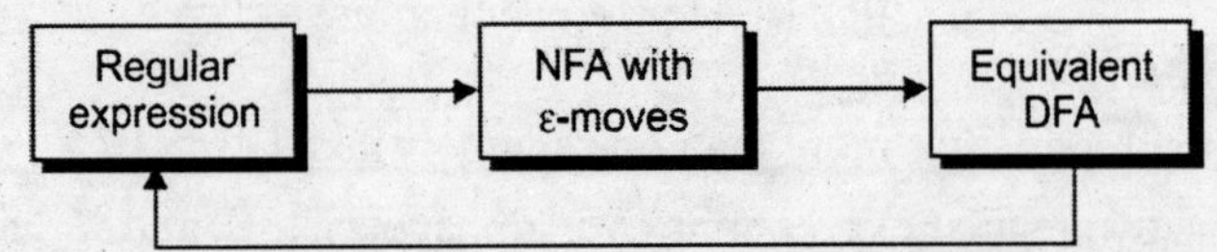

Fig. 5.1: Equivalence of regular expressions and finite automata

First let us see, what is the relation between regular expression and corresponding regular language. *If r is a regular expression, then L(r) is the language denoted by this expression.* It should be noted that a regular language might be represented by one or more regular expressions. Some identities for regular languages and regular expressions as given below:

(a) If r, r_1, and r_2 are regular expressions such that $r = r_1 + r_2$, then $L(r) = L(r_1 + r_2) = L(r_1) + L(r_2)$

(b) If r, r_1, and r_2 are regular expressions such that $r = r_1r_2$, then $L(r) = L(r_1r_2) = L(r_1)L(r_2)$

(c) If r, and r_1 are regular expressions such that $r = r_1{}^*$ then $L(r) = L(r_1{}^*) = L((L(r_1))^*)$

(d) If r, r_1, and r_2 are regular expressions such that $r = r_1{}^* \cup r_2{}^*$ then $L(r) = L(r_1{}^* \cup r_2{}^*) = L((L(r_1))^*) + L((L(r_2))^*)$

Theorem 5.1 (Kleene's Theorem Part 1): If r be a regular expression then there exists a NFA with ε-moves, which recognizes $L(r)$.

Proof: First, we will discuss the construction of NFA M with ε-moves for r and then prove that $L(M) = L(r)$. *Let* r be the regular expression over the alphabet Σ.

Construction of NFA with ε-moves:

Case 1: Regular expression r has zero or one symbol.

(i) Let $r = \phi$, and NFA $M = (\{s, f\}, \Sigma, \delta, s, \{f\})$ as shown in Fig. 5.2(a) recognizes r.

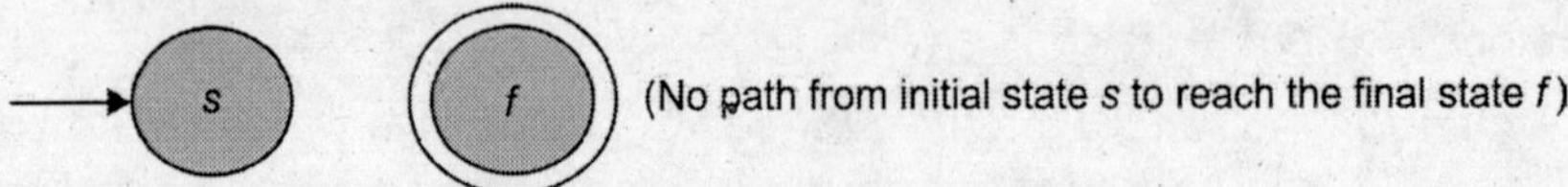

Fig. 5.2(a): NFA for regular expression $r = \phi$

(ii) Let $r = \varepsilon$, and NFA $M = (\{s\}, \Sigma, \delta, s, \{s\})$ as shown in Fig. 5.2(b) recognizes r.

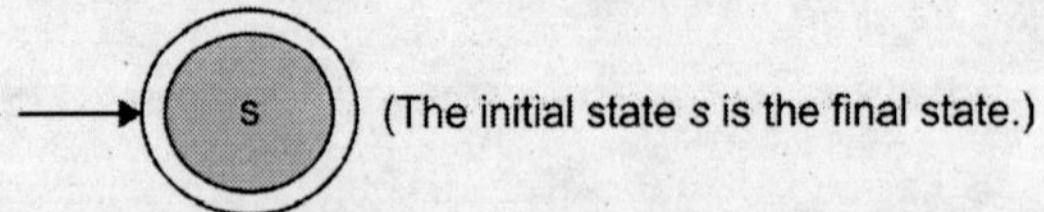

Fig. 5.2(b): NFA for regular expression $r = \varepsilon$

(iii) Let $r = a$, for all $a \in \Sigma$, and NFA $M = (\{s, f\}, \Sigma, \delta, s, \{f\})$ as shown in Fig. 5.2(c) recognizes r.

Fig. 5.2(c): NFA for regular expression $r = a$

Case 2: Regular expression has more than one symbols i.e., $|r| > 1$.

Let r_1 and r_2 be the two regular expressions over alphabets Σ_1, Σ_2 and N_1 and N_2 are two NFA for r_1 and r_2 respectively as shown in Fig. 5.3(a).

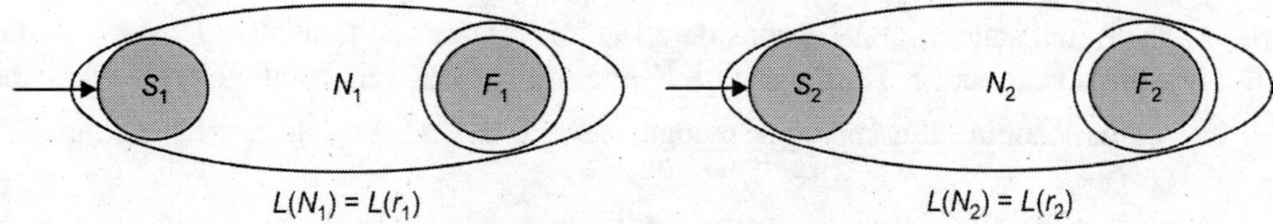

Fig. 5.3: (a) NFA for regular expression r_1 and r_2

Regular expression r has more than one symbols and we can break $\boldsymbol{r}$ into two parts $\boldsymbol{r_1}$ and $\boldsymbol{r_2}$ or we can represent in term of r_1 or r_2 such that $\boldsymbol{\Sigma = \Sigma_1 \cup \Sigma_2}$. There are four possibilities for regular expression as given below:

- $r = r_1 + r_2$ or $r_1 \mid r_2$ or $r_1 \cup r_2$ (Union of r_1 and r_2)
- $r = r_1 r_2$ (Concatenation of r_1 and r_2)
- $r = r_1^*$ (Transitive Closure of r_1)
- $r = r_1+$ (Positive Closure of r_1)

Rule 1: Constructing NFA M for $\boldsymbol{r = r_1 + r_2}$ **or** $\boldsymbol{r_1 \mid r_2}$ **or** $\boldsymbol{r_1 \cup r_2}$**:** Let s and f are the starting state and final state respectively of M. The transition diagram of M is shown in Fig. 5.3(b). We combine N_1 and N_2 in **parallel** to form NFA M.

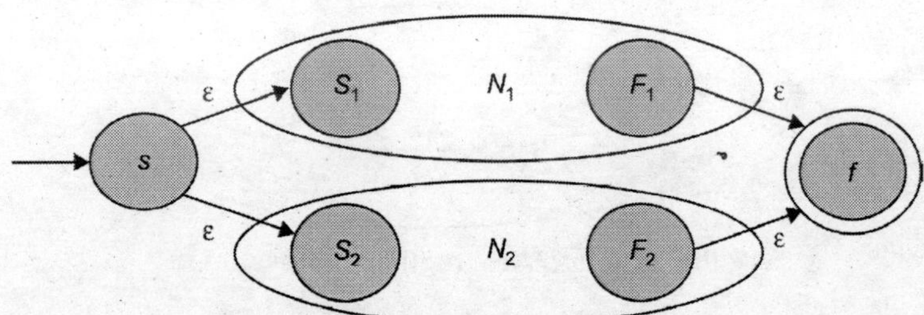

Fig. 5.3(b): NFA for regular expression $r_1 + r_2$

Now, let us see the language $L(M)$ recognized by the NFA M. Let regular expression recognized by M is r, i.e. $L(M) = r$.

$L(M) = \varepsilon L(N_1)\varepsilon$ or $\varepsilon L(N_2)\varepsilon = L(N_1)$ or $L(N_2) = L(r_1)$ or $L(r_2)$

So, $r = r_1 + r_2$

$\boldsymbol{M = (Q \cup \{s, f\}, \Sigma_1 \cup \Sigma_2, \delta, s, \{f\})}$, where Q contains all the states of N_1 and N_2.

Rule 2: Constructing NFA for regular expression $\boldsymbol{r = r_1 r_2}$**:**

We combine N_1 and N_2 in series such that N_1 is followed by N_2. NFA M shown in Fig. 5.3(c). NFA N_1 for $L(r_1)$ and NFA N_2 for $L(r_2)$ are **combined in series** to form M.

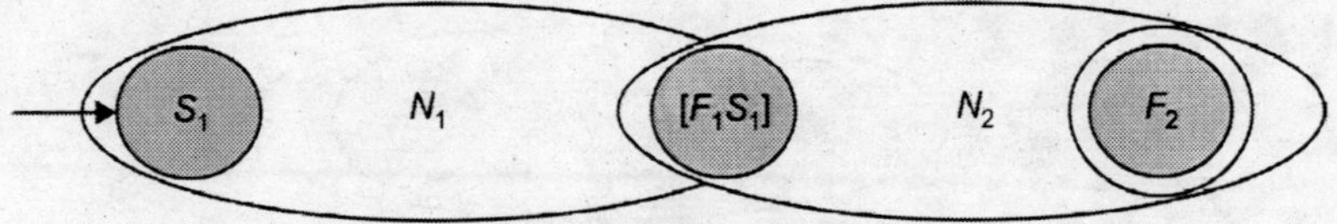

Fig. 5.3(c): NFA for regular expression $r_1 r_2$

The initial state S_1 of N_1 is considered as initial state and final state F_2 of N_2 is considered as final state for M. The final state F_1 and initial state S_2 is combined into one state for M.

Let us examine the language recognized by NFA M. Let language recognized by M is $L(M) = L(r)$,

So, $L(M) = L(N_1)$ followed $L(N_2) = L(N_1)L(N_2) = L(r_1r_2)$

Therefore, $r = r_1r_2$

$\boldsymbol{M = (Q, \Sigma_1 \cup \Sigma_2, \delta, S_1, \{F_2\})}$, where Q contains all the states of N_1 and N_2 such that final state(s) of N_1 is merged with initial state of N_2.

Rule 3: Constructing NFA for regular expression $\boldsymbol{r = r_1*}$:

Let NFA M shown in Fig. 5.3(d) recognizes $L(r)$, i.e., $L(M) = L(r)$. We add two addition states with NFA N_1, which recognizes $L(r_1)$. Additional states $\boldsymbol{s}$ and $\boldsymbol{f}$ are initial and final state respectively. The final state $\boldsymbol{F_1}$ of N_1 is made as non-final state. There is a path with label ε from state $\boldsymbol{s}$ to reach initial state $\boldsymbol{S_1}$ of N_1 and another path with label ε from state $\boldsymbol{F_1}$ of N_1 to final state $\boldsymbol{f}$. There are two arches with label ε; one from state $\boldsymbol{F_1}$ to $\boldsymbol{S_1}$ as a loop and another from initial state **s** to reach final state $\boldsymbol{f}$.

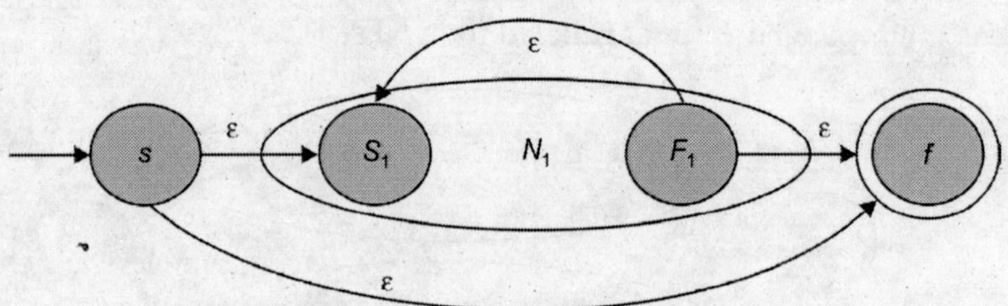

Fig. 5.3(c): NFA for regular expression r_1

Now, let us see the language $L(M)$ recognized by NFA M.

$$L(M) = \{\varepsilon, L(N_1), L(N_1)L(N_1), L(N_1)L(N_1)L(N_1), \ldots\}$$
$$= L(N_1)^* = L(r_1^*)$$

Therefore, $\quad r = r_1*$

We have, $\boldsymbol{M = (\{s, f\} \cup Q_1, \Sigma_1, \delta, S, \{f\})}$, where Q_1 is the set of states of N_1.

Rule 4: Constructing NFA for regular expression $\boldsymbol{r = r_1^+}$:

Let NFA M shown in Fig. 5.3(e) recognizes $L(r) = r_1^+$. We take help from the NFA shown in Fig. 5.3(d), which recognizes $L(r) = r_1*$. We remove one arch with label from initial state $\boldsymbol{s}$ to final state $\boldsymbol{f}$.

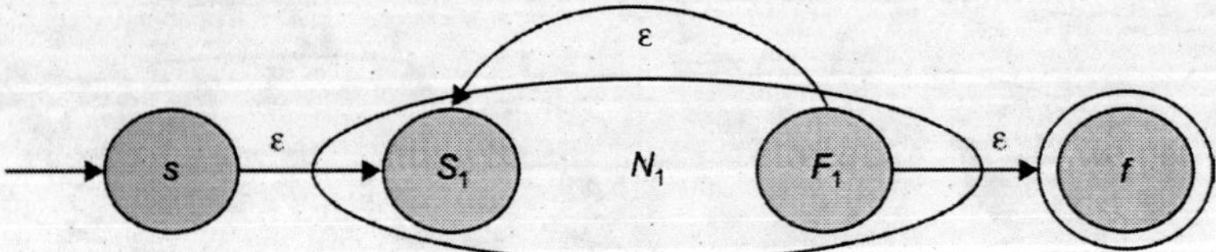

Fig. 5.3(e): NFA for regular expression for r_1^+

The language recognized by M is described as follows:

$$L(M) = \{L(N_1), L(N_1)L(N_1), L(N_1)L(N_1)L(N_1), \ldots\}$$
$$= L(N_1)^+ = L(r_1^+)$$

Therefore, $r = r_1^+$

So, we have, $\boldsymbol{M = (\{s, f\} \cup Q_1, \Sigma_1, \delta, S, \{f\})}$, where Q_1 is the set of states of NFA N_1.

Let us see some **examples** using the above rules to construct NFA for given regular expressions.

Example 1: Construct NFA for regular expression $r = a \mid b$.

Solution: First we break the regular expression r into sub-regular expressions. Let $\boldsymbol{r_1 = a}$ and $\boldsymbol{r_2 = b}$, and corresponding non-deterministic finite automata (NFA) are N_1 and N_2 respectively. Regular expression r is represented as $r_1 \mid r_2$. NFA M for regular expression $a \mid b$ is shown in Fig. 5.4. First we construct NFA N_1 and N_2 for r_1 and r_2 using Case 1 (iii) as discussed earlier. Now, we construct NFA M using Case 2 rule 1.

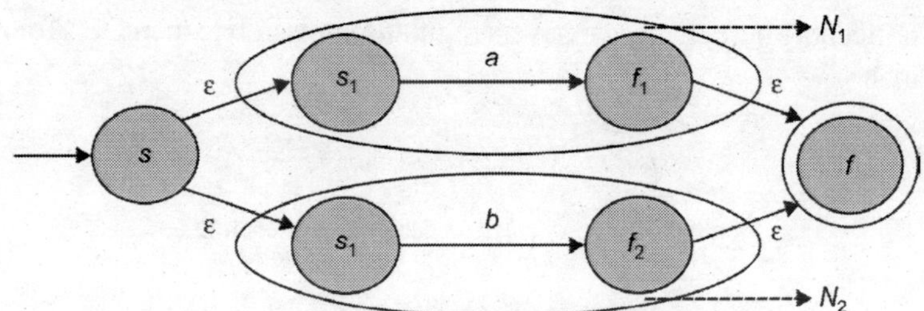

Fig. 5.4: NFA for regular expression ***a*** **|** ***b***

The language recognized by NFA M is described as follows:

$$L(M) = \varepsilon a \varepsilon + \varepsilon b \varepsilon = a + b$$

Therefore, $L(M) = L(r)$

Example 2: Construct NFA for the regular expression $(a \mid b)^*$.

Solution: First we break regular expression r into sub-regular expressions. Let NFA M recognizes regular expression $r = (a \mid b)^*$ and regular expressions $r_1 = a$ and $r_2 = b$. So, r is equal to $(r_1 \mid r_2)^*$. Now, we construct NFA for r_1 and r_2 using Case 1 (iii) and then we construct NFA for $r_1 \mid r_2$ using Case 2 rule 1. Finally, we construct M from N_1 and N_2 for regular expression $r_1 \mid r_2$ using Case 2 rule 3. NFA M is shown in Fig. 5.5(a).

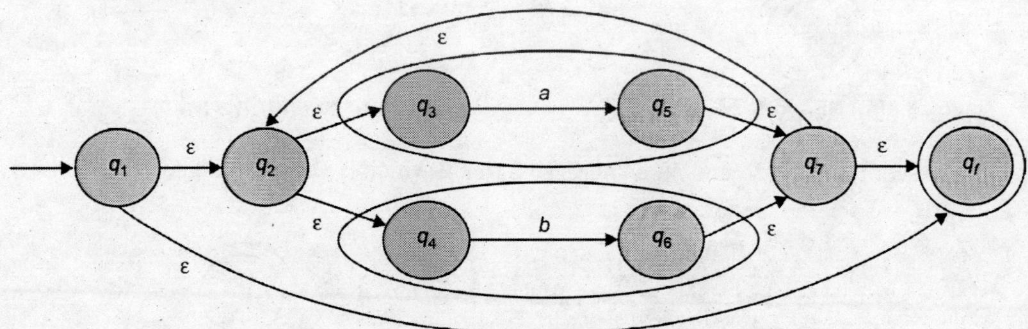

Fig. 5.5(a): NFA for regular expression (*a*| *b*)*

Let NFA, $M = (\{q_1, q_2, q_3, q_4, q_6, q_7, q_f\}, \{a, b\}, \delta, q_1, \{q_f\})$. The language recognized by M is described as follows:

$$L(M) = \varepsilon(r_1 \mid r_2)^* = \varepsilon(a + b)^* = (a + b)^*$$

Therefore, $L(M) = (a \mid b)^*$

Removing the ε-transitions from NFA M, we have DFA shown in Fig. 5.5(b).

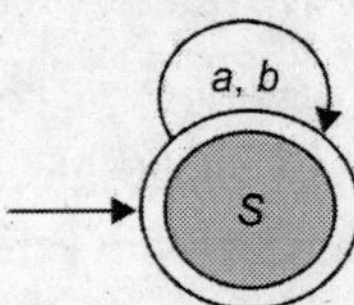

Fig. 5.5(b): NFA without ε-moves for $(a + b)^*$

One thing is noticeable here that if we have a regular expression r, then DFA for r^* is represented as shown in Fig. 5.5(c):

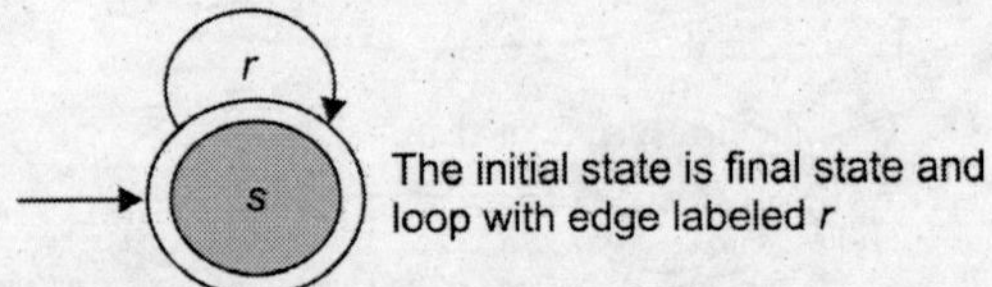

Fig. 5.5(c): DFA for regular expression r^*

Example 3: Draw NFA for regular expression: $r = (a \mid b)^*abb$.

Solution: First, we try to break regular expression r into sub-regular expressions. Let $r = r_1r_2$, where $r_1 = (a \mid b)^*$, and $r_2 = abb$. Now, we construct NFA for sub-regular expressions r_1 and r_2 as shown in Fig. 5.6(a) and Fig. 5.6(b).

(See the previous example (2) for $r_1 = (a \mid b)^*$)

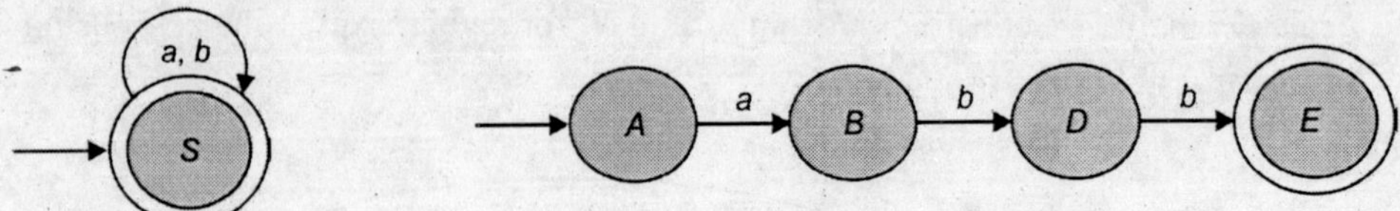

Fig. 5.6(a): NFA for *abb*

Fig. 5.6(b): NFA for $r_1 = (a \mid b)^*$

Now, we combine the N_1 and N_2 using Case 2 rule 2 which is shown in Fig. 5.6(c).

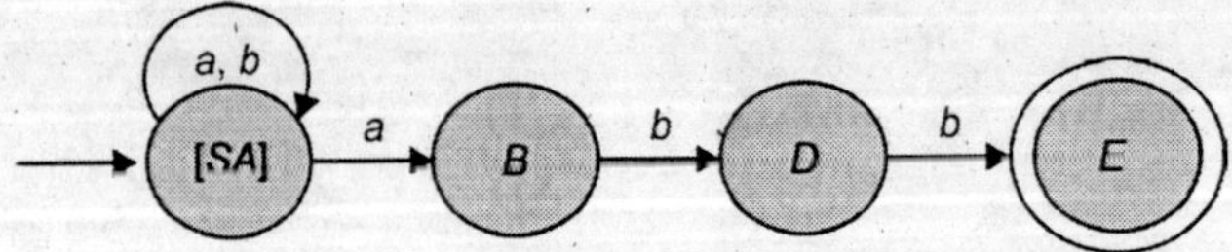

Fig. 5.6(c): NFA for regular expression $(a \mid b)^*abb$

Example 4: Construct NFA for regular expression: $ba^* \mid ab^*$.

Solution: Let $r = r_1 \mid r_2$, where $r_1 = ba^*$, and $r_2 = ab^*$. We construction NFA for r_1 and r_2 following the Case 2 rules 1, 2, 3, as shown in Fig. 5.7.

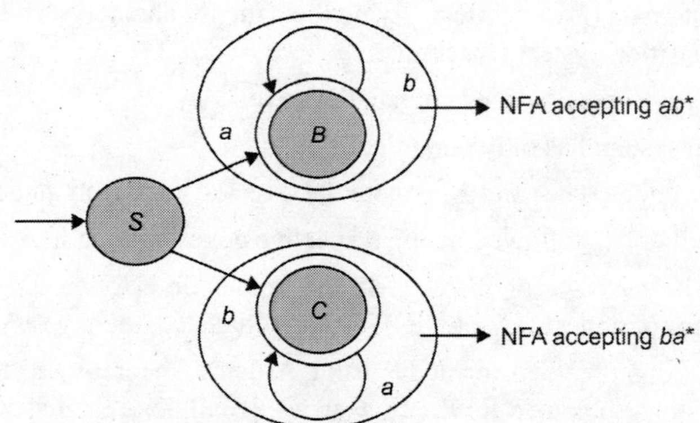

Fig. 5.7: NFA for regular expression $ba^* \mid ab^*$

Theorem 5.2 (Kleene's Theorem Part 2): If a finite automaton recognizes the regular language L, then there exists regular expression(s), which describe L.

We have discussed earlier that how a regular language is expressed using regular expression.

Theorem 5.3 (Arden's Theorem): If P and Q are two regular expressions over an alphabet Σ such that P does not represent a null string (ε), then the following equation in R: $\boldsymbol{R = Q + RP}$ has unique solution (only one solution) which is $R = QP^*$.

Proof: We know that regular expression $P \neq \varepsilon$. Let us put value of R ($R = QP^*$) in right-hand side of Arden's equation repeatedly.

$$R = Q + RP$$
$$= Q + (Q + RP)P \quad \text{(Replacing } R \text{ by } Q + RP \text{ in right-hand side.)}$$
$$= Q + QP + RP^2 \quad \text{(Replacing } R \text{ by } Q + RP \text{ in right-hand side.)}$$
$$= Q + QP + (Q + RP)P^2 \quad \text{(Replacing } R \text{ by } Q + RP \text{ in right-hand side.)}$$
$$= Q + QP + QP^2 + RP^3 \quad \text{(Replacing } R \text{ by } Q + RP \text{ in right-hand side.)}$$
$$\ldots$$
$$= Q + QP + QP^2 + QP^3 + \ldots. + QP^n + RP^{n+1}$$
$$\text{(Replacing } R \text{ by } Q + RP \text{ in right-hand side } n\text{-times.)}$$
$$= Q(\varepsilon + P + P^2 + P^3 + \ldots + P^n) + RP^{n+1}$$
$$= QP^* + RP^{n+1} \quad \text{(If } n \text{ tends toward infinite.)}$$

Therefore, it is clear that $R = QP^*$ is a solution for Arden's equation. Now, let us see, is there another solution. We put the above solution ($R = QP^*$) in the Arden's equation and examine the right-hand side of the equation.

$$R = Q + QP^*P = Q + QP^* \quad \text{(Since, } P^*P = P\text{)}$$
$$= Q(\varepsilon + P^*) = QP^* \quad \text{(Since, } \varepsilon + P^* = P^*\text{)}$$

After putting $R = QP^*$ in Arden's equation, equation is fully satisfied, i.e. the right-hand side is equivalent to QP^*. Therefore, we conclude that Arden's equation has solution $R = QP^*$, which is unique.

Application of Arden's Theorem: We use Arden's Theorem to find out the regular expression recognized by finite automata (FA). While applying the Arden's Theorems, following **assumptions** are made regarding the transition system (diagram):

1. The transition system (FA) does not have ε-moves.
2. The transition system has only one initial state.
3. V_i denotes the node (state) and E_{ij} denote the directed edge from node V_i to node V_j.

   V_i = Sum of all nodes followed by the respective edges coming into V_i

or $V_i = \Sigma V_i E_{ji}$ Where E_{ji} is a coming edge into V_i from node V_j for some $i, j = 0, 1, 2, \ldots, n$, where n is the number of nodes. If the node V_i is the initial state then we add ε in its equation.

We solve the equations obtained for nodes using Arden's Theorem and find the union of all the results (regular expressions) obtained for the final states. If only one final state is there then the result corresponding to final state is the final result i.e. regular expression recognized by the transition system.

Example 1: Consider the DFA shown in Fig. 5.8 and find the regular expression recognized by this.

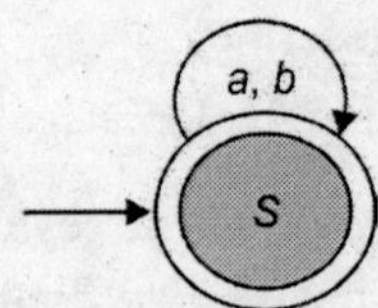

Fig. 5.8: DFA

Solution: Let DFA $M = (\{S\}, \{a, b\}, \delta, S, \{S\})$, which is shown in Fig. 5.8. We find equation for state S, which is initial and final state.

$S = Sa + Sb + \varepsilon$ (One edge with two labels a, b coming into S, and since, it is initial state, so addition of ε is there.)

$S = \varepsilon + S(a + b)$

$S = \varepsilon(a + b)^*$ (Using Arden's equation $R = Q + RP$ and its solution $R = QP^*$, where $R = S$, $O = \varepsilon$, $P = a + b$)

$= (a + b)^* \equiv (a \mid b)^*$

So, the regular expression $(\boldsymbol{a} \mid \boldsymbol{b})^*$ is recognized by DFA.

Hence, $L(M) = (a + b)^* \equiv (a \mid b)^*$

Example 2: Find the regular expression recognized by the NFA shown in Fig. 5.6(c).

Solution: Let NFA $M = (\{[SA], B, D, E\}, \{a, b\}, \delta, [SA], \{E\})$, which is shown in Fig. 5.6(c). There are four states and final state is E. We find equations are all the states, which are given below:

For initial state $[SA]$:

$$[SA] = [SA]a + [SA]b + \varepsilon \quad (1)$$

(One edge with two labels a, b coming into the state $[SA]$, and since it is initial state, so addition of ε is there.)

For states B, D, E:

$$B = [SA]a \quad (2)$$

$$D = Bb \quad (3)$$

$$E = Db \quad (4)$$

E is the only one final state and we have four equations. So we solve the equations for E. For equation (4), value of D should be there, for equation (3), value of B should be there, and for equation (2), value of $[SA]$ should be there. So, from the equation (1), we get:

$[SA] = \varepsilon(a + b)^* \equiv (a + b)^*$(Using Arden's Theorem, $R = [SA]$, $Q = \varepsilon$, $P = a + b$)

Now, putting value of $[SA]$ into equation (2), we get

$$B = (a + b)^*a$$

Putting value of B into equation (3), we get

$$D = (a + b)^*ab$$

Putting value of D into equation (4), we get

$$E = (a + b)^*abb$$

Since, E is the only final state, so regular expression recognized by NFA is $\boldsymbol{(a + b)^*abb}$.

Example 3: Find the regular expression recognized by DFA shown in Fig. 5.9.

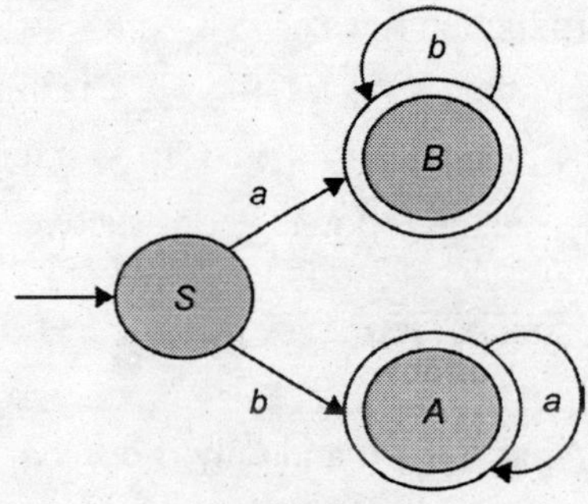

Fig. 5.9

Solution: Let DFA $M = (\{S, A, B\}, \{a, b\}, \delta, S, \{A, B\})$ is shown in Fig. 5.9. Following are the equations find for three states A, B, and S.

$$S = \varepsilon \quad (1)$$

$$A = Sb + Aa \quad (2)$$

$$B = Sa + Bb \quad (3)$$

Putting the value of S into equations (2), we get:

$$A = \varepsilon b + Aa = b + Aa$$

So, $A = ba^*$ (Using Arden's Theorem, $R = A$, $Q = b$, $P = a$)

Putting the value of S into equations (3), we get:

$$B = \varepsilon a + Bb = a + Bb$$

So, $B = ab^*$ (Using Arden's Theorem, $R = B, Q = a, P = b$)

Since, both A and B states are final states. Therefore, regular expression for M is union of regular expressions for A and B states.

$$\boldsymbol{L(M) = ba^* + ab^*}$$

5.3 EQUIVALENCE OF REGULAR GRAMMARS AND FINITE AUTOMATA

In this section, we will discuss how to convert a regular grammars into finite automata (FA) and finite automata into a regular grammars.

Theorem 5.4: If L is a regular language recognized by finite automaton (FA) M then there exists a regular grammar G, which generates L, that is, $\boldsymbol{L(G) = L}$.

Proof: We construct a regular grammar G *based* on the transitions of finite automaton M. We assume that all the productions of G are right linear.

Let $M = (Q, \Sigma, \delta, A_0, F)$, where $Q = \{A_0, A_1, A_2, \ldots, A_n\}$

Let grammar $G = (V_n, \Sigma, P, A_0)$, where

1. $\boldsymbol{V_n = \{A_0, A_1, A_2, \ldots, A_n\}}$,
2. $\boldsymbol{\Sigma}$ is same for both M and G,
3. P includes following production rules:
   (i) If $\delta(A_i, a) = A_j \notin F$, then $A_i \to aA_j$ for $a \in \Sigma$ is in P.
   (ii) If $\delta(A_i, a) = A_j \in F$, then $A_i \to aA_j$ and $A_i \to a$ for $a \in \Sigma$ are in P.

To prove $L(G) = L(M) = L$, we see the following constructive aspect:

$$A_0 \overset{n-1}{\underset{G}{\Rightarrow}} a_1a_2a_3\ldots a_{n-1}A_n \text{ (Using } A_0 \to a_1A_1 \to a_1a_2A_2\ldots \to a_1a_2a_3\ldots A_n\text{, for } a_1, a_2, a_3\ldots,a_{n-1} \in \Sigma)$$

$$A_0 \underset{G}{\Rightarrow} a_1a_2a_3\ldots a_{n-1}a_n \text{ (Using } A_na_n) \text{ if and only if } \delta(A_0, a_1) = A_1, \delta(A_1, a_2) = A_3, \ldots, \text{ and}$$

$\delta(A_n, a_n) = A_j \in F$. So, $L(G)$ and L are equivalent language.

Example 1: Construct a regular grammar for NFA shown in Fig. 5.10.

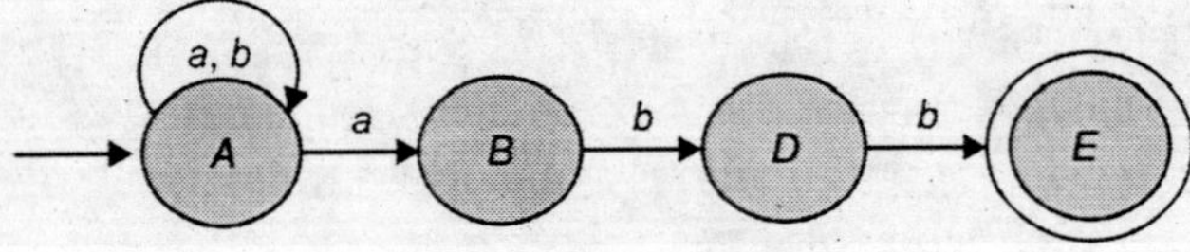

Fig. 5.10: NFA for $(a|b)^*abb$

Solution: Let regular grammar $\boldsymbol{G = (V_n, \Sigma, P, A)}$, where $\boldsymbol{V_n = \{A, B, D, E\}, \Sigma = \{a, b\}}$. State A has two transitions for input symbol 'a'; first on itself and second on state B. State E is only final state. The set of production rules P includes following production rules:

Transition	Production Rule (P)
$\delta(A, a) = \{A, B\}$	$A \rightarrow aA$, $A \rightarrow aB$
$\delta(A, b) = A$	$A \rightarrow bA$
$\delta(B, b) = D$	$B \rightarrow bD$
$\delta(D, b) = E$	$D \rightarrow bE$, $D \rightarrow b$

The regular grammar obtained for NFA has a flaw because of multiple transitions for single input symbol 'a' as: $\boldsymbol{A \rightarrow aA}$ and $\boldsymbol{A \rightarrow aB}$. This flaw is known as *left factoring*. We will discuss in next chapter. Let us find out the remedy. The equivalent DFA M_1 for above NFA is shown in Fig. 5.11.

Production rules based on transition of M_1 have no left factoring problem becuase M_1 has only one transition for input a or b.

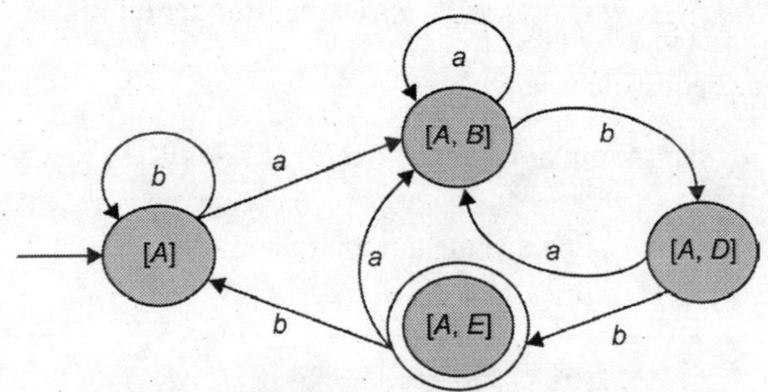

Fig. 5.11: Deterministic finite automata (DFA)

Let $G_1 = (V_1, \Sigma, P_1, [A])$, such that $L(M_1) = L$, where $V_1 = \{[A], [A, B], [A, D], [A, E]\}$, and transitions and corresponding production rules are given in following table:

Transition	Production Rule (P)
$\delta([A], a) = [A, B]$	$[A] \rightarrow a[A, B]$
$\delta([A], b) = [A]$	$[A] \rightarrow b[A]$
$\delta([A, B], a) = [A, B]$	$[A, B] \rightarrow a[A, B]$
$([A, B], b) = [A, D]$	$[A, B] \rightarrow b[A, D]$
$\delta([A, D], a) = [A, B]$	$[A, D] \rightarrow a[A, B]$
$\delta([A, D], b) = [A, E]$	$[A, D] \rightarrow b[A, E]$, $[A, D] \rightarrow b$
$\delta([A, E], a) = [A, B]$	$[A, E] \rightarrow a[A, B]$
$\delta([A, E], b) = [A]$	$[A, E] \rightarrow b[A]$

Theorem 5.5: If L is a regular language generated by some regular grammar G then there exists a finite automaton (FA) M which recognizes L, that is, $\boldsymbol{L(M) = L(G)}$.

Proof: We construct finite automaton M based on productions of the regular grammar G. We assume that all the productions of G are right linear.

Let $G = (V_n, \Sigma, P, A_0)$, where $V_n = \{A_0, A_1, A_2, \ldots, A_n\}$,

Let $M = (Q, \Sigma, \delta, A_0, \{A_f\})$, where

1. $\boldsymbol{Q = \{A_0, A_1, A_2, \ldots, A_n, A_f\}}$,
2. $\boldsymbol{\Sigma}$ is same for finite automaton M and grammar G,

3. δ includes following transitions:
   (a) $\boldsymbol{\delta(A_i, a) = A_j \notin F}$, if production rule $\boldsymbol{A_i \to aA_j}$ for $a \in \Sigma$ is in P.
   (b) $\boldsymbol{\delta(A_i, a) = A_j \in F}$, if production rule $\boldsymbol{A_i \to a}$ for $a \in \Sigma$ is in P.
4. A_0 is the initial state, and
5. A_f is the only final state.

To prove $L(G) = L(M) = L$, we use following constructive aspect:

$\delta'(A_0, a_1a_2a_3 \ldots a_{n-1}a_n) = \delta'(A_1, a_2a_3 \ldots a_{n-1}a_n) = \ldots \delta(A_n, a_n) = A_j \in F$ if and only if

$\delta(A_0, a_1) = A_1$, $\delta(A_1, a_2) = A_3$, ..., and $\delta(A_n, a_n) = A_f$ and $A_0 \overset{n-1}{\underset{G}{\Rightarrow}} a_1a_2a_3 \ldots a_{n-1}A_n$

(Using rules $A_0 \to a_1A_1 \to a_1a_2A_2 \ldots \to a_1a_2a_3 \ldots A_n$, for $a_1, a_2, a_3 \ldots, a_{n-1} \in \Sigma$)

So, $$A_0 \overset{*}{\underset{G}{\Rightarrow}} a_1a_2a_3 \ldots a_{n-1}a_n \text{ (Using production rule } A_n \to a_n)$$

Hence, $L(G)$ and L are equivalent languages.

Example 1: Consider a regular grammar $G = (\{S\}, \{a, b\}, \{S \to aS \mid b\}, S)$, construct a finite automaton M such that $L(M) = L(G)$.

Solution: Let $M = (Q, \Sigma, \delta, S, \{A_f\})$ be a finite automaton, where

$Q = \{S, A_f\}$, $\Sigma = \{a, b\}$, δ is defined as following:

Production rule	Transition	Transition diagram
$S \to aS$	$\delta(S, a) = S$	
$S \to b$	$\delta(S, b) = A_f$	Fig. 5.12: FA

5.4 REGULAR AND NON-REGULAR LANGUAGES

In this section, we will discuss how to prove a language non-regular. **Pumping Lemma** is a useful tool for this purpose. We use Pumping Lemma to prove that a certain language is not regular language. Pumping Lemma is introduced by **Yehoshua Bar-Hillel**, **Micha *A.* Perles**, and **Eliahu Shamir** in 1961.

Since, the number of states in a finite automata is finite, let us say it is $\boldsymbol{n}$ (for some fixed value of n), and then it can recognize all the words of length less than n without any loop. Suppose, a regular language L has infinite number of words and the length of these words may or may not be equal to n. So, how can finite automata recognize the L? It is not possible for finite automata without loop(s). Finite automata can recognize a language L having some loop(s) whenever the length of a given word is greater than or equal to n, where n is the number of states of finite automata. So, we conclude that the loop in finite automata makes it able to accept those strings, which have length greater than or equal to its total number of states.

When a string $\boldsymbol{w}$ has bigger length (greater than number of states in finite automata) then we can break this string in to three parts, say $\boldsymbol{x}$, $\boldsymbol{y}$ (y should not be null string), and z. Let finite automata has a loop for substring y, and $w = xyz \in L$ is being accepted. So, $\boldsymbol{w = xy^iz}$ for $i = 0, 1, 2, \ldots$ is also accepted by finite automata. This is the main concept used in Pumping Lemma.

5.4.1 Pumping Lemma for Regular Sets

Pumping Lemma is useful because of the following reasons:

1. It gives a method for pumping (generating) many substrings from a given long string. In other words, we say that it provides means to break a given sufficient long input string into several substrings.
2. It gives necessary condition(s) to prove a set of strings is not regular.

Theorem 5.6: Let $M = (Q, \Sigma, \delta, q_0, F)$ be a finite automaton (*FA*) having n states. Finite automaton *M* recognizes the language *L*. *A* long string $\boldsymbol{w \in L}$ such that $|\boldsymbol{w}| \geq \boldsymbol{n}$ and $\boldsymbol{w = xyz}$, where $\boldsymbol{y \neq \varepsilon}$, then $\boldsymbol{xy^iz} \in L$ for $i \geq 0$.

Proof: Finite automaton *M* recognizes *L* and hence *L* is a regular language. If $w \in L$ such that $w = xyz$. We have substring *y* optional in *w* and $|w| \geq n$, where *n* is the number of states in finite automata. Consider general conceptual transition diagram of finite automaton *M* as shown in Fig. 5.13.

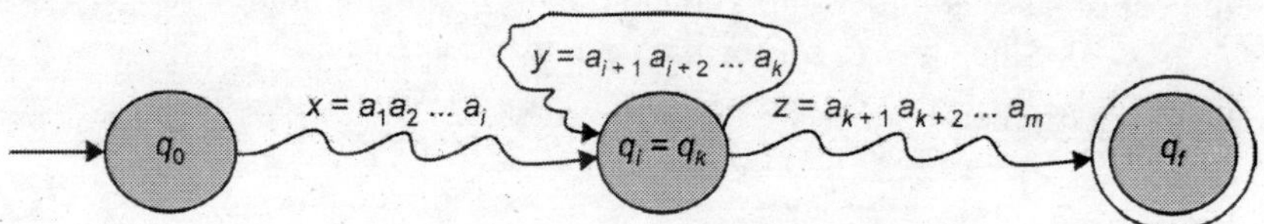

Fig. 5.13: Finite automata for xy^iz

Let us examine the strings recognized by *M*. String $\boldsymbol{w = xy^iz}$ for $n \geq 0$ is accepted by *M*. It is also obvious that substring *y* is optional and obtained by traveling the loop in state q_i. State q_f is the final state. When loop is not traveled, we get $\boldsymbol{w = xz}$ accepted by *M*.

Let $w = a_1a_2a_3 \dots a_ia_{i+1} \dots a_ka_{k+1} \dots a_m$, where substrings $x = a_1a_2a_3 \dots a_i$, $y = a_{i+1} \dots a_k$ and $z = a_{k+1} \dots a_m$. The length of *w* is *m* and $m \geq n$. It means, when $\boldsymbol{m > n}$, it indicates that there is some loop in transition diagram of *M*. Let *y* be the string obtained from the edges involved in looping as shown in Fig. 5.13.

Case 1: When $w = xy^0z \equiv xz$ for $i = 0$,

xz is accepted and $xz \in L$

Case 2: $w = xy^iz$ for $i \geq 1$, it means the control of finite automaton *M* decides to go *i*-times into the loop with label *y* and xy^iz is accepted. Following are the list of the strings accepted by *M*:

$$L(M) = \{xz, xyz, xy^2z, xy^3z, \dots\} = \{xy^0z, xy^1z, xy^2z, xy^3z, \dots\}$$
$$= \{xy^iz : i \geq 0\}$$

So, for all value of $i \geq 0$, $w = xy^iz$ is accepted by *M*. Hence, the statement of the theorem is true.

Application of pumping lemma

Pumping Lemma is used to prove certain sets are not regular sets (certain languages are not regular) using following steps:

Step 1: We assume that given set is regular and accepted by *FA M* having n states.

Step 2: Choose a string *w* such that $|w| \geq n$ and use Pumping Lemma to write $w = xy^iz$ for $i \geq 0$, such that $y \notin \varepsilon$, and $|xz| \leq n$.

Step 3: Find a suitable integer *i* such that $xy^iz \notin L$ and this contradicts our assumption made in step 1 and hence *L* is not regular.

The **result** of Pumping Lemma **is always negative**, which is a negative point of this lemma. **For example**, prove that $L = \{a^n b^n : n \geq 1\}$ is not regular.

Proof: In given language the number of a's is equal to number of b's. This is the one clue to find the contradiction.

Step 1: Let L is regular and accepted by DFA M with n states.

Step 2: String $w \in L$ such that $|w| \geq n$ and $w = xy^iz \in L$ for $i \geq 0$, $y \notin \varepsilon$, and $xz \leq n$

Step 3: Selecting substring y **($y \notin \varepsilon$):**

Let $w = xy^iz$ for $i = 0$, that is, $w = xz$

Case 1: When $y = a^p$, then

$$w = a^{n-p}b^n$$

Number of a's $= n - p$, and number of b's $= n$

Number of a's = Number of b's if and only if $p = 0$ and number of a's and b's is not equal when $q > 0$. Since, $y \neq \varepsilon$, so, for $p > 0$, $w = xy^iz \notin L$

Case 2: When $y = b^q$, then

$$w = a^nb^{n-q}$$

Number of a's $= n$, and number of b's $= n - q$

Number of a's = Number of b's if and only if $q = 0$ and number of a's and b's is not equal when $q > 0$. Since, $y \neq \varepsilon$, so, for $q > 0$, $w = xy^iz \notin L$

Case 3: When $y = a^pb^q$, then

$$w = a^{n-p}\,b^{n-q}$$

Number of a's $= n - p$, and number of b's $= n - q$

Number of a's = Number of b's if and only if $q = p$.

For $p = q$, we have number of a's and b's equal, but this case may or may not be. So, for $\boldsymbol{p \neq q}$, $w = xy^iz \notin L$

Since, we get contradiction in all the cases, therefore L is not regular.

(**Note:** We can choose any other value of $i \geq 0$.)

5.4.2 The Myhill-Nerode's Theorem

We have seen that Pumping Lemma for regular sets is negative in its application. So, it is used exclusively to show that certain languages are not regular because they cannot meet its requirements. But, there is another theorem known Myhill-Nerode theorem, which tells that the given language might be not regular and it has constructive aspect. This theorem is used in proving certain language is regular or not. In constrast with the Pumping Lemma for regular set, this theorem is almost exclusively used in order to prove that a given language is not regular. We will see this in this section. First let us see some terminologies.

Class and society: Each language whether regular or not regular creates its own classes of strings. **For example**, consider a language L consisting of all the strings over $\{a, b\}$ ending in a. The accepting finite automaton is shown in Fig. 5.14(a).

That is, $L = \{a, aa, ba, bba, aaa, \ldots\} = (a + b)^*a$

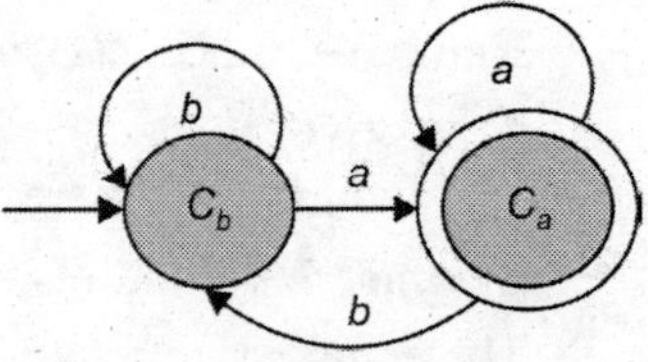

Fig. 5.14(a)

Here, L creates two classes, namely C_a and C_b such that

$C_a = (b + aa^*b)^*aa^*$ (All strings ending in a), and

$C_b = (b + aa^*b)^*$ (All strings ending in b)

Only the strings of the class C_a are acceptable by some finite automaton, which is equivalent to L. Now, let us think about finite automaton. States (final and non-final) of finite automata create some society of strings. **For example,** see the FA shown in Fig. 5.14(b).

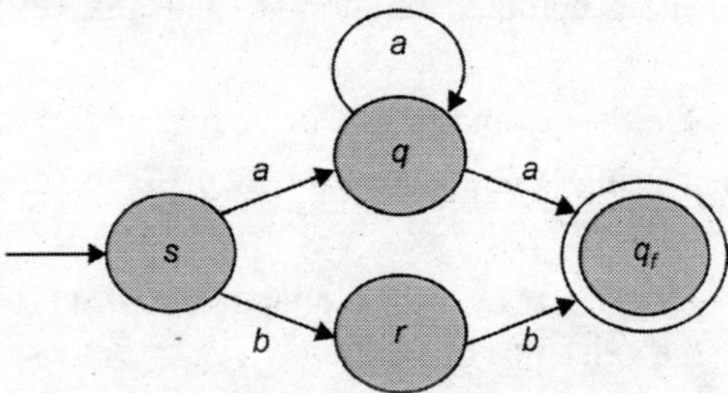

Fig. 5.14(b): Finite automaton

Let us consider four societies, S_s, S_q, S_r, S_{qf}, for states s, q, r, and q_f respectively. We use the Arden's equation in deciding the societies but we do not consider any variable. Following are the societies of finite automaton.

$$S_s = \{\varepsilon\} = \varepsilon,$$
$$S_q = \{a, aa, aaa, \ldots\} = a^+,$$
$$S_r = \{b\} = b, \text{ and}$$
$$S_{qf} = S_q a \cup S_r b = a^+a \cup bb = aa^+ \cup bb$$

We see that only the strings of society Sq_f are acceptable by finite automaton. In general, the societies formed for final states of finite automaton are acceptable societies and other are not. Can we minimize finite automata using the concepts of class and society? Yes, we can; *if the two states are equivalent (societies are equal) then we merge these into one state* and this way we minimize finite automata. One thing here, classes are dependent on language and these are mutually exclusive (we will prove this in our next theorem). So, *FA based on only the classes of a regular language will be minimum state FA and FA based on societies may or may not be minimum state FA.* Another thing is also noticeable here that *two or more societies may be used to define one class of a language.*

Equivalence class: We have discussed about the equivalence relation in Chapter 1. A binary relation is said to equivalence relation if and only if it is:

(a) Reflexive,

(b) Transitive, and

(c) Symmetric

There is a natural equivalence relation between the strings of finite automata. Suppose, DFA $M = (Q, \Sigma, \delta, s, F)$. For $x, y \in \Sigma^*$, a relation R_m is defined as follows:

$\boldsymbol{xR_my}$ if and only if $\delta(s, x) = \delta(s, y)$

In other words, we say that same state is reachable from initial state (s) on both inputs x and y. Since, R_m satisfies all the three conditions to be equivalence that is given below:

Reflexive: Since, $\delta(s, x) = \delta(s, x)$ for all strings $x \in \Sigma^*$. So, R_m is reflexive.

Transitive: If $\delta(s, x) = \delta(s, y)$ and $\delta(s, y) = \delta(s, z)$, where $z \in \Sigma^*$, then $\delta(s, x) = \delta(s, z)$. It means, if $\boldsymbol{xR_m y}$, and $\boldsymbol{yR_m z}$ are there, then $\boldsymbol{xR_m z}$ is also. So, R_m is transitive.

Symmetric: Since, $\delta(s, x) = \delta(s, y)$ and $\delta(s, y) = \delta(s, x)$, so R_m is symmetric.

The equivalence relation R_m divides the set Σ^* into classes of equivalent strings. *The number of classes is known as index and it is finite always for regular languages*.

Let us think about some more complex relation R_L with respect to language over an alphabet Σ defined as follows:

$x\ R_L\ y$ if and only if $\forall z \in \Sigma$ either xz and $yz \in L$ or both xz and $yz \notin L$

In other words, we say that strings x and y are equivalent and belong to the same class.

For examples,

1. Consider the language $L = (10)^*$ over the alphabet $\Sigma = \{0, 1\}$. Now, consider two strings $x = 1$, and $y = 101$ and see the existence of relation R_L:

z	$x\ R_L\ y$	Status
ε	1 R_L101	Both not in L
0	10 R_L 1010	Both in *L*
1	11 R_L1011	Both not in *L*
00	100 R_L10100	Both not in *L*
01	101 R_L10101	Both not in *L*
10	110 R_L10110	Both not in *L*
11	111 R_L10111	Both not in *L*
...	...	...
010	1010 R_L101010	Both in *L*
...	...	...

2. Consider the language L over $\{a, b\}$ defined as:

$$L = \{w : w \in (a + b)^* \text{ such that } |w| \bmod 3 = 1\}$$

There are three equivalence classes:

$$C_0 = \{\text{All strings } w \text{ such that } |w| \bmod 3 = 0\}$$
$$C_1 = \{\text{All strings } w \text{ such that } |w| \bmod 3 = 1\}$$
$$C_2 = \{\text{All strings } w \text{ such that } |w| \bmod 3 = 2\}$$

The finite automaton for language L is shown in Fig. 5.14(c).

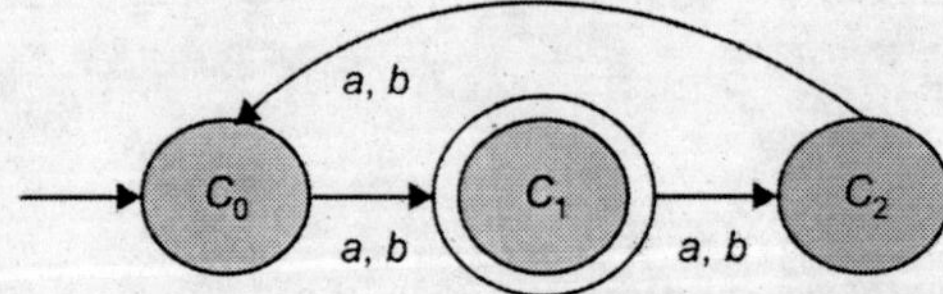

Fig. 5.14(c): Finite automaton

We can see that strings $x = aba$ and $y = aaa$ are equivalent and belong to same class C_0. But strings $x = ab$ and $y = a$ are not equivalent because x belongs to class C_2 and y belongs to class C_1.

3. Consider the language $L = \{a^n b^n : n \geq 0\}$ over $\{a, b\}$. We have following classes depending on the nature of language:
   $C_0 = \{\varepsilon\}$, $C_1 = \{ab\}$, $C_2 = \{aabb\}$, $C_3 = \{aaabbb\}$, ...
   The number of classes of L is infinite.
4. Consider the language $L = (00)^+$ over $\{0\}$. We have three classes depending on the nature of L. Finite automata for L is shown in Fig. 5.14(d).

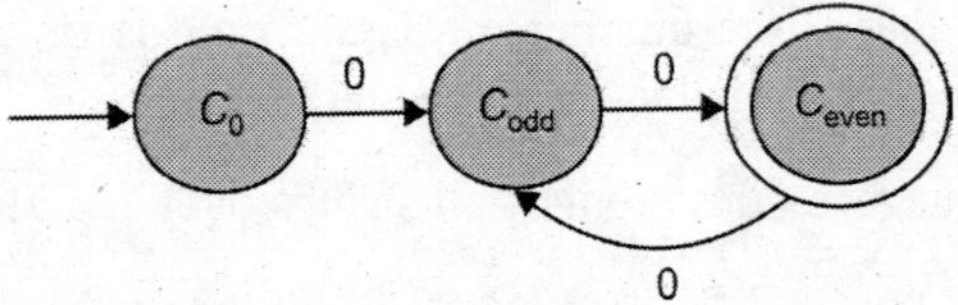

Fig. 5.14(d): FA accepting $(00)^+$

$C_0 = \{\varepsilon\}$, C_{odd} = {All strings of odd length}, and C_{even} = {All strings of even length excluding null string}.

Theorem 5.7 (*The Myhill-Nerode Theorem*): A given language L is a regular language if and only if the set of equivalence classes of L is finite.

or

Following statements are equivalent:

1. Language L can be divided into set of all possible strings into separate (mutually exclusive) classes.
2. If L is a regular language then number of classes created is finite.
3. If number of classes that L has, is finite then L is regular language.

Proof:

1. **Classes are mutually exclusive:** Let z be a string over Σ^* and finite automaton $M = (Q, \Sigma, \delta, s, F)$, which recognizes L then for strings $x, y \in L$,
   $x\, R_L\, y$ if and only if $\forall\, z \in \Sigma$ either xz and $yz \in L$ or both xz and $yz \notin L$
   Let us consider finite automaton M as DFA in which there is only one transition for an valide input. So, if two strings $x, y \in L$ and belong to one class, that is,
   $$\delta(s, x) = \delta(s, y)$$
   For some string $Z \in \Sigma^*$, $\delta(s, xz) = \delta(s, yz)$ and thus belong to same class (transition on same state). In other words, strings xz and yz belong to same class if $\delta(s_1 x) = \delta(s_1 y)$ and $xz, yz \in \Sigma^*$ are valid input.
   Hence, classes are mutually exclusive.
2. **If L is a regular language then the number of classes created is finite:** The language L is a regular language, so some FA M recognizes it. We know that FA has finite number of states. So, the number of societies it creates is finite. It may be there, some societies are equivalent, and so if we combine these equivalent societies into one and we can have minimum state DFA and then the societies are disjoint. These disjoint societies are called classes of the language L. Hence, if L is a regular language then the number of classes, it has, is finite.

3. **If number of classes is finite, then L is regular language:** Let finite classes be C_0, C_1, C_2, ..., C_n for some fixed value of n. We think these classes as the states of finite automaton (FA) such that:
   (a) The class containing ε (null string) is initial state,
   (b) For all $w_i \in L$ the class having w_i is the final state,
   (c) A transition (edge or arch) from the state C_i to C_j with label a is there if $x \in C_i$ and $xa \in C_j$.

   Now, we conclude that if the number of classes of L is finite then there is a DFA, which accepts it and hence L is a regular language and vice-versa

Example 1: Consider a language L consisting of all strings over $\{a, b\}$ ending in a. Prove that L is a regular language.

Proof: Let DFA $M = (Q, \Sigma, \delta, q_0, F)$ recognizes L.

$$L = \{a, aa, ba, bba, aaa, aba, ...\} = (b + aa^*b)^*aa^*$$

We have two classes C_0 and C_1 defined as follows:

$$C_0 = \{\text{All strings that end in } b\} = \{b, ab, bb, ...\}$$
$$= (b + aa^*b)^* \quad \text{(Rejected Strings)}$$
$$C_1 = \{\text{All strings that end in } a\} \quad \text{(Accepted Strings)}$$
$$= \{a, ba, aa, aaa, bba, ...\} = (b + aa^*b)^*aa^*$$

Transition diagram for DFA is shown in Fig. 5.15.

If can verify the above by applying Arden's theorem:

$$q_0 = q_0b + q_1b + \varepsilon, \; q_1 = q_0a + q_1a$$

Solving the above equations, we have

$$q_0 = (b + aa^*b)^* \text{ and } q_1 = (b + aa^*b)^*aa^*$$

We can select the two class of the above DFA as:

$$C_0 = (b + aa^*b)^*, \text{ and}$$
$$C_1 = (b + aa^*b)^*aa^*$$

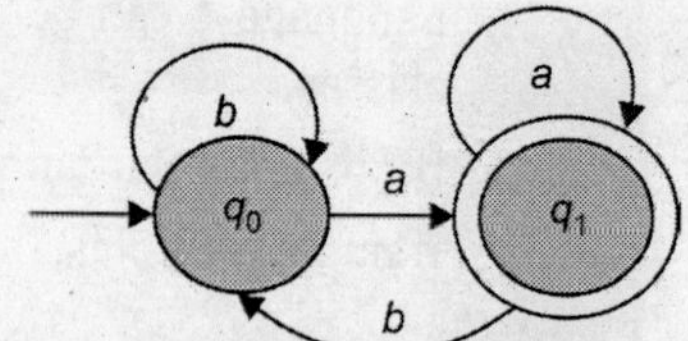

Fig. 5.15: DFA accepting $(a + b)^* a$

Classes C_0 and C_1 are corresponding to states q_0 and q_1 respectively. We have, L is equivalent to C_1. Now, let us apply Myhill-Nerode theorem:

(a) Two classes C_0 and C_1 are mutually exclusive.
(b) L is regular and it creates finite classes (two classes).
(c) The number of classes created by DFA is finite.

Since, all three statements of the Myhill-Nerode theorem are satisfied, hence L is regular.

Example 2: Show that $L = \{a^nb^n : n \geq 1\}$ is not regular using Myhill-Nerode theorem.

Solution: In the given language the number of a's is equal to number of b's.

So, $\quad L = \{ab, aabb, aaabbb, ...\}$

Depending on the value of n, classes are C_1, C_2, C_3, ..., C_n

So, if value of n in finite then number of classes is finite. **For example,** consider $n = 3$, then

$$C_1 = \{ab\}, C_2 = \{aabb\}, \text{and } C_3 = \{aaabbb\}$$

If value of n is very large (say tends toward the infinite), then the number of classes is infinite and it does not satisfy the Myhill-Nerode Theorem's statement. So, L is not regular.

5.5 MINIMIZATION OF FINITE AUTOMATA (FA)

In this section, we will discuss how to minimize a DFA. In the following theorem, we will discuss how to decide whether two states are equivalent or not. If two states are equivalent then we merge these two states into one state in order to minimize the number of states of a DFA.

Minimization of DFA

As we have seen in Myhill-Nerode Theorem that classes are mutually exclusive. But two or more societies of finite automata may be equivalent. So, if two or more societies are equivalent of a DFA then these can be merged into one in order to minimize the DFA. If a DFA has minimum states then each state is corresponding to a class and classes would be mutually exclusive. If a finite automaton has not minimum number of states then it results in wastage of the resources and often results in bad performance. **For example,** suppose a finite automaton is implemented as program and used to decide the validity of login name of an user for a website. But it has not minimum number of states. It means it may take longer time in deciding the validity of login name and requires more storage. So, response the users will not be speedy and results in bad performance. For minimization, we use the following method:

Minimization Method

Step 1: Construct transition table for DFA $M = (Q, \Sigma, \delta, q_0, F)$.

Step 2: Divide the Q into two groups G_1 and G_2 containing final states and non-final states i.e., F and Q-F respectively. Final groups are considered states of M. Group containing initial state is initial state.

Step 3: (Initialize counters) $i = 2, j = 1$

Step 4: Repeat step 5 until possibility of dividing a group is there.

Step 5: Repeat for $j <= i$

(a) Select the group G_j.

(b) If group G_j contain one state, then goto (e).

(c) (Repeat for all input symbols)

If transitions of all members of G_j belong to the same group, then G_j cannot be divided; goto step (e).

Else if transitions of members of G_j belong to n ($n \geq 2$) different groups, then partition the group G_j into n groups: G_j, G_{i+1}, G_{i+2} ... G_{i+n-1} such that a group contains those states having transitions on a same group.

(d) $i = i + n - 1$ and goto step (c)

(e) $j = j + 1$

(End of loop of step 5)

(End of loop of step 4)

Step 6: Exit

Example 1: Consider the following transition table of a DFA $M = (Q, \Sigma, \delta, q_0, \{q_3\})$. Construct minimum state DFA.

Present state	Next state	
	a	b
$\rightarrow q_0$	q_1	q_0
q_1	q_0	q_2
q_2	q_3	q_1
(q_3)	q_3	q_0
q_4	q_3	q_5
q_5	q_6	q_4
q_6	q_5	q_6
q_7	q_6	q_3

Solution: Q is divided into two groups G_1 and G_2, where

$G_1 = \{q_3\}$ and $G_2 = \{q_0, q_1, q_2, q_4, q_5, q_6, q_7\}$

G_1 has only one state, so it can't be partitioned further.

Applying input a on group G_2

States q_2 and q_4 have transition on state q_3 i.e. on group G_1 and remaining states $\{q_0, q_1, q_5, q_6, q_7\}$ have transitions on states q_0, q_2, q_4, q_6, q_3 respectively and these states belong to group G_2. So, the old group G_2 is partitioned into two new groups G_2 and G_3 as given below:

$G_2 = \{q_2, q_4\}$ (Transition on input a belong to group G_1)

$G_3 = \{q_0, q_1, q_5, q_6, q_7\}$ (Transition on input b belong to group G_2)

Applying input a on new formed group G_2

Both transitions belong to same group G_1, so division on input a is not possible.

Applying input b on new formed group G_2

Both transitions belong to same group G_3, so division on input b is not possible.

Applying input a on group G_3

All transitions belong to group G_3, so partition is not possible.

Applying input b on group G_3

Transitions from states q_1 and q_5 belong to group G_2 and transitions from states q_0 and q_6 belong to group G_3 and transition from q_7 belongs to group G_1. Since, all transitions belong to three different groups ($n = 3$), so the old group G_3 is partitioned into three different new groups as given below:

$G_3 = \{q_1, q_5\}$ (Transition on b input belong to the group G_2)

$G_4 = \{q_0, q_6\}$ (Transition on b input belong to the group old group G_3)

$G_5 = \{q_7\}$ (Transition on b input belong to the group G_1)

Now, no group can be partitioned further. So, constructing the new transition table considering a group as a single state:

Present state	Next state	
	a	*b*
→ q_0	q_1	q_0
$[q_0, q_6]$	$[q_1, q_5]$	$[q_0, q_6]$
$[q_1, q_5]$	$[q_0, q_6]$	$[q_2, q_4]$
$[q_2, q_4]$	q_3	$[q_1, q_5]$
(final) q_3	q_3	$[q_0, q_6]$
q_7	$[q_0, q_6]$	q_3

Example 2: Consider the finite automaton shown in Fig. 5.16(a). Construct minimum states finite automaton for this automaton.

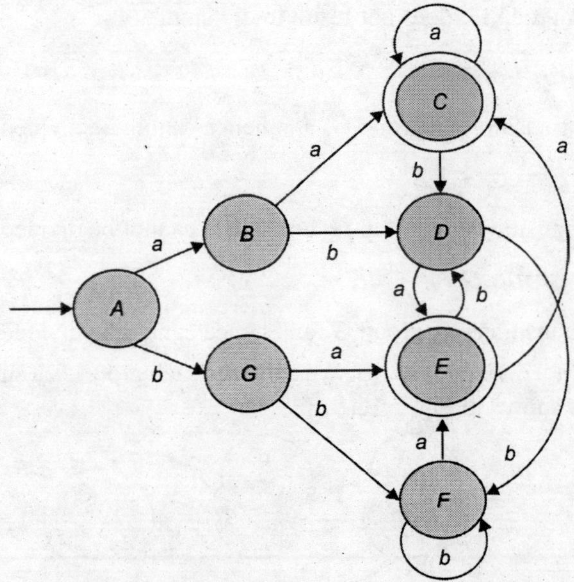

Fig. 5.16(a): Finite automaton for $(a + b)^* ba$

Solution: Transition table for given finite automaton is given below:

Present state	Next state	
	a	*b*
→ *A*	*B*	*G*
B	*C*	*D*
C	*C*	*D*
D	*E*	*F*
(*E*)	*C*	*D*
F	*E*	*F*
G	*E*	*F*

Let finite automaton $M = (Q, \Sigma, \delta, A, \{E\})$. Set of states Q is divided as:

$$G_1 = \{E\}, G_2 = \{A, B, C, D, F, G\}$$

Since, G_1 has only one state so it cannot be divided further.

Applying input a on group G_2

States *D*, *F*, and *G* have transition on group G_1 and states *A*, *B*, and *C* have transition on group G_2. So, group G_2 is divided into two groups as given below:

$G_2 = \{D, F, G\}$ (New group G_2, transition on group G_1)

$G_3 = \{A, B, C\}$ (Transition on old group G_2)

So, three groups are: $G_1 = \{E\}$, $G_2 = \{D, F, G\}$, $G_3 = \{A, B, C\}$

Applying input ***a*** on group G_2 does not result in division.

Applying input b on group G_2

States *D*, *F*, and *G* have transition on group G_2 and hence cannot be divided further.

Applying input a on group G_3

Sates *A*, *B*, and *C* have transitions on group G_3 and hence cannot be divided further.

Applying input b on group G_3

Sates *A*, *B*, and *C* have transitions on group G_2 and hence cannot be divided further.

Now, all groups are not divisible further. We consider each group as a state and draw the minimum state finite automaton as shown in Fig. 5.16(b).

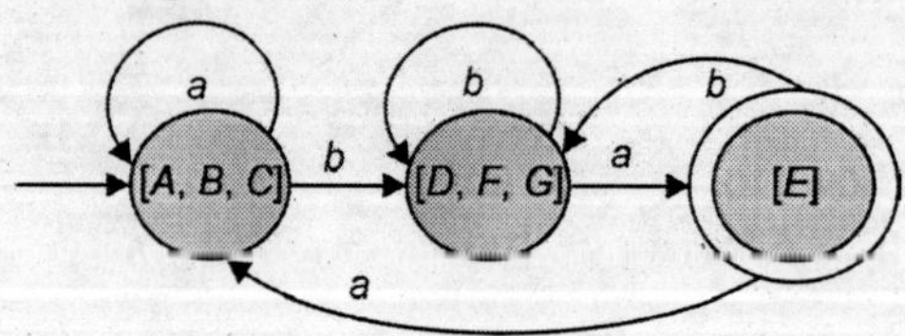

Fig. 5.16(b): Minimum state FA for (*a* + *b*)* *ba*

5.6 PROPERTIES OF REGULAR SETS AND LANGUAGES

Regular sets (or languages) are closed under following:

1. Union
2. Concatenation
3. Kleene Closure
4. Complementation
5. Transpose
6. Intersection

1. **Union:** Class of two regular sets S_1 and S_2 are closed under union operation. In other words, if S_1 and S_2 are two regular sets then union of these denoted by $\boldsymbol{S_1 + S_2}$ or $\boldsymbol{S_1 \cup S_2}$ is also a regular set.

   Proof: Let S_1 and S_2 be recognized by non-deterministic finite automaton N_1 and N_2 respectively as shown Fig 5.17(a) and Fig. 5.17(b).

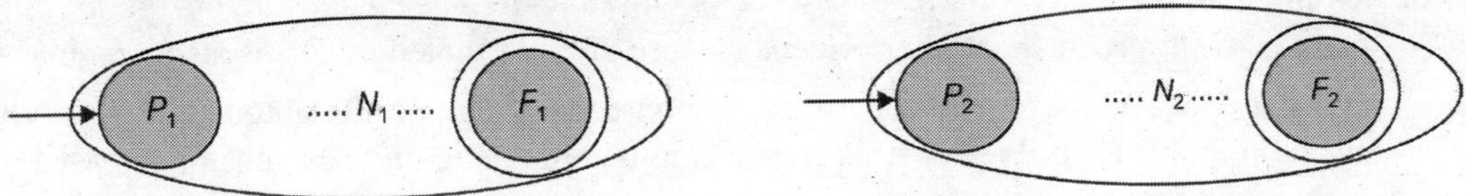

Fig. 5.17(a): NFA for regular set S_1 **Fig. 5.17(a): NFA for regular set S_1**

Now, we construct a new non-deterministic finite automaton (NFA) N based on union of N_1 and N_2 as shown in Fig. 5.17(c).

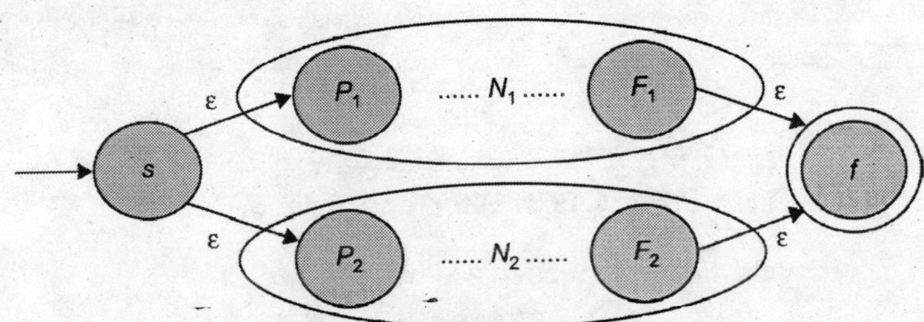

Fig. 5.17(c): NFA for $S_1 + S_2$

Let us verify the acceptance of N:

$$L(N) = \varepsilon L(N_1)\varepsilon + \varepsilon L(N_2)\varepsilon$$

(Where $L(N_1)$and $L(N_2)$ are recognized languages by NFA N_1 and N_2 respectively.)

$$= \varepsilon S_1\varepsilon + \varepsilon S_2\varepsilon = S_1 + S_2$$

Therefore, the language $L(N)$ is equivalent to regular set $\boldsymbol{S_1 + S_2}$. Since, N is finite automaton, hence $L(N)$ is a regular set (language). Therefore, $S_1 + S_2$ is a regular set.

2. **Concatenation:** Class of two regular sets S_1 and S_2 are closed under concatenation operation. In other words, if S_1 and S_2 are two regular sets then concatenation of these denoted by $\boldsymbol{S_1S_2}$ is also a regular set.

Proof: Let regular sets S_1 and S_2 be recognized by non-deterministic finite automata N_1 and N_2 respectively as shown in Fig 5.17(a) and Fig. 5.17(b). We construct a new non-deterministic finite automaton N based on concatenation of N_1 and N_2 as shown in Fig. 5.18.

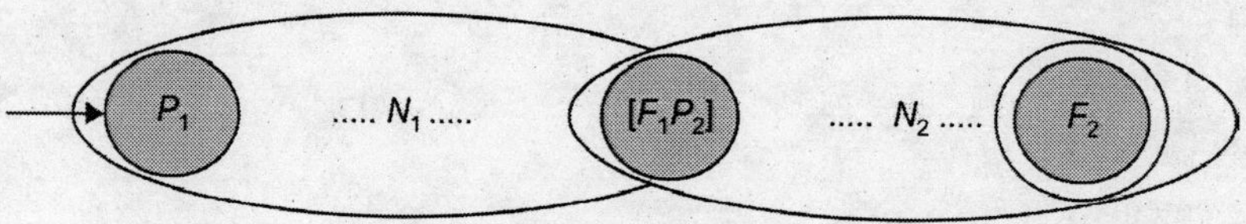

Fig. 5.18: NFA for regular set S_1S_2

Now, let us verify the language recognized by N:

$$L(N) = (\text{Language recognized by } N_1)\ (\text{Language recognized by } N_2)$$
$$= S_1S_2$$

Therefore, NFA recognized the set S_1S_2. Since, $L(N)$ is a regular language, hence S_1S_2 is also a regular set (language).

3. **Kleene Closure:** Class of a regular set S_1 is closed under Kleene closure operation. In other words, if S_1 is a regular set, then Kleene closure of this denoted by $\boldsymbol{S_1}$* is also a regular set.

   Proof: Let regular set S_1 is recognized by non-deterministic finite automaton (NFA) N_1 as shown in Fig. 5.17(a). We construct a new non-deterministic finite automaton N based on N_1 as shown in Fig. 5.19.

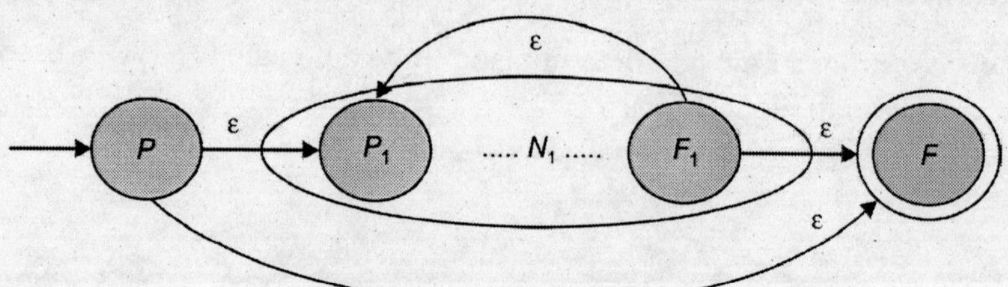

Fig. 5.19: NFA for regular set S_1^*

Now, let us verify the language recognized by N:

$$L(N) = \{\varepsilon, S_1, S_1S_1, S_1S_1S_1, \ldots\} = S_1^*$$

Since, $L(N)$ is a regular set, therefore S_1^* is also a regular set.

4. **Complement:** If S is a regular set over some alphabet Σ, then complement of S is denoted by $\boldsymbol{\Sigma^* - S}$ or $\overline{S}$, is also a regular set.

   Proof: Let S be recognized by non-deterministic finite automaton (NFA) $M = (Q, \Sigma, \delta, p, F)$ as shown in Fig. 5.20(a). It means, $\boldsymbol{L(M) = S}$.

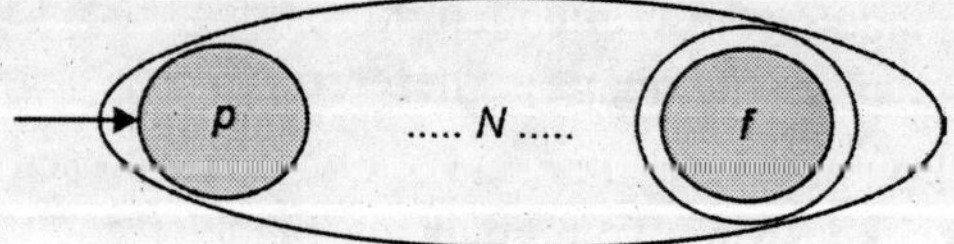

Fig. 5.20(a): NFA for regular set S

We construct new non-deterministic finite automaton (NFA) ***M′*** based on *M* as follows:

(a) Change all final states to non-final states.

(b) Change all non-final states to final states.

M′ is shown in Fig. 5.20(b).

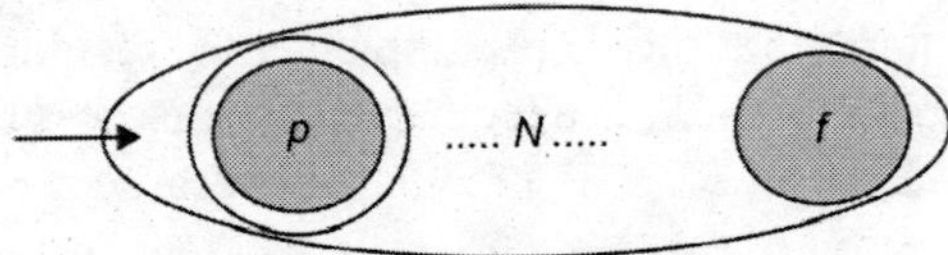

Fig. 5.20(b): NFA

Now, let us verify the language recognized by NFA *M′*:

$$L(M') = \{\text{All the words which are not accepted by NFA } M\}$$
$$= \{\text{All the rejected words by NFA } M\} = \Sigma^* - S$$

Since, $L(M')$ is a regular set, therefore $(\Sigma^* - S)$ is also a regular set.

5. **Transpose:** If *S* is a regular set then transpose of *S* is denoted by S^R, is also a regular set.

   Proof: *L*et regular set *S* be recognized by non-deterministic finite automaton $M = (Q, \Sigma, \delta, p, F)$ as shown in Fig. 5.20(a).

   If *w* is a word in regular set *S* then transpose (reverse) is denoted by w^R. **For example,** if $w = a_1a_2 \ldots a_n$ then $w^R = a_na_{n-1} \ldots a_1$

   We construct a new NFA *N* based on *M* using following rules:

   (a) Change the all final states into non-final states and merge all these into one state and make it initial state.

   (b) Change initial state to final state.

   (c) Reverse the direction of all edges or arches and maintain labels.

   N is shown in Fig. 5.21.

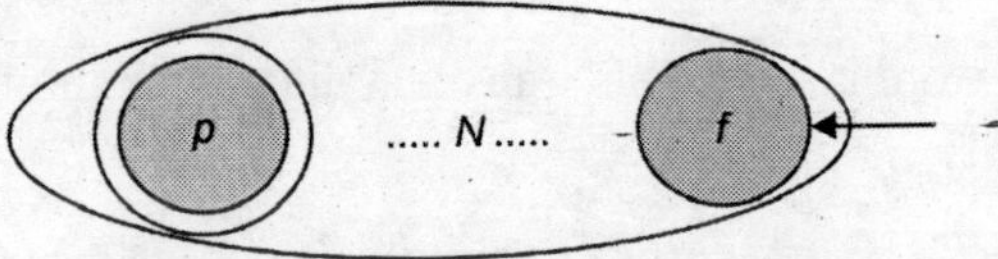

Fig. 5.21: NFA *N* for regular set *SR*

F Let $w = a_1a_2 \ldots a_n$ be a string in regular set *S* then it is recognized by *M* and $w^R = a_na_{n-1} \ldots a_1$ is recognized by *N* as shown in Fig. 5.21 by construction rules for *N*. In general, we say that if a word *w* in *S* is accepted by *M*, and then *N* accepts w^R. Since, $L(N)$ is a regular set containing w^R; it means $L(N) = S^R$ and S^R is also a regular set.

6. **Intersection**: Classes of two regular sets S_1 and S_2 are closed under intersection operation, in other words, if S_1 and S_2 are two regular sets over Σ, then intersection of these denoted by $S_1 \cap S_2$ is also a regular set.

Proof: We use **De Morgan's law** for two sets A and B over S. We know that

$$A \cap B = S^* - ((S^* - A) \cup (S^* - B))$$

So, $$S_1 \cap S_2 = \Sigma^* - ((\Sigma^* - S_1) \cup (\Sigma^* - S_2))$$

Let $$\boldsymbol{S_3 = (\Sigma^* - S_1)} \text{ and } \boldsymbol{S_4 = (\Sigma^* - S_2)}$$

So, S_3 and S_4 are regular sets as these are complement of regular sets S_1 and S_2. We have proved this earlier. Let $\boldsymbol{S_5 = S_3 \cup S_4}$, so, S_5 is a regular set because it is the union of two regular sets S_3 and S_4. Now, let $\boldsymbol{S_6 = \Sigma^* - S_5}$, so, S_6 is a regular set because it is the complement of regular set S_5. Therefore, intersection of two regular sets is also regular set.

5.7 REGULAR EXPRESSION AND DFA

We have discussed about equivalence of regular expression and finite automata with ε-moves (NFA with null moves) and how to convert NFA with e-moves into equivalent deterministic finite automata (DFA) in Chapter 2. One question is here; can we construct DFA directly for a regular expression? The answer is "YES", we can, but the need is that we should be aware about the format of words in given regular set to be recognized. In this section, we will try to explore this thing in details. Let us consider following **example**:

Example 1: Consider a regular language $L = (a + b)^* abb$ and construct a DFA, which recognizes L.

Solution: Let DFA $M = (Q, \Sigma, \delta, q_0, F)$ recognizes L.

$$L = (a + b)^* abb = \{\varepsilon, a, b, aa, bb, ab, ba, \ldots\} abb$$

$$= \{abb, aabb, babb, aaabb, bbabb, \ldots\}$$

$$= \text{All the words over } \{a, b\} \text{ ending in } abb$$

It means, the words that are in L and accepted by M end in substring "*abb*". This is the clue for constructing the DFA M.

Step 1: Select the first smallest length word from L and draw the transition diagram.

The smallest word is "*abb*" and transition diagram is shown in Fig. 5.22(a).

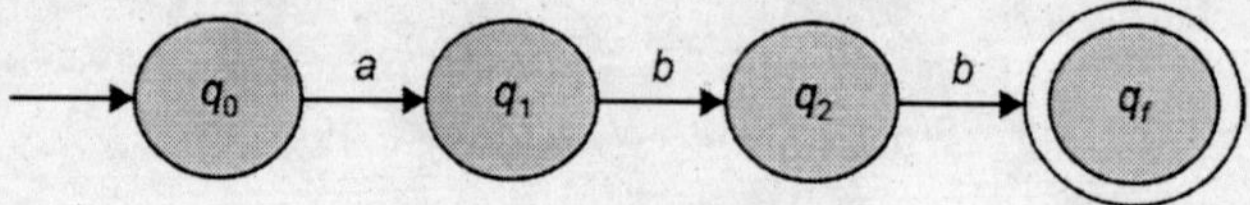

Fig. 5.22(a): DFA for *abb*

Step 2: We define transitions for each state for each input symbol such that the accepting words belong to L.

For state q_0: We have transition for input symbol a, but not for ***b***. So, we have to define transition for input symbol ***b***. It is obvious that all b's should be exhausted before the substring "*abb*". So, there is a loop for b in state q_0 as shown in Fig. 5.22(b).

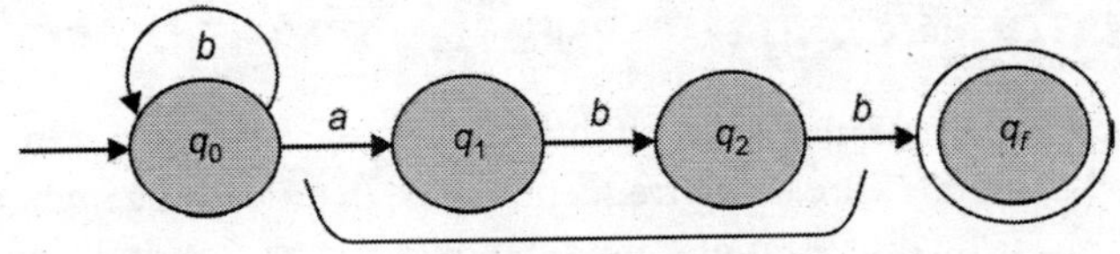

Fig. 5.22(b): DFA

For state q_1: We have transition for input symbol ***b***, but not for ***a***. So, we have to define transition for input symbol ***a***. We see that after state q_1, substring *bb* is following. So, all a's should be exhausted before substring "*bb*" as shown in Fig. 5.22(c).

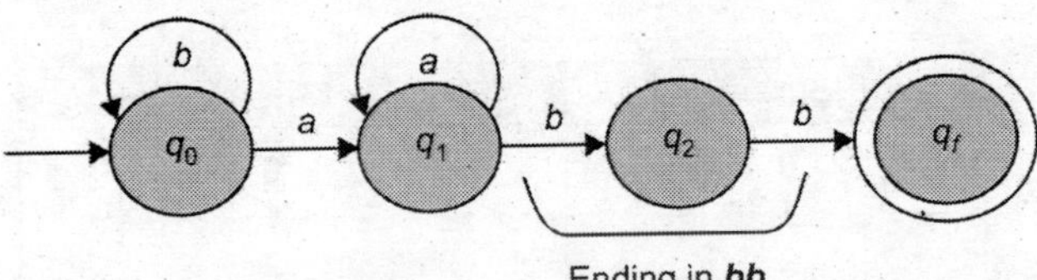

Fig. 5.22(c): DFA

For state q_2: We have transition for input symbol ***b***, but not for ***a***. So, we have to define transition for input symbol ***a***. We see that after state q_2, substring "*b*" is following. So, all a's should be exhausted before substring "*bb*" and "*bb*" is obtained from state q_1. So, for input **a**, transition is on q_1 as shown in Fig. 5.22(d).

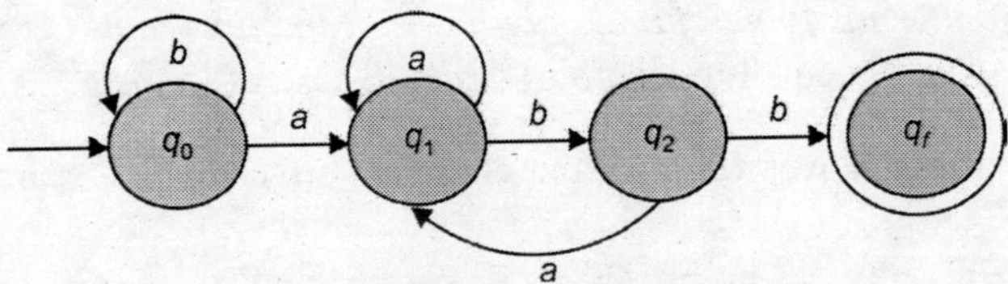

Fig. 5.22(d): DFA

For state q_f: We have no transition. So, we have to define transitions for input symbols ***a*** and ***b***. If input ***a*** is there, then for accepting word, "*bb*" substring should be there as a suffix and "*bb*" is obtained from state q_1. So, for input ***a***, transition is on state q_1. For input ***b***, we require "*abb*" substring as suffix, so transition is on state q_0 as shown in Fig. 5.22(e). The transition diagram shown in Fig. 5.22(e) is the final transition diagram.

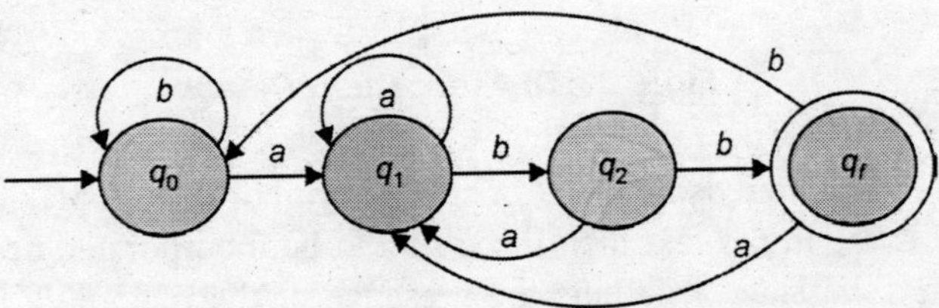

Fig. 5.22(e): DFA for $(a + b)^*$ *abb*

5.8 PATTERN MATCHING AND FINITE AUTOMATA (FA)

Finite automata are used in pattern matching. In this section, we will try to explore how DFA is used in pattern matching. Today computers are being frequently used in processing numbers, characters, records, arithmetic calculations etc. In all organizations, multinational companies, and institutions word processing is widely used. In word processing, **pattern matching** is a process to find a word or string in a given text and also known as **string matching**. The string or word to be matched in the given text is known as **pattern**. Let ***T*** is the given text and pattern is ***w*** to be searched. Both *T* and *w* are formed from the same alphabet Σ. States of DFA are named as 0, 1, 2, 3… *m*, where 0 is the initial state, *m* is final state, and ***m*** is the length of pattern *w*. In processing, when final state is reached then match is there otherwise not. These states also indicate the length of the substring of the *w* as given below:

State	Length of the substring
0	0
1	1
2	2
3	3
...	...
m	*m*

DFA is implemented as program and it has time and space complexities. We can use non-deterministic finite automata (NFA) also, which require less space but time requirement is more as compare to DFA. DFA processes the input string character by character and hence requires the time proportional to the length of the input. *A pattern is found if and only if one of the final states is reached.* The number of states of DFA is not necessarily equal to length of string in case of loop.

Example 1: Consider a text *T* over $\{a + b\}$ and construct a DFA which searches the presence of the pattern $P = abb$.

Solution: Let DFA $M = (Q, \Sigma, \delta, 0, F)$ is used as pattern matcher. DFA *M* is shown in Fig. 5.23. We have, $Q = \{0, 1, 2, 3\}$ and $\Sigma = \{a, b\}$, $F = \{3\}$

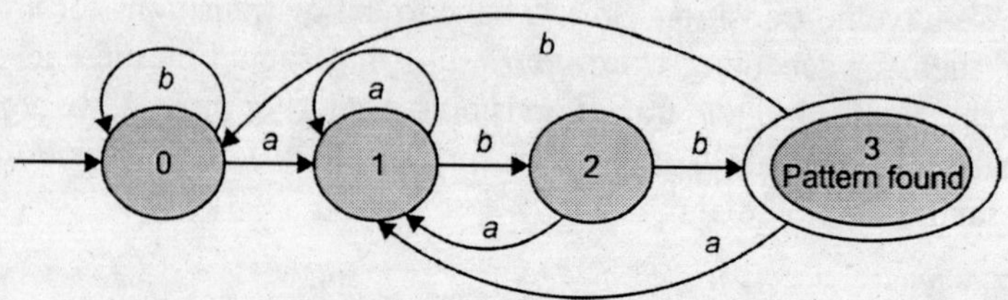

Fig. 5.23: DFA for pattern *P* = *abb*

It has been assumed that there is no blank or special symbols like dot (.), question mark (?), colon (:), etc. If such symbols are in the text then these should be incorporated accordingly. In the above transition diagram, the final state 3 outputs the presence of the pattern *P*. Let us consider the text $y = aabbbabb$ and $P = abb$. Following is the processing done by DFA *M*:

Symbol	Next State	Output
a	1	Nothing
a	1	Nothing
b	2	Nothing
b	3	Pattern found
b	0	Nothing
a	1	Nothing
b	2	Nothing
b	3	Pattern found

Point to Remember:

A **regular language** is a formal language (i.e. a possibly infinite set of finite sequences of symbols from a finite alphabet) that satisfies the following equivalent properties:

1. It can be accepted by a deterministic finite state automata (DFA)
2. It can be accepted by a non-deterministic finite state automata (NFA)
3. It can be described by a regular expressions.
4. It can be generated by a regular grammars.
5. It can be accepted by a read-only only Turing machines.
6. All **finite languages** are regular language, **For example,** $L_1 = \{a^n b^n : n = 1, 2, 3, ..., 100\}$, $L_2 = \{a^n b^n c^n : n = 1, 2, 3, ...,10\}$

5.9 SOLVED EXAMPLES

Example 5.1: Define regular expressions for following languages:

(a) Language containing all the words over $\{a, b, c\}$ ending in a.
(b) Language containing all the words over $\{a, b\}$ starting with "*aa*" and ending in "*bb*".
(c) Language containing all the words over $\{a, b\}$ having even number of a's and b's.
(d) Language containing all the words over $\{0, 1\}$ not having "00" as a substring.
(e) Language containing all the words over $\{0, 1\}$ such that some two 0's are separated by a string whose length is $4i$, for $i \geq 0$.

Solution:

(a) Regular expression $R = (a + b + c)^*a$
(b) Regular expression $R = aa(a + b)^*bb$
(c) Regular expression $R = (aa + bb + (ab + ba)\ (aa + bb)^*(ab + ba))^*$
(d) Regular expression $R = (1 + 01)^*$ or $(1 + 10)^*$
(e) Regular expression $R = (0 + 1)^*0((0 + 1)\ (0 + 1)\ (0 + 1)\ (0 + 1))^*0(0+ 1)^*$

Example 5.2: Construct NFA for the following regular expressions:

(a) $aa(a + b)^*bb$
(b) $(1 + 01)^*$

(c) $(0 + 1)^*0((0 + 1)(0 + 1)(0 + 1)(0 + 1))^*0(0 + 1)^*$

(d) $(a + b)^*(a + b)(a + b)(a + b)$

Solution:

(a) Let regular expression $R = aa(a + b)^*bb = R_1R_2R_3$, where $R_1 = aa$, $R_2 = (a + b)^*$, and $R_3 = bb$. NFA is shown in Fig. 5.24.

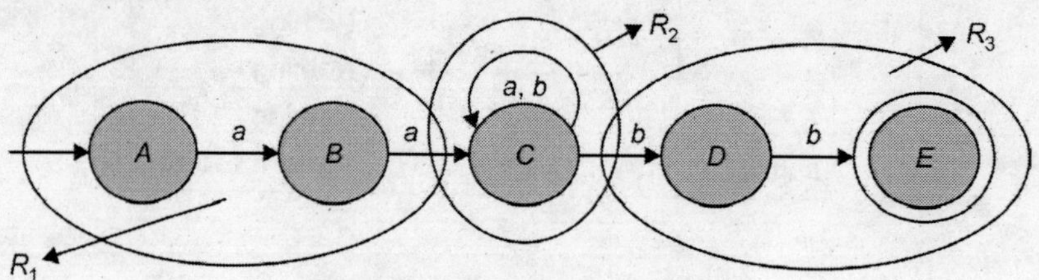

Fig. 5.24: NFA for *aa*(*a* + *b*)* *bb*

(b) Let regular expression P is $(1 + 01)^*$ and X is $1 + 01$, then $P = X^*$.

NFA for $P = X^*$ is shown in Fig. 5.25(a).

Since, initial state ***s*** has loop for input **1 + 01**, so rearranging the loop, we have final NFA shown in Fig. 5.25(b).

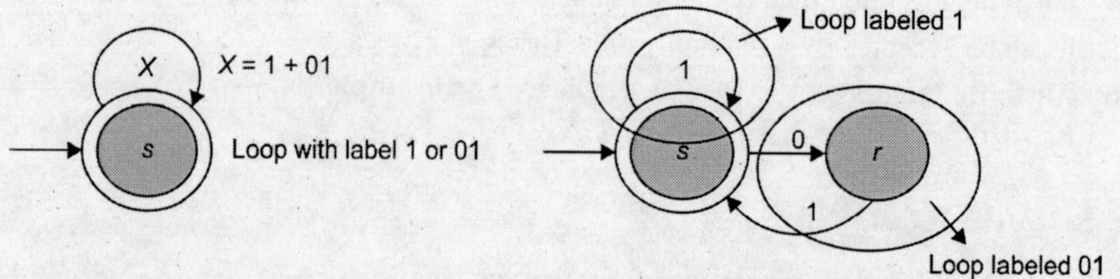

Fig. 5.25(a) NFA for $X = 1 + 01$ **Fig. 5.25(b): NFA for $P = (1 + 01)^*$**

(c) Let regular expression $R = (0 + 1)^*0((0 + 1)(0 + 1)(0 + 1)(0 + 1))^*0(0 + 1)^*$ and Let $R = R_1{}^*0R_2{}^*0R_1{}^*$, where $R_1 = (0 + 1)$, and $R_2 = (0 + 1)(0 + 1)(0 + 1)(0 + 1)$

The transition diagram of NFA accepting R is shown in Fig. 5.26.

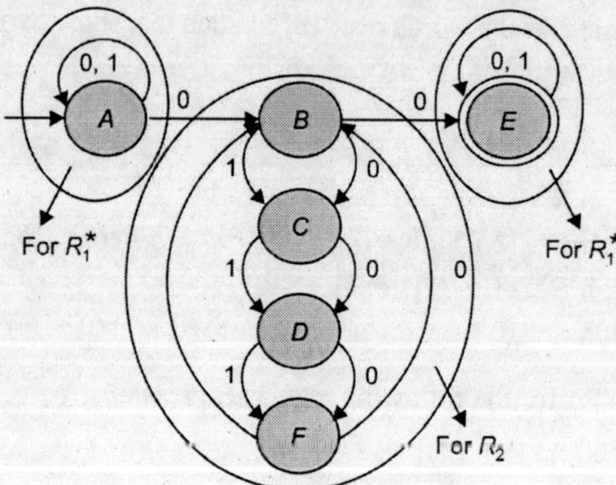

Fig. 5.26: NFA

(d) Let regular expression $\boldsymbol{R = (a + b)^*(a + b)(a + b)(a + b) = R_1{}^*R_1R_1R_1}$, where $\boldsymbol{R_1 = (a + b)}$. NFA accepting R is shown in Fig. 5.27.

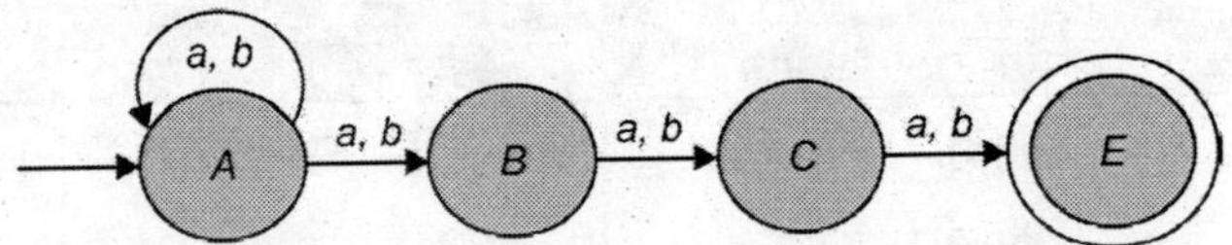

Fig. 5.27: NFA for $(a + b)^*(a + b)(a + b)(a + b)$

Example 5.3: Show that following pairs of regular expressions over $\{a, b\}$ define the same language.

(a) $(a^* + b)^*$ and $(a + b)^*$

(b) $(ab)^*a$ and $a(ba)^*$

(c) $(a^* + b^*)^*$ and $(a + b)^*$

Solution: We show the equivalence of two regular expressions by two methods:

- Constructing FA and comparing, and
- Finding the regular sets for regular expressions.

(a) Let $r_1 = (a^*+b)^*$ and $r_2 = (a + b)^*$

$$r_1 = (a^*+b)^* = (\{\varepsilon, a, aa, aaa, \ldots \cup b\})^*$$
$$= (\varepsilon + a + aa + aaa + \ldots + b)^*$$
$$= \{\varepsilon, a, b, aa, bb, ab, ba, aaa, \ldots\}$$
$$= (a + b)^* = r_2$$

So, r_1 and r_2 are equivalent regular expressions and hence define the same regular lanaguage.

(b) Let $r_1 = (ab)^*a$ and $r_2 = a(ba)^*$. Suppose, DFA N_1 accepts r_1 and DFA N_2 accepts r_2 as shown in Fig. 5.28(a) and Fig 5.28(b).

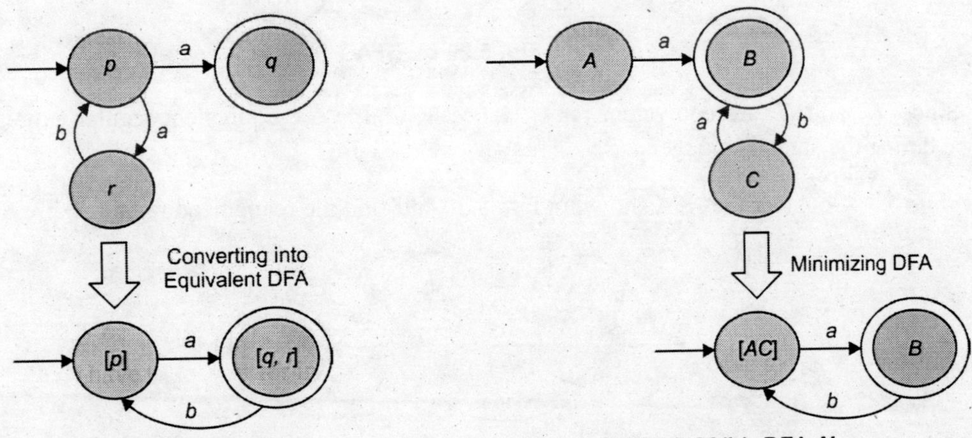

Fig. 5.28(a): DFA N_1

Fig. 5.28(b): DFA N_2

Let us compare the transition diagrams for N_1 and N_2.

DFA N_1		DFA N_2	
State	Transition	State	Transition
[*p*]	δ([*p*], *a*) = [*q*, *r*], δ([*p*], b) = φ	[*A*, *C*]	δ([*A*, *C*], *a*) = *B*, δ([*A*, *C*], *b*) = φ
[*q*, *r*]	δ([*q*, *r*], *a*) = φ, δ([*q*, *r*], *b*) = [*p*]	*B*	δ(*B*, *a*) = φ, δ(*B*, *b*) = [*A*, *C*]
States [*p*] ≡ [*A*, *C*], and [*q*, *r*] ≡ *B*			

Since, both DFA N_1 and N_2 are equivalent DFA, hence r_1 and r_2 are equivalent and define the same language.

(c) Let regular $r_1 = (a^* + b^*)^*$ accepted by DFA N_1 and and regular expression $r_2 = (a + b)^*$ accepted by DFA N_2 as shown in Fig. 5.29(a) and Fig 5.29(b). Let $r_1 = X^*$, where $\boldsymbol{X = (a^* + b^*)}$ and $\boldsymbol{r_2 = Y^*}$, where $\boldsymbol{Y = (a + b)}$

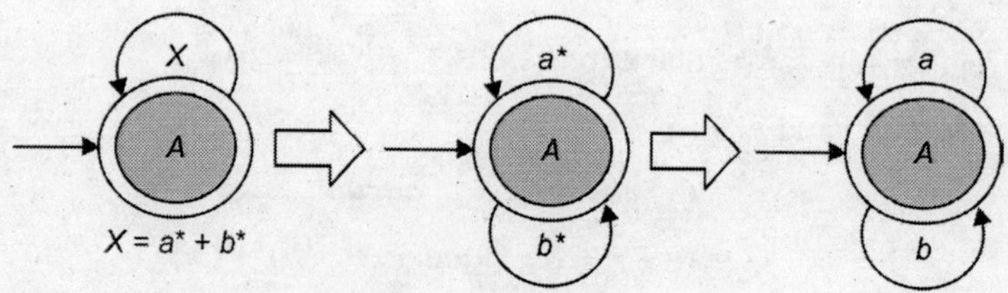

Fig. 5.29(a): DFA

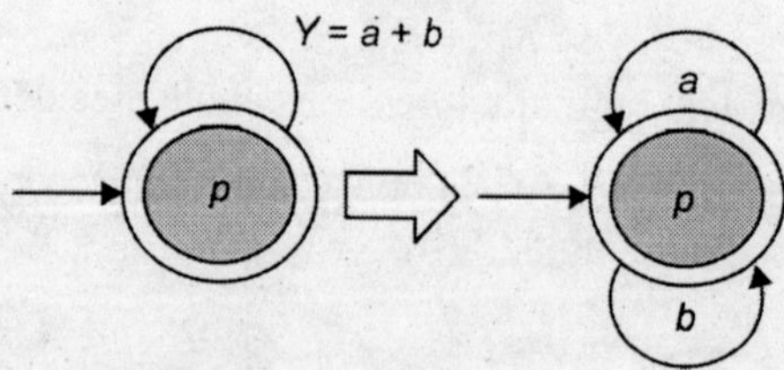

Fig. 5.29(b): DFA

Since, N_1 and N_2 are equivalent DFA. Hence, r_1 and r_2 are equivalent regular expressions and hence define the same language.

Example 5.4: Consider the *N*FA shown in Fig. 5.30 and find the recognized regular expression.

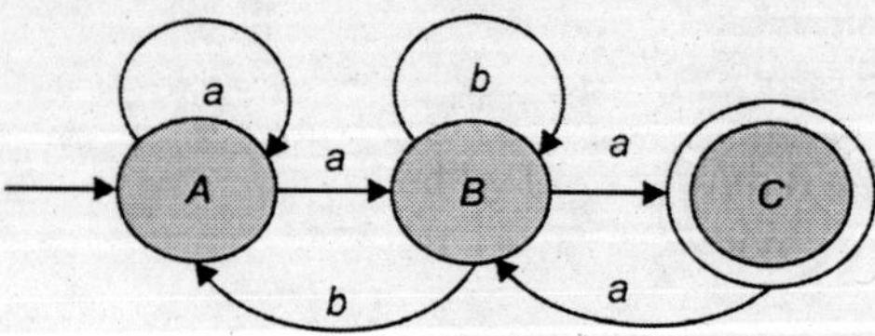

Fig. 5.30: NFA

Solution: We have no null-moves in NFA, so we apply Arden's Theorem directly.

$A = Aa + Bb + \varepsilon$ (A is the initial state.)

$B = Bb + Aa + Ca$, and $C = Ba$

Since, C is the final state, so we have to find the expression for state C. For C, B is required first. So, solving A equation, we have

$A = Bb + \varepsilon + Aa$ (Arden's equation: $R = Q + RP$, $R = A$, $Q = Bb + \varepsilon$, and $P = a$)

$A = (Bb + \varepsilon)\, a^*$

$= Bba^* + a^*$

Putting the value of A in B equation, we have

$B = Bb + Bba^*a + a^*a + Ca$

$= Ca + a^*a + B(b + ba^*a)$

So, $B = (Ca + a^*a)\,(b + ba^*a)^*$ ($R = B$, $Q = Ca + a^*a$, and $P = b + ba^*a$)

Putting the value of B into C equation, we have

$C = (Ca + a^*a)\,(b + ba^*a)^*a$

$= a^*a(b + ba^*a)^*a + Ca(b+ba^*a)^*a$

So, $C = a^*a(b + ba^*a)^*a\,(a(b + ba^*a)^*a)^*$

So, regular expression recognized by NFA is $\boldsymbol{a^*a(b + ba^*a)^*a\,(a(b + ba^*a)^*a)^*}$.

Example 5.5: Consider the NFA shown in Fig. 5.31 and find the recognized regular expression.

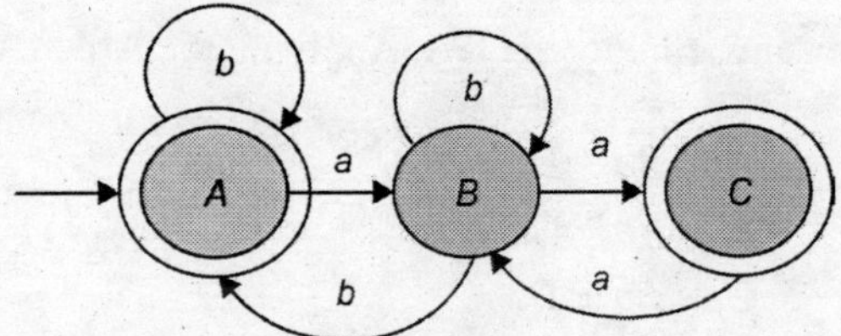

Fig. 5.31: NFA

Solution: We have two final states in NFA. We apply Arden's theorem and find the following equations:

$A = Ab + Bb + \varepsilon$ (A is the initial state), $B = Bb + Aa + Ca$, and $C = Ba$

Since, ***A*** and ***C*** are the final states, so we have to find the expression for states A and C. Solving A-equation, we have

$A = Bb + \varepsilon + Ab$ (Arden's equation: $R = Q + RP$, $R = A$, $Q = Bb + \varepsilon$, and $P = b$)

$A = (Bb + \varepsilon)b^* = Bbb^* + b^*$

Putting value of A in B equation, we have

$B = Bb + Bbb^*a + b^*a + Ca = Ca + b^*a + B(b + bb^*a)$

So, $B = (Ca + b^*a)\,(b + bb^*a)^*$ ($R = B$, $Q = Ca + b^*a$, and $P = b + ba^*a$)

Putting value of B into C equation, we have

$C = (Ca + b^*a)\,(b + bb^*a)^*a = Ca(b + bb^*a)^*a + b^*a(b + bb^*a)^*a$

So, $C = b^*a(b + bb^*a)^*a\,(a(b + bb^*a)^*a)^*$

Putting the value of C into B equation, we have

$$B = (b^*a(b + bb^*a)^*a\,(a(b+bb^*a)^*a)^*a + b^*a)\,(b+bb^*a)^*$$

Putting the value of B into A equation, we have

$$A = (b^*a(b + bb^*a)^*a\,(a(b + bb^*a)^*a)^*a + b^*a)(b + bb^*a)^*bb^* + b^*$$

So, regular expression recognized by NFA is union of values of A and C. So, reconized regular expression is:

$$(b^*a(b + bb^*a)^*a\,(a(b + bb^*a)^*a)^*a + b^*a)\,(b + bb^*a)^*bb^* + b^* + b^*a(b + bb^*a)^*a\,(a(b + bb^*a)^*a)^*$$

Example 5.6: Find the regular expression reconized by DFA shown in Fig. 5.32.

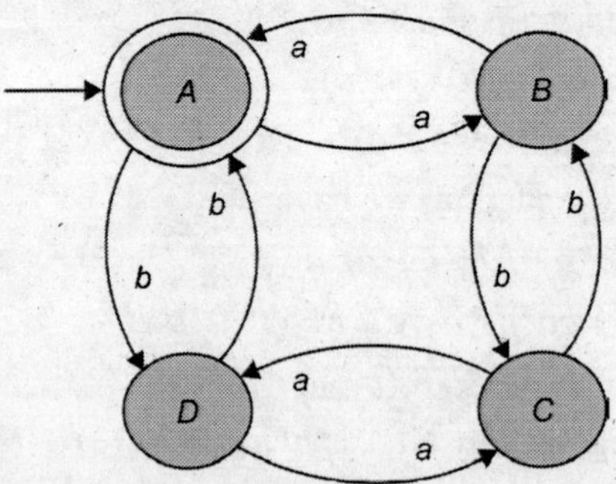

Fig. 5.32: DFA

Solution: We have one final state A in given DFA. Applying the Arden's Theorem, we have following equations:

$$A = Ba + Db + \varepsilon \quad (1)$$

$$B = Aa + Cb \quad (2)$$

$$C = Bb + Da \quad (3)$$

$$D = Ab + Ca \quad (4)$$

Putting value of D and B in equation (1), we get

$$A = Aaa + Cba + Abb + Cab + \varepsilon$$

$$= A(aa + bb) + C(ab + ba) + \varepsilon$$

Putting the value of D and B in equation (3), we get

$$C = Aab + Cbb + Aba + Caa = A(ab+ba) + C(aa + bb)$$

So, solving for C, we get

$$C = A(ab + ba)(aa + bb)^*$$

Putting the value of C into A equation, we get

$$A = A(aa + bb) + A(ab + ba)\,(aa + bb)^*(ab + ba) + \varepsilon$$

Now, solving for A, we get

$$A = \varepsilon(aa + bb + (ab + ba)\,(aa + bb)^*(ab + ba))^*$$

$$= (aa + bb + (ab + ba)(aa + bb)^*(ab + ba))^*$$

Therefore, regular expression for DFA is $\mathbf{(aa + bb + (ab + ba)\,(aa + bb)^*(ab + ba))^*}$.

Example 5.7: Construct DFA which accepts each of the following languages:

(a) $L = \{w: w \in (a + b)^*$ and has "*abab*" as a substring$\}$

(b) $L = \{w: w \in (a + b)^*$ and has even number of a's and odd number of b's$\}$

(c) $L = \{w: w \in (a + b)^*$ and each '*a*' is immediately preceded and immediately followed by a '*b*'$\}$

(d) $L = \{w: w \in (a + b)^*$ has either "*aa*" or "*bb*" as a substring$\}$

(e) $L = \{w: w \in (a + b)^*$ and has neither "*aa*" nor "*bb*" as a substring$\}$

Solution:

(a) Let DFA, $M = (Q, \Sigma, \delta, A, F)$ accepts $L = \{w: w(a + b)^*$ and has *abab* as a substring$\}$

$L = \{abab, aabab, babab, aababa, \ldots\} = (a + b)^*abab(a + b)^*$

M is shown in Fig. 5.33.

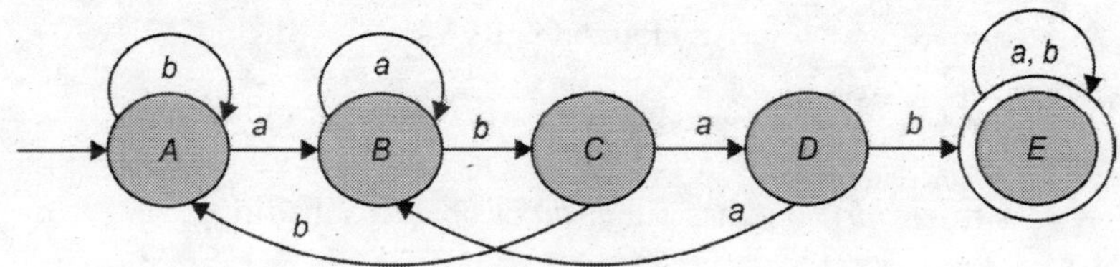

Fig. 5.33

(b) Let DFA $M = (Q, \Sigma, \delta, A, F)$ accepts $L = \{w: w \in (a + b)^*$ and has even number of a's and odd number of b's$\}$. *M* is shown in Fig. 5.34.

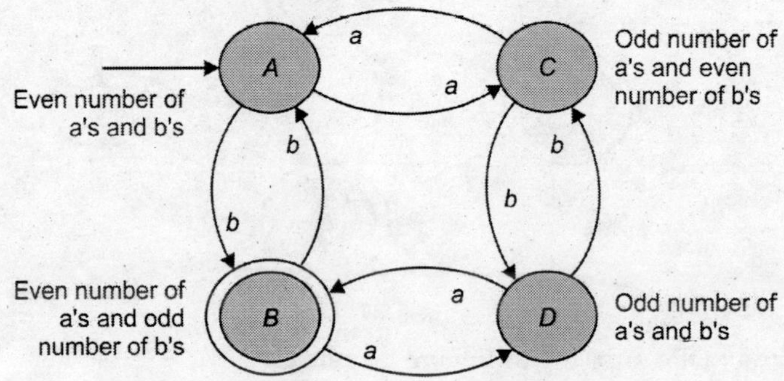

Fig. 5.34: DFA accepting even a's and odd b's

(c) Let DFA $M = (Q, \Sigma, \delta, A, F)$ accepts $L = \{w: w \in (a + b)^*$ and each '*a*' is immediately preceded and immediately followed by a '*b*'$\}$. *M* is shown in Fig. 5.35.

$L = \{\varepsilon, b, bb, bbb, \ldots, bab, babab, babbb, \ldots\} = b^*(ba)^*b^+ + b^+(ab)^*b^*$

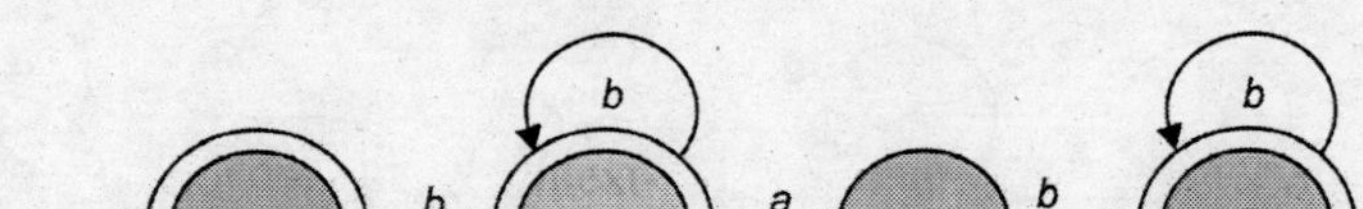

Fig. 5.35: DFA

(d) Let DFA $M = (Q, \Sigma, \delta, A, F)$ accepts $L = \{w: w(a + b)^*$ has either "*aa*" or "*bb*" as a substring}. M is shown in Fig. 5.36.

$$L = \{aa, aaa, baa, abaa, \ldots, bb, abb, bbb, abbb, \ldots\}$$
$$= (a + b)^*(aa + bb)(a + b)^*$$

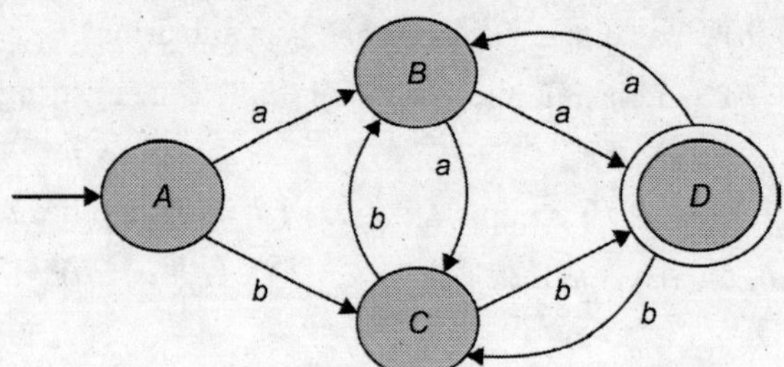

Fig. 5.36: DFA

(e) Let DFA $M = (Q, \Sigma, \delta, A, F)$ accepts $L = \{w: w(a + b)^*$ and has neither "*aa*" nor "*bb*" as a substring}

Let $L_1 = \{w: w \in (a + b)^*$ and has either *aa* or *bb* as a substring}

So, $L = \Sigma^* - L_1$

Thus, changing the all final state to non-final state and all non-final states to final states of DFA shown in Fig. 5.36, we construct DFA for $L = \Sigma^* - L_1$. M for L is shown in Fig. 5.37.

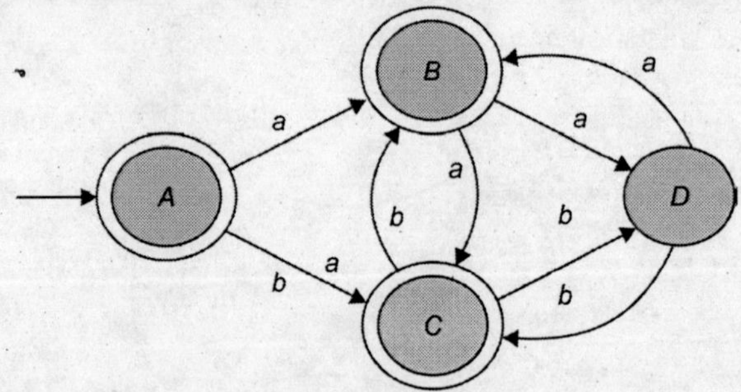

Fig. 5.37: DFA

Example 5.8: Construct DFA's for the following languages: **(GATE 2001)**

(a) $L = \{w: w \in (a + b)^*$, w has *baab* as a substring}

(b) $L = \{w: w \in (a + b)^*$, w has odd number of a's and odd number of b's}

Solution:

(a) Let DFA $M = (Q, \Sigma, \delta, A, F)$ accepts $L = \{w: w \in (a + b)^*$, w has "*baab*" as a substring}. M is shown in Fig. 5.38.

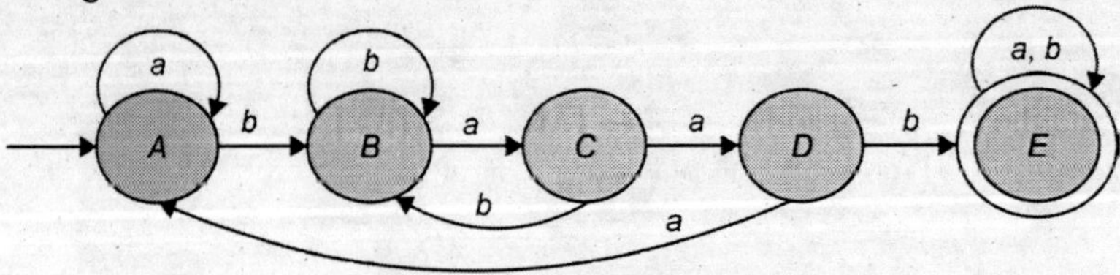

Fig. 5.38: DFA

(b) Let DFA $M = (Q, \Sigma, \delta, A, F)$ accepts $L = \{w: w(a + b)^*$, w has odd number of a's and odd number of b's$\}$. M is shown in Fig. 5.39.

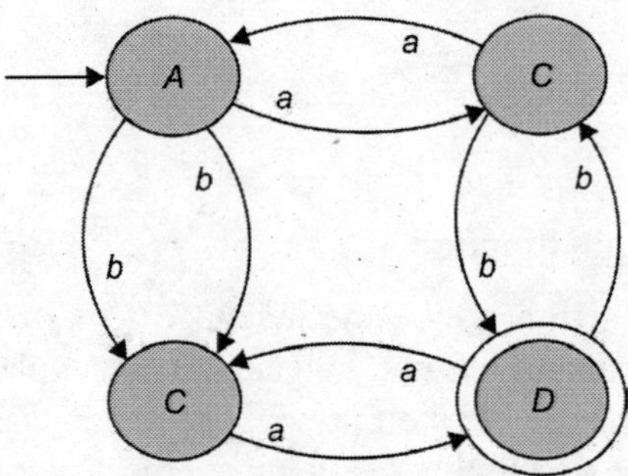

Fig. 5.39: DFA

Example 5.9: Prove that $L = \{ a^{i^2} : i \geq 1\}$ is not regular language.

Proof: (Using Pumping Lemma for regular sets)

In the given language L, all words have their lengths in perfect square and this is the clue for proving non-regular.

Step 1: Let L be regular and accepted by DFA M with n states.

Step 2: String $w \in L$ such that $|w| \geq n$ and $w = xy^iz \in L$ for $i \geq 0$, $y \notin \varepsilon$, let $|w| = n^2 \geq n$, and $|xz| \leq n$, (n is the number of states).

Step 3: Since, length of y can't exceed n (the number of states), it means, $|y| \leq n$

Let $i = 2$, so $w = xy^2z \in L$, and

$$|w| = |xyz| + |y| = n^2 + |y|$$

So, $n^2 \leq |w| \leq n^2 + n$ (Since, $|y| \leq n$)

or, $n^2 \leq |w| \leq n^2 + n + (n + 1)$ (Adding $n + 1$ to make perfect square)

or, $n^2 \leq |w| \leq (n + 1)^2$

It means, the length of w is between n^2 and $(n + 1)^2$ and is not a perfect square. Therefore, L is not regular.

Example 5.10: Prove that C language is not regular.

Proof: We can prove language C is not regular in many ways. Let us consider the main function construct:

```
void main( )
{
...             //Statements
        {
        ...     //Statements
        }
                //Statements
...
}       //End of main function
```

All opening curly brackets should be equal to closing curly brackets and vice-versa. It means, the main function looks like following:

```
void main( )
{ⁿ
..          //Statements
}ⁿ          //End of the main function, n ≥ 1
```

The format of the main function is like the language $L = \{a^n w b^n : n \geq 1 \text{ and } w \in (a + b)^*\}$. Obviously, L is not a regular language. Hence, C language is not regular. As we know that finite automata have finite memory and cannot remember their previous read inputs. So, for C language, the number of opening curly brackets should match with closing curly brackets and it is beyond the power of finite automata. So, *C language is not a regular language*.

Example 5.11: Consider the following production rules of a regular grammar G and construct DFA.

$$S \rightarrow \varepsilon, S \rightarrow aA, S \rightarrow bB, A \rightarrow a, A \rightarrow aS, A \rightarrow bD, B \rightarrow b, B \rightarrow bS, B \rightarrow aD, D \rightarrow bA, D \rightarrow aB\}$$

Solution: Let DFA $M = (\{S, A, B, D\}, \Sigma, \delta, S, \{S\})$ accepts $L(G)$. Since, S is the only final state because $S \rightarrow \varepsilon$. M is shown in Fig. 5.40.

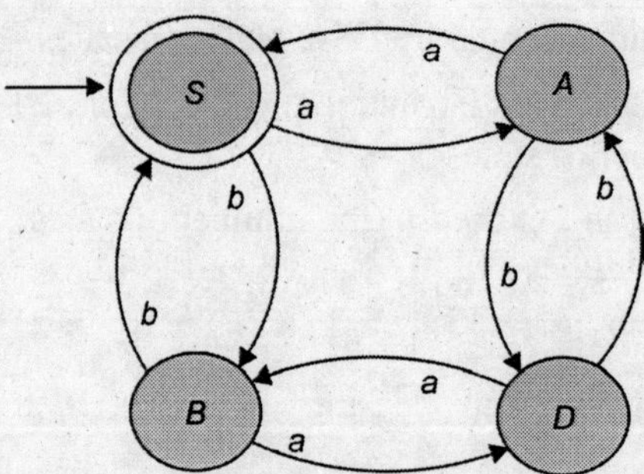

Fig. 5.40: DFA

Example 5.12: Consider the regular grammar G having productions: $A \rightarrow aA, A \rightarrow a, A \rightarrow bB, A \rightarrow b, B \rightarrow bC, B \rightarrow b, B \rightarrow aA, B \rightarrow a, C \rightarrow aB$, and $C \rightarrow a$. A is the starting symbol.

Construct DFA accepting $L(G)$.

Solution: Let DFA $M = (\{A, B, C\}, \Sigma, \delta, A, F)$ accepts $L(G)$. Since, $A \rightarrow aA, A \rightarrow a, B \rightarrow bC, B \rightarrow b, C \rightarrow aB, C \rightarrow a$ are productions in G, so A, B, C are three final states. DFA M is shown in Fig. 5.41.

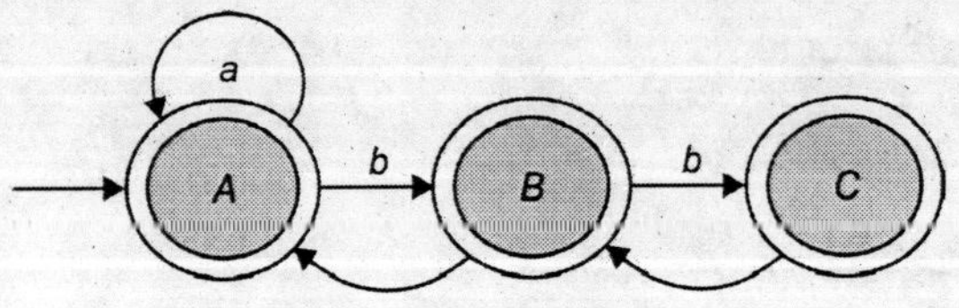

Fig. 5.41: DFA

Example 5.13: Construct a minimum state DFA for the following regular expressions:

(a) $(a + b)^*a(a + b)$ (All strings over $\{a, b\}$ ending in "*aa*" or "*ab*"}

(b) $(a + b)^*a(a + b)\,(a + b)$

Solution:

(a) Let DFA $M = (Q, \Sigma, \delta, 1, F)$ recognizes $(a + b)^*a(a + b)$ shown in Fig. 5.42(b).

(**Note:** The numbers of states are four when the number of $(a + b)$'s at the end of the regular expression is one.)

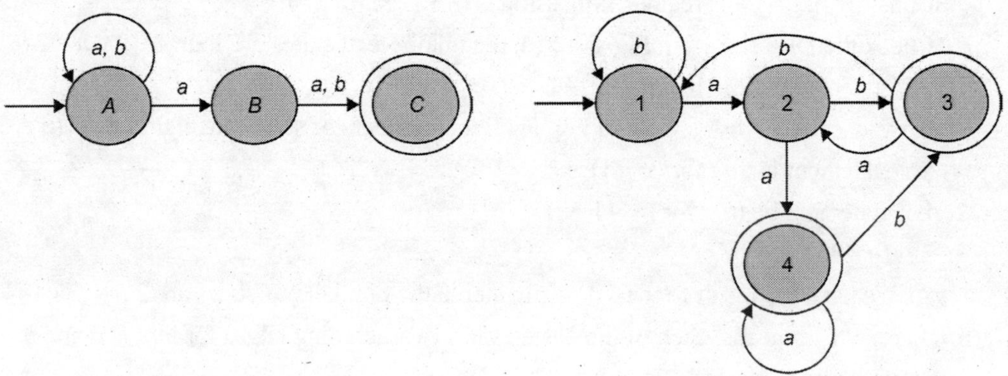

Fig. 5.42(a): NFA for $(a + b)^*a(a + b)$ **Fig. 5.42(b): DFA for $(a + b)^*a(a + b)$**

(b) Let DFA $M = (Q, \Sigma, \delta, 1, F)$ recognizes $(a + b)^*a(a + b)(a + b)$ as shown in Fig. 5.43.

(**Note:** The numbers of states are eight when the number of $(a + b)$'s at the end of the regular expression is two.)

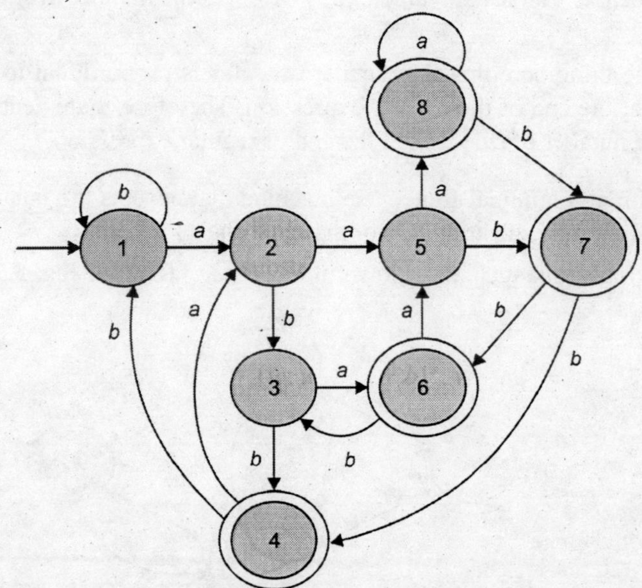

Fig. 5.43: DFA for $(a + b)^*a(a + b)(a + b)$

Example 5.14: Show that any DFA for regular expression $(a + b)^*a(a + b)(a + b).....(a + b)$ must have at least 2^n states, where $(n - 1)$ is the number of $(a + b)$'s at the end of regular expression.

Solution: We use mathematical induction method to prove the given statement.

Step 1: Let number of $(a + b)$'s is zero i.e $(n - 1)=0$, so $n = 1$. The numbers of states are two as shown in Fig. 5.44.

So, statement is true for $(n - 1)=0$

Fig. 5.44: DFA

Consider $(n - 1) = 1$, regular expression is $(a + b)^*a(a + b)$

Check the DFA shown in Fig. 5.42(b), the numbers of states are four i.e. 2^n $(n = 2)$.

So, statement is true for $(n - 1) = 1$.

Now, check the DFA shown in Fig. 5.43, the numbers of states are eight i.e. 2^n $(n = 3)$.

So, statement is true for $(n - 1) = 2$.

Step 2: Let statement be true for $(n - 1) = i$

Step 3: Let $(n - 1) = i + 1$

As we have the result for $(n - 1) = i$ in step 2,the numbers of states are 2^i.

As, $(n - 1) = i + 1$, it means, each of the 2^i states has two outgoing edges for inputs a and b.

So, numbers of states $= 2^*2^i$

$= 2^{i+1}$

Putting $i = n$ in the above result, we have the number of states are 2^{n+1}

Hence, statement is true for $n + 1$ number of $(a + b)$'s.

Therefore, statement is true for all value of n, where n is the number of $(a + b)$'s at the end of the regular expression.

(We conclude one thing here that the number of states is proportional to 2^{m+1}, where m is the number of $(a + b)$'s at the end of the regular expression. Therefore, statement is true for all value of $m \geq 0$, where m is the number of $(a + b)$'s at the end of regular expression.)

Example 5.15: Construct a minimal finite state machine that accepts the language over {0, 1} of all strings that contain neither the substring 00 nor the substring 11. **(GATE 2000)**

Solution: The DFA for given language is shown in Fig. 5.45. (See the Fig. 5.37 for help)

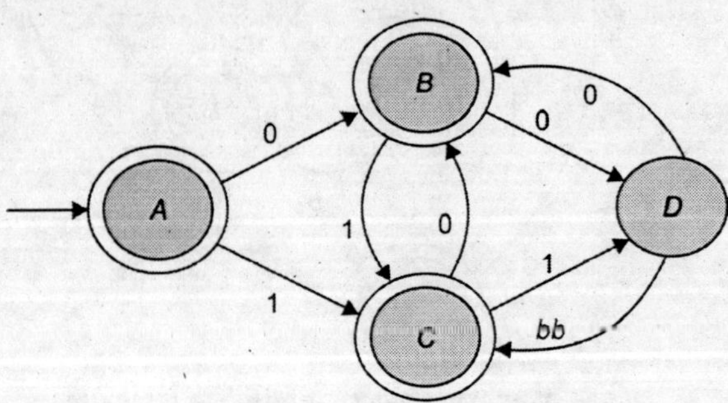

Fig. 5.45: DFA

Example 5.16: The regular language $L = 0(10)^*$ is generated by the right-linear grammar $S \rightarrow 0 \mid 0A$, $A \rightarrow 10 \mid 10A$. Construct a DFA for L and also find the left-linear grammar.

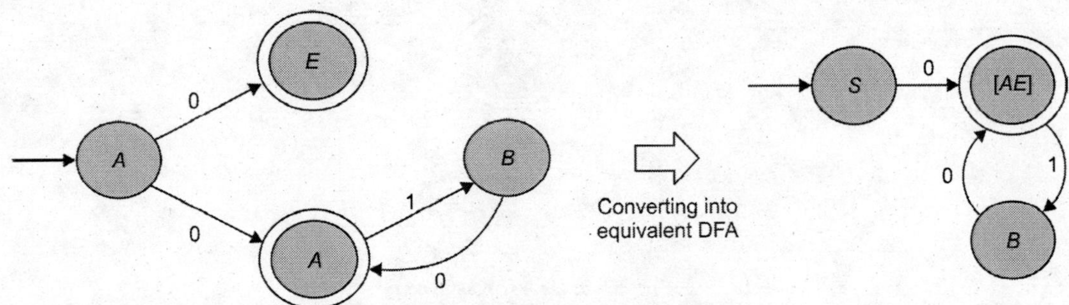

Fig. 5.46: DFA for $L = 0(10)^*$

Solution: Let DFA $M=(Q, \Sigma, \delta, S, F)$ recognizes $L = 0(10)^*$ shown in Fig. 5.46.

Finding left-linear grammar: Reversing the direction of all edges and changing the initial state to final state and final state to initial state of DFA shown in Fig. 5.46, the new DFA is shown in Fig. 5.47.

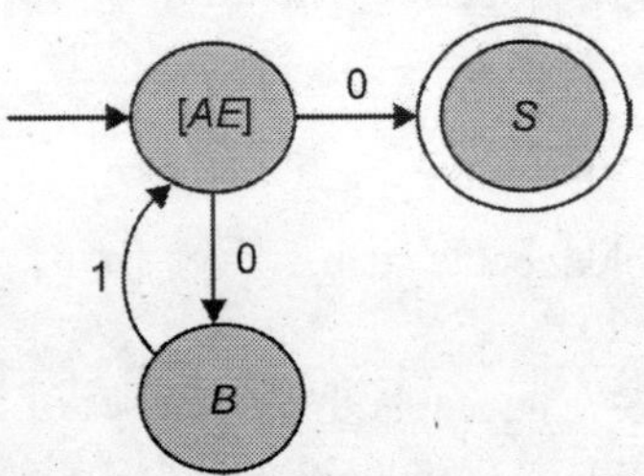

Fig. 5.47: DFA

The right-linear regular grammar for DFA shown in Fig. 5.47 is as follows:

$[AE] \rightarrow 0$

(We do not include $[AE] \rightarrow 0S$, because S has no transition.)

$[AE] \rightarrow 0B$

$B \rightarrow 1[AE]$

Replacing B in above production, we get

$[AE] \rightarrow 01[AE]$

Now, reversing both productions ($[AE] \rightarrow 0$, $[AE] \rightarrow 01[AE]$),

we get a new grammar G':

$[AE] \rightarrow 0$, $[AE] \rightarrow [AE]^{10}$(For reverse production: if $A \rightarrow a$ is in a G' if and only if $A \rightarrow a^R$ is in G)

Hence, $G' = (\{[AE]\}, \{0, 1\}, \{[AE] \rightarrow 0, [AE] \rightarrow [AE]10\}, \{[AE]\}$ is the desired left-linear grammar.

Example 5.17: Consider the DFA shown in Fig. 5.48 for $L = a(ba)^*$. Construct a regular grammar.

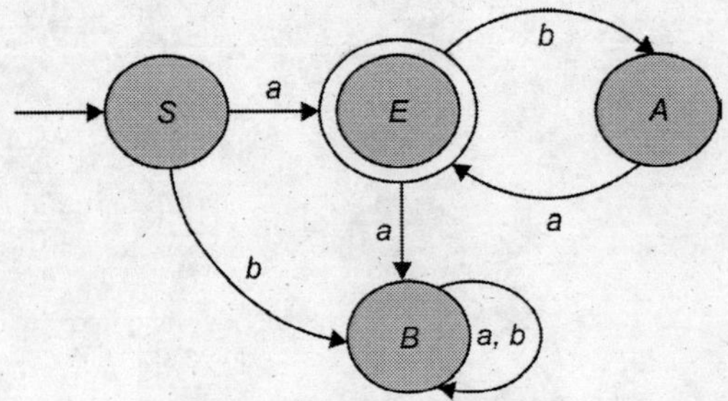

Fig. 5.48: DFA for L=a(ba)*

Solution: Let regular grammar G is corresponding to given DFA and let S, E, A, and B are variables of G.

$S \rightarrow a \mid aE \mid bB$, $E \rightarrow bA \mid aB$, $A \rightarrow a \mid aE$, and $B \rightarrow aB \mid bB$

In given DFA, B is the useless state because there is no path available to reach the final state from state B. So, all productions of B and productions including B should be removed from G.

Therefore, grammar G includes following productions:

$S \rightarrow a \mid aE$, $E \rightarrow bA$, and $A \rightarrow a \mid aE$

Example 5.18: Design a DFA which accepts strings over $\{a, b\}$ and counts the number of b's modulo 2.

Solution: Let DFA $M = (Q, \Sigma, \delta, S, F)$ accepts the given set of strings over $\{a, b\}$. As it is given that M counts number of b's modulo 2, it means, it accepts those strings which have number of b's multiple of 2 including all the strings of a's. M is shown in Fig. 5.49.

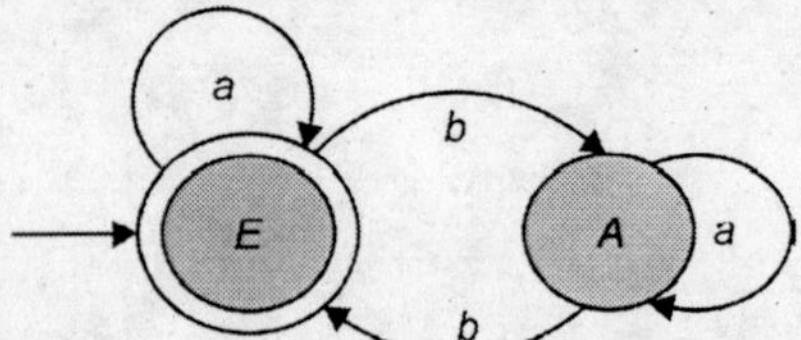

Fig. 5.49: DFA for $(a + ba^* b)^*$

So, accepted set of strings: $R = \{\varepsilon, a, aa, aaa, \ldots., bb, abab, abb, bba, \ldots\} = (a + ba^*b)^*$

Example 5.19: Construct a minimum state DFA for the following DFA:

Present state	Next state	
	0	1
→ q_0	q_1	q_5
q_1	q_6	q_2
(q_2)	q_0	q_2
q_3	q_2	q_6
q_4	q_7	q_5
q_5	q_2	q_6
q_6	q_6	q_4
q_7	q_6	q_2

Solution: The set of states is divided into two groups:

$G_1 = \{q_2\}$ (Final sates)

$G_2 = \{q_0, q_1, q_3, q_4, q_5, q_6, q_7\}$ (Non final states)

G_1 can not be divided, because it has one element, so we have to check for G_2.

Applying input 0 on G_2

$$G_2 \rightarrow \begin{cases} \text{For } \{q_0, q_1, q_4, q_6, q_7\} \text{ transitions belong to } G_2 \\ \text{For } \{q_3, q_5\} \text{ transitions belong to } G_1 \end{cases}$$

So, G_2 is divided into two groups. Total groups are:

$G_1 = \{q_2\}$

$G_2 = \{q_0, q_1, q_4, q_6, q_7\}$

and $G_3 = \{q_3, q_5\}$

Applying input 0 on G_2

All transitions belong to group G_2, so G_2 can't be divided on input 0.

Applying input 1 on G_2

$$G_2 \rightarrow \begin{cases} \text{For } \{q_6\} \text{ transitions belong to } G_2 \\ \text{For } \{q_0, q_4\} \text{ transitions belong to } G_3 \\ \text{For } \{q_1, q_7\} \text{ transitions belong to } G_1 \end{cases}$$

So, G_2 is divided into three groups. Total groups are:

$G_1 = \{q_2\}$

$G_2 = \{q_6\}$

$G_3 = \{q_3, q_5\}$

$G_4 = \{q_0, q_4\}$

and $G_5 = \{q_1, q_7\}$

Now, no group can be divided further. So, considering a group as a single state and G_4 as the initial state, the transition table for reduced DFA is as follows:

Present state	Next state	
	0	1
→ $[q_0, q_4]$	$[q_1, q_7]$	$[q_3, q_5]$
$[q_1, q_7]$	$[q_6]$	$[q_2]$
$[q_2]$ (final)	$[q_0, q_4]$	$[q_2]$
$[q_3, q_5]$	$[q_2]$	$[q_6]$
$[q_6]$	$[q_6]$	$[q_0, q_4]$

Example 5.20: Minimize the DFA shown in Fig. 5.50 using Myhill-Nerode Theorem.

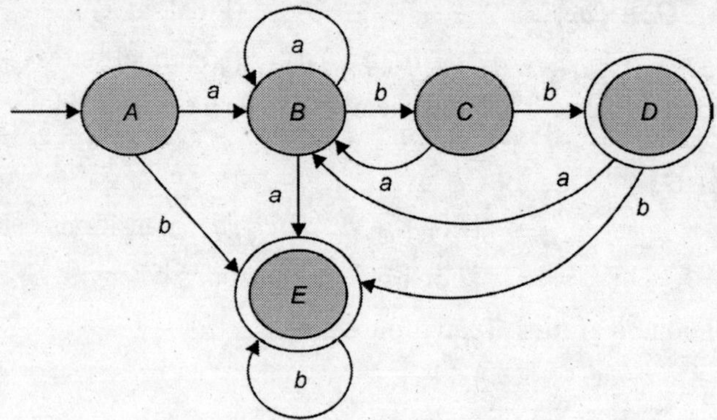

Fig. 5.50: DFA for $L = (a + b)^*abb$

Solution: Using Myhill-Nerode Theorem, we have to select the equivalent states and these states are merged to get the minimum state DFA.

We have following pairs of states to be checked for equivalent states:

(A, B), (A, C), (A, D), (A, E), (B, C), (B, D), (B, E), (C, D), (C, E), (D, E)

Let $\Sigma = \{a, b\}$

Selecting the pair [*A*, *B*]:

Let string $w = abb \in \Sigma^*$, then $\delta'(A, abb) = \delta'(B, abb) = D$

Let string $w = bb \in \Sigma^*$, then $\delta'(A, bb) = E$ and $\delta'(B, bb) = D$

So, *A* and *B* are not equivalence states.

Similarly, we check for the pairs (A, C), (A, D), (B, C), (B, D), (B, E), (C, D), (C, E), (D, E), and these are not equivalent states.

Now, **selecting the pair (*A*, *E*):** These states accept all the strings of the form aa^*bb and b^*a^*bb. So, these are equivalent states. We merge these states into one state and maintain all the transitions from *A* and *E* in order to get the minimum states DFA. The minimum states DFA is shown in Fig. 5.51.

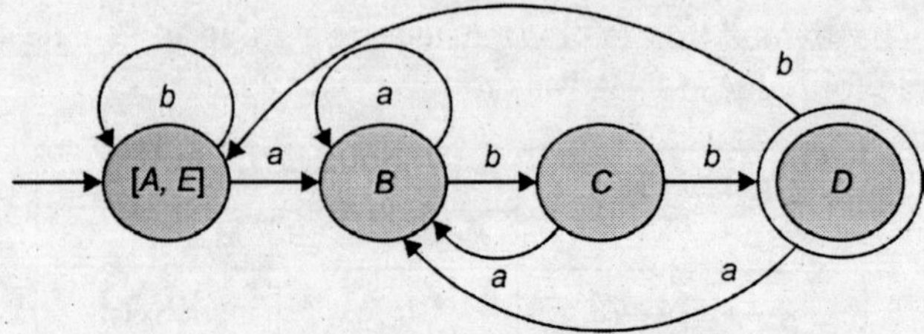

Fig. 5.51: Minimum states DFA for $L = (a + b)^*abb$

Example 5.21: Write regular expression for the following language over the alphabet {0, 1}- "The set of all strings not containing 101 as substring."

Solution: First we construct finite automaton for the language *L*, which is complement of the given language, that is

"The set of all strings containing 101 as substring."

Let DFA $M = (Q, \Sigma, \delta, A, \{D\})$ accepts $L = \{w: w \in (0 + 1)^*, w$ has "101" as a substring$\}$. M is shown in Fig. 5.52(a). Now, we complement the DFA M which is shown in Fig. 5.52(b).

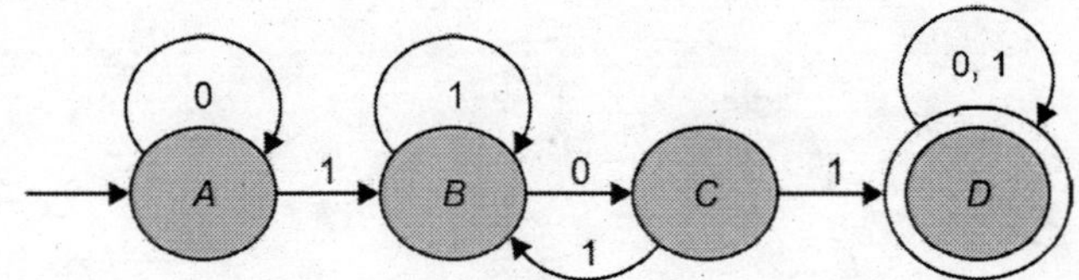

Fig. 5.52(a): DFA

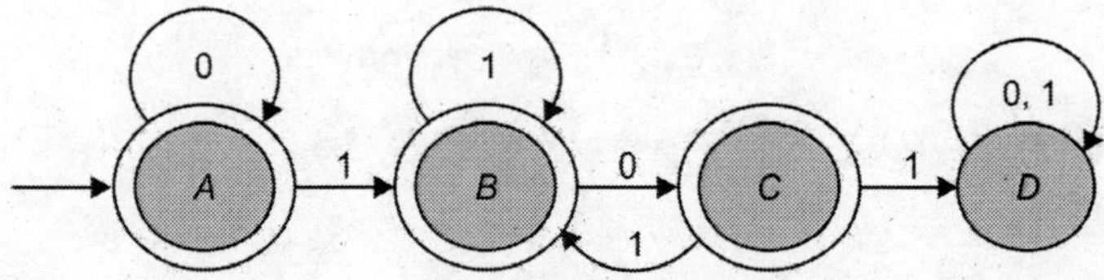

Fig. 5.52(b): DFA

Using Arden's Theorem, we find the regular expression for DFA shown in Fig. 5.52(b):

$A = A0 + \varepsilon$, $B = A1 + B + C1$, $C = B0$

Solving the above equations, we have:

$A = 0^*$, $B = 0^*11^* + (0^*11^*0)(11^*0)^*11^*$, $C = (0^*11^*0)(11^*0)^*$

Thus, the regular expression for DFA shown in Fig. 5(b), i.e. the desired regular expression for the given language is:

$0^* + 0^*11^* + (0^*11^*0)(11^*0)^*11^* + (0^*11^*0)(11^*0)^*$

Example 5.22: Prove or disprove the following for regular expressions r, s, and t

(i) $(r + s)^* = r^* + s^*$

(ii) $s(rs + s)^*r = rr^*s(rr^*s)^*$

Solution: (i)

$$\begin{aligned} \text{LHS} &= (r + s)^* = \{\varepsilon, r, s, rr, ss, rs, sr, rrr, sss \ldots\} \\ &= \{\text{All strings over } \{r, s\}\} \\ \text{RHS} &= r^* + s^* = \{\varepsilon, r, rr, rrr, \ldots\} \cup \{\varepsilon, s, ss, sss, \ldots\} \\ &= \{\varepsilon, r, s, rr, ss, rrr, sss, \ldots\} \\ &= \{\text{All strings over } \{r\} \text{ or All strings over } \{s\}\} \end{aligned}$$

It is obvious that regular expression $r^* + s^*$ has not the strings like rs, sr, rsr, ssr..., i.e. the combination of r and s. Therefore, the given statement is false.

(ii)

$$\begin{aligned} \text{LHS} &= s(rs + s)^*r = s(\varepsilon + s + rs + \ldots)r \\ &= \{sr, ssr, \ldots\} \\ \text{RHS} &= rr^*s(rr^*s)^* = r(\varepsilon + r + rr + \ldots)s\,(rr^*s)^* \\ &= \{rs, rr, \ldots\} \end{aligned}$$

We can see the smallest string in the regular expression $s(rs + s)^*r$ (LHS) is "sr" and other strings start with s and end in r. The smallest string in the second regular expression $rr^*s(rr^*s)^*$ (RHS) is "rs" and all the strings start with r. Therefore, the given statement is false.

Example 5.23: Construct NFA for $(a/b)^+$ and derive DFA through subset construction algorithm.

Solution: NFA for regular expression using ε-moves is shown in Fig. 5.53.

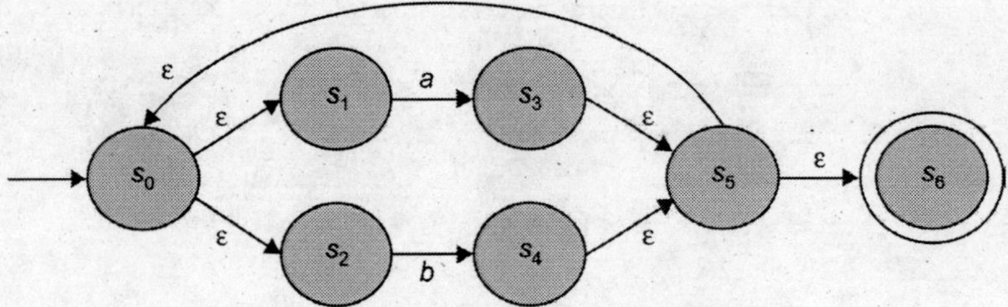

Fig. 5.53: NFA with ε-moves

Let equivalent DFA $M = (Q, \Sigma, \delta, s, F)$ as shown in Fig. 5.54.

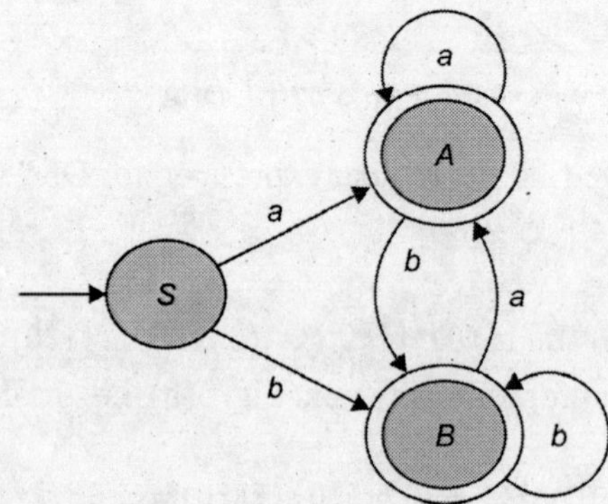

Fig. 5.54: DFA

Now, S = ε-closure (starting state of NFA) = ε-closure (s)

= {States reachable from state s_0 on input ε including state s_0}

= $\{s_0, s_1, s_2\}$

$\delta(s, a)$ = ε-closure(move($\{s_0, s_1, s_2\}, a$))

= ε-closure(s_3) = $\{s_3, s_5, s_6, s_0, s_1, s_2\}$ (Next state)

Let $A = \{s_0, s_1, s_2, s_3, s_5, s_6\}$

$\delta(s, b)$ = ε-closure(move($\{s_0, s_1, s_2\}, b$))

= ε-closure(s_4) = $\{s_4, s_5, s_6, s_0, s_1, s_2\}$ (Next state)

Let $B = \{s_0, s_1, s_2, s_4, s_5, s_6\}$

Here, we have two next states A and B, so we have to define the possible transitions from these states and we continue the process until no next states remain to be considered for defining its transition.

$\delta(A, a)$ = ε-closure (move($\{s_0, s_1, s_2, s_3, s_5, s_6\}, a$) = ε-closure ($s_3$) = A

$\delta(A, b)$ = ε-closure (move($\{s_0, s_1, s_2, s_3, s_5, s_6\}, b$)) = ε-closure ($s_4$) = B

$\delta(B, a)$ = ε-closure (move($\{s_0, s_1, s_2, s_4, s_5, s_6\}, a$)) = ε-closure ($s_3$) = A

$\delta(B, b)$ = ε-closure (move($\{s_0, s_1, s_2, s_4, s_5, s_6\}, b$)) = ε-closure ($s_4$) = B

Now, we tabularize the all transitions:

Present state	Next state	
	a	*b*
→ *s*	*A*	*B*
(*A*)	*A*	*B*
(*B*)	*A*	*B*

We have, $Q = \{s, A, B\}$, $\Sigma = \{a, b\}$, and $F = \{A, B\}$

Example 5.24: Construct DFA accepting the following languages over the alphabet {0, 1}

(i) The set of all strings with three consecutive zeros.

(ii) The set of alls strings such that every block of 05 consecutive symbols contains at least two zeros.

Solution: (i) Let a DFA $M = (Q, \{0, 1\}, \delta, q_0, F)$ accepts the given language. DFA is shown in Fig. 5.55.

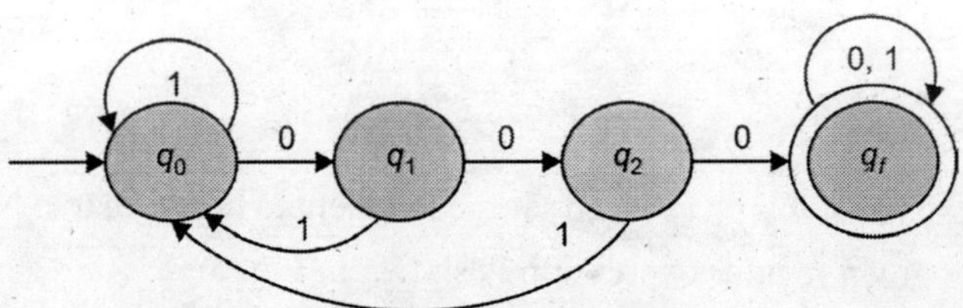

Fig. 5.55: DFA

(ii) Let a DFA $N = (Q, \{0, 1\}, \delta, q_0, F)$ accepts the given language. DFA is shown in Fig. 5.56. In the given language number of zeros is at least two, it means, number of zeros may be two, three, four, and five in a string of length five.

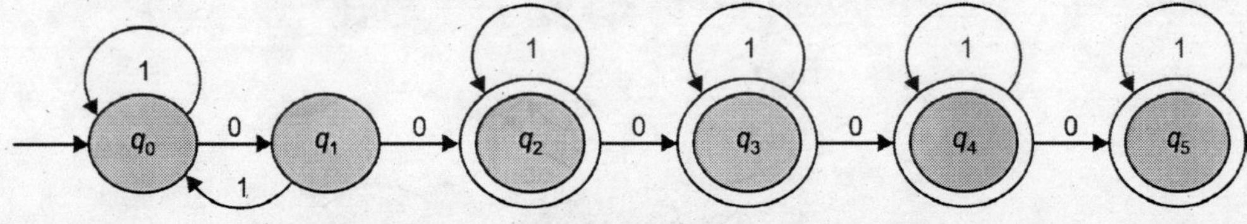

Fig. 5.56: DFA

Example 5.25: Write regular expression for the following language:

(i) A set of strings 0's and 1's with at most one pair or consecutive 1's

(ii) Set of all strings of 0's and 1's such that every pair of adjacent 0's appear before any pair of adjacent 1's.

Solution:

(i) Regular expression the set of strings over {0, 1} with no pair of 1's is: (10 + 0)* + (01 + 0)*

Now, the desired regular expression is: **(10 + 0)* + (01 + 0)* + (01 + 0)*11(10 + 0)***

(ii) Regular expression for pair of 0's appears before pair of 1's is: (0011)*

Regular expression for the strings without pair of 0's is: (1 + 01)* + (1 + 10)*

Thus, the desired regular expression is: **(1 + 01)* + (1 + 10)* + (1 + 01)* (0011)* (1 + 10)***

Example 5.26: Design NFA to recognize the following sets of strings *abc, abd, aacd*. Assume the alphabet is {*a, b, c, d*}.

Solution: Let NFA $M = (\{q_0, q_1, q_2, q_3, q_4, q_5, q_6, q_7, q_f\}, \{a, b, c, d\}, d, q_0, \{q_f\})$ shown in Fig. 5.57.

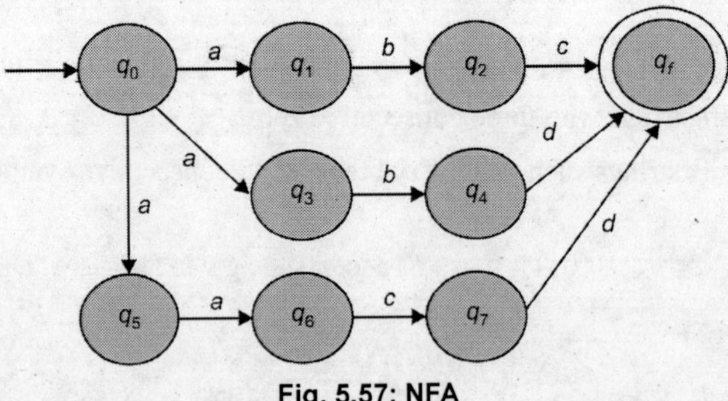

Fig. 5.57: NFA

Example 5.27: Construct a DFA with reduced sates equivalent to the regular expression 10 + (0 + 11)0*1

Solution: NFA for the given regular expression is shown in Fig. 5.58.

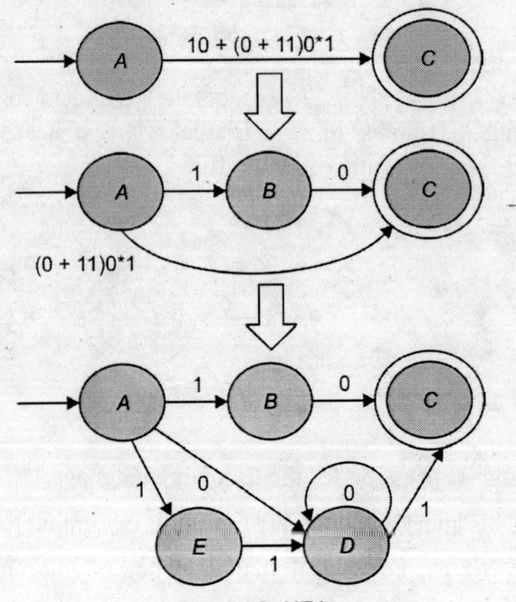

Fig. 5.58: NFA

Let equivalent DFA $M = (Q, \Sigma, \delta, [A], F)$, which is shown in Fig. 5.59.

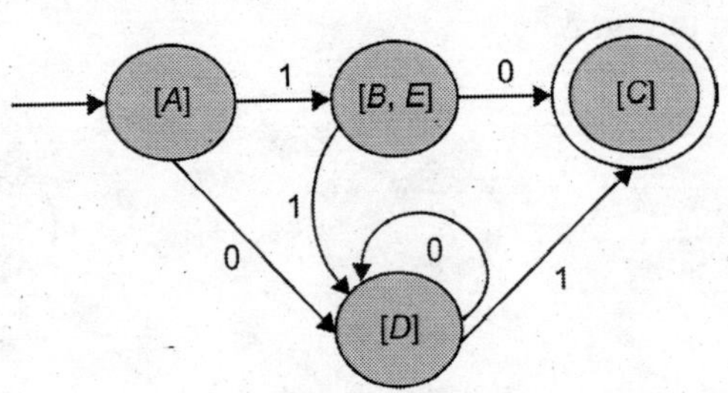

Fig. 5.59: DFA

Example 5.28: Find regular expressions corresponding to each of the following subsets of {0, 1}*.

(i) The language of strings containing exactly two 0's.

(ii) The set of all strings over $\{a, b\}$ in which the number of occurrences of a is divisible by 3.

(iii) The set of all strings over $\{a, b\}$ in which there are at least two occurrences of b between any two occurrences of a's.

Solution:

(i) Regular expression is: 1*01*0*

(ii) Regular expression is: $b^*(b^*ab^*ab^*ab^*)^*b^*$

(iii) Regular expression is: $b^*(abb(b^*)a)^*b^*$

Example 5.29: Show that the following languages are regular:

(i) $L = \{a^n \mid n > 4\}$

(ii) $L = \{vwv \mid v, w \in (a + b)^*, |v| = 2\}$

Solution:

(i) The given language is infinite and the shortest length string is of length 5 i.e.

$$L = \{aaaaa, aaaaaa, aaaaaaa, \ldots\}$$

We can represent the given language as regular expression: $aaaaa(a)^*$. Therefore, language L is regular language.

(ii) In the given language L, the string v has length two and L can be expressed as regular expression:

$$L = (aa + bb + ab + ba)\,(a + b)^*(aa + bb + ab + ba),$$

where $$v = (aa + bb + ab + ba) \text{ and } w \in (a + b)^*$$

Since, L can be represented as regular expression and therefore L is a regular language.

Example 5.30: Draw DFA for following over the set $\Sigma = \{0, 1\}$:

(i) $L = \{w: |w| \bmod 3 = 0\}$

(ii) $L = \{w: |w| \bmod 3 > 0\}$

Note: $|w|$ represents the length of string w.

Solution:

(i) The DFA is shown in Fig. 5.60.

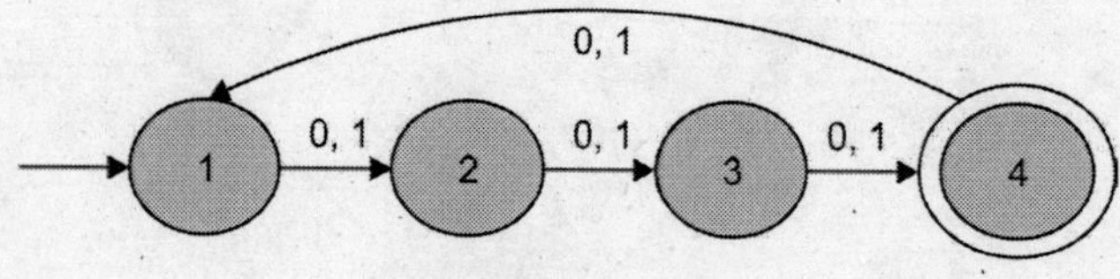

Fig. 5.60: DFA

(ii) The DFA is shown in Fig. 5.61.

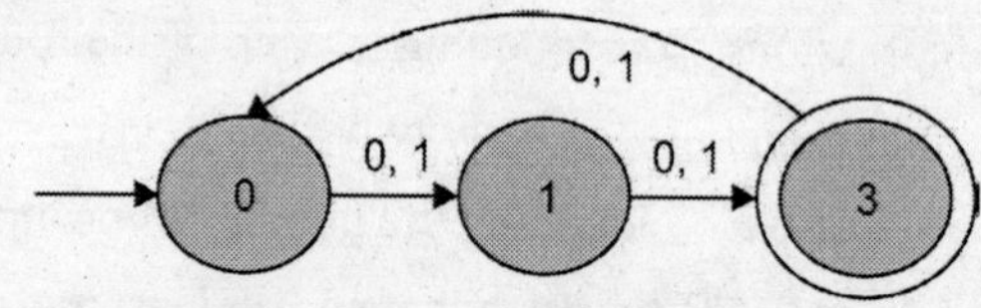

Fig. 5.61: DFA

Example 5.31: Let $\Sigma = \{a, b\}$, for each of the following language over Σ, find a regular expression representing it:

(i) All strings that exactly contain one '*a*'.

(ii) All strings beginning with "*ab*".

(iii) All strings that contain either the substring "*aaa*" or "*bbb*".

Solution:

(i) Regular expression is: b^*ab^*

(ii) Regular expression is: $ab(a + b)^*$

(iii) Regular expression is: $(a + b)^*(aaa + bbb)(a + b)^*$

Example 5.32: Define deterministic finite automata accepting the following languages over the alphabet {0,1}:

(i) The set of all strings ending in 00.

(ii) The set of all strings such that every block of five consecutive symbols contains at least two 0's.

Solution:

(i) Let DFA $M = (Q, \Sigma, \delta, q_1, \{q_3\})$ accepts the given language $(0 + 1)^*00$ as shown in Fig. 5.62.

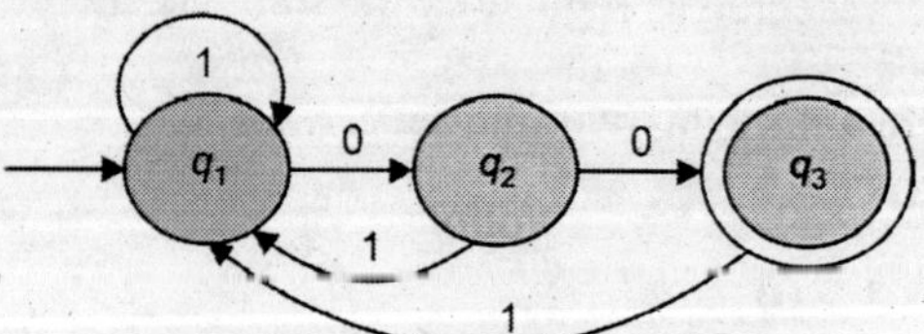

Fig. 5.62: DFA for {0 + 1)*00

(ii) Let DFA $M = (Q, \Sigma, \delta, 1, \{6\})$ accepts the given language. It is obvious from the given language that each block of five consecutive symbols contains atleast two 0's, i.e. two 0's, three 0's, four 0's, and five 0's. DFA is shown in Fig. 5.63.

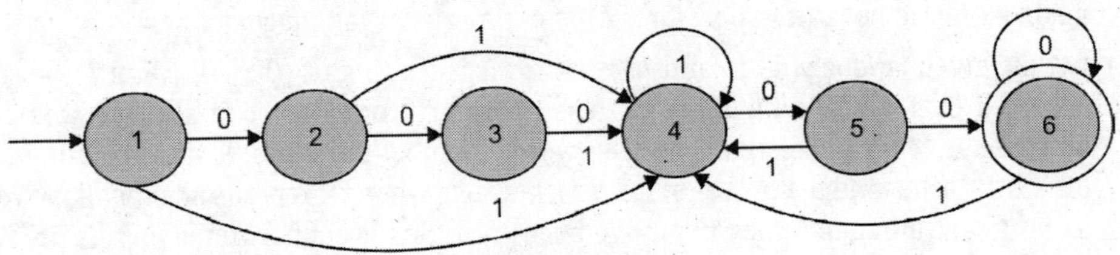

Fig. 5.63: DFA

Example 5.33: Let L_1 be a CFL and L_2 be a regular language, then prove that $L_1 \cap L_2$ is context-free language.

Proof: Consider the context-free language $L_1 = \{a^n b^n : n \geq 1\}$ and regular language $L_2 = \{a^p b^q : p, q \geq 1\}$ then intersection of L_1 and L_2 is a context-free language. Let us express the strings of languages L_1 and L_2.

$$L_1 = \{ab, aabb, aaabbb, \ldots\} \text{ and}$$

$$L_2 = \{ab, aab, aabb, abbb, aabbb, \ldots\}$$

So, $$L_1 \cap L_2 = \{ab, aabb, aaabbb, \ldots\} = \{a^k b^k : k \geq 1\}$$

So, obviously $L_1 \cap L_2$ is a context-free language.

(**Note:** L_1 is CFL and L_2 is regular language. Since, all regular languages are context- free language.)

Example 5.34: Draw non-deterministic finite automaton (NFA) with four states for all strings over {0, 1} in which third symbol from right end is '0'.

Solution: NFA $M = (\{A, B, C, D\}, \{0, 1\}, \delta, \{A\}, \{D\})$ shown in Fig. 5.64.

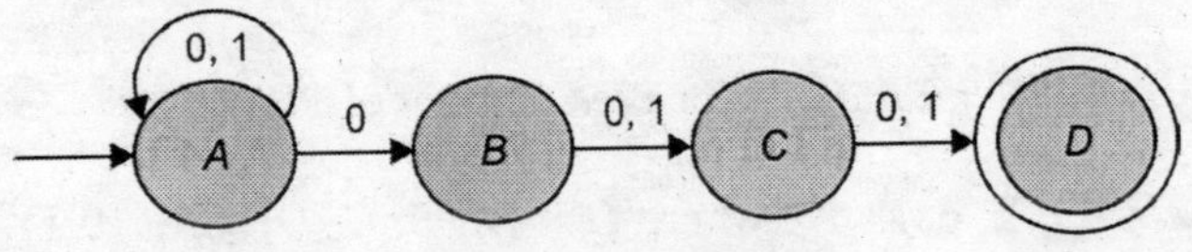

Fig. 5.64: NFA

Example 5.35: Prove or disprove whether following languages are regular or not?

(i) The set of all strings over the alphabet {0} of the form 0^n, where n is not a prime.

(ii) The set of all binary strings that read backwards the same as forwards (palindromes).

Proof:

(i) Let the given language is L_1 and $L_1 = \{0^m : m \text{ is not a prime number}\}$. Let L_1 be regular and accepted by DFA M with n states. String $w \in L$ such that $|w| \geq n$ and $w = xy^iz \in L$ for $i \geq 0$, $y \notin \varepsilon$, let $|w| = m$, where m is not a prime number and $|xz| \leq n$, (n is the number of states and $n <= m$).

Let $y = 0^j$, where $j = 0, 1, 2, 3, \ldots$, that is, y is considered as string 0^j

Now, $|w| = |xyz| = |xz| + |y| = n + j$, where n is number of states of DFA

The length of string w is $n + j$, which may or not be prime depending on the value of n and j. In other words, length of strings of L_1 may or may not be prime and hence the assumption made earlier is not true. Therefore, L_1 is not a regular language.

(ii) Let the given language is L_2 and $L_2 = \{ww^R: w \text{ is a string of } (0 + 1)^*\}$. Let L_2 be regular and accepted by DFA M with n states. It is necessary for M to read string w and then string w^R (reverse of w) and also it is necessary to remember the symbols of w to assure the reverse of w. This is beyond the power of DFA M, because when DFA reads an input it moves forward to read next input and does not move backward. So, M cannot remember its previous input and that is why it cannot decide the existence of palindromes. In other words, assumption made earlier about L_2 is incorrect and therefore, L_2 is not a regular language.

Example 5.36: Draw DFA for the following languages over {0, 1}:

(i) All string with even number of 0's and even number of 1's.

(ii) All string of length of at most five.

Solution:

(i) DFA for the even number of 0's and even number of 1's is shown in Fig. 5.65.

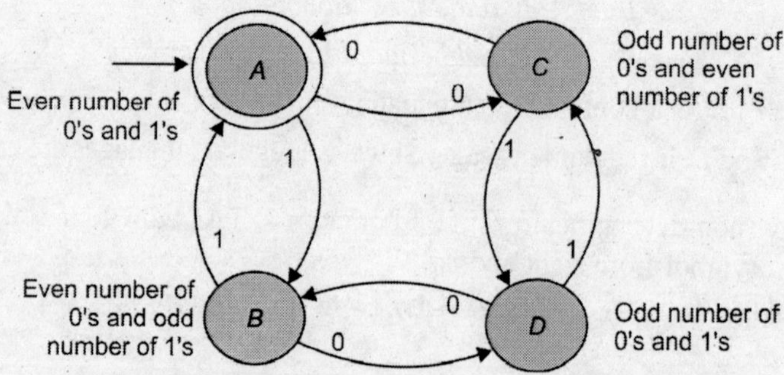

Fig. 5.65: DFA for even number of 0's and 1's

Let DFA $M = (Q, \Sigma, \delta, A, F)$, where $Q = \{A, B, C, D\}$, $\Sigma = \{0,1\}$, A is starting state, and $F = \{A\}$.

(ii) Let DFA $M = (Q, \Sigma, \delta, A, F)$, where $Q = \{A, B, C, D, E, H\}$, $\Sigma = \{0,1\}$, A is starting state, and $F = \{A, B, C, D, E\ H\}$.

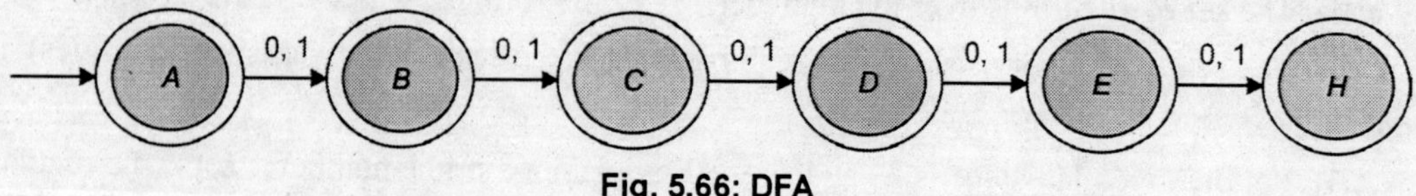

Fig. 5.66: DFA

Example 5.37: Write regular expression for the set of all strings over {0, 1} in which every pair of adjacent zero's appears before any pair of adjacent one's.

Solution: Regular expression is: $(01)^*(0011)^*(01)^*$

TEST YOUR SKILLS

Supplementary Problems

5.1 Describe the languages associated by following regular expressions:

(a) $(a + b)^*a(\varepsilon + bbb)$ (b) $(ab)^*a$

5.2 Design NFA and DFA for the language $L = (ab + aba)^*$.

5.3 Design FA for the following regular expressions over $\{a, b, c\}$:

(a) $((ab + aab)^*a^*)^*$ (b) $(a^*b^*c^*)^*b$

(c) $(ab)^*(ba)^* + aa^*$ (d) $(ab + aab + aba)^*$

(e) $(aa + bb + ab + ba)^*$ (f) $aa(a + b)(a + b)bb$

5.4 Prove that $L = \{a^{2n}: n \geq 1\}$ is regular.

5.5 Check following languages are regular or not:

(a) $L = \{a^n b^{2n}: n \geq 0\}$

(b) $L = \{a^n b^m: n > m\}$

(c) $L = \{a^n b^n: n = 0, 1, 2, 3, 4, 5, 6, 7, 8, ..., 100\}$

(d) $L = \{a^n b^n: n \geq 0\}(a + b)^*$

5.6 Construct a DFA equivalent to the grammar having production rules:

$S \to aS \mid bS \mid bA,\ A \to bB,\ B \to aC,\ C \to \varepsilon$

5.7 Design DFA which counts number of b's modulo3 over $\{a, b\}$.

5.8 If G is a regular grammar derives $L(G)$ over $\{a, b\}$. Prove that $L(G^R) = (L(G))^R$, where $A \to a$ is in G^R if and only if $A \to a^R$ is in G.

5.9 Construct a minimum state DFA for the following DFA:

Present state	Next state	
	0	1
$\to q_0$	q_0	q_3
q_1	q_2	q_5
q_2	q_3	q_4
q_3	q_0	q_5
q_4	q_0	q_6
q_5	q_1	q_4
(q_6)	q_1	q_3

5.10 Prove the following:

(a) $L = L_i$ is regular language, where L_i is a regular language for $i = 1, 2, ..., n$.

(b) $L = L_1 \mid L_2 \mid ... \mid L_n$ is regular language, where $L_1, L_2, ..., L_n$ are regular language.

5.11 Design FA for two operations; EX-OR and EX-NOR defined below. FA gives output either YES or NO.

EX-OR Operation: If $w_1 \in L_1$ and $w_2 \in L_2$, where L_1 and L_2 are regular language, then output is YES if and only if one of the strings w_1 and w_2 is accepted and other is rejected and output is NO if and only if both strings are accepted or rejected.

EX-NOR Operation: If $w_1 \in L_1$ and $w_2 \in L_2$, where L_1 and L_2 are regular language, then output is YES if and only if both the strings are accepted or rejected and output NO if and only if one of the two strings is accepted and other is rejected.

5.12 Show that if L is a regular language then the language L^n for $n \geq 0$ is regular.

5.13 Suppose r_1 and r_2 are two regular expressions over some alphabet Σ. Simplify the following regular expressions and find the corresponding languages:

(a) $(r_1 + \varepsilon)^*$
(b) $(r_1 + r_2 + \varepsilon)^*$
(c) $(r_1^* + \varepsilon)^* + r_2$
(d) $(r_1 + r_2 + r_1r_2 + r_2r_1)^*$
(e) $(r_1^* + r_2^*)^*$
(f) $(r_1^* + \varepsilon + r_2 + f)^*$

5.14 Suppose r_1 and r_2 are two regular expressions over some alphabet Σ. Show that the following expressions are regular:

(a) $(r_1 + \varepsilon + f)^*$
(b) $(r_1 + r_2)^* + \varepsilon)^*$
(c) $r_1 + r_2 + r_1r_2 + r_2r_1$
(d) $(r_1^* + r_2^*)^*$
(e) $(r_1^* + \varepsilon + r_2 + f)^*$

5.15 Consider the following regular expressions over {0, 1}. Find the regular set for each of the following expression.

(a) $(0 + 1 + 0)^*00$
(b) $(11 + 01 + 10 + 00)^*$
(c) $00(11 + 00)^*00$
(d) $(0^* + 1^*)^*(0 + 1)^*$
(e) $1^*(000)^*(111)^*0$
(f) $(0 + 1)^3$
(g) $(0 + 1)(0^* + 1^*)^*$

5.16 Find the regular expressions for the following regular sets over $\{a, b\}$:

(a) All strings containing exactly one '*a*'
(b) All strings containing "*aa*" as substring
(c) All strings starting with '*bb*" and ending with "*aa*"
(d) All strings starting with "*aa*" or ending with "*bb*"
(e) All strings containing even number of a's and b's
(f) All strings containing even number of a's and odd number of b's
(g) All strings containing odd number of a's and odd number of b's
(h) All strings containing odd number of a's and even number of b's
(i) All strings not containing "*aa*" or "*bb*" as substring
(j) All strings containing "*aaa*" as prefix
(k) All strings containing "*ab*" or "*ba*" as suffix

5.17 Consider the following text:

> *TWINKLE, TWINKLE LITTLE STAR*
> *HOW I WONDER WHAT YOU ARE*
> *UP ABOVE THE WORLD SO HIGH*
> *LIKE A DIAMOND IN THE SKY*
> *WHEN THE BURNING SUN IS SET*
> *AND THE GRASS WITH DUE IS WET*
> *THEN YOU SHOW YOUR LITTLE LIGHT*
> *TWINKLE, TWINKLE ALL THE NIGHT*

Design finite automata for finding the pattern "TWINKLE". Assume that number of characters used in the text is finite.

5.18 Consider the regular languages L_1, L_2, and L_3 over $\{a, b, c\}$. Show that following languages are regular:

(a) $L_1L_2L_3$
(b) $L_1L_1L_3$
(c) $(L_1 + L_2)^* + L_3$
(d) $(a + b + c)^* - L_1L_2$
(e) $(a + b + c)^* - L_2 + L_3$
(f) $(a + b + c + L_1)^*$
(g) $(a + b + c + L_1L_3)^*$
(h) $(L_1^* + L_2^* + L_3^*)^*$

5.19 Consider the regular languages over {0, 1} given below. Find the complement of each language.

(a) L_1 = {All strings starting with 0 and ending with 00}
(b) L_2 = {All strings starting with 000 and ending with 111}
(c) L_3 = {All strings containing at most two 0's}
(d) L_4 = {All strings containing "00" or "11" as substring}
(e) L_5 = {All strings containing "00" and "11" as substring}
(f) $L_6 = (0 + 1)^*011$
(g) $L_7 = 0(11 + 00)^*00$
(h) $L_8 = (00 + 11 + 10 + 01)^*$
(i) L_9 = {All strings containing exactly two 0's}
(j) L_{10} = {All strings containing exactly three consecutive 0's}

5.20 Prove that finite languages are regular language.

5.21 Prove or disprove the following statements about regular expressions:

(i) $(R + S)^* = R^* + S^*$ (ii) $(RS + R)^*RS = (RR^*S)^*$

5.22 Minimize the DFA shown in Fig. 5.67.

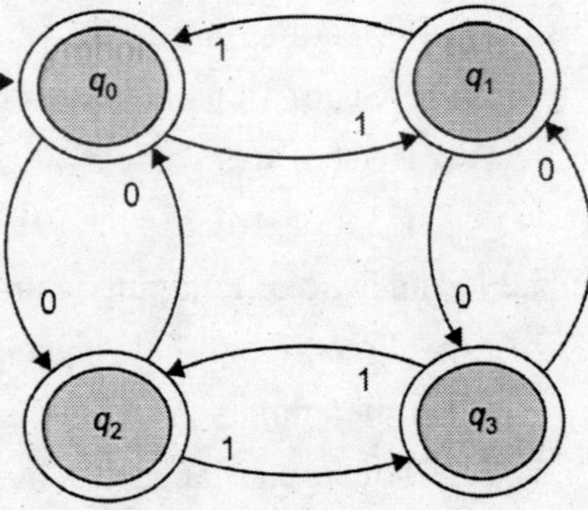

Fig. 5.67

5.23 Minimize the DFA given below:

Present state	Next state	
	0	1
→ *a*	*a*	*b*
b	*c*	*d*
c	*a*	*f*
d	*e*	*f*
e	*a*	*f*
f	*g*	*f*
g	*a*	*f*

Multiple Choice Questions

5.24 Regular languages are recognized by
(a) Finite automata (b) Pushdown automata
(c) Turing machines (d) All

5.25 Regular expressions are
(a) Compact representation of strings (b) Representation of strings over some alphabet
(c) Compact representation of certain set of strings in algebraic fashion
(d) None

5.26 Pumping Lemma is used for proving
(a) A given language is regular (b) A given grammar is regular
(c) A given language is not regular (d) All of the above

5.27 Which pair is equivalent regular expression?
(a) $(ab)^*$ and a^*b^* (b) $r(rr)^*$ and $(rr)^*r$
(c) r^+ and r^*r (d) (b) & (c)

5.28 Which one is regular?
(a) Set of strings of a's whose length is a perfect square
(b) Set of all palindromes over $\{a, b\}$
(c) Set of strings over $\{0, 1\}$ having length a prime number
(d) Set of strings over $\{0\}$ having odd number of zeros

5.29 The logic of Pumping lemma is a good example of
(a) The Pigeon-hole principle (b) Divide and conquer method
(c) Iteration (d) Recursion

5.30 Set of regular languages over certain alphabet is not closed under
(a) Complement (b) Iteration
(c) Union (d) None

5.31 Which of the following pairs of regular expression are not equivalent?

(a) $(a^* + b^*)^*$ and $(a + b)^*$ (b) $(a^* + b)^*$ and $(a + b)^*$

(c) $(ab)^*a$ and $a(ba)^*$ (d) None of the above

5.32 Choose the correct statement. A class of languages that is closed under

(a) Intersection and complementation has not to be closed under union

(b) Union and complementation has to be closed under intersection

(c) Union and intersection has to be closed under complementation

(d) Both (b) and (c)

5.33 Let $A = \{a, b\}$, $L = \{a^nb^n: n \geq 1\}$, and $R = A^*$, then the languages $R \cup L$ and R are

(a) Regular, regular (b) Regular, not regular

(c) Not regular, regular (d) Not regular, not regular

5.34 P, Q and R are three languages. P and R are regular languages and $R = PQ$, then

(a) Q can't be regular (b) Q has to be regular

(c) Q has to be CFL (d) Q need not be regular

5.35 Myhill-Nerode theorem is useful over Pumping Lemma because

(a) It has constructive aspect (b) Its result is negative

(c) Its result may be negative (d) (a) and (c)

5.36 Myhill-Nerode theorem is used for

(a) Finding equivalence classes

(b) Minimization of FA

(c) Proving regular and not regular languages

(d) All of the above statements

5.37 The result of Pumping Lemma is

(a) Negative always (b) Sometime negative

(c) Positive sometime (d) Positive always

5.38 Choose the correct statement

(a) For every regular language, there is right linear and left linear grammar

(b) For every regular language, there is right linear or left linear grammar but not both

(c) Transpose of a regular language is regular

(d) Both (a) and (c)

5.39 Consider the following grammar G: **(GATE 2004)**

$S \rightarrow bS \mid aA \mid b,$

$A \rightarrow bA \mid aB,$

$B \rightarrow bB \mid aS \mid a$

Let $N_a(w)$ and $N_b(w)$ denote the number of a's and b's in a string w respectively. The language $L(G) \subseteq (a + b)^+$ generated by G is

(a) $\{w \mid N_a(w) > 3\ N_b(w)\}$ (b) $\{w \mid N_b(w) > 3\ N_a(w)\}$

(c) $\{w \mid N_a(w) = 3k, k \in \{0, 1, 2, 3, \ldots\}\}$ (d) $\{w \mid N_b(w) = 3k, k \in \{0, 1, 2, 3, \ldots\}\}$

5.40 A language containing all the words over $\{a, b\}$ having even number of a's and b's is

(a) $(aa + bb + (ab+ba)\ (aa + bb)^*(ab + ba))^*$

(b) $(ab + ba + (ab + ba)(aa + bb)^*(ab + ba))^*$

(c) $(aa + bb + ab + ba)^*$

(d) None

5.41 Which one of the following regular expressions pair not define the same language?

(a) $(a^* + b)^*$ and $(a + b)^*$ (b) $(ab)^*a$ and $a(ba)^*$

(c) $(a^* + b^*)^*$ and $(a + b)^*$ (d) None

5.42 Consider the following deterministic finite state automata:

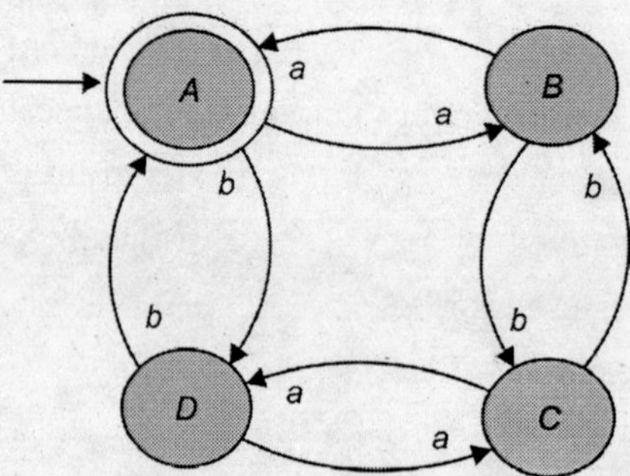

Fig. 5.68: DFA

The language accepted by the above automata is

(a) The words over $\{a, b\}$ having even number of a's and odd number of b's.

(b) The words over $\{a, b\}$ having odd number of a's and odd number of b's.

(c) The words over $\{a, b\}$ having even number of a's and even number of b's.

(d) The words over $\{a, b\}$ having odd number of a's and even number of b's.

5.43 Consider the DFA shown in Fig. 5.70.

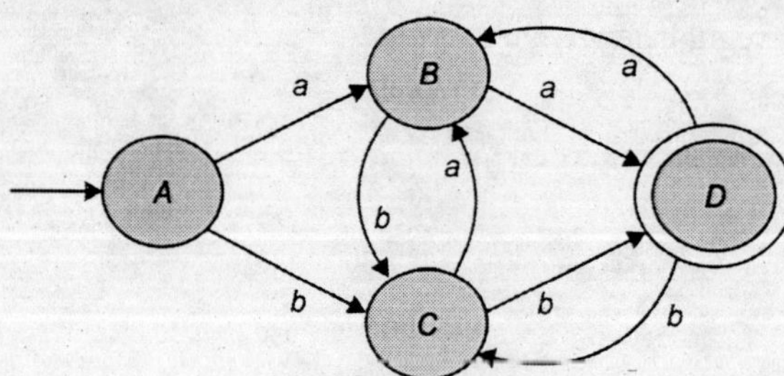

Fig. 5.69: DFA

Which one of the following languages is accepted by DFA?

(a) $L = \{w: w \in (a + b)^*$ has either *aa* or *bb* as a substring$\}$

(b) $L = \{w: w \in (a + b)^*$ has both *aa* and *bb* as substring$\}$

(c) $L = \{w: w \in (a + b)^*$ has neither *aa* nor *bb* as a substring$\}$

(d) None

5.44 Consider the finite automata shown in Fig. 5.71.

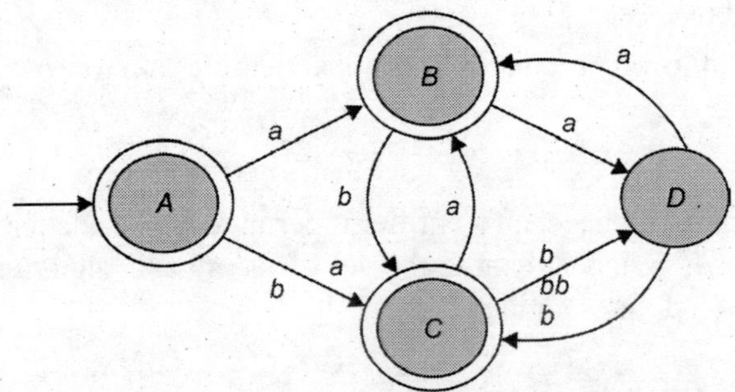

Fig. 5.70: FA

Which one of the following languages is accepted by DFA?

(a) $L = \{w: w \in (a + b)^*$ has either *aa* or *bb* as a substring$\}$

(b) $L = \{w: w \in (a + b)^*$ has both *aa* and *bb* as substring$\}$

(c) $L = \{w: w \in (a + b)^*$ has neither *aa* nor *bb* as a substring$\}$

(d) None

5.45 Which one of the following languages is regular?

(a) $L = \{a^n b^m: n > m \geq 0\}$

(b) $L = \{a^n b^n: 0 < n \leq k$, where k is fixed natural number$\}$

(c) $L = \{a^n b^n c^m: m, n0\}$

(d) None

5.46 Which one of the following languages is not regular?

(a) $L = \{a^n b^m: n, m \geq 0$

(b) $L = \{a^n b^n: n \in \{1, 2, 3, \ldots\}\}$

(c) $L = \{a^p b^q c^r: p, q, r \geq 0\}$

(d) None

5.47 Which one is incorrect?

(a) $L = L_i$ is regular language, where L_i is a regular language for $i = 1, 2, \ldots, n$.

(b) $L = L_1 \cap L_2 \cap \ldots \cap L_n$ is regular language, where $L_1, L_2, \ldots, L_n$ are regular language.

(c) $L = \Sigma - L_1 - L_2 - \ldots - L_n$ is regular language, where $L_1, L_2, \ldots, L_n$ are regular language over Σ.

(d) None

5.48 If L_1 and L_2 are two regular languages, then concatenation of L_1 and L_2 is
(a) L_1L_2 (b) $L_1.L_2$
(c) $L_1 \times L_2$ (d) None

5.49 Let $r = 1(1 + 0)^*$, $s = 11^*0$, and $t = 1^*0$ be three regular expressions. Which one of the following is true? **(GATE 1991)**
(a) $L(s) \subseteq L(r)$ and $L(s) \subseteq L(t)$ (b) $L(r) \subseteq L(s)$ and $L(s) \subseteq L(t)$
(c) $L(s) \subseteq L(t)$ and $L(s) \subseteq L(r)$ (d) $L(t) \subseteq L(s)$ and $L(s) \subseteq L(r)$
(e) None of the above

5.50 Which one of the following regular expressions identities are true? **(GATE 1992)**
(a) $(r^*)^* = r^*$ (b) $(r^* + s^*)^* = (r + s)^*$
(c) $(r + s)^* = r^* + s^*$ (d) $r^*s^* = r^* + s^*$

5.51 In some programming language, an identifier is permitted to be a letter following by any number of letters or digits. If L and D denote the set of letters and digits respectively, which of the following expression defines an identifier? **(GATE 1995)**
(a) $(L \cup D)^+$ (b) $L(L \cup D)^*$
(c) $(LD)^*$ (d) $L(LD)^*$

5.52 Consider a grammar with the following productions: $S \rightarrow a\alpha b \mid b\alpha c \mid aB$, $B \rightarrow aS \mid a$, $aS \rightarrow bab$
The grammar is
(a) Context-free (b) Regular
(c) Context-sensitive (d) None

5.53 A grammar G can be described by
(a) (V_n, Σ, P, S) (b) (V_n, P, S)
(c) (Σ, V_n, P, S) (d) both (a) & (c)

5.54 The word "FORMAL" in formal languages means
(a) No meaning
(b) The symbols used have well-defined meaning
(c) Only strings are significant
(d) None of the above

5.55 If $G = (\{S\}, \{a\}, \{S \rightarrow SS\}, S)$, then language $L(G)$ is
(a) ϕ (b) $aa(a)^*$
(c) $(aa)^*$ (d) None

5.56 The regular grammer G, $S \rightarrow aS \mid bS \mid a \mid b$ generates
(a) $(a + b)^+$ (b) $(a + b)(a + b)^*$
(c) $(a + b)^*(a + b)$ (d) All the above

5.57 The grammar $S \rightarrow aSb \mid \varepsilon$ generates
(a) $\{a^nb^n\text{: } n \geq 0\}$ (b) $\{a^nb^n\text{: } n \geq 1\}$
(c) $\{a^nb^m\text{: } m \geq 1, n \geq 0\}$ (d) $\{a^nb^m\text{: } m \geq 0, n \geq 1\}$

5.58 The regular language are accepted by

(a) Finite automata (b) Pushdown automata only

(c) Turing machines only (d) None

5.59 The CFLs are accepted by

(a) Finite automata (b) Pushdown automata

(c) Turing machines only (d) None

5.60 The CSLs are accepted by

(a) Finite automata (b) Pushdown automata only

(c) Turing machines only (d) Linear bounded Automata

5.61 The regular grammer $S \to aB \mid bA, A \to aSa, B \to bS \mid b$ generates

(a) Odd number of a's and b's (b) Equal number of a's and b's

(c) Even number of a's and b's (d) Even number of a's and odd number of b's

5.62 Choose the regular productions

(a) $S \to aS \mid a$ (b) $S \to aaSbb \mid \varepsilon$

(c) $S \to aA \mid bB, A \to c \mid aS, B \to c \mid bS$ (d) Both (a) & (c)

5.63 If for a grammar G and a language L, $L = L(G)$, then

(a) All the words of $L(G)$ are in L

(b) All words of L are in $L(G)$

(c) All words of $L(G)$ are in L and all words of L are in $L(G)$

(d) All words generated by G are in L

5.64 Choose the correct statement

(a) All regular grammars are CFG

(b) All CFGs are CSG

(c) Regular grammars are most restricted grammars

(d) All the above

5.65 The regular expression for the language recognized by the following finite state automata is **(GATE 1994)**

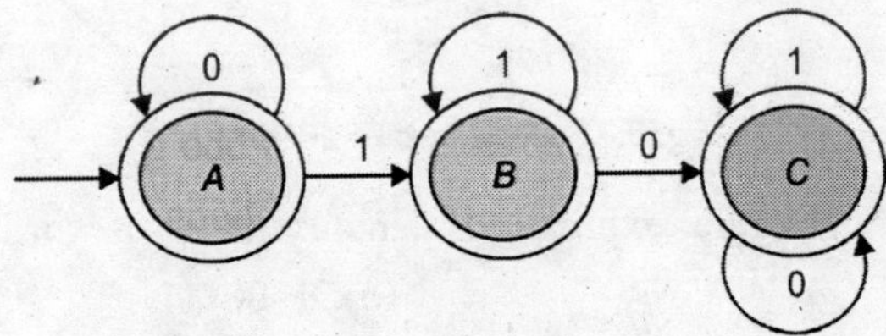

Fig. 5.71: DFA

(a) $0^* \mid 0^*1^+$ (b) $0^* \mid 0^*1^+ \mid 0^*1^+(0 + 1)^*$

(c) $0^* \mid 11^*$ (d) None

5.66 Which of the following definitions below generates the same language as L, where $L = \{x^n y^n$ such that $n \geq 1\}$? **(GATE 1995)**

(I) $E \to xEy \mid xy$

(II) $xy \mid (x^+xyy^+)$

(III) x^+y^+

(a) (I) only (b) (I) and (II)

(c) (II) and (III) (d) (II) only

5.67 Let $L \subseteq \Sigma^*$, where $\Sigma = \{a, b\}$. Which of the following is true? **(GATE 1996)**

(a) $L = \{x \mid x$ has an equal number of a's and b's$\}$ is regular

(b) $L = \{a^n b^n \mid n \geq 1\}$ is regular

(c) $L = \{x \mid x$ has more a's than b's$\}$ is regular

(d) $L = \{n^m b^n \mid m, n \geq 1\}$ is regular

5.68 Match the pairs given following:

(A) Finite Automata (P) Type 0 language

(B) Turing Machine (q) Type 1 language

(C) Pushdown Automata (R) Type 3 language

(D) Linear Bounded automata (S) Type 2 language

(a) $(A, R), (B, P), (C, S), (D, Q)$ (b) $(A, S), (B, P), (C, R), (D, Q)$

(c) $(A, R), (B, S), (C, P), (D, Q)$ (d) $(A, R), (B, P), (C, Q), (D, S)$

5.69 The following grammar $S \to bS \mid b \mid Aa, Aabc$ is

(a) Type 3 (b) Type 2

(c) Type 1 (d) Type 0

5.70 Consider the following finite state automaton M.

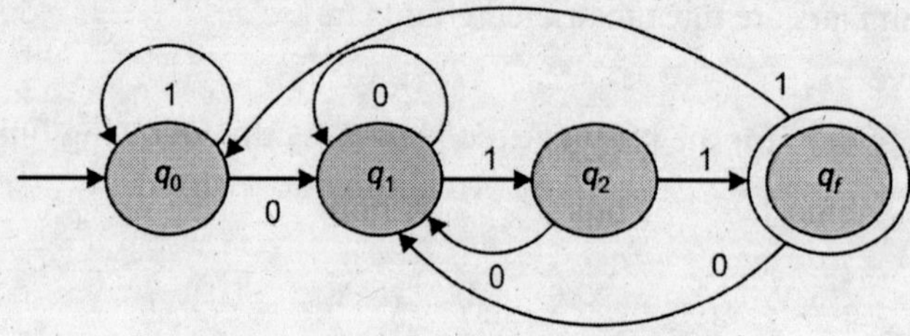

Fig. 5.72: Finite state automaton

Which of the following regular expressions denotes the set of words accepted by M?

(a) $011(0 + 1)^*$ (b) 1^*00^*11

(c) $(0 + 1)^*011$ (d) None

5.71 Choose the incorrect statement.

(a) A-productions $A \to a_1a_2a_3 \ldots a_nA \mid a_1a_2a_3 \ldots a_n$, where a_i is terminal for $i = 1, 2, 3, \ldots, n$ is right linear grammar

(b) S-productions $S \to wS \mid w \mid Sw$, where w is a terminal string such that $1 \leq |w| \leq n$ for some fixed $n \geq 1$ is regular grammar

(c) C language is regular language

(d) Both (b) and (c) are incorrect

5.72 Which one of the following languages is not regular?

(a) $L = \{a^{2n}: n \geq 0\}$

(b) $L = \{(ab)^n: n \geq 1\}$

(c) $L = \{a^n b^n: n = 1, 2, 3, \ldots, 1000\}$

(d) None

5.73 Which one of the following languages is not regular?

(a) $L = \{w: w \in (a + b)^*$ and has even number of a's and odd number of b's$\}$

(b) $L = \{w: w \in (a + b)^*$ and has either "*aaa*" or "*bb*" as substring$\}$

(c) $L = \{w: w \in (a + b)^*$ and has neither "*aa*" nor "*bb*" as substring$\}$

(d) None

Answers

5.24 (d)	5.25 (c)	5.26 (c)	5.27 (d)	5.28 (d)
5.29 (a)	5.30 (d)	5.31 (d)	5.32 (d)	5.33 (a)
5.34 (d)	5.35 (d)	5.36 (d)	5.37 (a)	5.38 (d)
5.39 (c)	5.40 (a)	5.41 (d)	5.42 (c)	5.43 (a)
5.44 (c)	5.45 (b)	5.46 (b)	5.47 (d)	5.48 (a)
5.49 (a)	5.50 (a), (b)	5.51 (b)	5.52 (c)	5.53 (d)
5.54 (c)	5.55 (a)	5.56 (d)	5.57 (a)	5.58 (a)
5.59 (b)	5.60 (d)	5.61 (b)	5.62 (d)	5.63 (c)
5.64 (d)	5.65 (a)	5.66 (a)	5.67 (d)	5.68 (a)
5.69 (a)	5.70 (c)	5.71 (c)	5.72 (d)	5.73 (d)

CHAPTER 6

Context-free Grammars and Languages

We will discuss context-free grammars (CFGs), leftmost and rightmost derivations, derivation tree, ambiguity, left recursion, left factoring, simplifications of context-free grammars, normal forms (**Chomsky** and **Greibach**), properties of context-free languages, and other related topics also in this chapter. It is noticeable that most of the programming languages are described by context-free grammars. Context-free grammars are very much useful in lexical analysis, which is a part of compilation and discussed in Chapter 7.

6.1 CONTEXT-FREE GRAMMAR (CFG)

Grammar $G = (V_n, \Sigma, P, S)$ is said to be context-free grammar (CFG) if the production rules of G are of the form:

$$A \to \alpha, \text{ where } \alpha \in (V_n \cup S)^*$$

The right hand side of a context-free grammar is not restricted and it may be null or a combination of variable and terminals from $(V_n + \Sigma)^*$. As we know that a context-free grammar has no context, neither left nor right. This is why, it is known as CONTEXT-FREE. *Many programming languages have recursive structure that can* be *defined by context-free grammars (CFGs)*. Right-hand side of the production rules in context-free grammars can be restricted in many ways and that result in many normal forms. We will see two important normal forms (Chomsky and Greibach) later on in this chapter. Let us consider a context-free grammar $G = (V_n, \Sigma, P, S)$ having production rules: $S \to aSb \mid bSb \mid \varepsilon$. Check the production rules for their type and find the language generated.

Solution: Let

$P_1 : S \to aSa$ (RHS is terminal variable terminal)

$P_2 : S \to bSb$ (RHS is terminal variable terminal)

$P_3 : S \to \varepsilon$ (RHS is null string)

Obviously production rules P_1 and P_2 are type 2 and production rules P_3 is type 3 and hence grammar G is type 2 grammar (context-free grammar) All production rules are of the form $A \to \alpha$, where $\alpha \in (V_n \cup \Sigma)^*$.

Language Generated:

$$\begin{aligned} S &\Rightarrow aSa && \text{(Using rule } P_1\text{)} \quad \text{or} \quad bSb && \text{(Using rule } P_2\text{)} \\ &\Rightarrow a^nSa^n && \quad\quad \text{or} \quad b^nSb^n && \text{(Using } n \text{ step derivation)} \\ &\Rightarrow a^nb^mSb^ma^n && \text{(Using rule } P_2\text{)} \quad \text{or} \quad b^na^mSa^mb^n && \text{(Using rule } P_1\ m\text{-steps)} \\ &\Rightarrow a^nb^mb^ma^n && \quad\quad \text{or} \quad b^na^ma^mb^n && \text{(Using } S \to \varepsilon\text{)} \end{aligned}$$

So, $\qquad L(G) = \{ww^R: w \in (a+b)^*\}$

6.1.1 Leftmost and Rightmost Derivations

We categorize the derivation of context-free grammars in two categories: leftmost and rightmost derivations. This categorization is based on the variable replacement in derivation. If leftmost variable is replaced in right hand side of derivation then derivation is known as leftmost derivation and if rightmost variable replacement is there then rightmost derivation. Sometimes we use both types of derivations in production of single string.

Leftmost derivation: If $G = (V_n, \Sigma, P, S)$ is a context-free grammar (CFG) and $w \in L(G)$, then a derivation $S \overset{*}{\underset{L}{\Rightarrow}} w$ is called leftmost derivation if and only if all steps involved in derivation have leftmost variable replacement. The sign L with production sign ($\Rightarrow$) indicates the leftmost variable replacement.

Rightmost derivation: If $G = (V_n, \Sigma, P, S)$ is a context-free grammar (CFG) and $w \in L(G)$, then a derivation $S \overset{*}{\underset{R}{\Rightarrow}} w$ is called rightmost derivation if and only if all steps involved in derivation have rightmost variable replacement. The sign R with production sign ($\Rightarrow$) indicates the rightmost variable replacement.

Example 1: Consider the production rules: $S \to S + S \mid S^*S \mid a \mid b$. Find the type of grammar and find leftmost and rightmost derivations for string w = a*$a + b$.

Solution: Let

$P_1: S \to S + S$ (RHS is variable terminal variable; type 2)

$P_2: S \to S^*S$ (RHS is variable terminal variable; type 2)

$P_3: S \to a$ (RHS is terminal; type 3)

$P_4: S \to b$ (RHS is terminal; type 3)

Hence, the given grammar is type 2 grammar or context-free grammar (CFG).

Leftmost derivation for $w = a^*a + b$:

$$\begin{aligned} S &\underset{L}{\Rightarrow} \underline{S}^*S && \text{(Using } S \to S^*S\text{)} \\ &\underset{L}{\Rightarrow} a^*\underline{S} && \text{(The first left hand symbol is `}a\text{', so using } S \to a\text{)} \\ &\underset{L}{\Rightarrow} a^*\underline{S} + S && \text{(Using } S \to S + S\text{, in order to get } a + b\text{)} \\ &\underset{L}{\Rightarrow} a^*a + \underline{S} && \text{(Third symbol from the left is `}a\text{', so using } S \to a\text{)} \\ &\underset{L}{\Rightarrow} a^*a + b && \text{(The last symbol from the left is `}b\text{', so using } S \to b\text{)} \end{aligned}$$

(**Note:** Leftmost variable is underlined in each step.)

Rightmost derivation for $w = a*a + b$:

$\underset{R}{\Rightarrow} S*\underline{S}$ (Using rule $S \rightarrow S*S$)

$\underset{R}{\Rightarrow} S*S + \underline{S}$

(Since, in the above sentential form second symbol from the right is *. So, we cannot use rules $S \rightarrow a \mid b$. Therefore, using $S \rightarrow S + S$)

$\underset{R}{\Rightarrow} S*\underline{S} + b$ (Using rule $S \rightarrow b$)

$\underset{R}{\Rightarrow} \underline{S}*a + b$ (Using rule $S \rightarrow a$)

$\underset{R}{\Rightarrow} a*a + b$ (Using rule $S \rightarrow a$)

(**Note:** Rightmost variable is underlined in each step.)

Example 2: Consider production rules: $S \rightarrow bA \mid aB$, $A \rightarrow aS \mid aAA \mid a$, $B \rightarrow bS \mid aBB \mid b$. Find leftmost and rightmost derivations for string $w = aaabbabbba$.

Solution: **Leftmost derivation for $w = aaabbabbba$:**

$S \Rightarrow a\underline{B}$ (Using $S \rightarrow aB$ to generate first symbol of w)

$\Rightarrow aa\underline{B}B$ (Since, second symbol is 'a', so we use $B \rightarrow aBB$)

$\Rightarrow aaa\underline{B}BB$ (Since, third symbol is 'a', so we use $B \rightarrow aBB$)

$\Rightarrow aaab\underline{B}B$ (Since, fourth symbol is 'b', so we use $B \rightarrow b$)

$\Rightarrow aaabb\underline{\mathbf{B}}$ (Since, fifth symbol is 'b', so we use $B \rightarrow b$)

$\Rightarrow aaabba\underline{B}B$ (Since, sixth symbol is 'a', so we use $B \rightarrow aBB$)

$\Rightarrow aaabbab\underline{\mathbf{B}}$ (Since, seventh symbol is 'b', so we use $B \rightarrow b$)

$\Rightarrow aaabbabb\underline{\mathbf{S}}$ (Since, third last symbol is 'b', so we use $B \rightarrow bS$)

$\Rightarrow aaabbabbb\underline{\mathbf{A}}$ (Since, ninth symbol is 'b', so we use $S \rightarrow bA$)

$\Rightarrow aaabbabbba$ (Since, the tenth last symbol is 'a', so using $A \rightarrow a$)

(**Note:** Leftmost variable is underlined in each step.)

Rightmost derivation for $w = aaabbabbba$:

$S \Rightarrow a\underline{\mathbf{B}}$ (Using $S \rightarrow$ aB to generate first symbol of w)

$\Rightarrow aaB\underline{B}$ (We need 'a' as the rightmost symbol and second symbol from the left side. So, we use $B \rightarrow aBB$)

$\Rightarrow aaBb\underline{S}$ (We need 'a' as a rightmost symbol and this can be obtained from A only. So, we use $B \rightarrow bS$)

$\Rightarrow aaBbb\underline{\mathbf{A}}$ (Using $S \rightarrow bA$)

$\Rightarrow aa\underline{\mathbf{B}}bba$ (Using $A \rightarrow a$)

$\Rightarrow aaaB\underline{B}bba$ (We need 'b' as the fourth symbol from the right,

$\Rightarrow aaa\underline{\mathbf{B}}bbba$ (Using $B \rightarrow b$)

$\Rightarrow aaab\underline{S}bbba$ (Using $B \rightarrow bS$)

$\Rightarrow aaabb\underline{A}bbba$ (Using $S \rightarrow bA$)

$\Rightarrow aaabbabbba$ (Using $A \rightarrow a$)

It appears that getting rightmost derivation is slightly difficult as compare to leftmost derivation. Is there any other approach to make derivation simple? We will see another approach in derivation trees.

6.1.2 Derivation Tree

Let $G = (V_n, \Sigma, P, S)$ be a context-free grammar (CFG). Each production rule of G can be represented with a tree satisfying the following:

1. If $A \rightarrow \alpha_1\alpha_2\alpha_3...\alpha_n$ is a production rule in P, then A becomes the parent of nodes labeled $\alpha_1, \alpha_2, \alpha_3, ..., \alpha_n$, and
2. The collection of children of a derivation tree from left to right yields $\alpha_1\alpha_2\alpha_3...\alpha_n$, where $\alpha_1, \alpha_2, \alpha_3, ...,$ and α_n are labels of children nodes.

Example 1: Consider production rules of a context-free grammar: $S \rightarrow S + S \mid S*S \mid a \mid b$ and represent each production rule by tree.

Solution:

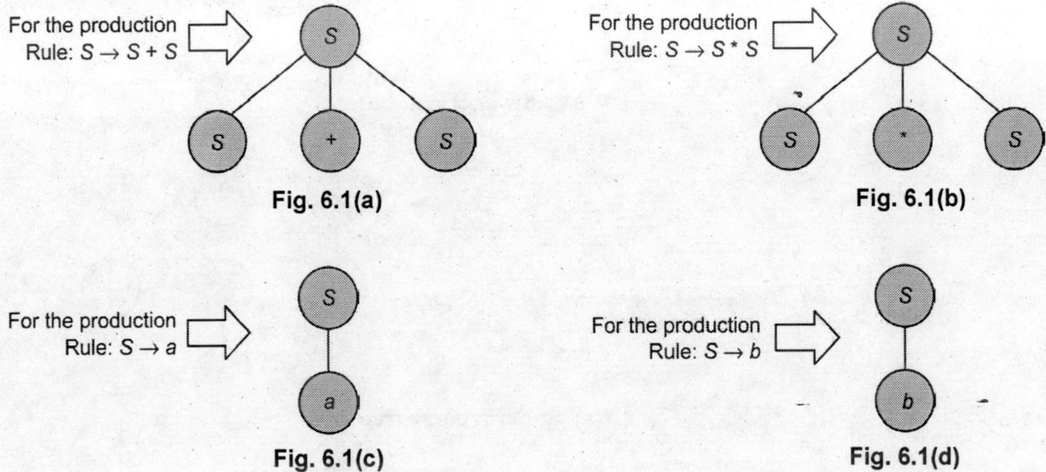

Fig. 6.1(a) Fig. 6.1(b) Fig. 6.1(c) Fig. 6.1(d)

Now, let us see what derivation tree is. If $w \in L(G)$, where G is a context-free grammar then w is represented by a tree known **derivation tree** or **parse tree** satisfying the following:

1. The root has label S (the starting symbol of grammar),
2. All internal vertices (or nodes) are labeled with variables,
3. The leaves or terminal nodes are labeled with ε or terminal symbols,
4. If $A \rightarrow \alpha_1\alpha_2\alpha_3...\alpha_n$ is a production rule in G then variable A becomes the parent of nodes labeled $\alpha_1, \alpha_2, \alpha_3, ..., \alpha_n$, and
5. The collection of leaves from left to right yields the string w.

Example 1: Consider production rules of a context-free grammar: $S \rightarrow S + S \mid S{*}S \mid a \mid b$. Construct derivation tree for string $w = a{*}a + b$.

Solution: The derivation tree or parse tree for w is shown in Fig. 6.2(b).

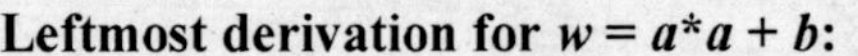

Leftmost derivation for $w = a{*}a + b$:

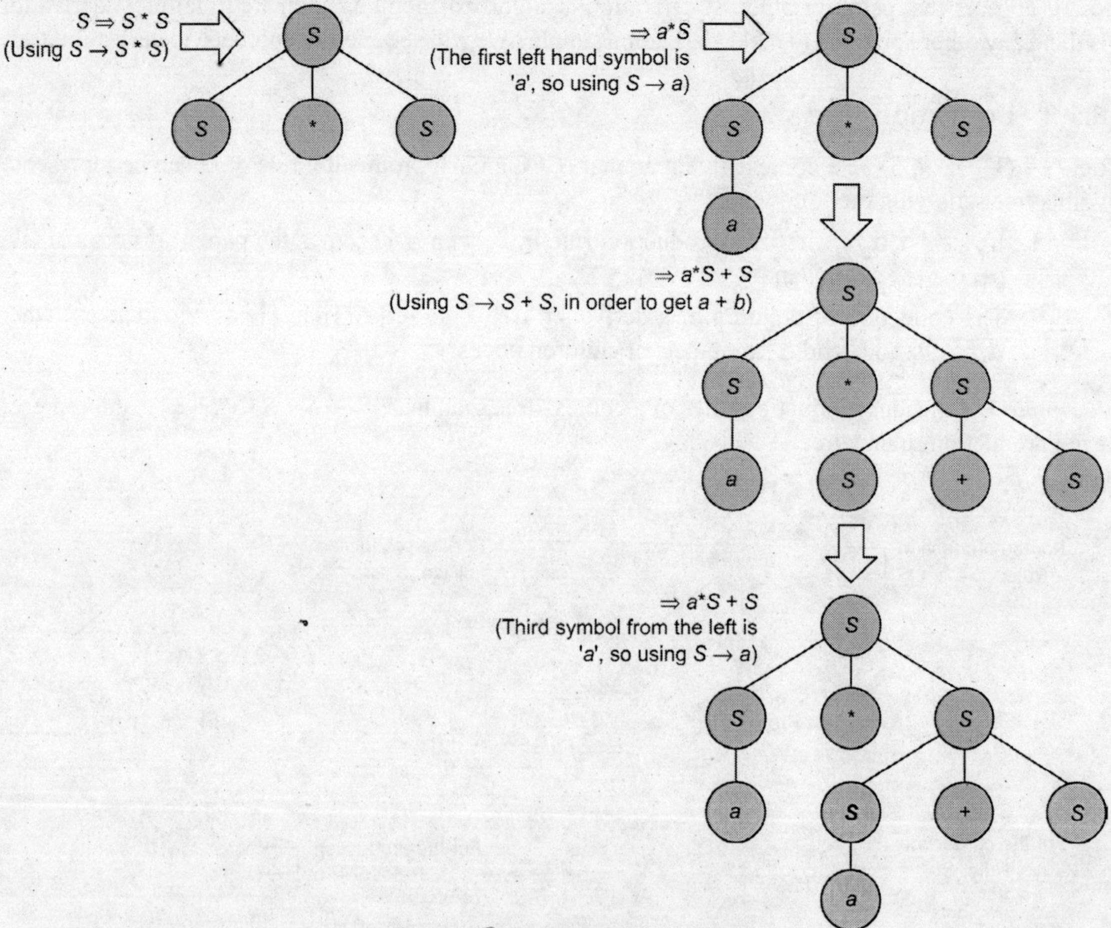

$S \Rightarrow S * S$
(Using $S \rightarrow S * S$)

$\Rightarrow a{*}S$
(The first left hand symbol is 'a', so using $S \rightarrow a$)

$\Rightarrow a{*}S + S$
(Using $S \rightarrow S + S$, in order to get $a + b$)

$\Rightarrow a{*}S + S$
(Third symbol from the left is 'a', so using $S \rightarrow a$)

Fig. 6.2(a): Steps in parse tree

$\Rightarrow a{*}S + b$
(The last symbol from the left is 'b', so using $S \rightarrow b$)

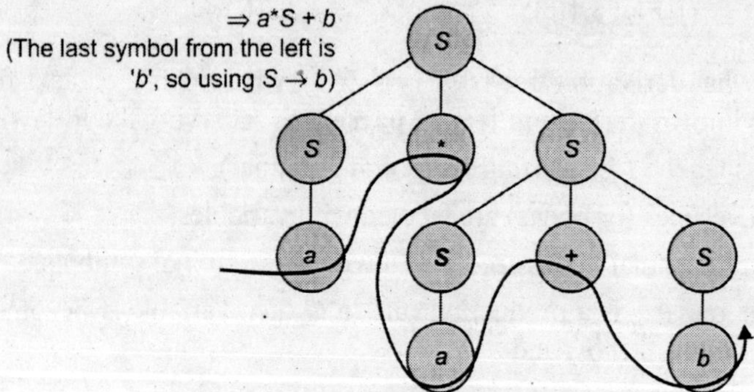

Fig. 6.2(b): Parse tree for $a{*}a + b$

6.1.3 Ambiguity and Context-free Grammars

A grammar G is said to be *ambiguous* if there exists some string $w \in L(G)$ for which *there are two or more distinct derivation trees*, or *there are two or more distinct leftmost derivations.* The main application of the context-free grammars is in compiler design. Ambiguous grammars are undesirable because multiple derivation trees provide multiple information about a certain string. Ambiguity is a negative property of a grammar. It is usually (but not always) possible to find an equivalent unambiguous grammar. The language generated by an ambiguous context-free grammar is known as ambiguous language. An **inherently ambiguous language** is a language for which no unambiguous grammar exists.

Example 1: consider the production rules of a context-free grammar: $S \rightarrow S + S \mid S*S \mid a \mid b$ and string $w = a*a + a$. Check whether grammar is ambiguous or not?

Solution: Let us see how many leftmost derivations are there for string w.

First leftmost derivation for $w = a*a + a$:

$$\begin{aligned} S &\Rightarrow S*S && \text{(Using rule } S \rightarrow S*S) \\ &\Rightarrow a*S && \text{(Using rule } S \rightarrow a) \\ &\Rightarrow a*S + S && \text{(Using rule } S \rightarrow S + S) \\ &\Rightarrow a*a + S && \text{(Using rule } S \rightarrow a) \\ &\Rightarrow a*a + a && \text{(Using rule } S \rightarrow a) \end{aligned}$$

Second leftmost derivation for $w = a*a + a$:

$$\begin{aligned} S &\Rightarrow S + S && \text{(Using rule } S \rightarrow S + S) \\ &\Rightarrow S*S + S && \text{(Using rule } S \rightarrow S*S) \\ &\Rightarrow a*S + S && \text{(Using rule } S \rightarrow a) \\ &\Rightarrow a*a + S && \text{(Using rule } S \rightarrow a) \\ &\Rightarrow a*a + a && \text{(Using rule } S \rightarrow a) \end{aligned}$$

So, we have two distinct leftmost derivations, which are given above and two distinct parse trees are shown in Fig. 6.3(a) and Fig. 6.3(b). In other words, there is ambiguity in given grammar for string w and grammar is ambiguous.

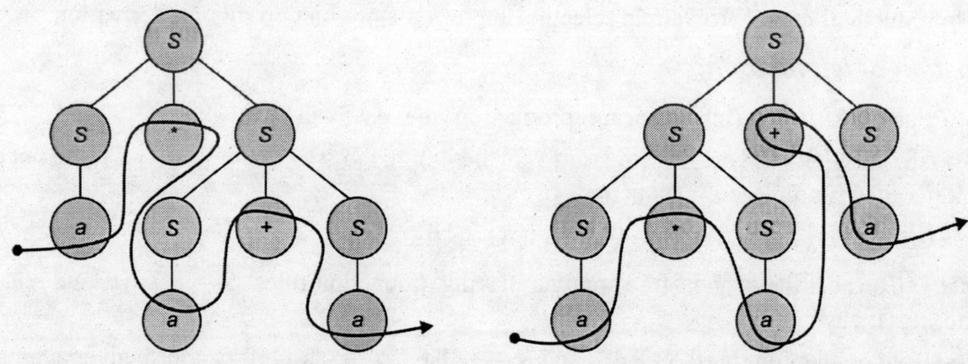

Fig. 6.3(a): Parse tree for $a*a + a$

Fig. 6.3(b): Parse tree for $a*a + a$

6.1.4 Left Recursion

A production rule of the grammar $G = (V_n, \Sigma, P, S)$ is said to be left recursive if it is of the form $A \to Aa$, where A is a variable and $a \in (V_n \cup \Sigma)^*$. For example, production rules $S \to Sa$, $A \to Aaa$, $S \to S^*S$ are left recursive. Sometimes left recursive production rules lead to the ambiguous grammar. We will see later on how left recursive production rules make a grammar ambiguous.

Elimination of left recursion

Let the variable A has left recursive productions as follows:

$A \to A\alpha_1 | A\alpha_2 | A\alpha_3 | \ldots | A\alpha_n | \beta_1 | \beta_2 | \beta_3 | \ldots | \beta_m$, where $\beta_1, \beta_2, \beta_3, \ldots, \beta_m$ do not begin with A, then we replace A-productions by following production rules:

$A \to \beta_1 A' | \beta_2 A' | \ldots | \beta_m A'$, **where** $A' \to \alpha_1 A' | \alpha_2 A' | \alpha_3 A' | \ldots. | \alpha_n A' | \varepsilon$

Example 1: consider the production rules of a context-free grammar (CFG) G: $E \to E + T | T$, $T \to T^*F | F$, $F \to id$, where $\boldsymbol{E}$ is the starting symbol and $\boldsymbol{id}$ is the only terminal. Remove the left recursion (if any).

Solution: Recursive production rules are:

$$E \to E + T, T \to T^*F$$

Eliminating left recursion

Production rule: $\boldsymbol{E \to E + T}$ can be replaced by: $\boldsymbol{E \to TE'}$, where $\boldsymbol{E' \to +TE'} | \varepsilon$

Production rule: $\boldsymbol{T \to T^*F}$ can be replaced by: $\boldsymbol{T \to FT'}$, where $\boldsymbol{T' \to *FT'} | \varepsilon$

So, production rules of G without left recursion are: $E \to TE'$, $E' \to +TE' | \varepsilon$, $T \to FT'$, $T' \to *FT' | \varepsilon$, $F \to id$

6.1.5 Left Factoring

Two or more production rules of a variable $\boldsymbol{A}$ of the grammar $G = (V_n, \Sigma, P, S)$ are said to have left factoring if A-productions are of the form $A \to \alpha\beta_1 | \alpha\beta_2 | \ldots | ab_n$, where $\beta_i \in (V_n \cup \Sigma)^*$ and does not start (prefix) with α. All these A-productions have common left factor, that is, α and this is why these production rules are called left factoring. Left factoring production rules are not healthy for derivation because these provide multiple options for a variable to be replaced. In other words, the common factor (α) in A-productions create problem in selecting appropriate production rule for derivation.

Elimination of left factoring

Let the variable $A \in V_n$ has (left factoring) production rules as given follows:

$A \to \alpha\beta_1 | \alpha\beta_2 | \beta_3 | \ldots | \alpha\beta_n | \gamma_1 | \gamma_2 | \ldots. | \gamma_m$, where $\beta_1, \beta_2, \beta_3, \ldots, \beta_n$ and $\gamma_1, \gamma_2, \ldots, \gamma_m$ do not contain α as a prefix then we replace A-productions by:

$A \to \alpha A' | \gamma_1 | \gamma_2 | \ldots. | \gamma_m$, where $A' \to \beta_1 | \beta_2 | \ldots | \beta_n$

Example 1: Consider the context-free grammar having production rules: $S \to aSa | aa$ and remove the left factoring (if any).

Solution: Both production rules: $S \to aSa$ and $S \to aa$ have $\alpha = a$ as a left factor, so given grammar has left factoring. We have, left (common) factor $\boldsymbol{\alpha = a}$, $\boldsymbol{\beta_1 = Sa}$, **and** $\boldsymbol{\beta_2 = a}$.

After removing the left factor, we get the production rules: $S \rightarrow aS', S' \rightarrow Sa \mid a$.

The problem associated with left factoring grammars is **backtracking**. We find a as a prefix in right-hand side in many ways and a string having a as a prefix can create problem. In worst condition, to get appropriate remaining part of the string we have to search the entire production list. What we do, we take the first production if it is not suitable then take second production then third and so on. This situation is known as **backtracking**. This problem is well known in compiler designing. We ensure the absence of left factoring production rules in a context-free grammar before using in lexical analysis (compiler design). **For example**, consider the above *S*-productions $S \rightarrow aSa \mid aa$ and a string $w = aa$. Both production rules look suitable if we consider the first symbol of the string. But, if we consider the next symbol in the string, that is '*a*', then only first production rule is suitable, not the second rule. Let us see how string *w* is derived:

Iteration first	Iteration second
$S \Rightarrow aSa$	$S \Rightarrow aa = w$
$\Rightarrow aaaa \neq w$	

So, if we follow the iteration first, then we cannot get the string w and will have to select the second iteration. This problem is known as backtracking. In backtracking, we proceed further and do not get the desired string then come to previous step and try the next production rule. One thing is clear here that if we look at one symbol in the string then we face problem in selecting the appropriate production rule but when two symbols are considered then there is no problem. This is due to the length of the left factor, which is one. So, this is concluded that if we look $n + 1$ symbols in the string, where n is length of the left factor, we do not face backtracking problem even there is left factoring in the grammar.

6.1.6 Removal of Ambiguity

We have no specific rule or method defined for removing ambiguity as we have for left recursion and left factoring. So, we will have to concentrate on heuristic approach most of the time. Let us consider the production rules of an ambiguous grammar: $S \rightarrow S{+}S \mid S{*}S \mid a \mid b$. If we analyze the production rules then we find that two production rules are left recursive. So, first we try to remove the left recursion:

$S \rightarrow S + S$ and $S \rightarrow S{*}S$ are replaced by $S \rightarrow aS' \mid bS' \mid, S' \rightarrow +SS' \mid {*}SS' \mid \varepsilon$

Now, we check the derivation for string $w = a{*}a + a$ and we have only one leftmost derivation given below:

$$S \Rightarrow aS' \Rightarrow a{*}SS' \Rightarrow a{*}aS'S' \Rightarrow a{*}a + SS'S' \Rightarrow a{*}a + aS'S'S'$$

$$\Rightarrow a{*}a + a\varepsilon S'S' \Rightarrow a{*}a + a\varepsilon S' \Rightarrow a{*}a + a\varepsilon \qquad (\equiv a{*}a + a)$$

So, *we see that removal of left recursion helps in removal of ambiguity in the ambiguous grammars*. We also conclude that proving a context-free grammar ambiguous is dependent upon the selection of a string, which has two distinct leftmost derivations or two distinct parse trees and selection of such string is totally heuristic; we have to be dependent on hit and trial method. Can we find such string for a given grammar? Yes, we can, but it is uncertain; sometime it can be found, sometime not because we have no straightforward procedure to search such string. This type of problem is known as *undecidable problem*. We will discuss this in Chapter 10.

Now, consider another ambiguous grammar G: $S \rightarrow aSb \mid aabS \mid \varepsilon$. We can see that the grammar G has fact factoring (left factor $\alpha = a$). Let us remove the left factoring from G and see whether G is still ambiguous or not. The production rules of G without left factoring is: $S \rightarrow aS' \mid \varepsilon$, $S' \rightarrow Sb \mid abS$

Consider the ambiguous string $w = aaabb$, now it has only one leftmost derivation given below:

$$
\begin{aligned}
S &\underset{L}{\Rightarrow} aS' && \text{(Using } S \rightarrow aS'\text{)} \\
&\underset{L}{\Rightarrow} aSb && \text{(Using } S' \rightarrow Sb\text{)} \\
&\underset{L}{\Rightarrow} aaS'b && \text{(Using } S \rightarrow aS'\text{)} \\
&\underset{L}{\Rightarrow} aaabSb && \text{(Using } S' \rightarrow abS\text{)} \\
&\underset{L}{\Rightarrow} aaabb && \text{(Using } S \rightarrow \varepsilon\text{)}
\end{aligned}
$$

Similarly, we can see for other ambiguous strings also. We can conclude here that the removal of left factoring from the ambiguous grammar helps in removing the ambiguity from the grammar. In general, we conclude that removal of left recursion and left factoring helps in removing the ambiguity from the ambiguous grammars. Let us see some more examples given below:

Example 1: Remove the ambiguity from the grammar: $S \rightarrow SS \mid a \mid b$.

Solution: The given grammar has left recursion in production $S \rightarrow SS$. So, removing left recursion from the grammar, we get: $S \rightarrow aS' \mid bS'$, $S' \rightarrow SS' \mid \varepsilon$

Consider the ambiguous string $w = aaa$, now it has only one leftmost derivation given below:

$$
\begin{aligned}
S &\underset{L}{\Rightarrow} aS' && \text{(Using } S \rightarrow aS\text{)} \\
&\underset{L}{\Rightarrow} SS' && \text{(Using } S' \rightarrow SS'\text{)} \\
&\underset{L}{\Rightarrow} aaS'S' && \text{(Using } S \rightarrow aS'\text{)} \\
&\underset{L}{\Rightarrow} aaSS'S' && \text{(Using } S' \rightarrow SS'\text{)} \\
&\underset{L}{\Rightarrow} aaaS'S'S' && \text{(Using } S \rightarrow aS'\text{)} \\
&\underset{L}{\Rightarrow} aaa && \text{(Using } S' \rightarrow \varepsilon \text{ three times)}
\end{aligned}
$$

Example 2: Remove the ambiguity from the grammar $G = \{S \rightarrow ASb \mid AS \mid \varepsilon, A \rightarrow aA \mid \varepsilon\}$.

Solution: The given grammar has left recursion, so let us remove the it from the grammar, we have the simplified grammar: $S \rightarrow AB \mid \varepsilon$, $B \rightarrow Sb \mid S$, $A \rightarrow aA \mid \varepsilon$. Now, variable B has left factoring and let us remove it, we have:

$$S \rightarrow AB \mid \varepsilon,\ B \rightarrow SD,\ A \rightarrow aA \mid \varepsilon,\ D \rightarrow b \mid \varepsilon$$

Consider an ambiguous string $w = b$ and let us see the leftmost derivation using the simplified grammar: $S \Rightarrow AB \Rightarrow \varepsilon B \Rightarrow SD \Rightarrow \varepsilon D \Rightarrow b$

6.2 SIMPLIFICATIONS OF CONTEXT-FREE GRAMMARS (CFGs)

We will discuss how to remove null productions, unit productions, and useless symbols from a grammar and how to find equivalent grammar for a given grammar if original grammar is simplified. We will consider the removal of left recursion and left factoring in simplification of grammar.

6.2.1 How to Remove of Null Productions

We have already seen the recursive production rules. Now, let us see what null production is. A production rule $A \rightarrow \varepsilon$ is called a **null production**, where A is a variable and variable B having production such that $B \overset{*}{\Longrightarrow} \varepsilon$ is called **nullable variable.** There may be one or more production rules that help B in producing null string. Suppose, a grammar G has null production(s) and $L(G) = \{\varepsilon\} + L(G')$ then there exists a simplified grammar G', which derives: $L(G') = L(G) - \{\varepsilon\}$ and G' has no null production rule.

Removing null production(s)

We will discuss two versions of null production removal method. The first seems, at first sight, to be correct but it has a serious flaw, which is corrected in the second version.

Proof (Version 1)

Consider a context-free grammar $G = (V_n, \Sigma, P, S)$, containing a null production of the form $X \rightarrow \varepsilon$, where X is any non-terminal. We perform the following transformation in order to remove null production $N \rightarrow \varepsilon$:

For all productions of the form: $X \rightarrow aNb$, where N is any non-terminal and a and b are terminals, then

(a) **Add** the production $X \rightarrow ab$, and

(*b*) **Delete** the production $N \rightarrow \varepsilon$, but **do not delete** the production $X \rightarrow aNb$

Example 1: Consider the following production rules and remove null production(s). $S \rightarrow aNbNa$, $N \rightarrow \varepsilon$.

Solution: We have one null production rule: $N \rightarrow \varepsilon$ and variable N appears in S-production $S \rightarrow aNbNa$. Let us delete occurrence of N, one occurrence at a time and then both the occurrences:

$S \rightarrow abNa$ (Deleting first occurrence of N)

$S \rightarrow aNba$ (Deleting second occurrence of N)

$S \rightarrow aba$ (Deleting both occurrences of N)

So, we have productions: $S \rightarrow aNbNa \mid abNa \mid aNba \mid aba$

Example 2: Consider the following production rules and remove null production(s):

$S \rightarrow aSa | bSb | \varepsilon$

Solution: After deleting the occurrences of S and including original non-null production rules, we have production rules:

$S \rightarrow aSa \mid bSb \mid aa \mid bb$

Example 3: Consider the following production rules and remove the null production(s).

$S \to a \mid Xb \mid aYa, X \to Y \mid \varepsilon, Y \to b \mid X$

Solution: We have only one null production rule: $X \to \varepsilon$. Now, let us delete the occurrence of X in the production rules:

$S \to b$ (From $S \to Xb$), and

$Y \to \varepsilon$ (From $Y \to X$, Null production)

Now, consider the null production rule: $Y \to \varepsilon$ and let us remove it, we get

$S \to aa$ (From $S \to aYa$), and

$X \to \varepsilon$ (From $X \to Y$)

What we find? We could not remove the null production $X \to \varepsilon$. It means, this version of the null-removal method does not work. We need to eliminate *all null production rules at once*. The other version of the above method is given below:

Proof (Version 2: Delete all null production rules)

Consider the null production rule $X \to \varepsilon$ and for every non-null production $Y \to \alpha X\beta$, where $\alpha, \beta \in (V_n + \Sigma)^*$,

(a) **Add** new production rules of the form $Y \to \alpha\beta$ such that $\alpha\beta \neq \varepsilon$.

(b) **Delete** the null production $X \to \varepsilon$.

Example 3 (revisited):

In given production rules: $S \to a \mid Xb \mid aYa, X \to Y \mid \varepsilon, Y \to b \mid X$, when we delete null production rule $X \to \varepsilon \mid$, we have to see what new production rules to be added as given in the following table:

Old null production rules	New non-null production rule to be added
$X \to Y$	No Production Rule
$X \to \varepsilon$	No Production Rule
$Y \to X$	No Production Rule
$S \to Xb$	$S \to b$
$S \to aYa$	$S \to aa$

The transformed context-free grammar (CFG) has production rules:

$S \to a \mid Xb \mid aYa \mid b \mid aa, X \to Y, Y \to b \mid X$

This has no null productions and generates the same language not including null string.

Example 4: Consider a context-free grammar G having production rules: $S \to \varepsilon \mid aSa \mid bSb$, remove the null production rules and find the equivalent grammar G' such that $L(G') = L(G) - \{\varepsilon\}$.

Solution: G has one null production rule, that is, $S \to \varepsilon$. So, replacing occurrences of variable S in right-hand side of production rules by ε, we get following new production rules: $\boldsymbol{S \to a}$ **and** $\boldsymbol{S \to bb}$.

So, collecting the new and old production rules except the null production, we get the simplified grammar G', which production rules are: $S \to aa \mid bb \mid aSa \mid bSb$

Equivalence of G and G':

$$L(G) = \{\varepsilon, aa, bb, abba, \ldots\} = \{ww^R: w \in (a + b)^*\}$$

$$L(G') = \{aa, bb, abba, \ldots\} = L(G) - \{\varepsilon\}$$

So, grammar G' is the desired simplified grammar.

Example 5: Consider a grammar having production rules: $S \rightarrow aS \mid aA \mid \varepsilon, A \rightarrow \varepsilon$ and remove the null production(s) and find the equivalent grammar.

Solution: In given grammar, we have two null production rules: $\boldsymbol{S \rightarrow \varepsilon}$**, and** $\boldsymbol{A \rightarrow \varepsilon}$

First, let us consider the production rule: $S \rightarrow \varepsilon$. Variable S appears in S-production $S \rightarrow aS$, so replacing S in right-hand side by null, we get new production rule: $S \rightarrow a$. Now, consider the second null production rule: $A \rightarrow \varepsilon$. Variable A appears in right-hand side of S-production $S \rightarrow aA$. So, replacing A by null, we get the new production rule: $S \rightarrow a$. So, removing the two null production rules and collecting new and old productions, we get the simplified grammar whose production rules are: $\boldsymbol{S \rightarrow a \mid aS}$.

Old production rules	New production rule to be added
$S \rightarrow aS$	$S \rightarrow a$
$S \rightarrow \varepsilon$	No production rule
$S \rightarrow aA$	$S \rightarrow a$
$A \rightarrow \varepsilon$	No production rule

The given grammar generates language $L = \{a^n : n \geq 0\}$ and the simplified grammar generates language $L' = \{a^n : n \geq 1\}$.

6.2.2 How to Remove Unit Production

In the previous section, we discussed how to remove null production rules and find the equivalent simplified grammar. Now, let us see what unit production rule is and how we overcome of it. A production rule of the type $\boldsymbol{A \rightarrow B}$, where A, B are variables is called unit production rule. Unit production rules create indirection and result into requirement of extra steps involved in deriving the terminal strings. Let us see example, which illustrates how unit production rules involved in extra steps in production of string. Consider a grammar having production rules: $S \rightarrow aA \mid a, A \rightarrow B, B \rightarrow C, C \rightarrow aS$. It is obvious that we find string **"aS"** in following derivation: $\boldsymbol{S \Rightarrow aA \Rightarrow aB \Rightarrow aC \Rightarrow aaS}$, after two intermediate steps, that is, $\boldsymbol{A \Rightarrow B \Rightarrow C \Rightarrow aS}$. So, we should have production rule: $\boldsymbol{S \rightarrow aS}$, instead of having of production rules: $A \rightarrow B, B \rightarrow C, C \rightarrow aS$, which create indirection.

Let grammar $G = (V_n, \Sigma, P, S)$ has unit production rule(s). We follow the following steps to remove the unit production rule:

Removing Unit Production Rule

Step 1: Collect all the unit production rules.

Step 2: Consider all the variables having unit production rules one by one. Suppose $\boldsymbol{A \Rightarrow A_1 \Rightarrow A_2 \Rightarrow \ldots \Rightarrow A_n \Rightarrow \alpha}$, where $A, A_1, A_2 \ldots A_n$ are variables and $\boldsymbol{\alpha}$ is string over $(V_n + \Sigma)^*$ then remove all A-productions by production rule: $\boldsymbol{A \rightarrow \alpha}$.

Example 1: Consider a grammar having production rules: $S \rightarrow aS \mid bS \mid A \mid B, A \rightarrow a, B \rightarrow b$ and remove the unit production rules (if any).

Solution: We have two unit production rules: $S \rightarrow A$ and $S \rightarrow B$. From variable A and B we get terminals 'a' and 'b' respectively. So, replacing the occurrences of A and B variables in S-productions, we get simplified production rules: $S \rightarrow aSbS \mid a \mid b$. A-production and B-production are removed. The production capability of given grammar and simplified grammar is same because both generate language $L = (a + b)^+$.

6.2.3 Removal of Useless Symbols (Variables and Terminals)

The symbols that cannot be used in derivation due to their unavailability in the production rules or inability in deriving the terminal(s) are known as useless symbols. **For example,** consider the production rules: $\boldsymbol{S \rightarrow aS \mid bS \mid a \mid b, A \rightarrow a, B \rightarrow b}$. Two variables A and B cannot be used because there is no link with S-productions and we cannot reach the variables A and B from the starting symbol S. So, variables A and B are useless and production rules including A, B variables are useless. These useless variables should be removed from the grammar. After removing variables A and B, the simplified production rules are: $\boldsymbol{S \rightarrow aS \mid bS \mid a \mid b}$

Now, let us consider grammar $G = (\{S\}, \{a, b, c\}, \{S \rightarrow aSa \mid bSb \mid a \mid b\}, S)$. Is there any useless symbol? There is no useless variable but there is a useless terminal, that is, $\boldsymbol{c}$. Grammar G generates language $L(G)$ over $(a + b)^*$. This is why terminal c is useless. So, after removing useless symbol 'c', the simplified grammar $G' = (\{S\}, \{a, b\}, \{S \rightarrow aSa \mid bSb \mid a \mid b\}, S)$. We can easily show that both grammars G and G' generate equivalent language.

6.3 NORMAL FORMS

As we have discussed earlier in this chapter that we have no restriction on right-hand side of context-free production rules. So, if we restrict the right-hand side of the production rules in different manner, this results into different normal forms. If G is a context-free grammar (CFG) and production rules of G satisfy certain restrictions then G is said to in a normal form. There are several normal forms depending on restrictions applied. There are two popular and important normal forms:

1. Chomsky Normal Form (**CNF**), and
2. Greibach Normal Form (**GNF**)

6.3.1 Chomsky Normal Form (CNF)

We have two types of production rules in Chomsky normal form (CNF):

<variable> → <terminal> For example, $A \rightarrow a$
<variable> → <variable><variable> For example, $A \rightarrow XY$

For example, grammar $G = (\{S\}, \{a, b, c\}, \{S \rightarrow SA \mid SB \mid c \mid b, A \rightarrow SA \mid a, B \rightarrow SB \mid b\}, S)$ is in Chomsky normal form (CNF).

Theorem 6.1: If a context-free language (CFL) L without ε is generated by a context-free grammar (CFG) G then there exists a context-free grammar G' which also generates L and production rules of G are of types: $A \to a$, and $A \to XY$, where A, X, and Y are variables and 'a' is the terminal i.e., G' is in Chomsky normal form (CNF).

Proof: We will discuss a constructive algorithm to convert all the production rules of G into form: $A \to a$, and $A \to XY$ and these production rules are in G'. We assume that G = (V_n, Σ, P, S) is free from null and unit production rules and $G' = (V_n, \Sigma, P', S)$.

Let $A \to a_1a_2a_3...a_n$ is a production rule of G and a_i for $i = 1, 2... n$ may be a terminal or a variable or combination of both. We construct the production rules of G' as follows:

Case 1: (Right-hand side of A-production has single symbol)

If $A \to \alpha_1$ for $i = 1$ then α_1 must be a terminal, because if it is a variable, then production rule becomes a unit production rule and it is not allowed in G. So, it is already in CNF.

(**Note**: We assume earlier that G has no unit production rule, so $A \to a_1$, where a_1 is a variable is not in G).

Case 2: (Right-hand side of A-production has two or more symbols)

If $A \to \alpha_1\alpha_2\alpha_3...\alpha_n$ is a production rule in G. If α_i is a terminal then replace all α_i by X_i, where X_i is a variable for some $i = 1, 2, 3, ..., n$. Now, the right-hand side symbols of A-production are variables and looks like: $A \to \beta_1\beta_2\beta_3...\beta_n$, where β_i for $i = 1, 2, ..., n$ are variables. Now, consider the new formed A-production: $A \to \beta_1\beta_2\beta_3...\beta_n$

(a) For $A \to \beta_1\beta_2$ for $i = 1, 2$ is in CNF.

(*b*) If $A \to \beta_1\beta_2\beta_3...\beta_n$, where $n > 2$ then replace all $\beta_2\beta_3...\beta_n$ by a new variable Y_1 and now the production rule becomes $A \to \beta_1 Y_1$ which is in CNF. Consider production rule: $Y_1 \to \beta_2\beta_3...\beta_n$, replace $\beta_3\beta_4 ...\beta_n$ by a new variable Y_2, the production rule becomes $Y_1 \to \beta_2 Y_2$ which is in CNF and so on. So, we have following production rules, which are in CNF:

$$A \to \beta_1 Y_1,$$
$$Y_1 \to \beta_2 Y_2,$$
$$Y_2 \to \beta_3 Y_3,$$
$$Y_3 \to \beta_4 Y_4,$$
$$\dots$$
$$Y_{n-2} \to \beta_{n-1}\beta_n$$

Equivalence of Grammars *G* and *G'*

We will use induction method to prove the equivalence of both grammars G and G'. Let w is a string in L and $|w| \geq 1$.

Case 1: If $w = a$, where $a \in \Sigma$, then $S \to a$ is a production rule in both grammars. So, string w is derived by both grammars.

Case 2: Assume that $w = a_1a_2... a_n$, where $a_i \in \Sigma$ for $i = 1, 2, ..., n$ and $n \geq 2$ is generated by both grammars.

Case 3: Let $w = a_1a_2... a_na_{n+1}$, where $a_i \in \Sigma$ for $i = 1, 2, ..., n, n + 1$ and $x = a_1a_2... a_n$

For Grammar *G*:

$$S \underset{L}{\Rightarrow} \alpha_1\alpha_2\alpha_3\ldots\alpha_m \quad (\alpha_i \in (V_n + \Sigma)^+ \text{ for } i = 1, 2, \ldots, n)$$

$$\overset{*}{\underset{G}{\Rightarrow}} xA_i$$

$$\Rightarrow xa_{n+1} \quad (\text{Let } A_i \to a_{n+1} \text{ is a production rule in } G \text{ and also in CNF})$$

So, $w \in L(G)$

For Grammar *G′*:

$$S \Rightarrow \alpha_1 X_j \quad (\text{If } \alpha_1 \text{ is a variable then by constructive proof of } G'.)$$

$$\overset{*}{\Rightarrow} \alpha_1\alpha_2\alpha_3\ldots\alpha_m \quad (\text{By constructive proof of } G')$$

$$\overset{*}{\underset{G}{\Rightarrow}} xA_i \quad (\text{As given in } G)$$

$$\Rightarrow xa_{n+1} \quad (\text{As given in } G\text{: } A_i \to a_{n+1})$$

So, $w \in L(G')$

Thus, it is proved that, $L(G') \subseteq L(G)$. In the same way, we can prove that $L(G) \subseteq L(G')$. Hence, we conclude that the grammars G and G' are equivalent.

Example 1: Consider a context-free grammar G having production rules: $S \to aSa \mid bSb \mid a \mid b$. Convert G it into CNF.

Solution: Grammar G generates language **$L = \{wcw: w \in (a + b)^*$, and $c \in (a + b)\}$**. Let us see which production rules are in CNF and which are not.

$P_1: S \to aSa$ (Not in CNF)

$P_2: S \to bSb$ (Not in CNF)

$P_3: S \to a$ (In CNF)

$P_4: S \to b$ (In CNF)

Consider P_1: Replace the terminal a *by* a new variable A, we get production rule: $S \to ASA$. Now, replace SA by a new variable X_1. So, new production rules: $S \to AX_1$, where $X_1 \to SA$, $A \to a$ are in CNF.

Consider P_2: Replace the terminal b by a new variable B, we get production rule: $S \to BSB$, Now, replace SB by a new variable X_2. So, new production rules: $S \to BX_2$, where $X_2 \to SB$, $B \to b$ are in CNF.

Now, all production rules of grammar G are in CNF, which are:

$S \to AX_1 \mid BX_2 \mid a \mid b$, $A \to a$, $B \to b$, $X_1 \to SA$, $X_2 \to SB$

Verification of language generated:

$$S \Rightarrow AX_1 \Rightarrow ASA \Rightarrow AAX_1A \Rightarrow AASAA \Rightarrow \ldots \Rightarrow A^nSA^n$$

$$S \Rightarrow BX_2 \Rightarrow BSB \Rightarrow BBX_2B \Rightarrow BBSBB \Rightarrow \ldots \Rightarrow B^nSB^n$$

So, $L_1 = \{wcw: w \in (a + b)^*, \text{ and } c \in (a + b)\}$
$= \{a, b, aaa, bbb, aba, bab, aabaa, babba, baaba, \ldots\}$

So, $L(G)$ is equivalent to the language L, the generated by the given grammar G.

One thing is noticeable in the given list of production rules that $S \to a \mid b$. So, why not to use variable S in place of terminals 'a' and 'b'? Let us use variable S to replace terminal 'a' and 'b' as given below and examine the resulting production rules:

$$S \to SSS \mid SSS$$

Now, we have only one S-production $S \to SSS$, which is not in Chomsky normal form. Let us replace SS by variable A, We have

$$S \to SA, \text{ where } A \to SS$$

So, production rules of G in CNF are:

$$S \to a \mid b \mid SA, A \to SS$$

Verification of language generated:

$$S \Rightarrow a$$
$$S \Rightarrow b$$
$$S \Rightarrow SA \Rightarrow SSS$$

From SSS, we can get strings: ***aaa, bbb, aba, bab, aab, bba***

So, $L_2 = \{a, b, aaa, bbb, aba, bab, aab, bba, \ldots\}$

But, strings ***aab, bba*** are not in the language generated by the given grammar G. We can see that all the strings which are in language L are also in L_2. But, why this happened? There are four S-productions given and we have tried to replace right-hand side of the two S-productions by S itself. After placing variable S in place of terminals a and b, resulting S-productions become less restrictive ($S \to SSS$) as compared to the original S-productions ($S \to aSa \mid bSb$). This is why language L_2 has all strings of language L and some other strings. So, it is advisable to not make such replacement as used above when there are other production rules for the replacing variable.

6.3.2 Greibach Normal Form (GNF)

A context-free grammar $G = (V_n, \Sigma, P, S)$ is said to in Greibach normal form (GNF) if its all production rules are of type $A \to a\alpha$, where $\alpha \in V_n^*$ (string of variables including null string) and $a \in \Sigma$. A *grammar in GNF is the* **natural generalization of a regular grammar** *(right-linear)*. We can see the reasons:

- If $\alpha = \varepsilon$, then $|\alpha| = 0$ and A-production becomes $A \to a$, which is type 3 production rule (regular production).
- If $\alpha = B$, where B is a variable in V_n then $|\alpha| = 1$ and A-production $A \to aB$ is type 3 production rule (right-linear).
- If $|\alpha| \geq 2$, then $A \to aB_1B_2\ldots B_n$, where B_i is a variable for $i = 1, 2, 3, \ldots, n$ and n is the length of α.

Advantages of GNF

1. Avoids left recursion.
2. Always has terminal in leftmost position in RHS of each production rule.

3. Helps in selecting the suitable production in derivation of a string.
4. Guarantees derivation length no longer than string length.

Theorem 6.2: Every context-free language L without ε can be generated by grammar, whose production rules are of type $A \rightarrow a\alpha$, where $\alpha \in V_n^*$ and $a \in \Sigma$, in other words, L can be generated by a context-free grammar whose production rules are in Greibach normal form (GNF).

We will discuss a method for converting a context-free grammar into Greibach normal form (GNF). Removal of left recursion plays important role in converting a grammar into Geibach normal form. We have already discussed removal of left recursion. There is no null string in language L mentioned in Theorem 6.2. So, we will see how to remove left recursion without null production rule in simplified grammar. We use removal of left recursion (without null production) as given below:

Let the variable A has left recursive productions as follows:

$A \rightarrow A\alpha_1 \mid A\alpha_2 \mid A\alpha_3 \mid \ldots \mid A\alpha_n \mid \beta_1 \mid \beta_2 \mid \mid \beta_3 \mid \ldots \mid \beta_m$, where $\beta_1, \beta_2, \beta_3, \ldots, \beta_m$ do not begin with A, then we replace A-productions by:

$A \rightarrow \beta_1 A' \mid \beta_2 A' \mid \ldots \mid \beta_m A' \mid \beta_1 \mid \beta_2 \mid \beta_3 \mid \ldots \mid \beta_m$, where

$A' \rightarrow a_1 A' \mid \alpha_2 A' \mid \alpha_3 A' \mid \ldots. \mid \alpha_n A' \mid \alpha_1 \mid \alpha_2 \mid \alpha_3 \mid \ldots. \mid \alpha_n$

Now, let us see how a context-free grammar is converted into Greibach normal form:

Method for Converting a CFGs into GNF

We consider CFG $G = (V_n, \Sigma, P, S)$.

Step 1: Rename all the variables like $A_1, A_2, A_3, \ldots, A_n$

Step 2: Repeat Step 3 and Step 4 for $i = 1, 2, \ldots, n$, where n is number of variables

Step 3: If $A_i \rightarrow a\alpha_1\alpha_2\alpha_3\ldots\alpha_m$, where $a \in \Sigma$, and α_j is a variable or terminal symbol for some
$i = 1, 2, 3, \ldots, n$ and
$j = 1, 2, 3, \ldots, m$

(a) Repeat for $j = 1, 2, \ldots, m$
If α_j is a terminal then replace it by a variable A_{n+1} and add production $A_{n+1} \rightarrow \alpha_j$,

(b) Increment n by one, that is, $n = n + 1$. Consider the next A_i-production and go to step 3.

Step 4: If $A_i \rightarrow \alpha_1\alpha_2\alpha_3\ldots\alpha_m$, where α_1 is a variable, then perform the following:
If α_1 is same as A_i, then remove the left recursion and go to Step 3.
Else replace α_1 by all right-hand side of α_1-productions one by one. Consider the remaining A_i-productions, which are not in GNF and go to Step 3.

Step 5: Exit.

Example 1: Consider the production rules of a context-free grammar: $S \rightarrow S + S \mid S{*}S \mid a \mid b$ and find an equivalent grammar in Greibach normal form (GNF).

Solution: Let G_1 is the equivalent grammar in GNF. Renaming the variable, we have following production rules:

$P_1: S_1 \rightarrow S_1 + S_1$ (Not in GNF)

$P_2: S_1 \rightarrow S_1 * S_1$ (Not in GNF)

$P_3: S_1 \rightarrow a$ (IN GNF)

$P_4: S_1 \rightarrow b$ (IN GNF)

P_1 and P_2 are left recursive production rules, so removing the left recursion, we get following production rules:

$$S_1 \rightarrow aS_2 \mid bS_2 \mid a \mid b, \text{ where}$$
$$S_2 \rightarrow +S_1S_2 \mid * S_1S_2 \mid + S_1 \mid *S_1$$

All the production rules are in GNF, which are:

$$S_1 \rightarrow aS_2 \mid bS_2 \mid a \mid b,\ S_2 \rightarrow +S_1S_2 \mid * S_1S_2 \mid + S_1 \mid *S_1$$

Verification of language generated:

$S_1 \Rightarrow a,$

$S_1 \Rightarrow aS_2 \Rightarrow a + S_1 \Rightarrow a + a,$

$S_1 \Rightarrow aS_2 \Rightarrow a + S_1 \Rightarrow a + b,$

$S_1 \Rightarrow bS_2 \Rightarrow b + S_1 \Rightarrow b + b,$

$S_1 \Rightarrow bS_2 \Rightarrow b + S_1 \Rightarrow b + a,$

$S_1 \Rightarrow aS_2 \Rightarrow a + S_1S_2 \Rightarrow a + aS_2 \Rightarrow \ldots,$

$S_1 \Rightarrow aS_2 \Rightarrow a*S_1S_2 \Rightarrow a*aS_2 \Rightarrow \ldots,$

$S_1 \Rightarrow bS_2 \Rightarrow b + S_1S_2 \Rightarrow b + bS_2 \Rightarrow \ldots,$

$S_1 \Rightarrow bS_2 \Rightarrow b*S_1S_2 \Rightarrow b*bS_2 \Rightarrow \ldots$

$S_1 \Rightarrow b,$

$S_1 \Rightarrow aS_2 \Rightarrow a*S_1 \Rightarrow a*a,$

$S_1 \Rightarrow aS_2 \Rightarrow a+S_1 \Rightarrow a*b,$

$S_1 \Rightarrow bS_2 \Rightarrow b*S_1 \Rightarrow b*b,$

$S_1 \Rightarrow bS_2 \Rightarrow b*S_1 \Rightarrow b*a,$

Therefore, we conclude that production rules in GNF generate the same language, which is generated by given grammar.

Now, let us see one simple heuristic method. Suppose terminal symbols +, * are produced by variable S_2 and replace the terminals +, and * by S_2.

$P_{11}: S_1 \rightarrow S_1S_2S_1$ (Not in GNF)

$P_{22}: S_1 \rightarrow S_1S_2 S_1$ (Not in GNF)

$P_5: \mathbf{S_2} \rightarrow + \mid *$ (In GNF)

Production rules P_{11} and P_{22} are same, so we select one of these. We know that we have two terminal substitutions for variable S_1, that are, *a* and b. So, replacing the leftmost S_1 by *a* and *b*, we have following production rules:

$P_{11}: S_1 \rightarrow aS_2S_1$ (In GNF)

$P_{12}: S_1 \rightarrow bS_2S_1$ (In GNF)

Now, production rules in Greibach normal form (GNF) are:

$$P_{11}: S_1 \rightarrow aS_2S_1,\ P_{12}: S_1 \rightarrow bS_2S_1,\ P_3: S_1 \rightarrow a,\ P_4: S_1 \rightarrow b,\ P_5: S_2 \rightarrow + \mid *$$

Verification of language generated:

$S_1 \Rightarrow a,$

$S_1 \Rightarrow aS_2S_1 \Rightarrow a + S_1 \Rightarrow a + a,$

$S_1 \Rightarrow b,$

$S_1 \Rightarrow aS_2S_1 \Rightarrow a*S_1 \Rightarrow a*a,$

$S_1 \Rightarrow aS_2S_1 \Rightarrow a + S_1 \Rightarrow a + b,$ $S_1 \Rightarrow aS_2S_1 \Rightarrow a*S_1 \Rightarrow a*b,$

$S_1 \Rightarrow bS_2S_1 \Rightarrow b + S_1 \Rightarrow b + b,$ $S_1 \Rightarrow bS_2S_1 \Rightarrow b*S_1 \Rightarrow b*b,$

$S_1 \Rightarrow bS_2S_1 \Rightarrow b + S_1 \Rightarrow b + a,$ $S_1 \Rightarrow bS_2S_1 \Rightarrow b*S_1 \Rightarrow b*a,$

$S_1 \Rightarrow aS_2S_1 \Rightarrow aS_2aS_2S_1 \Rightarrow \ldots,$

$S_1 \Rightarrow bS_2S_1 \Rightarrow bS_2bS_2S_1 \Rightarrow \ldots,$

Now, we can conclude that above production rules generated the same language, which is generated by the given grammar.

Example 2: Consider the grammar $G = (\{A_1, A_2, A_3\}, \{a, b\}, P, A_1)$, where P consists of $A_1 \to A_2A_3$, $A_2 \to A_3A_1 \mid b$, $A_3 \to A_1A_2 \mid a$.

Convert G into Greibach normal form (GNF).

Solution: We have three variables $\{A_1, A_2, A_3\}$, so, renaming of variables is not required. Let us see consider all production rules one by one.

Consider A_1-productions:

$A_1 \to A_2A_3$ (Not in GNF)

Replacing variable A_2 by its right-hand side, we get

$\mathbf{A_1 \to bA_3}$ (In GNF)

$A_1 \to A_3A_1A_3$ (Not in GNF)

Now, consider $A_1 \to A_3A_1A_3$, and replacing variable A_3, we get

$\mathbf{A_1 \to aA_1A_3}$ (In GNF)

$A_1 \to A_1A_2\,A_1A_3$ (Not in GNF)

Now, consider production rule: $A_1 \to A_1A_2A_1A_3$ and after removing left recursion, we get production rules:

$\mathbf{A_1 \to bA_3A_4 \mid bA_3}$ (In GNF)

$\mathbf{A_1 \to aA_1A_3A_4 \mid aA_1A_3}$ (In GNF),

Where $A_4 \to A_2A_1A_3A_4 \mid A_2A_1A_3$

A_4 is a new variable and A_4-production is not in GNF. Now all A_1-productions are in GNF.

Consider A_2-productions:

$\mathbf{A_2 \to b}$ (In GNF)

$A_2 \to A_3A_1$ (Not in GNF)

Now, consider $A_2 \to A_3A_1$ and after replacing variable A_3 by its right-hand side, we get following production rules:

$\mathbf{A_2 \to aA_1}$ (In GNF)

$A_2 \to A_1A_2A_1$ (Not in GNF)

Now, consider $A_2 \to A_1A_2A_1$ and after replacing variable A_1 by its right-hand side, we get following production rules:

$A_2 \to bA_3A_4A_2A_1,$ (In GNF)

$A_2 \rightarrow bA_3A_2A_1$, (In GNF)

$A_2 \rightarrow aA_1A_3A_4A_2A_1$, (In GNF)

$A_2 \rightarrow aA_1A_3A_2A_1$ (In GNF)

So, all A_2-productions are in GNF.

Consider A_3-productions:

$A_3 \rightarrow a$ (In GNF)

$A_3 \rightarrow A_1A_2$ (Not in GNF)

Now, consider $A_3 \rightarrow A_1A_2$ and after replacing variable A_1 by its right-hand side, we get following production rules:

$$A_3 \rightarrow bA_3A_4A_2 \mid bA_3A_2 \mid aA_1A_3A_4A_2 \mid aA_1A_3A_2$$

(In GNF)

Consider A_4-productions:

$A_4 \rightarrow A_2A_1A_3A_4 \mid A_2A_1A_3$ (Not in GNF)

Replacing variable A_2 by its right-hand side, we get following production rules:

$A_4 \rightarrow bA_1A_3A_4 \mid bA_1A_3 \mid aA_1A_1A_3A_4 \mid aA_1A_1A_3$,

$A_4 \rightarrow bA_3A_4A_2A_1A_1A_3A_4$,

$A_4 \rightarrow bA_3A_4A_2A_1A_1A_3$,

$A_4 \rightarrow bA_3A_2A_1A_1A_3A_4$,

$A_4 \rightarrow bA_3A_2A_1A_1A_3$,

$A_4 \rightarrow aA_1A_3A_4A_2A_1A_1A_3A_4$,

$A_4 \rightarrow aA_1A_3A_4A_2A_1A_1A_3$,

$A_4 \rightarrow aA_1A_3A_2A_1A_1A_3A_4$, and

$A_4 \rightarrow aA_1A_3A_2A_1A_1A_3$

Now, all A_4-productions are in GNF.

Production rules of grammar G in GNF are:

$A_1 \rightarrow aA_1A_3 \mid bA_3A_4 \mid bA_3 \mid aA_1A_3A_4 \mid aA_1A_3$,

$A_2 \rightarrow b \mid aA_1 \mid bA_3A_4A_2A_1 \mid bA_3A_2A_1 \mid aA_1A_3A_4A_2A_1 \mid aA_1A_3A_2A_1$,

$A_3 \rightarrow a \mid bA_3A_4\ A_2 \mid bA_3A_2 \mid aA_1A_3A_4A_2 \mid aA_1A_3A_2$,

$A_4 \rightarrow bA_1A_3A_4 \mid bA_1A_3 \mid aA_1A_1A_3A_4 \mid aA_1A_1A_3 \mid bA_3A_4A_2A_1A_1A_3A_4$,

$A_4 \rightarrow bA_3A_2A_1A_1A_3A_4 \mid aA_1A_3A_4A_2A_1A_1A_3A_4 \mid aA_1A_3A_2A_1A_1A_3A_4$,

$A_4 \rightarrow bA_3A_4A_2A_1A_1A_3 \mid bA_3A_2A_1A_1A_3 \mid aA_1A_3A_4A_2A_1A_1A_3 \mid aA_1A_3A_2A_1A_1A_3$

6.4 DECISION ALGORITHMS FOR CONTEXT-FREE LANGUAGES

Here we will discuss some decision algorithms for context-free languages (CFLs). These decision algorithms are used to determine emptiness, and finiteness of a context-free language and membership of a given string with some context-free language.

Theorem 6.3: There are algorithms to determine following for a context-free language (CFL) L:

(a) Empty: Is there any word in L? This is the question of emptiness.

(b) Finite: Is L finite? This is the question of finiteness.

(c) Infinite: Is L infinite? This is another question of finiteness.

(d) Membership: For a given string w, is $w \in L$? This is the question of membership.

Proof:

(a) Emptiness: Let context-free grammar $G = (V_n, \Sigma, P, S)$ generates L. We convert this grammar into Chomsky normal form (CNF) and let the new grammar in CNF is $G_1 = (V_{n1}, \Sigma, P_1, S)$ such that: $L(G_1) = L(G) - \{\varepsilon\} = L - \{\varepsilon\}$. We follow the following steps to decide the emptiness of language L.

Consider the S-productions of grammar G_1:

Step 1: If $S \Rightarrow a$, where $a \in \Sigma$, then $a \in L(G_1)$, and so $a \in L$. Thus, L is nonempty; otherwise go the Step 2.

Step 2: If $S \overset{*}{\Longrightarrow} \alpha_1 \alpha_2 \alpha_3 \ldots \alpha_n$, where α_i is a variable for $i = 1, 2, \ldots, n$, then replace all variables by possible terminal(s). Now, if $S \overset{*}{\Longrightarrow} a_1 a_2 \ldots a_m$, where $\boldsymbol{a_1, a_2, \ldots, a_m}$ are terminals, so $L(\mathrm{G}_1)$ is nonempty and hence L is nonempty, otherwise L is empty.

(b) & (c) Finiteness: Let $G = (V_n, \Sigma, P, S)$ be a context-free grammar for L. Let us convert this grammar into CNF and let the new grammar in CNF is $G_1 = (V_{n1}, \Sigma, P_1, S)$ such that:

$$L(G_1) = L(G) - \{\varepsilon\} = L - \{\varepsilon\}$$

We draw a directed graph with a vertex for each variable. An edge from vertex A to vertex B is there if and only if we have production rule: $A \to Ba$ or $A \to aB$, where $\in V_{n1}$ and $a \in \Sigma$. $L(G_1)$ is finite if and only if the graph has no cycles and so language L. We define the **rank** of a variable A to be the length of the longest path in graph beginning at A. *Absence of cycle implies that the rank of A is finite*. If cycle is there then rank is infinite. It also shows that if a grammar has recursive production rule(s) then language generated is infinite otherwise finite.

(d) Membership: (The **CYK algorithm**): CYK algorithm is suggested by John **C**ocke and subsequently published by Daniel H. **Y**ounger and Tadao **K**asami in 1965. The letters C, Y, and K are taken from the names of the inventors.

Let us see how membership of a string with a context-free language is decided. Let $G = (V_n, \Sigma, P, A_1)$ be a CFG for CFL L. We convert this grammar into CNF and let the new grammar in CNF is $G_1 = (V_{n1}, \Sigma, P_1, A_1)$ such that:

$$L(G_1) = L(G) - \{\varepsilon\} = L - \{\varepsilon\}$$

Let $V_{n1} = \{A_1, A_2, \ldots, A_n\}$, $\Sigma = \{a_1, a_2, \ldots, a_m\}$, and w is string over Σ. Consider the all substrings of w. If w_j is a substring of w and $\boldsymbol{A_i \overset{*}{\Longrightarrow} w_j}$, then A_i is the producing variable of w_j, and there may be other variables also that produce w_j. We make a list of such variables as given below:

Length of substrings of *w*	Substrings	Producing variables
One	$a_1, a_2, \ldots$	$A_i, A_j, \ldots$
Two	$a_1a_2, a_2a_3, \ldots$	$A_p, A_q, \ldots$
Three	$a_1a_2a_3, \ldots$	$A_k, \ldots$
...	...	...

Now, consider the final substring of w having the same length as w has and list of producing variables. If starting symbol is there then w is in L, otherwise w is not in L.

Example 1: Consider a context-free grammar (CFG) G whose production rules are $S \to XY$, $X \to AX$, $X \to AA$, $A \to a$, $Y \to BY$, $Y \to BB$, $B \to b$

Check whether $L(G)$ is empty or not.

Solution: $S \Rightarrow XY \Rightarrow AAY \Rightarrow aAY \Rightarrow aaY \Rightarrow aaBB \Rightarrow aabB \Rightarrow aabbb \in L(G)$

So, $L(G)$ is nonempty.

Example 2: Consider the production rules of a grammar: $S \to AB$, $A \to BC \mid a$, $B \to CC \mid b$, $C \to a$, check the finiteness of language generated by this grammar.

Solution: The production rules: $S \to AB$, $A \to BC \mid a$, $B \to CC \mid b$, $C \to a$ are in CNF. The directed graph is shown in Fig. 6.4 for given grammar. Now, consider the ranks of the variables:

Rank(S) = 2 ($S \to B \to C$),

Rank(A) = 1 ($A \to C$),

Rank(B) = 1 ($B \to C$), and

Rank(C) = 0 (No outgoing edge/arch)

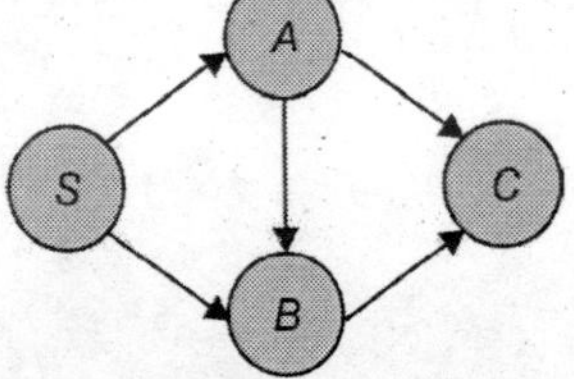

Fig. 6.4: Directed graph

Ranks of variables are finite or we have no cycle. So, language generated by given grammar is finite, that is, grammar has no recursive production rule.

Example 3: Consider a context-free grammar G whose production rules are: $S \to AB \mid BC$, $A \to BA \mid a$, $B \to CC \mid b$, $C \to AB \mid a$, check the membership of string w = ***baaba*** **with** $L(G)$.

Solution: List of all substrings of w is listed below:

Length	Substring	Producing variable(s)	
1	*b*	*B*	($B \Rightarrow b$)
	a	*C*, *A*	($A \Rightarrow a$, $C \Rightarrow a$)
2	*ba*	*S*, *A*	($S \Rightarrow BC \Rightarrow bC \Rightarrow ba$, $A \Rightarrow BA \Rightarrow bA \Rightarrow ba$)
	aa	*B*	($B \Rightarrow CC \Rightarrow aC \Rightarrow aa$)
	ab	*S*, *C*	($S \Rightarrow AB \Rightarrow aB \Rightarrow ab$, $C \Rightarrow AB \Rightarrow aB \Rightarrow ab$)
	ba	*S*, *A*	($S \Rightarrow BC \Rightarrow bC \Rightarrow ba$, $A \Rightarrow BA \Rightarrow bA \Rightarrow ba$)
3	*baa*	ϕ	(No variable leads to "*baa*")
	aab	*B*	($B \Rightarrow CC \Rightarrow aC \Rightarrow aAB \Rightarrow aaB \Rightarrow aab$,
	aba	*B*	($B \Rightarrow CC \Rightarrow ABC \Rightarrow aBC \Rightarrow abC \Rightarrow aba$)

4	*baab*	ϕ	(No variable leads to "*baab*")
	aaba	*S, A, C*	($S \Rightarrow AB \Rightarrow aB \Rightarrow aCC \Rightarrow aABC \Rightarrow aaBC$ $\Rightarrow aabC \Rightarrow aaba$, $A \Rightarrow BA \Rightarrow CCA \Rightarrow aCA$ $\Rightarrow aABA \Rightarrow aaBA \Rightarrow aabA \Rightarrow aaba$, $C \Rightarrow AB \Rightarrow aB \Rightarrow aCC \Rightarrow aABC \Rightarrow aaBC$ $\Rightarrow aabC \Rightarrow aaba$)
5	*baaba*	*S, A, C*	($S \Rightarrow AB \Rightarrow BAB \Rightarrow bAB \Rightarrow baB \Rightarrow baCC$ $\Rightarrow baABC \Rightarrow baaBC \Rightarrow baabC \Rightarrow baaba$, $A \Rightarrow BA \Rightarrow bA \Rightarrow bBA \Rightarrow bCCA \Rightarrow baCA$ $\Rightarrow baABA \Rightarrow baaBA \Rightarrow baabA \Rightarrow baaba$, $C \Rightarrow AB \Rightarrow BAB \Rightarrow bAB \Rightarrow baB \Rightarrow baCC$ $\Rightarrow baABC \Rightarrow baaBC \Rightarrow baabC \Rightarrow baaba$)

Final substring "*baaba*" is produced by variables *S*, *A*, and *C*. So, in final list of variables, we have starting symbol *S*, so $w = baaba \in L(\boldsymbol{G})$.

We tabularize the above decision steps as following:

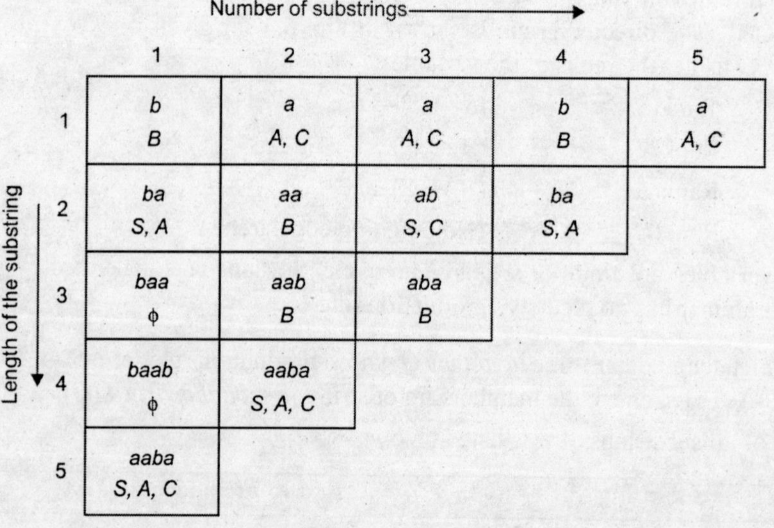

6.5 PUMPING LEMMA FOR CONTEXT-FREE LANGUAGES

We have discussed Pumping Lemma for regular languages (sets) in the previous chapter which states that every sufficiently long string in a regular set contains a short substring that can be pumped many times as we like and the result is a string in the same regular set. The pumping lemma for context-free languages (CFLs) states for every sufficiently long string in a context-free language, there are always two short substrings close together that can be pumped same number of times and the result is a string in the same context-free language.

Lemma 6.1 (For context-free Languages)

Let L be a context-free language and a long string z is in L then there exists a constant n such that $|z| \geq n$ and z can be written as ***uvwxy*** and

(i) $|vx| \geq 1$

(ii) $|vwx| \leq n$, and

(iii) uv^iwx^iy is in L for $i = 0, 1, 2, \ldots$

Proof: Let G is a context-free grammar in Chomsky normal form (CNF) and generates L-{ε}. Since, string z is a long string, so parse tree for z must contain a long path. Suppose the longest path in parse tree for string z has length $\boldsymbol{h}$. In the parse tree no string can be greater than the length $\mathbf{2^{h-1}}$ or in other words, the maximum length word would of length 2^{h-1}. Now, let us see how this happens.

Since, the grammar G is in CNF (that is, production rules are of types $A \rightarrow a$ or $A \rightarrow XY$, where a is terminal and X, Y are variables), so parse tree for z is a binary tree. The parse tree yields longest word if and only if its all levels, except the last level, contain two children as shown in Fig. 6.5.

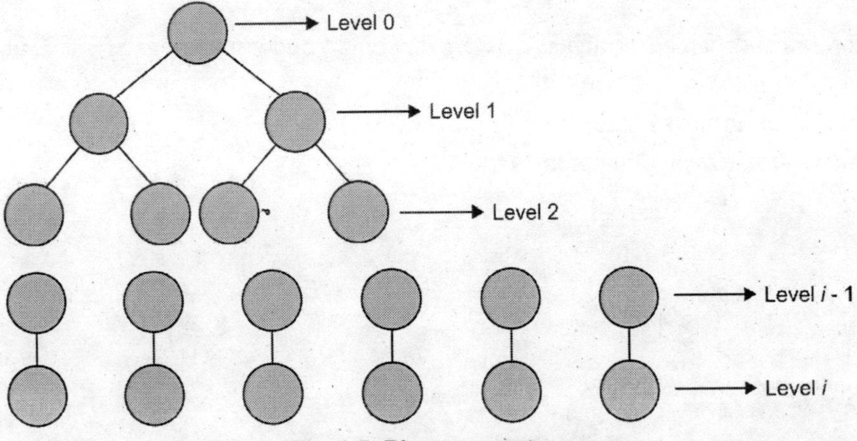

Fig. 6.5: Binary parse tree

The number of leaves in the parse tree is the length of longest string and it is equal to the number of nodes at level ***i*-1** as shown in Fig. 6.5.

The number of nodes at level $i - 1 = 2^{i-1}$

So, the longest word has the length 2^{h-1}, where h is the longest path length. In other words, we say that no word can be greater than $\mathbf{2^{h-1}}$.

Let grammar G has $\boldsymbol{k}$ variables and $\boldsymbol{n = 2^k}$. If z is in $L(G)$ and $|z| \geq 2^k$. So, the longest path in the parse tree for string z has length greater than equal to $\boldsymbol{k+1}$ and this path contains $\boldsymbol{k+2}$ vertices ($k+1$ internal vertices and one leaf labeled terminal). Since, all the vertices (up to $k+1$ label) except the terminal (label $k+2$) are variables, so the longest path contains $\boldsymbol{k+1}$ variables. It means, one variable appears twice in the longest path for string z. Let variable A appears twice, so $A \overset{*}{\underset{G}{\Rightarrow}} z_3 Az_4 \overset{*}{\underset{G}{\Rightarrow}} (z_3)^i A(z_4)^i$, where z_3 and z_4 are two substrings of string z. Let $A \overset{*}{\underset{G}{\Rightarrow}} z_2$, then $A \overset{*}{\underset{G}{\Rightarrow}} (z_3)^i z_2(z_4)^i$ and say z_3 and z_4 can be pumped same number of times as we like.

Now, consider production rules of a context-free grammar: $S \to SS \mid a$ and string $z = aaaa$. The parse tree for z is shown in Fig. 6.6(a). Consider the subtree shown in Fig. 6.6(b), we have:

$$S \Rightarrow SS \Rightarrow aS \Rightarrow aSS \Rightarrow aaS \equiv \boldsymbol{aaS\varepsilon}$$

So, we can write, $S \overset{*}{\Rightarrow} z_3Sz_4$, where $z_3 = aa$ and $z_4 = \varepsilon$. Now, consider the subtree shown in Fig. 6.6(c), we have:

$$S \Rightarrow a$$

So, we can write, $S \overset{*}{\Rightarrow} z_2$

The subtree shown in Fig. 6.6(b) can be added many times as we like in the parse tree for string z shown in Fig. 6.6(a). So, $S \overset{*}{\Rightarrow} z_3^i\, Sz_4^i \overset{*}{\Rightarrow} z_3^i z_2 z_4^i$

Therefore, string z can be written as $uz_3z_2z_4y$ for some u and y substrings of z and substrings z_3 and z_4 can be pumped many times as we like. Replacing z_3, z_2 and z_4 by v, w and x respectively we get, $z = uvwxy$ and $S \overset{*}{\Rightarrow} \boldsymbol{uv^iwx^iy}$ for some $i = 0, 1, 2, \ldots, n$

Therefore, the statement of theorem is true.

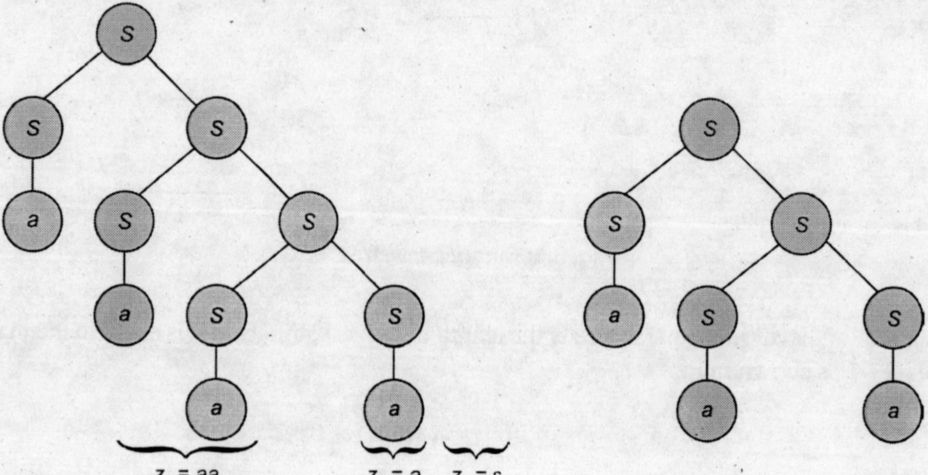

Fig. 6.6(a): Parse tree for z = *aaaa*

Fig. 6.6(b): Parse tree for "*aaa*"

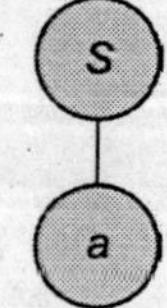

Fig. 6.6(c): Parse tree for "*a*"

Application of pumping lemma for CFLs

We use the Pumping Lemma to prove certain languages are not context-free language. We proceed as we have seen in application of Pumping Lemma for regular sets and get contradiction. *The result of this lemma is always negative.*

Example 1: Consider the language $L = \{a^n b^n c^n : n \geq 1\}$ and prove that L is not context-free language (CFL).

Proof: All the strings in L contain equal number of a's, b's and c's. Let L is a CFL and z is a long string in L such that $|z| \geq n$. Using Pumping Lemma for L, we write $z = uvwxy$ and uv^iwx^iy is in L for some $i = 0, 1, 2, \ldots$ such that $|vx| \geq 1$ and $|wvx| \leq n$.

The substring vx may be a^p, b^q, c^r, $a^p b^q$, $b^q c^r$ but not $a^p c^r$.

Consider $i = 0$, so uwy is in L.

Case 1: $vx = a^p$, so $z = uwy = a^{n-p} b^n c^n$ is in L.

The number of a's is fewer than the number of b's and c's for $p \geq 1$, which is a contradiction.

Case 2: $vx = b^q$, so $z = uwy = a^n b^{n-q} c^n$ is in L.

The number of b's is fewer than the number of a's and c's for $q \geq 1$, which is a contradiction.

Case 3: $vx = c^r$, so $z = uwy = a^n b^n c^{n-r}$ is in L.

The number of c's is fewer than the number of a's and b's for $r \geq 1$, which is a contradiction.

Case 4: $vx = a^p b^q$, so $z = uwy = a^{n-p} b^{n-q} c^n$ is in L.

The number of a's and b's are fewer than the number of c's for $p, q \geq 1$, which is a contradiction.

Case 5: $vx = b^q c^r$, so $z = uwy = a^n b^{n-q} c^{n-r}$ is in L.

The number of b's and c's are fewer than the number of a's for $q, r \geq 1$, which is a contradiction.

Since, we get contradiction for all values of substring vx, so L is not a context-free language (CFL).

6.6 CLOSURE PROPERTIES OF CONTEXT-FREE LANGUAGES (CFLs)

Context-free languages are closed under following properties:

1. Union
2. Concatenation and
3. Kleene Closure

   (Context-free languages **may** or **may not** close under following properties.)

4. Intersection
5. Complementation

Theorem 6.4: If L_1 and L_2 are two context-free languages then union of L_1 and L_2 denoted by $\boldsymbol{L_1 + L_2}$ or $\boldsymbol{L_1 \cup L_2}$ is also a context-free language. In other words, context-free languages (CFLs) are closed under union operation.

Proof: Let context-free grammar $G_1 = (V_{n1}, \Sigma_1, P_1, S_1)$ generates L_1, context-free grammar $G_2 = (V_{n2}, \Sigma_2, P_2, S_2)$ generates L_2 and grammar $G = (V_n, \Sigma, P, S)$ generates $L = L_1 + L_2$. We construct grammar G as follows:

Step 1: Rename the variables of G_1:

Let $V_{n1} = \{S, A, B, ..., X\}$ then the renamed variables are $\{S_1, A_1, B_1, ..., X_1\}$. This modification should be reflected in production rules also.

Step 2: Rename the variables of G_2:

Let $V_{n2} = \{S, A, B, ..., X\}$ then the renamed variables are: $\{S_2, A_2, B_2, ..., X_2\}$. This modification should be reflected in production rules also.

Step 3: Union of the production rules of G_1 and G_2:

We introduce S-production as: $\boldsymbol{S \rightarrow S_1 \mid S_2}$, where S_1 and S_2 are starting symbols of grammars G_1 and G_2 respectively and S_1-productions and S_2-productions are remain unchanged.

Set of terminals $\Sigma = \Sigma_1 \cup \Sigma_2$, and

Set of variables $V_n = \{S_1, A_1, B_1, ... X_1\} \cup \{S_2, A_2, B_2, ... X_2\} \cup \{S\}$

Since, all production rules of G_1 and G_2 including $S \rightarrow S_1 \mid S_2$ are in context-free form, so grammar G is a context-free grammar (CFG).

Verification of language generated by *G*:

$$L(G) = \text{Language generated from } S_1\text{-productions } \textbf{or } S_2\text{-productions}$$
$$= L(G_1) \text{ or } L(G_2)$$

(Since, S_1 and S_2 are starting symbols of G_1 and G_2 respectively and G_1 produces L_1 and G_2 produces L_2)

$$= L_1 + L_2$$

Hence, statement of the theorem is true.

Example 1: Consider the production rules of context-free grammars $S \rightarrow aSb \mid ab$ and $S \rightarrow cSdd \mid cdd$ which generate languages L_1 and L_2 respectively. Construct grammar for language $L = L_1 + L_2$.

Solution: Let context-free grammar G_1 generates L_1 and context-free grammar G_2 generates L_2 and grammar $G = (V_n, \Sigma, P, S)$ generates $L = L_1 + L_2$.

Renaming the variables of grammars G_1 and G_2, we get

$\boldsymbol{V_{n1} = \{S_1\}}$**, and** $\boldsymbol{V_{n2} = \{S_1\}}$, where S_1-productions are: $\boldsymbol{S_1 \rightarrow aS_1b \mid ab}$, and

S_2-productions are: $\boldsymbol{S_2 \rightarrow cS_2dd \mid cdd}$

We define grammar G as follows:

$\boldsymbol{V_n = \{S, S_1, S_2\}}$, $\Sigma = \{\text{Terminals of } G_1 \text{ or } G_2\} = \{a, b, c, d\}$,

P includes: $S \rightarrow S_1 \mid S_2$, $S_1 \rightarrow aS_1b \mid ab$, and $S_2 \rightarrow cS_2dd \mid cdd$

Language generated by grammar *G*:

$$L(G) = \text{Language generated by } G_1 + \text{Language generated by } G_2$$
$$L = L_1 + L_2$$
$$= \{a^nb^n: m, n \geq 1\} \cup \{c^nd^{2n} : n \geq 1\}$$

Theorem 6.5: If L_1 and L_2 are two context-free languages then concatenation of L_1 and L_2 denoted by $\boldsymbol{L_1L_2}$ is also a context-free language. In other words, context-free languages are closed under concatenation operation.

Proof: Let context-free grammar $G_1 = (V_{n1}, \Sigma_1, P_1, S_1)$ generates language L_1 and context-free language $G_2 = (V_{n2}, \Sigma_2, P_2, S_2)$ generates language L_2 and $G = (V_n, \Sigma, P, S)$ generates L_1L_2. We construct grammar G as follows:

Step 1: Rename the variables of CFG G_1:

Let $V_{n1} = \{S, A, B, ..., P\}$ then the renamed variables are $\{S_1, A_1, B_1, ..., X_1\}$. This modification is reflected in production rules also.

Step 2: Rename the variables of CFG G_2:

Let $V_{n2} = \{S, A, B, ..., X\}$ then the renamed variables are: $\{S_2, A_2, B_2, ..., X_2\}$. This modification is reflected in production rules also.

Step 3: The productions of G_1 are followed by the productions of G_2 to get production rules of grammar G as follows:

$\boldsymbol{S \rightarrow S_1S_2}$, where S_1 and S_2 are starting symbols of grammars G_1 and G_2 respectively and S_1-productions and S_1-productions are remain unchanged.

$\boldsymbol{\Sigma = \Sigma_1 \cup \Sigma_2, V_n = \{S_1, A_1, B_1, ..., X_1\} \cup \{S_2, A_2, B_2, ..., X_2\} \cup \{S\}}$

Since, all production rules of G_1 and G_2 including $S \rightarrow S_1S_2$ are in context-free form, so G is a context-free grammar.

Verification of language generated by *G*:

$L(G)$ = Language generated by G_1 followed by language generated by G_2

$= L(G_1)L(G_2)$ (Since, S_1 and S_2 are starting symbols of G_1 and G_2 respectively.)

$= L_1L_2$ (Since, G_1 produces L_1 and G_2 produces L_2.)

Hence, statement of the theorem is true.

Example 1: Consider the production rules of context-free grammars $S \rightarrow aSb \mid ab$ and $S \rightarrow cSdd \mid cdd$, which generate languages L_1 and L_2 respectively. Construct grammar for language $L = L_1L_2$.

Solution: Let G_1 generates L_1 and G_2 generates L_2 and grammar $G = (V_n, \Sigma, P, S)$ generates $L = L_1L_2$. Renaming the variables of G_1 and G_2, we get

$V_{n1} = \{S_1\}$, and $V_{n2} = \{S_1\}$, where S_1-productions are: $S_1 \rightarrow aS_1b \mid ab$, and S_2-productions are: $S_2 \rightarrow cS_2dd \mid cdd$

We define G as follows:

$V_n = \{S, S_1, S_2\}$, Σ = {Terminals of G_1 or G_2} = $\{a, b, c, d\}$,

P includes: $S \rightarrow S_1S_2$, $S_1 \rightarrow aS_2b \mid ab$, and $S_2 \rightarrow cS_2dd \mid cdd$

Verification of language Generated by *G*:

$L(G)$ = Language generated by G_1 followed by language generated by G_2

$= L_1L_2$

$= \{a^nb^n: m, n \geq 1\}\{c^nd^{2n}: n \geq 1\}$

Theorem 6.6: If L is a context-free language generated by context-free grammar $G = (V_n, \Sigma, P, S)$ then Kleene closure of L denoted by L^* is also a context-free language. In other words, context-free languages are closed under Kleene closure operation.

Proof: Let grammar $G' = (V_n, \Sigma, P', S')$ generates L^*, where L is generated by context-free grammar G. We define grammar G' based on given grammar G.

$L^* = \{\varepsilon, L, LL, LLL, \ldots\}$, since language L^* includes null string, so G' has production rule: $S' \to \varepsilon$ and from other production rules, G' has to generate multiple of language L like LL, LLL, etc. So, we have two recursive S'-productions: $S' \to SS' \mid S'S$, where S is the starting symbol of G and terminal production rule is $S' \to \varepsilon$ defined above.

So, $P' = \{S' \to \varepsilon \mid SS' \mid S'S\} \cup \{S\text{-productions of grammar } G\}$

Since, all productions of G' are in context-free form, so G' is a context-free grammar.

Verification of language generated by *G*:

$$L(G') = \{\varepsilon, L, LL, LLL, \ldots\} = L^*$$

Thus, statement of theorem is true.

Example 1: Consider the production rules of a context-free grammar G: $S \to aSa \mid aa$, which generates $L = \{a^{2n}: n \geq 1\}$. Construct a grammar, which generates L^*.

Solution: Let $G' = (V_n, \Sigma, P', S')$ generates language L^*. We define the production rules of G' as follows:

$\boldsymbol{S' \to \varepsilon \mid SS' \mid S'S}$**, where** $\boldsymbol{S \to aSa \mid aa}$

Verification of language generated by *G′*:

We have production: $S \Rightarrow \varepsilon$,

So, null string e is in $L(G')$.

We have production:

$$
\begin{aligned}
S &\Rightarrow S'S && (\text{Using } S' \to S'S)\\
&\Rightarrow S'SS && \ldots\\
&\Rightarrow S'SS\ldots n \text{ times} && (\text{Using } S' \to S'S\ n \text{ times})\\
&\Rightarrow \varepsilon SS\ldots n \text{ times} && (\text{Using } S' \to \varepsilon)\\
&\Rightarrow aaS\ldots && (\text{Using } S \to aa)\\
&\Rightarrow aaaaS\ldots && (\text{Using } S \to aa)\\
&\ldots\\
&\Rightarrow aa\ldots n \text{ times} && (\text{Using } S \to aa,\ n \text{ times})\\
&\equiv (aa)^n \text{ for } n = 1, 2, 3, \ldots
\end{aligned}
$$

So, $$L(G') = \{\varepsilon, aa, aaaa, \ldots\} = L^*$$

Theorem 6.7: If L_1 and L_2 are two context-free languages then intersection of L_1 and L_2 denoted by $\boldsymbol{L_1 \cap L_2}$ may or may not be a context-free language. In other words, context-free languages may or may not be closed under intersection operation.

We will discuss some examples, which show the statement of the theorem true.

Example 1: Consider the context-free languages $L_1 = \{a^n b^n c^m: m, n \geq 1\}$ and $L_2 = \{a^m b^n c^n: m, n \geq 1\}$, then intersection of L_1 and L_2 is not a context-free language.

Proof: Let us express the strings of languages L_1 and L_2.

$$L_1 = \{abc, aabbc, aaabbbc, ...\} \text{ and}$$

$$L_2 = \{abc, abbcc, aabbcc, aabbbbccc, aaabbbccc, ...\}$$

So, $$L_1 \cap L_2 = \{abc, aabbcc, aaabbbccc, ...\}$$

$$= \{a^n b^n c^n : n \geq 1\}$$

So, obviously $L_1 \cap L_2$ is not a context-free language.

(**Note**: Both the languages L_1 and L_2 are non-regular.)

Example 2: Consider the context-free languages $L_1 = \{a^n b^n : n \geq 1\}$ and $L_2 = \{a^p b^q : p, q \geq 1\}$ then intersection of L_1 and L_2 is a context-free language.

Proof: Let us express the strings of languages L_1 and L_2.

$$L_1 = \{ab, aabb, aaabbb, ...\} \text{ and}$$

$$L_2 = \{ab, aab, aabb, abbb, aabbb, ...\}$$

So, $$L_1 \cap L_2 = \{ab, aabb, aaabbb, ...\}$$

$$= \{a^k b^k : k \geq 1\}$$

So, obviously $L_1 \cap L_2$ is a context-free language.

(**Note:** L_1 is CFL and L_2 is regular language. Since, all regular languages are context-free language).

Theorem 6.8: If L is a context-free language over some alphabet Σ then complement of L is denoted by $\Sigma^* - L$ may or may not be a context-free language. In other words, context-free languages may or may not be closed under complement operation.

Proof: We will discuss some mathematical identities to prove this theorem. Let us assume that complement of a context-free language is also context-free language. It means, $\overline{L} = \Sigma^* - L$ is a context-free language.

Let R and S are two context-free languages over Σ then we know that

$$R \cap S = \Sigma^* - (\overline{R} \cup \overline{S}) \qquad \text{(De Morgan's law)}$$

Since, we have assumed that complement of context-free language is context-free language, so $\overline{R}$ and $\overline{S}$ are context-free languages. Let language $P = \overline{R} \cup \overline{S}$ and P is a context-free language (P is union of two CFLs).

So, $$R \cap S = \Sigma^* - P$$

or, $$R \cap S = \overline{P}$$

Since, P is a context-free language and so complement of P, that is, $\overline{P}$ is also context-free language. In other words, $R \cap S$ is a context-free language i.e., intersection of context-free languages R and S is a context-free language. But, according to Theorem 6.7, $R \cap S$ may or may not be a context-free language. So, our assumption about complement of context-free languages is not hundred percent correct.

We know that intersection and complement are interchangeable using De Morgan's law, so whatever the truth about intersection is there, it is also applicable to complement. Therefore, we conclude that complement of a context-free language may or may not be a context-free language.

6.7 SOLVED EXAMPLES

Example 6.1: Find a reduced grammar equivalent to the grammar G whose production rules are:

$S \to AB \mid CA,\ B \to BC \mid AB,\ A \to a,\ C \to aB \mid b.$

Solution: The given grammar G has no null or unit production rule but it has recursive production rules: $B \to BC \mid AB$. We can see that variable B has two recursive production rules but no terminating production i.e. variable B does not derive string of terminals $\{a, b\}$. So, variable B is not useful in any production and it should be removed from the grammar along with its productions rules and the production rules containing B.

The reduced grammar is given below:

$S \to CA,\ A \to a,\ C \to b$

Example 6.2: Consider a grammar G having production rules: $S \to aAS \mid a,\ A \to SbA \mid SS \mid ba$. Show that *Saabbaa* and construct a derivation tree whose yield is *aabbaa*.

Solution: $S \Rightarrow a\boldsymbol{A}S \Rightarrow a\boldsymbol{S}bAS \Rightarrow aab\boldsymbol{A}S \Rightarrow aabba\boldsymbol{S} \Rightarrow aabbaa$

Hence, $\qquad S \overset{*}{\Rightarrow} aabbaa$

Parse tree is shown in Fig. 6.7.

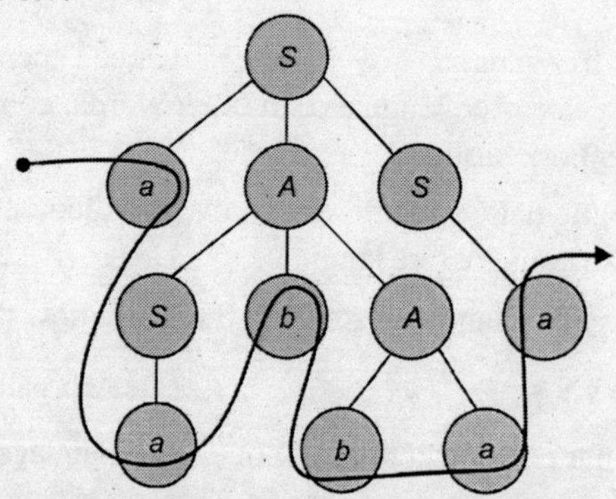

Fig. 6.7: Parse tree yielding *aabbaa*

Example 6.3: Consider a grammar G whose production rules are: $S \to 0B \mid 1A,\ A \to 0 \mid 0S \mid 1AA,\ B \to 1 \mid 1S \mid 0BB$. Find (a) leftmost and (b) rightmost derivation for string 00110101, and construct a derivation tree.

Solution:

(a) Leftmost derivation:

$$S \Rightarrow 0\boldsymbol{B}$$
$$\Rightarrow 00BB$$
$$\Rightarrow 001\boldsymbol{B}$$
$$\Rightarrow 0011S$$
$$\Rightarrow 00110\boldsymbol{B}$$

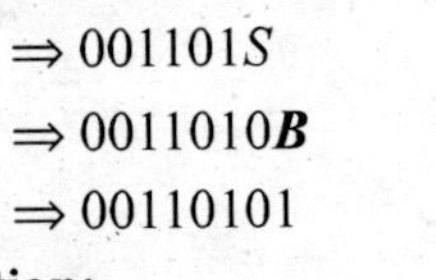

$\Rightarrow 001101S$

$\Rightarrow 0011010\boldsymbol{B}$

$\Rightarrow 00110101$

(b) Rightmost derivation:

$$
\begin{aligned}
S &\Rightarrow 0\boldsymbol{B} \\
&\Rightarrow 00B\boldsymbol{B} \\
&\Rightarrow 00\boldsymbol{B}1 \\
&\Rightarrow 001S1 \\
&\Rightarrow 0011\boldsymbol{A}1 \\
&\Rightarrow 00110S1 \\
&\Rightarrow 001101\boldsymbol{A}1 \\
&\Rightarrow 00110101
\end{aligned}
$$

(c) Derivation tree is shown in Fig. 6.8.

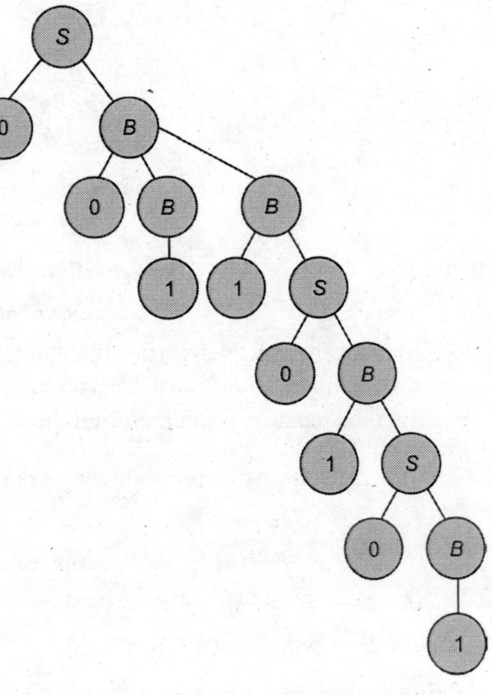

Fig. 6.8: Derivation tree for 00110101

Example 6.4: Consider the parse tree for w = *aaab babbba* shown in Fig. 6.9. Construct the rightmost derivation for w.

Solution: We scan the parse tree starting from the root and use the rightmost and leftmost variables for replacement to find rightmost and leftmost derivations respectively.

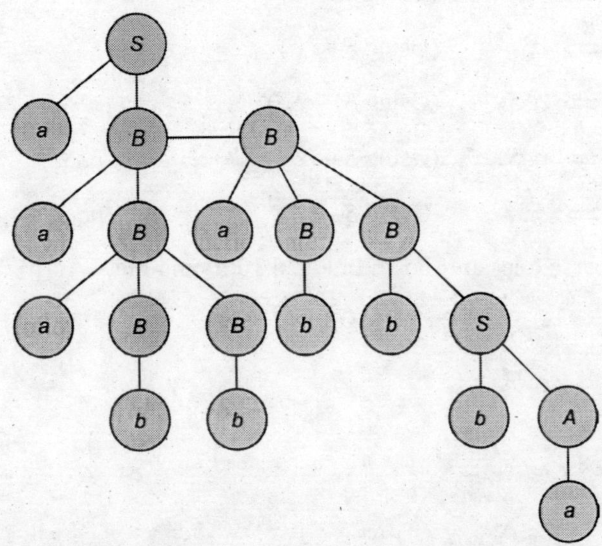

Fig. 6.9: Derivation tree for *aaabbabbba*

So, rightmost derivation is given below:

$$
\begin{aligned}
S &\Rightarrow a\boldsymbol{B} \\
&\Rightarrow aaB\boldsymbol{B}
\end{aligned}
$$

$$\Rightarrow aaBaB\mathbf{B}$$
$$\Rightarrow aaBaBb\mathbf{S}$$
$$\Rightarrow aaBaBbb\mathbf{A}$$
$$\Rightarrow aaBa\mathbf{B}bba$$
$$\Rightarrow aa\mathbf{B}abbba$$
$$\Rightarrow aaaBBabbba$$
$$\Rightarrow aaa\mathbf{B}babbba$$
$$\Rightarrow aaabbabbba$$

It has been indicated earlier that sometimes finding rightmost derivation of a given string is not easier as compare to leftmost derivation. So, for simplicity, we first find the leftmost derivation and construct the parse tree and then find the rightmost derivation using the parse tree as discussed above.

Example 6.5: Show that the following grammars are ambiguous.

(a) $S \to SS \mid a \mid b$

(*b*) $S \to A \mid B \mid b,\ A \to aAB \mid ab,\ B \to abB \mid \varepsilon$

(c) $S \to aSb \mid aaSb \mid \varepsilon$

(d) $S \to aSb \mid abS \mid \varepsilon$

Solution:

(a) Consider the string $\boldsymbol{w} = aaa$, two distinct leftmost derivations are as follows:

$S \underset{L}{\Rightarrow} SS$	(Using $S \to SS$)	$S \underset{L}{\Rightarrow} SS$	(Using $S \to SS$)
$\underset{L}{\Rightarrow} aS$	(Using $S \to a$)	$\underset{L}{\Rightarrow} SSS$	(Using $S \to SS$)
$\underset{L}{\Rightarrow} aSS$	(Using $S \to SS$)	$\underset{L}{\Rightarrow} aSS$	(Using $S \to a$)
$\underset{L}{\Rightarrow} aaS$	(Using $S \to a$)	$\underset{L}{\Rightarrow} aaS$	(Using $S \to a$)
$\underset{L}{\Rightarrow} aaa$	(Using $S \to a$)	$\underset{L}{\Rightarrow} aaa$	(Using $S \to a$)

Two distinct parse trees are shown in Fig. 6.10(a) and Fig. 6.10(b). So, the given grammar is ambiguous.

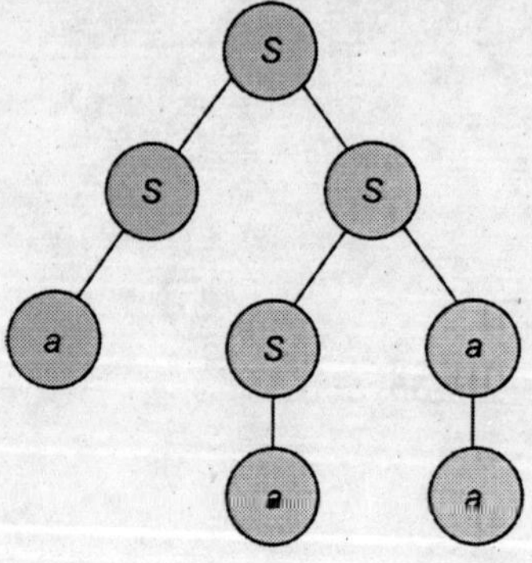

Fig. 6.10(a): Parse tree for *aaa*

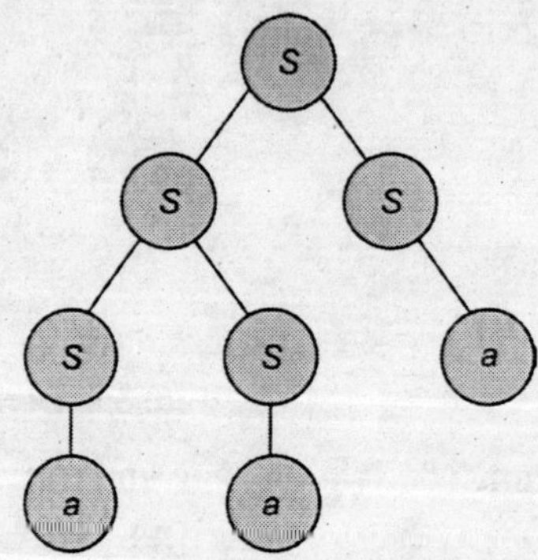

Fig. 6.10(b): Parse tree for *aaa*

(b) Consider the string $\boldsymbol{w} = \boldsymbol{ab}$, we get two leftmost derivations for w as follows:

$$S \underset{L}{\Rightarrow} A$$
$$\underset{L}{\Rightarrow} ab \quad \text{(Using } A \to ab\text{)}$$

$$S \underset{L}{\Rightarrow} B$$
$$\underset{L}{\Rightarrow} abB \quad \text{(Using } B \to abB\text{)}$$
$$\underset{L}{\Rightarrow} ab \quad \text{(Using } B \to \varepsilon\text{)}$$

Two parse trees are shown in Fig 6.11 (a) and Fig. 6.11(*b*).

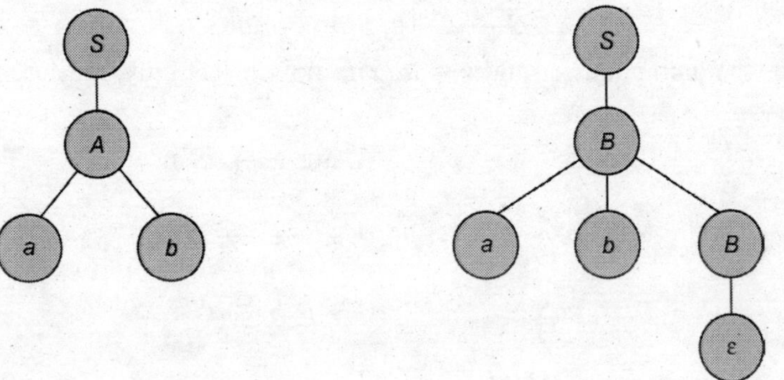

Fig. 6.11(a): Parse tree for *w*= *ab* **Fig. 6.11(b): Parse tree for *w*= *ab***

So, the given grammar is ambiguous.

(c) Consider the string $\boldsymbol{w} = \boldsymbol{aaabb}$, we get two leftmost derivations as follows:

$$S \underset{L}{\Rightarrow} aSb \quad \text{(Using } S \to aSb\text{)}$$
$$\underset{L}{\Rightarrow} aaaSbb \quad \text{(Using } S \to aaSb\text{)}$$
$$\underset{L}{\Rightarrow} aaabb \quad \text{(Using } S \to \varepsilon\text{)}$$

and

$$S \underset{L}{\Rightarrow} aaSb \quad \text{(Using } S \to aaSb\text{)}$$
$$\underset{L}{\Rightarrow} aaaSbb \quad \text{(Using } S \to aSb\text{)}$$
$$\underset{L}{\Rightarrow} aaabb \quad \text{(Using } S \to \varepsilon\text{)}$$

So, the given grammar is ambiguous.

(d) Consider the string $\boldsymbol{w} = \boldsymbol{ab}$, we have two leftmost derivations as follows:

$$S \underset{L}{\Rightarrow} aSb \quad \text{(Using } S \to aSb\text{)}$$
$$\underset{L}{\Rightarrow} ab \quad \text{(Using } S \to \varepsilon\text{)}$$

and

$$S \underset{L}{\Rightarrow} abS \quad \text{(Using } S \to abS\text{)}$$
$$\underset{L}{\Rightarrow} ab \quad \text{(Using } S \to \varepsilon\text{)}$$

So, the given grammar is ambiguous.

Example 6.6: Remove the ambiguity from the following grammars:

(a) $S \to aSb \mid aabS \mid \varepsilon$

(b) $E \to E + E \mid E*E \mid (E) \mid id$

(c) $S \to SS \mid a \mid b$

Solution:

(a) The given grammar has left factoring in productions $\boldsymbol{S \to aSb \mid aabS}$, so removing the left factoring, we get

$$S \to aS' \mid \varepsilon,\ S' \to Sb \mid abS$$

Consider the ambiguous string $w = aaabb$, now it has only one leftmost derivation given below:

$$\begin{aligned} S &\underset{L}{\Rightarrow} aS' && \text{(Using } S \to aS'\text{)} \\ &\underset{L}{\Rightarrow} aSb && \text{(Using } S' \to Sb\text{)} \\ &\underset{L}{\Rightarrow} aaS'b && \text{(Using } S \to aS'\text{)} \\ &\underset{L}{\Rightarrow} aaabSb && \text{(Using } S' \to abS\text{)} \\ &\underset{L}{\Rightarrow} aaabb && \text{(Using } S \to \varepsilon\text{)} \end{aligned}$$

Similarly, we can see for other ambiguous strings also.

(b) The given grammar has left recursion in productions $E \to E + E \mid E*E$. So removing left recursion, we get

$$E \to (E)E' \mid idE',\ E' \to +EE' \mid *EE' \mid \varepsilon$$

Consider the ambiguous string $id + id*id$, now it has only one leftmost derivation given below:

$$\begin{aligned} E &\underset{L}{\Rightarrow} idE' && \text{(Using } E \to idE'\text{)} \\ &\underset{L}{\Rightarrow} id + EE' && \text{(Using } E' \to +EE'\text{)} \\ &\underset{L}{\Rightarrow} id + idE'E' && \text{(Using } E \to idE'\text{)} \\ &\underset{L}{\Rightarrow} id + id*EE'E' && \text{(Using } E' \to *EE'\text{)} \\ &\underset{L}{\Rightarrow} id + id*idE'E'E' && \text{(Using } E \to idE'\text{)} \\ &\underset{L}{\Rightarrow} id + id*id && \text{(Using } E' \to \varepsilon \text{ three times)} \end{aligned}$$

(c) The given grammar has left recursion in production $S \to SS$. So, removing left recursion from the grammar, we get

$$S \to aS' \mid bS',\ S' \to SS' \mid \varepsilon$$

Consider the ambiguous string $w = aaa$, now it has only one leftmost derivation given below:

$$S \underset{L}{\Rightarrow} aS' \qquad \text{(Using } S \to aS'\text{)}$$

$$\underset{L}{\Rightarrow} aSS' \qquad \text{(Using } S' \to SS'\text{)}$$

$$\underset{L}{\Rightarrow} aaS'S' \qquad \text{(Using } S \to aS'\text{)}$$

$$\underset{L}{\Rightarrow} aaSS'S' \qquad \text{(Using } S' \to SS'\text{)}$$

$$\underset{L}{\Rightarrow} aaaS'S'S' \qquad \text{(Using } S \to aS'\text{)}$$

$$\overset{*}{\underset{L}{\Rightarrow}} aaa \qquad \text{(Using } S' \to \varepsilon \text{ three times)}$$

Example 6.7: Consider the following grammar and remove left recursion if any.

$S \to Aa \mid b, A \to Ac \mid Sd \mid \varepsilon$ **(GATE 1998)**

Solution: One thing noticeable here that the given grammar has not immediate left recursion. So, replacing variable S in A-productions, we have

$A \to Ac \mid Aad \mid bd \mid \varepsilon$

Now, the A-productions have immediate left recursion. So, removing left recursion from the A-productions, we get

$\boldsymbol{A \to bdA' \mid A', A' \to cA' \mid adA' \mid \varepsilon}$

(Note: $\boldsymbol{\varepsilon A' \equiv A'}$**)**

Now, the grammar without left recursion is following:

$S \to Aa \mid b, A \to bdA \mid A', A' \to cA' \mid adA' \mid \varepsilon$

Example 6.8: Remove the useless symbols and find the reduced and equivalent grammar for the following grammars:

(a) $S \to AB \mid CA, B \to BC \mid AB, A \to a, C \to aB \mid b$

(b) $S \to aAa, A \to Sb \mid bCC \mid DaA, C \to DD \mid ab, E \to a \mid aA, D \to aDA$

Solution:

(a) In the given grammar G, $S \to AB \mid CA$, $B \to BC \mid AB$, $A \to a$, $C \to aB \mid b$, variable B has recursion but no terminating production rule. So, variable B cannot be used in production. So, removing all the B occurrences, we get following production rules for reduced grammar G':

$$S \to CA, A \to a, C \to b$$

We see that string $w = ba$ is the only terminal string produced by both grammar G and G', so these are equivalent grammar. Hence, G' is the reduced and equivalent grammar.

(b) In the given grammar G, $S \to aAa$, $A \to Sb \mid bCC \mid DaA$, $C \to DD \mid ab$, $E \to a \mid aA$, $D \to aDA$, variables D has recursion but no terminating production rule and variable E is not reachable from the starting symbol S. So, removing all the occurrences of variables D and E, we get following production rules for reduced grammar G':

$S \to aAa, A \to Sb \mid bCC, C \to ab$

We see that production of G and G' are equivalent because in both grammars useful productions are: $S \to aAa, A \to Sb \mid bCC, C \to ab$

So, G' is the reduced and equivalent grammar.

Example 6.9: Remove null, unit and useless productions (if any) from the following grammar:

(a) $S \to aS \mid AB, A \to \varepsilon, B \to \varepsilon\ D \to a$

(b) $S \to AB, A \to a, B \to C \mid b, C \to D, D \to E, E \to a, F \to a$

Solution:

(a) In the given grammar G, two null production rules are $A \to \varepsilon$, $B \to \varepsilon$ and variable D is not reachable from the starting symbol. So, removing null productions and useless variable D, we get $S \to aS \mid \varepsilon$, which has null production obtained by removing AB. Further, removing null production from the S-production, we get desired grammar G′ whose production rules are: $S \to aS \mid a$

(b) In the given grammar G, $S \to AB, A \to a, B \to C \mid b, C \to D, D \to E, E \to a, F \to a$, unit productions are $B \to C$, $C \to D$, $D \to E$ and variable F is not reachable from the S. So, removing the unit production and useless variable F, we get the production rules of grammar G':

$S \to AB, A \to a, B \to a \mid b$ (Since, $B \overset{*}{\Rightarrow} a$)

Example 6.10: Show that following languages are not context-free language.

(a) $L = \{a^p : p \text{ is a prime number}\}$

(b) $L = \{a^n b^m c^n d^m : m, n \geq 1\}$

(c) $L = \{a^n b^n c^m : m \geq n\}$

Solution:

(a) All the words of L have length prime. Let L is a context-free language and z is a long string in L. Using Pumping Lemma for L, we write $z = uvwxy$ and uv^iwx^iy is in L for some $i = 0, 1, 2, \ldots$ and $|vx| = m$ amd $|uwy| = n$ where n is a prime number then $|uv^nwx^ny| = n + mn$. As $n + mn$ is not a prime number, so $uv^nwx^ny \notin L$ and this is a contradiction. Therefore, L is not a CGL.

(b) Let L is a CFL and z is a long string in L such that $z = uvwxy$ for $|vx| \geq 1$ and $|vwx| \leq k$, where k is some constant.

In L, all words have equal number of a's and c's and equal number of b's and d's. The value of vx may be combination of two consecutive symbols like a^pb^q, b^qc^r, c^rd^s. According to Pumping Lemma uv^iwx^iy is in L for some $i = 0, 1, 2, \ldots$

Consider $i = 0$, then $z = uwy$ is in L.

Case 1: $vx = a^pb^q$, then

$$z = a^{n-p}b^{m-q}c^nd^m$$

The number of a's and b's are fewer than number of c's and d's for $p, q \geq 1$, which is a contradiction.

Case 2: $vx = b^q c^r$, then

$$z = a^n b^{m-q} c^{n-r} d^m$$

The number of b's and c's are fewer than number of d's and a's for q, $r \geq 1$, which is a contradiction.

Case 3: $vx = c^r d^s$, then

$$z = a^n b^m c^{n-r} d^{m-s}$$

The number of c's and d's are fewer than number of a's and b's for r, $s \geq 1$, which is a contradiction.

Since, we are getting contradiction in all cases, so L is not a context-free language.

(c) All the words of L contain equal number of a's, b's and number of c's is greater than number of a's (or b's). Let L is a CFL and z is a long string in L such that $|z| \geq n$. Using pumping lemma for L, we write $z = uvwxy$ and uv^iwx^iy, which are in L for some $i = 0, 1, 2, \ldots$ and $|vx| \geq 1$ & $|wvx| \leq n$.

The substring vx may be a^p, b^q, c^r, a^pb^q, b^qc^r but not a^pc^r.

Consider $i = 0$, so uwy is in L

Case 1: $vx = a^p$, so $z = uwy = a^{n-p}b^nc^n$ is in L.

The number of a's is fewer than the number of b's for $p \geq 1$, which is a contradiction.

Case 2: $vx = b^q$, so $z = uwy = a^nb^{n-q}c^n$ is in L.

The number of b's is fewer than the number of a's for $q \geq 1$, which is a contradiction.

Case 3: $vx = c^r$, so $z = uwy = a^nb^nc^{n-r}$ is in L.

The number of c's is may be equal or less than the number of a's (or b's) for $r \geq 1$, which is a contradiction.

Since, we are getting contradiction in all cases, so L is not a context-free language.

Example 6.11: Find equivalent grammar in Greibach normal form (GNF) for each of following grammar.

(a) $S \rightarrow aB \mid bA$, $A \rightarrow aS \mid bAA \mid a$, $B \rightarrow bS \mid aBB \mid b$

(*b*) $S \rightarrow abSb \mid \mathrm{a} \mid aAb$, $A \rightarrow bS \mid aAAb$

(c) $S \rightarrow AA \mid 0$, $A \rightarrow SS \mid 1$

Solution:

(a) Renaming S, A, and B by A_1, A_2, and A_3 respectively, we get the following production rules:

$$A_1 \rightarrow aA_3 \mid bA_2,\ A_2 \rightarrow aA_1 \mid bA_2A_2 \mid a,\ A_3 \rightarrow bA_1 \mid aA_3A_3 \mid b$$

Since, all productions are in GNF, so there is no need of any modification.

(*b*) Renaming S, and A by A_1, and A_2 respectively, we get the following production rules:

$A_1 \rightarrow abA_1b \mid a \mid aA_2b$, $A_2 \rightarrow bA_1 \mid aA_2A_2b$

Consider the A_1-productions one by one:

$$A_1 \rightarrow abA_1b \qquad \text{(Not in GNF)}$$

Replacing all the RHS terminals except the first by new variables, we get:

$A_1 \to aA_3A_1A_3$ where $A_3 \to b$ (In GNF)

Considering the next A_1-production:

$A_1 \to a$ (In GNF)

Considering the next A_1-production:

$A_1 \to aA_2b$ (Not in GNF)

Replacing b by variable A_3 (since, we have already defined $A_3 \to b$) we get:

$A_1 \to aA_2A_3$ (In GNF)

Consider the A_2-productions:

$A_2 \to bA_1$ (In GNF)

Considering the next A_2-production:

$A_2 \to aA_2A_2b$ (Not in GNF)

Replacing b by variable A_3 (since, we have already defined $A_3 \to b$) we get:

$A_2 \to aA_2A_2A_3$ (In GNF)

Now, all productions given following are in GNF:

$$A_1 \to aA_2A_1A_3 \mid a \mid aA_2A_3,\ A_2 \to bA_1 \mid aA_2A_2A_3, \text{ and } A_3 \to b$$

(c) Renaming S, and A by A_1, and A_2 respectively we get the following productions:

$$A_1 \to A_2A_2 \mid 0,\ A_2 \to A_1A_1 \mid 1$$

Consider the A_1-productions one by one:

$A_1 \to A_2A_2$ (Not in GNF)

Replacing leftmost A_2 by A_1A_1 and 1, we get:

$$A_1 \to A_1A_1A_2 \mid 1A_2$$

Considering the production $A_1 \to A_1A_1A_2$, this is not in GNF and has left recursion. Considering the all A_1-productions $A_1 \to A_1A_1A_2 \mid 1A_2 \mid 0$ and removing left recursion from the production $A_1 \to A_1A_1A_2$, we get

$A_1 \to 1A_2A_3 \mid 0A_3$ (In GNF), where $A_3 \to A_1A_2A_3 \mid A_1A_2$

Considering A_2-production $A_2 \to A_1A_1$ and replacing leftmost A_1 by $1A_2A_3$ and $0A_3$, we get:

$A_2 \to 1A_2A_3A_1 \mid 0A_3A_1$ (In GNF)

Considering A_3-productions $A_3 \to A_1A_2A_3 \mid A_1A_2$ and replacing A_1 by $1A_2A_3$ and $0A_3$, we get:

$A_3 \to 1A_2A_3A_2 \mid 0A_3A_2 \mid 1A_2A_3A_2A_3 \mid 0A_3A_2A_3$ (In GNF)

Now, the production rules in GNF are:

$$A_1 \to 1A_2A_3 \mid 0A_3,\ A_2 \to 1A_2A_3A_1 \mid 0A_3A_1 \mid 1,$$

and $A_3 \to 1A_2A_3A_2 \mid 0A_3A_2 \mid 1A_2A_3A_2A_3 \mid 0A_3A_2A_3$

Example 6.12: Let G be a CFG, where $G = (\{S, A, B, C\}, \{a, b, d\}, P, S)$ with the production rules in P are given below:

$$S \to ABAC \mid C, A \to aA \mid \varepsilon, B \to bB \mid \varepsilon, C \to d$$

Transform the grammar G to an equivalent CFG that has no ε-productions and unit production rules. **(GATE 1996)**

Solution: Since, A and B variables have null production rules. So, considering $A \to \varepsilon$, $B \to \varepsilon$ productions and removing these production rules, we get

$S \to BAC$ (Removing leftmost A)
$S \to ABC$ (Removing rightmost A)
$S \to AAC$ (Removing B)
$S \to AC$ (Removing leftmost A and B)
$S \to AC$ (Removing rightmost A and B)
$S \to BC$ (Removing both occurrences of A)
$S \to C$ (Removing both A and B)

And $A \to a$, $B \to b$

Now, removing the unit production $S \to C$:

$S \to d$ (Since, $C \to d$)

Now, the productions without null and unit production rules are following:

$$S \to ABAC \mid BAC \mid ABC \mid AAC \mid AC \mid BC \mid d,$$
$$A \to aA \mid a, B \to bB \mid b, \text{ and } C \to d$$

Example 6.13: Consider the context-free grammar whose productions are:

$S \to ABS \mid aa$, $S \to A$, $A \to aA \mid \varepsilon$, $B \to ab \mid bB \mid \varepsilon$

Remove the null and unit productions (if any).

Solution: Variables A, and B have null and S is nullable variable. Now, removing null productions, we get following additional productions:

$S \to BS$ (Removing A from ABS)
$S \to AS$ (Removing B from ABS)
$S \to AB$ (Removing S from ABS)
$S \to S$ (Removing A and B, has no meaning)
$S \to A$ (Removing B and S form ABS, result is unit production)
$S \to B$ (Removing A and S from ABS, result is unit production)
$A \to$ a (Removing A from aA)
$B \to b$ (Removing B from bB)

And $A \to a$, $B \to b$

Now, removing the unit productions, we get,

$S \to a \mid aA$ (Since, $A \to a \mid aA$)
$S \to b \mid ab \mid bB$ (Since $B \to b \mid ab \mid bB$)

Now, the productions without null and unit productions are following:

$S \rightarrow ABS \mid BS \mid AS \mid AB \mid aA \mid a \mid bB \mid b \mid ab \mid aa$, $A \rightarrow aA \mid a$, and $B \rightarrow ab \mid bB \mid b$.

Example 6.14: Consider a context-free grammar G given below:

$S \rightarrow XY, X \rightarrow a \mid b \mid XA, Y \rightarrow a \mid AY, A \rightarrow a$

Check whether the terminal string $w = babaa \in L(G)$ or not ?

Solution: All given production rules are in CNF. Checking the substrings of w and their related variables:

	1	2	3	4	5
1	*b* *X*	*a* *X, A, Y*	*b* *X*	*a* *X, A, Y*	*a* *X, A, Y*
2	*ba* *X, S*	*ab* ϕ	*ba* *X, S*	*aa* *S, X, Y*	
3	*bab* ϕ	*aba* ϕ	*baa* *S, X*		
4	*baba* ϕ	*abaa* ϕ			
5	*abaa* ϕ				

Since, in the final list of producing variables for substring "*abaa*", S is not there. Hence, $w = babaa \in L(G)$.

Example 6.15: Convert the grammar into Chomsky Normal Form (CNF).

$S \rightarrow ABa, A \rightarrow aab, B \rightarrow AC.$

Solution: The Chomsky normal form is:

1. <variable> $\rightarrow$ <terminal> For example, $\boldsymbol{A \rightarrow a}$
2. <variable> $\rightarrow$ <variable><variable> For example, $\boldsymbol{A \rightarrow XY}$

First let us see which productions rules of the given grammar are not in Chomsky normal form (CNF):

$P_1: S \rightarrow ABa$ (Not in CNF)

$P_2: A \rightarrow aab$ (Not in CNF)

$P_3: B \rightarrow AC$ (In CNF)

Let $X \rightarrow a$ and $Y \rightarrow b$ and replace the terminals of productions rules P_1 and P_2. We get

$S \rightarrow ABX$ and $A \rightarrow XXY$

Now, replace the variables BX and XY by new variables D and E respectively, we get

$S \rightarrow AD$, and $A \rightarrow XE$, where $D \rightarrow BX$ and $E \rightarrow XY$

Now, all the production rules are in CNF:

$S \rightarrow AD, A \rightarrow XE, D \rightarrow BX, E \rightarrow XY, B \rightarrow AC, X \rightarrow a$, and $Y \rightarrow b$

Example 6.16: Prove or disprove whether the following language is context-free or not?

$\{a^n b^n a^n : n \geq 0\}$

Proof:

(i) All the strings in given language $L = \{a^n b^n a^n : n \geq 0\}$ contain equal number of a's, b's and a's at the right side. Let L is a CFL and z is a long string in L such that $|z| \geq n$. Using Pumping Lemma for L, we write $z = uvwxy$ and uv^iwx^iy is in L for some $i = 0, 1, 2, \ldots$ such that $vx| \geq 1$ and $|wvx| \leq n$.

The substring $\boldsymbol{vx}$ may be $\boldsymbol{a^p}$, $\boldsymbol{b^q}$, $\boldsymbol{a^r}$, $\boldsymbol{a^p b^q}$, $\boldsymbol{b^q a^r}$.

Consider $i = 0$, so uwy is in L.

Case 1: $vx = a^p$, so $z = uwy = a^{n-p} b^n a^n$ is in L.

The number of a's is fewer than the number of b's and a's at the right side for $p \geq 1$, which is a contradiction.

Case 2: $vx = b^q$, so $z = uwy = a^n b^{n-q} a^n$ is in L.

The number of b's is fewer than the number of a's at the left side and a's at right side for $q \geq 1$, which is a contradiction.

Case 3: $vx = a^r$, so $z = uwy = a^n b^n a^{n-r}$ is in L.

The number of a's at the right side is fewer than the number of a's at the left and b's for $r \geq 1$, which is a contradiction.

Case 4: $vx = a^p b^q$, so $z = uwy = a^{n-p} b^{n-q} a^n$ is in L.

The number of a's at the left side and b's are fewer than the number of a's at the right side for $p, q \geq 1$, which is a contradiction.

Case 5: $vx = b^q a^r$, so $z = uwy = a^n b^{n-q} c^{n-r}$ is in L.

The number of b's and a's at the right side are fewer than the number of a's at the left side for $q, r \geq 1$, which is a contradiction.

Since, we get contradiction for all values of substring vx, so L is not a context-free language (CFL).

Example 6.17: What is ambiguity? Show that $S \to aS \mid Sa \mid a$ is an ambiguous grammar.

Solution: A grammar G is said to be *ambiguous* if there exists some string $w \in L(G)$ for which *there are two or more distinct derivation trees*, or *there are two or more distinct leftmost derivations.*

Consider an ambiguous string $w = aaa$ and let us see the leftmost derivation using the given grammar.

(i) $S \Rightarrow aS \Rightarrow aaS \Rightarrow aaa$

(ii) $S \Rightarrow Sa \Rightarrow Saa \Rightarrow aaa$

There are two leftmost derivations and two distinct derivation trees shown Fig. 6.11(a) and Fig. 6.11(*b*).

Therefore, the given grammar is an ambiguous grammar.

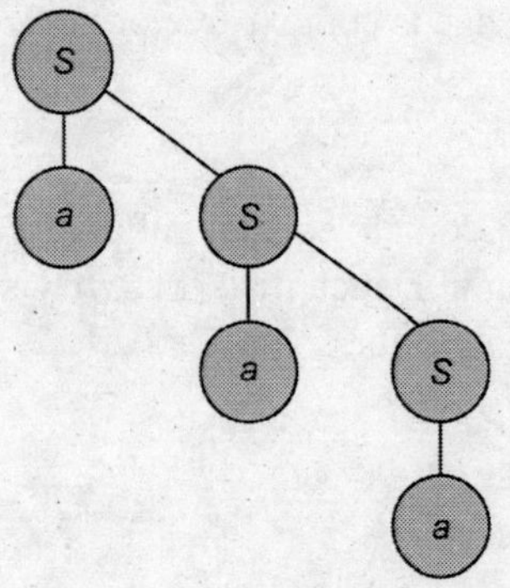

Fig. 6.11(a): Derivation tree

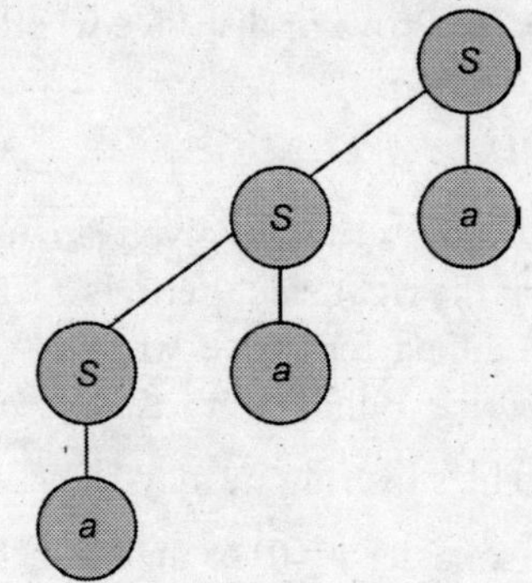

Fig. 6.11(b): Derivation tree

Example 6.18: Show the derivation tree for string "*aabbbb*" with the following grammar:

$S \to AB \mid \varepsilon,\ A \to aB,\ B \to Sb.$

Solution: The leftmost derivation for the given string is below and derivation tree is shown in Fig. 6.12.

Leftmost derivation

$$
\begin{aligned}
S &\Rightarrow AB\\
&\Rightarrow aBB\\
&\Rightarrow aSbB\\
&\Rightarrow aABbB\\
&\Rightarrow aaBBbB\\
&\Rightarrow aaSbBbB\\
&\Rightarrow aa\varepsilon bBbB\\
&\Rightarrow aabSbbB\\
&\Rightarrow aab\varepsilon bbB\\
&\Rightarrow aabbbSb\\
&\Rightarrow aabbb\varepsilon b\\
&\equiv aabbbb
\end{aligned}
$$

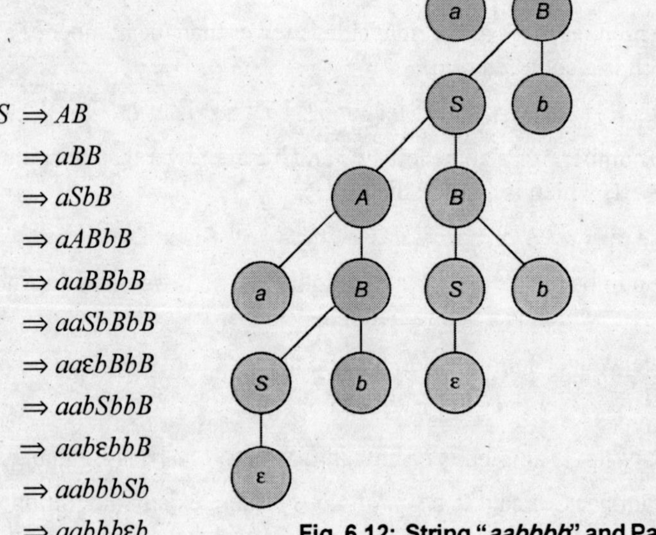

Fig. 6.12: String "*aabbbb*" and Parse tree

Example 6.19: Consider the grammar $G = \{S \to ASb \mid AS \mid \varepsilon,\ A \to aA \mid \varepsilon\}$. State True/False for the following:

(i) The string "*ababb*" is generated by the grammar G.

(ii) Every string of the form $a^n b^m$, $n, m \geq 0$ is generated by G.

(iii) The grammar is ambiguous.

(iv) The language generated by G is regular.

Solution:

(i) False: Let us try the derivation for the string "*ababb*":

$$S \Rightarrow AS \Rightarrow aAS \Rightarrow a\varepsilon S \Rightarrow aAS \Rightarrow aaAS \Rightarrow aa\varepsilon S\ldots$$

$$S \Rightarrow ASb \Rightarrow aASba\varepsilon Sb\ldots$$

$$S \Rightarrow ASb \Rightarrow \varepsilon Sb\ldots$$

$$S \Rightarrow AS \Rightarrow \varepsilon S\ldots$$

But we cannot get the symbol '*b*' after symbol '*a*' at the beginning of the given string. Therefore, the given string is not generated by the given grammar.

(ii) True: The string generated by the grammar *G* is of the form $a^n b^m$, $n, m \geq 0$.

(iii) True: Consider the ambiguous string $w = b$, the two distinct derivation trees are shown in Fig. 6.13(a) and Fig. 6.13(b).

(iv) True: The language generated by the grammar *G* is $\{a^n b^m: n, m \geq 0\}$, which is a regular language.

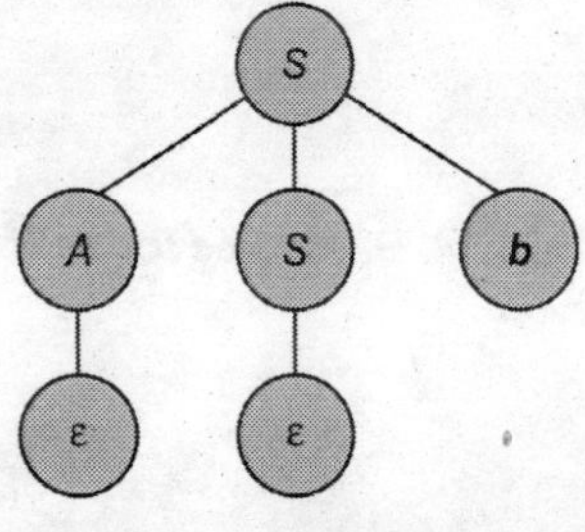

Fig. 6.13(a): Derivation tree

Fig. 6.13(b): Derivation tree

Example 6.20: Consider the following production rules $S \rightarrow aB \mid bA$, $A \rightarrow aS \mid bAA \mid a$, $B \rightarrow bS \mid aBB \mid a$. For the string *aaabbabbba*, find the following:

(i) The leftmost derivation

(ii) The rightmost derivation, and

(iii) Parse tree

Solution:

(i) Leftmost derivation:

$$S \Rightarrow aB \Rightarrow aaBB\ aaaBBB \Rightarrow aaabBB$$

$$\Rightarrow aaabbSB \Rightarrow aaabbaBB \Rightarrow aaabbabB$$

$$\Rightarrow aaabbabbS \Rightarrow aaabbabbbA$$

$$\Rightarrow aaabbabbba$$

(ii) Rightmost derivation:

$$S \Rightarrow aB \Rightarrow aaBB \Rightarrow aaBbS \Rightarrow aaBbbA$$

$$\Rightarrow aaBbba \Rightarrow aaaBBbba$$
$$\Rightarrow aaaBbSbba \Rightarrow aaaBbaBbba$$
$$\Rightarrow aaaBbabbba \Rightarrow aaabbabbba$$

(iii) Parse Tree is shown in Fig. 6.14.

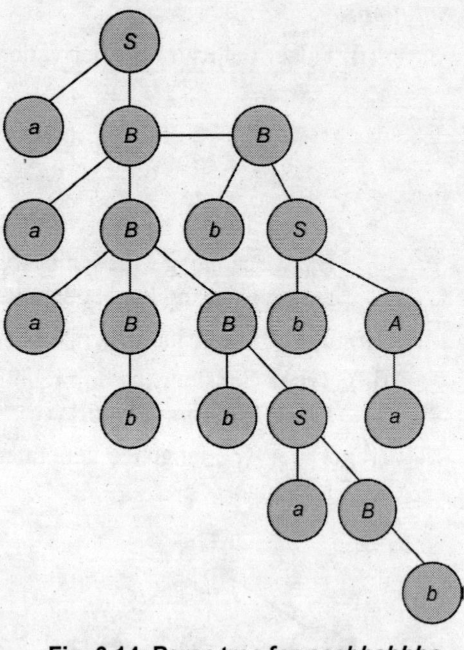

Fig. 6.14: Parse tree for *aaabbabbba*

Example 6.21: Let G be the CFG generating well-defined formulas of prepositional calculus with predicates p and q:

$$S \to \sim S \mid [S \supset S] \mid p \mid q$$

The terminals are p, q, ~, [,], and ⊃. Find a Chomsky normal form grammar generating $L(G)$.

Solution: **Chomsky Normal Form (CNF) of *G*:**

Let $A \to \sim$, $B \to \supset$, $C \to [$, and $D \to]$ and replacing the terminal ~, ⊃, [, and] by variable A, B, C, and D respectively in the given production rules, we have:

$S \to AS$ (in CNF), $S \to CSBSD$ (Not in CNF)

Now, Replacing $SBSD$ by X in production rule $S \to CSBSD$, we have:

$S \to CX$ (In CNF), where $X \to SBSD$ (Not in CNF)

Now, replacing BSD by Y in production rule $C \to SBSD$, we have:

$X \to SY$ (In CNF), where $Y \to BSD$ (Not in CNF)

Now, replacing SD by Z in production rule $Y \to BSD$, we have:

$Y \to BZ$ (in CNF), where $Z \to SD$ (In CNF)

So, production rules in CNF are:

$S \to AS \mid CX \mid p \mid q$, $A \to \sim$, $B \to \supset$, $C \to [$, $D \to]$, $X \to SY$, $Y \to BZ$, $Z \to SD$

Example 6.22: Design a context-free grammar for the following languages:

(a) The set $\{0^n1^n \mid n \geq 1\}$ i.e., the set of all strings of one or more 0's followed by an equal number of 1's.

(b) A set $\{a^ib^jc^k \mid i \neq j \text{ or } j \neq k\}$ i.e., the set of strings of a's followed by b's followed c's such that there are either a different number of a's and b's or a different number of b's and c's or both.

Solution:

(a) Let the desired grammar is G and G is defined as:

$$G = (\{S\}, \{0, 1\}, \{S \to 0S1, S \to 01\}, S)$$

(b) Let the given language is $L = \{a^ib^jc^k\ \ddot{\imath} \neq j \text{ or } j \neq k\} = L_1 \cup L_2$, where

$$L_1 = \{a^ib^Jc^k \mid i \neq J\} \text{ and } L_2 = \{a^ib^Jc^k \mid J \neq k\}$$

Let the grammars $G_1 = (V_{n1}, \{a, b, c\}, P_1, S_1)$ and $G_2 = (V_{n2}, \{a, b, c\}, P_2, S_2)$. For language L_1, we have two conditions:

(i) $i > j$ and (ii) $i < j$

For language L_2 has two conditions:

1. $j > k$ and 2. $j < k$

Set of production rules P_1 has following rules:

$S_1 \to A_1B_1, A_1 \to C_1D_1 | E_1D_1, C_1 \to aC_1 | a, D_1 \to aD_1b | \varepsilon, E_1 \to bE_1 | b, B_1 \to cB_1 | \varepsilon$

Set of production rules P_2 has following rules:

$S_2 \to A_2B_2, A_2 \to aA_2 | \varepsilon, B_2 \to C_2D_2 | E_2D_2, C_2 \to bC_2 | b, D_2 \to bD_2c | \varepsilon, E_2 \to cE_2 | c$

Now, let the desired grammar $G = (V_{n1}, \{a, b, c\}, P, S)$, where P has following production rules:

$S \to S_1 | S_2$, where S_1 and S_2 are starting symbols of grammar G_1 and G_2 and all the production rules of G_1 and G_2 are also included in G.

Example 6.23: The following grammar generates the language of regular expression 0*1(0 + 1)*:

$S \to A1B, A \to 0A | \varepsilon, B \to 0B | 1B | \varepsilon$

Give the leftmost and rightmost derivation of the following strings:

(i) 00101 (ii) 1001

Solution:

(i) Leftmost Derivation for string 00101:

$S \Rightarrow A1B \Rightarrow 0A1B \Rightarrow 00A1B \Rightarrow 00\varepsilon 1B \Rightarrow 0010B \Rightarrow 00101B \Rightarrow 00101\varepsilon \equiv 00101$

Rightmost Derivation for string 00101:

$S \Rightarrow A1B \Rightarrow A10BA101B \Rightarrow A101\varepsilon \Rightarrow 0A101 \Rightarrow 00A101 \Rightarrow 00\varepsilon 101 \equiv 00101$

(ii) Leftmost Derivation for string 1001:

$S \Rightarrow A1B \Rightarrow \varepsilon 1B \Rightarrow 10B \Rightarrow 100B \Rightarrow 1001B \Rightarrow 1001\varepsilon \equiv 1001$

Rightmost Derivation for string 1001:

$S \Rightarrow A1B \Rightarrow A10B \Rightarrow A100B \Rightarrow A1001B \Rightarrow A1001 \Rightarrow \varepsilon 1001 \equiv 1001$

Example 6.24: Consider the grammar ({S, A, B}, {a, b}, P, S) that has the production rules are: $S \to bA | aB, A \to bAA | aS | a, B \to aBB | bS | b$

Find an equivalent grammar in CNF.

Solution: First let us see which productions are not in CNF(Chomsky Normal Form):

$S \to bA$	(Not in CNF),	$S \to aB$	(Not in CNF),	$A \to bAA$	(Not in CNF)
$A \to aS$	(Not in CNF),	$A \to a$	(in CNF),	$B \to aBB$	(Not in CNF)
$B \to bS$	(Not in CNF),	$B \to b$	(in CNF)		

Only two productions are in CNF.

Now, consider the production:

$$S \to bA$$

Let $X \to b$ and replace the terminal 'b' by X, we have,

$$S \to XA \qquad \text{(In CNF)}$$

Now, consider production: $S \rightarrow aB$

Let $Y \rightarrow a$ and replace terminal 'a' by Y, we have,

$S \rightarrow YB$ (In CNF)

Now, consider the production: $A \rightarrow bAA$. We have a new production $X \rightarrow b$, so replacing b by X, we have production $A \rightarrow XAA$, which is not in CNF.

Let $Z \rightarrow XA$ and replacing "XA" of the production: $A \rightarrow XAA$, we have

$A \rightarrow ZA$ (In CNF)

Now, consider production: $A \rightarrow aS$ and replacing terminal 'a' by Y, we have

$A \rightarrow YS$ (In CNF),

where $Y \rightarrow a$ is defined already.

Now, consider the production: $B \rightarrow aBB$, and replacing terminal 'a' by Y, we have

$B \rightarrow YBB$, which is not in CNF, where $Y \rightarrow a$ is defined already.

Now, replacing "YB" by C, we have,

$B \rightarrow CB$ (in CNF),

where $C \rightarrow YB$

Now, consider the production: $B \rightarrow bS$ and replacing terminal 'b' by X, we have

$B \rightarrow XS$ (In CNF),

where $X \rightarrow b$ is defined already.

So, productions in CNF are:

$$S \rightarrow XA \mid YB,\ X \rightarrow b,\ Y \rightarrow a,\ A \rightarrow ZA \mid YS \mid a,\ Z \rightarrow XA,\ B \rightarrow CB \mid XS \mid b,\ C \rightarrow YB$$

TEST YOUR SKILLS

Supplementary Problems

6.1 Construct grammar in Chomsky normal form (CNF) generating each of the following language:

(a) $\{a^n b^n c^m: m, n = 1, 2, \ldots\}$ (b) $\{a^n b^m c^m d^n: m, n = 1, 2, \ldots\}$

(c) $\{\#x\#x^R\#: x \in (a + b)^*\}$

6.2 Construct grammar in Greibach normal form (GNF) generating each of the following language:

(a) $(a + b)^*abb(a + b)^*$ (b) $\{a^m b^n c^p: m, n, p = 1, 2, \ldots, \text{ and } n = m + p\}$

(c) $\{a^m b^n c^p: m, n, p = 1, 2, \ldots, \text{ and } m = n \text{ or } m = p\}$

6.3 Show that the following grammars are ambiguous and find an unambiguous grammar for each of the grammar.

(a) $E \rightarrow E^*E \mid E + E \mid id$, where E is variable and *, +, *id* are terminals

(b) Stmt → If (condition) then Stmt | If (condition) then Stmt Else Stmt | Other, where "Stmt", "condition", and "Other" are variables

(c) $S \rightarrow A \mid B$, $A \rightarrow aAb \mid ab$, $B \rightarrow abB \mid \varepsilon$, where S, A, B are variables

(d) $S \rightarrow SS \mid 0 \mid 1$, where S is variable

6.4 Consider the following grammar and convert it into Chomsky normal form (CNF).

$S \to AACD, A \to aAb \mid \varepsilon, C \to aC \mid a, D \to aDa \mid bDb \mid \varepsilon$

6.5 Show the language $L = \{xcx: x \in (0 + 1)^*$, c is terminal symbol not 0 or 1$\}$ in not CFL.

(GATE 1999)

6.6 Prove that following languages are not context-free language (CFL):

(a) $L = \{ww: w \in (a + b)^*\}$ (*b*) $L = a^n b^m c^n d^m: m, n \geq 1\}$

6.7 Prove the following:

(a) Union of a regular and a CFL is CFL.

(*b*) Intersection of a regular language and a CFL is CFL.

6.8 Consider the context-free grammar G which productions are: $E \to E + T \mid T$, $T \to T^*F \mid F$, $F \to a \mid b$. Convert grammar G into Chomsky normal form (CNF).

6.9 Consider the following grammars and remove useless production rules, unit production rules, and null production rules if any.

(a) $S \to aAa, A \to S \mid bC \mid DA, C \to DD \mid ab, E \to a \mid Aa, D \to aDA$

(*b*) $SaSAa, A \to Sb \mid bCC \mid \varepsilon, C \to aD \mid ab$

(c) $S \to aSaB, B \to Sb \mid bCD, C \to ab$

(d) $S \to aSa \mid \varepsilon \mid aa, A \to Sb \mid bCC, C \to ab, E \to a \mid Aa$

6.10 Define the leftmost and rightmost derivations with examples. Which one is easier to find for some given string?

6.11 What is ambiguous grammar? Is there any well-defined method to show that a grammar is ambiguous or not?

6.12 Define parse tree with some examples.

6.13 Explain the following:

(a) Left factoring and its side effect (b) Left recursion

(c) Unit production rule (d) Null production rule and Nullable variable

(e) Backtracking

6.14 Consider the following two context-free languages:

$L_1 = \{a^n b^n c^m: m, n \geq 1\}$ and $L_2 = \{a^n b^m c^m: m, n \geq 1\}$

Prove that languages L_1 and L_2 are closed under following:

(a) Union (b) Concatenation

(c) Kleene Closure

6.15 Find the context-free grammar for following languages:

(a) $L_1 = \{a^n b^n c^m: m, n \geq 1\}$ (*b*) $L_2 = \{a^n b^m c^m: m, n \geq 1\}$

(c) $L_3 = \{a^n b^m: m + 1 = n\}$ (d) $L_4 = \{a^m b^n c^m: m, n \geq 1\}$

(e) $L_5 = \{a^n b^n c^m: m, n \geq 1\} \cup \{a^m b^n c^m: m, n \geq 1\}$

(f) $L_6 = \{a^n b^n: n \geq 1\}\{b^m c^m: m \geq 0\}$

(g) $L_7 = \{b^n c^m: m \neq 2n\}$

(h) $L_8 = \{w \in (0 + 1)^*: |w|_a = 2|w|_b\}$

(i) $L_9 = \{a^n b^n c^m d^m: m, n \geq 0\}$

6.16 Consider language $L = \{0^n 1^n: n \geq 1\}$.

(a) Show that L^2 is context-free language.

(b) Show that L^* is context-free language.

(c) Show that $(a + b)^*L(a + b)^*$ is context-free language.

(d) Show that $00L11$ is context-free language.

6.17 Construct context-free grammar for language $L = \{0^n ww^R 1^n: w \in (a + b)^* \text{ and } n \geq 1\}$.

6.18 Construct context-free grammar for language $L = \{0^n 1^n ww^R: w \in (a + b)^* \text{ and } n \geq 0\}$

6.19 Construct context-free grammar for language
$L = \{0^n 1^n ww^R 0^m 1^m: w \in (a + b)^* \text{ and } n \geq 0\}$

6.20 Construct context-free grammar for language $L = \{0^n 1^n 0^{2n}: n \geq 0\}$.

6.21 Show that a context-free grammar G in Greibach normal form (GNF) produces a terminal string w in at most n steps, where n is the number of symbols in w.

6.22 Consider production rules of a context-free grammar (CFG): $S \to bA \mid aB$, $A \to aS \mid aAA \mid a$, $B \to bS \mid aBB \mid b$. Show that string $w = \boldsymbol{aaabbabbba}$ is produced by G.

6.23 Prove or disprove whether the following language is context-free or not?
$\{a^n a^n b^n: n \geq 0\}$.

Multiple Choice Questions

6.24 Productions in Context-free Grammars are of the form

(a) $A \to a, a \in (V_n \cup \Sigma)^*$
(b) $A \to a, a \in V_n^*$
(c) $A \to a, a \in (V_n^* \cup \Sigma^*)^*$
(d) Both (a) and (c)

6.25 The length of the right-hand side of the CFG productions is

(a) Finite
(b) Infinite
(c) 0 to ∞
(d) None

6.26 Production rules in Chomsky normal form are

(a) $A \to \alpha$, $B \to C$, where $a \in \Sigma$, $A, B, C \in V_n$
(b) $A \to \alpha$, $A \to BC$, where $a \in \Sigma$, $A, B, C \in V_n$
(c) $A \to \alpha$, $A \to BC$, $A \to \varepsilon$, where $a \in \Sigma$, $A, B, C \in V_n$
(d) None

6.27 Productions in Greibach normal form are

(a) $A \to a\alpha$, where $a \in \Sigma$, $a \in V_n^*$
(b) $A \to a\alpha$, where $a \in \Sigma$, $\alpha \in (V_n \cup \Sigma)^*$
(c) $A \to \alpha$, where $a \in (V_n \cup \Sigma)^*$
(d) None

6.28 Pumping Lemma for the CFLs is used

(a) To prove certain language is not CFL
(b) To prove certain language is CFL or not
(c) To prove certain language is CFL
(d) Both (a) and (c)

6.29 $L = \{a^n b^n : n = 1, 2, \ldots, 100\}$ is

(a) CFL but not regular
(b) Regular language
(c) Not regular language
(d) None

6.30 $L = \{a^n b^n : n = 1, 2, \ldots\}$ can be generated by the grammar

(a) $S \rightarrow \varepsilon \mid aSb$
(b) $S \rightarrow ab \mid aSb$
(c) $S \rightarrow ab \mid aabb \mid aSb$
(d) Both (b) and (c)

6.31 $L = \{a^n b^n c^n : n = 1, 2, \ldots\}$ is

(a) CFL
(b) Regular language
(c) Not regular
(d) None

6.32 Which one of the following is correct?

(a) All languages can be generated by CFG
(b) All regular languages are CFL
(c) All not regular languages are CFL
(d) Some regular languages can't be generated by CFG

6.33 Which one of the following is incorrect?

(a) Any regular language has an equivalent CFG
(b) All CFLs can be converted in CNF
(c) CNF is natural generalization of regular grammar
(d) GNF is natural generalization of regular grammar

6.34 CFLs are closed under

(a) Union
(b) Concatenation
(c) Kleene Closure
(d) All **(GATE 1999)**

6.35 CFLs are not closed under

(a) Kleene Closure
(b) Complementation
(c) Product
(d) Union

6.36 If L is a CFL, then complementation of L

(a) is CFL
(b) is not CFL
(c) may or may not CFL
(d) None

6.37 $L = \{a^n b^n c^n : n = 1, 2, \ldots, 10\}$ is

(a) CFL *b*ut not regular
(b) Not CFL
(c) CSL but not CFL
(d) Regular

6.38 If $L_1 = \{a^n b^n c^n : n = 1, 2, \ldots\}$, $L_2 = \{a^n b^n c^m : m, n = 1, 2, \ldots\}$, then $L = L_1 \cap L_2$ is

(a) $\{a^n b^n c^n : n = 1, 2, \ldots\}$
(b) $\{a^n b^n : n = 1, 2, \ldots\}$
(c) $\{a^n b^n c^m : m, n = 1, 2, \ldots\}$
(d) None

6.39 If $L_1 = \{a^n b^n c^n: n = 1, 2, \ldots\}$, $L_2 = \{a^m b^n c^m: m, n = 1, 2, \ldots\}$, then $L = L_1 \cap L_2$ is

(a) $\{a^n b^n c^n: n = 1, 2, \ldots\}$ (b) $a^n b^n: n = 1, 2, \ldots\}$

(c) $\{a^n b^n c^m: m, n = 1, 2, \ldots\}$ (d) None

6.40 If $L_1 = \{a^n b^n c^n: n = 1, 2, \ldots\}$, $L_2 = \{a^n b^n c^m: m, n = 1, 2, \ldots$, and $m \neq n\}$, then $L = L_1 \cap L_2$ is

(a) $\{a^n b^n c^n: n = 1, 2, \ldots\}$ (b) $a^n b^n: n = 1, 2, \ldots\}$

(c) $\{a^n b^n c^m: m, n = 1, 2, \ldots\}$ (d) ϕ

6.41 Let G be a CFG in CNF and G derives a terminal string w such that $|w| \geq 2$. The number of productions used is

(a) $2|w|$ (b) $2|w|+1$

(c) $2|w|-1$ (d) $2|w|+2$

6.42 Let G be a CFG in GNF and derives a terminal string w such that $|w| \geq 2$. The number of productions used in derivation of w is

(a) $2|w|$ (b) $2|w|+1$

(c) $2|w|-1$ (d) $|w|$ **(GATE 1992)**

6.43 If w is a terminal string derived by the CFGs G_1 and G_2, which are in CNF and GNF respectively. If number of productions used in derivation of w is n by grammar G_1, then the number of productions used by G_2 in derivation of w is

(a) $\lceil n/2 \rceil$ (b) $\lfloor n/2 \rfloor + 1$

(c) $(n + 1)/2$ (d) All

6.44 CFLs are accepted by

(a) TM (b) PDA

(c) LBA (d) All

6.45 The intersection of a CFL and a regular language is

(a) Regular language (b) Not CFL

(c) Always CFL (d) None

6.46 The language $\{a^m b^n c^{m+n} | m, n \geq 1\}$ is **(GATE 2004)**

(a) Regular (b) Context-free but not regular

(c) Context sensitive but not context free (d) Type 0 but not context sensitive

6.47 Which one of the following languages is context-free language?

(a) $L = \{a^p: p$ is a prime number$\}$ (b) $L = \{a^n b^m c^n d^m: m \geq n \geq 1\}$

(c) $L = \{a^n b^n c^m: m \geq n1\}$ (d) None

6.48 Consider the grammar G and its productions: $S \rightarrow aa \mid bb \mid aSa \mid bSb$, then $L(G)$ is

(a) $\{xy: x, y \in (a + b)^*$ and y is mirror image of $x\}$

(b) $\{xy: x, y \in (a + b)^*$ and $x = y\}$

(c) $\{w; w \in (a + b)^*$ having aa or bb substring$\}$

(d) Both (a) and (c)

6.49 A context-free grammar is ambiguous if **(GATE 1987)**

(a) The grammar contains useless terminals

(b) It produces more than one parse tree for some sentence

(c) Some production has two non-terminals side by side on right hand side

(d) None of the above

6.50 Context-free and regular languages are both closed under the operation(s) of

(a) Union (b) Intersection

(c) Concatenation (d) Complementation **(GATE 1989)**

6.51 Consider a context-free grammar G and its production: $S \to \varepsilon \mid ASA \mid BSB$, $A \to a$, $B \to b$, then $L(G)$ is

(a) $\{x: x \in (a + b)^*\}$ (b) $\{xx: x \in \{a, b\}\}$

(c) $\{xy: x, y \in (a + b)^*$ such that $x = y^R\}$ (d) None

6.52 A context-free grammar is ambiguous if there exist

(a) Left recursion in the production rules

(b) Left factoring in the production rules

(c) Two or more distinct parse trees for some string

(d) All the above

6.53 Context-free languages are **(GATE 19992)**

(a) Closed under union (b) Closed under complementation

(c) Closed under intersection (d) Closed under Kleene closure

6.54 The problem associated with left recursion and left factoring is

(a) Backtracking (b) Ambiguity

(c) Useless symbols (d) None

6.55 Consider the context-free grammar G which productions are

$E \to E + T \mid T$, $T \to T^*F \mid F$, $F \to (id)$

After removing the left recursion (if any), the equivalent grammar G' such that $L(G) = L(G')$ is

(a) $E \to TE'$, $E' \to + TE' \mid \varepsilon$, $T \to FT'$, $T' \to {}^*FT' \mid \varepsilon$, $F \to (id)$

(b) $E \to TE' \mid T$, $E' \to + TE' \mid \varepsilon$, $T \to FT' \mid F$, $T' \to {}^*FT' \mid \varepsilon$, $F \to (id)$

(c) $E \to TE' \mid T$, $E' \to +TE' \mid +T$, $T \to FT' \mid F$, $T' \to {}^*FT' \mid {}^*F$, $F \to (id)$

(d) Both (a) and (c)

6.56 Consider the following grammars:

(I) $S \to aSb \mid aabS \mid \varepsilon$ (II) $E \to E^*E \mid E + E \mid (E) \mid id$

(III) $S \to a \mid b \mid SS$

(a) (II) is ambiguous only (b) (I) is ambiguous but not (III)

(c) (II) is ambiguous but (III) (d) All are ambiguous

6.57 Every context-free language over $\{a\}$ is

(a) Regular (b) Context-free but not regular

(c) Finite (d) None

6.58 Let L be a context-free language over some alphabet Σ such that

(i) For each $u \in \Sigma^*$, there exists $av \in \Sigma^*$ such that $uv \in L$, and

(ii) $\Sigma^* - L$ is not context-free

Then

(a) L is regular

(b) L is not deterministic context-free

(c) Both (a) and (b)

(d) None

6.59 Which one of the following languages is context-free?

(a) $\{a^m b^n c^p d^q : m, n, p, q \geq 1 \text{ and } m + n = p + q\}$

(b) $\{www : w \in (a + b)^*\}$

(c) $\{: n \geq 0\}$

(d) None

6.60 Which one of the following is reduced and equivalent grammar of the following grammar: $S \to aAa, A \to Sb \mid bCC \mid DaA, C \to DD \mid ab, E \to a \mid Aa, D \to aDA$

(a) $SaAa, A \to Sb \mid bCC \mid DaA, C \to DD \mid ab, D \to aDA$

(b) $S \to aAa, A \to Sb \mid bCC, C \to ab$

(c) $S \to aAa, A \to Sb \mid bCC, C \to ab, E \to a \mid Aa$

(d) None

6.61 Consider the following grammar

$S \to AB, A \to a, B \to C \mid b, C \to D, D \to E, E \to a, F \to a$

Which one of the following the equivalent grammar that has no unit production, no null production, and useless symbols?

(a) $SAB, A \to a, B \to a \mid b$ (b) $S \to AB, A \to a, B \to b$

(c) $S \to AB, A \to a, B \to a \mid b, F \to a$ (d) None

6.62 The membership algorithm for context-free languages is suggested by

(a) Church

(b) John Cocke, D.H. Younger, and T. Kasmi

(c) Allan Turing

(d) None of above

6.63 Which one of the following is in decision algorithm for context-free languages?

(a) Emptiness (b) Finiteness

(c) Membership (d) All

Answers

6.24 (d)	6.25 (c)	6.26 (b)	6.27 (a)	6.28 (a)
6.29 (b)	6.30 (d)	6.31 (c)	6.32 (b)	6.33 (c)
6.34 (d)	6.35 (b)	6.36 (c)	6.37 (d)	6.38 (a)
6.39 (a)	6.40 (d)	6.41 (c)	6.42 (d)	6.43 (d)
6.44 (d)	6.45 (c)	6.46 (b)	6.47 (d)	6.48 (a)
6.49 (b)	6.50 (a, c)	6.51 (b)	6.52 (c)	6.53 (a, d)
6.54 (d)	6.55 (d)	6.56 (d)	6.57 (a)	6.58 (b)
6.59 (a)	6.60 (b)	6.61 (a)	6.62 (b)	6.63 (d)

CHAPTER 7

Pushdown Automata and Parsing Techniques

In this chapter, we will discuss pushdown automata (PDA) and their acceptability and parsing techniques. Pushdown automata are nondeterministic device and recognize context-free languages. The deterministic version of pushdown automata recognize only a subset of context-free languages, but positive thing is that this subset, known as deterministic context-free languages (DCFLs), are able to describe most of the programming languages. Context-free grammars are generally based on recursive structure, which is very useful in describing the syntax of the programming languages. We will see later on, how syntax of programming languages is described by context-free grammars using pushdown automata. Pushdown automata (PDA) are enhanced version of finite automata (FA); finite automata with a stack memory can be viewed as pushdown automata. Additional stack memory enhances the capability of pushdown automata as compared to finite automata. The stack memory is potentially infinite and its operation is based on **last-in-first-out** (LIFO) manner. It means the last object pushed on the stack is popped first. It is just like array of plates kept together in the kitchen and we add or remove a plate from the top only. In practical, we assume that a stack memory is long enough and linearly arranged so that we can add or remove objects at the left end. Stack memory is also known as **pushdown store** (PDS). At the end of this chapter, we see the parsing techniques which are based on use of pushdown automata.

7.1 MODEL OF PUSHDOWN AUTOMATA (PDA)

A model of pushdown automata is shown in Fig. 7.1. It consists of a finite tape, a reading head, which reads from the tape, a stack memory, which is read/write and operated in last-in-first-out (LIFO) fashion.

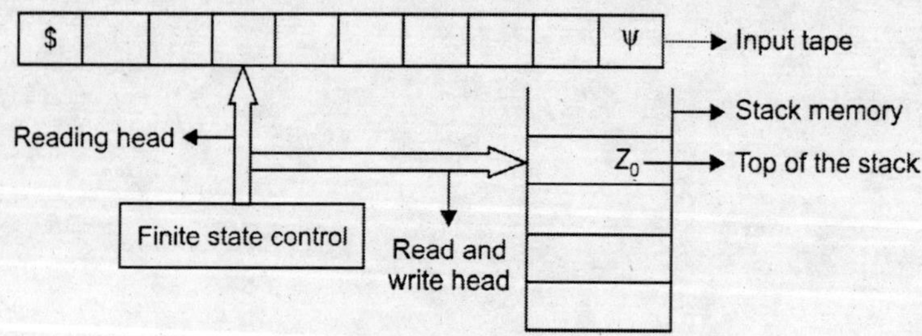

Fig. 7.1: Model of pushdown automata

There are two alphabets for input symbols to be read; one for input tape and another for stack memory. The Stack alphabet is denoted by Γ and input alphabet is denoted by Σ. Pushdown automata reads from the both alphabets; one symbol from the input and one symbol from the top of the stack. After reading the inputs from tape and stack, pushdown automata moves in next state and write zero or more symbols on the stack. After writing on the stack, the pointer to the top of stack is automatically adjusted and it points to the top of the stack. This operation is carried out for entire inputs on the tape. At the end of operation, the content on the stack memory is considered as output produced by pushdown automata.

7.2 MATHEMATICAL DESCRIPTION OF PUSHDOWN AUTOMATA

A pushdown automata is described by 7-tuple $(Q, \Sigma, \Gamma, \delta, s, Z_0, F)$, where

1. $\boldsymbol{Q}$ is finite and nonempty set of states,
2. Σ is input alphabet,
3. Γ is finite and nonempty set of pushdown symbols,
4. δ is the transition function which maps
   From $\boldsymbol{Q} \times (\Sigma \cup \{\varepsilon\}) \times \Gamma$ **to (finite subset of)** $\boldsymbol{Q} \times \Gamma^*$,
5. $\boldsymbol{s} \in \boldsymbol{Q}$, is the starting states,
6. $\mathbf{Z_0} \in \Gamma$, is the starting (top most or initial) stack symbol, and
7. $\boldsymbol{F} \subseteq \boldsymbol{Q}$, is the set of final states and sometimes $F = \phi$

There are two additional parameters; alphabet for pushdown symbols (Γ), starting or initial stack symbol (Z_0), as compared to the parameters of finite automata. The set of final states may or may not be empty. We will see when $F = \phi$ later on. The transition function is slightly different from the transition function of finite automata. Input for pushdown automata is considered from tape as well as stack including null string. Transition function maps (present state, input on tape, input on stack) to the (next state, string on stack symbols). Starting state $\boldsymbol{s}$ is similar to the starting state of finite automata.

7.3 WORKING (MOVES) OF PUSHDOWN AUTOMATA

We define the processing of pushdown automata in terms of move. A move indicates the present state, inputs (tape and stack), possible next state(s), and string to be written on stack. If pushdown automata is deterministic then possible next state is zero or one, otherwise there may be zero, one or more possible next states for non-deterministic pushdown automata. Move of a pushdown automaton indicates the options to proceed further after reading inputs in some state. **Move** of pushdown automata will be of two types:

1. In the first type of move, an input symbol is read from tape, it means, the head is advanced and depending upon the topmost symbol on the stack and present state, PDA has number of choices to proceed further.
2. In the second type of move, the input symbol is not read from the tape, it means head is not advanced and the topmost symbol of stack is used. The topmost of stack is modified without reading the input symbol. It is also known as an **ε-move**.

Mathematically **fist type of move** is defined as:

$$\delta(q, a, Z) = \{(p_1, \beta_1), (p_2, \beta_2) \ldots (p_n, \beta_n)\},$$

Where for $1 \le i \le n$, q, p_i are states in Q, $a \in \Sigma$, $Z \in \Gamma$, and $\beta_i \in \Gamma^*$

Pushdown automata read an input symbol a and one stack symbol Z in present state q and for any value(s) of i, enters state p_i, replaces stack symbol Z by string $\beta_i \in \Gamma^*$, and head is advanced one cell on the tape. Now, the leftmost symbol of string β_i is assumed to be the topmost symbol on the stack.

Mathematically **second type of move** is defined as:

$$\delta(q, \varepsilon, Z) = \{(p_1, \beta_1), (p_2, \beta_2) \ldots (p_n, \beta_n)\},$$

Where for $1 \le i \le n$, q, p_i are states in Q, $a \in \Sigma$, $Z \in \Gamma$, and $\beta_i \in \Gamma^*$

Pushdown automata do not read input symbol on the tape and it reads stack symbol Z in present state q and for any value(s) of i, enters state p_i, replaces stack symbol Z by string $\beta_i \in \Gamma^*$, and head is not advanced on the tape. Now, the leftmost symbol of string β_i is assumed to be the topmost symbol on the stack.

The **string β_i** to be written on the stack can be any one of the following:

1. $\beta_i = \varepsilon$, in this case the topmost stack symbol Z_{i+1} is erased and second topmost symbol Z_i becomes the topmost symbol in the next move. It is shown in Fig. 7.2(a).

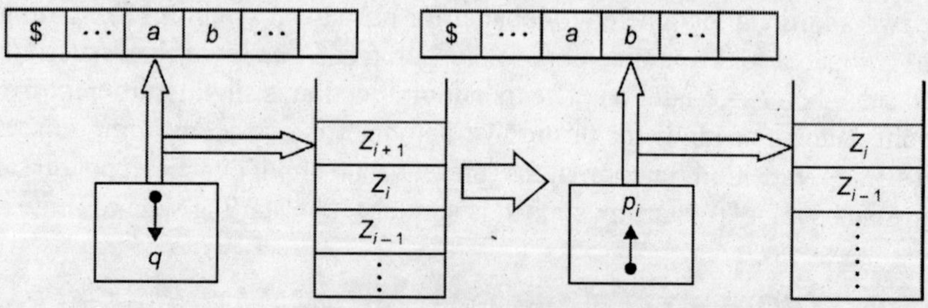

Fig. 7.2(a): Move of PDA

2. $\beta_i = c, c \in \Gamma$, in this case the topmost stack symbol Z_{i+1} is replaced by symbol c. It is shown in Fig. 7.2(b).

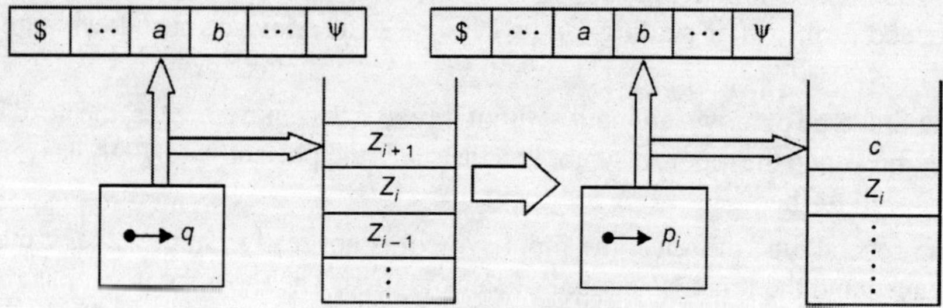

Fig. 7.2(b): Move of PDA

3. $\beta_i = c_1c_2\ldots c_m$, in this case the topmost stack symbol Z_{i+1} is replaced by string $c_1c_2\ldots c_m$. It is shown in Fig. 7.2(c).

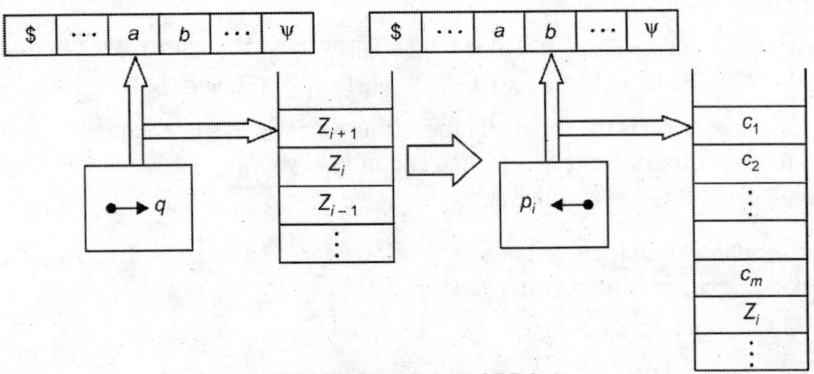

Fig. 7.2(c): Move of PDA

7.4 INSTANTANEOUS DESCRIPTION (ID) OF PUSHDOWN AUTOMATA

Let a pushdown automata $M = (Q, \Sigma, \Gamma, \delta, s, Z_0, F)$, then its *configuration* at a given instant can be defined by instantaneous description (ID). An **ID** includes state, remaining input string, and remaining stack string (symbols). So, an ID is (q, x, β), where $q \in Q, x \in \Sigma^*, \beta \in \Gamma^*$. The relation between two consecutive IDs can be represented with sign $\vdash$. We say that:

$(q, ax, Z\gamma) \vdash_{M} (p, x, \beta\gamma)$ if $\delta(q, a, Z)$ contains (p, β),

where $Z, \gamma, \beta \in \Gamma^*$, symbol '$a$' may be null or $a \in \Sigma, p, q \in Q$ for M.

The reflexive and transitive closure of the relation $\vdash_M$ is denoted by $\vdash^*_M$

Properties

1. If $(q, x, \beta) \vdash^*_M (p, \varepsilon, \beta)$, where $\beta \in \Gamma^*, x \in \Sigma^*$, and $p, q \in Q$, then
   for all $y \in \Sigma^*$, $(q, xy, \beta) \vdash^*_M (p, y, \beta)$
2. If $(q, xy, \beta) \vdash^*_M (p, y, \beta)$, where $\beta \in \Gamma^*, x, y \in \Sigma^*$, and $p, q \in Q$, then
   $(q, x, \beta) \vdash^*_M (p, \varepsilon, \beta)$
3. If $(q, x, \beta) \vdash^*_M (p, \varepsilon, \gamma)$, where $\beta, \gamma \in \Gamma^*, x \in \Sigma^*$, and $p, q \in Q$, then
   $(q, x, \beta\eta) \vdash^*_M (p, \varepsilon, \gamma\eta)$, where $\gamma \in \Gamma^*$

7.5 ACCEPTANCE BY PUSHDOWN AUTOMATA

Let M be a pushdown automata. The language recognized by M is represented by $N(M)$. We defined the acceptance by M in two ways:

1. Let $M = (Q, \Sigma, \Gamma, \delta, s, Z_0, F)$, then $w \in N(M)$ is accepted by final state such that

   $N(M) = \{w: (s, w, Z_0) \vdash^*_M (q_f, \varepsilon, \gamma)$, where $s \in Q, w \in \Sigma^*, Z_0, \gamma \in \Gamma^*$, and $q_f \in F\}$

It is similar to the acceptance by finite automata (FA). We define some final states and the accepted language $N(M)$ is the set of all inputs strings for which some choice of moves leads to some final state.

2. Let $M = (Q, \Sigma, \Gamma, \delta, s, Z_0, \phi)$, then $w \in N(M)$ is accepted by empty stack or null stack such that

$$N(M) = \{w: (s, w, Z_0) \overset{*}{\underset{M}{\vdash}} (q, \varepsilon, \varepsilon), \text{ where } s, q \in Q, w \in \Sigma^*\}$$

The language $N(M)$ is the set of all input strings for which some sequence of moves causes the PDA to empty its stack. If acceptance is defined by empty stack then there is no meaning of final state and it is represented by ϕ.

Example 1: Consider a pushdown automata $M = (\{s, p, q\}, \{a, c\}, \{a, Z_0\}, \delta, s, Z_0, \{p\})$ shown in Fig. 7.3. Check the acceptability of string "***aacaa***".

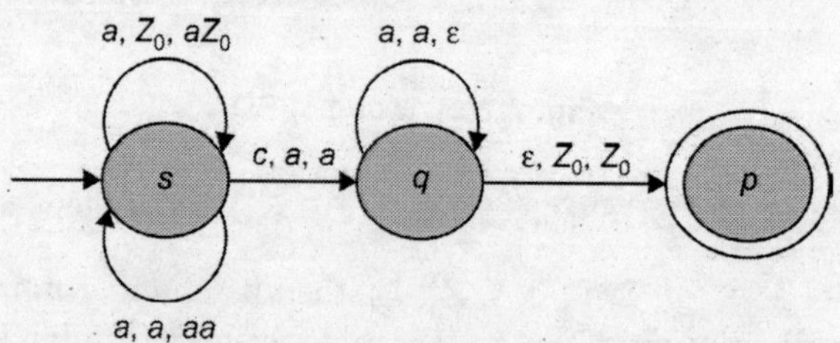

Fig. 7.3: PDA accepting $\{a^n ca^n : n \geq 1\}$

(**Note:** Edges/Arches are labeled with Input symbol, stack symbol, written symbol on the stack.)

Solution: The transition function δ is defined following:

$\delta(s, a, Z_0) = \{(s, aZ_0)\}$, $\delta(s, a, a) = \{(s, aa)\}$, $\delta(s, c, a) = \{(q, a)\}$,

$\delta(q, a, a) = \{(q, \varepsilon)\}$, and $\delta(q, \varepsilon, Z_0) = \{(p, Z_0)\}$

Following moves are carried out in order to check acceptability of string "*aacaa*":

$$\begin{aligned}(s, aacaa, Z_0) &\vdash (s, acaa, aZ_0)\\ &\vdash (s, caa, aaZ_0)\\ &\vdash (q, aa, aaZ_0)\\ &\vdash (q, a, aZ_0)\\ &\vdash (q, \varepsilon, Z_0)\\ &\vdash (p, \varepsilon, Z_0)\end{aligned}$$

Hence, $(s, aacaa, Z_0) \overset{*}{\vdash} (p, \varepsilon, Z_0)$

Therefore, the string "*aacaa*" is accepted by M by final state.

7.6 DETERMINISTIC AND NONDETERMINISTIC PUSHDOWN AUTOMATA

In this section, we will discuss about the deterministic and nondeterministic behavior of pushdown automata.

7.6.1 Nondeterministic PDA (NPDA)

Like nondeterministic finite automata (NFA), nondeterministic pushdown automata PDA (NPDA) have finite number of choices for next state for some input. As we have discussed in the mathematical description that transition function d which maps from $Q \times (\Sigma \cup \{\varepsilon\}) \times \Gamma$ to (**finite subset** of) $Q \times \Gamma^*$. A nondeterministic PDA accepts an input if some sequence of choices leads to some final state or causes PDA to empty its stack memory. Since, sometime it has more than one choice to move further on a particular input; it means, PDA has to guess the right choice always, otherwise it will be failed and it will be in hang state.

Example 1: Consider a nondeterministic PDA $M = (\{q\}, \{a, b\}, \{a, b, S\}, \delta, q, S, \phi)$, for the language $L = \{a^nb^n: n \geq 1\}$, where δ is defined following:

$\delta(q, \varepsilon, S) = \{(q, ab), (q, aSb)\}$ (Two possible moves for input ε on the tape and S on the stack),

$\delta(q, a, a) = \{(q, \varepsilon)\}$, and $\delta(q, b, b) = \{(q, \varepsilon)\}$

Check whether string $w = aabb$ is accepted or not?

Solution: Initial configuration is **(*q*, *aabb*, *S*)**. Following moves are possible:

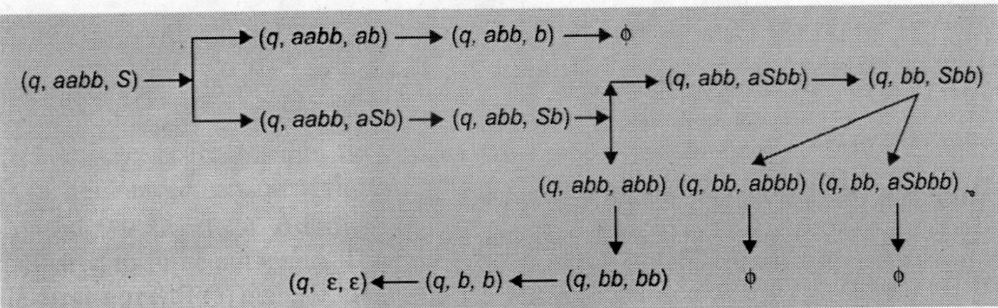

Hence, string $w = aabb$ is accepted by empty stack. One thing is noticeable here that only one move sequence leads to empty store and other don't. In other words, we say that some move sequence(s) leads to accepting configuration and other lead to **hang state.**

7.6.2 Deterministic PDA (DPDA)

Deterministic PDA (DPDA) is just like DFA, which has *at most one choice* to move for certain input. A PDA $M = (Q, \Sigma, \Gamma, \delta, s, Z_0, F)$ is deterministic if it satisfies both the conditions given following:

1. For any $q \in Q$, $a \in (\Sigma \cup \{\varepsilon\})$, and $Z \in \Gamma$, $\delta(q, a, Z)$ has at most one choice of move.
2. For any $q \in Q$, and $Z \in \Gamma$, if $\delta(q, \varepsilon, Z)$ is defined i.e. $\delta(q, \varepsilon, Z) \neq \phi$, then $\delta(q, a, Z) = \phi$ for all $a \in \Sigma$.

Example 1: Consider a DPDA $M = (\{p, q\}, \{a, c\}, (a, Z_0\}, \delta, p, Z_0, \phi)$ accepting the language $\{a^nca^n: n \geq 1\}$, where δ is defined following:

$\delta(p, a, Z_0) = \{(p, aZ_0)\}$, $\delta(p, a, a) = \{(p, aa)\}$, $\delta(p, c, a) = \{(q, a)\}$,

$\delta(q, a, a) = \{(q, \varepsilon)\}$, and $\delta(q, \varepsilon, Z_0) = \{(q, \varepsilon)\}$

Check whether the string $w = aacaa$ is accepted by empty stack or not?

Solution: We see, in each transition DPDA has at most one move. Initial configuration is $(p, aacaa, Z_0)$. Following are the possible moves:

$$(p, aacaa, Z_0) \longrightarrow (p, acaa, aZ_0) \longrightarrow (p, caa, aaZ_0) \longrightarrow (q, aa, aaZ_0)$$

$$\downarrow$$

$$(q, \varepsilon, \varepsilon) \longleftarrow (q, \varepsilon, Z_0) \longleftarrow (q, a, aZ_0)$$

Hence, the string $w = aacaa$ is accepted by empty stack.

The language recognized by DPDA: The language recognized by DPDA is known as **deterministic context-free language** (DCFL) and it is noticeable that not all CFLs are DCLs. **For example**, following languages are DCFLs:

1. $L = \{a^n b^n: n \geq 0\}$ but not $L = \{a^n b^n: n \geq 0\} \cup \{a^n b^{2n}: n \geq 0\}$
2. $L = \{a^n c b^n: n \geq 0\}$
3. $L = \{wcw^R: w \in (a + b)^*\}$ but not $L = \{ww^R: w \in (a + b)^*\}$
4. $L = \{a^n b^m: m \neq n \geq 0\}$
5. $L = \{ca^n b^n: n \geq 0\} \cup \{da^n b^{2n}: n \geq 0\}$
6. $L = \{a^n c b^n: n \geq 0\} \cup \{a^n d b^{2n}: n \geq 0\}$
7. $L = \{w_1 c w_1^R w_2 c w_2^R \ldots w_k c w_k^R: k \geq 1, w_i \in (a + b)^*$ for $i = 1, 2, 3, \ldots, k$

Some useful results

1. If L_1 is a DCFL and L_2 is a regular language, then $L_1 \cup L_2$ is also DCFL.
2. If L_1 is a DCFL and L_2 is a regular language, then $L_1 \cap L_2$ is also DCFL.
3. Every regular language is DCFL.
4. The union of a DCFL and a regular language is DCFL.

As we have discussed in earlier chapter that DFA and NFA are equivalent with respect to the language acceptance, but the same is not true for the NPDA and DPDA. **For example**, language $L = \{ww^R: w \in (a \cup b)^*\}$ is accepted by nondeterministic PDA, not by any deterministic PDA. A nondeterministic PDA can not be converted into equivalent deterministic PDA, but all DCFLs recognized by DPDA are also recognized by NPDA. So, we say that deterministic PDA is a proper subset of nondeterministic PDA and *the power of nondeterministic PDA is more as compare to deterministic PDA*.

Relation among CFLs, DCFLs and regular languages: The relation among CFLs, DCFLs, and regular languages is shown in Fig. 7.4.

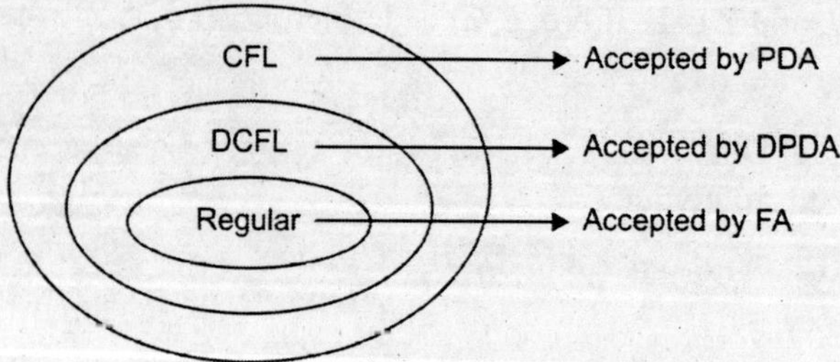

Fig. 7.4: Relation among languages

7.7 EQUIVALENCE OF EMPTY STORE AND FINAL STATE ACCEPTANCE

In this section we will discuss how an empty store PDA can be converted into equivalent final state PDA and vice-versa.

Theorem 7.1: If $M = (Q_m, \Sigma, \Gamma_m, \delta_m, P_m, Z_m, \phi)$ is a pushdown automaton recognizing context-free language L by empty store then there exists another pushdown automaton $N = (Q_n, \Sigma, \Gamma_n, \delta_n, P_n, Z_n, \{q_f\})$ which recognizes language L by final state.

Proof: First we construct PDA N based on PDA M and then we prove that both accept L.

Step 1: Construction of PDA N based on given PDA M: Input alphabet Σ is same for both pushdown automata. We add a new initial state and a final state with given PDA M.

So, $\quad \boldsymbol{Q_n = Q_m \cup \{P_n \cup q_f\}}$

(Two additional states)

The stack alphabet Γ_n of N contains one additional symbol Z_n and all symbols of Γ_m.

So, $\quad \Gamma_n = \Gamma_m \cup \{\boldsymbol{Z_n}\}$

The transition function λ_n contains all the transitions of given PDA M and two additional transitions (R_1 and R_3) as defined following:

$\boldsymbol{R_1}$: $\delta_n(P_n, \varepsilon, Z_n) = \{(P_m, Z_mZ_n)\}$,

$\boldsymbol{R_2}$: $\delta_n(q, a, Z) = \delta_m(q, a, Z)$ for all (q, a, Z) in $Q_m \times (\Sigma \cup \{\varepsilon\}) \times \Gamma_m$

(The original transitions of M), and

$\boldsymbol{R_3}$: $\delta_n(q, \varepsilon, Z_n) = \{(q_f, \varepsilon)\}$ for all $q \in Q_m$

By the transition R_1, pushdown automata N moves from its initial ID (P_n, ε, Z_n) to the initial ID of given pushdown automata M. By transition R_2, pushdown automata N uses all the transitions of M, the given pushdown automata. After reaching the initial ID of M and by using transition R_3, N reaches the final state q_f. The block diagram is shown following in Fig. 7.5.

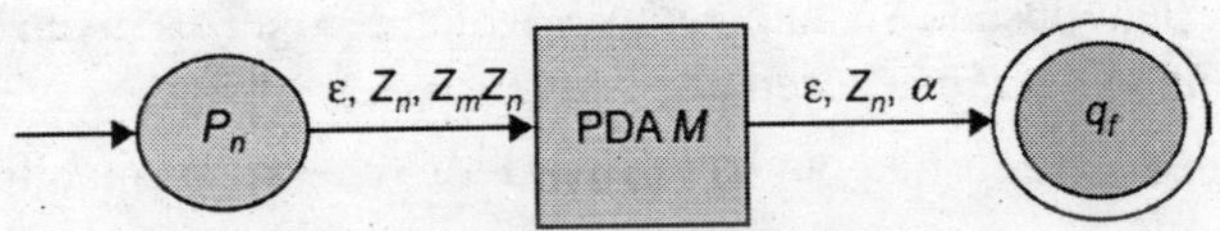

Fig. 7.5: Block diagram of PDA *N*

Step 2: The language accepted by PDA M and PDA N: The behaviors of pushdown automata M and N are same except the two ε-moves defined in transitions R_1 and R_3. Let string $w \in L$ and accepted by M, then

$$(P_m, w, Z_m) \overset{*}{\underset{M}{\vdash}} (q, \varepsilon, \varepsilon), \text{ where } q \in Q_m \textbf{ (Result 1)}$$

For N, the initial ID is (P_n, w, Z_n) and it can be written as $(P_n, \varepsilon w\varepsilon, Z_n)$.

So,

$$(P_n, \varepsilon w\varepsilon, Z_n) \underset{N}{\vdash} (P_m, w, Z_mZ_n) \qquad \text{(The initial ID of } M\text{) by Using } R_1$$

$$\overset{*}{\underset{N}{\vdash}} (q, \varepsilon, Z_n) \qquad \text{(By using } R_2 \text{ and Result 1)}$$

$\vdash_N (q_f, \varepsilon, \alpha), \alpha \in \Gamma_n^*$ (By using R_3)

Thus, if M accepts w, then N also accepts it.

It means, $L(N) \subseteq L(M)$ **(Result 2)**

Let string $w \in L$ and accepted by pushdown automaton N, then

$(P_n, \varepsilon w \varepsilon, Z_n) \vdash_N (P_m, w, Z_m Z_n)$ (By using R_1) **(Result 3)**

$\vdash_N^* (q, \varepsilon, Z_n)$ (By using R_2) **(Result 4)**

$\vdash_N (q_f, \varepsilon, \alpha), \alpha \in \Gamma_n^*$ (By using R_3)

The Result 3 is the initial ID of pushdown automaton M and the Result 4 shows the empty store for M if symbol Z_n is not there. Thus, for M the initial ID is (P_m, w, Z_m).

So, $(P_m, w, Z_m) \vdash_N^* (q, \varepsilon, \varepsilon)$, where $q \in Q_m$ **(By Result 3 and Result 4)**

Thus, if pushdown automaton N accepts w then pushdown automaton M also accepts it.

It means, $L(M) \subseteq L(N)$ **(Result 5)**

Therefore, $L = L(N) = L(M)$ **(From Result 2 and Result 5)**

Hence, the statement of theorem is true.

Example 1: Consider a nondeterministic pushdown automaton $M = (\{q\}, \{a, b\}, \{a, b, S\}, \delta, q, S, \phi)$ which recognizes the language $L = \{a^n b^n : n \geq 1\}$ by empty store, where transition function δ is defined below:

$\delta(q, \varepsilon, S) = \{(q, ab), (q, aSb)\}$ (Two possible moves),

$\delta(q, a, a) = \{(q, \varepsilon)\}$, and

$\delta(q, b, b) = \{(q, \varepsilon)\}$

Construct an equivalent pushdown automaton N which recognizes given language L by final state and check whether string $w = aabb$ is accepted or not?

Solution: Following moves are carried out by M in order to check acceptability of $w = aabb$:

$(q, aabb, S) \vdash (q, aabb, aSb)$

$\vdash (q, abb, Sb)$

$\vdash (q, abb, abb)$

$\vdash (q, bb, bb)$

$\vdash (q, b, b)$

$\vdash (q, \varepsilon, \varepsilon)$

Hence, $(s, aabb, S) \vdash_M^* (q, \varepsilon, \varepsilon)$

Therefore, string $w = aabb$ is accepted by M.

Construction of PDA N based on given PDA M

Let pushdown automaton $N = (Q_n, \Sigma, \Gamma_n, \delta_n, P_n, Z_n, \{q_f\})$, where $Q_n = \{q, q_f, P_n\}$, $\Sigma = \{a, b\}$, $\Gamma_n = \{a, b, S, Z_n\}$, and transition function δ_n defined following:

$$\delta_n(P_n, \varepsilon, Z_n) = \{(q, SZ_n)\} \quad \text{(Using } R_1\text{)},$$
$$\delta_n(q, \varepsilon, S) = \{(q, ab), (q, aSb)\} \quad \text{(Using } R_2\text{)},$$
$$\delta_n(q, a, a) = \{(q, \varepsilon)\} \quad \text{(Using } R_2\text{)},$$
$$\delta_n(q, b, b) = \{(q, \varepsilon)\} \quad \text{(Using } R_2\text{), and}$$
$$\delta_n(q, \varepsilon, Z_n) = \{(q_f, \varepsilon)\} \quad \text{(Using } R_3\text{)}$$

Following moves are carried out by N in order to check acceptability of $w = aabb$:

$$\begin{aligned}(P_n, aabb, Z_n) &\vdash (q, aabb, SZ_n)\\ &\vdash (q, aabb, aSbZ_n)\\ &\vdash (q, abb, SbZ_n)\\ &\vdash (q, abb, abbZ_n)\\ &\vdash (q, bb, bbZ_n)\\ &\vdash (q, b, bZ_n)\\ &\vdash (q, \varepsilon, Z_n)\\ &\vdash (q_f, \varepsilon, Z_n)\end{aligned}$$

Hence $(P_n, aabb, Z_n) \overset{*}{\underset{N}{\vdash}} (q_f, \varepsilon, Z_n)$

The pushdown automata N is shown in Fig. 7.6.

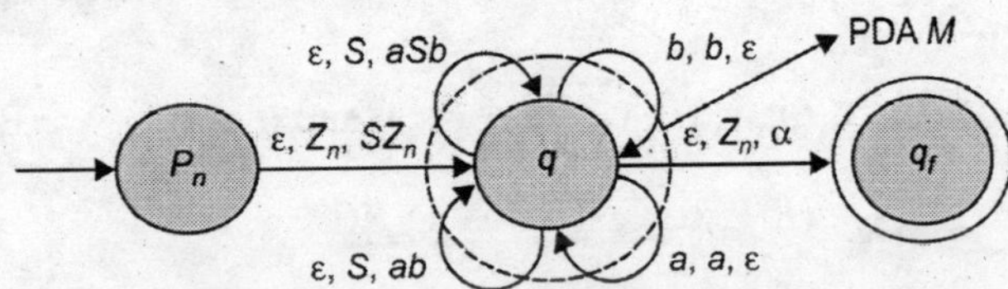

Fig. 7.6: PDA *N* recognizing language $\{a^n b^n : n \geq 1\}$

Theorem 7.2: If $M = (Q_m, \Sigma, \Gamma, \delta_m, q_0, Z_0, F)$ is a pushdown automaton recognizing context-free language L by final state then there exists another pushdown automaton $N = (Q_n, \Sigma, \Gamma, \delta_n, q_0, Z_0, \phi)$ which recognizes language L by empty store.

Proof: First we construct PDA N based on PDA M and then we prove that both accept L.

Step 1: Construction of PDA *N* based on given PDA *M*: The input alphabet Σ, stack alphabet Γ, initial state q_0, and initial symbol on the stack Z_0 are same for both pushdown automata. We add a new state with states of given pushdown automata M while converting all final states of M into non-final states.

So, $$Q_n = Q_m \cup \{E\}$$

The transition function δ_n contains all the transitions of given pushdown automata M and additional transitions (R_2 and R_3) as defined below:

$\boldsymbol{R_1}$: $\delta_n(q, a, Z) = \delta_m(q, a, Z)$ for all (q, a, Z) in $Q_m \times (\Sigma \cup \{\varepsilon\}) \times \Gamma_m^*$ (the original transitions of M),

$\boldsymbol{R_2}$: $\delta_n(p, \varepsilon, \alpha) = \{(E, \alpha)\}$ for all $p \in F$ and $\alpha \in \Gamma$, and

$\boldsymbol{R_3}$: $\delta_n(E, \varepsilon, \alpha) = \{(E, \varepsilon)\}$ for all $\alpha \in \Gamma$ and $E \in Q_n$

By using R_1 pushdown automaton N uses all the transitions of given pushdown automaton M. By using R_2 pushdown automaton N reaches state E from some final state of the M. After reaching state E and by using R_3, pushdown automaton N erases all the stack symbols (a). Transition R_3 provides a loop incase of stack is not empty. The block diagram of pushdown automaton N is shown following in Fig. 7.7.

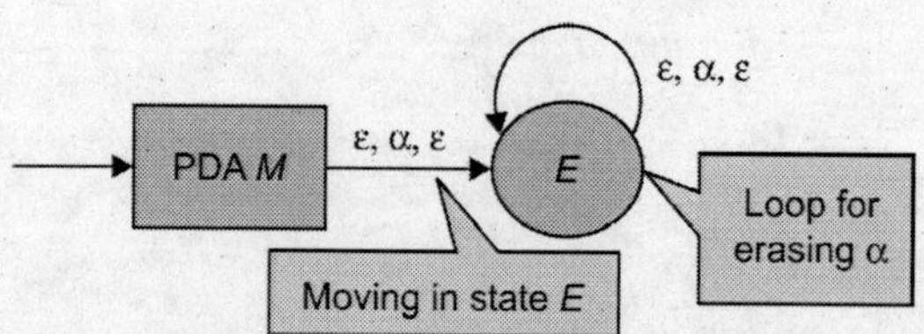

Fig. 7.7: Block diagram of PDA *N*

Step 2: The language accepted by Pushdown Automata *M* and *N*: The behavior of pushdown automata M and N is similar except the two ε-moves defined in transitions R_2 and R_3. Let string $w \in L$ and accepted by M, then

$(q_0, w, Z_0) \vdash^*_M (q_f, \varepsilon, \alpha)$, where $q_f \in F$ and $\alpha \in \Gamma^*$ **(Result 1)**

For pushdown automaton N, the initial ID is (q_0, w, Z_0). We have following moves carried out by N in processing of string w:

$(q_0, w, Z_0) \vdash^*_N (q_f, \varepsilon, \alpha)$, where $q_f \in Q_n$ and $\alpha \in \Gamma^*$ (By using R_1 and Result 1)

$\vdash_N (E, \varepsilon, \alpha)$ (By using R_2)

$\vdash^*_N (E, \varepsilon, \varepsilon)$ (By using R_3)

Therefore, if pushdown automaton M accepts string w then pushdown automaton N also accepts. It means,

$\boldsymbol{L(N) \subseteq L(M)}$ **(Result 2)**

Let string $w \in L$ and accepted by pushdown automaton N. For N, the initial ID is (q_0, w, Z_0). Following are the moves carried out by N in processing of string w:

$(q_0, w, Z_0) \vdash^*_N (q_f, \varepsilon, a)$, for some $q_f \in Q_n$ and $\alpha \in \Gamma^*$ **(Result 3)**

$\vdash_N (E, \varepsilon, \alpha)$ (By using R_2)

$\vdash^*_N (E, \varepsilon, \varepsilon)$ (By using R_3)

For pushdown automaton M, the initial ID is (q_0, w, Z_0). Following are the moves carried out by M in processing of string w:

$$(q_0, w, Z_0) \overset{*}{\underset{M}{\vdash}} (q_f, \varepsilon, \alpha) \text{ where } q_f \in Q_n \text{ and } \alpha \in \Gamma^* \quad \textbf{(By Result 3)}$$

Therefore, if pushdown automaton N accepts string w then pushdown automaton M also accepts. It means,

$$\boldsymbol{L(M) \subseteq L(N)} \qquad \textbf{(Result 4)}$$

Therefore, $\quad \boldsymbol{L = L(N) = L(M)}$ $\quad$ (From Result 2 and Result 4)

Hence, the statement of theorem is true.

(**Note:** If PDA is deterministic PDA having acceptance by either empty store or final state then its equivalent PDA is also deterministic having acceptance by final state or empty store and vice-versa.)

Example 1: Consider a pushdown automaton $M = (\{s, p\}, \{a, c\}, \{a, Z_0\}, \delta, s, Z_0, \{p\})$, which accepts a string by final state. Convert M into pushdown automaton N whose acceptance is by empty store. Check the acceptability of string $\boldsymbol{w = aacaa}$. The transition function δ is given below:

$\delta(s, a, Z_0) = \{(s, aZ_0)\}$, $\delta(s, a, a) = \{(s, aa)\}$, $\delta(s, c, a) = \{(q, a)\}$, $\delta(q, a, a) = \{(q, \varepsilon)\}$, and $\delta(q, \varepsilon, Z_0) = \{(p, Z_0)\}$

Solution: Following moves are carried out by pushdown automaton M in order to check acceptability of string $w = aacaa$:

$$\begin{aligned}(s, aacaa, Z_0) &\vdash (s, acaa, aZ_0)\\ &\vdash (s, caa, aaZ_0)\\ &\vdash (q, aa, aaZ_0)\\ &\vdash (q, a, aZ_0)\\ &\vdash (q, \varepsilon, Z_0)\\ &\vdash (p, \varepsilon, Z_0)\end{aligned}$$

Hence, $\quad (s, aacaa, Z_0) \overset{*}{\underset{M}{\vdash}} (p, \varepsilon, Z_0)$

Therefore, pushdown automaton M accepts the given string "*aacaa*" by final state. Let us define the transitions for pushdown automaton N whose acceptance is by empty store. The transition function δ_n for N is defined below:

$$\begin{aligned}
\delta_n(s, a, Z_0) &= \{(s, aZ_0)\} && \text{(Using } R_1\text{)},\\
\delta_n(s, a, a) &= \{(s, aa)\} && \text{(Using } R_1\text{)},\\
\delta_n(s, c, a) &= \{(q, a)\} && \text{(Using } R_1\text{)},\\
\delta_n(q, a, a) &= \{(q, \varepsilon)\}, && \text{(Using } R_1\text{)},\\
\delta_n(q, \varepsilon, Z_0) &= \{(p, Z_0)\} && \text{(Using } R_1\text{)},\\
\delta_n(p, \varepsilon, a) &= \{(E, a)\} && \text{(Using } R_2\text{)},\\
\delta_n(p, \varepsilon, Z_0) &= \{(E, Z_0)\} && \text{(Using } R_2\text{)},\\
\delta_n(E, \varepsilon, a) &= \{(E, \varepsilon)\} && \text{(Using } R_3\text{), and}\\
\delta_n(E, \varepsilon, Z_0) &= \{(E, \varepsilon)\} && \text{(Using } R_3\text{)}
\end{aligned}$$

Following moves are carried out by pushdown automata N in order to check the acceptability of the string $w = aacaa$:

$$\begin{aligned}(s, aacaa, Z_0) &\vdash (s, acaa, aZ_0)\\ &\vdash (s, caa, aaZ_0)\\ &\vdash (q, aa, aaZ_0)\\ &\vdash (q, a, aZ_0)\\ &\vdash (q, \varepsilon, Z_0)\\ &\vdash (p, \varepsilon, Z_0)\\ &\vdash (E, \varepsilon, Z_0)\\ &\vdash (E, \varepsilon, \varepsilon)\end{aligned}$$

Hence $(s, aacaa, Z_0) \overset{*}{\underset{N}{\vdash}} (E, \varepsilon, \varepsilon)$

7.8 PUSHDOWN AUTOMATA AND CONTEXT-FREE LANGUAGES

As we have discussed earlier that context-free languages are recognized by pushdown automata. We will see how context-free languages are recognized by pushdown automata and acceptance of pushdown automata is context-free language in this section. First, we will see how to construct pushdown automata for a given context-free grammar and then in second step we will see how to construct context-free grammar for a given PDA. We can also construct pushdown automata for a given language based on the format of the strings in the language.

Every context-free language can be derived by some context-free grammar. So, based on this fact we assume that for a given context-free language we have some context-free grammar. The approach in designing pushdown automata for some context-free grammar is to simulate the derivation of a string produced by context-free grammar. In other words, pushdown automata attempt to simulate a derivation of an arbitrary string derived by grammar. This approach can be categorized into two categories:

1. **Top-down approach**, and
2. **Bottom-up approach**

The leftmost derivation for a given string is one example of top-down approach. We use this approach in designing lexical analyzer. The input tape will contain the input string and the stack memory will contain all the right hand sides (RHS) of production rules involved in leftmost derivation of a given string. Pushdown automata read one input symbol on the tape and matches with the topmost symbol on the stack. If it is the same symbol (terminal) then erases it and move forward. If pushdown automata find a variable symbol on top of the stack then variable is replaced by its right-hand side, which is used in leftmost derivation without moving the head on the tape. Empty store acceptance method is used to recognize the given language, but no confusion should be here about the acceptance, as we have already discussed the equivalence of empty store and final state pushdown automata. In the Theorem 7.3 and Theorem 7.4 we will discuss the equivalence of pushdown automata and context-free languages.

Example 1: Consider a context-free grammar $G = (\{S\}, \{a, b, c\}, \{S \to c \mid aSb\}, S)$ for the language $L = \{a^n cb^n : n \geq 0\}$. The string $w = aacbb$ is in L. Let pushdown automaton $M = (\{q\}, \Sigma, \Gamma, \delta, s, S, \phi)$ recognizes L. Following are the steps in leftmost derivation and corresponding moves of M:

Leftmost derivation	Moves of PDA
$S \Rightarrow aSb$	$(q, aacbb, S) \vdash (q, aacbb, aSb)$
$\Rightarrow aaSbb$	$\vdash (q, acbb, Sb)$
$\Rightarrow aacbb$	$\vdash (q, acbb, aSbb)$
	$\vdash (q, cbb, Sbb)$
	$\vdash (q, cbb, cbb)$
	$\vdash (q, bb, bb)$
	$\vdash (q, b, b)$
	$\vdash (q, \varepsilon, \varepsilon)$

The above example can be easily understood by following:

Input tape	State	Stack
a a c b b ↑ (under 1st a)	q	S ↑
a a c b b ↑ (under 1st a)	q	a S b ↑
a a c b b ↑ (under 2nd a)	q	S b ↑
a a c b b ↑ (under 2nd a)	q	a S b b ↑
a a c b b ↑ (under c)	q	S b b ↑
a a c b b ↑ (under c)	q	c b b ↑
a a c b b ↑ (under 1st b)	q	b b ↑
a a c b b ↑ (under 2nd b)	q	b ↑
a a c b b ε ↑ (under ε)	q	ε ↑

Theorem 7.3: If L is a context-free language generated by context-free grammar G then there exists pushdown automaton M, which recognizes language L by empty store.

Proof: We construct pushdown automaton M based on the production rules of the given grammar G.

Step 1: Construction of Pushdown Automaton M: Let grammar $G = (V_n, \Sigma, P, S)$ and pushdown automaton $M = (\{q\}, \Sigma, \Gamma, \delta, q, S, \phi)$, where

$G = V_n \cup \Sigma$, the starting symbol S of grammar G is the initial symbol of stack, ϕ indicates the acceptance by empty store, and transition function δ is defined by following two rules:

$\mathbf{R_1}$: $\delta(q, \varepsilon, A) = \{(q, \alpha_1), (q, \alpha_2), \ldots, (q, \alpha_n)\}$, where $\forall A \in V_n$, and $\alpha_i \in (V_n \cup \Sigma)^*$ for $i = 1, 2, \ldots, n$ such that $A \to \alpha_1 \mid \alpha_2 \mid \ldots \mid \alpha_n$, and

$\mathbf{R_2}$: $\delta(q, a, a) = \{(q, \varepsilon)\}$, where $\forall\ a \in \Sigma$

Initially, pushdown automaton M searches right production rule and places the right-hand side of S-production on the stack without reading the input symbol. For all other variables pushdown automaton M does the same thing; it keeps on e-moves and places the right right-hand side on the stack. If M reads a terminal symbol rather than a variable on the stack then it compares with present input symbol on the tape and if match is there, then stack symbol is erased and M moves to next input symbol. This process is going on for entire input symbols on the tape and finally stack is empty if input on the tape is accepted.

If w is a string in the language $L(G)$, then we have some leftmost derivation for w and that should be attempted by pushdown automaton M always. It means if M does not follow that sequence which is in leftmost derivation of given string w then M will be failed. So, pushdown automaton guesses the right moves always.

Step 2: Proof for $N(M) = L(G)$: We use induction method to show the above. Let string w is in language $L(G)$. Based on the construction method of pushdown automaton M, we have:

Case 1: Let $|w| = 0$, it means $w = \varepsilon$ and $S \to \varepsilon$ is in P.

$$(q, \varepsilon, S) \vdash_{M} (q, \varepsilon, \varepsilon) \qquad (w \text{ is accepted.})$$

Case 2: Let $|w| = 1$, it means $w = a$, where $a \in \Sigma$ and $S \overset{*}{\underset{L}{\Rightarrow}} a$, then

$$(q, \varepsilon, S) \overset{*}{\vdash}_{M} (q, \varepsilon, \varepsilon) \qquad (w \text{ is accepted.})$$

Case 3: Let $|w| > 1$, it means $w = a_1a_2\ldots a_n$, where $a_i \in \Sigma$ for $i = 1, 2 \ldots n$ and $S \overset{*}{\underset{L}{\Rightarrow}} w$, then

$$(q, \varepsilon, S) \overset{*}{\vdash}_{M} (q, \varepsilon, \varepsilon) \qquad (\text{Using Rules } R_1 \text{ and } R_2)$$

Hence, all strings w in $L(G)$ are recognized by pushdown automaton M using rules R_1 and R_2 if there is a leftmost derivation for w.

Therefore, $\qquad N(M) = L(G)$ or $N(M) = L$

Example 1: Consider the grammar $G = (\{S\}, \{a, b\}, \{S \to aSa \mid bSb \mid \varepsilon\}, S)$ generating the even length palindromes over $\{a, b\}$. The corresponding pushdown automaton $M = (\{q\}, \{a, b\}, \{a, b, S\}, \delta, q, S, \phi)$, where transition function δ is defined following:

Production	Transition (Using rule R_1)
$S \rightarrow aSa$	$\delta(q, \varepsilon, S) = \{(q, aSa)\}$
$S \rightarrow bSb$	$\delta(q, \varepsilon, S) = \{(q, bSb)\}$
$S \rightarrow \varepsilon$	$\delta(q, \varepsilon, S) = \{(q, \varepsilon)\}$

And two additional transitions using rule R_2 for terminals 'a' and 'b' are:

$$\delta(q, a, a) = \{(q, \varepsilon)\}$$

and

$$\delta(q, b, b) = \{(q, \varepsilon)\}$$

Theorem 7.4: If $M = (Q, \Sigma, \Gamma, \delta, s, Z_0, \phi)$ is a pushdown automaton which recognizes the language L then there exists a context-free grammar $G = (V_n, \Sigma, P, S)$ such that $L(G) = N(M)$ or $L(G) = L$.

Proof: We will discuss the proof in two steps, in first step how to construct the grammar from given pushdown automaton M and the equivalence of language recognized by M and the language generated by grammar G in the second step.

Step 1: Construction of grammar G from given pushdown automaton: $V_n = \{S\} \cup \{[p, Z, q] : p, q \in Q$ and $Z \in \Gamma\}$, input alphabet Σ is same for both G and M, P includes following productions:

P_1: $S \rightarrow [s, Z_0, q]$ is in P for every $q \in Q$,

P_2: $[p, Z, q] \rightarrow a$ is in P for every $p, q \in Q$, $a \in \Sigma \cup \{\varepsilon\}$, and $Z \in \Gamma$ such that $\delta(p, a, Z) = \{(q, \varepsilon)\}$, and

P_3: $[p, Z, q_{m+1}] \rightarrow a[q_1, B_1, q_2][q_2, B_2, q_3]\ldots[q_m, B_m, q_{m+1}]$ is in P for every $p, q_i \in Q$, $a \in (\Sigma \cup \{\varepsilon\})$, and $Z, B_i \in \Gamma$, where $1 \leq i \leq m$ such that $\delta(p, a, Z) = \{(q_1, B_1B_2\ldots B_m)\}$ and If $m = 0$, then $[p, Z, q_1] \rightarrow a$

Step 2: Equivalence of language generated by G and acceptance of M: The purpose of $[p, A, q] \rightarrow x$, where $x \in \Sigma^*$, is that pushdown automaton M erases the string x from the stack by some right sequence of moves starting in state p and ending in state q. In reaching state q from the state p, M may have several moves erasing the terminal symbols or loading some variable or doing both. But, finally M uses right moves and erases the symbols of string x.

To prove $L(G) = N(M)$, we use following induction method as given below:

If $[p, Z_0, q] \overset{*}{\underset{G}{\Rightarrow}} x$, where $x \in \Sigma^*$ if and only if $(p, x, Z_0) \overset{*}{\underset{M}{\vdash}} (q, \varepsilon, \varepsilon)$

Case 1: If $|x| \geq 1$ and let $x = a$, where $a \in (\Sigma \cup \{\varepsilon\})$, then $(p, a, Z_0) \underset{M}{\vdash} (q, \varepsilon, \varepsilon)$ and using the P_2, we have $[p, Z_0, q] \rightarrow a$ in grammar G and therefore, $[p, Z_0, q] \underset{G}{\Rightarrow} a$ and $a \in L(G)$

Case 2: If $|x| \geq 2$ and let $x = ay$, where $y = y_1y_2\ldots y_n$, then

$(p, ay, Z_0) \underset{M}{\vdash} (q_1, y, Z_1Z_2\ldots Z_n) \overset{*}{\underset{M}{\vdash}} (q, \varepsilon, \varepsilon)$ **(Result 1)**

The stack symbols $\boldsymbol{Z_1, Z_2, Z_3, \ldots Z_n}$ cause the erase of substrings $\boldsymbol{y_1, y_2, y_3, \ldots, y_n}$ respectively.

So, we have the production rule like $[q_i, Z_i, q_{i+1}] \overset{*}{\underset{G}{\Rightarrow}} y_i$, for $1 \leq i \leq n$ such that

$(\boldsymbol{q_i, y_i, Z_i}) \overset{*}{\underset{M}{\vdash}} (\boldsymbol{q_{i+1}, \varepsilon, \varepsilon})$ **(Result 2)**

We know from the construction rule P_2 that $[p, Z, q_{m+1}] \rightarrow a[q_1, B_1, q_2]\,[q_2, B_2, q_3]\ldots[q_m, B_m, q_{m+1}]$ is in P for every $p, q_i \in Q$, $a \in (\Sigma \cup \{\varepsilon\})$, and $Z, B_i \in \Gamma$, where $1 \leq i \leq m$ such that $\delta(p, a, Z) = \{(q_1, B_1B_2\ldots B_m)\}$. So, from the Result 1, we have production rule:

$$[p, Z_0, q] \rightarrow a[q_1, Z_1, q_2]\,[q_2, Z_2, q_3]\ldots[q_m, Z_m, q] \text{ and}$$

From the Result 2, we have production rule:

$$[q_1, Z_1, q_2] \rightarrow y_1[q_2, Z_2, q_3] \text{ and } [q_2, Z_2, q_3] \rightarrow y_2[q_3, Z_3, q_4], \ldots[q_n, Z_n, q] \rightarrow y_n$$

The above production rules in grammar G cause the erase of substrings $y_1, y_2, \ldots, y_n$. Thus

$$[p, Z_0, q] \overset{*}{\underset{G}{\Longrightarrow}} ay \in L(G)$$

So, for all strings $x \in \Sigma^*$, if $x \in N(M)$ then $x \in L(G)$. That is, $N(M) = L(G) = L$

We conclude from the Theorem 7.3 and Theorem 7.4 that any context-free language is recognized by some pushdown automaton and acceptance of pushdown automata is context-free language.

Example 1: Consider the pushdown automaton $M = (\{p, q\}, \{a, b\}, \{a, Z_0\}, \delta, p, Z_0, \phi)$ recognizing the language $L = \{a^nb^ma^n: m, n \geq 1\}$. M has following transitions:

$\delta(p, a, Z_0) = \{(p, aZ_0)\}$, $\delta(p, a, a) = \{(p, aa)\}$, $\delta(p, b, a) = \{(q, a)\}$, $\delta(q, b, a) = \{(q, a)\}$,

$\delta(q, a, a) = \{(q, \varepsilon)\}$, and $\delta\,|\,(q, \varepsilon, Z_0) = \{(p, \varepsilon)\}$

Construct a context-free grammar G which generates language L.

Solution: Let context-free grammar $G = (V_n, \Sigma, P, S)$, where

$V_n = \{[p, Z_0, p], [p, Z_0, q], [q, Z_0, p], [q, Z_0, q], [p, a, p], [p, a, q], [q, a, p], [q, a, q], S\}$

The number of states are two and stack symbols are two then number of combination of states and stack symbols in triplet form is $2 \times 2 \times 2$ ($= 2^3 = 8$.)

$\Sigma = \{a, b\}$, S is the start symbol, and P consists of following production rules:

Using construction rule P_1:

$$P_1: S \rightarrow [p, Z_0, p], \text{ and } P_2: S \rightarrow [p, Z_0, q]$$

For transition $\delta(p, a, Z_0) = \{(p, aZ_0)\}$:

$P_3: [p, Z_0, p] \rightarrow a[p, a, p]\,[p, Z_0, p]$ (Using construction rule P_3)

$P_4: [p, Z_0, p] \rightarrow a[p, a, q]\,[q, Z_0, p]$ (Using construction rule P_3)

$P_5: [p, Z_0, q] \rightarrow a[p, a, p]\,[p, Z_0, q]$ (Using construction rule P_3)

$P_6: [p, Z_0, q] \rightarrow a[p, a, q]\,[q, Z_0, q]$ (Using construction rule P_3)

For transition $\delta(p, a, a) = \{(p, aa)\}$:

$P_7: [p, a, p] \rightarrow a[p, a, p]\,[p, a, p]$ (Using construction rule P_3)

$P_8: [p, a, p] \rightarrow a[p, a, q]\,[q, a, p]$ (Using construction rule P_3)

$P_9: [p, a, q] \rightarrow a[p, a, p]\,[p, a, q]$ (Using construction rule P_3)

$P_{10}: [p, a, q] \rightarrow a[p, a, q]\,[q, a, q]$ (Using construction rule P_3)

For transition $\delta(p, b, a) = \{(q, a)\}$:

$P_{11}: [p, a, p] \rightarrow b[q, a, p]$ (Using construction rule P_3)

$P_{12}: [p, a, q] \rightarrow b[q, a, q]$ (Using construction rule P_3)

For transition $\delta(q, b, a) = \{(q, a)\}$:

P_{13}: $[q, a, p] \rightarrow b[q, a, p]$ (Using construction rule P_3)

P_{14}: $[q, a, q] \rightarrow b[q, a, q]$ (Using construction rule P_3)

For transition $\delta(q, a, a) = \{(q, \varepsilon)\}$:

P_{15}: $[q, a, q] \rightarrow a$ (Using construction rule P_2)

For transition $\delta(q, \varepsilon, Z_0) = \{(q, \varepsilon)\}$:

P_{16}: $[q, Z_0, q] \rightarrow \varepsilon$ (Using construction rule P_2)

7.9 PARSING TECHNIQUES

In the previous two chapters we have discussed about the grammars. The importance of a grammar is that it provides the platform to describe (generate or produce) certain language. We also know the fact that context-free grammars are able to describe almost all programming languages. In this section, we will discuss about the main application of context-free grammar that is parsing.

In all programming languages, the construction rules, symbols used, and other aspects are well defined. One question is here; if some program is developed using certain programming language, then *how we can say that the program is correctly developed*? In saying a program is correctly developed, we have two aspects:

1. **Syntax:** It means, the grammatical construct of a program, and
2. **Semantics:** It means, the meaning of statements in a program. It is all about the operations that are to be carried out by some means.

We look into first aspect only, that is, syntax of a program developed in some programming language. Let us see one example of a small program developed in C language which is given below:

```
1: #include<stdio.h>
2: void main( )
3: {
4: printf(" Welcome to Automata Theory"):
5: }
```

If we see the syntax of above program line by line then we find that in line four colon is there at the end instead of semicolon. C compiler raises this syntax error. Now, the question is that how C compiler will detect this error? C compiler knows that a semicolon should terminate each statement in C language and it is done based on the grammar defined for C language. Now, let us define parsing. Parsing is a technique to construct a parse (derivation) tree or to check whether there is some leftmost derivation or not for a given string using certain grammar.

Example 1: Consider a grammar *G*, which describes the if-else statement construction in a programming language:

Stmt → if (Condition) then Statement else Statement | Other-statement

Condition → S_1 | S_2 | ... | S_n

Statement → Read Automata Theory | Do some other thing

Other-statement → Something more

(S_1, S_2, ..., S_n are statements and provide the value TRUE or FALSE.)

Suppose a string "**if (S_2) then Read Automata Theory else Something more**" is given. Check whether the given string is generated by the grammar G or not?

Solution: For given string following is the leftmost derivation:

$$\text{Stmtif} \underset{L}{\Rightarrow} \underline{\text{(Condition)}} \text{ then Statement else Statement}$$

$$\underset{L}{\Rightarrow} \text{if } (S_2) \text{ then } \underline{\text{Statement}} \text{ else Statement}$$

$$\underset{L}{\Rightarrow} \text{if } (S_2) \text{ then Read Automata Theory else } \underline{\text{Statement}}$$

$$\underset{L}{\Rightarrow} \text{if } (S_2) \text{ then Read Automata Theory else Something more}$$

The parse tree is shown in Fig. 7.8.

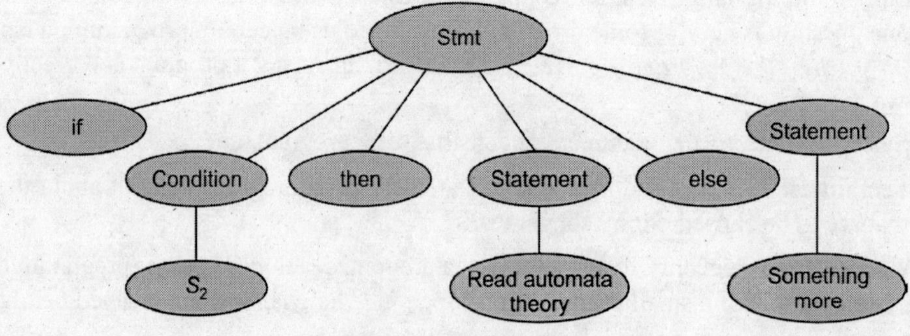

Fig. 7.8: Parse tree

Hence, the given string is correctly constructed. In other words, the syntax of given string is fine. If the syntax of a given string is correct then the answer is "YES" otherwise the answer is "NO". Parser performs parsing, which is a program (a part of a compiler). We will discuss how a deterministic PDA can be used as a parser. We can enhance the parser to do some modification in input and this is known as smart parser. Presently almost all parsers available in different compilers are able to remove some errors based on their capability. In general, parsing can be categorized into two categories:

1. Top-down parsing, and
2. Bottom-up parsing

7.9.1 Top-down Parsing

We have discussed about leftmost derivation of given string in which we start with initial symbol and replace the leftmost variable in each step. This approach is known as top-down parsing. In the parse tree, start symbol is root, terminal are leaves (input symbols), and other intermediate nodes are variables. We start from the top of the parse tree, that is root, and replace the intermediate nodes one by one from left to right by terminals. This is the reason why this approach is known as top-down approach. This approach is also known as **recursive descent** parsing. **For example**, consider a context-free grammar $G = (\{S, A, B\}, \{a, b\}, P, S)$ and a string $w = aabb$ in $L(G)$, where P is defined below:

$P_1: S \to aA$, $P_2: S \to bB$, $P_3: S \to \varepsilon$, $P_4: A \to aS$, and $P_5: B \to bS$

We have a leftmost derivation for string ***w*** considering following steps by looking one symbol ahead in the input:

1. From the start symbol S, we have a production rule $S \to aA$,
2. From the variable A, we have production rule $A \to aS$,
3. Using above (1) and (2), we get substring "*aa*" and substring "*bb*" is remaining, so we use the production rule $S \to bB$,
4. Now, we have only one symbol '*b*' to be derived from variable B, so we use production rule $B \to bS$ and get the sentential *aabbS*,
5. Finally we use $S \to \varepsilon$ and get the string "*aabb*".

So, $S \underset{L}{\Rightarrow} aA \underset{L}{\Rightarrow} aaS \underset{L}{\Rightarrow} aab\text{B} \underset{L}{\Rightarrow} aabbS \underset{L}{\Rightarrow} aabb$

Here, we have constructed the leftmost derivation looking ahead one symbol in the given string. A grammar having this property is known as ***LL*(1)** grammar. In general, if one leftmost derivation is constructed for some string w by looking k symbols ahead in the given string w then the grammar is known as ***LL*(*k*)** grammar. Due to the non-determinism problem in the grammar, we have to use $LL(k)$ approach in the parsing. We reduce the non-determinism at some extent by converting a grammar in CNF and removing left recursion and left factoring. Once again we consider the above grammar and see these following:

If first symbol of input string is '*a*' then we use production rule $S \to aA$ and if symbol is *b* then we use production rule $S \to bB$. It means we are looking ahead one symbol in the input string to decide which production will be used and this is because we have more than one *S*-production (that is two *S*-productions). We have discussed context-free grammar and we have seen the effect of left-factoring and left recursion.

We prepare a table known as **parsing table** for above grammar considering $LL(1)$ grammar as following:

Parsing table 1 for *LL*(1) grammar

Variable	Symbols			
	ε	*a*	*b*	
S	P_3	P_1	P_2	
A	*E*	P_4	*E*	(*E* stands for error.)
B	*E*	*E*	P_5	

Sometime, we face problem in case of ambiguity or left factoring or left recursion in context-free grammars. We can see in the above table that what the variables, which produce terminal, are. **For example,** we if want symbol '*a*' from variable *S* then P_1 is correct production rule to be used. Similarly, if symbol *b* is to be derived by variable A then there is no such production rule in the grammar and it is indicated by E (stands for error). **For example,** consider the grammar $G = (\{S\}, \{\text{id}, *, +\}, P, S)$, where P includes following production rules:

$P_1: S \rightarrow S + S$, $P_2: S \rightarrow S*S$, $P_3: S \rightarrow \text{id}$

Suppose a string $w = \text{id} + \text{id}*\text{id}$ is to be parsed. Parsing table for $LL(1)$ grammar is given below:

Parsing Table 2 for *LL*(1) Grammar				
Variable	**Symbols**			
	ε	**id**	*****	**+**
S	***E***	P_3	***E***	***E***

If we use $LL(1)$ parsing table, then we have problem in selecting the suitable production rule for derivation of string w as given below:

Suitable production	Not suitable production
$S \underset{L}{\Rightarrow} S + S$ $\underset{L}{\Rightarrow} \text{id} + S$ $\underset{L}{\Rightarrow} \text{id} + S*S$ $\underset{L}{\Rightarrow} \text{id} + \text{id}*S$ $\underset{L}{\Rightarrow} \text{id} + \text{id}*\text{id}$ or $S \underset{L}{\Rightarrow} S*S$ $\underset{L}{\Rightarrow} S + S*S$ $\underset{L}{\Rightarrow} \text{id} + S*S$ $\underset{L}{\Rightarrow} \text{id} + \text{id}*S$ $\underset{L}{\Rightarrow} \text{id} + \text{id}*\text{id}$	$S \underset{L}{\Rightarrow} S*S$ $\underset{L}{\Rightarrow} \text{id}*S$ or $S \underset{L}{\Rightarrow} S + S$ $\underset{L}{\Rightarrow} S*S + S$ $\underset{L}{\Rightarrow} \text{id}*S + S$

How we will be able to select the suitable production rules? This question is to be answered. If we are looking at one symbol ahead then we cannot get the suitable production rule. So, let us look at more than one symbol (two symbols) ahead in the input string and then select the suitable production rule. This is known as $LL(2)$ parsing as shown in the following table:

Table 3													
	Symbols												
Variable	**ε**	**id**	**+**	*****	**id +**	**id***	**+ id**	***id**	**idid**	**+ +**	******	*** +**	**+ ***
S	***E***	P_3	***E***	***E***	P_1	P_2	***E***	***E***	***E***	***E***	***E***	***E***	***E***

(**Note:** *E* stands for error.)

A grammar G having the property to look at k ($k \geq 1$) symbols ahead in the given string to parse that given string is known as LL(k) grammar. The above grammars shown in Table 1 and Table 3 are $LL(1)$ and $LL(2)$ respectively.

As we have discussed above about LL(k) grammars. One problem is arising in case of $k \geq 2$ that is reading the input in advance. But this can be solved using suitable data structure like queue. Another problem is non-determinism. Suppose parser is looking k symbols ahead and gets more than one production suitable. It means more than one choices of productions to use. **For example**, consider grammar G having production rules $S \rightarrow$ if <Expr> then S | if <Expr> then S else S | a, <Expr> $\rightarrow$ TRUE | FALSE. If we look up to the string "if <Expr> then S" in the S-productions then we have two production rules $S \rightarrow$ if <Expr> then S | if <Expr> then S else S to be used. This is known as non-determinism and this is due to left factoring here. Ambiguity and left recursion may create the same problem. So, before constructing the parsing table we remove these problems. If we use a grammar having non-determinism problem then parser may have processing (searching of suitable production for leftmost derivation) back and forth i.e., if one production is unsuitable then left it and come to that point from where it had started to use this unsuitable production. This problem of moving back and forth due to non-determinism in the grammar is known as **backtracking.** It is a fundamental concern in designing of a parser.

7.9.2 How to Implement a Parser?

A parser is a program and part of a compiler, which reads input string, using certain context free grammar finds a leftmost derivation or constructs a parse tree. In other words, parser checks the syntax of input. The translation discussed in the previous examples is not very useful in the design of such a program because of the non-determinism. There are many parsers:

1. **General parsers:** These are too inefficient for production, but they can parse any string.
2. **Top down parser:** Construct parse tree from root (start symbol) toward leaves.
3. **Bottom up parser:** Construct parse tree from leaves to root.

Both top-down and bottom-up parsers scan the input from left to right. ***LL* parsers** (Left to right scan using Leftmost derivation) usually are top-down parsers, and ***LR* parser** (Left to right scan; Rightmost in reverse order) usually are bottom-up parsers.

7.9.3 What is a *LL*(1) Grammar?

The basic idea of a recursive descent parser is to use the current input symbol to decide which alternative replacement to choose in parsing. Grammars which have the property to look at k symbols ahead into the input string are called $LL(k)$ grammars. We add a end marker (#) to the input string to fixed the end of the string. The end marker is also incorporated into context-free grammar. We modify a given grammar $G = (V_n, \Sigma, P, S)$ as following:

$$G_{\#} = (V'_n, \Sigma, P', S'), \text{ where}$$

$$V'_n = V_n \cup \{S'\},$$

$$\Sigma' = \Sigma \cup \{\#\},$$

$$P' = \mathbf{P} \cup \{S' \rightarrow S\#\}, \text{ and } S', \# \notin (V_n \cup \Sigma)$$

The purpose of modification of grammar is to define $L(G_{\#}) = \{w\# \mid w \in L(G)\}$. We have seen in the parsing table that a variable deriving terminal x is entered into table under this terminal by placing the production rule identification like $P_1, P_2 \ldots$ We are interested in $LL(k)$ grammars. So, we are looking forward to calculate the first generated symbol and symbol(s) followed by a variable and for this we define FIRST(A) and FOLLOW(A) for variable A such that

$$\textbf{FIRST(A)} = \{a \mid a \in \Sigma \text{ and } A \overset{*}{\underset{G}{\Rightarrow}} a\beta \text{ for } \beta \in (V \cup \Sigma)^*\}, \text{ and}$$

$$\textbf{FOLLOW(A)} = \{a \mid a \in \Sigma \text{ and } S' \overset{*}{\underset{G}{\Rightarrow}} \alpha A a \beta \text{ for } \alpha, \beta \in (V \cup \Sigma)^*\}$$

The FIRST(A) is the set of terminal symbols with which substring is derived from variable A may start and FOLLOW(A) is the set of symbols which may occur directly after the variable A. We use the above-modified grammar to have a marker for the end of the each input string.

Let a context-free grammar $G = (V_n, \Sigma, P, S)$. For each production rule $A \to \alpha \in P$, we define the set **Lookahead($A \to \alpha$)** which is the set of symbols and indicates that how many alternatives A has.

$$\textbf{Lookahead } (A \to B_1\ B_2 \text{ and } B_n) = \begin{cases} \{\text{FIRST } (B_i \mid \forall 1 \le k \le i\ B_k \overset{*}{\Rightarrow} \varepsilon, i \le n\}, \text{ or} \\ \{\text{Follow } (A) \text{ if } B_1\ B_2 \ldots B_n \overset{*}{\Rightarrow} \varepsilon\}, \text{ or} \\ \phi \text{ otherwise} \end{cases}$$

Now, we define a grammar G as a $LL(1)$ grammar if and only if for each pair of A-production $A \to \alpha$, and $A \to \beta$, where $\alpha \ne \beta$ such that:

$$\textbf{Lookahead } (A \to \alpha) \cap \textbf{Lookahead } (A \to \beta) = \phi$$

Computing FIRST( ) Set

To compute FIRST(a) for all grammar symbols a (terminals and variables), apply the following rules until no more terminals or e can be added to any FIRST set.

Rule 1: If a is a terminal, then FIRST(a) = $\{a\}$.

Rule 2: If A is a variable and $A \to \varepsilon$ is a production rule then add ε to FIRST(A).

Rule 3: If A is a variable and $A \to Y_1Y_2 \ldots Y_k$ is a production rule then place 'a' in FIRST(A) if for some i, a is in FIRST(Y_i), and ε is in all of FIRST(Y_1)...FIRST(Y_{i-1}); that is, $Y_1 \ldots Y_{i-1} \overset{*}{\Rightarrow} \varepsilon$.

If ε is in FIRST(Y_j) for all $j = 1, 2, \ldots, k$, that is $Y_1Y_2 \ldots Y_k \overset{*}{\Rightarrow} \varepsilon$ then add ε to FIRST(A). If Y_1 does not derive ε then we add FIRST(Y_1) to FIRST(A) , but if Y_1 derives ε, then add FIRST(Y_2) and so on. If nothing is derived by $Y_1Y_2 \ldots Y_k$, then nothing is added to the FIRST(A).

Rule 4: To compute FIRST for any string $X_1X_2 \ldots X_n$

(a) Add all the non-null symbols of FIRST(X_1) to FIRST($X_1X_2 \ldots X_n$). If ε is in FIRST(X_1), add all the non-null symbols of FIRST(X_2). If ε is in both FIRST(X_1) and FIRST(X_2), add all the non-null symbols of FIRST(X_3), and so on.

(b) Add ε to FIRST($X_1X_2 \ldots X_n$) if, for all i, FIRST(X_i) contains ε that is $X_1X_2 \ldots X_n \overset{*}{\Rightarrow} \varepsilon$.

Computing FOLLOW( ) Set

To compute FOLLOW(A) for all variables A, apply the following rules until nothing can be added to any FOLLOW set.

Rule 1: Add # in set FOLLOW(S), where S is the start symbol and # is the end marker.

Rule 2: If there is a production rule $A \to aB\beta$, then everything in FIRST(β) except for ε is added to FOLLOW(B).

Rule 3: If there is a production rule $A \to \alpha B$, or a production rule $A \to \alpha B\beta$, where FIRST(β) contains ε (i.e. $\beta \overset{*}{\Longrightarrow} \varepsilon$), then everything in FOLLOW(A) is in FOLLOW(B).

(**Note:** *If* $A \to \varepsilon$, *then we need FOLLOW(A)*, otherwise it is not necessary to calculate.)

Example 1: Consider context-free grammar $G = (\{E, T, F\}, \{a, +, *, (,)\}, P, E)$ defined for arithmetic expression, where P includes following production rules:

$$E \to T \mid E + T,\ T \to F \mid T{*}F,\ F \to a \mid (E)$$

Check whether G is $LL(1)$ or not?

Solution: We donnot need the set FOLLOW( ) because no variable derives null string. So, we calculate the set FIRST( ) for all the variables.

FIRST(E) = {a, (} (Since $E \Rightarrow T \Rightarrow F \Rightarrow a$ and $E \Rightarrow T \Rightarrow F \Rightarrow (E)$)

FIRST(T) = {a, (} (Since $T \Rightarrow F \Rightarrow a$ and $T \Rightarrow F \Rightarrow (E)$)

FIRST(F) = { a, (} (Since $F \Rightarrow a$ and $F \Rightarrow (E)$)

We can easily say that FIRST(E) includes everything whatever in the set FIRST(T) looking the production rule $E \to T$ and FIRST(T) includes everything whatever is in FIRST(F) looking the production rule $T \to F$.

The set Lookahead( ) is calculated following:

Lookahead($E \to T$) = {a, (},
Lookahead($E \to E + T$) = {a, (},
Lookahead($T \to F$) = {a, (},
Lookahead($T \to T{*}F$) = {a, (},
Lookahead($E \to a$) = {a}, and
Lookahead($E \to (E)$) = {(},

We see here that:

Lookahead($E \to T$) $\cap$ Lookahead($E \to E + T$) = {a, (},
Lookahead($T \to F$) $\cap$ Lookahead($T \to T{*}F$) = {a, (},
Lookahead($F \to a$) $\cap$ Lookahead($F \to (E)$) = ϕ

Hence, the grammar G is not $LL(1)$ grammar.

Example 2: Consider the above grammar and remove left recursion we get the following production rules: $E \to TE'$, $E' \to +TE'$, $E' \to \varepsilon$, $T \to FT'$, $T' \to *FT'$, $T' \to \varepsilon$, $F \to (E)$, and $F \to a$. Now, check whether G is $LL(1)$ or not?

Solution: We have following sets:

FIRST(E) = FIRST(T) = FIRST(F) = {(, a},

FIRST(E') = { + , ε},
FIRST(T') = {*, ε},
FOLLOW(E) = FOLLOW(E') = {), #},
FOLLOW(T) = FOLLOW(T') = FIRST(E') ∪ FOLLOW(E') = { + ,), #} (Excluding null)
FOLLOW(F) = FIRST(T') ∪ FOLLOW(T) = { + , *,), #}

We simply say that FIRST(E) includes everything whatever in the set FIRST(T) looking the production rule $E \rightarrow T$ and FIRST(T) includes everything whatever is in FIRST(F) looking the production rule $T \rightarrow F$.

The set Lookahead( ) is calculated following:

Lookahead($E \rightarrow TE'$) = FIRST(T) = {a, (},
Lookahead($E' \rightarrow + TE'$) = { + },
Lookahead($E' \rightarrow \varepsilon$) = FOLLOW($E'$) = {), #},
Lookahead($T \rightarrow FT'$) = FIRS(F) = {a, (},
Lookahead($T' \rightarrow *FT'$) = {*},
Lookahead($T' \rightarrow \varepsilon$) = FOLLOW($T'$) = { + ,), #},
Lookahead($F \rightarrow a$) = {a}, and
Lookahead($F \rightarrow (E)$) = {(},

We have two variables E' and T' which have more than one production rule. So, finding the intersection of Lookahead ( ) sets of these variables, we get

Lookahead($E' \rightarrow + TE'$) ∩ Lookahead($E' \rightarrow \varepsilon$) = φ, and
Lookahead($T' \rightarrow *FT'$) ∩ Lookahead($T' \rightarrow \varepsilon$) = φ

Therefore, grammar is $LL(1)$ grammar.

7.9.4 Construction of Top-down Parser

Following steps are involved in designing of a top-down parser:

Designing of Top-down Parser

Step 1: Eliminate left recursion (if any) from the given grammar

Step 2: Eliminate left factoring (if any) from the given grammar

Step 3: If resulting grammar is $LL(k)$ for some $k \geq 1$, then construct parsing table as discussed in the earlier examples.

Example 1: Consider the context-free grammar G having production rules: $E \rightarrow E + T \mid T$, $T \rightarrow T*F \mid F$, $F \rightarrow a \mid (E)$, where E is the starting symbol and **id** is the terminal. Construct top-down parser.

Solution: Grammar G has left recursion. So, we have to remove this then we construct top-down parser. Recursive productions are: $E \rightarrow E + T$, $T \rightarrow T*F$

Eliminating left recursion:

Production rule $E \rightarrow E + T$ can be replaced by: $E \rightarrow TE'$, where $E' \rightarrow + TE' \mid \varepsilon$
Production rule $T \rightarrow T*F$ can be replaced by: $T \rightarrow FT'$, where $T' \rightarrow *FT' \mid \varepsilon$

So, now the production rules of G are:

$P_1: E \to TE'$, $P_2: E' \to +TE'$, $P_3: E' \to \varepsilon$, $P_4: T \to FT'$, $P_5: T' \to *FT'$,
$P_6: T' \to \varepsilon$, $P_7: F \to a$, and $P_8: F \to (E)$

Calculating sets FIRST( ) and FOLLOW( ):

FIRST(E) = FIRST(T) = FIRST(F) = {(, a},
FIRST(E') = { + , ε},
FIRST(T') = {*, ε},
FOLLOW(E) = FOLLOW(E') = {), #},
FOLLOW(T) = FOLLOW(T') = FIRST(E') ∪ FOLLOW(E') = { + ,), #}, and
FOLLOW(F) = FIRST(T') ∪ FOLLOW(T) = { + , *,), #}

Parsing table: *LL*(1) grammar							
Variable	**Symbols**						
	ε	*a*	+	*	(	)	#
E	Error	P_1	Error	Error	P_1	Error	Error
E'	P_3	Error	P_2	Error	Error	P_3	P_3
T	Error	P_4	Error	Error	P_4	Error	Error
T'	P_6	Error	P_6	P_5	Error	P_6	P_6
F	Error	P_7	Error	Error	P_8	Error	Error

7.9.5 Deterministic Pushdown Automata (DPDA) and Top-down Parsing

We have discussed in earlier sections that the behavior of deterministic PDA is deterministic and it is used in top-down parsing. A deterministic PDA simulates the leftmost derivation of certain string. As compared to non-deterministic PDA (NPDA), deterministic PDA takes lesser time due to its deterministic approach. We will discuss a heuristic approach for designing of deterministic PDA for deterministic CFLs based on the sets FIRST( ) and FOLLOW( ). Let L be a deterministic CFL and grammar $G = (V_n, \Sigma, P, S)$ generates it. We follow the following steps to design a deterministic PDA, $M = (\{p, q_a, q_\#, q\}, \Sigma, \Gamma, \delta, p, S, \phi)$ for all $a \in \Sigma$:

Step 1: 1. Remove left recursion (if any).

2. Remove left factoring (if any).

3. Calculate FIRST( ) set for all variables and FOLLOW( ) set for those variable that have null production.

Step 2: Define following transition rules for M:

$\boldsymbol{R_1}$: $\delta(\text{p}, \varepsilon, S) = \{(q, S)\}$,

$\boldsymbol{R_2}$: $\delta(q, a, \varepsilon) = \{(q_a, \varepsilon)\}$ for all $a \in (\Sigma \cup \{\#\})$ (The symbol # is the end marker.),

$\boldsymbol{R_3}$: $\delta(q_a, \varepsilon, a) = \{(q, \varepsilon)\}$ for all $a \in \Sigma$,

$\boldsymbol{R_4}$: $\delta(q_a, \varepsilon, A) = \{(q_a, a)\}$ for $a \in$ FIRST(A), and $A \overset{*}{\Rightarrow} a\alpha$, and

$\boldsymbol{R_5}$: If $A \to \varepsilon$, then $\delta(q_b, \varepsilon, A) = \{(q_b, \beta)\}$ for all $b \in$ (FOLLOW(A) - FIRST(A)), and $A \overset{*}{\Rightarrow} b\beta$

Example 1: consider the context-free language $L = \{a^n b^n : n \geq 1\}$ and corresponding grammar G having production rules: $S \to aSb \mid ab$. Design a parser (deterministic PDA) for language L.

Solution: Let deterministic PDA $M = (\{p, q, q_a, q_b, q\}, \{a, b\}, \{a, b, S\}, \delta, p, S, \phi)$ for the given language L. Transitions are defined as given below:

Using **Step 1**, Given grammar G has left factoring, so removing left factoring we get the new production rules: $S \to aA$, $A \to Sb \mid b$

Using **Step 2**: Transitions are given below:

$\delta(p, \varepsilon, S) = \{(q, S)\}$ (Using rule R_1),

$\delta(q, a, \varepsilon) = \{(q_a, \varepsilon)\}$ (Using rule R_2),

$\delta(q, b, \varepsilon) = \{(q_b, \varepsilon)\}$ (Using rule R_2),

$\delta(q, \#, \varepsilon) = \{(q_\#, \varepsilon)\}$ (Using rule R_2, # is the end marker),

$\delta(q_a, \varepsilon, a) = \{(q, \varepsilon)\}$ (Using rule R_3),

$\delta(q_b, \varepsilon, b) = \{(q, \varepsilon)\}$ (Using rule R_3),

$\delta(q_a, \varepsilon, S) = \{(q_a, aA)\}$ (Using rule R_4, since FIRST(S) = $\{a\}$),

$\delta(q_a, \varepsilon, A) = \{(q_a, Sb)\}$ (Using rule R_4, since FIRST(A) = $\{\boldsymbol{a}, b\}$ and $A \Rightarrow Sb \Rightarrow aAb$),

and $\delta(q_b, \varepsilon, A) = \{(q_b, b)\}$ (Using rule R_4, since FIRST(A) = $\{a, \boldsymbol{b}\}$)

Now, consider the string $\boldsymbol{w} = \boldsymbol{ab\#}$ (including end marker #) then the leftmost derivation for w is simulated by M as following:

Step	State	Input	Stack
1.	p	$ab\#$	$\underline{S}$
2.	q	$\underline{a}b\#$	S
3.	q_a	$b\#$	$\underline{S}$
4.	q_a	$b\#$	$\underline{a}A$
5.	q	$\underline{b}\#$	A
6.	q_b	$\#$	$\underline{A}$
7.	q_b	$\#$	$\underline{b}$
8.	q	$\underline{\#}$	ε
9.	$q_\#$	ε	ε

So, deterministic PDA M simulates the leftmost derivation for string $w = ab\#$ (where # is the end marker) and M is called **top-down parser**. The designing of M can be easily understood by diagram shown in Fig. 7.9.

7.10 BOTTOM-UP PARSING

The basic characteristic of a bottom-up parser is that it starts with input string and replaces the terminal(s) by some variable such that replacement(s) lead to the starting symbol of the grammar. So, in each step we reduce the input string to reach the starting symbol. This approach is reverse of the top-down approach.

A bottom-up parser reads the input from left and uses rightmost derivation in reverse order. Like predictive parsing with tables, bottom-up parsers use stack to push symbols. If the first few symbols (sentential form) at the top of the stack match the right-hand side of some variable then sentence pop out from the stack and variable is pushed on the stack. This is called a **reduction. For example,** if the stack is $a*E + E$ (where a symbol is at the bottom of the stack) and there is a production rule: $E \to E + E$, then string $E + E$ is popped out from the top of the stack and variable E is pushed on the top of the stack and now the stack contains string $a*E$. The string $E + E$ on the stack is called a ***handle***. But, suppose that there is another production rule $S \to E$, and then E is also a handle. Now, question is which one to choose as a handle? Also what happens if there is no handle? The latter question is easy to answer; we push one more symbol on the stack from the input stream and check again for a handle. This is called ***shifting***. So another name for bottom-up parsers is **shift-reduce (SR) parsers**. We have several variations of SR parser. Readers are advice to concert some compiler design books for these variations. For the first question, we will try to answer in the following discussion.

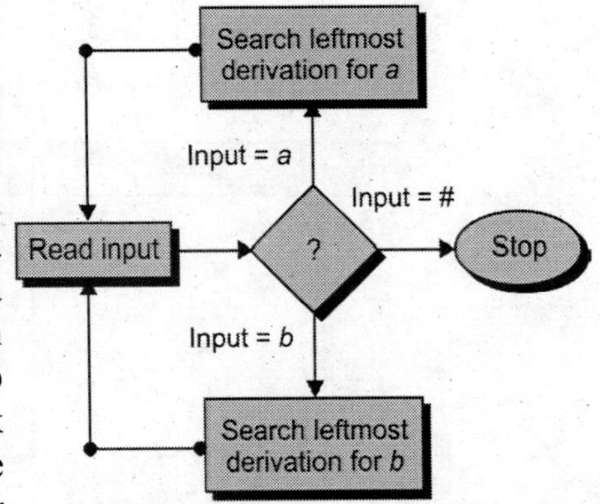

Fig. 7.9: Parsing of $L = \{a^n b^n : n \geq 1\}$

Let us define handle. A Handle is the sequences (terminals and variables or both) on the stacks that match with some right-hand side of production rule in the given grammar and replacements of handles lead to the start symbol. If replacement does not lead to the starting symbol then sequence considered is not categorized as a handle.

There three actions in bottom-up parsing:

1. **Shift** the current input (token) on the stack and read the next token,
2. **Reduce** by some suitable left-hand side of production rule, and
3. **Acceptance:** Final reduction, which leads to starting symbol.

Consequently, the problem is to recognize when to shift and when to reduce each time, and, if reduction is there then by which variable? Thus, we need a smart recognizer for handles so that by scanning the stack recognizer can decide the proper action. The recognizer for handles is actually a finite state machine discussed in Chapter 3. But here the sequence on the stack includes both terminals and variables (so state transitions can be for any symbol from the stack alphabet) and the final states indicate either reduction by some variable or a final acceptance. Deterministic finite automata (DFA) can only be used if there is one choice for each symbol. But this is not the case here, as it is obvious from the previous example that there are multiple options in recognizing handles on the stack. In the previous example, the handle can either be $E + E$ or E. This ambiguity will hopefully be resolved later when we read more symbols (also known as tokens). This implies that if there are multiple choices and each choice denotes a valid potential for reduction then instead of a DFA, we must use a NFA as recognizer for handles.

For example, consider the grammar G whose production rules are following:

P_0: $S \to E\#$, P_1: $E \to E + T$, P_2: $E \to E - T$, P_3: $E \to T$, P_4: $T \to T*F$,
P_5: $T \to T/F$, P_6: $T \to F$, P_7: $F \to \text{num}$, P_8: $F \to \text{id}$

Consider the input string **x – 2*y**, where *x*, *y* are identifiers (id) and 2 is the number (num). Following is a trace of the bottom-up parsing of the input **x – 2*y** # (id-num*id#):

	Stack	Rest of the input	Action
1.		id-num* id#	Shift
2.	id	-num*id#	Reduce by P_8
3.	*F*	-num*id#	Reduce by P_6
4.	*T*	-num*id#	Reduce by P_3
5.	*E*–	num*id#	Shift
6.	*E*-num	*id#	Shift
7.	*E* – *F*	*id#	Reduce by P_7
8.	*E* – *T*	*id#	Reduce by P_6
9.	*E* – *T**	id#	Shift
10.	*E* – *T** id	#	Shift
11.	*E* – *T**F	#	Reduce by P_8
12.	*E* – *T*	#	Reduce by P_4
13.	*E*	#	Reduce by P_2
14.	*E*#		Shift
15.	*S*		Accept (reduce by P_0)

Bottom-up parser starts with an empty stack and finishes when the stack contains the non-terminal *S* (starting symbol) only. Every time shifting is there, the current symbol (token) is pushed onto the stack and the next symbol (token) from the input string is read. When reduction by using a production rule is there, the top symbols of the stack (the handle) must match the right-hand side of the production rule *exactly* and then handle is replaced by a variable. **For example,** in the line number 11 and 12 as mentioned above, parser reduces *T**F* and places variable *T* on the top of the stack by using production rule P_4 ($T \to T*F$). In other words, parser pops the symbols *F*, *, and *T* (in order) and pushes the variable T on the stack. At each instance, the stack (from bottom to top) concatenated with the rest of the input (the unread input) forms a valid bottom-up derivation from the input sequence. That is, the derivation sequence is given below:

1.	id-num*id#
3.	⇒ *F* – num*id#
4.	⇒ *T* – num*id#
5.	⇒ *E* – num*id#
8.	⇒ *E* – *F** id#
9.	⇒ *E* – *T** id#
12.	⇒ *E* – *T** *F*#
13.	⇒ *E* – *T*#
14.	⇒ *E*#
15.	⇒ *S*

The purpose of the above example is to show how bottom-up parser works. It involves a lot of good predictions from the parser.

7.10.1 Designing of Bottom-up Parser

Let $G = (V_n, \Sigma, P, S)$ be a context-free grammar and pushdown automata $M = (\{p, q\}, \Sigma, \Gamma, \delta, p, Z, \{q\})$ recognizes L(G), where $G = \Sigma \cup V_n$, and transition function d is defined by following rules:

$\boldsymbol{R_1}: \delta(p, a, Z) = \{(p, aZ)\}$ for all $a \in \Sigma$,

$\boldsymbol{R_2}: \delta(p, a, \varepsilon) = \{(p, a)$ for all $a \in \Sigma$,

$\boldsymbol{R_3}: \delta(p, \varepsilon, \alpha^R) = \{(p, A)\}$ for each $A \to \alpha$ in P, α^R is reverse of α, and

$\boldsymbol{R_4}: \delta(p, \varepsilon, S) = \{(q, \varepsilon)\}$

Example 1: consider the following grammar G for arithmetic expression $E \to E + T \mid T$, $T \to T*F \mid F$, $F \to (E) \mid x1 \mid x2$, E is the starting symbol and +, *, (,), $x1$, $x2$ are terminals. Construct a bottom-up parser.

Solution: Let pushdown automata $M = (\{p, q\}, \Sigma, \Gamma, \delta, p, Z, \{q\})$ recognizes $L(G)$, where $\Sigma = \{ +, *, (,), x, 1, 2\}$, $G = \{E, T, F, +, *, (,), x, 1, 2\}$, and transition function δ is defined below:

$\delta(p, a, Z) = \{(p, aZ)\}$ for all $a \in \Sigma$ (Using rule R_1),

$\delta(p, a, \varepsilon) = \{(p, a)\}$ for all $a \in \Sigma$ (Using rule R_2),

$\delta(p, \varepsilon, T + E) = \{(p, E)\}$ (Using rule R_3 for $E \to E + T$),

$\delta(p, \varepsilon, T) = \{(p, E)\}$ (Using rule R_3 for $E \to T$),

$\delta(p, \varepsilon, F*T) = \{(p, T)\}$ (Using rule R_3 for $T \to T*F$),

$\delta(p, \varepsilon, F) = \{(p, T)\}$ (Using rule R_3 for $T \to F$),

$\delta(p, \varepsilon,)E( ) = \{(p, F)\}$ (Using rule R_3 for $F \to (E)$),

$\delta(p, \varepsilon, 1x) = \{(p, F)\}$ (Using rule R_3 for $F \to x1$),

$\delta(p, \varepsilon, 2x) = \{(p, F)\}$ (Using rule R_3 for $F \to x2$), and

$\delta(p, \varepsilon, E) = \{(q, \varepsilon)\}$ (Using rule R_4 for $F \to x1$)

Pushdown automata M accepts string $x1 + x2$ and does following processing:

Step	State	Rest of the input	Stack	Production used
1.	p	$\underline{x}1 + x2$	Z	
2.	p	$\underline{1} + x2$	xZ	$\delta(p, x, Z) = \{(p, xZ)\}$
3.	p	$+ x2$	$\underline{1x}Z$	$\delta(p, 1, \varepsilon) = \{(p, 1)\}$
4.	p	$+ x2$	FZ	$\delta(p, \varepsilon, 1x) = \{(p, F)\}$
5.	p	$+ x2$	$\underline{T}Z$	$\delta(p, \varepsilon, F) = \{(p, T)\}$
6.	p	$\underline{+} x2$	EZ	$\delta(p, \varepsilon, T) = \{(p, E)\}$
7.	p	$\underline{x}2$	$+ EZ$	$\delta(p, +, \varepsilon) = \{(p, +)\}$
8.	p	$\underline{2}$	$x + EZ$	$\delta(p, x, \varepsilon) = \{(p, x)\}$
9.	p	ε	$\underline{2x} + EZ$	$\delta(p, 2, \varepsilon) = \{(p, 2)\}$
10.	p	ε	$\underline{F} + EZ$	$\delta(p, \varepsilon, 2x) = \{(p, F)\}$
11.	p	ε	$\underline{T + E}Z$	$\delta(p, \varepsilon, F) = \{(p, T)\}$
12.	p	ε	$\underline{E}Z$	$\delta(p, \varepsilon, T + E) = \{(p, E)\}$
13.	q	ε	Z	$\delta(p, \varepsilon, E) = \{(q, \varepsilon)\}$

7.11 SOLVED EXAMPLES

Example 7.1: Construct a pushdown automat*a*, which recognizes language

$$L = \{a^n c^m b^n : m, n \geq 1\}.$$

Solution: Suppose pushdown automaton $M = (\{q\}, \{a, b\}, \{a, b, Z_0\}, \delta, q, Z_0, f)$ recognizes language L by empty store. There is restriction apposed on number of a's and b's in given language; it should be e*q*ual but not on the number of c's. So, M stores all a's on the stack and when c's encounter then keeps the stack unchanged and when b's encounters then matches with a's stored on the stack. Transition function δ is defined following:

$\delta(q, a, Z_0) = \{(q, aZ_0)\}$, (To store first a on the stack)

$\delta(q, a, a) = \{(q, aa)\}$, (To store remaining a's on the stack)

$\delta(q, c, a) = \{(q, a)\}$, (To read all c's on the input tape and keep stack contents unchanged)

$\delta(q, b, a) = \{(q, \varepsilon)\}$, (To match input b with a on the stack)

$\delta(q, \varepsilon, Z_0) = \{(q, \varepsilon)\}$ (To empty the stack)

Example 7.2: Construct a pushdown automataon which recognizes the set of strings over $\{a, b\}$ with e*q*ual number of a's and b's such that all a's and b's are consecutive.

Solution: We construct pushdown automaton M, which recognizes the given language by

(a) Empty store, and (*b*) Final state

(a) By empty store: Let $M = (\{q\}, \{a, b\}, \{a, b, Z_0\}, \delta, q, Z_0, \phi)$ as shown in Fig. 7.10(a). We know that the given language contains all the words over $\{a, b\}$ that have equal number of consecutive a's and b's. So, the given language $L = \{a^n b^n : n \geq 0\} \cup \{b^n a^n : n \geq 0\}$. We use stack to hold either a's to match with b's or b's to match with a's. Transition function δ is defined as:

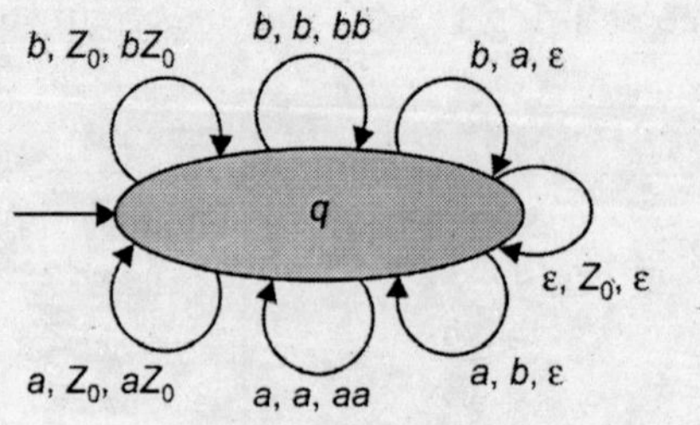

Fig. 7.10(a)

$\delta(q, a, Z_0) = \{(q, aZ_0)\}$, (To store first a on the stack)

$\delta(q, a, a) = \{(q, aa)\}$, (To store remaining a's on the stack)

$\delta(q, b, Z_0) = \{(q, bZ_0)\}$, (To store first b on the stack)

$\delta(q, b, b) = \{(q, bb)\}$, (To store remaining b's on the stack)

$\delta(q, b, a) = \{(q, \varepsilon)\}$, (To match input b with a on the stack in case of language $\{a^n b^n : n \geq 0\}$

$\delta(q, a, b) = \{(q, \varepsilon)\}$, (To match input a with b on the stack in case of language $\{b^n a^n : n \geq 0\}$)

$\delta(q, \varepsilon, Z_0) = \{(q, \varepsilon)\}$ (To make the stack empty)

(b) By final state: Let $M = (\{q, q_f\}, \{a, b\}, \{a, b, Z_0\}, \delta, q, Z_0, \{q_f\})$ as shown in Fig. 7.10(b). Following are the transitions:

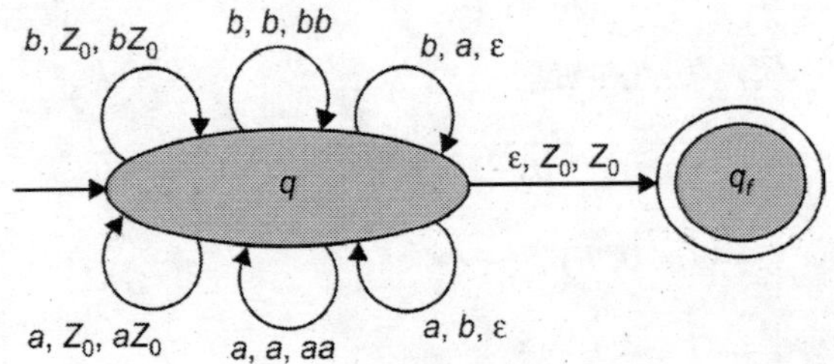

Fig. 7.10(b)

$\delta(q, a, Z_0) = \{(q, aZ_0)\}$, (To store first a on the stack)

$\delta(q, a, a) = \{(q, aa)\}$, (To store remaining a's on the stack)

$\delta(q, b, Z_0) = \{(q, bZ_0)\}$, (To store first b on the stack)

$\delta(q, b, b) = \{(q, bb)\}$, (To store remaining b's on the stack)

$\delta(q, b, a) = \{(q, \varepsilon)\}$, (To match input b with a on the stack)

$\delta(q, a, b) = \{(q, \varepsilon)\}$, (To match input a with b on the stack)

$\delta(q, \varepsilon, Z_0) = \{(q_f, Z_0)\}$ (To reach the final state)

Example 7.3: Construct pushdown automaton M equivalent to the context-free grammar whose production rules are: $S \rightarrow 0BB$, $B \rightarrow 1S \mid 0S \mid 0$ and check whether $\mathbf{010^4}$ is in $N(M)$ or not.

Solution: Let pushdown automaton $M = (\{q\}, \{a, b\}, \{S, B, 0, 1\}, \delta, q, S, \phi)$ as shown in Fig. 7.11. Transition function is defined as:

$\delta(q, \varepsilon, S) = \{(q, 0BB)\}$ (For the production $S \rightarrow 0BB$),

$\delta(q, \varepsilon, B) = \{(q, 1S)\}$ (For the production $B \rightarrow 1S$),

$\delta(q, \varepsilon, B) = \{(q, 0S)\}$ (For the production $B \rightarrow 0S$),

$\delta(q, \varepsilon, B) = \{(q, 0)\}$ (For the production $B \rightarrow 0$),

$\delta(q, 0, 0) = \{(q, \varepsilon)\}$ (For terminal 0), and

$\delta(q, 1, 1) = \{(q, \varepsilon)\}$ (For terminal 1)

For string $w = 010^4$ M has following moves:

$(q, 010000, \underline{S}) \vdash (q, \underline{0}10000, \underline{0}BB)$

$\vdash (q, 10000, \underline{B}B)$

$\vdash (q, \underline{1}0000, \underline{1}SB)$

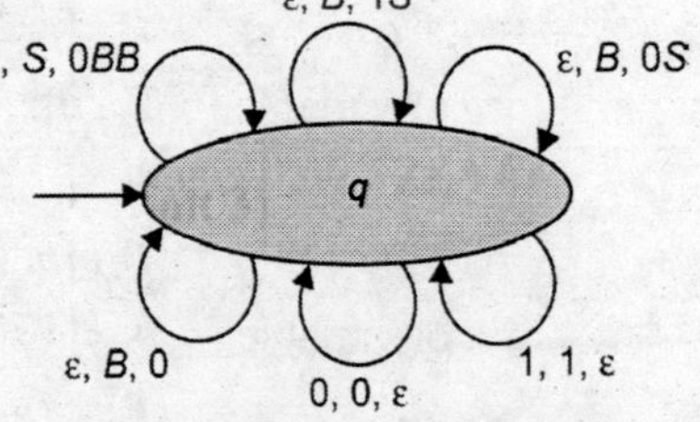

Fig. 7.11: Pushdown automata

$\vdash (q, 0000, \underline{S}B)$

$\vdash (q, \underline{0}000, \underline{0}BBB)$

$\vdash (q, 000, \underline{B}BB)$

$\vdash (q, \underline{0}00, \underline{0}BB)$

$\vdash (q, 00, \underline{B}B)$

$\vdash (q, \underline{0}0, \underline{0}B)$

$\vdash (q, 0, \underline{B})$

$\vdash (q, \underline{0}, \underline{0})$

$\vdash (q, \varepsilon, \varepsilon)$

Hence, $010^4 \in N(M)$.

Example 7.4: Let $M = (\{p, q\}, \{a, b\}, \{c, Z_0\}, \delta, p, Z_0, \phi)$ is a pushdown automaton and transition function δ is defined following:

$\delta(p, a, Z_0) = \{(p, cZ_0)\}$, $\delta(p, a, c) = \{(p, cc)\}$, $\delta(p, b, c) = \{(q, \varepsilon)\}$, $\delta(q, b, c) = \{(q, \varepsilon)\}$, $\delta(q, \varepsilon, c) = \{(q, \varepsilon)\}$, and $\delta(q, \varepsilon, Z_0) = \{(q, \varepsilon)\}$

Construct context-free grammar G that generate $N(M)$.

Solution: Let grammar $G = (V_n, \Sigma, P, S)$, where

1. V_n contains elements from the set $\{S, [p, c, p], [p, c, q], [p, Z_0, p], [p, Z_0, q], [q, c, q], [q, c, p], [q, Z_0, q], [q, Z_0, p]\}$,
2. $\Sigma = \{a, b\}$,
3. S is the starting symbol, and
4. P includes following production rules:

For variable S: $P_1: S \rightarrow [p, Z_0, p]$, and

$P_2: S \rightarrow [p, Z_0, q]$

For variable $[p, Z_0, p]$ using transition $\boldsymbol{\delta(p, a, Z_0) = \{(p, c\, Z_0)\}}$:

$P_3: [p, Z_0, p] \rightarrow a[p, c, p]\ [p, Z_0, p]$, and

$P_4: [p, Z_0, p] \rightarrow a[p, c, q]\ [q, Z_0, p]$

For variable $[p, Z_0, q]$:

$P_5: [p, Z_0, q] \rightarrow a[p, c, p]\ [p, Z_0, q]$, and

$P_6: [p, Z_0, q] \rightarrow a[p, c, q]\ [q, Z_0, q]$

For variable $[p, c, p]$ using transition $\boldsymbol{\delta(p, a, c) = \{(p, cc)\}}$:

$P_7: [p, c, p] \rightarrow a[p, c, p]\ [p, c, p]$, and

$P_8: [p, c, p] \rightarrow a[p, c, q]\ [q, c, p]$

For variable $[p, c, q]$:

$$P_9: [p, c, q] \rightarrow a[p, c, p]\,[p, c, q], \text{ and}$$
$$P_{10}: [p, c, q] \rightarrow a[p, c, q]\,[q, c, q]$$

For variable $[p, c, q]$ using transition $\boldsymbol{\delta(p, b, c) = \{(q,)\}}$:

$$P_{11}: [p, c, q] \rightarrow b$$

For variable $[q, Z_0, q]$ using transition $\boldsymbol{\delta(q, \varepsilon, Z_0) = \{(q, \varepsilon)\}}$:

$$P_{12}: [q, Z_0, q] \rightarrow \varepsilon$$

For variable $[q, c, q]$ using transition $\boldsymbol{\delta(q, \varepsilon, c) = \{(q, \varepsilon)\}}$:

$$P_{13}: [q, c, q] \rightarrow \varepsilon$$

For variable $[q, c, q]$ using transition $\boldsymbol{\delta(q, b, c) = \{(q, \varepsilon)\}}$:

$$P_{14}: [q, c, q] \rightarrow b$$

We have no production rule for the variable $[q, Z_0, p]$ and $[q, c, p]$. So these are useless variables and discarded with their associated productions. So, now we have following productions:

$$P_1: S \rightarrow [p, Z_0, p],$$
$$P_2: S \rightarrow [p, Z_0, q],$$
$$P_3: [p, Z_0, p] \rightarrow a[p, c, p]\,[p, Z_0, p],$$
$$P_5: [p, Z_0, q] \rightarrow a[p, c, p]\,[p, Z_0, q],$$
$$P_6: [p, Z_0, q] \rightarrow a[p, c, q]\,[q, Z_0, q],$$
$$P_7: [p, c, p] \rightarrow a[p, c, p]\,[p, c, p],$$
$$P_9: [p, c, q] \rightarrow a[p, c, p]\,[p, c, q],$$
$$P_{10}: [p, c, q] \rightarrow \mathrm{a}[p, c, q]\,[q, c, q]\,,$$
$$P_{11}: [p, c, q] \rightarrow b,$$
$$P_{12}: [q, Z_0, q] \rightarrow \varepsilon,$$
$$P_{13}: [q, c, q] \rightarrow \varepsilon,$$
$$P_{14}: [q, c, q] \rightarrow b$$

In production P_3, and P_7, variables $[p, Z_0, p]$ and $[p, c, p]$ have right and left recursion respectively but have no terminating production rule is there i.e., no terminal from these variables are produced directly or indirectly. So, these are useless production rules and all the production rules that include these variables including P_3 and P_7 are discarded. Now, we have following production rules included in P:

For variable S:

$P_2: S \rightarrow [p, Z_0, q]$, $\quad P_6: [p, Z_0, q] \rightarrow a[p, c, q]\,[q, Z_0, q]$,

$P_{10}: [p, c, q] \rightarrow a[p, c, q]\,[q, c, q]$, $\quad P_{11}: [p, c, q] \rightarrow b$,

$P_{12}: [q, Z_0, q] \rightarrow \varepsilon$, $\quad P_{13}: [q, c, q] \rightarrow \varepsilon$, $P_{14}: [q, c, q] \rightarrow b$

Example 7.5: Construct context-free grammar G for the pushdown automaton whose transitions are given below:

$\delta(q, a, Z_0) = \{(q, aZ_0)\}$, $\delta(q, a, a) = \{(q, aa)\}$, $\delta(q, c, a) = \{(q, a)\}$,

$\delta(q, b, a) = \{(q, \varepsilon)\}$, and $\delta(q, \varepsilon, Z_0) = \{(q, \varepsilon)\}$

Solution: Let grammar $G = (V_n, \Sigma, P, S)$, $V_n = \{[q, Z_0, q], [q, a, q]\}$, $\Sigma = \{a, b, c\}$, P consists of following production rules:

$$S \rightarrow [q, Z_0, q],$$

For transition $\delta(q, a, Z_0) = \{(q, aZ_0)\}$:

$$[q, Z_0, q] \rightarrow a[q, a, q]\,[q, Z_0, q]$$

For the transition $\delta(q, a, a) = \{(q, aa)\}$:

$$[q, a, q] \rightarrow a[q, a, q]\,[q, a, q]$$

For the transition $\delta(q, c, a) = \{(q, a)\}$:

$$[q, a, q] \rightarrow c[q, a, q]$$

For the transition $\delta(q, b, a) = \{(q, \varepsilon)\}$:

$$[q, a, q] \rightarrow b$$

For the transition $\delta(q, \varepsilon, Z_0) = \{(q, \varepsilon)\}$:

$$[q, Z_0, q] \rightarrow \varepsilon$$

Example 7.6: Construct a pushdown automaton M, which recognizes language:

$$L = \{a^n b^m c^m d^n : m, n \geq 1\}$$

Solution: We can construct M by using the grammar of given language L. But, if we see the format of strings in language L then it is clear that each word of language L contains number of a's at the starting is equal to number of d's at the end and in the middle number of b's is followed by equal number of c's. So, all the starting a's and following b's are loaded on to the stack. After this stack will contains b's at the top and a's at the bottom (*LIFO*) and on the input tape $c^m d^n$ is remaining. Now, M can match the number of c's with b's and d's with a's. This is shown in the Fig. 7.12.

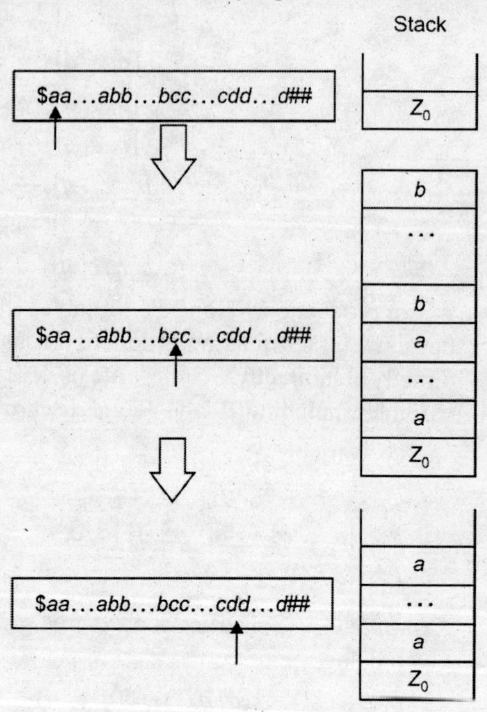

Fig. 7.12: Moves of pushdown automata

Let pushdown automata $M = (\{p, q\}, \{a, b\}, \{a, b, Z_0\}, \delta, p, Z_0, \{q\})$. Transition function δ is defined below:

$\delta(p, a, Z_0) = \{(p, aZ_0)\}$

(To store first a on the stack),

$\delta(p, a, a) = \{(p, aa)\}$

(To store remaining a's on the stack),

$\delta(p, b, a) = \{(p, ba)\}$

(To store first b on the stack and keeping stack contents unchanged),

$\delta(p, b, b) = \{(p, bb)\}$

(To store remaining b's on the stack),

$\delta(p, c, b) = \{(p, \varepsilon)\}$

(To match c's on the tape with b's on the stack),

$\delta(p, \delta, a) = \{(p, \varepsilon)\}$ (To match d's on the tape with a's on the stack), and

$\delta(p, \varepsilon, Z_0) = \{(q, Z_0)\}$ (To reach the final state)

Example 7.7: Construct context-free grammar and parser for each of the following languages:

(a) $\{a^n b^n: n \geq 1\} \cup \{a^m b^{2m}: m \geq 1\}$

(b) $\{a^n b^m a^n: m, n \geq 1\} \cup \{a^m c^m: m \geq 1\}$

Solution:

(a) Let language $L = L_1 \cup L_2$, where $L_1 = \{a^n b^n: n \geq 1\}$ and $L_2 = \{a^m b^{2m}: m \geq 1\}$. Context-free grammars $G = (V_n, \{a, b\}, P, S\}$ generates L, $G_1 = (\{S_1\}, \{a, b\}, P_1, S_1)$ generates L_1, and $G_2 = (\{S_2\}, \{a, b\}, P_2, S_2)$ generates L_2, where

P_1 includes following production rules:

$$S_1 \rightarrow aS_1b \mid ab$$

P_2 includes following production rules:

$$S_2 \rightarrow aS_2bb \mid abb$$

Since, $G = G_1 \cup G_2$, hence $G = (\{S, S_1, S_2\}, \{a, b\}, \{S \rightarrow S_1 \mid S_2\}, S)$, where S_1 and S_2 are given above. Let corresponding pushdown automaton $M = (\{q\}, \{a, b\}, \{S, S_1, S_2, a, b\}, \delta, q, S, \phi)$ and transition function δ includes following transitions:

$$\delta(q, \varepsilon, S) = \{(q, S_1), (q, S_2)\},$$
$$\delta(q, \varepsilon, S_1) = \{(q, aS_1b), (q, ab)\},$$
$$\delta(q, \varepsilon, S_2) = \{(q, aS_2bb), (q, abb)\},$$
$$\delta(q, a, a) = \{(q, \varepsilon)\}, \text{ and } \delta(q, b, b) = \{(q, \varepsilon)\}$$

(b) Let language $L = L_1 \cup L_2$, where $L_1 = \{a^n b^m a^n: m, n \geq 1\}$and $L_2 = \{a^m c^m: m \geq 1\}$. Context-free grammars $G = (V_n, \{a, b\}, P, S\}$ generates L, $G_1 = (\{S_1\}, \{a, b\}, P_1, S_1)$ generates L_1, and $G_2 = (\{S_2\}, \{a, b\}, P_2, S_2)$ generates L_2, where

P_1 includes following production rules:

$$S_1 \rightarrow aS_1a \mid A, A \rightarrow b \mid bA$$

P_2 includes following production rules:

$$S_2 \rightarrow aS_2c \mid ac$$

Since, $G = G_1 \cup G_2$, hence $G = (\{S, S_1, S_2\}, \{a, b\}, \{S \rightarrow S_1 \mid S_2\}, S)$

Let corresponding pushdown automaton $M = (\{q\}, \{a, b\}, \{S, S_1, S_2, A, a, b\}, \delta, q, S, \phi)$ and transition function δ includes following transitions:

$$\delta(q, \varepsilon, S) = \{(q, S_1), (q, S_2)\},$$
$$\delta(q, \varepsilon, S_1) = \{(q, aS_1a), (q, A)\},$$
$$\delta(q, \varepsilon, A) = \{(q, b), (q, bA)\},$$
$$\delta(q, \varepsilon, S_2) = \{(q, aS_2c), (q, ac)\},$$
$$\delta(q, a, a) = \{(q, \varepsilon)\},$$
$$\delta(q, b, b) = \{(q, \varepsilon)\}, \text{ and}$$
$$\delta(q, c, c) = \{(q, \varepsilon)\}$$

Example 7.8: The Language L is defined as the set of all strings over $\{a, b\}$ consisting of twice as many a's as b's. Construct a construct-free grammar for language L and a pushdown automata recognizing language L by empty store.

Solution: According to the given statement of language L,

$$L = \{aab, aba, baa, aaaabb, \ldots\}$$

Let context-free grammar $G = (V_n, \{a, b\}, P, S\}$ generates L, where P consists of following production rules:

$$S \to SaSaSbS \mid SbSaSaS \mid SaSbSaS \mid \varepsilon$$

Let pushdown automata $M = (\{q\}, \{a, b\}, \{a, b, S\}, \delta, q, S, \phi)$ recognizes L, where transition function δ is defined following:

$$\delta(q, \varepsilon, S) = \{(q, SaSaSbS), (q, SbSaSaS), (q, SaSbSaS), (q, \varepsilon)\},$$
$$\delta(q, a, a) = \{(q, \varepsilon)\}, \text{ and}$$
$$\delta(q, b, b) = \{(q, \varepsilon)\}$$

Example 7.9: Consider the following grammar with terminal alphabet $\Sigma = \{a, *, +, (,)\}$ and start symbol E. The production rules of the grammar are:

P_1: $E \to (E)$, P_2: $E \to aA$, P_3: $A \to +E$, P_4: $A \to *E$, and P_5: $A \to \varepsilon$

(a) Compute the FIRST and FOLLOW sets for E and A.

(b) Compute the $LL(1)$ parse table for the grammar. **(GATE 2001)**

Solution:

(a) FIRST(E) = $\{a, (\}$, FIRST(A) = $\{+, *\}$,
FOLLOW(E) = $\{\#\} \cup \{)\} = \{\#,)\}$ (Using the production $E \to (E)$, $A \to +E$, $A \to *E$), and
FOLLOW(A) = FOLLOW(E) = $\{\#,)\}$ (Using the production $E \to aA$)

(b) $LL(1)$ parse table is given below:

Parsing table: $LL(1)$ grammar						
Variable	**Symbols**					
	ε	**+**	*****	**(**	**)**	***a***
E	Error	Error	Error	P_1	Error	P_2
A	P_5	P_3	P_4	Error	P_5	Error

Example 7.10: Give a deterministic PDA for the language $L = \{a^n c b^{2n} : n \geq 1\}$ over the alphabet $\Sigma = \{a, b, c\}$. Specify the acceptance state. **(GATE 2001)**

Solution: Let deterministic PDA $M = (\{q_a, q_b, q_f\}, \{a, b, c\}, \{a, Z_0\}, \delta, q_a, Z_0, \{q_f\})$ recognizes the given language L. We see that in the given L, in each word, double of number of a's at the starting is equal to the number of b's at the end and there is no restriction on the number of c's in relation with number of a's or b's. So, one '***a***' is read on the tape and stored as "***aa***" on the stack and when b's encounter then match with a's on the stack.

In state q_a all a's are read and stored on the stack and when c is read then M moves in the state q_b and in the state q_b b's are read on the tape and matched with a's on the stack. When symbol Z_0 is on the tape then M moves to the final state q_f. The transition function δ is defined following:

$\delta(q_a, a, Z_0) = \{(q_a, aaZ_0)\}$ (To store the first a as *aa* on the stack),

$\delta(q_a, a, a) = \{(q_a, aaa)\}$ (To store the remaining a's as double on the stack),

$\delta(q_a, c, a) = \{(q_b, a)\}$ (To read c and move to state q_b),

$\delta(q_b, b, a) = \{(q_b, \varepsilon)\}$ (To match the b's and a's stored on the stack), and

$\delta(q_b, \varepsilon, Z_0) = \{(q_f, Z_0)\}$ (To reach the final state)

The acceptance state is q_f and deterministic PDA M is shown in Fig. 7.13.

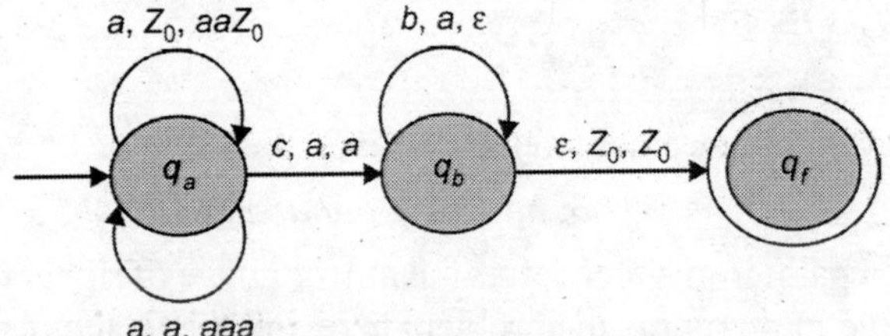

Fig. 7.13: PDA accepting $\{a^n cb^{2n}: n \geq 1\}$

Example 7.11: Let $M = (\{q_0, q_1\}, \{0, 1\}, \{Z_0, X\}, \delta, q_0, Z_0, \phi)$ be a pushdown automaton where transition function δ is given below:

$\delta(q_0, 1, Z_0) = \{(q_0, XZ_0)\}$, $\delta(q_0, \varepsilon, Z_0) = \{(q_0, \varepsilon)\}$, $\delta(q_0, 1, X) = \{(q_0, XX)\}$,
$\delta(q_1, 1, X) = \{(q_1, \varepsilon)\}$, $\delta(q_0, 0, X) = \{(q_1, X)\}$, and $\delta(q_1, 0, Z_0) = \{(q_0, Z_0)\}$

(a) What is the language accepted by this PDA by empty store?

(b) Describe informally the working of the PDA. **(GATE 1998)**

Solution: (a) & (b)

Let R_1: $\delta(q_0, 1, Z_0) = \{(q_0, XZ_0)\}$, R_2: $\delta(q_0, \varepsilon, Z_0) = \{(q_0, \varepsilon)\}$,
R_3: $\delta(q_0, 1, X) = \{(q_0, XX)\}$, R_4: $\delta(q_1, 1, X) = \{(q_1, \varepsilon)\}$,
R_5: $\delta(q_0, 0, X) = \{(q_1, X)\}$, and R_6: $\delta(q_1, 0, Z_0) = \{(q_0, Z_0)\}$

From the given transitions, we analyze following things:

1. Using R_1 terminal 1 is stored as X on the stack in the state q_0.
2. Using R_2 with no input PDA makes the stack empty in the state q_0.
3. Using R_3 remaining 1's are stored as X's on the stack in the state q_0.
4. Using R_4 input 1's are matched with X's stored on the stack in state q_1.
5. Using R_5 PDA reads 0 and moves to the state q_1 while maintaining X on the stack.
6. Using R_6 PDA reads 0 on the tape and moves to the state q_0 while maintaining Z_0 on the stack.

So, PDA reads 1's on the tape and loads these on to stack as X's (R_1& R_3) and when 0 is read in state q_0 then moves to the state q_1(R_5). In the state q_1, 1's on the tape are matched with X's on the stack (R_4) and when 0 is read on the tape then PDA changes its state to q_0 (R_6) and in the state q_0 if no input is remaining on the tape and Z_0 is on the stack then PDA makes the stack empty (R_2).

So, the accepted language $\boldsymbol{L = \{1^n01^n0: n \geq 0\}}$.

Example 7.12: Let $Q = (\{q_1, q_2\}, \{a, b\}, \{a, b, Z\}, \delta, q_1, Z, \phi)$ be a PDA accepting by empty stack for the language which is the set of all nonempty even palindromes over the set $\{a, b\}$. Below is an incomplete specification of the transition function δ. Complete the specification. The top of the stack is assumed to be at the right end of the string representing stack contents.

1. $\delta(q_1, a, Z) = \{(q_1, Za)\}$,
2. $\delta(q_1, b, Z) = \{(q_1, Zb)\}$,
3. $\delta(q_1, a, a) =$ ....,
4. $\delta(q_1, b, b) =$ ....,
5. $\delta(q_2, a, a) = \{(q_2, \varepsilon)\}$,
6. $\delta(q_2, b, b) = \{(q_2, \varepsilon)\}$, and
7. $\delta(q_2, \varepsilon, Z) = \{(q_2, \varepsilon)\}$ **(GATE 1996)**

Solution: Let the set of even palindromes over $\{a, b\}$ is L, then

$$L = \{\varepsilon, aa, bb, abba, baba, aaaa, bbbb, \ldots\}$$

If we find the mid of a palindrome then left is the mirror image of right and right is the mirror image of the left. So, deciding the mid point is the problem here and this is the reason that we cannot design deterministic PDA for given set.

In the given example either terminal symbol is stored on the stack to be matched later on after the mid point or if the corresponding match is there then PDA popped the stack symbol.

In the given transitions using (1) & (2) PDA loads symbol '*a*' or '*b*' on the stack, using (5) & (6) PDA matches the input with stack symbol and using (7) PDA makes the stack empty. So, if more a or *b* symbols are there then PDA will use (3) & (4) and in these either symbol will be loaded on the stack and remain in the state q_1 or matched with the same symbol and moved to state q_2. So, (3) & (4) solve the non-determinism problem to select the mid point into the palindromes.

So, transitions are:

1. $\delta(q_1, a, Z) = \{(q_1, Za)\}$,
2. $\delta(q_1, b, Z) = \{(q_1, Zb)\}$,
3. $\delta(q_1, a, a) = \boldsymbol{\{(q_1, aa), (q_2, \varepsilon)\}}$,
4. $\delta(q_1, b, b) = \boldsymbol{\{(q_1, bb), (q_2, \varepsilon)\}}$,
5. $\delta(q_2, a, a) = \{(q_2, \varepsilon)\}$,
6. $\delta(q_2, b, b) = \{(q_2, \varepsilon)\}$, and
7. $\delta(q_2, \varepsilon, Z) = \{(q_2, \varepsilon)\}$

Example 7.13: Consider the grammar having production rules: $S \to SS \mid aSb \mid bSa \mid \varepsilon$ and string $w = aabb$. Show the exhaustive search parsing method for w.

Solution: Exhaustive search parsing is a form of top-down parsing in which all the productions are consider round by round as given following:

Round one:

1. $S \Rightarrow SS$ 2. $S \Rightarrow aSb$ 3. $S \Rightarrow bSa$ 4. $S \Rightarrow \varepsilon$

Round second:

1.1 $S \Rightarrow \underline{S}S \Rightarrow SSS$ (*S* is replaced by *SS*)

1.2 $\Rightarrow aSbS$ (*S* is replaced by *aSb*)

1.3 $\Rightarrow bSaS$ (*S* is replaced by *bSa*)

1.4 $\Rightarrow S$ (*S* is replaced by ε)

2.1 $S \Rightarrow aSb \Rightarrow aSSb$ (*S* is replaced by *SS*)

2.2 $\Rightarrow aaSbb$ (*S* is replaced by *aSb*)

2.3 $\Rightarrow abSab$ (*S* is replaced by *bSa*)

2.4 $\Rightarrow ab$ (*S* is replaced by ε)

3.1 $S \Rightarrow bSa \Rightarrow bSSa$ (*S* is replaced by *SS*)

3.2 $\Rightarrow baSba$ (*S* is replaced by *aSb*)

3.3 $\Rightarrow bbSaa$ (*S* is replaced by *bSa*)

3.4 $\Rightarrow ba$ (*S* is replaced by ε)

Similarly, in the third round we find the target string;

$$S \Rightarrow aSb \Rightarrow aaSbb \Rightarrow aabb$$

So, in the round one number of production used = 4,

In the second round the number of production used = 4 × 4,

In the third round the number of production used = 4 × 4 × 4, and so on, where 4 is the number of production rules given. What is the total number of rounds and sentential forms used for a given string? The answer we will see in the next problem.

Example 7.14: Suppose $G = (V_n, \Sigma, P, S)$ is a context-free grammar and does not have any production rule of the form $A \rightarrow \varepsilon$ (null production) or $A \rightarrow B$ (unit production), where *A*, *B* are variables. Show that for a given string $w \in L(G)$ the total number of rounds involved in derivation cannot exceed $2 \times |w|$ and the total number of sentential forms cannot exceed *M*, where *M* is given by following equation:

$$M \leq |P| + |P|^2 + |P|^3 + \ldots + |P|^{2 \times |w|}$$

Solution: Since, the given grammar *G* doesn't have null and unit productions, so it has production of type $A \rightarrow \alpha$, where $|\alpha| \geq 1$, if $|\alpha| = 1$, then $\alpha \in \Sigma$, otherwise $\alpha \in (\Sigma \cup V_n)^+$.

We use mathematical induction approach show the above identities. One thing is clear here about the size of sentential forms, which cannot exceed $|w|$.

If $|w| = 1$, then total round involved can't exceed $2 \times |w|$, so identity is true for $|w| = 1$.

If $|w| = 2$, then

Case 1: We can get both the symbols of *w* in first round.

Case 2: We get one symbol of *w* and one variable and in the second round variable is replaced by the remaining symbol of *w*.

Case 3: We get two variables in the first round and second round involved the Case 2 and in the third round we get *w*.

So, the total rounds involved can't exceed $2 \times |w|$.

For the $|w| = n$ for $n > 2$, in worst case, we get

$$S \Rightarrow A_1X_1 \Rightarrow A_1A_2X_2 \Rightarrow A_1A_2A_3X_3$$
$$\ldots$$
$$\Rightarrow A_1A_2\ldots A_{n-2}X_{n-2}$$
$$\Rightarrow A_1A_2\ldots A_{n-2}A_{n-1}A_n, \text{ where } X_i \in V_n \text{ for } i = 2, 3, \ldots, n-2$$

So, using $(n-2)$ rounds we get $S \overset{n-2}{\underset{G}{\Longrightarrow}} A_1A_2 \ldots A_n$, and variable A_i's are replaced by terminals one by one in further n rounds. So, $S \overset{n-2+n}{\underset{G}{\Longrightarrow}} a_1a_2 \ldots a_n$, where $a_i \in \Sigma$ for $i = 1, 2, \ldots, n$. Therefore, total rounds involved is $n - 2 + n = 2 \times n - 2$, where n is the length of given string w. So, for $n > 2$, the total number of rounds involved can't exceed $2 \times w$.Thus, the given identity is true.

The total number of sentential forms derived in derivation of w cannot exceed the total sentential forms derived in $2\times |w|$ *rounds.*

So, $M \leq$ total sentential forms in round first + total sentential forms in round second + ... + total sentential forms in round $2 \times |w$

Since, we have seen in the previous problem that total sentential form in round i^{th} is less than equal to $|P|^i$, where $|P|$ is the total production rules given.

So, $M \leq |P| + |P|^2 + |P|^3 + \ldots + |P|^{2\times|w|}$

Example 7.15: Design a top-down parser for the grammar $G = (V_n, \{+, *, x, 1, 2,), (\}, P, E)$, where P includes $E \to TE_1$, $E_1 \to +TE_1 | \varepsilon$, $T \to FT_1$, $T_1 \to *FT_1 | \varepsilon$, $F \to (E) | xN$, $N \to 1 | 2$ and show the parsing of string $x1 + x2$.

Solution: Let pushdown automata $M = (\{p, q, q_1, q_2, q+, q_*, q_(, q_), q_\#\}, \{+, *, x, 1, 2,), (\}, \{+, *, x, 1, 2,), (, E, T, F, N, E_1, T_1\}, \delta, p, E, \}$ accepts $L(G)$, where transition function δ is defined below:

$\delta(p, \varepsilon, E) = \{(q, E)\}$, $\delta(q, 1, \varepsilon) = \{(q_1, \varepsilon)\}$, $\delta(q, 2, \varepsilon) = \{(q_2, \varepsilon)\}$, $\delta(q, +, \varepsilon) = \{(q+, \varepsilon)\}$,
$\delta(q, *, \varepsilon) = \{(q_*, \varepsilon)\}$, $\delta(q, (, \varepsilon) = \{(q_(, \varepsilon)\}$, $\delta(q,), \varepsilon) = \{(q_), \varepsilon)\}$, $\delta(q, \#, \varepsilon) = \{(q_\#, \varepsilon)\}$,
$\delta(q_1, \varepsilon, 1) = \{(q, \varepsilon)\}$, $\delta(q_2, \varepsilon, 2) = \{(q, \varepsilon)\}$, $\delta(qx, \varepsilon, x) = \{(q, \varepsilon)\}$, $\delta(q+, \varepsilon, +) = \{(q, \varepsilon)\}$,
$\delta(q_*, \varepsilon, *) = \{(q, \varepsilon)\}$, $\delta(q_(, \varepsilon, () = \{(q, \varepsilon)\}$, $\delta(q_), \varepsilon,)) = \{(q, \varepsilon)\}$,

Since, FIRST(E) = FIRST(T) = FIRST(F) = $\{x, (\}$, so we have:

$\delta(q_x, \varepsilon, E) = \{(q_x, TE_1)\}$ (Using $E \Rightarrow TE_1 \Rightarrow FT_1E_1 \Rightarrow xNT_1E_1$),
$\delta(q_(, \varepsilon, E) = \{(q_(, TE_1)\}$ (Using $E \Rightarrow TE_1 \Rightarrow FT_1E_1 \Rightarrow (E)T_1E_1$),
$\delta(q_x, \varepsilon, T) = \{(q_x, FT_1)\}$ (Using $T \Rightarrow FT_1 \Rightarrow xNT_1E_1$),
$\delta(q_(, \varepsilon, T) = \{(q(, FT_1)\}$ (Using $T \Rightarrow FT_1 \Rightarrow (E)T_1E_1$),
$\delta(q_x, \varepsilon, F) = \{(q_x, xN)\}$ (Using $F \Rightarrow xN$),
$\delta(q_(, \varepsilon, F) = \{(q_(, (E))\}$ (Using $F \Rightarrow (E)$),

Since, FIRST(T_1) = $\{*, \varepsilon\}$, FOLLOW(T_1) = FOLLOW(T) = FIRST(E_1) $\cup$ FOLLOW(E) = $\{+,), \#\}$,

So we have:

$$\delta(q_*, \varepsilon, T_1) = \{(q_*, *FT_1)\} \qquad \text{(Using } T \Rightarrow *FT_1\text{)},$$
$$\delta(q_+, \varepsilon, T_1) = \{(q_+, \varepsilon)\} \qquad \text{(Using } T \Rightarrow \varepsilon\text{)},$$
$$\delta(q_), \varepsilon, T_1) = \{(q_), \varepsilon)\} \qquad \text{(Using } T \Rightarrow \varepsilon\text{)},$$
$$\delta(q_\#, \varepsilon, T_1) = \{(q_\#, \varepsilon)\} \qquad \text{(Using } T \Rightarrow \varepsilon\text{)},$$

Since, FIRST(E_1) = { + , ε}, FOLLOW(E_1) = {#,)}, so we have:

$$\delta(q_+, \varepsilon, E_1) = \{(q_+, +TE_1)\} \qquad \text{(Using } E_1 \Rightarrow +TE_1\text{)},$$
$$\delta(q_), \varepsilon, E_1) = \{(q_), \varepsilon)\} \qquad \text{(Using } E_1 \Rightarrow \varepsilon\text{)},$$
$$\delta(q_\#, \varepsilon, E_1) = \{(q_\#, \varepsilon)\} \qquad \text{(Using } E_1 \Rightarrow \varepsilon\text{)},$$

Since, FIRST(N) = {1, 2), so we have:

$$\delta(q_1\ \varepsilon, N) = \{(q_1, \varepsilon)\} \qquad \text{(Using } N \Rightarrow 1\text{)},$$
$$\delta(q_2, \varepsilon, N) = \{(q_2, \varepsilon)\} \qquad \text{(Using } N \Rightarrow 2\text{)},$$

Followings are the steps involved in parsing of string **x1 + x2:**

Step	State	Input	Stack	Rule
1.	p	$x1 + x2\#$		
2.	q	$\underline{x}1 + x2\#$		$\delta(p, \varepsilon, E) = (q, E)$
3.	q_x	$1 + x2\#$	$\underline{E}$	$\delta(q, x, \varepsilon) = (q_x, \varepsilon)$
4.	q_x	$1 + x2\#$	$\underline{T}E_1$	$\delta(q_x, \varepsilon, E) = (q_x, TE_1)$
5.	q_x	$1 + x2\#$	FT_1E_1	$\delta(q_x, \varepsilon, T) = (q_x, FT_1E_1)$
6.	q_x	$1 + x2\#$	xNT_1E_1	$\delta(q_x, \varepsilon, T) = (q_x, xNT_1E_1)$
7.	q	$\underline{1} + x2\#$	NT_1E_1	$\delta(q_x, \varepsilon, x) = (q, \varepsilon)$
8.	q_1	$+ x2\#$	$\underline{N}T_1E_1$	$\delta(q, 1, \varepsilon) = (q_1, \varepsilon)$
9.	q_1	$+ x2\#$	$\underline{1}T_1E_1$	$\delta(q_1, \varepsilon, N) = (q_1, 1)$
10.	q	$\underline{+} x2\#$	T_1E_1	$\delta(q_1, \varepsilon, 1) = (q, \varepsilon)$
11.	q_+	$x2\#$	$\underline{T_1}E_1$	$\delta(q, +, \varepsilon) = (q_+, \varepsilon)$
12.	q_+	$x2\#$	$\underline{E_1}$	$(q_+, \varepsilon, T_1) = (q_+, \varepsilon)$
13.	q_+	$x2\#$	$\underline{+}\ TE_1$	$\delta(q_+, \varepsilon, E_1) = (q_+, + TE_1)$
14.	q	$x2\#$	TE_1	$\delta(q_+, \varepsilon, +) = (q, \varepsilon)$
15.	q_x	$2\#$	$\underline{T}E_1$	$\delta(q, \varepsilon, x) = (q_x, \varepsilon)$
16.	q_x	$2\#$	FT_1E_1	$\delta(q_x, \varepsilon, T) = (q_x, FT_1)$
17.	q_x	$2\#$	xNT_1E_1	$\delta(q_x, \varepsilon, F) = (q_x, xN)$
18.	q	$\underline{2}\#$	NT_1E_1	$\delta(q_x, \varepsilon, x) = (q, \varepsilon)$
19.	q_2	$\#$	$\underline{N}T_1E_1$	$\delta(q, 2, \varepsilon) = (q_2, \varepsilon)$
20.	q_2	$\#$	$\underline{2}T_1E_1$	$\delta(q_2, \varepsilon, N) = (q_2, 2)$
21.	q	$\underline{\#}$	T_1E_1	$\delta(q_2, \varepsilon, 2) = (q, \varepsilon)$
22.	$q_\#$	ε	$\underline{T_1}E_1$	$\delta(q, \#, \varepsilon) = (q_\#, \varepsilon)$
23.	$q_\#$	ε	$\underline{E_1}$	$\delta(q_\#, \varepsilon, T_1) = (q_\#, \varepsilon)$
24.	$q_\#$	ε	ε	$\delta(q_\#, \varepsilon, E_1) = (q_\#, \varepsilon)$

Example 7.16: Design a PDA to accept the following language. PDA may accept either by final state or by empty stack. $L = \{a^n b^n : n \geq 1\}$

Solution: Let $M = (\{q\}, \{a, b\}, \{a, b, Z_0\}, \delta, q, Z_0, \phi)$ be PDA as shown in Fig. 7.14(*a*). We know that the given language contains all the words over $\{a, b\}$ that have ε*q*ual number of consecutive a's and b's.

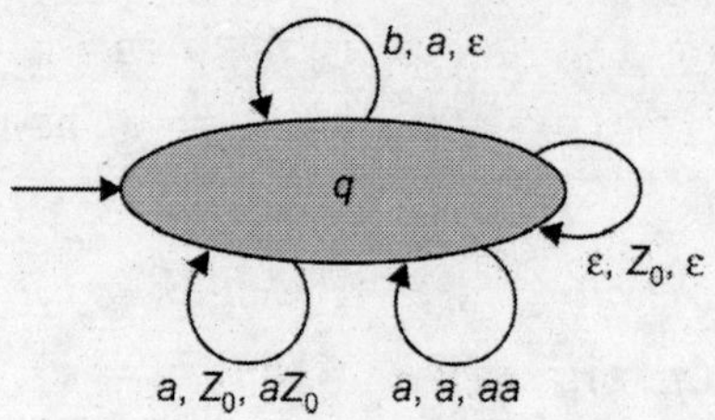

Fig. 7.14(a): PDA for $\{a^n b^n : n \geq 1\}$

(a) By empty store: We use stack to hold a's to match with b's. Transition function δ is defined as:

$\delta(q, a, Z_0) = \{(q, aZ_0)\}$, (To store first *a* on the stack)

$\delta(q, a, a) = \{(q, aa)\}$, (To store remaining a's on the stack)

$\delta(q, b, a) = \{(q, \varepsilon)\}$, (To match input *b* with a on the stack)

$\delta(q, \varepsilon, Z_0) = \{(q, \varepsilon)\}$ (To make the stack empty)

(b) By final state: Let $M = (\{q, q_f\}, \{a, b\}, \{a, b, Z_0\}, \delta, q, Z_0, \{q_f\})$ be PDA as shown in Fig. 7.14(b). Following are the transitions:

$\delta(q, a, Z_0) = \{(q, aZ_0)\}$, (To store first *a* on the stack)

$\delta(q, a, a) = \{(q, aa)\}$, (To store remaining a's on the stack)

$\delta(q, b, a) = \{(q, \varepsilon)\}$, (To match input *b* with a on the stack)

$\delta(q, \varepsilon, Z_0) = \{(q_f, Z_0)\}$ (To reach the final state)

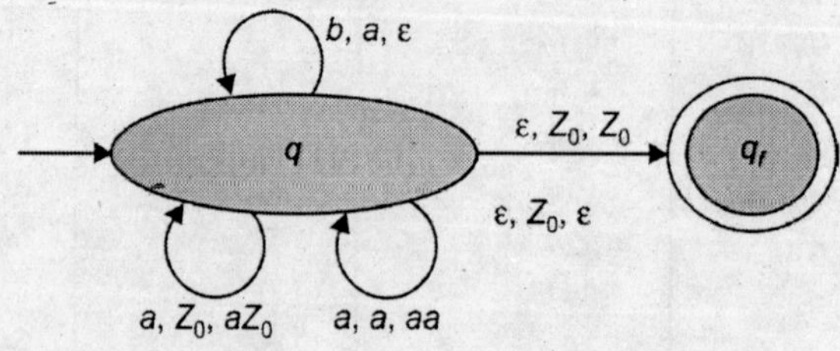

Fig. 7.14(b): PDA For language $\{a^n b^n : n \geq 1\}$

Example 7.17: Construct pushdown acceptors for the following languages:

(i) $L_1 = \{0^n \subset 0^m \mid n, m > 0, nm\}$

(ii) $L_2 = \{0^n \subset 0^m \mid n > 0, m = 3n\}$

Solution:

(i) We construct grammar $G_1 = (V_n, \{0\}, P, S)$ for the given language L_1, where *P* consists of following production rules:

$$S \rightarrow 0S0,\ S \rightarrow 0A,\ A \rightarrow 0A,\ A \rightarrow \subset$$

We construct PDA $M_1 = (\{q\}, \{0\}, \{0, S, A\}, \delta, q, S, f)$ based on the above production rules of grammar G_1:

Production	Transition
$S \rightarrow 0S0$	$\delta(q, \varepsilon, S) = \{(q, 0S0)\}$
$S \rightarrow 0A$	$\delta(q, \varepsilon, S) = \{(q, 0A)\}$
$A \rightarrow 0A$	$\delta(q, \varepsilon, A) = \{(q, 0A)\}$
$A \rightarrow \subset$	$\delta(q, \varepsilon, A) = \{(q, \subset)\}$
And there are two transitions for terminals 'a' and '$\subset$':	
	$\delta(q, 0, 0) = \{(q, \varepsilon)\}$, and
	$\delta(q, \subset, \subset) = \{(q, \varepsilon)\}$

(ii) We construct grammar $G_2 = (V_n, \{0\}, P, S)$ for the given language L_2, where P consists of following production rules:

$$S \rightarrow 0S000,\ S \rightarrow 0 \subset 000$$

We construct PDA $M_2 = (\{q\}, \{0\}, \{0, S\}, \delta, q, S, \phi)$ based on the above production rules of grammar G_2:

Production	Transition
$S \rightarrow 0S000$	$\delta(q, \varepsilon, S) = \{(q, 0S000)\}$
$S \rightarrow 0 \subset 000$	$\delta(q, \varepsilon, S) = \{(q, 0 \subset 000)\}$
And there are two transitions for terminals '0' and '$\subset$':	
	$\delta(q, 0, 0) = \{(q, \varepsilon)\}$, and
	$\delta(q, \subset, \subset) = \{(q, \varepsilon)\}$

Example 7.18: Let G be the grammar with the following productions:

$$\Sigma \rightarrow aAA,\ A \rightarrow bB,\ A \rightarrow aB,\ A \rightarrow a,\ B \rightarrow aAA$$

Describe informally $L(G)$, construct a pushdown acceptor M such that

$$L(M) = L(G)$$

Solution: The given grammar G generates two types of strings:

(i) $\Sigma \Rightarrow aAA \Rightarrow aaa, \Rightarrow aAA \Rightarrow aaBA \Rightarrow aaaAAA \ldots \Rightarrow aaaaaa$

That is, $0^{3n} \in L(G)$ for $n = 1, 2, 3, \ldots$

(ii) $\Sigma \Rightarrow aAA \Rightarrow abBAabaAAA \ldots \Rightarrow abaaaa$

$\Sigma \Rightarrow aAA \Rightarrow abBAabaAAA \ldots \Rightarrow ababaaaaa$

$\Sigma \Rightarrow aAA \Rightarrow abBAabaAAA \ldots \Rightarrow abababaaaaaa$

That is, $(ab)^m a^{3+m} \in L(G)$ for $m = 0, 1, 2, \ldots$

Therefore, $L = \{0^{3n} \cup (ab)^m a^{3+m} : n > 0, m \geq 0\}$

We construct PDA $M = (\{q\}, \{0\}, \{0, S\}, \delta, q, S, \phi)$ based on the above production rules of grammar G:

Production	Transition
$S \to aAA$	$\delta(q, \varepsilon, S) = \{(q, aAA)\}$
$A \to aB$	$\delta(q, \varepsilon, A) = \{(q, aB)\}$
$A \to bB$	$\delta(q, \varepsilon, A) = \{(q, bB)\}$
$A \to a$	$\delta(q, \varepsilon, A) = \{(q, a)\}$
$B \to aAA$	$\delta(q, \varepsilon, B) = \{(q, aAA)\}$
And there are two transitions for terminals '*a*' and '*b*':	
	$\delta(q, a, a) = \{(q, \varepsilon)\}$, and
	$\delta(q, b, b) = \{(q, \varepsilon)\}$

Example 7.19: Convert the PDA, $P = (\{p, q\}, \{0, 1\}, \{x, z_0\}, \delta, q, z_0)$ to CFG if δ is given as $\delta(q, 1, z_0) = \{(p, xz_0)\}$

Solution: Let context-free grammar $G = (V_n, \Sigma, P, S)$, where

$$V_n = \{[p, z_0, p], [p, z_0, q], [q, z_0, p], [q, z_0, q], [p, x, p], [p, x, q], [q, x, p], [q, x, q], S\}$$

The number of states are two and stack symbols are two then number of combination of states and stack symbols in triplet form is $2 \times 2 \times 2$ ($= 2^3 = 8.$), $\Sigma = \{a, b\}$, S is the start symbol, and P consists of following production rules:

$$P_1: S \to [q, z_0, q], \text{ and}$$
$$P_2: S \to [q, z_0, p]$$

For transition $\delta(q, 1, z_0) = \{(p, xz_0)\}$:

$$P_3: [q, z_0, q] \to 1[q, x, q]\,[q, z_0, q]$$
$$P_4: [q, z_0, q] \to 1[q, x, p]\,[p, z_0, q]$$
$$P_5: [q, z_0, p] \to 1[q, x, q]\,[q, z_0, q]$$
$$P_6: [q, z_0, p] \to 1[q, x, p]\,[p, z_0, q]$$

Example 7.20: Convert the grammar $S \to 0S1 \mid A,\ A \to 1A0 \mid S \mid \varepsilon$.

To PDA that accepts the same language by empty stack.

Solution: The corresponding pushdown automaton $M = (\{q\}, \{0, 1\}, \{0, 1, S, A\}, \delta, q, S, \phi)$, where transition function δ is defined following:

Production	Transition
$S \to 0S1$	$\delta(q, \varepsilon, S) = \{(q, 0S1)\}$
$S \to A$	$\delta(q, \varepsilon, S) = \{(q, A)\}$
$A \to 1A0$	$\delta(q, \varepsilon, A) = \{(q, 1A0)\}$
$A \to S$	$\delta(q, \varepsilon, A) = \{(q, S)\}$
$A \to \varepsilon$	$\delta(q, \varepsilon, A) = \{(q, \varepsilon)\}$
And two additional transitions for terminals '0' and '1' are:	
	$\delta(q, 0, 0) = \{(q, \varepsilon)\}$, and
	$\delta(q, 1, 1) = \{(q, \varepsilon)\}$

Example 7.21: Design a PDA equivalent to the following grammar $S \to aAA, A \to aS \mid bS \mid a$

Solution: The corresponding pushdown automata $M = (\{q\}, \{a, b\}, \{a, b, S, A\}, \delta, q, S, \phi)$, where transition function δ is defined following:

Production	Transition
$S \to aAA$	$\delta(q, \varepsilon, S) = \{(q, aAA)\}$
$A \to aS$	$\delta(q, \varepsilon, A) = \{(q, aS)\}$
$A \to bS$	$\delta(q, \varepsilon, A) = \{(q, bS)\}$
$A \to a$	$\delta(q, \varepsilon, A) = \{(q, a)\}$
And two aδditional transitions for terminals '*a*' and '*b*' are:	
	$\delta(q, a, a) = \{(q, \varepsilon)\}$, and
	$\delta(q, b, b) = \{(q, \varepsilon)\}$

Example 7.22: Design a PDA accepting the language $\{a^i b^j c^k \mid i \neq j \text{ or } j \neq k\}$

Solution: Let grammar $G = (V_n, \{a, b, c\}, P, S)$ generates the given language. The production rules for the G are:

$$S \to A_1B_1, A_1 \to C_1D_1 \mid E_1D_1, C_1 \to aC_1 \mid a, D_1 \to aD_1b \mid \varepsilon, E_1 \to bE_1 \mid b, B_1 \to cB_1 \mid \varepsilon$$
$$S \to A_2B_2, A_2 \to aA_2 \mid \varepsilon, B_2 \to C_2D_2 \mid E_2D_2, C_2 \to bC_2 \mid b, D_2 \to bD_2c \mid \varepsilon, E_2 \to cE_2 \mid c$$

The corresponding pushdown automaton $M = (\{q\}, \{a, b, c\}, \{a, b, c, S, A_1, A_2, B_1, B_2, C_1, C_2, D_1, D_2, E_1, E_2\}, \delta, q, S, \phi)$, where transition function δ is defined following:

Production	Transition
$S \to A_1B_1$	$\delta(q, \varepsilon, S) = \{(q, A_1B_1)\}$
$S \to A_2B_2$	$\delta(q, \varepsilon, S) = \{(q, A_2B_2)\}$
$A_1 \to C_1D_1$	$\delta(q, \varepsilon, A_1) = \{(q, C_1D_1)\}$
$A_1 \to E_1D_1$	$\delta(q, \varepsilon, A_1) = \{(q, E_1D_1)\}$
$C_1 \to aC_1$	$\delta(q, \varepsilon, C_1) = \{(q, aC_1)\}$
$C_1 \to a$	$\delta(q, \varepsilon, C_1) = \{(q, a)\}$
$D_1 \to aD_1b$	$\delta(q, \varepsilon, D_1) = \{(q, aD_1b)\}$
$D_1 \to \varepsilon$	$\delta(q, \varepsilon, D_1) = \{(q, \varepsilon)\}$
$E_1 \to bE_1$	$\delta(q, \varepsilon, E_1) = \{(q, bE_1)\}$
$E_1 \to b$	$\delta(q, \varepsilon, E_1) = \{(q, b)\}$
$B_1 \to cB_1$	$\delta(q, \varepsilon, B_1) = \{(q, cB_1)\}$
$B_1 \to \varepsilon$	$\delta(q, \varepsilon, B_1) = \{(q, \varepsilon)\}$
$A_2 \to aA_2$	$\delta(q, \varepsilon, A_2) = \{(q, aA_2)\}$
$A_2 \to \varepsilon$	$\delta(q, \varepsilon, A_2) = \{(q, \varepsilon)\}$
$B_2 \to C_2D_2$	$\delta(q, \varepsilon, B_2) = \{(q, C_2D_2)\}$
$B_2 \to E_2D_2$	$\delta(q, \varepsilon, B_2) = \{(q, E_2D_2)\}$
$C_2 \to bC_2$	$\delta(q, \varepsilon, C_2) = \{(q, bC_2)\}$
$C_2 \to b$	$\delta(q, \varepsilon, C_2) = \{(q, b)\}$
$D_2 \to bD_2c$	$\delta(q, \varepsilon, D_2) = \{(q, bD_2c)\}$
$D_2 \to \varepsilon$	$\delta(q, \varepsilon, D_2) = \{(q, \varepsilon)\}$
$E_2 \to cE_2$	$\delta(q, \varepsilon, E_2) = \{(q, cE_2)\}$
$E_2 \to c$	$\delta(q, \varepsilon, E_2) = \{(q, c)\}$

TEST YOUR SKILLS

Supplementary Problems

7.1 Construct pushdown automata for the following languages:

(a) $L = \{0^n1^n2^m: m, n \geq 0\}$
(b) $L = \{a^nb^m: m > n \geq 0\}$
(c) $L = \{ww^R: w \in (a + b + c)^*\}$
(d) $L = \{w: w \in (a + b)^* \text{ and } w = w^R\}$
(e) $L = \{a^nb^m: m \leq n \leq 2m\}$

7.2 Show that following languages are deterministic context-free:

(a) $L = \{wcw^R: w \in (a + b)^*\}$
(b) $L = \{a^nb^m: m \neq n \geq 0\}$
(c) $L = \{a^ncb^n: n \geq 0\} \cup \{a^mdc^{2m}: m \geq 0\}$
(d) $L = \{a^nb^mc^pd^q: m, n, p, q \geq 1\}$
(e) $L = \{(ab)^m: m \geq 1\}$
(f) $L = \{a^nb^nc^md^n: m, n \geq 1 \text{ and } m = 2n\}$

7.3 Construct pushdown automata for the following grammar having production rules: $S \to AA, A \to AAA \mid bA \mid Ab \mid a$ and check the acceptance of the string "*babbab*".

7.4 Consider the context-free grammar whose production rules are: $S \to S + S \mid S{*}S \mid a \mid b$. Design a top-down parser.

7.5 Consider following grammar:

Stmt $\to$ if(Condition) then Statement | if(Condition) then Statement else statement | While-statement, Condition $\to S_1 \mid S_2 \mid \ldots \mid S_n$, Statement $\to$ Read Automata Theory | Enjoy *C* language, While-statement $\to$ while (Condition) {Statement}

($S_1, S_2, \ldots, S_n$ statements give the value TRUE or FALSE)

Design top-down and bottom-up parser for the above grammar.

7.6 Show that context-free grammar *G* having production rules: $S \to S + S \mid S{*}S \mid a \mid b$ is not *LL*(1) grammar.

7.7 Consider the pushdown automata designed in solved examples (1) and check the acceptability of the following strings:

(a) *aabb*
(b) *aaabba*
(c) *bbbaaa*

7.8 Design pushdown automata that recognizes language $L = \{0^n1^m2^n: m, n \geq 0)$ by

(a) Empty store
(b) Final state

7.9 Consider the following grammars and find out which is *LL*(1).

(a) $S \to Aa \mid b, A \to bdA' \mid A', A' \to cA' \mid adA' \mid \varepsilon$
(b) $S \to aS' \mid bS', S' \to SS' \mid \varepsilon$
(c) $S \to aAa, A \to Sb \mid bCC, C \to ab$
(d) $S \to abSb \mid a \mid aAb, A \to bS \mid aAAb$

7.10 Consider a context-free grammar having production rules:

$S \to ABAC \mid BAC \mid ABC \mid AAC \mid AC \mid BC \mid d, A \to aA \mid a, B \to bB \mid b$, and $C \to d$

Design bottom-up parser for the given grammar.

7.11 Consider a context-free grammar G given below:

$S \to XY, X \to a \mid b \mid XA, Y \to a \mid AY, A \to a$

Design a bottom-up parser for G and show the parsing of the string $w = babaa$.

7.12 Consider the following grammar:

$S \to aY \mid bY \mid aX, X \to a \mid b, Y \to a \mid aYbY$

Design a top-down parser the given grammar.

7.13 Consider the following production rules of grammar G in Greiback normal form (GNF). Design top-down and bottom-up parsers for G.

$A_1 \to 1A_2A_3 \mid 0A_3$, $A_2 \to 1A_2A_3A_1 \mid 0A_3A_1 \mid 1$, and $A_3 \to 1A_2A_3A_2 \mid 0A_3A_2 \mid 1A_2A_3A_2A_3 \mid 0A_3A_2A_3$

7.14 Design pushdown automata for the following grammars:

(a) $L_1 = \{a^n b^n c^m: m, n \geq 1\}$

(b) $L_2 = \{a^n b^m c^m: m, n \geq 1\}$

(c) $L_3 = \{a^n b^m: m + 1 = n\}$

(d) $L_4 = \{a^m b^n c^m: m, n \geq 1\}$

(e) $L_5 = \{a^n b^n c^m: m, n \geq 1\} \cup \{a^m b^n c^m: m, n \geq 1\}$

(f) $L_6 = \{a^n b^n: n \geq 1\}\{b^m c^m: m \geq 0\}$

(g) $L_7 = \{b^n c^m: m \neq 2n\}$

(h) $L_8 = \{w \in (0 + 1)^*: |w|_a = 2|w|_b\}$

(i) $L_9 = \{a^n b^n c^m d^m: m, n \geq 0\}$

7.15 Consider pushdown automaton M which recognizes the language $L = \{0^n 1^n: n \geq 1\}$. Design pushdown automata for following languages:

(a) L^* (b) L^2

(c) $00L11$ (d) $0 + L1^*$

7.16 Define the following for pushdown automata:

(a) Moves (b) Instantaneous description

(c) Pushdown store (d) Transition function

7.17 What is parsing? How many parsers are used in compilation?

7.18 What are differences between top-down and bottom-up parsers?

7.19 What is deterministic context-free language (DCFL)? Explain with some examples.

7.20 What is $LL(k)$ grammar? Why a parser has to look k symbols ahead in the input stream? Give some examples.

7.21 What is handle in bottom-up parsing? How bottom-up parser select handle?

7.22 Discuss the model of pushdown automata.

7.23 Discuss the acceptance of pushdown automata by

(a) Final state

(b) Empty store

7.24 Show that context-free languages are recognized by pushdown automata.

7.25 Show that pushdown automata having acceptance by final state and empty sore have equivalent language recognizing power.

7.26 Discuss the deterministic and nondeterministic pushdown automata and their language recognization.

7.27 Construct DPDA for the following languages:

(a) $L = \{wcw^R: w \in (0 + 1)^*\}$

(b) $L = \{a^nb^m: m \neq n \geq 0\}$

(c) $L = \{a^ncb^n: n \geq 0\} \cup \{a^mdc^{2m}: m \geq 0\}$

(d) $L = \{a^nb^mc^pd^q: m, n, p, q \geq 1\}$

(e) $L = \{(00)^m: m \geq 1\}$

(f) $L = \{a^nb^nc^md^n: m, n \geq 1 \text{ and } m = 2n\}$

Multiple Choice Questions

7.28 A pushdown automaton recognizes

(a) Regular language
(b) CFL
(c) CSL
(d) Both (a) & (b)

7.29 What is additional in pushdown automata as compare to finite automata?

(a) Stack memory
(b) Tape
(c) Head
(d) None

7.30 Pushdown automaton behaves like an finite state machine when the number of auxiliary memory it has, is

(a) One
(b) Zero
(c) Two
(d) Can't behave like FSM

7.31 PDA behaves like Turing Machine when it has the number of auxiliary memory

(a) One or more
(b) Two or more
(c) Zero
(d) Can't behave like TM

7.32 Choose the correct statement

(a) The power of nondeterministic PDA and deterministic PDA is same
(b) The power of nondeterministic PDA and deterministic PDA is not same
(c) A nondeterministic PDA can be converted into an equivalent deterministic PDA
(d) None

7.33 Choose the correct statement

(a) A FSM with one stack is more powerful than FSM without stack
(b) A FSM with one stack is more powerful than PDA
(c) A FSM with two stacks is equal powerful as PDA
(d) All statements are correct

7.34 Choose the correct statement

(a) A FSM with two stacks is more powerful than Turing machine

(b) A FSM with one stack is more powerful than PDA

(c) A FSM with two stacks is equal powerful as Turing machine

(c) All statements are correct

7.35 Top-down parsers use

(a) Leftmost derivation (b) Rightmost derivation

(c) Rightmost derivation in reverse order (d) None

7.36 Bottom-up parsers use

(a) Leftmost derivation (b) Rightmost derivation

(c) Rightmost derivation in reverse order (d) None

7.37 Top-down parsing is also known as

(a) Shift-reduce parsing (b) Predictive descent parsing

(c) Both (a) & (b) (d) None

7.38 Bottom-up parsing is also known as

(a) Shift-reduce parsing (b) Predictive descent parsing

(c) Both (a) & (b) (d) None

7.39 Top-down parsers use the grammar

(a) $LL(k)$ (b) $LR(k)$

(c) SLR(k) (d) All the above

7.40 The grammar G having productions $S \rightarrow aSb \mid ab$ is

(a) $LL(1)$ grammar (b) $LL(2)$ grammar

(c) $LL(0)$ (d) None

7.41 The grammar G having productions $S \rightarrow ab \mid ba$ is

(a) $LL(1)$ grammar (b) $LL(2)$ grammar

(c) $LL(0)$ (d) None

7.42 Consider L_1 is context-free language and L_2 is a regular language. Which of the following is/are false?

(a) $L_1 - L_2$ is not CFL (b) $L_1 \cap L_2$ is CFL

(c) $\overline{L}_2$ is CFL (d) $\overline{L}_1$ is regular **(GATE 1999)**

7.43 Which of the following is the most powerful parsing method?

(a) $LL(1)$ (b) Canonical LR

(c) SLR (d) LALR **(GATE 1999)**

7.44 Let L_D be the set of all languages recognized by a PDA by final state and L_E be the set of all languages recohnized by empty stack. Which of the following is true?

(a) $L_D = L_E$ (b) $L_D \supset L_E$

(c) $L_D \subset L_E$ (d) None of the above **(GATE 1999)**

7.45 Which of the following language over $\{a, b, c\}$ is recognized by a DPDA?

(a) $\{wcw^R: w \in (a + b)^*\}$
(b) $\{ww^R: w \in (a + b + c)^*\}$
(c) $\{a^n b^n c^n: n \geq 0\}$
(d) $\{w: w$ is a palindrome over $\{a, b, c\}\}$

(GATE 1997)

7.46 NPDA recognize

(a) DCFL
(b) CFL
(c) Regular language
(d) Both (a) & (c)

7.47 NDPDA recognize

(a) DCFL
(b) CFL
(c) Regular language
(d) ALL the above

7.48 Which one of the following languages is not deterministic context-free?

(a) $L = \{a^n b^n: n \geq 0\}$
(b) $L = \{a^n b^n: n \geq 0\} \cup \{a^n b^{2n}: n \geq 0\}$
(c) $L = \{a^n c b^n: n \geq 0\}$
(d) None

7.49 Which one of the following languages is deterministic context-free?

(a) $L = \{wcw^R: w \in (a + b)^*\}$
(b) $L = \{ww^R: w \in (a + b)^*\}$
(c) $L = \{x :$ x is a palindrome over $\{a, b\}\}$
(d) None

7.50 Choose one of the following languages that is not recognized by deterministic pushdown automata.

(a) $L = \{wcw^R: w \in (a + b)^*\}$
(b) $L = \{a^n b^m: m \neq n \geq 0\}$
(c) $L = \{a^n c b^n: n \geq 0\} \cup \{a^m d c^{2m}: m \geq 0\}$
(d) None of the above

7.51 If PDA M accepts language L by empty stack and it is deterministic then there is equivalent PDA N that accepts L by final state. Choose the right option.

(a) N is deterministic
(b) N is nondeterministic
(c) May be deterministic
(d) None

7.52 Suppose PDA M accepts language L by empty stack and it is nondeterministic then there is equivalent PDA N that accepts L by final state. Choose the right option.

(a) N is deterministic
(b) N is nondeterministic
(c) May be deterministic
(d) None

7.53 Consider a PDA N that recognizes L and has x, y number of states and stack symbols respectively. There is a context-free grammar G that is based on the transition function of N then how many possible variables are there?

(a) $x + y$
(b) x^*y
(c) x
(d) y

7.54 Pushdown automata are useful in

(a) Language recognization
(b) Parsing
(c) Computing
(d) None

7.55 Which of the following language is not recognized by pushdown automata?

(a) Regular (b) Context-free

(c) Context-sensitive (d) None

7.56 Which of the following language is recognized by pushdown automata?

(a) Regular (b) Context-free

(c) Context-sensitive (d) None

7.57 Consider the following languages:

1. $L = \{a^n b^m c^m d^n: m, n \geq 1\}$
2. $L = \{a^n b^n c^m d^n: m, n \geq 1 \text{ and } m = 2n\}$
3. $L = \{a^n b^m: m, n \geq 0\}$
4. $L = \{a^n b^m c^m: m, n \geq 1\}$

Select the correct statement:

(a) Language (1), (2), (3), and (4) are recognized by pushdown automata

(b) Language (1), (3), and (4) are recognized by pushdown automata

(c) Language (3) and (4) are recognized by pushdown automata

(d) Language (1), (2), and (3) are recognized by pushdown automata

7.58 Consider the languages:

1. $L = \{a^n b^m c^p d^q: m, n, p, q \geq 1\}$
2. $L = \{(ab)^m: m \geq 1\}$
3. $L = \{a^n b^m: m, n \geq 0\}$
4. $L = \{a^{2n} b^m c^m: m, n \geq 1\}$

Select the correct statement:

(a) Language (1), (2), (3), and (4) are recognized by pushdown automata

(b) Language (1), (3), and (4) are recognized by pushdown automata

(c) Language (3) and (4) are recognized by pushdown automata

(d) Language (1), (2), and (3) are recognized by pushdown automata

Answers

7.28 (d)	7.29 (a)	7.30 (b)	7.31 (b)	7.32 (b)
7.33 (a)	7.34 (c)	7.35 (a)	7.36 (c)	7.37 (b)
7.38 (a)	7.39 (a)	7.40 (b)	7.41 (a)	7.42 (a), (c)
7.43 (b)	7.44 (a)	7.45 (a)	7.46 (d)	7.47 (d)
7.48 (b)	7.49 (c)	7.50 (d)	7.51 (a)	7.52 (b)
7.53 (b)	7.54 (a), (b)	7.55 (c)	7.56 (a), (b)	7.57 (a)
7.58 (a)				

CHAPTER 8

Turing Machine

We have discussed the finite automata, which is the simple machine capable of doing recognization of regular languages only and it is abstract model of general-purpose computer system. We remove some limitations of finite automata and add one additional memory (stack memory) and this model is known as pushdown automaton. But again, pushdown automata do the same job as finite automata that are recognization, not computation. One thing is obvious that addition of memory enhances the power of automata. So, we concentrate on this fact and look for some more powerful machines. In our practical life, we need such machines that can perform recognization as well as computation. A machine is not much useful as desired without computational capability. At present, we have many machines like computer system, which are capable of doing recognization as well as computation. We will see the designing of an automaton (machine) that can solve our both objectives:

1. **Recognization** and
2. **Computation**

Let us see what the meaning of above objectives is. Consider one small program written in *C* language:

```
void main( )
{
    int number1, number2, result;
    number1 = 20;
    number2 = 15;
    result = number1 + number2;
    printf(" Addition of two number is: %d", result);
}
```

In the compilation of above code, the first work of C compiler is to check the syntax of program whether it is correctly developed or not and then second job is to check the operations defined in the program. The first job is known as **syntax analysis** and the second job is known as **semantic analysis**. If we see the above program code line-by-line then we find that all statements are grammatically developed and program code has no **syntax error**. Syntax error means missing of grammar rules like missing of semicolon, missing of parenthesis, curly brackets, etc. So, the syntax of the above program is fine.

The second job is computation defined in the program code. It means what are the computations defined in the program? Whether these are valid or not? Validity means the eligibility of computations defined for a compiler. All these questions are considered before actual operations carried out by a computer system.

A Turing machine (**TM**) is a generalization of pushdown automata, which uses a read-write tape instead of a read-only tape and stack storage. The potential (storage) of the tape is assumed to be infinite and divided into cells. Each cell can hold one input symbol. The head of Turing machine is capable of reading as well as writing on the tape and can move left or right or remain static. We know that practically all storage capacity is finite. So, keeping the potential of the tape infinite has theoretical interest more rather than practical interest.

Turing machine is an abstract version of a computer system; this has been used to define formally what is *computable*. There are number of alternative approaches to formalize the concept of computability (e.g., called the λ-calculus, or μ-recursive functions etc.) but these can be proved to be equivalent. One thesis called **Church's Thesis** support the fact that a Turing machine can simulate the behaviour of a general-purpose computer system. There is interesting debate over "Turing machine is more powerful over a computer system".

Concept of Turing machine is suggested by **Alan Turing**, an English mathematician in 1936. Alan Turing formulated an abstract machine and based on his name this machine is known as Turing machine. Alan Turing imagined a human-computer that was similar to a human who solves problems in a well-defined way. This well-defined way is known as algorithm. **For example**, if we consider *addition operation A + B, we think that A is incremented by B or B is incremented by A. Let us take multiplication operation A*B, we think A is added with itself B times or B is added with itself A times.* It means multiplication is converted into addition operation. Similarly division is converted into subtraction and so on. So, if we consider addition as a basic operation then a machine capable of doing addition can be used for multiplication and similarly for division and other operations also. Alan Turing used this concept and designed his machine.

Now, we discuss about the recognization of languages. We know that generalization of context-free grammars called phrase structure grammars in which we allow several symbols on the left hand side of a production e.g., we may define the context in which a rule is applicable. Turing machines recognize the languages definable by these grammars and these languages are called *Type 0 languages* or the **recursively enumerable** (r.e.) *languages*. Turing machines behave differently from the previous machine classes that we have discussed. To say that a Turing machine recognizes a language means that the Turing machine will stop eventually in a halting state for each word in the language. Halting state does not mean the final state (as we have been discussing earlier for finite automata and pushdown automata), but it is a special state in Turing machine similar to the final state. However, if the word is not in the language then Turing machine may stop in a halting or non-halting state. Obvious question is that will a Turing machine halt on an arbitrary input? There may be situation that a Turing machine runs forever on some input and never halts. Such Turing machine cannot produce result without coming to a halt state. This is known as halting problem of Turing machine.

We say a language is **decidable**, if there is a Turing machine, which always stops its processing in halting state. There are some *type 0 languages*, which are not decidable and Turing machine may stop its processing in non-halting state. This is most famous problem in Computer Science known as *halting problem* (**HP**). At first instant the halting problem looks confusing; it is not clear that why a Turing machine cannot recognize a given string. Although we have already discussed that Type 0 languages are recognized by Turing machines. Let us take a simple example. Suppose the given string is long enough to be processed within life span of a man. So, how can a Turing machine decide its acceptability? A Turing machine may take infinite time in deciding the acceptability. We will discuss the halting problem in detail in the next chapter.

There is not a single type of grammar, which captures all decidable languages. However, there is a subset of decidable languages, which are called *context-sensitive languages*, are generated by *context-sensitive grammars*. These are those grammars where the left hand side of a production is always shorter or equal to the right hand side. The context sensitive languages are correspond to linear bounded automata (LBA), these are those Turing machines that use only a tape whose length can be given by a linear function over the length of the input stream.

8.1 MODEL OF TURING MACHINE

A Turing machine consists of a tape, which is finite at the left end and infinite at the right end, a finite control to control the operations, and a read/write head as shown in Fig. 8.1. Turing machine reads input given on the tape and writes output on the tape. The reading and writing capability of Turing machine make it different and powerful from other class of machines. There is a left end marker \$ on the tape that indicates the left end of the tape and starting of input stream. The finite control is similar to the finite control of finite automata and it has finite control instructions used to control the operation of the Turing machine.

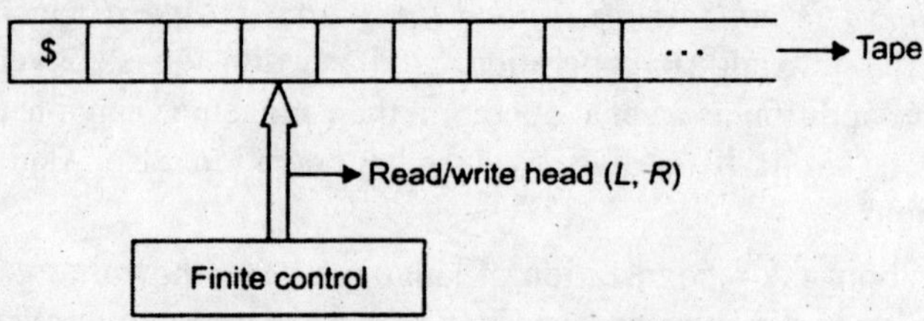

Fig. 8.1: Model of turing machine

8.1.1 Mathematical Description of Turing Machine

A Turing machine can be described by 4-tuples (Q, Σ, δ, s), where

1. Q is the finite set of states, not including the halt state (h),
2. Σ is the alphabet containing the blank symbol #, but not containing the symbols L (left), R (right), and symbols from this alphabet can be read or write on the tape,
3. δ is the transition function which maps from $Q \times \Sigma$ to $(Q \cup \{h\}) \times (\Sigma \cup \{L, R\})$, and
4. $s \in Q$ is the initial state or starting state.

A Turing machine may be deterministic or non-deterministic as per the transition defined. If Turing machine has at most one move in transition for all input symbols then it is called deterministic Turing machine (**DTM**), if one or more moves then non-deterministic Turing machine (**NTM**). A standard Turing machine reads one cell of the tape and changes its configuration and moves left or right one cell.

Turing machine for recognization looks very much similar to two-way finite automata. The difference between a Turing machine and two-way automata is the writing capability, not in the movement. A Turing machine has infinite length tape and writing capability and recognizes type 0 languages as compared to two-way automata.

Now, let us see what is halting or halt state in Turing machine. The halt state represented by ***h*** means the stopping point of processing by Turing machine. When Turing machine processes some input then it may fall into one of these following state:

(a) Halting state (h),

(b) Non-halting state (all the states of Q),

(c) Loop (infinite or finite),

(d) Crash, and

(e) Hang state (undefined transition)

When Turing machine reads input on the tape then it keeps write on the tape and when it halts or stops the processing then whatever written on the tape is the output of produced by it. When Turing machine does not stop it's processing and it is on for infinite time then this situation is known as infinite loop and when head damages the tape then it is known as crash. For some input, if Turing machine does not decide what to do then we will say that Turing machine is in hang state. Initially, Alan Turing suggested that the head can move any number of cells up to some fixed number of cells left (L) or right (R) in one transition, but restricting the head to move one cell in one step can also accomplish our objective and this restriction makes the operations easier to be understood. So, we restrict the head movement one cell left or right or sometimes static as required.

The transition function δ is defined as $\boldsymbol{\delta(p, a) = (q, b, D)}$, where p is the present state, q is the next state, $a, b \in \Sigma$, and D is the movement (left or right or static). We use L, R, and S for left movement, right movement, and static respectively. We will assume that input stored from the leftmost cell and after that remaining cells contain blank symbol (#). Sometime input is separated by blank symbol (blank cell) or special symbol like \$ for example, #w#, \$$w$##, etc., where w is the input. **For example,** consider the Turing machine $M = (Q, \{a, \#\}, \delta, s)$, where transition function δ is defined below:

Transition table		
Present state	**Input symbol**	
	a	**#**
s	(s, #, R)	(h, #, S)

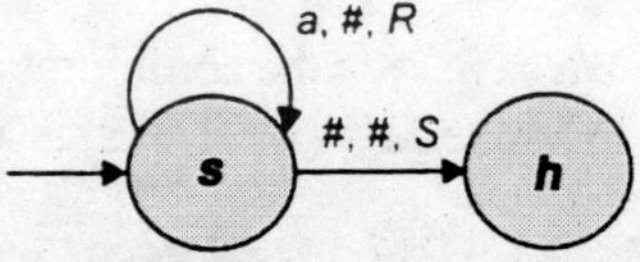

Fig. 8.2: Turing machine

The transition diagram is shown in Fig. 8.2. Each arrow and arch is labelled as (Present input symbol, Written symbol (s), Movement). There is only one state, which is ***s*** in the transition table. Turing machine reads input symbol a in state s, remains in state s and makes the cell blank (#) on the tape in place of read symbol a and moves right (R) one cell on the tape. When Turing machine reads blank cell (symbol #) in state s, it moves to the halting state ***h*** while keeping the read cell blank (#) and head remains static (S). Consider the input string $w = aaa$ and let us see the steps involved in processing. The initial state is s, so initially Turing machine is in state s and processes as following:

Step	Input	Written symbol	State	Tape content	Transiton used
1.	*aaa*	#	*s*	$#*aa*##...	$\delta(s, a) = (s, \#, R)$
2.	*aa*	#	*s*	$##*a*##...	$\delta(s, a) = (s, \#, R)$
3.	*a*	#	*s*	$#####...	$\delta(s, a) = (s, \#, R)$
4.	#	#	*h*	$#####...	$\delta(s, \#) = (h, \#, S)$

The tape contents initially and finally are shown in Fig. 8.3.

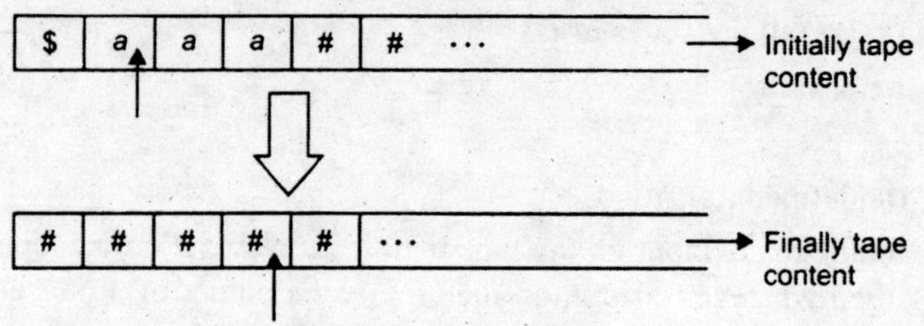

Fig. 8.3: Tape contents

Now, let us conclude the things. After reading an input $a \in \Sigma$, Turing machine does one of the following:

1. Write $b \in \Sigma$ and move right (R) as $\delta(p, a) = (q, b, R)$
2. Without write move right (R) as $\delta(p, a) = (q, a, R)$
3. Write $b \in \Sigma$ and move left (L) as $\delta(p, a) = (q, b, L)$
4. Without write move left (L) as $\delta(p, a) = (q, a, L)$
5. Write $b \in \Sigma$ and does not move i.e., remain static (S) as $\delta(p, a) = (q, b, S)$
6. Without write remain static but changes its state as $\delta(p, a) = (q, a, S)$

The change of state in (1) to (5) cases is optional i.e., Turing machine may or may not change its present state. A Turing machine cannot be inactive i.e., it cannot remain static without write something or changing its state, it will be hang situation. We will see these conditions in coming examples. One thing should be clear here that when Turing machine does not write it means it reads the input and head moves in specified direction or remain static. So, readers are advised to not think that Turing machine reads and write the same input in case of (2), (4), and (6) of the above.

8.1.2 Configuration of Turing Machine

We have seen the configuration of pushdown automata in Chapter 7. Similarly configuration of a Turing machine $M = (Q, \Sigma, \delta, s)$ is a member of

$(Q \cup \{h\}) \times \Sigma^* \times \Sigma \times ((\Sigma^* - \{\#\}) \cup \{e\})$, where *e* stands for end of the string

In other form, a configuration is: (**Present state, w_1, a, w_2**), where input string $w = w_1 a w_2$ and symbol '*a*' is the present input symbol. **For example,** (s, aa, a, e), $(q, abab, b, aba)$ are configurations shown in Fig. 8.4(*a*) and Fig. 8.4(b).

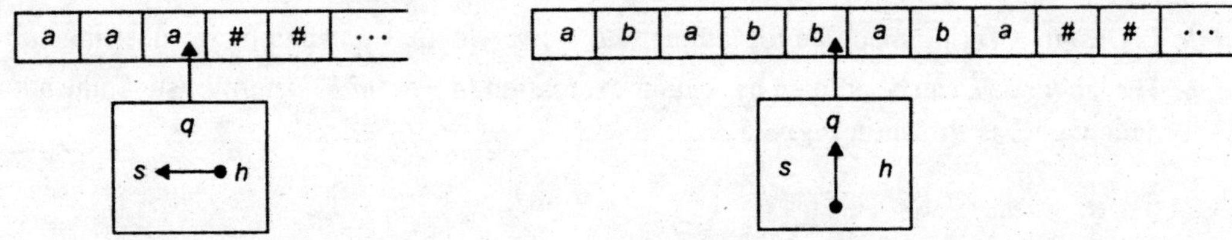

Fig. 8.4(a): Configuration **(*s*, *aa*, *a*, *e*)** **Fig. 8.4(b):** Configuration **(*q*, *abab*, *b*, *aba*)**

The relation between two consecutive configurations is denoted by $\vdash_M$ and reflexive-transitive closure is denoted by $\vdash_M^*$

For example, consider a Turing machine $M = (\{s\}, \{a, b, \#\}, \delta, s)$ whose transitions are $\delta(s, a) = (s, b, R)$, $\delta(s, \#) = (h, \#, S)$. M converts symbol 'a' into symbol 'b'. Consider the string $w = aaaa$, following are the configurations involved in processing:

(Initial configuration)

$$(s, \#, a, aaa\#) \vdash (s, b, a, aa\#)$$
$$\vdash (s, bb, a, a\#)$$
$$\vdash (s, bbb, a, \#)$$
$$\vdash (s, bbbb, \#, e)$$
$$\vdash (h, bbbb, \#, e)$$
$$(s, \#aaaa\#) \vdash_M^* (h, \#bbbb\underline{\#})$$

8.2 RECOGNIZATION AND TURING MACHINE

As we have discussed earlier that Turing machine is used as a language recognizer. So, in this section we will discuss how a Turing machine is used as a language recognizer. For regular languages, designing of Turing machine is similar to designing of finite automaton and Turing machine for context-free language similar to pushdown automata except some change in the configuration or label of edges in the transition diagram. All languages (regular language, CFL, CSL, Type 0 language) are recognized by Turing machines. A language L is recognized by Turing machine $M = (Q, \Sigma, \delta, s)$ if for each string $w \in L \subseteq (\Sigma^+ - \{\#\})$,

$$(s, \#, a_1, a_2a_2...a_n) \vdash_M^* (h, a_1a_2a_2...a_n, \#, e), \text{ where } w = a_1a_2a_2...a_n$$

A language that is recognized by some Turing machine is known as **recursively enumerable** (r.e.). Being enumerable means, some Turing machine precisely lists the all the strings of that language. We have discussed earlier that some type-0 languages are not decidable (not precisely listed) by any Turing machine. We select a subclass of type 0 languages, which is decidable by Turing machines, is known as **recursive set** (recursive language). For a recursive language, a Turing machine always halts for its member strings and rejects other.

Recursive set ⊂ recursively enumerable set (r.e.) (over same alphabet)

Example 1: Design a Turing machine for language $L = \{w: w \in (a + b)^*$ ending in substring "*abb*"}

Solution: The language L can be defined by regular expression $(a + b)^*abb$. Deterministic finite automata (DFA) for language L is shown in Fig. 8.5.

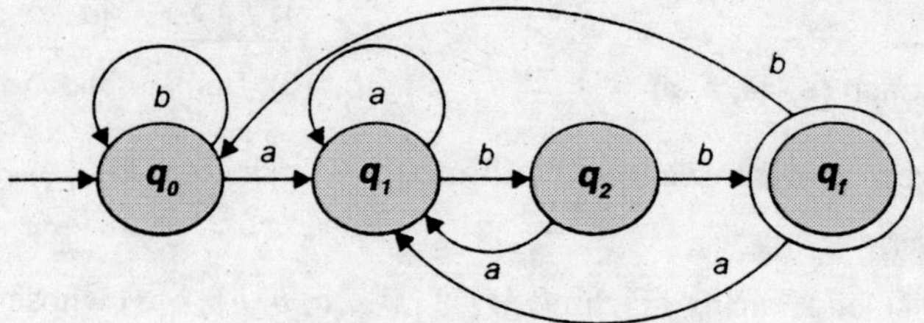

Fig. 8.5: DFA for $(a + b)^*abb$

Let Turing machine $M = (\{q_0, q_1, q_2, q_3\}, \{a, b, \#\}, \delta, q_0)$ recognizes language L, where transition function δ is defined below:

Transition for turing machine	Transition for DFA
$\delta(q_0, b) = (q_0, b, R)$	$\delta(q_0, b) = \{q_0\}$
$\delta(q_0, a) = (q_1, a, R)$	$\delta(q_0, a) = \{q_1\}$
$\delta(q_1, a) = (q_1, a, R)$	$\delta(q_1, a) = \{q_1\}$
$\delta(q_1, b) = (q_2, b, R)$	$\delta(q_1, b) = \{q_2\}$
$\delta(q_2, a) = (q_1, a, R)$	$\delta(q_2, a) = \{q_1\}$
$\delta(q_2, b) = (q_3, b, R)$	$\delta(q_2, b) = \{q_f\}$
$\delta(q_3, a) = (q_1, a, R)$	$\delta(q_f, a) = \{q_1\}$
$\delta(q_3, b) = (q_0, b, R)$	$\delta(q_f, b) = \{q_0\}$
$\delta(q_3, \#) = (h, \#, S)$	

The final state q_f of DFA is named as q_3 and halting state ***h*** is additional which is reachable from the state q_3 while reading # (blank cell). The transition diagram of Turing machine M is shown in Fig. 8.6.

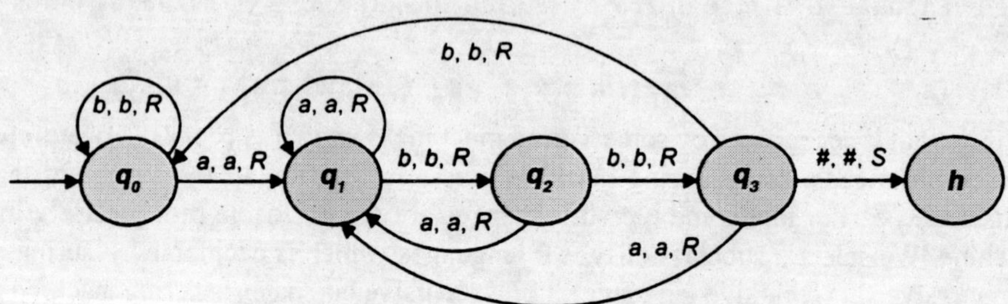

Fig. 8.6: TM for language $L = (a + b)^*abb$

Example 2: Design a Turing machine which recognizes all the words over $\{a, b\}$ which have even number of a's and b's (a's and b's are consecutive).

Solution: If we see the Fig. 5.34 of deterministic finite automata (DFA) for the given language then designing of Turing machine become easier. Let $M = (\{A, B, C, D\}, \{a, b, \#\}, \delta, A)$ be the Turing machine accepting the given language and shown in Fig. 8.7.

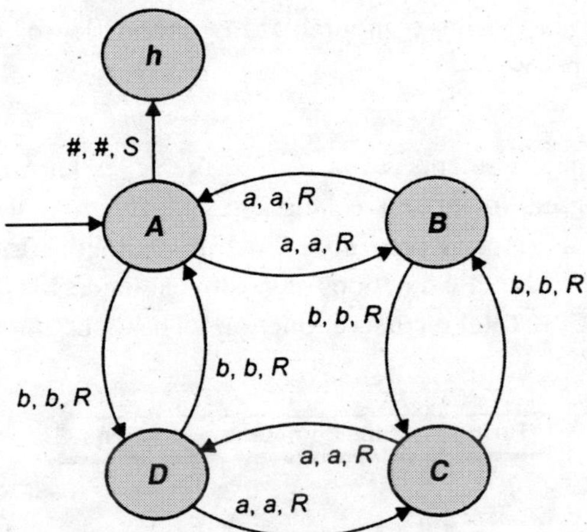

Fig. 8.7: TM for even number of a's and b's over $\{a, b\}$

8.3 COMPUTATION WITH TURING MACHINE

It has been discussed earlier that Turing machine can perform computation like addition, subtraction, multiplication, division etc. In this section, we will discuss how a Turing machine does computing. First thing is that if decimal digits like 0, 1, 2, ..., 9 are used in computations then how these number are stored on the tape. We require some coding system to code these numbers so that it is understood by Turing machine. We represent integer numbers on the tape in form of zeros. Suppose i is a positive integer, then $\mathbf{0}^i$ represents this integer. We assume that **1** separates two integer numbers. **For examples,**

1. Decimal digit **5** is represented by $\mathbf{0}^5$ as shown in Fig. 8.8(a).

0	0	0	0	0	#	#	#	#	#	...

Fig. 8.8(a): Representation integer 5

2. Digits **2** and **4** are represented by $\mathbf{0}^2\mathbf{1}\mathbf{0}^4$ as shown in Fig. 8.8(b).

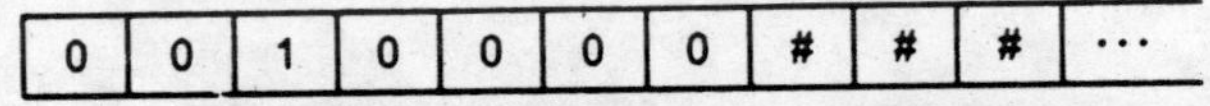

0	0	1	0	0	0	0	#	#	#	...

Fig. 8.8(b): Representation integers 2 & 4

In the above representation, the starting of tape is not marked i.e., the beginning of the input is not marked by symbol $. It is assumed or provided if necessary, the beginning and end of the input stream for Turing machine.

8.3.1 Turing Machine Computable Function

Suppose f is a function and it has arguments $a_1, a_2, ..., a_n$ such that $f(a_1, a_2, ..., a_n) = m$. where $a_1, a_2, ..., a_n$, and m are some natural numbers then f is said to be computed by Turing machine $M = (Q, \Sigma, \delta, s)$ if and only if

$$(s, \$0^{a_1}10^{a_2}1...10^{a_n}) \vdash^*_M (h, \$0^m\#)$$

The function f is said to be Turing computable. In general, Turing machine computes **integer to integer** function as defined below:

$$f_1(a_1, a_2, ..., a_n) \longrightarrow m$$

If f_1 is defined for all the arguments $a_1, a_2, ..., a_n$ then f_1 is known as **total recursive** function. The total function is analogous to recursive languages. A function $f(a_1, a_2, ..., a_n)$ computed by a Turing machine is known as **partial recursive** function analogous to the recursive enumerable set (r.e. languages). All common arithmetic functions on positive integers like addition, subtraction, division, multiplication, $n!$, $\log_2 n$, etc. are total recursive functions. The recursive function theory is discussed in the next chapter.

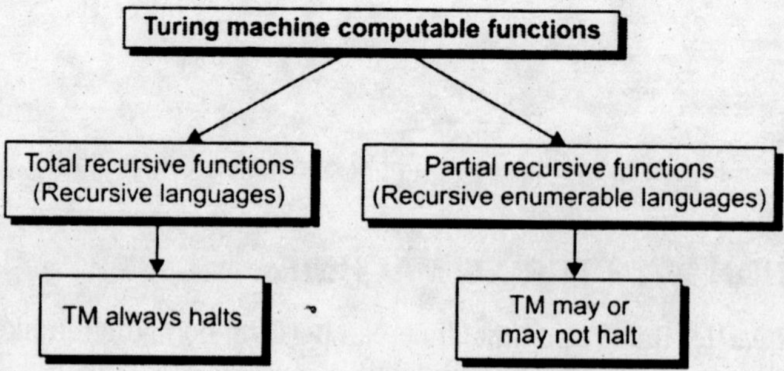

Example 1: Design a Turing machine which increments the input decimal integer number by one.

Solution: Let Turing machine $M = (Q, \{0, \#\}, \delta, s)$ increments the input integer number by one. It means, if m is the input decimal number then output is $m + 1$. Therefore we have a Turing computable function f such that, $f(m) = m + 1$

M reads input from left and reaches the end of input without write (successive right movement) and add one zero at the end to increment the input number by one. Since, the input is coded into zeros, so after passing the rightmost zero, M adds one zero and stops processing in halting state (h). The transition function δ is defined following:

$\delta(s, 0) = (s, 0, R)$ (Maintains all zeros and to reach the rightmost zero), and

$\delta(s, \#) = (h, 0, S)$ (Adds one zero while reading the first right blank symbol)

The transition diagram is shown in Fig. 8.9.

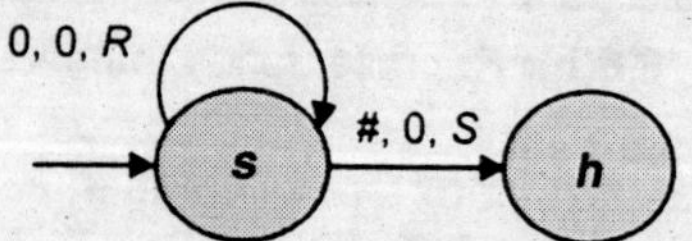

Fig. 8.9: Turing machine for $f(m) = m + 1$

Let us examine the computation of the Turing machine shown in Fig. 8.9. Consider decimal number $m = 3$, then following are the steps involved in computation:

$$(s, \$\underline{0}00\#) \vdash (s, \$0\underline{0}0\#) \vdash (s, \$00\underline{0}\#) \vdash (s, \$000\underline{\#}) \vdash (h, \$0000\underline{\#})$$

Example 2: Design a Turing machine which decrements the input decimal number m ($m \geq 1$) by one.

Solution: Let Turing machine $M = (Q, \{0, \#\}, \delta, s)$ decrements the input by one. The computed function is defined as:

$$f(m) = \begin{cases} m - 1 \text{ (If } m \geq 1) \\ 0 \text{ (Otherwise)} \end{cases}$$

We select one of the following options for function f:

1. M reads the leftmost zero, writes # and halt, or
2. M reads all the zeros, without write and reaches the right end moves one cell left and writes zero and halt.

The transition diagrams are shown in Fig. 8.10(a) and Fig. 8.10(b) for both the Turing machines.

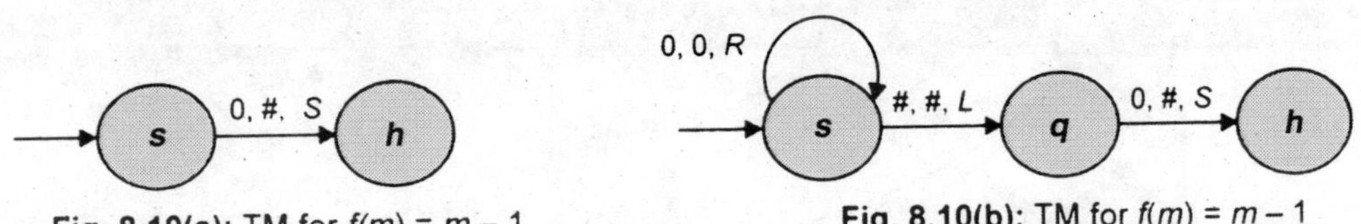

Fig. 8.10(a): TM for $f(m) = m - 1$

Fig. 8.10(b): TM for $f(m) = m - 1$

Let us see the computed function of Turing machines for $M = 4$, which are given below:

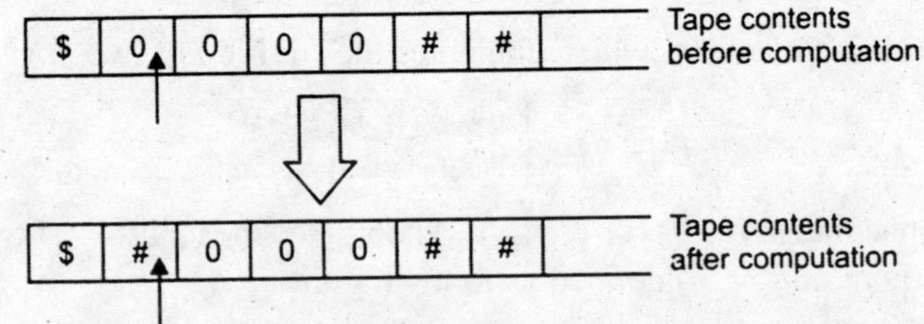

Fig. 8.10(c): Computation of turing machine shown in Fig. 8.10(a)

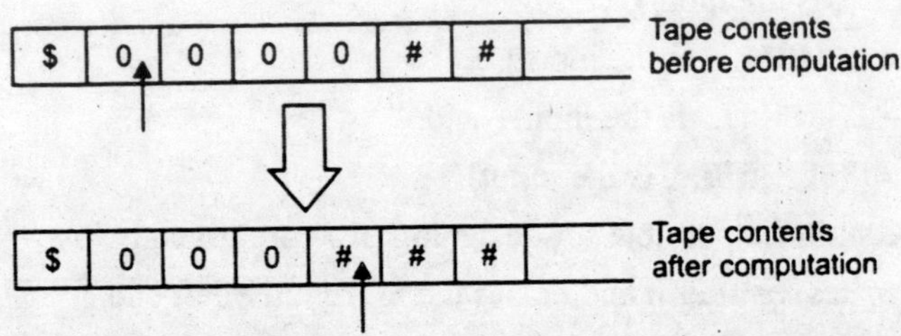

Fig. 8.10(d): Computation of turing machine shown in Fig. 8.10(b)

Example 3: Design a Turing machine $M = (Q, \{0, \#, 1\}, \delta, s)$ which computes the following:

$$(s, \#\, \boldsymbol{n}\#) \vdash_M^* (h, \#\, n\, \#\, n\, \underline{\#}), \text{ where } n \text{ is the input (positive integer)}$$

Solution: Turing machine *M* copies the input number but does not overwrite on the input i.e., the input on the tape is not modified and copies the number on the tape. The input and copied number is separated by blank symbol (#). Now, the question is how *M* will remember that how many zeros are copied and how many zeros are remaining? This is the real hurdle in designing of *M*. We use following technique in designing of *M*:

1. *M* reads one zero and writes 1 and reaches the end of input without write and on the second blank cell after the input (cell containing #) zero is written, and
2. Now, *M* returns from the right end to left, where it has written 1 in place of zero and 1 is replaced by 0 and moves right goes to step (1) until the end of the input.

Writing 1 in place of 0 provides the mark which indicates that all cells left to this been copied and also the returning point for *M* in step 1. Turing machine *M* is shown in Fig. 8.11.

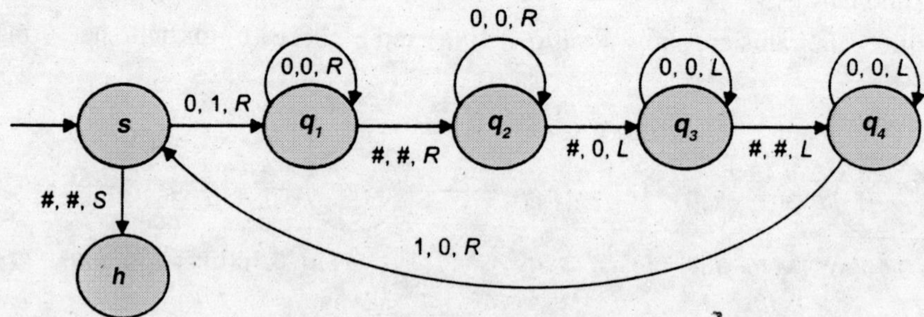

Fig. 8.11: TM for coping input

Example 4: Design a Turing machine, which computes the addition of two positive decimal integers.

$$f(m, n) = \begin{cases} m + n \text{ (If } m, n \geq 0) \\ 0\ (m = n = 0) \end{cases}$$

Solution: Let Turing machine $M = (Q, \{0, 1, \#\}, \delta, s)$ computes the addition of two positive integers *m* and *n*. The computed function *f*(*m*, *n*) defined as following:

Operands *m* and n are separated by 1 on the tape. Following values combinations are possible for *m* and n:

1. $m = n = 0$(**#1#**... is the input),
2. $m = 0$ and $n \neq 0$(**#10**^{n}**#**... is the input),
3. $m \neq 0$ and $n = 0$(**#0**^{m}**1#**... is the input), and
4. $m \neq 0$ and $n \neq 0$(**#0**^{m}**10**^{n}**#**... is the input)

Some of several techniques possible for designing of *M* are given below:

(a) *M* appends (writes) *m* after *n* and erases the *m* from the left end.

(b) *M* writes 0 in place of 1 and erases one zero from the right or left end. This is possible in case of $n \neq 0$ or $m \neq 0$ only. If $m = 0$ or $n = 0$ then 1 is replaced by #.

We use techniques (b) given above. First, M checks the operand n, whether n is zero or not. If $n = 0$ then M replaces 1 by blank symbol (#) and halts. If $n \neq 0$, M replaces one zero from right end and halts. Turing machine M is shown in Fig. 8.12.

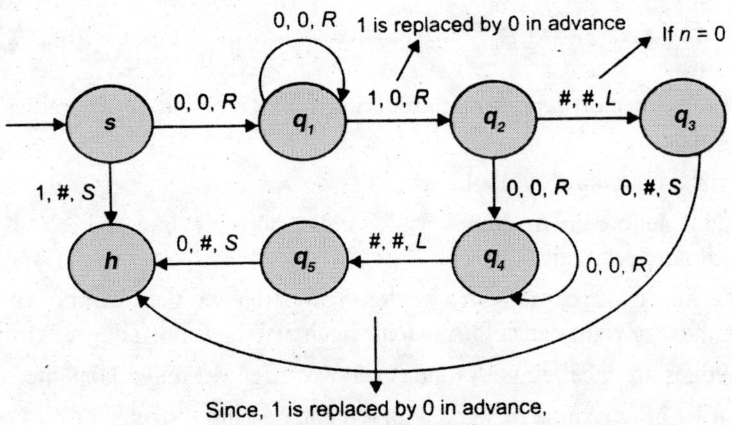

Fig. 8.12: TM for addition of two positive integers

8.4 SOME POWERFUL TURING MACHINES

As we have seen earlier that transition diagram of a Turing machine for a complex task requires a lot of space. So, now we discuss some powerful machine and their short representation that we will use in our examples later on.

For examples,

1. This Turing machine finds the first blank symbol right to the current head position. This is shown in Fig. 8.13(a). This is useful while searching right end of a string. This is represented by $R_{\#}$.
2. This Turing machine finds the first blank symbol left to the current head position. This is shown in Fig. 8.13(b). This is useful while searching left end of a string. This is represented by $L_{\#}$.

Fig. 8.13(a): TM $R_{\#}$ **Fig. 8.13(b):** TM $L_{\#}$

3. This Turing machine finds the first non-blank symbol right to the current head position. This is shown in Fig. 8.13(c). This is useful while searching the first non-blank symbol right to the current head position. This is represented by $R_{\bar{\#}}$.
4. This Turing machine finds the first non-blank symbol left to the current head position. This is shown in Fig. 8.13(d). This is useful while searching the first non-blank symbol left to the current head position. This is represented by $L_{\bar{\#}}$.

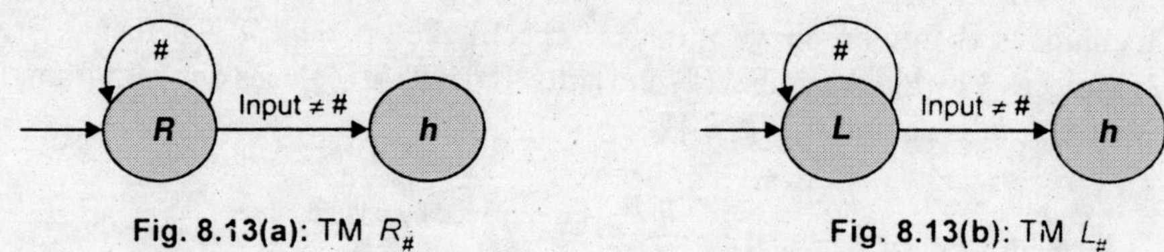

Fig. 8.13(a): TM $R_{\#}$ Fig. 8.13(b): TM $L_{\#}$

Now, we use the short representation of above machines in our examples. We use following notations also:

(a) σ denotes the input symbol.

(b) R and L denote the machines, which move one cell right and left from the current head position respectively.

(c) A machine can proceed with a written symbol like aR, the meaning is writing symbol a and then moving right one cell. A machine can also be followed by a written symbol like Ra.

(d) All edges are labelled with input(s) and an edge without a label means for all inputs.

5. Suppose a Turing machine M starts with left end of a input string and moves right one cell and if it reads symbol a then writes symbol b and repeats it until it reads #. Turing machine M is shown in Fig. 8.14.

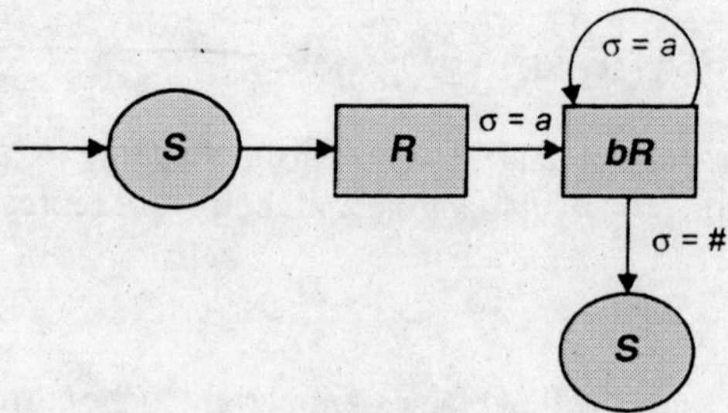

Fig. 8.14

Example 1: Design a Turing machine for language $L = \{a^n b^n : n \geq 1\}$.

Solution: Let Turing machine $M = (Q, \{a, b, \#\}, \delta, s\}$ recognizes the language L. We design M simply without using powerful Turing machines, which is shown in Fig. 8.15(a) and using powerful Turing machines, which is shown in Fig. 8.15(b).

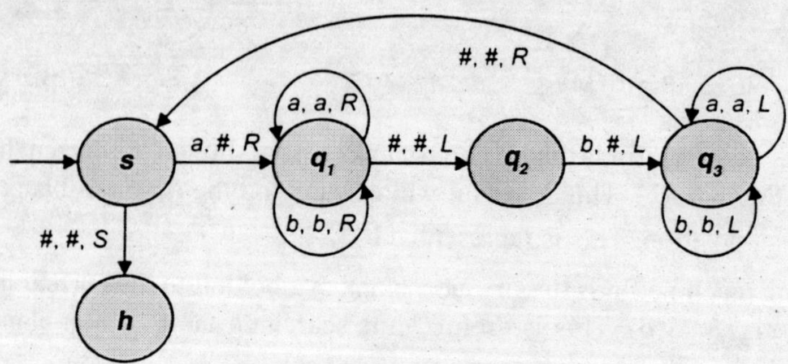

Fig. 8.15(a): TM for $L = \{a^n b^n : n \geq 1\}$

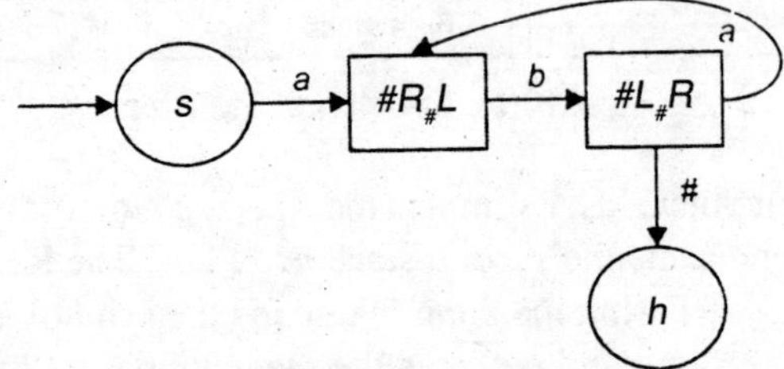

Fig. 8.15(b): TM for $L = \{a^n b^n : n \geq 1\}$

Consider input strings "*ab*", "*abb*" and see the steps involved in processing:

$$(s, \#\underline{a}b\#) \vdash^{\#R_\#} (\#, \#b\#) \vdash^{L} (\#\#\underline{b}\#) \vdash^{\#L_\#} (\#\underline{\#}\#\#) \vdash^{R} (\#\underline{\#}\#\#) \vdash (h, \#\#\#\underline{\#})$$

$$(s, \#\underline{a}bb\#) \vdash^{\#R_\#} (\#\#bb\#) \vdash^{L} (\#\#b\underline{b}\#) \vdash^{\#L_\#} (\#\#b\#\#) \vdash^{R} (\#\#\underline{b}\#\#) \vdash \text{Hang}$$

8.5 VARIATIONS OF TURING MACHINE

In this section, we will discuss about **variations** or **modifications** of a Turing machine. We will also discuss the power of Turing machine whether altered or not after modifications.

8.5.1 Two-Stack Pushdown Automaton (2PDA)

The pushdown automaton discussed in Chapter 7 has only one stack storage and can recognize only the context-free languages. We have one question here. Does addition of a second stack storage to a PDA alter its power? Pushdown automaton with two stacks is known as **2PDA**. The instruction set of a 2PDA has the same instruction format as simple PDA has. The only difference is the operation of the second stack. We separate the operations of first stack and second stack like WRITE_1, WRITE_2, READ_1 and READ_2. Operation WRITE_1 indicates the write on first stack and WRITE_2 indicates write on second stack. Similarly, operations READ_1 and READ_2 indicate reading on first and second stacks respectively. Now, the obvious question is about the power of 2PDA. Is there any non-context-free language like type 1 or type 0 recognizable by 2PDA? Yes, we have such languages. Let us see one **example** given below:

Consider the language $L = \{a^n b^n c^n : n \geq 1$, which is already proved to be non-context free. A 2PDA could recognise this language by performing the following steps:

1. Reads all the a's from the beginning of the input string and writes on the first stack (WRITE_1).
2. Reads all the b's from the input string and for each *b*, reads symbol '*a*' from the first stack and writes *X* on the second stack (WRITE_2), and
3. Reads all the c's from the input string and matches with *X*'s from the second stack.

So, we conclude that 2PDA recognizes $L = \{a^n b^n c^n : n \geq 1\}$.

Theorem 8.1: Some single tape Turing machine can simulate a 2PDA.

Proof: Here is a constructive algorithm that converts a 2PDA to a Turing machine that recognises the same language recognized by 2PDA. We simply divide the tape of the Turing machine into three regions separated by some distinguished symbols. The first region starts with \$, second region starts with ψ, and the third region starts with λ as shown in Fig. 8.16(a).

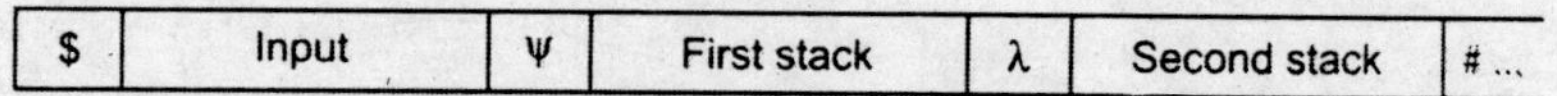

Fig. 816(a): Division of TM's tape

The first region represents the 2PDA's input tape, the second region represents the first stack of 2PDA and the third region represents the second stack of 2PDA. The READ instructions of the 2PDA is simulated by the instruction of Turing machine that reads the symbol at the corresponding cell from the corresponding region on the tape and replaces the read symbol by # symbol. The POP_1 and POP_2 instructions of the 2PDA are simulated by instructions of Turing machine that reads the symbol from the corresponding region and writes # at that position as shown in Fig. 8.16(b).

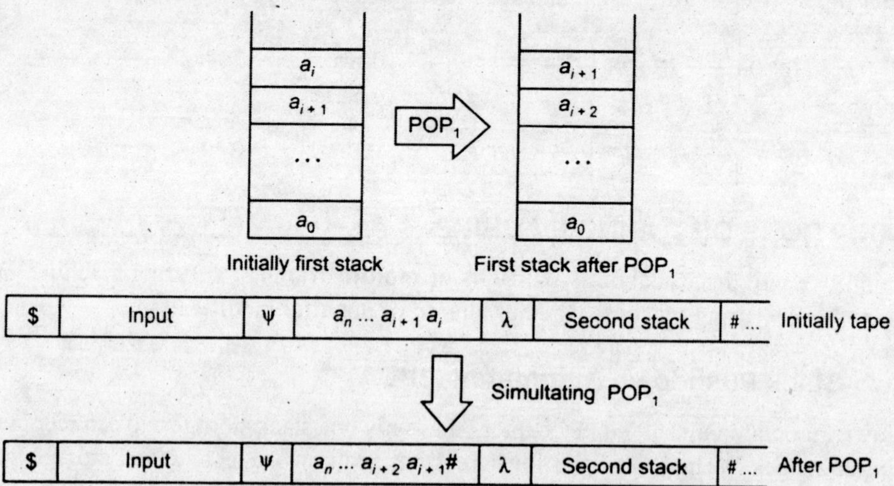

Fig. 8.16(b): Simulation of POP_1 operation by TM

The $PUSH_1$ and $PUSH_2$ instructions of the 2PDA are simulated by instruction of Turing machine that inserts the required symbol(s) at the end as shown in Fig. 8.16(c).

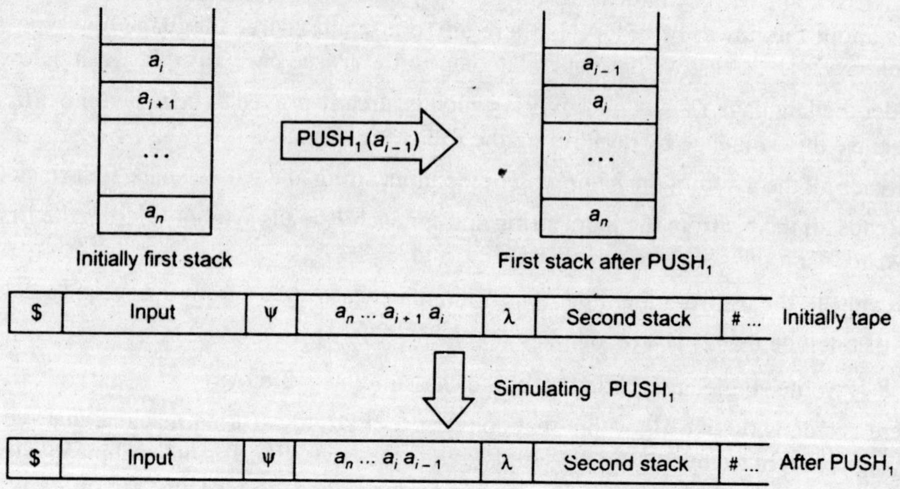

Fig. 8.16(c): Simulation of $PUSH_1$ operation by TM

Now, it is clear that a Turing machine can do whatever a 2PDA can do by simulating the read and write operations of 2PDA. So, we conclude that some Turing machine simulates a given 2PDA.

Theorem 8.2: Every single tape Turing machine is simulated by some 2PDA.

Proof: The proof of this theorem relies on the use of the two stacks of 2PDA to represent those parts of the TM's tape that lie on each side of its head. The content of left side of the tape from the head position is kept on the first stack and the remaining content of right hand side of the head is kept on the second stack of 2PDA. As the TM's head moves along, reading and writing symbols to its tape, the 2PDA simulates the operations of Turing machine by moving corresponding symbols from first stack to second stack or second stack to first stack along with doing the same operations whatever Turing machine does. When Turing machine halts in halting state then the contents of two stacks are considered as the output computed by Turing machine. Therefore, we conclude that some 2PDA can simulate the behaviour of a given Turing machine.

The Theorem 8.1 and Theorem 8.2 together assert that

$$\text{TM} = \text{2PDA}$$

Now, it is obvious that adding a second stack storage to pushdown automaton considerably increases the power. The recognizing power of 2PDA and Turing machines is equivalent. So, we might expect that adding a third stack, or fourth, fifth, etc., would generate even more powerful classes of pushdown automaton. But, this is not the truth. We cannot get more powerful machine while adding more than two stacks. So, the conclusion is

$$\textbf{2PDA} = \textbf{3PDA} = \textbf{4PDA} = \ldots = n\textbf{PDA} = \textbf{TM}$$

We may be able to see this intuitively by extending the same constructive algorithm developed for the 2PDA to simulate its behaviour by a single tape Turing machine. All we have to do is to make more regions on the tape of the Turing machine to represent the n ($n \geq 3$) stacks of the nPDA and simulate the nPDA's instructions accordingly. Thus, every nPDA for $n \geq 3$ can be simulated by some Turing machine. So, no increment in power of pushdown automaton is obtained and therefore the above conclusion is true.

8.5.2 Read-Only Turing Machines and Two-way Finite Automata

We will see what happen if we restrict a Turing machine to read only. The read-only Turing machine can read only, but cannot write on the tape. Clearly, such a Turing machines cannot write any output and therefore cannot compute any function that requires writing. But, such Turing machines can still recognise languages by coming to a halt state for acceptable strings. The read-only Turing machine may therefore be considered similar as finite automaton that has the additional property of being able to move its head in both directions (left and right) which is known as two-way finite automata. The additional thing is the length of the tape of Turing machine, which has infinite potential. Now, we have some questions here:

1. What class of languages is recognized by these Turing machines?
2. Does the restriction to the Turing machine decreases its power, or does the enhancement to the finite automaton increases power?

By the Kleene's Theorem that is any read-only Turing machine can be converted to regular expression. So, we conclude that the Read-Only Turing machines accept only the regular languages.

We have seen already the two-way finite automaton recognize the regular languages and have equivalent language recognizing power what read-only Turing machines have.

8.5.3 Multiple Tracks Turing Machines

As we have discussed that addition of stacks to pushdown automaton increases recognizing power. So, what about adding the more tracks to a Turing machine? A k-track (for some fixed $k > 0$) Turing machine (known as **kTM**) has k tracks and one read/write head that reads and writes all of them one by one. Its instruction set is appropriately modified so that each transition is labelled by a k-tuple that defines the symbols to be read from, and the (possibly different) symbols to be written to each of the k tracks as compared to single track Turing machine.

Theorem 8.3: A kTM for some fixed $k \geq 2$ can be simulated by a single track Turing machine.

For example, consider the 3-track TM shown in Fig. 8.17.

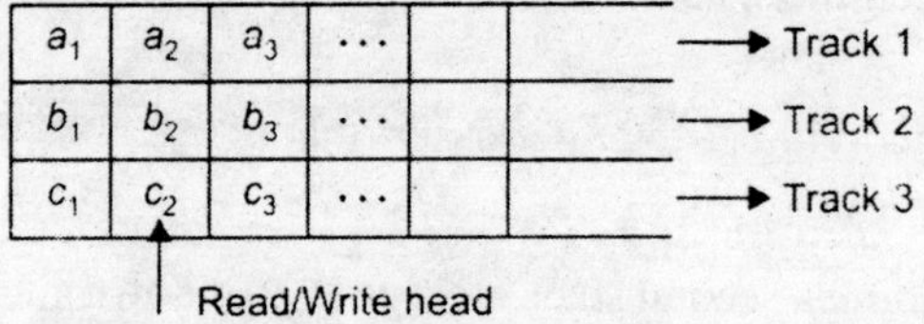

Fig. 8.17: Model of 3TM

The kTM relates easily to traditional manual operations, such as the addition of columns of numbers, where the calculation proceeds from right to left dealing with one column of digits at a time. Now, one question is here. Can any kTM simulated by some single track Turing machine? The clue to doing this is to see that each column of cells on the tape consists of a k-tuple of symbols. It is straightforward to encode each of the possible values of this tuple as a single symbol in some extended alphabet. **For example**, if the original Turing machine's alphabet $\Sigma = \{a, b, \#\}$ and two tracks are there then corresponding cells on the first track and second track may contain one of 9 (= 3^k for $k = 2$) combinations given following:

$$(a, a), (a, \#), (\#, a), (b, b), (b, \#), (\#, b), (a, b), (b, a), (\#, \#)$$

So, we define a new alphabet that contains the composite symbols (k-tuple) for single track Turing machine that has to simulate the behaviour of a kTM. This new alphabet contains total $|\Sigma|^k$ composite symbols. If the kTM's program is encoded using this new alphabet, the result will be an equivalent Turing machine with single track. So, we conclude that a kTM is simulated by some single track Turing machine.

8.5.4 Two-way Infinite Tape Turing Machines

Turing machine model as shown in Fig. 8.1 has a one-way-infinite tape. That is, the tape has an end at the left and beyond this the machine should not move. But it is unbounded (infinite) to the right end. Would there be any increase in power if the tape is made infinite to the left end as well? We will this in Theorem 8.4.

Theorem 8.4: A two-way infinite Turing machine can be simulated by some one-way infinite Turing machine and vice-versa.

Proof: To simulate a one-way infinite Turing machine on a two-way infinite Turing machine, we need to place a distinguished symbol on the tape of the two-way infinite Turing machine to mark the position corresponding to the starting point of the one-way infinite Turing machine's tape. The new program is almost the same as the old, except for some careful treatment of movement left out of the mark. The two-way program must use an explicit non-halt state to represent the one-way's possible crash after the leftmost cell of the tape.

To simulate a two-way infinite Turing machine by an one-way infinite Turing machine, we first construct a 3TM (a TM with three tracks) in which

1. The first track contains the right hand half of the two-way TM's tape,
2. The third track contains its left hand half, and
3. The centre (second) track contains some distinguished symbols that tell the one-way infinite Turing machine to which track to refer to and where the join occurs.

After completed the above translation, the 3TM is converted to the required one-way infinite Turing machine (Theorem 8.4). If two-way infinite Turing machine operates in its left region then one-way infinite Turing machine operates its third track in reverse direction applied by two-way infinite Turing M. Again we conclude that two-way infinite Turing machine is equivalent to one-way infinite Turing machine.

8.5.5 Multi-Tape Turing Machines

The multi-tape Turing machine differs from the kTM in that it has multiple tapes and it can have a separate tape head for each of its multiple tapes. On each move, such a machine reads the symbols under all the tape heads simultaneously, changes state according to the combination of symbols read and writes new symbols to each of the scanned cells independently. The heads movements on the each tape are independent; either one cell right or left and some time stationary also.

Theorem 8.5: A multi-tape Turing machine is equivalent to a single tape Turing machine.

8.5.6 Nondeterministic and Deterministic Turing Machines

A non-deterministic Turing machine (**NTM**) is similar to the Turing machine discussed earlier. The only difference is in transition function. For a given state and input symbol a NTM has at least one choice to move (finite number of choices for the next move), each choice consisting of a new state, a symbol to write and a direction of head movement. Like the nondeterministic finite automaton (NFA), NTM may have several choices of path that it might follow for a given input string. An input string is accepted by a NTM if any such path leads to a halting state, even if some choices of path lead to loop. Note that non-determinism adds no power to the NFA class; same is true for NTM. A deterministic Turing machine (DTM) has at most one move for input symbol and present state. DTM has similar transition function what deterministic finite automata have. Deterministic Turing machine is a kind of nondeterministic Turing machine with some restriction in transition function but power of both DTM and NTM is equivalent. The obvious question is whether:

$$\text{NTM} = \text{DTM?}$$

We will see the answer in the following theorem.

Theorem 8.6: A non-deterministic Turing machine (NTM) is equivalent to a deterministic Turing machine (DTM).

Proof: A NTM can do anything that a DTM can do simply by not exploiting its non-determinism. We construct a 3-tape DTM M_2 that recognizes the same language as a NTM M_1. For any state and symbol of M_1, there is finite number of choices for the next move. Suppose these choices are numbered 1, 2, 3, ... and let r be the maximum number of choices for some state and a symbol in M_1. Then any finite sequence of choices can be represented by a sequence of the digits 1, 2, ..., r. Not all such sequences represent r choices of moves, since there may be fewer than r choices in some situations. Deterministic Turing machine M_2 has three tapes. The first tape holds the input string, on the second tape M_2 generates sequences of the digits 1, 2, ..., r in a systematic manner, the shortest sequences appears first and sequences of equal length appearing in lexicographic order (that is, for example, [1, 2, 3] will appear before [1, 3, 2]). For each sequence generated on second tape, M_2 copies the input on the third tape and then simulates nondeterministic Turing machine M_1 running on the third tape, using the sequence on the second tape to dictate M_1's moves. If M_1 enters halt state then M_2 also. If there is a sequence of choices that leads M_1 to accept the input string then that sequence will eventually be generated by M_2 on second tape and will lead M_2 to accept that string. But, if there is no such sequence of moves then M_2 will not accept the input string.

Since, M_2 has at most one choice of move for all states and input symbols that simulates the behaviour of NTM M_1. It has been seen earlier that a DTM is considered as NTM. So, we conclude that a NTM is equivalent to some DTM and vice-versa.

8.5.7 The Off-line Turing Machines

Off-line Turing machines are similar to multi-tape Turing machines except the first tape (input tape), which is read-only and has two end markers for input stream. Symbol \$ is used for left end and symbol y is used for right end. The remaining tapes are two-way infinite tapes. These Turing machines do not allow their heads to move across the marked region on the input tape. These Turing machines are special type of multi-tape Turing machines, so this new arrangement does not increase the power of the off-line Turing machines. It is obvious that an off-line Turing machine is equivalent to a one-way infinite Turing machine (Theorem 8.5).

8.6 INTRODUCTION TO TURING MACHINE EFFICIENCY

So far, we have considered only the power of the machines; recognizing and computing. We have been investigating, in terms of their ability to recognize languages and computation they are performing. The relative efficiency of different machines recognizing the same language or computing the same task has not been an issue. Consider the following cases:

1. Consider the case that we have discussed earlier about the simulation of two-way infinite tape Turing machine by one-way infinite tape Turing machine. In this simulation, many moves of one-way infinite Turing machine are needed to simulate one move of two-way infinite Turing machine. In fact, to simulate k moves of two-way infinite Turing machine, one-way infinite Turing machine requires around $2k^2$ moves. So, obviously, two-way infinite Turing machines are better than one-way infinite Turing machines in view of computational speed.
2. Consider the language consisting of even length palindromes $L = \{ww^R : w \in (0 + 1)^*\}$ can be recognised on a single tape Turing machine by moving its head back and forth (left and right) to the input, comparing symbols from both ends. The number of moves that this Turing machine takes to accept any word of the language is approximately the square of the length of word.

To recognize this language on a two tapes Turing machine, the input is copied to the second tape and compare the first tape contents from the left end with the second tape contents from the right end of the input checking the input length whether it is even or not. For this Turing machine, the number of moves to accept a word is proportional to the length of word.

The efficiency (speed) difference between single tape and two tapes Turing machines varies as the square of the length of input. So, for word consisting of 5 symbols, one machine will take 25 moves while other takes 5 moves (approximately). For words of 100 symbols, the performance difference will be a factor of 10000 (approximate). Clearly, this factor of difference in efficiency rapidly outstrips the influence of any conceivable technological device.

So, efficiency measurement and comparison are very important for the machines before implementation. We will discuss these issues in the Chapter 11.

8.7 CHURCH'S THESIS

In automata theory, we give idea about the behaviour of automatic machines mathematically. Our abstract model of a computer system is finite automata. Finite automaton is a device having finite states and operates on a string of symbols with fixed and finite set of rules. Pushdown automaton and Turing machines are more powerful machines than finite automaton. Turing machines capture behaviours of finite automaton and pushdown automaton as well as general-purpose computer system. We consider a Turing machine to be equivalent to an algorithm. Nothing will be considered as algorithm if it cannot be implemented as a Turing machine.

"The principle that Turing machines are formal version of algorithms and no computational procedure will be considered an algorithm unless it can be implemented as a Turing machine is known as **Church's Thesis**."

According to the Church's Thesis, behaviour of a general-purpose computer can be simulated by some Turing machine. It is a thesis, not a theorem because it has no mathematical proof. A Turing machine can perform all the computations (recognization and computation), which are carried out by a general-purpose digital computer. We are very much aware that a large variety of complicated tasks are performed by digital computers. So, proving that Turing machines also perform these all tasks is not easier. We have also seen that some powerful Turing machines can be combined to solve some complicated task, but looking on the variety of tasks performed by a computer, we still not in position to prove the equivalence of Turing machines and computers. First thing is that "How we can define digital computer precisely?" If we could do this, then our work will be easier. Since proving equivalence of Turing machines and computers straightforward is not easier, so we choose the other way. We would like to search a counter example to disprove the Church's Thesis. But, if this were possible, then we would have a basis to reject the Church's Thesis. No one yet has been able to produce such a counter example. Still this is open debate for future that someday somebody could be able to produce some counter example and we could precisely conclude the debate....

Allan Turing also suggested in his Turing's Thesis that "Any computation that can be performed by mechanical means can also be performed by some Turing machine". Again, we have to define the terms "*mechanical means*". If we consider this, then the model of Turing machine shown in Fig. 8.1 comes true.

Some arguments for accepting the Church's Thesis are following:

1. No one has been able to suggest a counter example to disprove till now.
2. Some Turing machines can also perform any thing that can be performed by digital computers.
3. There are several alternative model of computation like random access machine (**RAM**), Post machine (**PM**) etc., but no one is more powerful than Turing Machine.

The above arguments do not prove the Church's Thesis but support the thesis. We think in another way also to accept the Church's Thesis. Consider the Newton's laws of motion defined in Physics that has no mathematical proof and still we consider these as laws. The reason is that we feel these and these can be observed practically. So, the conclusion is that we are agreed to accept the Church's Thesis as a basis law of Computer Science.

Definition of algorithm

After accepting the Church's Thesis we are in position to define the term algorithm precisely.

"An algorithm for a function $f: D \longrightarrow R$ is considered as a Turing machine which takes any input $\delta \in$ D and halts with the right answer $f(\delta) \in R$.

So, if Turing machine $M = (Q, \Sigma, \delta, s)$, then

$$(s, \#\underline{\delta}\#) \vdash_M^* (h, \# f(\delta) \underline{\#}) \text{ for all } \delta \in D, f(\delta) \in R$$

8.8 UNIVERSAL TURING MACHINE (UTM)

Each Turing machine is capable of performing a single algorithm. In this sense, Turing machines are analogous to computer programs (software) rather than hardware of a computer. This means that we might need to build a separate Turing machine for each and every algorithm that we would like to execute. This is highly impractical. A **Universal Turing machine** is a specific Turing machine that can simulate the behaviour of any Turing machine. Alan Turing described such machines. Its existence means that there is a machine (known as UTM), which is capable of running any algorithm. The key idea is to think of the description of a Turing machine itself as input (data) for some other machine. Universal Turing machines can run many algorithm one at a time. We think a UTM as a reprogrammable Turing machine. A universal Turing machine takes as input the description of a Turing machine along with the initial tape contents, and simulates the input on that Turing machine. Thus, the UTM can simulate the behaviour of any individual Turing machine. Building such a UTM appears to be a daunting task. Alan Turing described the first such Turing machine in his 1937 paper. In 1962, Minsky discovered a remarkable 7-state UTM that executes using a four-symbol alphabet, but it is rather complicated to describe here.

General-purpose computers and UTM

General-purpose computers are analogous to universal Turing machines. These are capable of running different algorithms without requiring any hardware modifications or addition. This is possible because modern day microprocessors are based upon the **von Neumann architecture**. In this model, computer programs and data are stored in the same memory (main memory). This means that the contents of memory can be treated as a machine instruction or data depending on the context. This is exactly analogous to the tape contents of the UTM that consists of both a program (description of TM) and its data (the tape contents). Alan Turing's work on UTM anticipated the development of general-purpose computers, and can be viewed as the invention of software.

8.9 SOME OTHER POWERFUL MACHINES

Let us discuss some other powerful machines other than Turing machines.

8.9.1 Random Access Machine (RAM)

As we know that Turing machine is the most powerful computing device we have discussed so far. But, its one limitation is that it cannot read its input randomly. A Turing machine reads its input one by one sequentially. Now, we think about a new type of machine, which access (read or write) its memory randomly. This type of machine is known as **random access machine** (RAM). Such machines have random access memory. A RAM consists of:

1. Infinite number of memory words each of which can hold any integer and can be accessed randomly,
2. A read/write head capable to access any word randomly,
3. A finite number of arithmetic registers capable of holding any integer, and
4. Finite control to control the operations of machine.

A model of RAM is shown in Fig. 8.18.

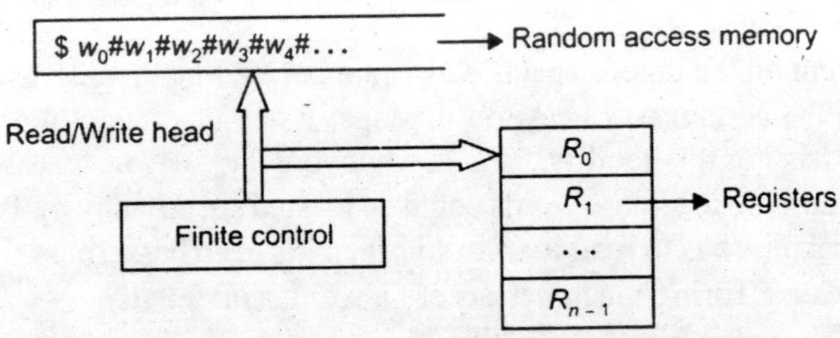

Fig. 8.18: Model of random access machine

Word w_i for $i \geq 0$ is of fixed length and R_j for some $j = 0, 1, \ldots, n-1$ is an arithmetic register. Total number of registers is $\boldsymbol{n}$, symbol **$** is the left end marker of random accessed memory. RAM starts reading the first instruction after positioning the **location counter** (LC) to the first instruction and decodes the instruction. After decoding whatever operations are defined in the instruction, are carried out by RAM. Now, location counter is incremented by one to point the next instruction and this is on for all the instructions that are to be executed. An instruction may consist of more than one word. When RAM decodes an instruction then the execution may require accessing of some other word(s). In other words, we say that execution of an instruction may require the accessing of other word(s). In such situations, RAM accesses that word(s) and final result is evaluated. The location counter holds the address of next instruction to be fetched and another counter called **memory address register** (MAR) holds the number of words in an instruction. An instruction has following format:

Opcode	**Operands(s)/Address**

First field contains the **opcode** (stands for operation code) which indicates the operation to be carried out after decoding and second field contains the necessary operand(s) or address(s) of operand(s). Different random access machines (RAMs) may have different instruction formats. Let us suppose that opcode contains ADD (addition operation) and second field contains R_0 and R_3, so instruction is: "ADD contents of register R_0 with register R_3 and store result into register R_0." Thus, a RAM executing this instruction, finds the contents of register R_0 and adds with register R_3 contents and stores the result into R_0 register.

Theorem 8.7: A Turing machine can simulate a Random access machine provided that Turing machine can itself simulate the elementary RAM's instructions.

Proof: We discuss a constructive algorithm to construct a Turing machine for a given random access machine (RAM). We use four tapes Turing machine to simulate a given RAM. Contents of different tapes are as follows:

Tape 1: Tape 1 consists of the input of RAM, as shown in Fig. 8.19(a).

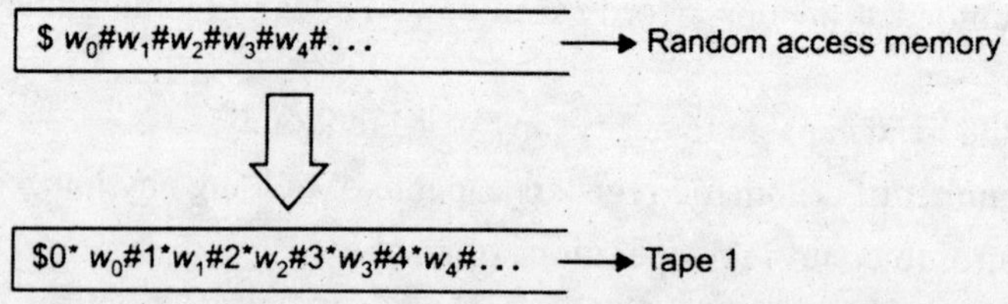

Fig. 8.19(a): Storage of RAM and turing machine

The content on the tape is specified by numbering like 0, 1, 2, ...These numbers are used to locate the certain word (w_i) on the tape. RAM has random access facility but Turing machine has not this facility. This is why words w_0, w_1, w_2, ... are preceded by numbers like 0, 1, 2, ... so that these words could be located specifically by Turing machine. Suppose Turing machine has to read the word w_i then it's head has to pass the words $w_0, w_1, w_2, \ldots, w_{i-1}$, because Turing machines access a word sequentially.

Tape 2: Second tape holds the registers contents as shown in Fig. 8.19(b).

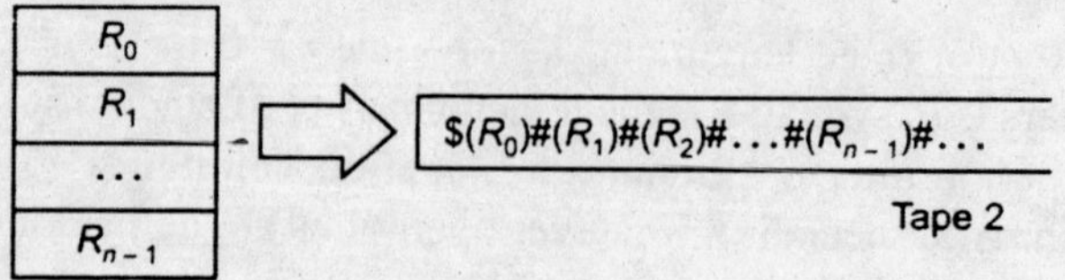

Fig. 8.19(b)

(Note that (R_i) indicates the contents of register R_i)

Register's content on the second tape is also identified by numbering as used for first tape. Turing machine moves sequentially to access any register's content. Whenever content of a register is changed by RAM then this change is reflected on the tape.

Tape 3: The location counter of RAM, which contains the next instruction's address is hold on the third tape as shown in Fig. 8.19(c).

$(LC)#...

Tape 3

Fig. 8.19(c)

(Note that (LC) indicates the content of location counter.)
Content of location counter is changed after execution of an instruction, that is, location counter is incremented by one to point the next instruction. This change is reflected on the third tape.

Tape 4: The fourth tape holds the contents of memory address register (MAR) as shown in Fig. 8.19(d).

$$(I_n)$#...

Tape 4

Fig. 8.19(d)

(Note that (I_n) indicates the number of words in n^{th} instruction.)
Content of memory address register indicates the number words to be accessed in order to execute the current instruction and it is changed after execution of an instruction. This change is reflected on the fourth tape.

Operation

Suppose initially location counter (LC) holds the value ***i***. Turing machine M searches the ith word (w_i) on the first tape looking for ***#i****. If this word is found then proceeds further otherwise halts. Word i^{th} is not found if and only if ***#i**** is followed by #. Suppose word w_i is found then whatever operation carried out by random access machine (RAM), those are also carried out by M. After completion of execution location counter (LC) is incremented by one and now RAM access the next instruction. According to the value of location counter (LC), Turing machine M also accesses the word(s) and whatever carried out by RAM; those are also carried out by M. The memory address register (MAR) content is taken as a counter and location counter (LC) content is taken as an index for searching the number of words in an instruction. That is, how many words are going to be access starting from the location indicated by location counter is estimated using memory address register and location counter. So, it is clear that four tapes Turing machine simulates the behaviour of a random access machine (RAM). As we have discussed earlier that a multi-tape Turing machine can be simulated by a single tape Turing machine. So, finally we conclude that a single tape Turing machine can simulate a random access machine (RAM).

8.9.2 POST Machine

Post machine was suggested by **Emil Post** in 1936, a kind of machine that is based on the notion of the program that later **von Neumann** studied in 1946. He was a mathematical logician and he is best known for his work on polyadic groups, recursively enumerable sets, and degrees of unsolvability, as well as for his contribution to the unsolvability of problems in combinatorial mathematics. He introduced the concepts of completeness and consistency in a paper on truth-table methods that developed from the work of his doctoral thesis. In 1941, Emil Post wrote:

> ... mathematical thinking is, and must be, essentially creative...
> but he said there are limitations and symbolic logic is:
> ... the indisputable means for revealing and developing these limitations.

Post machine is similar to a Turing machine but instead of a tape, it uses queue storage to hold the input and output. Potentially, queue storage is infinite as tape used in Turing machine. But operation manner is different for tape and queue. A queue is a storage, which operates in *first-in-first-out* (FIFO) manner. It means an item pushed on the queue first will be used first.

Model of post machine

A Post machine consists of queue storage, a Read/Write head, and finite control. Post machine model is shown in Fig. 8.20. (The symbol $ indicates the bottom of the queue.)

Fig. 8.20: Model of post machine

A Post machine can be described by 4-tuple (Q, Σ, δ, s), where

1. $\boldsymbol{Q}$ is the set of finite, non-empty read and write states,
2. Σ is input and output alphabet including #,
3. δ is the transition function which maps
   (a) For read state $R \in Q$: From $\boldsymbol{R} \times \Sigma(\boldsymbol{X}, \boldsymbol{R})$, where $X \in Q$ is a read or write state and moves right one cell,
   (b) For write (addition) state $A \in Q$: From $\boldsymbol{A} \rightarrow (\boldsymbol{X}, \boldsymbol{a}, \boldsymbol{R})$, where $X \in Q$ is a read or write state and $a \in \Sigma$ is a written symbol. Symbol 'a' is written after input stream leaving first cell blank after input stream and moves to the next input symbol.
4. $\boldsymbol{s} \in \boldsymbol{Q}$ is the starting state.

Post machine reads a symbol from the left side of the input and for writing it uses its write (adding) states and writes a symbol at the right end of the input. In other words, a Post machine appends a symbol whenever it writes. **For example,** consider the language $L = \{a^n b^n : n \geq 1\}$ and Post machine for this language is shown in Fig. 8.21.

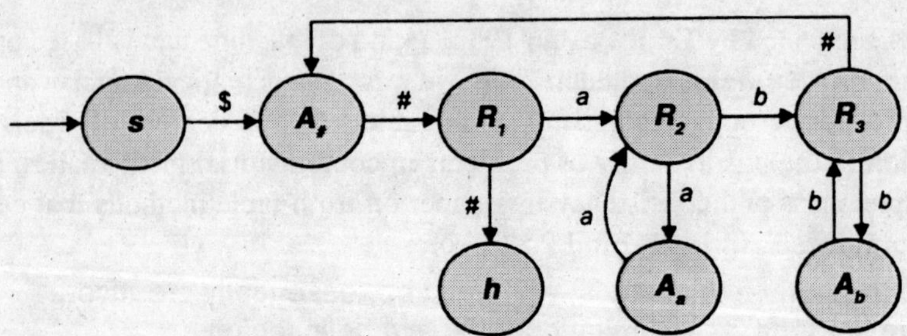

Fig. 8.21: Post machine for $L = \{a^n b^n : n \geq 1\}$

$A_\#$, A_a, A_b are write states which write #, a, and b respectively. R_1, R_2, and R_3 are read states. Consider a string ***w* = *aabb*** and let us see the processing given:

State	Content of queue
s	$aabb
$A_\#$	$aabb#
R_1	$aabb#
R_2	$aabb#
A_a	$aabb#a
R_2	$aabb#a
R_3	$aabb#a
A_b	$aabb#ab
R_3	$aabb#ab
$A_\#$	$aabb#ab#
R_1	$aabb#ab#
R_2	$aabb#ab#
R_3	$aabb#ab#
$A_\#$	$aabb#ab##
R_1	$aabb#ab##
h	$aabb#ab##

Theorem 8.8: Some Turing machine can simulate the behaviour of a Post machine.

Proof: We will discuss a constructive algorithm to construct a Turing machine M for given Post machine P. Let Turing machine $M = (Q, \Sigma, \delta, s)$, where

1. The starting state is same for both machines,
2. Simulation of reading operation of Post machine P by Turing machine M is shown in Fig. 8.22(a).

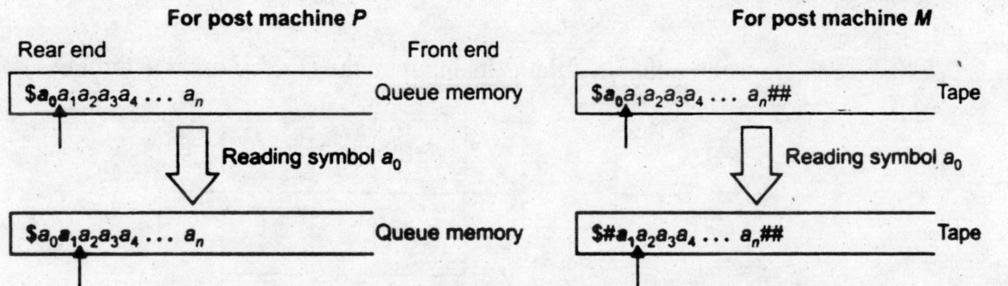

Fig. 8.22(a): Reading operation of post and turing machines

When Post machine starts reading from bottom (rear end) of the queue and reads symbol $\boldsymbol{a_i}$ then its moves the read/write head to next input symbol a_{i+1}. When Turing machine reads symbol $\boldsymbol{a_i}$ and makes the cell blank and then moves to the next input symbol a_{i+1}.

3. The simulation of writing operation of Post machine P by Turing machine M is shown in Fig. 8.22(b).

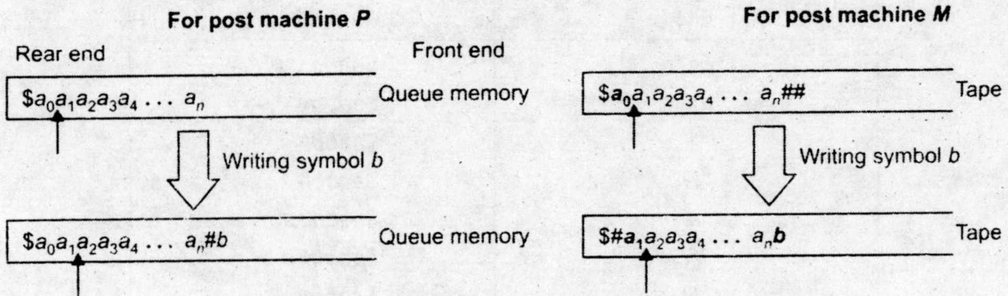

Fig. 8.22(b): Writing operation of post and turing machines

Post machine reads symbol a_0 and writes symbol b after the input steam and in the second blank cell at the front end on the queue. The first blank is considered as marker. Turing machine reads symbol a_0, makes the cell blank and moves to the first blank symbol to the right and writes symbol b on the tape.

4. Halting condition is same for both machines. So, we conclude that some Turing machine can simulate the behaviour of a Post machine.

$$(s,\#w\#) \vdash_M^* (h, \#w\#w\#)$$

8.10 SOLVED EXAMPLES

Example 8.1: Design a Turing machine, which performs the following:

$$\text{Input} = \#w\#$$
$$\text{Output} = \#w\#w\#, \text{ where } w \in (a+b)^*$$

Solution: Let Turing machine $M = (Q, \{a, b, \#\}, \delta, s)$ performs the given task:

$$(s,\#w\#) \vdash_M^* (h, \#w\#w\#)$$

M is just like a copier machine that maintains its input on the tape. M is shown in Fig. 8.23.

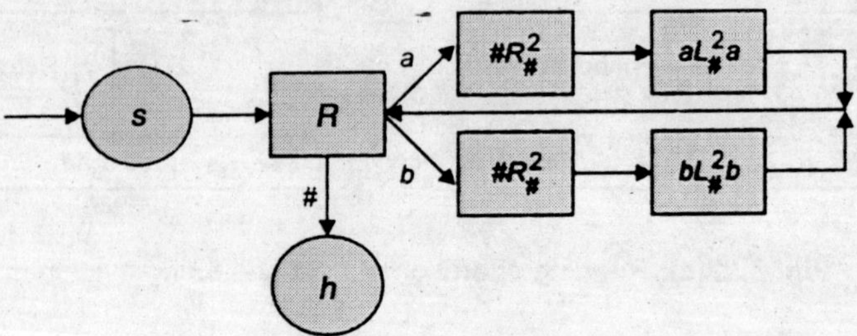

Fig. 8.23: Copier TM

(Note: $R_{\#}^{2}$ Denotes two machines of type)

Turing machine starts in initial state s and moves right and reads the input symbol. If symbol is '***a***' then it makes the present cell blank and moves to second rightmost blank cell (using Powerful Turing machine $R_{\#}^{2}$) and then writes symbol 'a'. After writing symbol 'a', Turing machine returns to the previous cell (cell containing blank in place of symbol a). Now, Turing machine returns to the next input symbol (using powerful Turing machine $L_{\#}^{2}$). The same process is there for input symbol b. The process of making the read symbol (a or b) blank provides the return point for Turing machine. Otherwise there is no way to remember how many symbols (a's or b's) have been read. When Turing machine reads blank then it stops it's processing in halting state h.

Example 8.2: Design a Turing machine, which reverses the input string over $\{a, b\}$ and maintains it input also. For example, if input is #w# then output is $\#w\#w^R\#$.

Solution: Let Turing machine $M = (Q, \{a, b, \#\}, \delta, s)$ performs the given task:

$$(s, \#w\#) \vdash_M^* (h, \#w\#w^R\#)$$

M is shown in Fig. 8.24.

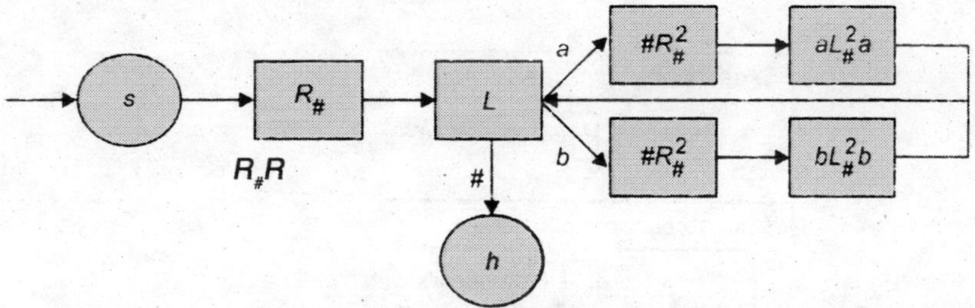

Fig. 8.24: TM for reversing the input string

The head of the Turing machine is assumed to be at the left end. M starts in initial state s and moves to the first blank cell to the right using $R_{\#}$ and after reading an input symbol (using left move L) moves to second rightmost blank cell using powerful Turing machine $\#R_{\#}^2$ and writes symbol (a or b) which has been read and returns to the present input symbol and write the read symbol a or b using $aL_{\#}^2a$ or $bL_{\#}^2b$. When a symbol is read then Turing machine makes it blank so that it can be used as return point after writing the symbol on right end of the input. Since Turing machine starts reading from the rightmost input symbol and copies at right end therefore copied stream is reverse of the input stream.

Example 8.3: Design a right shifting Turing machine that shifts the input one cell right. For example if input is #w# then output is ##w#.

Solution: Let Turing machine $M_R = (Q, \{a, b, \#\}, \delta, s)$ performs the given task:

$$(s, \#w\#) \vdash_M^* (h, \#\#w\#)$$

M_R is shown in Fig. 8.25.

Turing machine M moves to the first rightmost blank symbol and moves one cell left using ***R#*** and L. After reading a symbol (a or b) makes the present cell blank and moves to the first rightmost blank symbol. Now Turing machine writes the read symbol (a or b) using $\#R_{\#}a$ or $\#R_{\#}b$. Now, it is time to return to the next input symbol that is done by using $L_{\#}$ and L. This process is on for entire input stream and finally the input stream w is shifted one cell right.

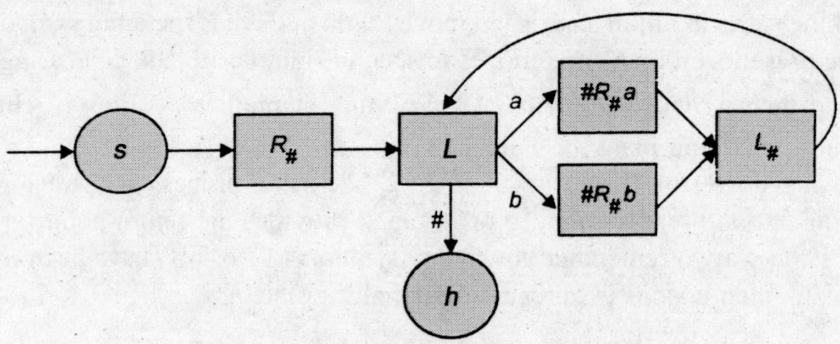

Fig. 8.25: Right shifting turing machine

Example 8.4: Design a Turing machine and a 2PDA for the language $L = \{a^n b^n c^n : n \geq 1\}$.

Solution: Let Turing machine $M = (Q, \{a, b, c, \#\}, \delta, s)$ recognizes language L. In the given language L, number of a's, b's, and c's is be equal. First, M copies the all a's after the c's and then it matches the all a's with the all b's and then all c's with all rightmost a's as shown in Fig. 8.26(a). Turing machine M is shown in Fig. 8.26(b).

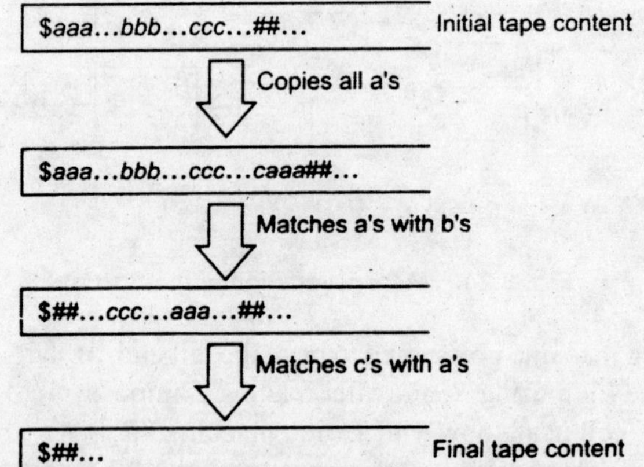

Fig. 8.26(a): Processing of turing machine

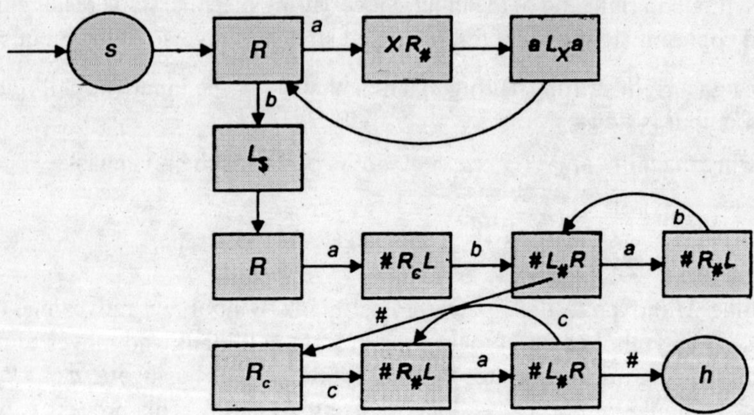

Fig. 8.26(b): TM for $L = \{a^n b^n c^n. n \geq 1\}$

It has been assumed that input stream starts with symbol \$ (marker). Turing machine starts in state s and moves right to read the input symbol. If input symbol is a then it writes symbol 'X' and moves to the first rightmost blank cell (using $XR_{\#}$) and writes symbol a. Now, M returns to present input cell that contains symbol 'X' and writes symbol 'a' in place of X (using $L_X a$). Using this process all a's are copied after c's on the tape. Now, M returns to the left end of the input stream using Turing machine $L_{\$}$. M starts matching a's and b's and then c's and a's as shown in Fig. 8.26(b).

Let 2PDA $N = (\{s, q_1, q_2, q_f\}, \{a, b, c\}, G_1, G_2, \delta, s, Z_1, Z_2, \{q_f\})$ recognizes language L, where $G_1 = \{Z_1, a\}$ is the stack$_1$ alphabet, $G_2 = \{Z_2, X\}$ is the stack$_2$ alphabet, Z_1 and Z_2 are topmost symbols on the stack$_1$ and stack$_2$ respectively, s is the starting state, q_f is the final state. We use the following format for representing transitions:

$$(Q \times \{a, b, c\} \times \Gamma_1 \times \Gamma_2) \longrightarrow (Q \times \Gamma_1 \times \Gamma_2)$$

The transition function for N is defined below:

$$\delta(s, a, Z_1, Z_2) = (s, aZ_1, Z_2),$$
$$\delta(s, a, a, Z_2) = (s, aa, Z_2),$$
$$\delta(s, b, a, Z_2) = (q_1, \varepsilon, XZ_2),$$
$$\delta(q_1, b, a, X) = (q_1, \varepsilon, XX),$$
$$\delta(q_1, c, Z_1, X) = (q_2, Z_1, \varepsilon),$$
$$\delta(q_2, c, Z_1, X) = (q_2, Z_1, \varepsilon), \text{ and}$$
$$\delta(q_2, \varepsilon, Z_1, Z_2) = (q_f, Z_1, Z_2)$$

Example 8.5: Design a Turing machine, which recognizes the set of all even length palindromes over $\{0, 1\}$.

Solution: Let Turing machine $M = (Q, \{0, 1, \#\}, \delta, s)$ recognizes the set of even length palindromes over $\{0, 1\}$. The set of even length palindromes $L = \{ww^R: w \in (0 + 1)^*\}$. M does the following:

Reads one symbol (not #) from the left end of the input and moves right end and matches with the read symbol. This is repeated for the whole input.

Turing machine M is shown in Fig. 8.27.

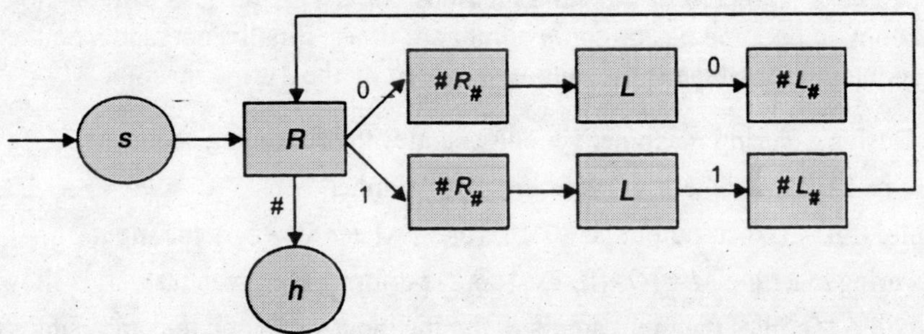

Fig. 8.27: TM for even length palindromes

Example 8.6: Design a Turing machine that performs the multiplication of two positive integers.

Solution: Let Turing machine $M = (Q, \{0,1, \#\}, \delta, s)$ performs multiplication of two positive integers. The multiplication function f over operands m and n positive integers is defined as following:

$$f(m,n)=\begin{cases} mn & \text{for } m,n\geq 1 \\ 0 & \text{(Otherwise)} \end{cases}$$

We have used the following steps in designing of *M*:

1. If $m = 0$ or $n = 0$ then $f(m, n) = 0$, it means, first *M* checks the values of m and n.
2. Considering the tape content $\$0^m10^n\#\#...$, for $m, n > 0$, *M* copies operand *n*, *m* times and writes blank in place of operands *m* and *n* and halts.

Turing machine *M* is shown in Fig. 8.28.

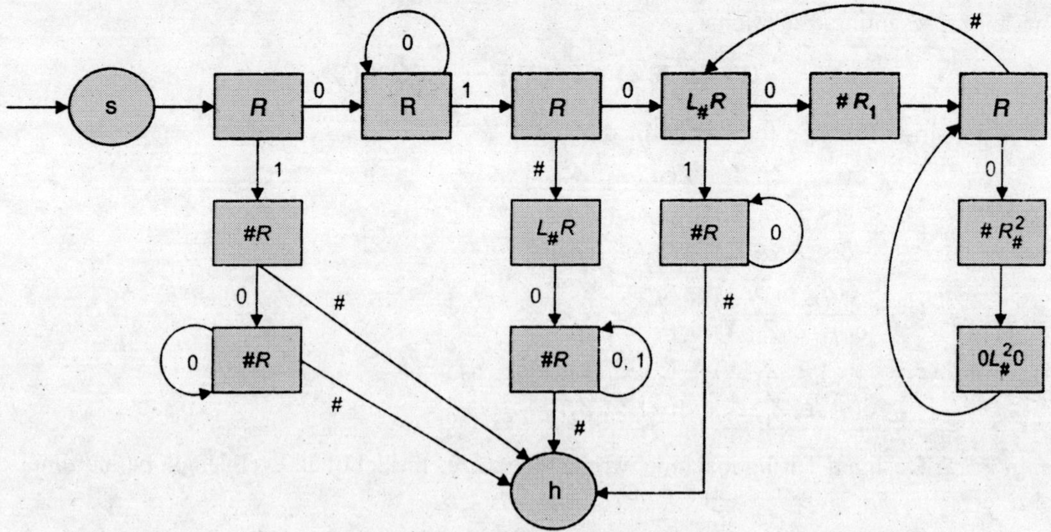

Fig. 8.28: TM for multiplication

Turing machines *M* checks the input numbers and if the numbers are not zero then it continues the multiplication operation. *M* copies the operand *n*, *m*-times, where *m* is operand to be multiplied with *n*. Turing machine reduces one zero of operand *m* when it copies *n*. Next time one zero is further reduces from *m* and operand *n* is appended after the previous copy. This process of reduction of zeros from operand *m* and copy of operand *n* is on for *m* number of times. Finally, operand *n* on the tape is deleted and remaining content of the tape is the output produced by the Turing machine *M*.

Example 8.7: Design a Turing machine, which generates the following sequence:

n, (*n* – 1), (*n* – 2), ..., 1, where $n \geq 1$ is the input number.

For example, if $n = 3$, then output is: $\$0^3 10^2 10\#...$, where $\$0^3\#...$ is the input.

Solution: Let Turing machine $M = (Q, \{0, 1, \#\}, \delta, s)$ performs the given task. *M* is shown in Fig. 8.29.

Turing machine *M* copies the input number after the input stream on the tape using $\#R_\#^2$ and $0L_\#^2 0$. Now, *M* makes the separator (1) between the two stream on the tape and reduces one zero from the rightmost zero of the copied stream using $1R_\# L$ and $\#L^2$. After this, *M* looks for terminating the process. If process has be continued further it moves to the separator mark (1) and moves right one cell to read the copied stream and copies this stream. This process is on until only one zero is to be copied.

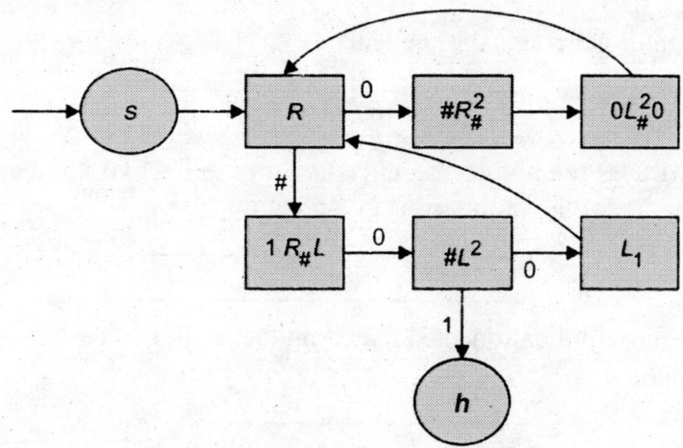

Fig. 8.29: Sequence generator TM

Example 8.8: Design a Turing machine that performs the proper division of two positive integers. For example, $Q = \lfloor M/N \rfloor$, where M is dividend, N is divisor, and Q is quotient.

Solution: Let Turing machine $M = (Q, \{0, 1, \#\}, \delta, s)$ performs the proper division of two positive integers. M is shown in Fig. 8.30. We use following technique.

1. First, M and N are checked whether these are zero or not and initially quotient $Q = 0$,
2. The devisor N is repeatedly subtracted from the dividend M,
3. On a successful subtraction the quotient is incremented by one i.e., $Q = Q + 1$,
4. The devisor N is kept as it is until the last possible subtraction, and
5. When no subtraction if possible further then N is erased and only quotient is remain on the

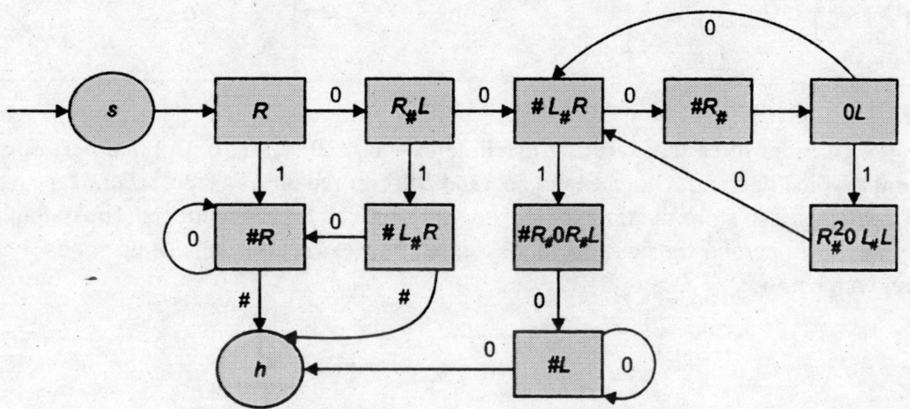

Fig. 8.30: Turing machine for division

Example 8.9: Design Turing machine for, where $n \geq 0$.

Solution: We know that, $n! = n \times (n-1) \times (n-2) \ldots \times 1$ and if $n = 0$ or 1 then $n! = 1$.

We use the Turing machine designed in solved problem (6) and (7). In first phase we use sequence generator and then multiplication repeatedly.

The sequence generator generates the sequence:

$\$0^n10^{n-1}\ldots10\#\ldots$

Now, multiplier TM uses the above sequence and multiplies two numbers from the left side and stores the result at right side of the numbers as given below.

$\$0^{n-2}10^{n-3}\ldots1010^{n(n-1)}\#\ldots$

The above process of multiplication and appending the result is repeated $n-1$ times and finally we get the result as given below:

$\$0^{n(n-1)(n-2)}\ldots1\#\ldots$

Example 8.10: Consider the following table for full adder for two binary numbers and one previous carry:

Operands			Sum (S)	Carry (C_i)
A	B	Previous carry (C_{i-1})		
0	0	0	0	0
0	0	1	1	0
0	1	0	1	0
0	1	1	0	1
1	0	0	1	0
1	0	1	0	1
1	1	0	0	1
1	1	1	1	1

Design a Turing machine for above binary addition.

Solution: We consider three tapes Turing machine $M = (Q, \{0, 1, \#\}, \delta, C_0)$ that performs the given binary addition. First operand A and second operand B are stored on first tape, second tape respectively. The third tape is used to store the output i.e., the sum of given binary numbers. The output carry C_i is considered as third operand for next operands' digits. **For example,** suppose operands A and B have n-digits as given below:

$$A = a_n a_{n-1} a_{n-2} \ldots a_2 a_1$$

and

$$B = b_n b_{n-1} b_{n-2} \ldots b_2 b_1$$

Carry C_{i-1} is generated by addition of digits a_i and b_i for some $i = 1, 2, 3, \ldots, n$ and initially carry is assumed to be 0 ($C_0 = 0$) and addition is carried out bit by bit as:

$$S_i = a_i + b_i + C_{i-1}$$

for some $i = 1, 2, 3, \ldots, n$

Turing machine M is shown in Fig. 8.31. The transitions are represented in the format: (First tape's input, Second tape's input, written symbol on third tape, movement)

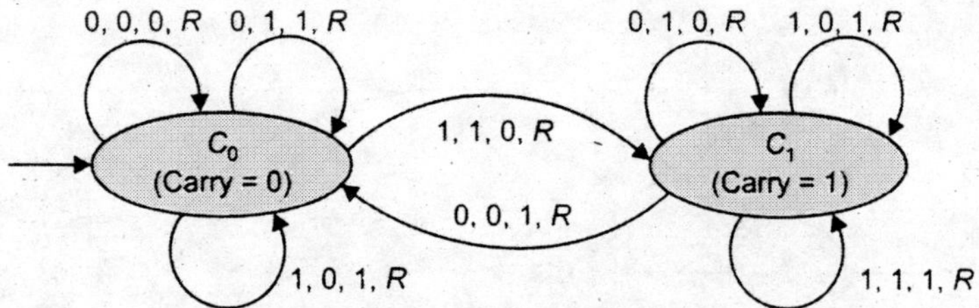

Fig. 8.31: Turing for binary addition

Example 8.11: Design turing machine to compute the function:

$$f(n) = n^2$$

Solution: Let Turing machine $M = (Q, \{0, \#, 1, X\}, \delta, s)$ computes the given function $f(n)$. Turing machine M adds the input multiple times, .i.e., if input is n then M adds n-times the input n to output n^2. Turing machine M is shown in Fig. 8.32. First M copies the input, i.e., the tape content is: #n#n###.... using transitions $s \to q_1 \to q_2 \to q_3 \to q_4$. Then leftmost input n is taken as index and M adds n-times the input.

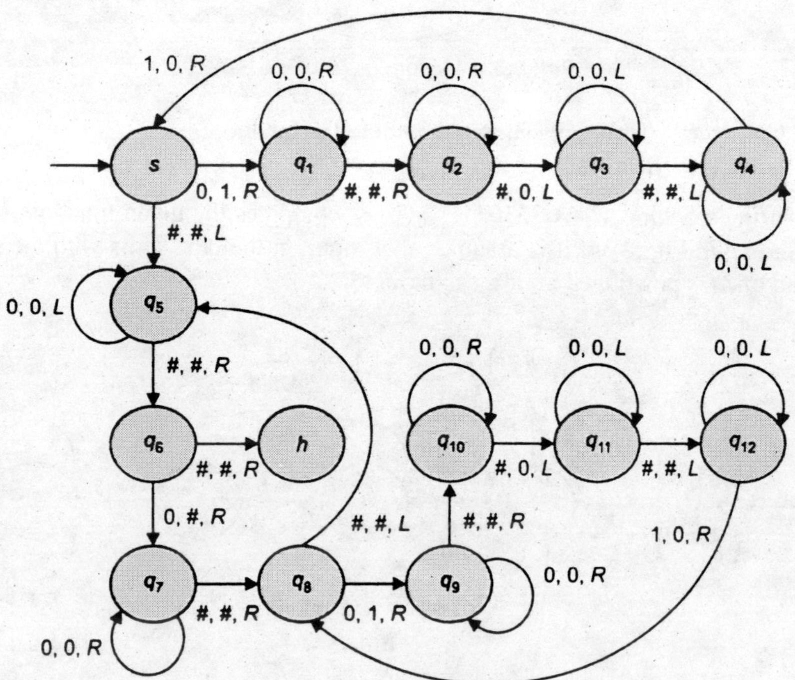

Fig. 8.32: TM for function $f(n) = n^2$

Example 8.12: Design a Turing machine that can accept the following language:

(i) $L = \{a^n b^{2n} \mid n > 0\}$

Solution: Let Turing machine $M = (Q, \{a, b, \#\}, \delta, s\}$ recognizes the language L. M is shown in Fig. 8.33. First Turing machine M reads symbol 'a' and writes as "aa" after b's on the tape ($s \to q_1 \to q_2 \to q_3$) and then matches the b's with a's ($s \to q_4 \to q_5 \to q_6$).

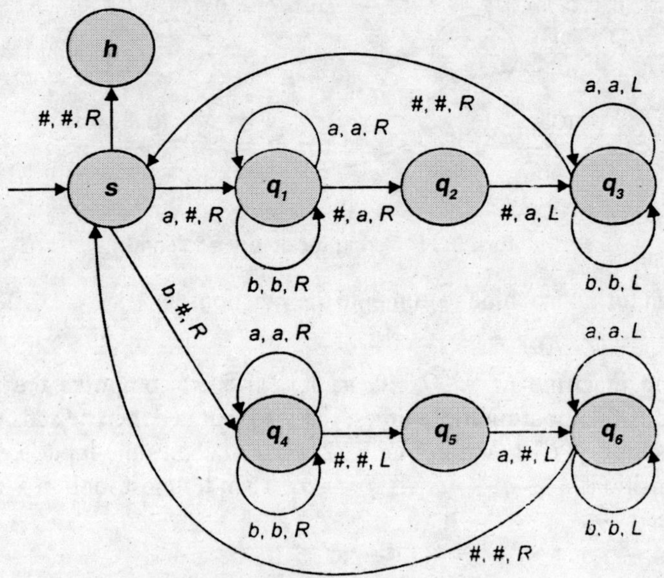

Fig. 8.33: TM for $L = \{a^n b^{2n}: n > 0\}$

Example 8.13: Construct a Turing machine to compute the function:

$f(w) = w^R$, where $w \in \{0, 1\}+$ and w^R is reverse of w

Solution: Let Turing machine $M = (Q, \{0, 1, \#\}, \delta, s\}$ computes the given function $f(w)$. The Turing machine M is shown in Fig. 8.34. It is assumed that input on the tape starts with the symbol '\$' and initially the head of M is positioned after the symbol '\$'.

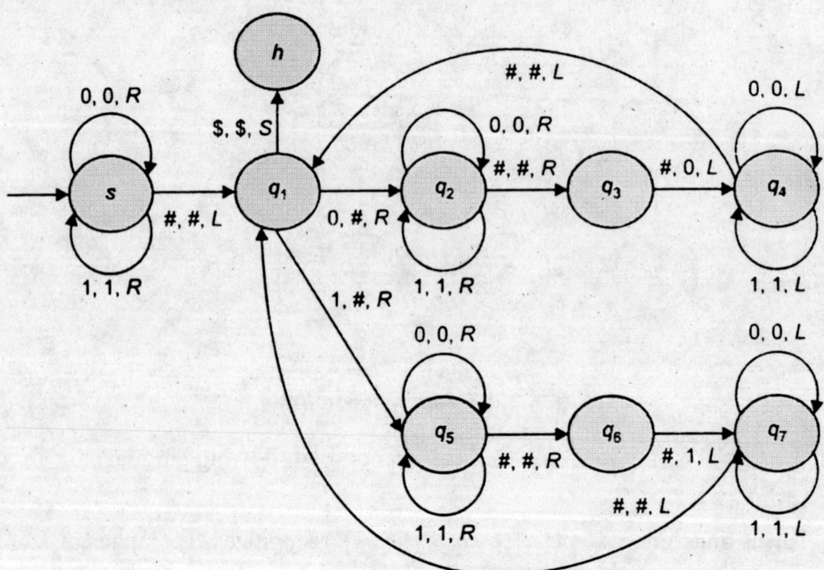

Fig. 8.34: TM for reversing input

Example 8.14: Design a TM that accepts the language $L = \{a^n b^{n+1}: n > 0\}$.

Solution: Let Turing machine $M = (Q, \{a, b, \#\}, \delta, s\}$ recognizes the language L. M is shown in Fig. 8.35.

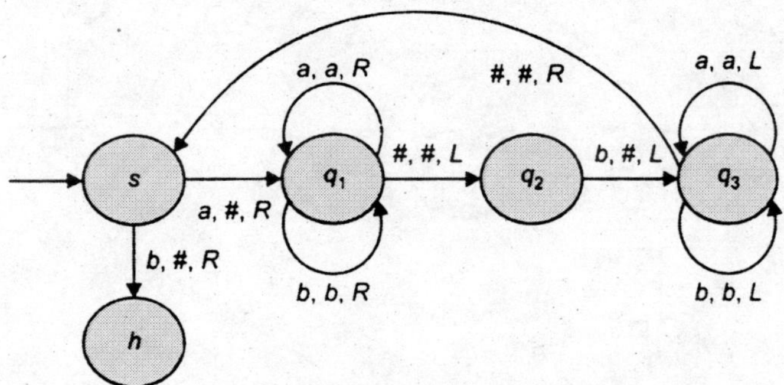

Fig. 8.35: *TM* for $L = \{a^n b^n: n \geq 0\}$

Example 8.15: Design a Turing machine (TM) that accepts the language of odd integers written in binary.

Solution: Let Turing machine $M = (Q, \{0, 1, \#\}, \delta, s\}$ recognizes the language L, which consists of odd integers written in binary. Language L can be expressed as:

$$L = \{1, 11, 101, 111, 1001, \ldots\}$$

One thing is noticeable about L is that each number in L ends with '1'. In other words, we can say that TM accepts all the words over $\{0, 1\}$ ending in '1'. Turing machine M is shown in Fig. 8.36. M reads all the input on the tape from left side and reaches the first blank cell in the tape and moves left $(s \rightarrow q_1)$. Now, if the rightmost input symbol on the tape is '1' then M moves to halt $(q_1 \rightarrow h)$ otherwise hang situation is there (state f).

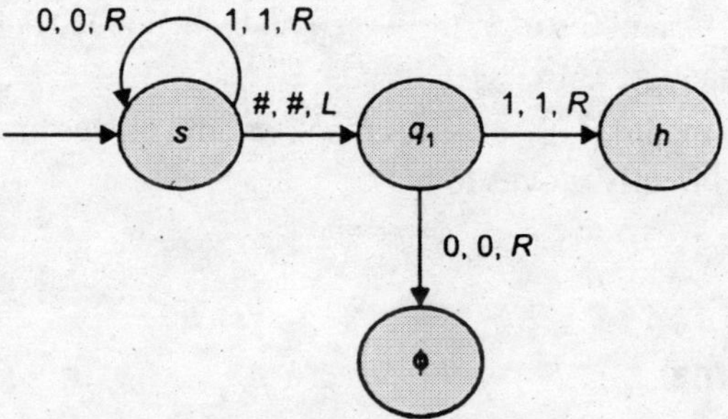

Fig. 8.36: TM for Odd integers written in Binary

Example 8.16: Design a TM that can compute proper subtraction i.e. $m + (-n)$, where m and n are positive integers, $m + (-n)$ is defined as $m - n$ is $m > n$ and 0 if $m <= n$.

Solution: Turing machine $M = (Q, \{a, b, \#\}, \delta, s\}$ for proper subtraction is shown in Fig. 8.37.

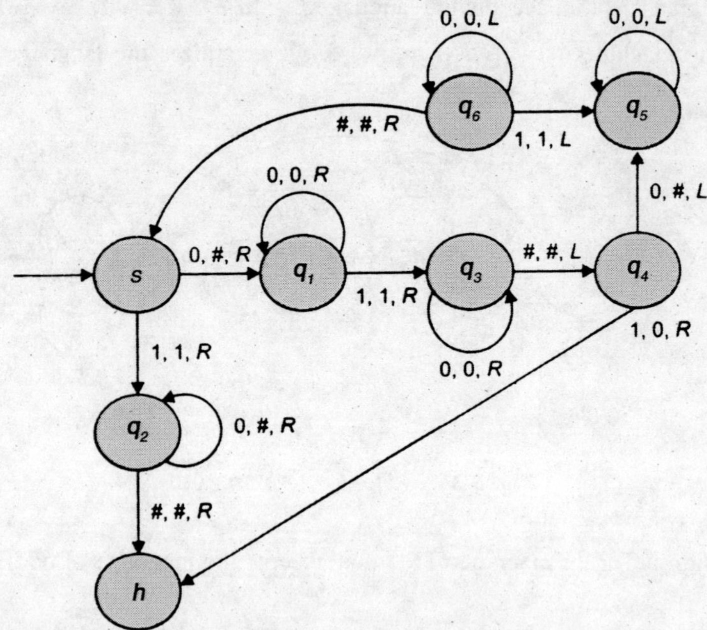

Fig. 8.37: TM for proper subtraction

Turing Machine M does following:

(i) Reads input symbol of m on the tape and makes the cell blank if $m > 0$ ($S \rightarrow q_1$).

(ii) Moves right side on the tape while reading m, the separation mark '1', and all n ($q_1 \rightarrow q_3$) and reaches the first blank cell on the right side and then moves one cell left ($q_3 \rightarrow q_4$).

(iii) Now, if present input symbol is '1' then writes symbol '0' and halts ($q_4 \rightarrow h$)

Else reads one symbol 0 and writes blank (#) ($q_4 \rightarrow q_5$) and moves left while reading 0's of n, separation mark '1', and 0's of m ($q_5 \rightarrow q_6$) and when reaches first blank (#), it moves right one cell ($q_6 \rightarrow s$) and goes to step (i).

(iv) In the state s, if M reads '1', then writes blank (#) and moves to state q_2. In the state q_2, makes 0's of n blank and finally moves to halt.

TEST YOUR SKILLS

Supplementary Problems

8.1 Design a Turing machine that shifts the input string one cell left.

8.2 Design Turing machine for

(a) $\text{Log}_2 n$, where n is a positive integer

(b) 2^n, where n is a positive integer

(c) n^2, where n is a positive integer

(d) Fibonacci sequence

8.3 Design a Turing machine and 2PDA that recognise the languages

$$L = \{a^n b^n a^n b^n : n \geq 1\}.$$

8.4 Design two tapes Turing machine for the language $L = \{ww^R : w \in (a + b)^*\}$.

8.5 Use following inputs and test the operation of Turing machine shown in Fig. 8.28.

(a) $m = 0, n = 3$

(b) $m = 3, n = 0$

(c) $m = 3, n = 2$

8.6 Use the following inputs and test the performance of Turing machine shown in Fig. 8.30.

(a) $M = 0, N = 2$

(b) $M = 5, N = 2$

(c) $M = 2, N = 3$

8.7 Design a Turing machine that works as a comparator. For example is X and Y are two positive integers then

(a) Output is "YES" if and only if $X \geq Y$,

(b) Output is "NO" otherwise.

8.8 Design Turing machine for the following functions for binary system.

(a) 1's complement

(b) 2's complement

(c) Subtraction of two binary numbers

(d) AND operation for two binary numbers having 4 bits

(e) OR operation for two binary numbers having 4 bits

(f) NOT operation for a binary number having 4 bits

(g) X-OR operation for two binary numbers having 4 bits

(h) X-NOR operation for two binary numbers having 4 bits

8.9 Design a Turing machine, which checks the input positive integer and find whether it is prime or not?

8.10 Design a Turing machine, which checks the input positive integer and find whether it is even or odd?

8.11 Design a Turing machine, which performs the following functions:

$F(r) = m - n^*Q(q)$, where $Q(q) = \lfloor m/n \rfloor$ for two positive integers m & n

8.12 Design Turing machines to recognization of following languages:

(a) L_1 = {All strings starting with 0 and ending with 000}

(b) L_2 = {All strings starting with 000 and ending with 1100}

(c) L_3 = {All strings containing at most two 0's}

(d) L_4 = {All strings containing "010" or "101" as substring}

(e) L_5 = {All strings containing "011" and "1010" as substring}

(f) $L_6 = (a + b)^*abb$

(g) $L_7 = 0(11 + 00)^*00$

(h) $L_8 = (aa + bb + ab + ba)^*$

8.13 Design a Turing machine, which outputs residue mod 3 for input binary number.

8.14 Construct a Turing machine which reads input from {0, 1} and outputs EVEN or ODD according to total number of 1's even or odd in the input stream over {0, 1}.

8.15 Design Turing machines as recognizer for following languages:

(a) $\{a^n b^n c^m : m, n \geq 1\}$

(b) $\{a^n b^m c^m : m, n \geq 1\}$

(c) $\{a^n b^m : m + 1 = n\}$

(d) $\{a^m b^n c^m : m, n \geq 1\}$

(e) $\{a^n b^n c^m : m, n \geq 1\} \cup \{a^m b^n c^m : m, n \geq 1\}$

(f) $\{b^n c^m : m \neq 2n\}$

(g) $\{w \in (0 + 1)^* : |w|_0 = 2|w|_1\}$

(h) $\{a^n b^n c^m d^m : m, n \geq 0\}$

(i) $\{a^n c^m b^{2n} : m, n \geq 1\}$

(j) $\{a^{2n} c b^n : m, n \geq 1\}$

8.16 Design a Turing machine that recognizes the language $L = \{ww^R 1^n : w \in (0 + 1)^* \text{ and } n \geq 1\}$.

8.17 Consider a Turing machine M that recognizes the language $L = \{0^n 1^n : n \geq 1\}$. Design Turing machines for following languages:

(a) L^*

(b) L^3

(c) $abLba$

(d) $0^+ L^*$

8.18 Discuss the model of a Turing machine.

8.19 What are the variations of a Turing machine? Are these variation lead to increase in the power of Turing machine?

8.20 How a Turing machine can be used as language recognizer? What kind of languages is recognized by Turing machines?

8.21 What is Church's Thesis? Discuss the importance of this thesis in Computer Science.

8.22 What is universal Turing machine? Compare with a general-purpose digital computer.

8.23 Show that single tape Turing machine and three tapes Turing machine have equivalent string recognization for language $L = \{a^n b^n c^n : n \geq 1\}$.

8.24 Compare the finite automaton, pushdown automaton, and Turing machines.

8.25 Show that 2PDA has equivalent string recognization power what a Turing machine has.

8.26 Show that nPDA for some $n \geq 2$ has equivalent string recognization power what a Turing machine has.

8.27 Show that

2PDA = 3PDA = 4PDA = ...nPDA, where $n \geq 2$

8.28 Write short note on following:

(a) Post Machine

(b) Random Access machine

(c) Universal Turing machine

(d) Read-only Turing machine and Two-way finite automata

8.29 Construct Turing machine to accept the following languages:

(i) $L_1 = \{0^n \subset 0^m \mid n, m > 0, n > m\}$

(ii) $L_2 = \{0^n \subset 0^m \mid n > 0, m = 3n\}$

8.30 Design Turing machine for the languages:

(i) $\{\phi^n 1^n \mid n \geq 1\}$

(ii) $\{0^n \mid n \text{ is a perfect square}\}$

8.31 Design Turing machine for the language:

"A set $\{a^i b^j c^k \mid i \neq j \text{ or } j \neq k\}$ i.e., the set of strings of a's followed by b's followed c's such that there are either a different number of a's and b's or a different number of b's and c's or both."

8.32 Design Turing machine for the following regular expressions:

(a) (01)*(0011)*(01)*

(b) (0 + 1)*00

(c) $(a + b)^*(aaa + bbb)(a + b)^*$

Multiple Choice Questions

8.33 Turing machine is more powerful than finite automaton because

(a) Head movement is confined to one direction

(b) Head movement is in both directions (L, R)

(c) It has capability to remember arbitrary long sequence of input string

(d) All the above

8.34 PDA behave like a Turing machine when it has number of auxiliary memory

(a) 0

(b) Exactly 2

(c) 2 or more

(d) Both (b) and (c)

8.35 The language $L = \{a^n b^n a^n : n \geq 1\}$ is recognized by

(a) TM

(b) 2PDA

(c) Post machine

(d) All the above

8.36 If Turing machine accepts all the words of the language L and rejects or loops for other words which are not in L, then L is said to be

(a) Recursive enumerable

(b) Recursive

(c) CFL

(d) None

8.37 If Turing machine halts for each and every word of a language L and rejects others, then L is said to be

(a) Recursive enumerable (b) Recursive

(c) CFL (d) None

8.38 Universal Turing Machine (UTM) influenced the concept of

(a) Computability

(b) Interpretive implementation of programming language

(c) Program and data is in same memory

(d) All the above

8.39 The number of symbols necessary to simulate a TM with m symbols and n states is

(a) $4m*n + m$ (b) $4m*n + n$

(c) $m + n$ (d) None

8.40 UTM is a

(a) Reprogrammable TM (b) Two-tape TM

(c) Single tape TM (d) None

8.41 The difference between a read-only TM and a two-way FA is

(a) Head movement (b) Finite control

(c) Storage capacity (d) Power

8.42 Off-Line TM is

(a) A special type of multi-tape TM (b) A kind of multi-tracks TM

(c) A kind of multi-head TM (d) None of the above

8.43 Choose the wrong statement

(a) Power of NTM and TM is same

(b) For $n \geq 2$, nPDA has same power as a TM

(c) For $n \geq 3$, nPDA and 2PDA have same power

(d) Power of NTM and TM is not same

8.44 Four pairs are following. In each pair both objects have some common thing. Choose the odd pair.

(a) (TM, 2PDA) (b) (Computer, UTM)

(c) (2PDA, nPDA) (d) (FA, PDA) (Assume $n \geq 3$)

8.45 We think Turing machine as a

(a) Computer system (b) Software

(c) Hardware (d) All the above

8.46 Church's Thesis supports

(a) TM as a general-purpose computer system

(b) TM as an algorithm and an algorithm as a TM

(c) Both (a) and (b)

(d) None

8.47 Random access machine (RAM) and a TM are different in

(a) Power (b) Accessing

(c) Storage (d) Both (b) and (c)

8.48 Choose the correct statement

(a) Recursive set $\subset$ recursive enumerable set

(b) Total function $\subset$ partial function

(c) Recursive sets are analogous to total functions

(d) All the above

8.49 Given $\Sigma = \{a, b\}$, which one of the following sets is not countable? **(GATE 1997)**

(a) The set all strings over Σ.

(b) The set of all language over Σ.

(c) The set of all regular language over Σ.

(d) The set of all languages over Σ accepted by Turing machines.

8.50 Choose the correct statement about the Post machine.

(a) It uses random-accessed memory (b) It uses sequential memory like tape

(c) It uses queue storage (d) None

8.51 Select the correct statement(s):

(a) Turing machine is invented by Allan Turing

(b) Random access machine is invented by Emil Post

(c) Post machine is invented by Charles Babbage

(d) None

8.52 3TM stands for

(a) Turing machine with three tapes

(b) Turing machine with three tracks

(c) Turing machine with three read/write heads

(d) Turing machine with three tapes and three tracks

Answers

8.33 (c)	8.34 (c)	8.35 (d)	8.36 (a)	8.37 (b)
8.38 (d)	8.39 (a)	8.40 (a)	8.41 (c)	8.42 (a)
8.43 (d)	8.44 (d)	8.45 (b)	8.46 (c)	8.47 (d)
8.48 (d)	8.49 (b)	8.50 (c)	8.51 (a)	8.52 (b)

CHAPTER 9

Computability and Recognizability of Turing Machine

We have discussed in the previous chapter that The Church–Turing Thesis was an idea put forward in 1936 by Alan Turing and Alonzo Church for computability of functions. In their thesis, they defined what is effective calculation (or computation). The idea of this Thesis is:

> **"If a function is effectively calculable then it is Turing-computable. Conversely, if a function is not Turing–computable, then it is not effectively calculable."**

An **effectively computable** function is one in which there is a *finite number of steps to find solution*, if there is no errors in the computation, it always has right output in a finite number of steps and it does not require any leaps of intuition or intelligence i.e., it is a mechanical process to derive the result. This was a great and very interesting idea because it suggests that the Turing machine is the appropriate model needed to describe computable problems. In other way, if a problem has effective solution then there is a Turing machine to solve the problem. The meaning of effective solution means the algorithm; that is, if solution is described as an algorithm then there is a Turing machine, which implements this algorithm.

Around the same time when the Church–Turing Thesis was being explored, there were many other models of computation that were studied as well by other mathematicians. These include Church's lambda calculus, Markov algorithms, Post computability, partially recursive functions, etc. Interestingly, these all-dissimilar systems describe the exact same class of computable functions that the Church-Turing Thesis describes. It turns out that Turing machines could model all of the functions that were included in these other models.

In brief, the Church–Turing Thesis says that a Turing machine can model all effectively computable functions and it has held up under close scrutiny by mathematicians. This thesis is an important method in designing of automatic machines that can be used to model computable problems. Since, it is not a mathematical result, so there is no way to prove this beyond the shadow of a doubt, but there is a growing body of evidence that it is true. The conclusion of this thesis is that if some problem has effective solution (that is algorithm) then there is an automatic machine known as Turing machine to solve the problem. The important thing in this thesis is the focus on effective solution; if effective solution is there then automatic machine is there.

9.1 EFFECTIVE CALCULATION (OR COMPUTATION)

In introduction part, we were discussing about the *effectively computable (or calculable) functions*. Effective calculation means calculation terminates in finite number of steps with some desired output (answer). Effective calculations are fully described in terms of algorithms. Allan Turing in his Thesis described the effective calculation and he claimed the following notion:

"A number-theoretic function *f* is effectively calculable if and only if *f* is Turing-computable"

The above notion of Allan Turing can be broken into following two parts:

1. If function *f* is effectively calculable, then *f* is Turing-computable. (Church-Turing Thesis)
2. If function *f* is Turing-computable, then *f* is effectively calculable.

The first part is not intuitively obvious but part two is obvious. All number based functions can be partitioned into part one and part two situations, either Turing-computable or not Turing-computable. All other known reasonable computation models, however there may be difference in concept or process, are equivalent computable to Turing machine computability. So, with regard to the Church-Turing Thesis, although it has not been proven, it remains true in the philosophical sense because no one has disapproved it yet. In other words, we say that no one is able to come up with another type of computation model that produces a function that cannot be classified as Turing-computable. Therefore, the class of Turing-computable functions is identical to the class of effectively calculable functions. The Church-Turing thesis states the following:

"If function *f* is effectively calculable, then *f* is Turing-computable. Equivalently, if a function *f* is not Turing-computable, then *f* is not effectively calculable."

9.2 TURING MACHINE RECOGNIZABLE LANGUAGES AND COMPUTABLE FUNCTIONS

We have seen in the previous chapter that the class of languages recognized by Turing machines is known as **recursively enumerable** (r.e.) and the class of functions computed is known as **partial recursive function.** The meaning of enumerable is *listing in certain steps*. There should not be infinite number of steps involved in listing a string of a Turing machine recognizable language. In other words, a Turing machines should not fall into infinite loop or hang up while listing a string. **For example,** consider the Turing machine shown in Fig. 9.1.

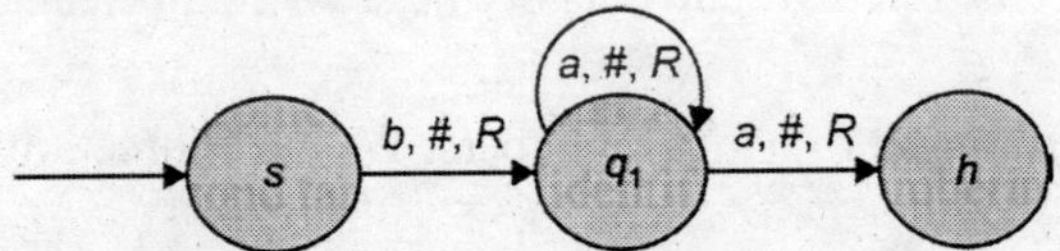

Fig. 9.1: Turing machine for $L = ba^*a$

Now, consider the input string $w = ba$, we have two conditions:

1. Processing halts in halting state h,
2. Processing halts in non-halting state q_1.

It means, for other strings also that belong to the language $L = ba^*a$, Turing machine may fall into loop in state q_1 and those would be understood as rejected. A string $w \in L$ is accepted if processing terminates in halting state h following the certain steps. In other words, L is enumerable by Turing machine if for all $w \in L$, Turing machine eventually halts in halting state.

In the above example, the rejection of a string that does not belong to recursively enumerable language is not definitive. So, we define a subclass of recursively enumerable class known as **recursive set**. We define language L as a **recursive set** if and only if, for this set there is some Turing machine that halts for all $w \in L$ and rejects $x \notin L$.

Let us define recursive languages. "A language is recursive if it is recursively enumerable and its complement is also recursive. An equivalent definition is that there is a Turing machine which halts in halting state only on members of the language and always halts." We will discuss the above in this chapter. First let us see what partial and total recursive functions are.

9.2.1 Recursive Functions Theory

Recursive function theory is one way to make formal and precise the intuitive, informal, and imprecise notion of an effective method. It identifies the class of functions which are Turing computable. Recursive function theory begins with some very elementary functions that are intuitively effective. These elementary functions are known as initial functions. Then it provides a few methods for building more complicated functions from simpler functions. The initial functions and the building operations are very few in number, and so simple in nature that one can simply inspect these on paper.

In this section, we will discuss about the partial and total functions. As we know that partial recursive functions are Turing machine computable and total recursive functions are subclass of partial function and for which Turing machine halts always and computation is made on all the input parameters. We define another subclass of partial recursive functions known as **primitive recursive** function that can be defined using **initial functions**. Initial functions are defined over set of natural numbers $N = \{0,1, 2, \ldots\}$ and some alphabet of symbols. So, first we discuss about the initial functions and then partial and total recursive functions.

9.2.1.1 Initial functions for natural numbers

The elementary functions are total, not partial because the total functions fit the intuitive sense of effective method. A partial function is not defined for some arguments; it is defined partially on its input arguments and hence computes no result for some arguments. It is part of the definition of an effective method that it will always produce the correct answer. The elementary functions are all functions of the natural numbers. Hence, they may take zero as input, but not a negative number, and not any rational or irrational fraction.

Let $N = \{0, 1, 2, \ldots\}$ is the set of natural numbers. We have three initial functions over N defined following:

1. **Zero function:** It is denoted by Z and defined as:

   $$Z(n) = 0 \text{ for every } n \in N,$$

2. **Successor function:** It is denoted by S and defined as:

   $$S(n) = n + 1 \text{ for every } n \in N, \text{ and}$$

3. **Projection function:** It is denoted by P_i^n and defined as:

   $P_i^n(a_1, a_2, \ldots, a_n) = a_i$, where $a_i \in N$ for i = 1, 2, ..., n and $i \leq n$.

   We think P_i^n as a linear array of ***n*** natural numbers and ***i*** is the index used to access ***i*^th^** element from set of *n* elements.

For examples,

1. $Z(2) = 0$, where $2 \in N$
2. $S(2) = 2 + 1 = 3$, where $2, 3 \in N$
3. $Z(0) = 0$, where $0 \in N$
4. $P_2^5(2, 4, 6, 8, 10) = 4$, where $|P_2^5| = 5$, and $2, 4, 6, 8, 10, 5 \in N$
5. $P_1^1(2) = 2$, where $1, 2 \in N$, in general $P_1^1(n) = n$ for every $n \in N$
6. $S(P_1^3(f(4, 3), 10, Z(20)))$, where $f(m, n) = m \times n$

   $= S(P_1^3(f(4, 3), 10, 0)) = S(P_1^3(12, 10, 0))$

   $= S(12) = 12 + 1 = 13$

The zero function returns zero regardless of its argument. It is the simplest intuitively computable function. The successor function returns the successor of its argument. Since successorship is a more primitive notion than addition. We will see how addition function is built using the initial functions. We have used the set of natural numbers *N*, so calculating the successor of a number is the next number in the set when the numbers of *N* are kept in ascending order. The projection function may take one or more arguments but it returns the projected argument as the result. So, all the above functions are very simple and considered as "ingredient" for other complex functions, which we will see later on. We will also see how the initial functions are Turing computable and how complex functions are Turing computable based on the initial functions.

9.2.1.2 *Initial functions for symbols (alphabet)*

Let Σ is some alphabet. Two initial functions are defined over Σ that are following:

1. **Null function:** It is abbreviated as *NUL* and defined as:

   $$NUL(x) = \varepsilon \text{ for all } x \in \Sigma^*, \text{ and}$$

2. **Concatenation function:** It is abbreviated as *CONCATE* and defined as:

   $$CONCATE\ a(x) = ax \text{ for } a, x \in \Sigma^* \text{ and } |x| \geq 0.$$

For examples, consider alphabet $\Sigma = \{a, b, c, \ldots, z\}$

1. $NUL(a) = \varepsilon$
2. *NUL*(automata) = ε
3. *CONCATE* A(utomata) = Automata
4. *CONCATE A*(*CONCATE U*(*CONCATE* T(*CONCATE* O(ε))))

   = *CONCATE* A(*CONCATE U*(*CONCATE* T(O)))

= *CONCATE* A(*CONCATE* U(TO)) = *CONCATE* A(UTO)

= AUTO

5. *CONCATE* a(*CONCATE* b(*NUL*(abc))) = *CONCATE* a(*CONCATE* $b(\varepsilon)$)

= *CONCATE* $a(b) = ab$

9.2.1.3 Composition of functions

We can combine two or more functions to define one more complex function by three methods: composition, primitive recursion and minimization. In composition method, the outputs of combined functions become the arguments (input) of the defined function. Let f be a function of n arguments and $f_1, f_2, \ldots, f_n$ are n functions, each having of k arguments. We define $f_1, f_2, \ldots, f_n$ as arguments of function f as following:

$$f(f_1(x_1, x_2, \ldots, x_k), f_2(a_1, a_2, \ldots, a_k), \ldots, f_n(y_1, y_2, \ldots, y_k))$$

For example, let $f(x, y) = x + y, f_1(x, y) = x^2 + y^2, f_2(x, y) = 2xy$, then

$$f(f_1(x, y), f_2(x, y)) = f(x^2 + y^2, 2xy)$$
$$= x^2 + y^2 + 2xy$$

9.2.1.4 Recursion

Recursion is well known word in Computer Science. We use this word to define recursive functions. Here we use this word to define the computable functions of Turing machines.

"A function which calls itself directly or indirectly and terminates after finite number of steps is known as recursive function."

One thing is noticeable here that a recursive function should be terminated after finite number of steps because calling a function infinite number of times leads to crash or hang the computing system. So, a recursive function will be good if it has terminating point and its call to itself should be nearer to its terminating point. The terminating point is also known as **base point.**

Let f is a function of $n + 1$ arguments, g is function of n arguments, and h is a function of m arguments where $m \leq n + 2$. We define the function f recursively using the functions g and h as following:

If $f(a_1, a_2, \ldots, a_n, 0) = g(b_1, b_2, \ldots, b_n)$,
then $f(a_1, a_2, \ldots, a_n, a_{n+1} + 1) = h(a_1, a_2, \ldots, a_n, a_{n+1}, f(a_1, a_2, \ldots, a_n, a_{n+1}))$,
where g **and** h **are defined functions.**

The function f is evaluated for all a_{n+1} and fixed $a_1, a_2, \ldots, a_n$. The function g is used as terminating point and h is used to call f indirectly. We can also define the function f recursive that calls itself directly.

Example 1: Define addition of two positive integers (m and n) recursively.

Solution: Let f is the addition function of two positive integers, so

$$f(m, n) = m + n$$

We define f to increment the argument m, n-times, one at a time.

So, $f(m, 0) = m$ (Terminating point)

$f(m, n+1) = f(m, n) + 1$ (For direct call)

Consider $f(5, 2)$, where $m = 5$, $n = 2$, so

$$f(5, 2) = f(5, 1+1) = f(5, 0+1) + 1 = 5 + 1 + 1 = 7$$

Example 2: Define recursively.

Solution: Let $f(n) = = n*(n-1)*(n-2)...*1$ We know that $0! = 1! = 1$,

So, $f(0) = 1$ (Terminating point)

$h(x, y) = x*y$,

$f(n+1) = h(n+1, f(n))$ (Indirect call)

Example 3: Define concatenation of two strings w_1 and w_2 over $\{a, b\}$ recursively.

Solution: Let f is the concatenation function of two strings over $\{a, b\}$,

So, $f(w_1, w_2) = w_1 w_2$

We know that concatenation of null string with any string is the same string,

So, $f(w_1, \varepsilon) = w_1$, (Terminating point)

$f(w_1, a_1 a_2 ... a_n) = f(w_1 a_1, a_2 a_3 ... a_n)$ (Direct call)

9.2.1.5 Primitive recursive function

A function is primitive recursive if

1. It is an initial function, or
2. It is obtained from recursion or composition of initial functions.

Most popular total functions are primitive recursive functions; however some total functions are not. **For example,** the **Ackermann function** is a total function but not primitive recursive. **For example,**

Example 1: Show that addition function of two positive integers is primitive recursive.

Proof: In the above example we have defined the addition function f for arguments m and n as $f(m, 0) = m, f(m, n+1) = f(m, n) + 1$

We can define function f using the initial functions as following:

$$f(m, 0) = m \equiv P_1^1(m),$$

and

$$f(m, n+1) = f(m, n) + 1 \equiv S(f(m, n))$$

For example consider $f(5, 2)$,

$$f(5, 2) = S(f(5, 1) = f(5, 1) + 1 = S(f(5, 0)) + 1$$
$$= f(5, 0) + 1 + 1$$
$$= 5 + 1 + 1 = 7$$

Hence, f is a primitive recursive function.

Example 2: Show that the concatenation of two strings over $\{a, b\}$ is primitive recursive.

Proof: We have defined the concatenation as:

$$f(\varepsilon, w_2) = w_2,$$

$$f(a_1a_2...a_n, w_2) = a_1f(a_2a_3...a_n, w_2), \text{ where } w_1, w_2 \in \Sigma^*.$$

We define function f using the initial functions as following:

$f(\varepsilon, w_1) \equiv CONCATE\ e(w_1) = w_1$, and

$f(a_1a_2...a_n, w_2) \equiv CONCATE\ a_1(f(a_2a_3...a_n, w_2))$

For example consider $f(ab, cd)$,

$$f(ab, cd) = CONCATE\ a(f(b, cd))$$
$$= af(b, cd) = aCONCATE\ b(f(\varepsilon, cd))$$
$$= abf(\varepsilon, cd) = abcd$$

(Since, $f(\varepsilon, w) = w$)

Hence, concatenation is primitive recursive function.

Theorem 9.1: Every primitive recursive function is Turing machine computable.

Proof: We discuss a constructive proof here to prove the theorem. We construct Turing machine for all the initial functions. As we know that primitive functions are defined using initial functions applying composition and recursion sometime.

1. **Turing machine for zero function $Z(n) = 0$, for $n \in N$:** Turing machine for $Z(n)$ is shown in Fig. 9.2.

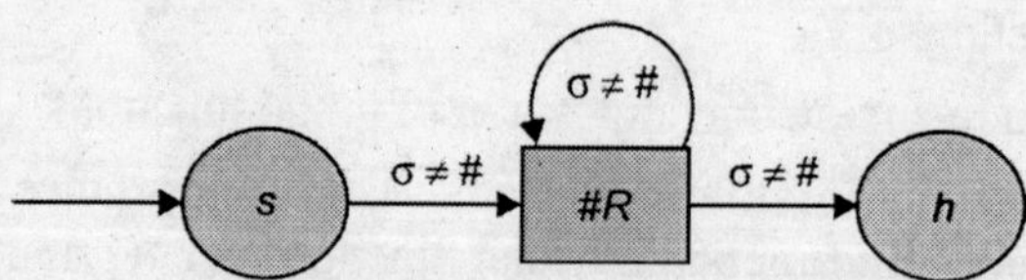

Fig. 9.2: TM for zero function

The above Turing machine erases the input number n by making the cells blank.

2. **Turing machine for successor function $S(n) = n + 1$, for $n \in N$:** Turing machine for $S(n)$ is shown in Fig. 9.3.

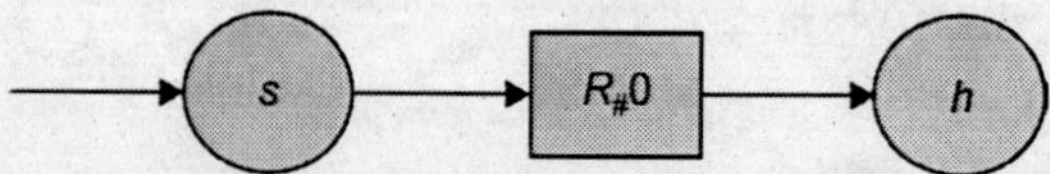

Fig. 9.3: Turing machine for successor function

The above Turing machine writes one zero after the input number to increment the input number by one.

3. **Turing machine for projection function:** Let the projection function, $P_i^n(a_1, a_2, ..., a_n) = a_i$, for $a_1, a_2, ..., a_n \in N$

The Turing machine for is P_i^n shown in Fig. 9.4. Let input and output are shown as following on the tape: **Input:** $\$0^{i_1}10^{i_2}1...10^{i_n}\#...$, where $i_1, i_2, ..., i_n$ are integers numbers

Output: $\$\#\#...0^{i_i}\#\#...$ (i_i is the output)

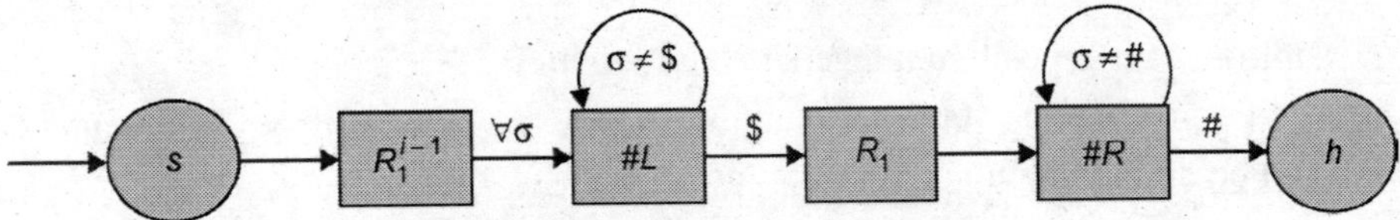

Fig. 9.4: TM for projection function

(**Note:** We assume that input is separated by 1 i.e. $\$0^{i_1}10^{i_2}1...10^{i_n}1\#\#...$)

For composition of initial functions, we design a Turing machine combining simple Turing machines designed for initial functions. For recursion, we design a Turing machine using multiple calls to a simple Turing machine designed for initial function with some fixed termination point. So, we combine our both the approaches (designing of Turing machine for composition and recursion) into one to design a Turing machine for composition and recursion together. So, the statement of the theorem is true.

9.2.1.6 Minimization

Let us take a function G(x). We want to find the *least* value of x which made $f(x) = 0$. There is an obviously effective method for doing so. We know that x is a natural number. So we set $x = 0$, and then compute $f(x)$; if we get 0 we stop, having found the least x which makes $f(x) = 0$; but if not, we try the next natural number 1 and consequently we try 0,1,2,3... until we reach the first value which makes $f(x) = 0$. When we know that *there is* such a value, then we know that this method will terminate in a finite time with the correct answer. If we say that $f(x)$ is a function that computes the least x such that $G(x) = 0$, then we know that f(x) is computable. We will say that G is produced from f by minimization.

Let us think about the value of x which makes $G(x)$ zero. It is obvious that we don't always know that there is any x which makes $G(x) = 0$. Hence, the function f(x) for testing 0,1,2,3... to find $G(x) = 0$ may never terminate. If we run the test anyway, that is called *unbounded minimization.* Obviously, when $f(x)$ is produced by unbounded minimization, it is not effectively computable. If we don't know whether there is any x which makes $G(x) = 0$, then there is still a way to make function $f(x)$ effectively computable. We can start testing 0, 1, 2, 3... and set an upper bound to our search. We search until we hit the upper bound and then stop. If we find a value before stopping which makes $G(x) = 0$, then $f(x)$ returns that value; if not, then f(x) returns 0. This is called *bounded minimization.*

Now, let us define the function G with one or more arguments. Let g is a function of n ($n \geq 1$) arguments then minimization of g with respect to the value of y is defined as following:

$$G_Y(g(x, y)) = \begin{cases} y, \text{ the least } y \text{ such that } G(x, y) = 0 \\ 0 \text{ otherwise} \end{cases}$$

For example, consider $g(x, y) = x + y - 2$,

So, putting $g(x, y) = 0$, we get $y = 2 - x$ if $x \leq 2$ is the result of minimization.

So, $\quad Gy(g(x, y) = 2 - x \quad \text{for } x \leq 2$

$\qquad\qquad = 0 \qquad \text{for } x = 2$

It means, the least value of y that is zero makes the function g minimum.

9.2.1.7 Total recursive function

Total functions are a subclass of partial functions. A function is called total function if it is defined for its all arguments. Let $f(a_1, a_2, ..., a_n)$ is a function and defined on function $g(b_1, b_2, ..., b_m)$, then f is total function if every element of f is assigned to some unique element of function g.

Example 1: Addition of two positive integers is total function.

Proof: Let $f(m, n) = m + n$ is the addition function *from* $N \times N$ *to* N of two positive integers m and n. This function can be defined recursively as:

$f(m, 0) = 1, f(m, n + 1) = f(m, n) + 1.$

Since, f is defined for all values of $m, n \in N$. So, f is total function.

Example 2: Multiplication of two positive integers is total function.

Proof: Let $g(m, n)$ is multiplication function *from* $N \times N$ *to* N of two positive integers m and n and can be defined recursively as: $g(m, 0) = 0$, $g(m, n + 1) = m + g(m, n)$. Since, g is defined for all $m, n \in N$, so g is total recursive function.

Example 3: Subtraction of two positive integers is not total function.

Proof: Let $h(m, n)$ is the subtraction function *from* $N \times N$ *to* N of two positive integers m and n and defined recursively as: $h(m, 0) = m$, $h(m, n + 1) = h(m, n) - 1$. Since, h is not defined for $m < n$, when it occurs then result is negative which is not in N. So, h is not total function.

A total function is recursive or primitive recursive if

(a) It is an initial function over N, or

(b) It is obtained by applying composition or recursion finite number of times to the initial function over N.

Example 4: How that multiplication of two positive integers is total recursive function (or primitive recursive function).

Proof: As we have discussed above that multiplication of two positive integers is total recursive function from $N \times N$ to N of two positive integers m and n and can be defined recursively as: $g(m, 0) = 0$, $g(m, n + 1) = m + g(m, n)$

Now, we define the function g by using initial functions as following:

$$g(m, 0) = 0 \equiv Z(m)$$

and

$$g(m, n + 1) = m + g(m, n) \equiv P_1^2(m, n) + P_1^1(g(m\ n))$$

Now, consider $g(2, 3)$ and see the evaluation given following:

$$\begin{aligned} g(2, 3) &= g(2, 2 + 1) \\ &= P_1^2(2, 2) + P_1^1(g(2, 2)) = 2 + g(2, 1 + 1) \\ &= 2 + P_1^2(2, 1) + P_1^1(g(2, 1)) = 2 + 2 + g(2, 0 + 1) \\ &= 2 + 2 + P_1^2(2, 0) + (g(2, 0)) = 2 + 2 + 2 + g(2, 0) \\ &= 2 + 2 + 2 + Z(2) = 2 + 2 + 2 + 0 = 6 \end{aligned}$$

Hence, function g is primitive recursive function.

Theorem 9.2: Not all total recursive functions are primitive recursive function.

Proof: Initially, we assume that all total recursive functions are primitive recursive function. We see a counter example (Ackerman's Function) to disprove our assumption.

Ackerman's Function: Let Ack is the Ackerman's function given below:

$$\text{Ack}(0, y) = y + 1$$
$$\text{Ack}(x + 1, 0) = \text{Ack}(x, 1)$$
$$\text{Ack}(x + 1, y + 1) = \text{Ack}(x, \text{Ack}(x + 1, y))$$

Consider Ack(1, 1):

$$\text{Ack}(1, 1) = \text{Ack}(0 + 1, 0 + 1)$$
$$= \text{Ack}(0, \text{Ack}(0 + 1, 0)) \quad (\text{Using Ack}(x + 1, y + 1) = \text{Ack}(x, \text{Ack}(x + 1, y)))$$
$$= \text{Ack}(0, \text{Ack}(0, 1)) \quad (\text{Using Ack}(x + 1, 0) = \text{Ack}(x, 1))$$

and $\text{Ack}(x + 1, 0) = \text{Ack}(x, 1))$

$$= \text{Ack}(0, 2) \quad (\text{Using Ack}(0, y) = y + 1)$$
$$= 3$$

One thing is clear about the Ackerman's function that taking the larger arguments the function Ack requires several recursive calls to reach the result. So, the growth rate is very high with larger arguments. It is clear that Ackerman's function is total and not good recursive function but due to the very higher growth rate with larger arguments, it is not primitive.

Theorem 9.3: All primitive recursive functions are total function but not all primitive recursive functions are total function.

(Using Theorem 9.1 and Theorem 9.2 we can prove it.)

9.2.1.8 Partial recursive function

A function is called partial function if it is defined for some of its arguments. Let $f(a_1, a_2, \ldots, a_n)$ is a function and defined on function $g(b_1, b_2, \ldots, b_m)$, then f is partial function if some elements of f is assigned to almost one element of function g.

A partial function is recursive if

1. It is an initial function over N, or
2. It is obtained by applying recursion or composition or minimization on initial functions over N.

For example, subtraction of two positive integers is partial recursive function. For proof we see the example (3) in the above section.

Theorem 9.4: The composition of partial (total) functions yields a partial (total) function.

Theorem 9.5: The minimization of a total recursive function is a partial recursive function.

9.2.2 Recursively Enumerable (R.E.) and Recursive Languages

When a Turing machine executes an input there are four possible outcomes of execution. The Turing machine

1. Halts and accepts the input,
2. Halts and rejects the input,
3. Never halts (fall into loop), or
4. Crash

We also know that the language recognized by Turing machine is known as recursively enumerable (r.e.) and the set of recursive languages is subset of recursively enumerable set. The set of recursively enumerable (r.e.) languages are precisely those languages that can be listed (enumerated) by a Turing machine. Basically, if a Turing machine can generate all the strings in a language, another Turing machine can accept all the strings. But, we don't know about rejection of strings that are not in the given language. (Strings that are not in the language may be rejected or may cause the Turing machine to go into an infinite loop.)

A language is **recursive** if there exists a Turing machine that accepts every string of the language and rejects every string that is not in the language.

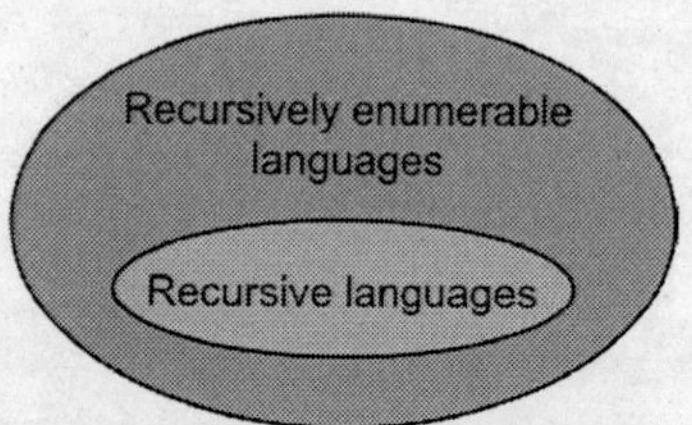

Fig. 9.5: Relation between recursive enumerable and recursive languages

Theorem 9.6: If a language L is recursive then it is recursively enumerable language.

Proof: A language is recursively enumerable if there exists a Turing machine that accepts every string of the language and a language is recursive is there is a Turing machine that accepts every string of the language and does not accept strings that are not in the language. So, every recursive language is also recursively enumerable. Hence, statement of the theorem is true.

9.2.2.1 Enumerating a language

We have used so far the word "enumerate" many times. Now, let us see what it means. To *enumerate* a language is to place the elements of the language in some sequence like 1, 2, 3, ..., n. In other words, there should be one-to-one correspondence with strings of the language and the natural numbers.

We have seen that the set of all possible strings over an alphabet is infinite. A language is a set of strings that may be finite or infinite over some alphabet. If L is a language over alphabet Σ then language L is a subset of Σ^*, that is, $L \subseteq \Sigma^*$. Let us see how strings in a language are enumerated. If a language is recursive then there exists a Turing machine that always halts for strings in the language. The strings of set Σ^* (all strings over Σ) are generated in a shortest-length-first order (to guarantee that every finite string will be generated). We test the string with a Turing machine and if the Turing machine accepts the string then a natural number from the set $N = \{0, 1, 2, \ldots\}$ is assigned to string. This process will ensure that all strings over some alphabet are in length increasing order.

Turing machine can also enumerate the recursively enumerable languages. A Turing machine will halt and accept any string that belongs to the enumerable language. But problem is how to avoid getting hung up on strings that cause the Turing machine to go into an infinite loop or crash sometimes. Turing machine can over come of this problem by switching among the strings of the enumerable language. Suppose Turing machine M_1 enumerates the string w_1, and then there is another Turing machine M_2 applies the first pass to the string w_1. Now, M_1 enumerates next string $\mathbf{w}_2$ and M_2 applies the second pass to w_1 and first pass to $\mathbf{w}_2$ and this process is carried out for other strings also. It means, a string w_i is enumerated by Turing machine M_1 and accepted by Turing machine M_2. So, using Turing machines M_1 and M_2, strings of a recursive enumerable language are precisely listed and accepted. When a string is accepted then it is collected in a set this set finally named as recursive enumerable set. We design a third Turing machine M_3 that is the combination of first and second Turing machines (M_1 and M_2) and this machine M_3 enumerates the strings of a recursively enumerable language. Hence, all recursively enumerable languages are Turing machine enumerable and hence recursive languages are also Turing enumerable (recursive languages are subset of recursive enumerable languages).

Theorem 9.7: All recursive enumerable languages are Turing machine enumerable.
(For proof see the above discussion)

Theorem 9.8: Turing machines are countable over some alphabet.

Proof: Let Σ is an alphabet. Then set of strings Σ^* has infinite number of strings of length zero, one, two, and so on.

Σ^* = (String of length zero, Strings of length one, Strings of length two, ...}

Let there is a Turing machine for each string in the set Σ^* and a Turing machine can be represented in binary notation. For example, the quintuple (q_5, a_2, a_3, R, q_7), where q_5 is the present state, a_2 is the present symbol, a_3 is the written symbol, R is the right movement, and q_7 is the next state can be represented in binary as:

$$11111011011101101111111$$

Each member of the set (q_5, a_2, a_3, R, q_7) is separated by single zero. For example, 11111 represents q_5, 11 represents a_2, 111 represents a_3, 11 represents R, and 1111111 represents q_7. The sequence of the member in the set is fixed and it is valid if it is predefined.

The set of quintuples $\{(q_5, a_2, a_3, R, q_7), (q_2, a_2, a_2, R, q_2)\}$ can be represented as:

$$111110110111011011111110110110110110 11$$

We have seen that the sequence of the member of the set (q_5, a_2, a_3, R, q_7) is fixed. So, not every binary number represents a Turing machine. **For example**, a Turing machine can move in two directions (L and R) only, so a sequence ...01110..., for direction (11 for R and 1 for L) would not be meaningful and it will be treated as non-existence of Turing machine.

Now, suppose we count in binary. We check each number to see whether it represents a valid Turing machine or not. We assign 1 to the first valid Turing machine, 2 to the second such Turing machine, 3 to third Turing machine, and so on. Since any Turing machine can be represented in binary. So, it is clear that this establishes a one-to-one correspondence between Turing machines and the natural numbers. Hence, Turing machines are enumerable over some alphabet. In other words, Turing machines are countable over certain alphabet.

Theorem 9.9: The power set of an infinite set is not countable.
(For proof, see the Appendix A)

Theorem 9.10: Not all languages are recursively enumerable.

Proof: As we have discussed that a Turing machine is powerful enough to recognize any language. So, considering the above statement the Theorem becomes confusing. But, there are some languages that are not recursively enumerable, because no Turing machine can enumerate these languages.

Let Σ is some alphabet and a language L is over Σ. Since any language over Σ is a subset of set Σ*. We have proved that Turing machines are countable (enumerable) and recursively enumerable languages are those whose strings are accepted by some Turing machine in previous theorems. So, the set of recursively enumerable languages is also enumerable.

Consider the set of Σ* which has infinite strings. We know that the power set of an infinite set is not countable (see the Theorem 9.9). Now, consider the power set of Σ* denoted by **powerset(Σ*)**. Each of these represents a language. Therefore, there are some languages that are not enumerable (computable) by any Turing machine. Hence, the statement of the theorem is true.

(According to Church-Turing's Thesis, a Turing machine can compute any effective procedure, that is, algorithm. Therefore, there are some languages that cannot be defined by any effective procedure (no well-defined grammars) and these are the languages that are not recursive enumerable and this is why there is no Turing machine for these languages.)

9.3 TURING MACHINE AND GRAMMARS

In the previous chapter, we have discussed about languages and their corresponding Turing machines. Now, we will discuss about Turing machines and grammars. As we know that Turing machine can enumerate recursive enumerable languages, so Turing machines can enumerate any type of grammar (type 0, type 1, type 2, and type 3) also. Because these grammars (type 0, type 1, type 2, and type 3) are based on effective procedure and these procedures are used to produce strings.

Definition of unrestricted (Type 0) grammars

The productions of an unrestricted (type 0) grammar G have the form:

$(V_n \cup \Sigma)^+ \rightarrow (V_n \cup \Sigma)^*$, where $G = (V_n, \Sigma, P, S)$

The other types of grammars (left linear, right linear, linear, context free) have restricted form of productions in one or another way but an **unrestricted grammar** does not. We will attempt to show that unrestricted grammars are equivalent to Turing machines. It has been proved that a language is *recursively enumerable* if there is a Turing machine, which accepts every string of the language. But about rejection of some strings, we are not sure whether the Turing machine could go into an infinite loop instead, and never get around to either accepting or rejecting the string. Our objective is to show that the languages generated by unrestricted grammars are precisely the recursively enumerable languages.

Theorem 9.11: Any language generated by an unrestricted grammar (Type 0) is recursively enumerable (r.e.) language.

Proof: We can break the statement of theorem into two parts:

1. The strings produced by an unrestricted grammar can be enumerated by a Turing machine, and
2. For each Turing machine, there is some unrestricted grammar.

• *From unrestricted grammar (type 0) to Turing Machine*

If an effective procedure exists for enumerating the strings of a language then the language is recursively enumerable, we have proved this earlier. There exists a procedure for enumerating all the strings in any language generated by an unrestricted grammar. We also know that all recursive enumerable languages are Turing machine enumerable (Theorem 9.7) and Turing machine lists all the string in some order (let's say in length increasing order). Now, we will focus on the notion that an unrestricted grammar (type 0) produces strings and strings can be put in length increasing order. If this could happen then there is one-to-one relationship between set of produced strings and set of natural numbers. But, how we will be sure about the production of unrestricted grammar that a particular production rule generates a shorter string in finite time? Some productions could make the sentential form shorter, but it might take a million steps to derive null (ε) or terminal symbol. So, instead of taking the strings of *shortest derivation first*, first we consider all the strings that can be generated from S-productions in one-step derivation, where *S* is the start symbol of the grammar, and see if any of them are composed entirely of terminals. We do this because there are only a finite number of production rules in the grammar. After this, we consider all the strings that can be derived in two-step derivation, three-step derivation, and so on. It means, the strings produced by an unrestricted grammar can be produced in step increasing derivation. Now, we design Turing machines for strings derived in first-step derivation, second-step derivation, third-step derivation, and so on. Now, these all Turing machines are combined into one Turing machine, which enumerates the strings produced by an unrestricted grammar. Hence, some Turing machine enumerates the strings generated by an unrestricted grammar.

• *From Turing Machine to production rule of grammar*

We have seen that a Turing machine can enumerate anything that an unrestricted grammar can produce. Now, we have to show that an unrestricted grammar can produce anything what a Turing machine can. We show that an unrestricted grammar can emulate the behaviour of a Turing machine. We will discuss only the notion of the proof. Recall that a *configuration* of a Turing machine written as a string:

$a_n...a_jq_ma_{j-1}...a_1$, where a_i is read input symbol for $i = j, j + 1, j + 2, ..., n$, and q_m is present state, and a_{j-1} is the present input symbol under head.

It makes sense that a grammar, which is a system for rewriting strings, can be used to manipulate configurations, which can easily be written as strings.

A Turing machine $M = (Q, \Sigma, \delta, s)$ accepts a string $w, x \in \Sigma^*$ if

$$(s, \underline{\#}w\#) \vdash_M^* (h, \#x\underline{\#})$$

And a grammar produces a string if $S \overset{*}{\Rightarrow} w$. Because the Turing machine starts with input *w* while the grammatical derivation ends with *w*, so, the grammar will run in reverse as compared to the Turing machine. Therefore a type 0 grammar can produce the string (*w*), which is accepted by Turing machine *M*.

9.4 GODELIZATION

We have concentrated on processing over symbols for automaton discussed so far. For computing, we have a code system that converted the positive integer numbers in form of zeros, but we had no such a system that could convert a string into number and number into string for some alphabet. Such an encoding system suggested by **Kurt Godel** (1906–1978).

> **"Godelization is an encoding technique which encodes a string as a number". This is also known *Godel numbering.***

Let Σ is an alphabet and $\beta = |\Sigma| + 1$. We fix the order of the symbols of alphabet Σ such as: $a_1, a_2, a_3, \ldots, a_{\beta-1}$, where $a_1, a_2, a_3, \ldots, a_{\beta-1}$ are integers for first symbol, second symbol, third symbol, ..., $(\beta - 1)^{st}$ symbol. The factor β is used as a base for representing the number corresponding to a string. We define Godelization as a function G_n from $\Sigma^* \rightarrow N$, where $N = \{0, 1, 2, \ldots\}$. If a string $w \equiv a_1a_2\ldots a_n$ (symbols are in their order, total n symbols), then

$$G_n(w) = \beta^{n-1} \times a_1 + \beta^{n-2} \times a_2 + \ldots + \beta \times a_{n-1} + a_n$$

$G_n(w)$ is the **Godel number** of the string w over some alphabet.

In particular, $G_n(\varepsilon) = 0$.

Example 1: Consider $\Sigma = \{a, b, c\}$ and find Godel numbers for the strings: *a*, *ab*, *ccc*.

Solution: Since, the number of symbols in given alphabet, that is, $|\Sigma| = 3$, so $\beta = 3 + 1 = 4$ (base for number system corresponding to Σ)

So, possible digits in this number system are four, that is, $\beta = \{0, 1, 2, 3\}$. Let $a \equiv 1$, $b \equiv 2$, $c \equiv 3$, and $\varepsilon \equiv 0$, then

$$G_n(a) = 4^0 \times 1 = 1,$$
$$G_n(ab) = 4^1 \times 1 + 4^0 \times 2 = 6, \text{ and}$$
$$G_n(ccc) = 4^2 \times 3 + 4^1 \times 3 + 4^0 \times 3 = 63$$

There is reverse Godel numbering also. It means, we can find the string for a given number also for certain alphabet. Let us see the inverse of the Godelization function represented as G_n^{-1}. We convert the given number at base β. Let us consider the above given alphabet $\Sigma = \{a, b, c\}$. Some reverse Godel numbering are given below:

$$G_n^{-1}(0)_{10} = G_n^{-1}(0)_4 = \varepsilon,$$
$$G_n^{-1}(1)_{10} = G_n^{-1}(1)_4 = a,$$
$$G_n^{-1}(2)_{10} = G_n^{-1}(2)_4 = b,$$
$$G_n^{-1}(3)_{10} = G_n^{-1}(3)_4 = c,$$
$$G_n^{-1}(13)_{10} = G_n^{-1}(31)_4 = ca \qquad \text{(Converting 13 at base 4)}$$

The above conversion is very simple. There are ten digits in decimal number system and there are four possible symbols (a, b, c, ε) in the alphabet. So, a decimal number is converted at base 4 number system and then symbols are placed. It has been assumed earlier that: $a \equiv 1$, $b \equiv 2$, $c \equiv 3$, and $\varepsilon \equiv 0$. Now, we can say that Godelization can work in both direction; string to integer and integer to string.

9.5 SOLVED EXAMPLES

Example 9.1: Show that following functions over alphabet $\Sigma = \{a_1, a_2, \ldots, a_n\}$ are primitive recursive.

(a) Concatenation of two strings

(b) Reverse or transpose of a string
(c) Proper prefix of a string
(d) Proper suffix of a string

Solution:

(a) Let concatenation function of two strings is H and defined as

$$H(w_1, w_2) = w_1w_2, \text{ where } w_1, w_2 \in \Sigma^*.$$

We define H by using initial functions as following:

$$H(\varepsilon,w_2) = w_2 \equiv CONCATE\ \varepsilon(w_2),$$
$$H(a_iw_1, w_2) = a_iw_1w_2 \equiv CONCATE\ a_i(H(w_1, w_2)),$$

where $w_1, w_2, a_i \in \Sigma^*$ for some $i = 1, 2, \ldots, n$.

Therefore, $H(w_1, w_2)$ is a primitive recursive function.

(b) Let reverse function of a string is Rev and defined as following:

$$\text{Rev}(w) = w^R, \text{ where } w \in \Sigma^*$$

We define Rev by using initial functions as following:

$$\text{Rev}(\varepsilon) = \varepsilon \neq NULL(\varepsilon),$$
$$\text{Rev}(wa_i) = a_iw^R \equiv CONCATE\ a_i(\text{Rev}(w)),$$

where $a_i, w \in \Sigma^*$ for some $i = 1, 2, \ldots, n$

Therefore, Rev(w) is primitive recursive function.

(c) Let proper prefix function is Pref and defined as following:

Pref(w) = Set of all strings obtained from w by deleting one or more trailing symbols

We define Pref by using initial functions as following:

$$\text{Pref}(\varepsilon) = \varepsilon \neq NULL(\varepsilon),$$
$$\text{Pref}(wa_i) = w + \text{Pref}(w)\ CONCATE\ \text{e(w)} + CONCATE\ \varepsilon(\text{Pref}(w)),$$

where $a_i, w \in \Sigma^*$ for some $i = 1, 2, 3, \ldots, n$

Therefore, Pref is a primitive function.

(d) Let proper suffix function is Suff and defined as following:

Suff(w) = Set of all strings obtained from w by deleting one or more leading symbols.

We define Suff by using initial functions as following:

$$\text{Suff}(\varepsilon) = \varepsilon \equiv NULL(\varepsilon),$$
$$\text{Suff}(a_iw) = w + \text{Suff}(w) \equiv CONCATE\ \text{e}(w) + CONCATE\ \varepsilon(\text{Suff}(w)),$$

where $a_i, w \in \Sigma^*$ for some $i = 1, 2, 3, \ldots, n$

Therefore, Suff is a primitive function.

Example 9.2: Compute minimal $(G(x, y))$ for the following:

(a) $G(x, y) = y - 3 + 2^x$,
(b) $G(x, y)$ = integer part of $(x - 1)/(y + 1)$

Solution: We know that $minimal_y(G(x, y))$ = minimum value of y for which $G(x, y) = 0$

(a) Putting $G(x, y) = 0$, we get

$$y - 3 + 2^x = 0$$

or, $$y = 3 - 2^x$$

Since, the value of y will be minimum and positive if $x = 0$ or 1, so domain of minimization is {0, 1}. Putting $x = 1$ in the equation we get

$$y = 3 - 2 = 1$$

So, $minimal_y(G(x, y)) = 1$

(**Note:** we can't calculate negative value for y and x)

(b) Putting $G(x, y) = 0$, we get integer part of $(x - 1)/(y + 1) = 0$

So, values of $x > 1$ can make y positive, so domain is {2, 3, …}. Since, we want minimum value for y, so putting $x = 2$ in the equation, we get

integer part of $(2 - 1)/(y + 1) = 0$

or, integer part of $1/(y + 1) = 0$

The minimum value of y, which can provide the quotient value 0 is 1, so $y = 1$.

Therefore, $minimal_y(G(x, y)) = 1$

Example 9.3: Show that $f(r)$ = integer part of $\sqrt{r}$ is partial recursive function.

Solution: It is obvious that f(r) is the smallest value of n such that

$$(n + 1)^2 > r$$

or, $$(n + 1)^2 - r > 0$$

So, $$f(r) = minimal_y((n + 1)^2 - r0)$$

Since, $(n + 1)^2 - r > 0$ can be defined by using initial functions i.e. proper subtraction of $(n + 1)^2$ and r. So, $f(r)$ can be defined by using initial functions and minimization.

Therefore, $f(r)$ is partial recursive function.

Example 9.4: Prove that following functions from N to N or $N \times N$ to N are primitive recursive function, where $N = \{0, 1, 2, ...\}$.

(a) The predecessor function $h(x)$ for positive integer x is defined as:

$h(x) = 0$ if $x = 0$ and $h(x) = x - 1$ if $x > 0$

(b) Proper subtraction function of two positive integers.

(c) Absolute value function over positive integers.

(d) The function, which finds the minimum of two positive integers.

(e) The function $f(x)$ defined as:

$$f(x) = \begin{cases} x/2 \text{ if } x \text{ is even} \\ (x-1)/2 \text{ if } x \text{ is odd} \end{cases}$$

(f) The function $g(n) = 2^n$, where n is an positive integer.

(g) The function $f(x, y) = x^y$, where x, y are positive integers.

(h) The division function of two positive integers defined on two functions Div and Rem as following:

Div$(x, y) = n$, where x^3ny and

Rem$(x, y) = x - ny$

Solution:

(a) The predecessor function $h(x)$ can be defined by using initial functions as following:

$$h(x) = 0 \equiv Z(x), \text{ and } h(x) = x - 1 \text{ can be converted into } h(x+1) = h(x) \equiv P_1^1(x)$$

Hence, $h(x)$ is primitive recursive function.

(b) The proper subtraction function for two positive integers m and n can be defined as following:

$$H(m, n) = \begin{cases} m - n \text{ if } m > n \\ 0 \text{ if } m \le n \end{cases}$$

We define the $H(m, n)$ by using initial functions as following:

$$H(m, 0) = m \equiv P_1^1(m),$$
$$H(0, n) = 0 \equiv Z(n),$$
$$H(0, 0) = 0 \equiv Z(0), \text{ and}$$
$$H(m+1, n+1) = H(m, n) \equiv P_1^1(H(m, n))$$

Hence, $H(m, n)$ is primitive recursive function.

(c) Let $G(x, y)$ is the absolute value function for two positive integers x and y defined as following:

$$G(x, y) = |x - y| = \begin{cases} x - y \text{ if } x \ge y \\ y - x \text{ if } x \le y \end{cases}$$

The $G(x, y)$ can be defined by initial functions as following:

$$G(0, 0) = 0 \equiv Z(0),$$
$$G(x, 0) = x \equiv P_1^2(x, y),$$
$$G(0, y) = y \equiv P_2^2(x, y), \text{ and}$$
$$G(x+1, y+1) = G(x, y) \equiv P_1^1(G(x, y))$$

Hence, $G(x, y)$ is a primitive recursive function.

(d) Let the function Min(m, n) finds the minimum of two positive integers m and n defined following:

$$\text{Min}(m, n) = \begin{cases} m \text{ if } m > n \\ n \text{ if } n > m \\ 0 \text{ if } m, n = 0 \end{cases}$$

We define the Min function by using the initial functions as following:

$$\text{Min}(m, 0) = 0 \equiv Z(0),$$
$$\text{Min}(0, n) = 0 \equiv Z(0),$$

$$\text{Min}(m, n) = m - H(m, n) \equiv P_1^1\,(m - H(m, n)),$$

where $H(m, n)$ is the proper subtraction function proved as a primitive recursive function earlier. Hence, $\text{Min}(m, n)$ is a primitive recursive function.

(e) The given function $f(x)$ is

$$f(x) = \begin{cases} x/2 \text{ if } x \text{ is even} \\ (x-1)/2 \text{ if } x \text{ is odd} \end{cases}$$

The function $f(x)$ can be defined by using the initial functions as following:

$$f(0) = 0 \equiv Z(0),$$

$$f(x+1) = f(x) + P_r(x) \equiv P_1^1\,(f(x) + P_r(x)),$$

where $P_r(x)$ is defined below:

$$P_r(2n) = 0 \equiv Z(2n) \text{ for } n = 0, 1, 2, \ldots, \text{ and}$$

$$P_r(2n+1) = 1 \equiv S(Z(2n+1)) \text{ for } n = 0, 1, 2, \ldots$$

Hence, $f(x)$ is primitive recursive function.

(f) The given function $f(n) = 2^n$, where $n = 0, 1, 2, \ldots$

The function $f(n)$ can be defined by using initial functions as following:

$$f(0) = 2^0 = 1 \equiv S(0), \text{ and}$$

$$f(n+1) = 2*f(n) \equiv P_1^1\,(2*f(n))$$

Hence, $f(n)$ is primitive recursive function.

(g) The given function $f(m\ n) = m^n$, where m & n are two positive integers. We defined $f(m, n)$ by using the initial functions as following:

$$f(m, 0) = m^0 = 1 \equiv S(Z(m)),$$

$$f(0, n) = 0 \equiv Z(n), \text{ and}$$

$$f(m, n+1) = m*f(m, n) \equiv P_1^1\,(m*f(m, n))$$

Hence, $f(m, n)$ is primitive recursive function.

(h) The given functions Div and Rem can defined by using the initial functions as following:

$$\text{Div}(0, 0) = 0 \equiv Z(0),$$

$$\text{Div}(0, y) = 0 \equiv Z(y),$$

$$\text{Div}(x, y) = \text{Div}(H(x, y), y) + 1 \equiv P_1^1\,(\text{Div}(H(x, y), y) + 1),$$

Where $H(x, y)$ is the proper subtraction function already proved as a primitive recursive function.

$$\text{Rem}(0, 0) = 0 \equiv Z(0),$$

$$\text{Rem}(x, 0) = x \equiv P_1^1\,(x),$$

$$\text{Rem}(0, y) = 0 \equiv Z(y), \text{ and}$$

$$\text{Rem}(x+1, y+1) = \text{Rem}(x, y) \equiv P_1^1\,(\text{Rem}(x, y))$$

Hence, the given functions are primitive recursive function.

Example 9.5: Design a Turing machine for the following function:

$$\text{Min}(m, 0) = 0,$$

$$\text{Min}(0, n) = 0,$$

$$\text{Min}(m, n) = m - H(m, n),$$

where $H(m, n)$ is the proper subtraction

Solution: The given function Min(m, n) finds the minimum of two positive integers. Turing machine, which computes Min(m, n) is shown in Fig. 9.5.

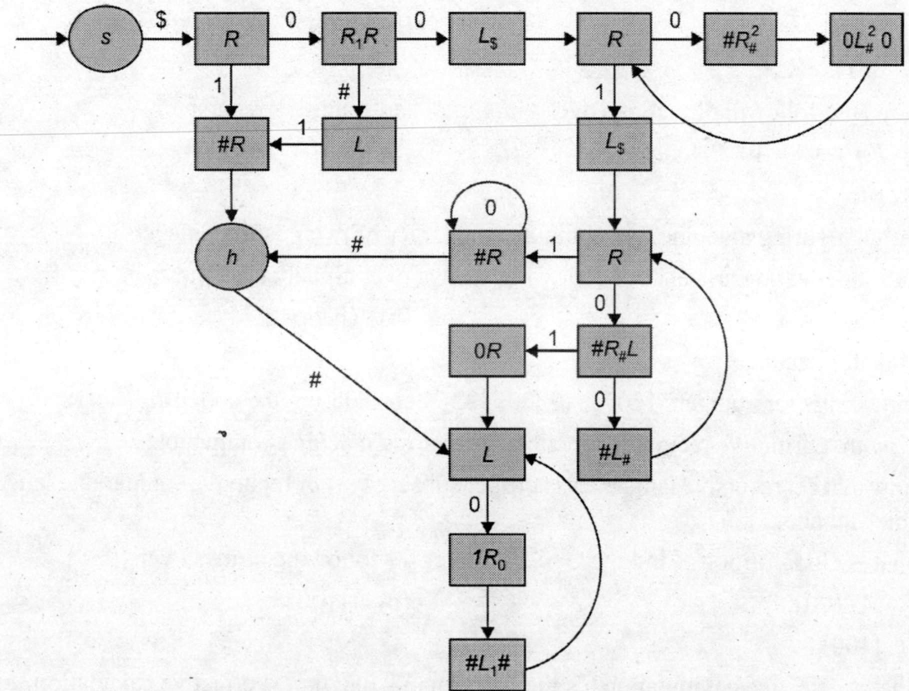

Fig. 9.5: TM for finding minimum of two positive integers

Initial tape contents:

$\$0^m10^n\#\#....$

When proper subtraction function is called first time:

$\$0^m10^n\#0^m\#\#....$

When proper subtraction function *H*(*m n*) is finished:

$\$0^{H(m,\,n)}\#0^m\#\#....$

Final tape contents:

$\$\#\#...0^{m\,-\,H(m,\,n)}\#\#....$, $H(m, n)$ is the proper subtraction function

TEST YOUR SKILLS

Supplementary Problems

9.1 Compute following for Ackerman's function

(a) Ack(3, 3) (b) Ack(2, 1)

(c) Ack(3, 2)

9.2 Show that Fibonacci number is generated by primitive recursive function.

9.3 Show that following logical operations are primitive recursive

(a) AND (b) OR

(c) NOT

9.4 Show that following functions over N are total and primitive recursive.

(a) $F(n) = 0 + 1 + 2 + \dots + n$ (b) $G(n) = 0 + 2 + 4 + \dots + 2n$

(c) $H(n) = 1 + 3 + 5 + \dots + 2n + 1$

9.5 Design a Turing machine that computes the larger of two positive integers.

9.6 Use Godelization and encode following strings over alphabet $\Sigma = \{a, b, c, \dots, z\}$.

(a) Automata (b) Theory

(c) Automatatheory

Find strings for numbers 12073, 12200, 33364 considering the above alphabet.

9.7 Show that primitive recursive functions are Turing machine computable.

9.8 Show that set recursive languages is proper subset of set of recursive enumerable languages over same alphabet.

9.9 What is Godelization? Find the Godel number for following strings over {0, 1}.

(a) 0111001 (b) 11100

(c) 110011

9.10 What is effective computation? Is the Ackerman's function is effective calculation?

9.11 Why some languages and problems are not Turing computable?

9.12 Discuss the following:

(a) Recursive enumerable languages (b) Partial recursive functions

(c) Total recursive functions (d) Primitive recursive functions

(e) Initial functions for natural numbers (f) Initial functions for some alphabet

(g) Type 0 grammar and Turing machine

9.13 Show that following functions are total and primitive recursive.

(a) Addition of three positive numbers

(b) Multiplication of n-positive integers, where $n \geq 2$

(c) Modulo operations for positive integers

Multiple Choice Questions

9.14 The word "enumerable" stands for

(a) Countable
(b) Able to be put in some order
(c) Calculable
(d) None

9.15 Recursive enumerable language is

(a) Accepted by TM
(b) Not accepted by TM
(c) Some times accepted and some time not
(d) None

9.16 For recursive enumerable language

(a) TM halts always
(b) TM does not halt
(c) Some time halts but some time not
(d) None

9.17 Suppose L is a recursive enumerable language and Turing machine M accepts L, then for $w \notin L$, M

(a) Halts always
(b) Does not halt
(c) May or may not halt
(d) Rejects

9.18 Suppose L is a recursive language and TM M accepts L, then for $w \notin L$, M

(a) Halts always
(b) Does not halt
(c) May or may not halt
(d) Rejects

9.19 Suppose L_1 and L_2 are recursive and recursive enumerable languages respectively over some alphabet Σ, then

(a) $L_1 \subset L_2$
(b) $L_2 \subset L_1$
(c) $L_1 \subset L_2$
(d) None

9.20 Choose the incorrect statement

(a) All recursive languages are recursive enumerable
(b) All recursive enumerable languages are recursive
(c) All recursive languages are TM computable
(d) None

9.21 Choose the correct statement

(a) Initial functions are primitive recursive function
(b) Primitive recursive functions are initial functions or based on initial functions using composition and recursion
(c) Both (a) and (b) statements
(d) None

9.22 Choose the correct statement

(a) All total functions are partial functions
(b) All partial functions are total functions
(c) All total functions are primitive recursive
(d) None

9.23 Which one is not a total function?

(a) Addition of two positive integers
(b) Multiplication of two positive integers
(c) Subtraction of two positive integers
(d) None

9.24 Which one is not a partial function?

(a) Addition of two positive integers
(b) Multiplication of two positive integers
(c) Subtraction of two positive integers
(d) None

9.25 Choose the correct statement

(a) The number of TMs for some alphabet is countable
(b) The number of TMs over some alphabet is countable but not enumerable
(c) Some languages are not TM computable
(d) Both (a) and (c)

9.26 Some languages are not Turing machine computable because

(a) No algorithm is there
(b) Algorithm is there but we can't implement
(c) These are not enumerable
(d) Both (a) and (c)

9.27 Partial recursive function is

(a) Total recursive function
(b) Primitive recursive function
(c) Primitive recursive function with minimization
(d) Total recursive function with minimization

9.28 If S is a finite set then

(a) $|2^S|$ is infinite but countable
(b) $|2^S|$ is finite but not countable
(c) $|2^{S^*}|$ is infinite but countable
(d) $|2^{S^*}|$ is infinite and not countable

9.29 Ackerman's function is

(a) Total recursive function and TM computable
(b) Primitive recursive function and TM computable
(c) Not primitive recursive function but TM computable
(d) Both (a) and (c) statements

9.30 Godelization is a/an

(a) Number system
(b) Encoding function
(c) String to integer function
(d) Both (b) and (c) statements

Answers

9.14 (b)	9.15 (a)	9.16 (a)	9.17 (c)	9.18 (d)
9.19 (a)	9.20 (b)	9.21 (c)	9.22 (a)	9.23 (c)
9.24 (d)	9.25 (d)	9.26 (d)	9.27 (d)	9.28 (d)
9.29 (d)	9.30 (b)			

CHAPTER 10

Decidability and Undecidability

We will discuss decidability and undecidability of the problems in this chapter. Decidability and undecidability are analogous to solvability and unsolvability. Decidability and solvability are related to decision and computable problems respectively. In our practical life, we have several problems and many of these have solution also, but some have not. Simply, we say a problem is solvable if there is a solution otherwise unsolvable. If the solution is restricted to the set {Yes, No} then problems are known as decision problems. **For example,** consider following decision problems and their answers:

1. Does the sun rise in the east? (answer is YES, decidable problem)
2. Does the earth move around the sun? (answer is YES, decidable problem)
3. What is your name? (answer is Automata, decidable problem)
4. Are you a Government servant? (answer is No)
5. Will tomorrow be a rainy day? (Do not know, undecidable problem)

We have solutions (answers) for all problems except the last one. The last problem has no answer, because we have no way to tell about the weather of tomorrow exactly, although at some extent we can predict only. So, the last problem is undecidable and remaining problems are decidable. If a problem is solved (or answered) based on some algorithm then it is known as decidable (decision problems) otherwise undecidable.

Each problem P is a pair consisting of a set and a question, where the question can be applied to each element in the set. The set is called the domain of the problem, and its elements are called the instances of the problem.

For example,

Domain: {All regular languages over some alphabet Σ},

Instance: $L = \{w : w$ is a word over Σ ending in $aa\}$,

Question: Is union of two regular languages regular?

So, decision problem P = ({All regular languages over some alphabet Σ}, Is union of two regular languages regular?)

10.1 DECIDABLE AND UNDECIDABLE PROBLEMS

A problem is said to be decidable (or solvable) if

1. Its language is recursive, or
2. It has solution or answer (algorithm)

Other problems those do not satisfy the above conditions are undecidable (or unsolvable). We restrict the answer of decidable problems to "YES" or "NO". If there is some algorithm for the problem then outcome of the algorithm is either "YES" or "NO", but not the both. Restricting the answers (Yes, No), we could not be able to cover the whole problems; still we can cover a lot of problems. One question is here. Why we are restricting our answers to only "Yes" or "No"? The answer is very simple; we want the solutions as simple as possible.

Now, we say: "If for a problem, there exists an algorithm which tells that the answer is either "Yes" or "No" then problem is decidable."

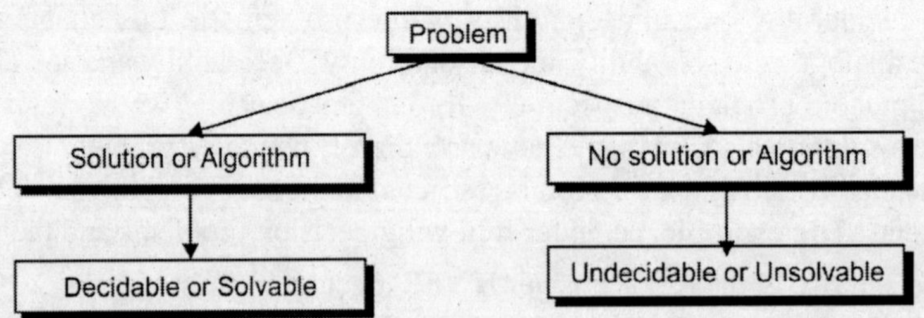

If a problem has both the answers; sometime "Yes" and sometime "No" then problem is undecidable. If solution is definite, either "Yes" or "No" then problem is said to be decidable.

10.2 DECIDABLE PROBLEMS FOR FINITE AUTOMATA, REGULAR GRAMMARS AND REGULAR LANGUAGES

We have discussed finite automaton, regular grammars, and regular languages. Whatever theorems and algorithms we have discussed for these, are solution for decidable problems. Some decidable problems are given below:

1. Does finite automaton accept regular language?
2. Is the power of nondeterministic finite automaton (NFA) and deterministic finite automaton (DFA) same?
3. L_1 and L_2 are two regular languages. Are these closed under following:
   (a) Union
   (b) Concatenation
   (c) Intersection
   (d) Complement
   (e) Transpose
   (f) Kleene Closure (positive transitive closure)

Example 1: For a given finite automaton *M* and string w over alphabet Σ, is $w \in L(M)$?

Proof: We assume that finite automaton *M* is DFA accepting all strings $w \in \Sigma^*$. We check the acceptability of string w by tracing on *M* for $|w|$ steps. If trace ends in some final state of *M* then string *w* is accepted otherwise not. So, we have some algorithm to check whether $w \in L(M)$ or not. Hence, the problem is decidable. (We can see the above result for nondeterministic finite automata also.)

Example 2: For a given finite automaton *M*, is $L(M) = \phi$?

Proof: We check whether a path starting from initial state of *M* ends in some final state or not. If such a path exists, then $L(M) \neq \phi$, otherwise $L(M) = \phi$. So, we have an algorithm to check whether $L(M) = \phi$ or not. Hence, the problem is decidable.

Example 3: For a given finite automaton *M* and alphabet Σ, is $L(M) = \Sigma^*$? This is a decidable problem.

Proof: We construct a another finite automata *M′* for $\Sigma^*\text{-}L(M)$ and check whether $L(M') = \phi$ or not. If $L(M') = \phi$, then $L(M) = \Sigma^*$ otherwise not. So, we have an algorithm to check whether $L(M) = \Sigma^*$ or not. Hence, the problem is decidable.

(**Note:** We have already prove that "Is $L(M) = \phi$ or not ?" is decidable)

Example 4: For given two finite automaton M_1 and M_2, such that $L(M_1), L(M_2) \in \Sigma^*$, is $L(M_1) = L(M_2)$? This is a decidable problem.

Proof: Since, two finite automata M_1 and M_2 are given. We construct a third finite automaton M_3 which recognizes the language $L = (\Sigma^* - L(M_1)) \cap L(M_2)$. Now, we check whether $L(M_3) = \phi$ or not. If $L(M_3) = \phi$, then $L(M_1) = L(M_2)$, otherwise not. So, we have an algorithm to check whether $L(M_1) = L(M_2)$ or not. Hence, the problem is decidable.

(**Note:** We have already prove that "Is $L(M) = \phi$ or not ?" is decidable)

Example 5: For given two regular languages L_1 and L_2 over some alphabet Σ, is $L_1 \subset L_2$? This is a decidable problem.

Proof: We know that $L_1 \subset L_2$ (proper subset) if and only if all strings of L_1 are in L_2 and at least one string of L_2 is not in L_1. It means, if we find the complement of L_1 and intersection with L_2, then result should not be ϕ.

So, $L_1 \subset L_2$ if and only if $\overline{L_1} \cap L_2 \neq \phi$. So, we have algorithm for deciding whether $L_1 \subset L_2$ or not. Hence, the problem is decidable.

10.3 DECIDABLE AND UNDECIDABLE PROBLEMS FOR CONTEXT-FREE LANGUAGES AND GRAMMARS

Whatever theorems and algorithms we have discussed so far for context-free languages and context-free grammars are solution for decidable problems. But, there are some undecidable problems also.

10.3.1 Decidable Problems

Some decidable problems about context-free languages and context-free grammars are given below:

1. If L_1 and L_2 are two context-free languages over some alphabet Σ then $\boldsymbol{L_1 \cup L_2}$ is context-free language.

2. If L_1 and L_2 are two context-free languages over some alphabet Σ then $\boldsymbol{L_1 L_2}$ is context-free language.
3. If L is a context-free language over some alphabet Σ, then $\boldsymbol{L^*}$ is a context-free language.
4. If L_1 is a regular language, L_2 is a context-free language then $L_1 \cup L_2$ is context-free language.
5. If L_1 is a regular language, L_2 is a context-free language over some alphabet Σ, then $L_1 \cap L_2$ is context-free language.
6. For a given context-free grammar G, finding whether $L(G)$ is finite or not, is decidable.

   (We have already discussed this in the Chapter 6, decision algorithms for CFLs and CFGs.)

Example 1: For a given context-free grammar G, is $L(G) = \phi$ or not?

Proof: We construct a new grammar G' such that $L(G') = L(G) - \{\varepsilon\}$. Now, we remove the useless symbols and useless production rules. After this, if there is at least one S-production, then $L(G') \neq \phi$, and hence $L(G) \neq \phi$, otherwise $L(G') = L(G) = \phi$. So, we have algorithm for deciding whether $L(G) = \phi$ or not. Hence, the problem is decidable.

Example 2: For a given context-free grammar G and a string w over alphabet Σ, checking whether $w \in L(G)$ or not is decidable.

Proof: We use membership (CYK) algorithm to check whether $w \in L(G)$ or not. So, problem is decidable.

10.3.2 Undecidable Problems

Following are some undecidable problem about context-free languages and grammars:

1. For two given context-free languages L_1 and L_2, whether $\boldsymbol{L_1 \cap L_2}$ is context-free language or not?

   (For proof, see the Theorem 6.7 in Chapter 6.)
2. For a given context-free language L over some alphabet Σ, whether complement of L i.e., * $-\boldsymbol{L}$ is context-free language?

   (For proof, see the Theorem 6.8 in Chapter 6.)
3. For a given context-free grammar G, is $\boldsymbol{L(G)}$ is ambiguous?
4. For two arbitrary context-free grammars G_1 and G_2, is $\boldsymbol{L(G_1) \cap L(G_2) = \phi}$**?**
5. For two arbitrary context-free grammars G_1 and G_2, is $\boldsymbol{L(G_1) \subseteq L(G_2)}$**?**

10.4 DECIDABILITY AND UNDECIDABILITY ABOUT TURING MACHINE

We have considered Turing machine as the most powerful machine that can compute any effective computation and it can recognize any recursive enumerable language. So, how undecidability comes and why? These questions are really interesting. According to Church-Turing Thesis, we have considered a Turing machine as an algorithm and an algorithm as a Turing machine. So, for a problem, if there is an algorithm (effective solution or procedure to find answer) then problem is decidable and some Turing machine can solve that problem. We have several problems related to computation and recognization that have no solution and these problems are undecidable.

10.4.1 Partial Decidable/Solvable and Decidable/Solvable Problems

A Turing machine M is said to **partially solve** a given problem P if it provides the solution for each instance of the problem and the problem is said to be partially solvable. P is analogous to recursive enumerable languages. If all the computations of the Turing machine are halting computations for P then the problem P is said to solvable. A Turing machine is said to partially decide a problem if the following two conditions are satisfied:

(a) The problem is a decision problem, and
(b) The Turing machine recognizes a given input if and only if the problem has an answer "YES" for the input, that is, the Turing machine recognizes the language $L = \{x : x$ is an instance of the problem, and the problem has the answer "YES" for $x\}$.

The main difference between a Turing machine M_1 that partially solves (partially decides) a problem and another Turing machine M_2 that solves (decides) the same problem is that M_1 might reject an input by a non-halting computation, whereas M_2 can reject the input only by a halting computation.

(Recall that on an input that is accepted by a Turing machine, the Turing machine has only accepting computations and halting computations. But, on an input that is not in the language, the Turing machine might have some computations, of which some may never halt.)

A computational problem is said to be **unsolvable** if no algorithm can solve it, and a problem is said to be **undecidable** if it is a decision problem and no algorithm can decide the solution.

10.4.2 Decidable Problems about Recursive and Recursive Enumerable Languages

As we have discussed that if a decision problem has solution then it is decidable. In this section, we will discuss some decidable problems about recursive and recursive enumerable languages.

Example 1: The complement of a recursive language L over some alphabet Σ is recursive.

Proof: We will discuss a constructive algorithm to prove that complement of a recursive language is also recursive i.e., recursive languages are closed under complementation. As we know, for all strings $w \in L$ Turing machine always halts and rejects those strings that are not in L. So, problem "Are all strings $w \in L$?" is always decidable.

We construct a Turing machine M, which recognizes the language L. Now, we construct another Turing machine M' based on first Turing machine M such that M' accepts those strings that are rejected by M. It means, if Turing machine M accepts then M' does not. In other words, Turing machine M' rejects those strings that are accepted by Turing machine M. It means, for all strings $x \notin L$ accepted by M' and for all strings $w \in L$ are rejected by M'. We can say that Turing machine M' also follows same kind of algorithm to decide whether a string $w \in L$ or not what Turing machine follows. Hence, complement of recursive language L i.e. $\Sigma^* - L$ is also recursive. The logic diagram of M' is shown in Fig. 10.1.

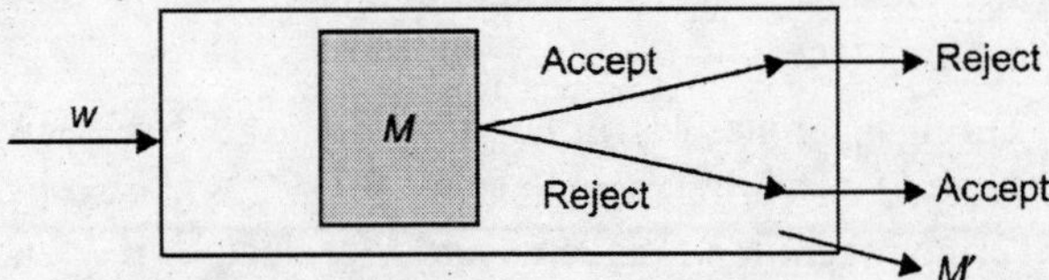

Fig. 10.1: TM for complement of a recursive language

Example 2: The union of two recursive languages is recursive.

Proof: Let L_1 and L_2 are two recursive languages and Turing machines M_1 and M_2 recognize L_1 and L_2 respectively as shown in Fig. 10.2(a) and Fig. 10.2 (b).

Fig. 10.2(a): Turing machine M_1 **Fig. 10.2(b): Turing machine M_2**

We construct a third Turing machine M_3, which follows either M_1 or M_2 as shown in Fig. 10.2(c).

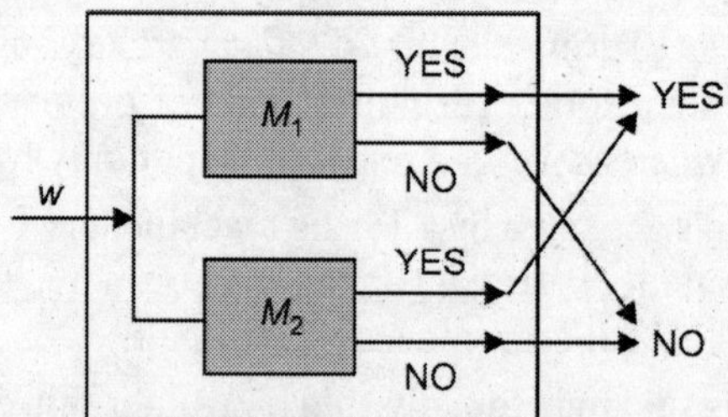

Fig. 10.2(c): Turing machine M_3

Turing machine M_3 accepts a string if either M_1 accepts or M_2 accepts that string and rejects if either M_1 rejects or M_2 rejects that string. Turing machines M_1 and M_2 are based on effective procedure (algorithm) and so Turing machine M_3 is also based on the same kind of procedure (algorithm). Thus, language recognizes by Turing machine M_3 is recursive that is union of L_1 and L_2 languages. Therefore, union of two recursive languages L_1 and L_2 is also recursive.

Example 3: A language is recursive if and only if its complement is recursive.

(For proof see the above discussion for complement and union of recursive languages.)

Example 4: The union of two recursively enumerable languages is recursive enumerable.

Proof: Let L_1 and L_2 are two recursively enumerable languages and recognized by Turing machines M_1 and M_2. We construct another Turing machine M_3, which recognizes either L_1 or L_2. Now, as we know the problem about recursive enumerable languages that if w is not in L_1 and L_2, then M_3 cannot decide whether it is accepted or rejected. So, the problem of recursive languages is persistent with M_3 also. So, $N(M_3)$ is recursive enumerable language and hence $L_1 \cup L_2$ is recursive enumerable language. In general, *recursive enumerable languages are closed under union operation.*

Example 5: If a language L over some alphabet Σ and its complement $\overline{L} = \Sigma^* - L$ is recursive enumerable, then L and $\overline{L}$ are recursive languages.

Proof: We construct two Turing machines M_1 for language L and M_2 for language $\overline{L}$. Now, we construct a third Turing machine M_3 based on Turing machines M_1 and M_2 as shown in Fig. 10.3. Turing machine M_3 accepts a string w if Turing machine M_1 accepts and M_3 rejects w if M_2 accepts. It means, if $w \in L$, then w is accepted and if $w \notin L$ then rejected. Since for all string w, either w is accepted or rejected by Turing machine M_3. In other words, Turing machine M_3 is based on algorithm and produces either

"YES" or "NO" for input string $w \in L$. It means M_3 decides acceptability all the strings over Σ. Hence, L is recursive. As we know that complement of a recursive language is also recursive and hence $\overline{L}$ is also recursive.

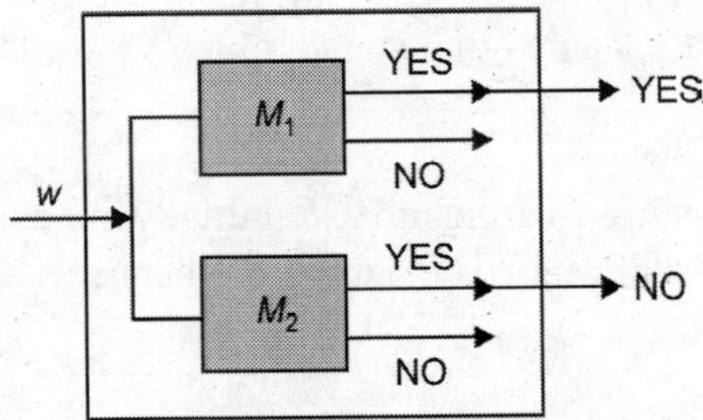

Fig. 10.3: Turing machine

Example 6: We have following co-theorem based on above discussion for recursive enumerable and recursive languages.

Proof: Let L and $\overline{L}$ are two languages, where $\overline{L}$ the complement of L, then one of the following is is true:

(a) Both L and $\overline{L}$ are recursive languages,

(b) Neither L nor $\overline{L}$ is recursive languages,

(c) If L is recursive enumerable but not recursive, then $\overline{L}$ is not recursive enumerable and vice versa.

(Co-theorem (a), (b), and (c) can be proved using the earlier discussion.)

10.4.3 Undecidable Problems of Turing Machines

First, we will discuss about halting problem in general and then we will see undecidable problems about Turing machines

10.4.3.1 Halting Problem (HP)

The **halting problem** is a decision problem which can be informally stated as following:

"Given a description of an algorithm and a description of its initial arguments (inputs), determine whether the algorithm, when executed with these arguments, ever halts. The alternative is that the given algorithm runs forever without halting."

Alan Turing proved in 1936 that there is no general method or algorithm which can solve the halting problem. An algorithm may contain loops which may be infinite or finite in length depending on the input and behaviour of the claimed algorithm. The amount of work done in an algorithm usually depends on the input size. Algorithms may consist of various numbers of loops, nested or in sequence. The HP asks the question:

Given a program and an input to the program, determine if the program will eventually stop when it is executed that input?

One thing, we can do here to find the solution of HP. Let the program run with the given input and wait for result. If the program stops and we would conclude that problem is solved. But if the program doesn't stop in a reasonable amount of time, we cannot conclude. The question is: "how long we can wait...? ". The waiting time may be long enough to exhaust the whole life. So, we cannot take it easier as it seems to be. We must have answer, either "YES" or "NO", and hence some algorithm to decide the exact answer. The importance of the halting problem lies in the fact that it is the first problem to be proved undecidable. Subsequently, many other such problems have been described.

Theorem 10.1: HP is undecidable.

Proof: This proof was devised by Alan Turing in 1936. Initially, we assume that HP is decidable and the algorithm (effective solution) for HP is ***H***. The halting problem solution *H* takes two inputs:

1. Description of Turing machine *M* i.e., program *P* and
2. Input *I* for the program *P*

Algorithm *H* generates an output "YES" if it determines that *P* stops for input ***I*** and it outputs "NO" if it determines that *P* loops as shown in Fig. 10.4(a).

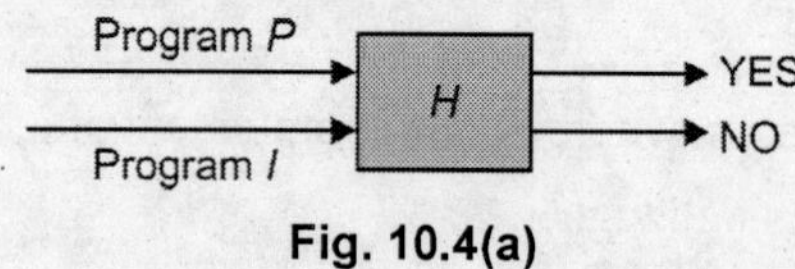

Fig. 10.4(a)

When an algorithm is coded, it is expressed as a string of characters. Input is also coded into the same format. So, after coding, a program and data have no difference in their format of representation on the storage and so, a program can be treated a data sometime and a data can be treated as a program sometime.

Now algorithm *H* can be modify to take *P* as both inputs (the program *P* and its input *I*) and *H* should be able to determine if *P* will halt on *P* as shown in Fig. 10.4(b). It very interesting; algorithm *H* has to process its program *P* as program and input.

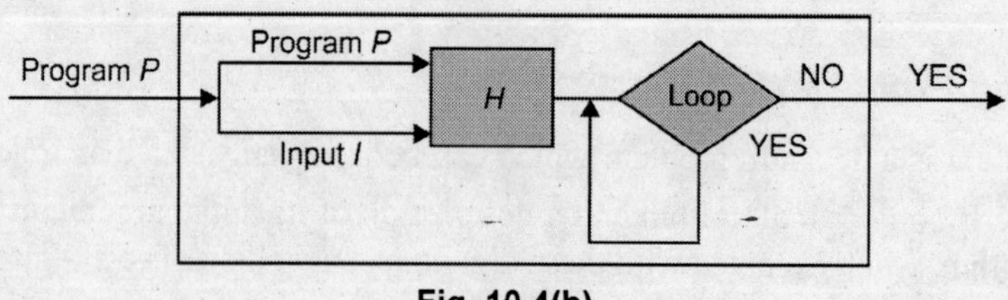

Fig. 10.4(b)

Let us construct a new, simple algorithm *K* that takes output of algorithm *H* as its input and does the following:

1. If *H* outputs "NO" then *K* outputs "YES" and halts,
2. Otherwise if *H* outputs "YES" then *K* loops forever.

It means, *K* does the opposite what algorithm *H* does. We define algorithm *K* as following:

```
Functlon K( )
{
if (Function H( ) = "NO")
```

```
{
return("YES");
}
else
{
while(1);                    //Loop for ever
}
}        //End of the function K
```

Since, algorithm K is a program (Turing machine), so let us use code of algorithm K as the input to itself as shown in Fig. 10.4(c).

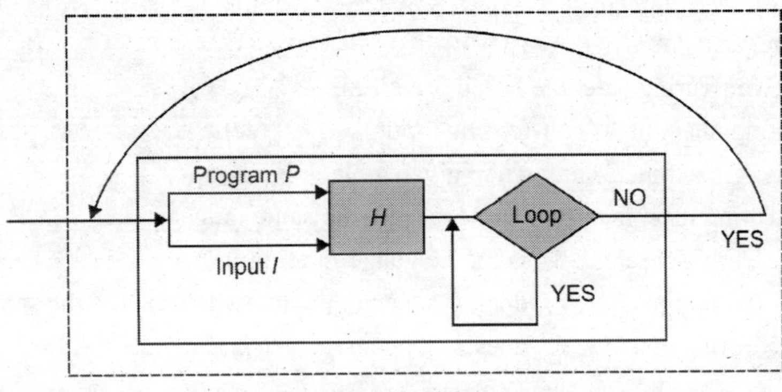

Fig. 10.4(c)

Now, we analyse the following:

1. If algorithm H outputs "YES" and tells that algorithm K halts then K itself would loop (that's how we constructed it).
2. If algorithm H outputs "NO" and tells that K loops then K outputs "YES" and halts.

Since, in either case algorithm H provides wrong answer for algorithm K. Therefore, H cannot work in all cases and hence cannot provide right solution for all the inputs. This contradicts our assumption made earlier for HP. Hence, HP is undecidable.

Theorem 10.2: HP of Turing machines is undecidable.

HP of Turing machine is stated as "To decide whether or not a Turing machine halts for arbitrary input w". We can prove this problem as undecidable by following the similar stepts discussed in Theorem 10.1.

10.4.3.2 Reduction of problems to halting problem of turing machine

We reduce a problem X to the HP of Turing machine as following:

1. Assume that we have an effective procedure (Turing machine M or any other kind of algorithm) to solve problem X.
2. Show how to use the program for X to solve the HP.
3. Since, HP cannot be solved i.e., undecidable, so conclude that problem X is also undecidable.

Example 1: consider the state-entry problem (also known as *dead code problem*) is to determine whether Turing machine M, when given input w, ever enters state q or not. This is undecidable.

Proof: We check whether a Turing machine M enters state q or not following the steps given below:

1. Define transition function $\delta(q, a) = \{h, \#)$, for all input symbols 'a',
2. Now, check whether M halts for w or not.

Now, the given problem is same as the HP problem of Turing machine that whether M halts for input w or not. Hence, the given problem is undecidable.

10.4.3.3 Other undecidable problems of turing machine

Following problems of Turing machine can be proved as undecidable by converting into halting problem of Turing machine.

1. Does a given Turing machine M halt on all inputs?
2. Does Turing machine M halt for *any* input, i.e., is $L(M) = \phi$?
3. Does Turing machine M halt when given a blank input tape?
4. Do two Turing machines M_1 and M_2 accept the same language i.e., $N(M_1) = N(M_2)$?
5. For some Turing machine M, is the language $L(M)$ finite?
6. For some Turing machine M, does $L(M)$ contain any two strings of the same length?
7. For some Turing machine M, does $L(M)$ contain a string of length k, for some given $k \geq 1$?

10.4.3.4 Implications for programming

It is important to understand that what the HP does and doesn't say, and how this applies to computer programming. First, every existing programming language, no one has more power than a Turing machine. Hence, this result applies directly to programming languages. *Theorem 10.1 does not say that whether or not a given program halts on a given input*. Most of the time, for most practical programs, we can do eliminate infinite loops from our programs and provide solution. We can even write a meta-program to check another program for potential infinite loops, and get this meta-program to work most of the time. Theorem 10.1 says that we cannot ever write such a meta-program that could work *all the time for all inputs.* Moreover, the result can be used to demonstrate that certain other problems are also undecidable. We do this as following:

1. If we could solve problem X, we could solve the HP,
2. We cannot solve the HP,
3. Therefore, we cannot solve problem X.

Sometime, we are able to solve a subset of problem X. However, unless we have proper understanding of X and its solution, it is better to avoiding problem X and we will say X is undecidable.

Some philosophers have tried to use the HP as an argument against the possibility of intelligent computers. Stripped to its basics, the argument goes like this:

1. There are several problems that computers can do,
2. But, a computer cannot do some problems,
3. We can do those problems,
4. Therefore, we must be superior to computers.

10.5 POST CORRESPONDENCE PROBLEM (PCP)

Post's correspondence problem is a combinatorial problem formulated by **Emil Post** in 1946. This problem has many applications in the field of theory of formal languages.

Definition: A correspondence system ***P*** is a finite set of ordered pairs of nonempty strings over some alphabet. Let be an alphabet, then P is finite subset of $\Sigma^+ \times \Sigma^+$. A match or solution of *P* is any string $w \in \Sigma$ such that pairs $(u_1, v_1), (u_2, v_2), \ldots, (u_n, v_n) \in P$ and

$$w = u_1u_2\ldots u_n = v_1v_2\ldots v_n \text{ for some } n > 0.$$

The selected pairs $(u_1, v_1), (u_2, v_2), \ldots, (u_n, v_n)$ are not necessarily distinct. Let strings $u_1, u_2, \ldots, u_m$ are in set ***U*** and strings $v_1, v_2, \ldots, v_m$ are in set ***V***, then

$$U = \{u_1, u_2, \ldots, u_m\} \text{ and } V = \{v_1, v_2, \ldots, v_m\} \text{ for some } m > 0.$$

PCP is to determine whether there is any match or not for a given correspondence system.

Theorem 10.3: PCP is undecidable.

PCP is undecidable problems like the HP problem of Turing machine. For **example,**

Example 1: A correspondence system $P = \{(b, a), (ba, ba), (bab^3, b^3)\}$. Is there any solution for *P*?

Solution: We represent the *P* as following:

i	u_i	v_i
1	b	a
2	ba	ba
3	bab^3	b^3

Here, $u_1 = b$, $u_2 = ba$, $u_3 = bab^3$, $v_1 = a$, $v_2 = ba$, $v_3 = b^3$.

We have a solution $w = u_3u_1u_1u_2 = v_2v_3v_3v_1 = bab^3b^3a$

Example 2: Consider a correspondence system $P = \{(b, ca), (a, ab), (ca, a), (abc, c)\}$. Find match (if there is any).

Solution: We represent the *P* as following:

i	u_i	v_i
1	b	ca
2	a	ab
3	abc	c

Here, $u_1 = b$, $u_2 = a$, $u_3 = abc$, $v_1 = ca$, $v_2 = ab$, $v_3 = c$.

We have a solution $w = u_3u_2 = v_2v_1 = abca$

Modified version of PCP (MPCP)

A modified version of correspondence system *P* is ***P′*** and defined as:

$P' = \{P, (x, y)\}$, where *P* is over $\Sigma^+ \times \Sigma^+$ and *x*, *y* are strings.

P' has a solution $\mathbf{w} = xu_1u_2 \dots u_n = yv_1v_2 \dots v_n$, for some $n > 0$, $(u_1, v_1), (u_2, v_2), \dots,$ $(u_n, v_n) \in P$ or $w = u_1u_2 \dots u_nx = v_1v_2 \dots v_ny$.

Theorem 10.4: MPCP is undecidable.

Application of PCP

PCP has very important role in formal languages and also in general life. It is used to prove certain problems are undecidable. **For example,**

Example 1: The problem "whether an arbitrary context-free grammar is ambiguous or not" is undecidable.

Proof: Let context-free grammar G is defined over Σ and two sets of strings over Σ are following:

$U = \{u_1, u_2, \dots, u_m\}$ and $V = \{v_1, v_2, \dots, v_m\}$ for some $m > 0$.

Let $\Sigma_1 = \{a_1, a_2, \dots, a_n\}$ for some $n > 0$ such that $\Sigma_1 \cap \Sigma = \phi$ and

Two languages, $L_A = \{u_1u_2 \dots u_m a_m a_{m-1} \dots a_1 : m \geq 1\}$, and

$L_B = \{v_1v_2 \dots v_m\, a_m a_{m-1} \dots a_1 : m \geq 1\}$

Let context-free grammar $G = (\{S, S_A, S_B\}, \Sigma \cup \Sigma_1, P, S)$, where P consists of following production rules:

$$S \to S_A \mid S_B,$$
$$S_A \to u_i S_A a_i \mid u_i a_i,$$
$$S_B \to v_i S_B a_i \mid v_i a_i, \text{ for } 1 \leq i \leq n$$

We can show that $L(G) = L_A \cup L_B$. Now, we define a correspondence system $P = \{(u_1, v_1), (u_2, v_2), \dots, (u_n, v_n)\}$. If modified P has a solution w for pairs $(u_1, v_1), (u_2, v_2), \dots, (u_m, v_m)$, where $m \leq n$, and

$w = u_1u_2 \dots u_m a_m a_{m-1} \dots a_1 = v_1v_2 \dots v_m\, a_m a_{m-1} \dots a_1$

We have $u_1u_2 \dots u_m a_m a_{m-1} \dots a_1 \in L_A$, and $v_1v_2 \dots v_m\, a_m a_{m-1} \dots a_1 \in L_B$ and hence $w \in L(G)$.

Since, string w is derived by two leftmost derivations:

1. $S \Rightarrow S_A \overset{*}{\Rightarrow} u_1u_2 \dots u_m a_m a_{m-1} \dots a_1$
2. $S \Rightarrow S_B \overset{*}{\Rightarrow} v_1v_2 \dots v_m a_m a_{m-1} \dots a_1$

Thus, G is ambiguous.

It means, grammar G is ambiguous if and only if P has a solution and hence we have a procedure to find the match for correspondence system P. But, we know that PCP is undecidable; it means "G is ambiguous" is not correct assumption. Since, $L(G)$ can be thought as a correspondence system, hence we conclude that problem "whether an arbitrary CFG G is ambiguous or not" is undecidable.

10.6 SOLVED EXAMPLES

Example 10.1: It is undecidable for any arbitrary context-free grammar G over alphabet Σ whether $L(G) = \Sigma^*$ or not.

Proof: We convert this problem into halting problem (HP) of Turing machine. Let there is a Turing machine M such that $L(G) = \Sigma^*$ if and only if $N(M) = \phi$. It means, not a single string of Σ^* is accepted by Turing machine M.

Let $L(G) = \Sigma^*$ is decidable. It means there is a Turing machine M' that accepts all strings over Σ and rejects others strings. Turing machine M accepts those strings that are not accepted by Turing machine M'. Therefore the language recognized by Turing machine M is empty i.e., $N(M) = \phi$ and it is also decidable because we can construct M by complementing M'. But, we know that "deciding $N(M) = \phi$ or not" is undecidable for arbitrary Turing machine M. So, our assumption about $L(G)$ is not correct. Since, we think "whether $L(G) = \Sigma^*$ or not" as HP of Turing machine. Hence, it is undecidable.

Example 10.2: For two arbitrary context-free grammars (CFGs) G_1 and G_2, deciding whether $L(G_1) \cap L(G_2) = \phi$ or not is undecidable.

Proof: Let grammar $G_1 = (\{S_1\}, \Sigma_1 \cup \Sigma_3, P_1, S_1)$, and grammar $G_2 = (\{S_2\}, \Sigma_2 \cup \Sigma_3, P_2, S_2)$, where $\Sigma_3 = \{a_1, a_2, \ldots, a_n\}$ and $\Sigma_1 \cap \Sigma_3 = \phi$, $\Sigma_2 \cap \Sigma_3 = \phi$.

$\boldsymbol{P_1}$ consists of $S_1 \rightarrow u_i S_1 a_i \mid u_i a_i$, and $\boldsymbol{P_2}$ consists of $S_2 \rightarrow v_i S_2 a_i \mid v_i a_i$ for some $1 \leq i\ n$.

Let $L(G_1) \cap L(G_2)$ is decidable and there is a common string $\boldsymbol{w}$ such that

$$w = u_i u_j \ldots u_k a_k \ldots a_j a_i = v_i v_j \ldots v_k a_k \ldots a_j a_i$$

We define a correspondence system P which contains the pairs (u_i, v_i), (u_j, v_j), ..., (u_k, v_k) and its solution would be $w = u_i u_j \ldots u_k a_k \ldots a_j a_i = v_i v_j \ldots v_k a_k \ldots a_j a_i$. It means, P has a solution and we have a procedure to find the solution of PCP, which is incorrect. Since, $L(G_1) \cap L(G_2)$ can be thought as a correspondence system and we know that PCP is undecidable. Hence, we conclude that "whether $L(G_1) \cap L(G_2) = \phi$ or not" is undecidable.

Example 10.3: For two arbitrary context-free grammars (CFGs) G_1 and G_2, deciding whether $L(G_1) = L(G_2)$ or not is undecidable.

Proof: Let grammar $G_1 = (\{S_1\}, \Sigma_1 \cup \Sigma_3, P_1, S_1)$, grammar $G_2 = (\{S_2\}, \Sigma_2 \cup \Sigma_3, P_2, S_2)$, where $\Sigma_3 = \{a_1, a_2, \ldots, a_n\}$ and $\Sigma_1 \cap \Sigma_3 = \phi$, $\Sigma_2 \cap \Sigma_3 = \phi$.

P_1 consists of $S_1 \rightarrow u_i S_1 a_i \mid u_i a_i$, P_2 consists of $S_2 \rightarrow v_i S_2 a_i \mid v_i a_i$ for some $1 \leq i \leq n$.

Let $L(G_1) = L(G_2)$ is decidable; it means for all $w = u_i u_j \ldots u_k a_k \ldots a_j a_i = v_i v_j \ldots v_k a_k \ldots a_j a_i$ is in languages $L(G_1)$ and $L(G_2)$.

Now, we define a correspondence system P which contains the pairs (u_i, v_i), (u_j, v_j), ..., (u_k, v_k) and its solution would be $w = u_i u_j \ldots u_k a_k \ldots a_j a_i = v_i v_j \ldots v_k a_k \ldots a_j a_i$. It means, P has a solution and we have a procedure to find the solution of PCP, which is not correct. Since, $L(G_1) = L(G_2)$ can be thought as a correspondence system and we know that PCP is undecidable. Hence, we conclude that "whether $L(G_1) = L(G_2)$ or not" is also undecidable.

Example 10.4: It is undecidable for an arbitrary context-free grammar G whether is $\overline{L(G)}$ context-free language or not.

Proof: We convert this problem into another undecidable problem about context-free grammars. Let "$\overline{L(G)}$ is context-free language" is decidable. We know that $L(G)$ and $\overline{L(G)}$ are complement of each other. So, $L(G) \cap \overline{L(G)} = \phi$, it means, deciding intersection of two arbitrary context-free languages is ϕ or not is decidable. But, we know that deciding intersection of two arbitrary context-free languages whether it is ϕ or not is undecidable. So, our assumption about $\overline{L(G)}$ is not correct. Since, the given problem can be thought as another undecidable problem; hence the given problem is also undecidable.

Example 10.5: Show that following are undecidable for a regular language L over some alphabet Σ.

(a) Is the prefix language L_1 regular for $L = L_1L_2$?

(b) Is the suffix language L_2 regular for $L = L_1L_2$?

(c) Is the sublanguage L_2 regular for $L = L_1L_2L_3$?

Solution: We will discuss some examples to prove the above.

(a) Let $\Sigma = \{a, b\}$ and $L = a^*b^* = L_1L_2$, where $L_1 = a^*$ and $L_2 = b^*$. Obviously, L_1 and L_2 are regular language.

Now, if $L_1 = \{a^nb^n: n \geq 0\}$, then $L_2 = b^*$, it means L_1 is a context-free language and L_2 is a regular language. So, we conclude that the prefix language L_1 may or may not be a regular language. Therefore, the problem "Is the prefix language L_1 regular for $L = L_1L_2$?" is undecidable.

(b) Let $\Sigma = \{a, b\}$ and $L = a^*b^* = L_1L_2$, where $L_1 = a^*$ and $L_2 = b^*$. Obviously, L_1 and L_2 are regular language. Now, if $L_2 = \{a^nb^n: n \geq 0\}$, then $L_1 = a^*$, it means L_1 is a regular language and L_2 is a CFL. So, we conclude that the suffix language L_2 may or may not be a regular language. Therefore, the problem "Is the suffix language L_2 regular for $L = L_1L_2$?" is undecidable.

(c) Let $\Sigma = \{a, b\}$ and $L = a^*b^* = L_1L_2L_3$, where $L_1 = a^*$, $L_2 = a^*$, and $L_3 = b^*$. Obviously, L_1, L_2, and L_3 are regular language. Now, if $L_1 = a^*$, $L_2 = \{a^nb^n: n \geq 0\}$, then $L_3 = b^*$, it means L_2 is a CFL and L_1 and L_3 are regular language. So, we conclude that the sublanguage L_2 may or may not be a regular language. Therefore, the problem "Is the sublanguage L_2 regular for $L = L_1L_2L_3$?" is undecidable.

Example 10.6: Let $A = \{001, 0011, 11, 101\}$ and $B = \{01, 111, 111, 010\}$. Does the pair (A, B) has a Post Correspondence solution?

Solution: Let $A = \{a_1, a_2, a_3, a_4\}$ and $B = \{b_1, b_2, b_3, b_4\}$ are the given pair. We have,

$a_1 = 001$, $a_2 = 0011$, $a_3 = 11$, $a_4 = 101$, $b_1 = 01$, $b_2 = 111$, $b_3 = 111$, $b_4 = 010$

We have Post correspondence solution:

$a_3a_4a_3a_4a_1a_3a_4a_2a_3 = b_2b_1b_3b_4b_1b_3b_4b_1b_2 = 111\ 01\ 111\ 010\ 01\ 111\ 010\ 01\ 111$

For other solutions, we can repeat the above sequence.

Example 10.7: Let $X = \{11, 111, 100\}$ and $Y = \{111, 11, 001\}$. Does the pair (X, Y) has Post Correspondence solution?

Solution: Let $X = \{u_1, u_2, u_3\}$ and $Y = \{v_1, v_2, v_3\}$ are the objects in the given pair, so we have: $u_1 = 11$, $u_2 = 111$, $u_3 = 100$, and $v_1 = 111$, $v_2 = 11$, $v_3 = 001$

We have Post Correspondence solution: $u_1u_3u_2 = v_1v_3v_2 = 11100111$

TEST YOUR SKILLS

Supplementary Problems

10.1 Show that if L_1 and L_2 are regular and CFL respectively over Σ, then deciding whether $L_1 \subseteq L_2$ or not, is undecidable.

10.2 Show that following are undecidable for two arbitrary CFGs, G_1 and G_2.

(a) $L(G_1) \cap L(G_2)$ is CFG

(b) $L(G_1) \subset L(G_2)$

(c) $L(G_1)$ is regular

10.3 Show that union of recursive enumerable and recursive languages is recursive enumerable language.

10.4 Show that for two regular languages L_1 and L_2, the problem of deciding whether L_1 and L_2 are disjoint or not, is decidable.

10.5 Show that "*an arbitrary TM M halts on every input*" is undecidable.

10.6 Show that the problem "*an arbitrary TM M halts on empty word or not*" also known as *empty word problem* is undecidable.

10.7 Let a decision problem X be defined as follows:

X: Given a TM M over Σ and any word $w \in \Sigma^*$, does M loops forever on w?

You may assume that the HP of TM is undecidable but partially decidable.

(a) Show that X is undecidable.

(b) Show that X is not even partially decidable. **(GATE 2001)**

10.8 Show that the following problems are partially decidable for type 0 grammars.

(a) Membership problem

(b) Emptiness problem

10.9 Show that the membership problem is decidable for type 1 grammars.

10.10 Show that following are decidable:

(a) Concatenation of two recursive enumerable languages is recursive enumerable.

(b) Concatenation of two recursive languages is recursive.

10.11 Show that following are decidable for finite automaton and regular languages:

(a) Emptiness problem for finite automata

(b) Complement of emptiness problem of finite automata

(c) Finiteness of regular language (or regular set)

(d) Equivalence of two regular sets (or regular languages)

Multiple Choice Questions

10.12 Some problem is decidable if there is

(a) An algorithm that answers either "YES" or "NO"

(b) An algorithm that answers both "YES" and "NO"

(c) A TM that computes it

(d) Both the (a) and (c)

10.13 PCP is first suggested by

(a) Allan turing
(b) Emil post
(c) Kurt godel
(d) None

10.14 PCP is to determine a

(a) String
(b) Match
(c) Undecidability
(d) None

10.15 If L_1 and L_2 are two regular languages then the problem "Is $L_1 \oplus L_2$ (L_1 EX-OR L_2) regular? is

(a) Decidable
(b) Undecidable
(c) Regular
(d) Both (a) and (c) statements.

10.16 PCP over {a} is

(a) Decidable always
(b) Undecidable always
(c) Some time decidable
(d) Undecidable some time

10.17 Let G_1 and G_2 are two grammars and G_1 is a regular grammar. The problem $L(G_1) = L(G_2)$ or not is decidable when

(a) G_2 is type 0 grammar
(b) G_2 is CFG
(c) G_2 is regular grammar
(d) G_2 is CSG

10.18 If $L_1, L_2, \ldots, L_n$ are regular languages, then $L = L_1 \cup L_2 \cup \ldots \cup L_n$ is regular. This is

(a) Undecidable
(b) Decidable
(c) Dependent on nature of $L_1, L_2, \ldots, L_n$
(d) Partially decidable

10.19 If $L_1, L_2, \ldots, L_n$ are regular languages, then $L = L_1 \cap L_2 \cap \ldots \cap L_n$ is regular. This is

(a) Undecidable
(b) Decidable
(c) Dependent on nature of $L_1, L_2, \ldots, L_n$
(d) Partially decidable

10.20 If $L_1, L_2, \ldots, L_n$ are regular languages, then $L = L_1 \oplus L_2 \oplus \ldots \oplus L_n$ is regular. This is

(a) Undecidable
(b) Decidable
(c) Dependent on nature of $L_1, L_2, \ldots, L_n$
(d) Partially decidable

10.21 Deciding ambiguity of a language generated by a CFG is

(a) Decidable
(b) Depend on nature of the grammar
(c) Undecidable
(d) None of the above

10.22 Choose the correct statement

(a) Recursive languages are closed under union and intersection
(b) $L = \{a^n b^n c^n : n \geq 1\}$ is recursive language
(c) Every recursive language is recursive enumerable
(d) All the above statements

10.23 If a language L and its complement $\overline{L}$ are regular then choose the correct statement

(a) L is recursive but not $\overline{L}$
(b) Both L and L are recursive
(c) $\overline{L}$ is recursive but not L
(d) None

10.24 Choose the correct statement

(a) Recursive languages are closed under complement

(b) Recursive enumerable languages are closed under union

(c) If language L and its complement is recursive enumerable then L and are recursive.

(d) All the above statements

10.25 If there is a Turing machine M for a problem set P. M is applied to any problem in the set P and terminates when answer is "YES" and may or may not terminate otherwise, them P is

(a) Solvable (b) Unsolvable

(c) Partially solvable (d) None

10.26 The statement "A Turing machine cannot solve HP" is

(a) False (b) True

(c) Still an open question (d) None

10.27 Consider the following problem X:

"Given a Turing machine M over the input alphabet Σ, any state q of M and a word $w \in \Sigma^*$, does the computation of M on w visit the state q?"

Which of the following statements about X is correct? **(GATE 2001)**

(a) X is decidable

(b) X is undecidable but partially decidable

(c) X is undecidable and not even partially decidable

(d) X is not a decision problem

Answers

10.12 (d)	10.13 (b)	10.14 (b)	10.15 (a)	10.16 (a)
10.17 (c)	10.18 (b)	10.19 (b)	10.20 (b)	10.21 (c)
10.22 (d)	10.23 (b)	10.24 (d)	10.25 (c)	10.26 (b)
10.27 (c)				

CHAPTER 11

Linear Bounded Automata and Context-Sensitive Languages

Linear bounded automata(LBA)are restricted form of Turing machines. The only difference is in the size of the input tape used by linear bounded automata. Turing machine has an infinite length input tape but linear-bounded automatause input tape whose length is **k×n** squares (cells) long, where **n** is the length of the initial input and k is particular constant associated with the linear-bounded automata. For the further processing, linear bounded automata use multi-track single tape. The number of tracks selected for some linear bounded automatondepends upon the kind of processing it requires.

First time in 1960, *John Myhill* introduced the notion of deterministic linear bounded automata (DLBA). In 1963, *Peter S. Landweber* proved that the languages accepted by DLBA are context-sensitive languages. In 1964, *S. Y. Kuroda*in his paper titled "*Classes of Languages of & Linear-Bounded Automata*", Information and Control Journal, Vol. 7, pages 207-223 introduced the more general model which is known as nondeterministic linear bounded automata (NLBA) and showed that the languages accepted by NLBAare precisely the context-sensitive languages. Later on so many research papers are published on LBA describing the decidability and undecidability problems. We will discuss some of these problems later on in this chapter.

Linear bounded automata are mainly non-deterministic machine but there is deterministic form also which perform what non-deterministic LBA but it is debatable till nowwhether non-deterministic form is more powerful than deterministic form. These were initially developed as models of actual computers rather than model of computational process. But these are not considered as much applicable what pushdown automata are. The positive part about the linear bounded automata is its finite storage and computers also have finite storage and perform the tasks in lesser complex manner as compared to what Turing machines do.

11.1 LINEAR BOUNDED AUTOMATA (LBA)

A linear bounded automaton(LBA) is a multi-track single tape Turing machine and its tape length is in proportion of the input. A model of linear bounded automata (LBA) is shown in Fig. 11.1. It possesses a single track tape made up of cells that can contain symbols from a finitealphabet, a head that can read from and write to on the tape and can move left or right on the tape utilizing finite number of states. A finite contiguous portion of the tape whose length is a linear function of the length of the initial input can be accessed by the read/write head. This limitation makes LBA a more accurate model of computers that actually exist than a Turing machine in some respects.

LBA is designed to use limited storage. So, as a safety feature, we shall employ end markers ($ on the left and ψ on the right) on tape and never allow the machine to go past them. This will ensure that the storage bounds are maintained and help keep our machines from leaving their tape. In case of multi-track tape, the first track is used for input always and other tracks are used for processing. It does not mean that first track is read-only. Linear bounded can read and write on either of the tracks of the tape.

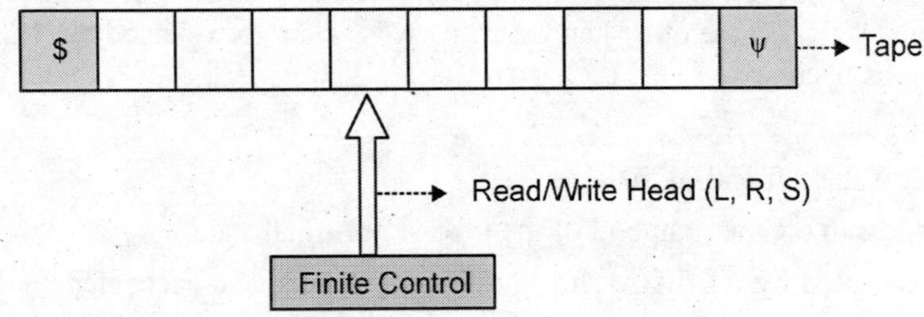

Fig. 11.1: Model of Linear Bounded Automata

Linear bounded automata can be described by 5-tuples (Q, Σ, δ, s, F), where

(1) **Q** is the finite set of states.

(2) Σ is the alphabet containing the blank symbol (#), two end markers symbols '$' and 'ψ', but not containing the symbols L (left), R (right), and S(static). Symbols from this alphabet can be read or write (excluding end markers) on the tape.

(3) **δ** is the transition function which maps from **Q×Σ(t_i) to (Q×(Σ(t_i) {L, R, S})**, where t_i is the track on which symbol is to be read and write.

(4) **s∈Q** is the initial state or starting state.

(5) F⊂Q, is the finite set of final states.

We have discussed the configuration of pushdown automata (PDA) in Chapter-7. Similarly configuration of a LBA, M=(Q, Σ, δ, s, F) defined as a member of

Q×Σ*×Σ×(Σ*-{#}), where **#** stands for blank

In other form, a configuration for single track LBAis: (**Presentstate, w_1, a, w_2**), where input string $w=w_1aw_2$ and symbol 'a' is the present input symbol under the head, w_1 is already read string, and w_2 is the string after the current head position. For **example**, (s, aa, a, ψ), (q, abab, b, aba) are two configurations. Suppose, if transition δ(s, a)=(q, b, R) then we have following relation:

$$(s, \$, a, bw\psi) \vdash_M (q, \$a, b, w\psi)$$

The above configurations are also known as consecutive configurations. We also use reflexive-transitive relation for two or more consecutive configurations by following representation: $\vdash_M^*$.

If string w is accepted by some LBA M if the head of M reaches the rightmost cell on the tape and processing ends in one of the final states. If the processing not ends in some of final states (F), the string is rejected. Such LBA are known as **deterministic LBA** (DLBA) by the definition given by *J. Myhill* (1960). The set of all strings accepted by M is known as language accepted by M also represented by L(M). The transition function of M is multivalued, in other words, for certain input symbol there is one or more transition. This is similar the transition function of the NFA as discussed in Chapter-3. Such LBA are known as **nondeterministic LBA** (NLBA). We then mean by a string accepted by NLBA M, for which there is a processing of M which, given the string as an input ends up off the right end of the tape in a final state. On the other hand, a string w is said to be rejected by NLBA M if one of the following conditions occurs:

(1) Processing never ends

(2) Ends up off the left end of the tape

(3) Finally ends up off the right end of the tape in non-final state

The strings accepted by NLBA M are known as the languages accepted by M and the strings rejected by M are called the languages rejected by M. It is important to know that *because of the non-determinacy characteristic of NLBA M, a certain string can be accepted or rejected both by M.* When we say LBA it means NLBA in the rest of this chapter. So, readers are advised not to be confused about this unless it is specified.

LBA are accepters for the class of context-sensitive languages. The only restriction placed on grammars for such languages is that no production maps a string to a shorter string. Thus no derivation of a string in a context-sensitive language can contain a sentential form longer than the string itself. Since there is a one-to-one correspondence between linear-bounded automata and such grammars, no more tape than that occupied by the original string is necessary for the string to be recognized by the automata. We will see the proof later on in this chapter.

Now let us see some reorganization done by LBA.

(1) Design a linear bounded automaton for the language $L=\{a^nb^n: n_1\}$.

Solution: Method 1: Let linear bounded automaton, M=(Q, {a, b, #}, δ, s, {h}) recognizes the language L. M is shown in Fig. 11.2(a). M is single track LBA. M goes back and forth while reading the input on the tape and compares a's from left with b's from the right hand of the tape. If number of a's in left hand side is equal to number of b's at right hand side then M halts in final state h and accepts the input. We assume that M starts in initial state s and current symbol is 'a' under the head. The symbol 'ψ' represent the right end the tape.

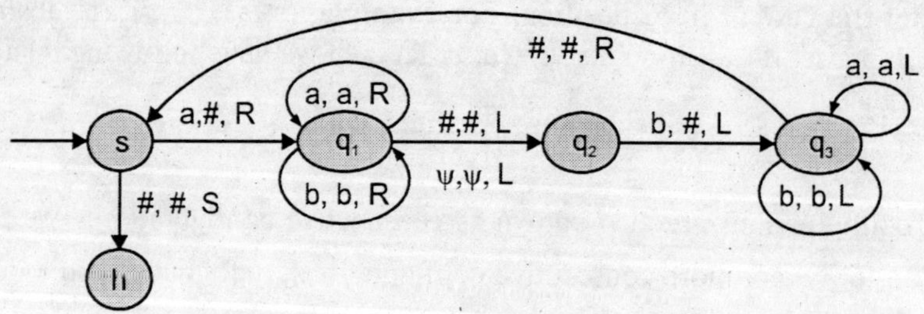

Fig. 11.2 (a): LBA for $L = \{a^nb^n: n \geq 1\}$

Method 2: Let linear bounded automaton, M=(Q, {a, b, #}, δ, s, {h}) recognizes the language L with two track tape. On the first track input is given and second track is blank initially. M copies a's on the second track and matches with b's on the first track. This is rather simpler automaton than earlier one. M is shown in Fig. 11.2(b). The t_1 and t_2 are track number of the tape. The transitions are labeled as [read symbol on track 1, write symbol of track 1, read symbol on track 2, write symbol on track 2, movement (R)]. [a/t_1, $\#/t_1$, $\#/t_2$, a/t_2, R] represents LBA reads symbol 'a' on track 1(a/t_1), writes blank on track 1 ($\#/t_1$), reads blank on track 2 ($\#/t_2$), writes symbol 'a' on track 2 (a/t_2), and moves one cell right on the tape. In this way all the 'a' symbols are copied on track 2. When LBA reads symbol 'b' on track 1, its reads symbol 'a' on track 2 and writes blank in place of both read symbols. In other words, all the 'b' symbols on track 1 are matched with 'a' symbols on track 2. When end of tape reached (ψ), LBA halts in final state h and input string w is accepted.

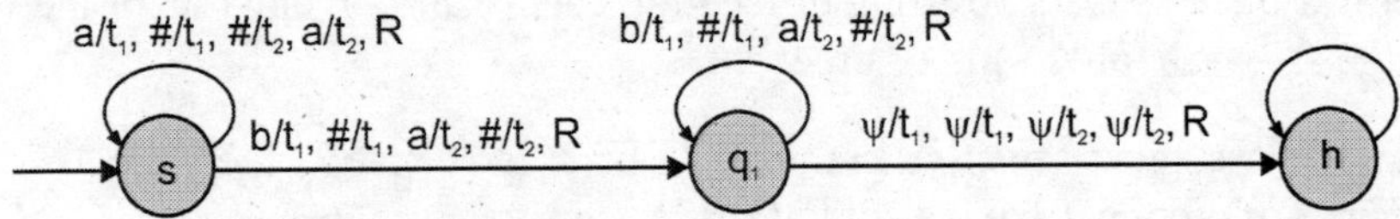

Fig. 11.2 (b): LBA for $L=\{a^nb^n: n \geq 1\}$

(2) Design LBA for the language $\{a^n \mid n \text{ is a perfect square}\}$.

Solution: Here LBAshall use a four track tape with the input written on the first track. The second and third tracks are used for processing work and the fourth track is used to hold strings of square length. The string on fourth track is to be matched against the input string on first track. First question is how to generate the strings of perfect square length. The second and third tracks are used for this purpose. On the second track, the strings of length k = 1, 2, 3, ... are generated. For each string on second track, we hold a counter (k) on third track and we constructa perfect square length string on fourth track. To do so the string on the second track is copiedon the fourth track exactly 'k' times. The third track is used to count down from 'k'. Then the input string on first track is compared with the string (perfect square length) on the fourth track. This process in on for next value of 'k' (k=k+1) and so on until overflow takes place on fourth track or input is matched. The algorithm is given below.

Algorithm to Recognize language $L=\{a^n \mid n \text{ is a perfect square}\}$

1. Select a Four Tracks Tape of the size of the input string
2. Make the 3rd and 4th tracks blank

   Repeat

   {

   (i) Write another symbol 'a' on the the 2nd track

   (ii) Copy the content of 2nd track to the 3rd track

   (iii) While (there are a's written on the 3rd track)

      (a) Make an 'a' blank from the 3rd track

      (b) Write the content of 2nd track on the 4th track

      (c) If overflow takes place, REJECT and EXIT

   (iv) Compare the contents of 1st and 4th tracks, if contents are matched, ACCEPT and EXIT.

   }

11.2 LINEAR BOUNDED AUTOMATA AND CONTEXT-SENSITIVE LANGUAGES

Our interest in nondeterministic LBA's stems from the fact that the class of sets accepted is precisely the class of context-sensitive languages. We will see some definitions regarding context-sensitive grammars and some lemmas. Later on we will see the relationship of context-sensitive languages and linear bounded automata. The closure properties of the context-sensitive languages are also discussed.

11.2.1 Length Preserving and Linear-Bounded Context-Sensitive Grammars

Definition: A context-sensitive grammar G = (V_n, Σ, P, S) has production rule of the form: αβ such that $|\alpha| \le |\beta|$ where α, β∈$(V_n \cup \Sigma)^*$ and α has at least one element from V_n. The grammar G is said to be of order n if there appears no string of length greater than n in any rule of the G. For example, G=({S}, {a, b}, {S→aSb | ab}, S) is of order n=3.

Lemma 11.1: For a context-sensitive grammar G of order n ($n \ge 3$) there exists another context-sensitive grammar of order n-1 equivalent to G.

Proof: Suppose the given context-sensitive grammar G=(V, Σ, P, S). The equivalent grammar of order n-1 is $G_1=(V_1, \Sigma, P_1, S)$. The production rules of G are of form

$\alpha \to \beta$ where α, ∈ $(V \cup \Sigma)^*$ such that $|\alpha| \le |\beta|$

It is fact that not all production rules of G are order of n. So, we select the production rules according to their order. We assume that no rule of G contains the terminal symbol unless it is of the form A→a where A∈V and a∈Σ. If terminals are there in production rules then we replace each terminal by new a variable.

Case 1: If $|\beta| < 3$ then all the production rules of G are in G_1.

Case 2: If $|\beta| \ge 3$

Suppose the production rule of G is of form

(1) $A \to BCD\beta'$ then $A \to A_1A_2$ and $A_1 \to BC$, $A_2 \to D\beta'$ where A_1 & A_2 are two new variables in V_1

(2) $A\alpha' \to BCD\beta'$ where $\alpha' = E\alpha''$ then this production rule is replaced by rules

$AE \to A'E'$, $A' \to B$, $E' \to CD\beta'$ where A′ and B′ two new variables in V_1

We can see that all the production rules of G_1 are order n-1 and equivalent to G. It should be noted that the above form and conversions of the production rules are given as per the proposal by S. Y. Kuroda (1964). There may be some different approach. For example, we can convert the given grammar into lower order equivalent grammar without replacing the terminals of production rules by some new variables.

For example, consider the context-sensitive grammar G=({S, A}, {a, b, c}, {S→abc | aSAc, cA→Ac, bA→bb}, S) of order 4. Find an equivalent grammar of order 3.

Solution: Suppose the equivalent grammar $G_1=(V_1, \{a, b, c\}, P_1, S)$. There should not be any terminal in the production rules of G unless it is of the form A→a. So, we introduce following new production rules in G_1:

$A_1 \to a$, $B_1 \to b$, and $C_1 \to c$

Now, the production rules of G are

$S \to A_1B_1C_1 \mid A_1SAC_1$, $C_1A \to AC_1$, $B_1A \to B_1B_1$

Case 1: All production rules of order 3 or less are in G_1. So following rules are in G_1:

$S \to A_1B_1C_1$, $C_1A \to AC_1$, $B_1A \to B_1B_1$

Case 2: Consider the production rules of G of higher order. There is only one production rule $S \to A_1SAC_1$ of order 4.

So, production rules $S \to A_2A_3$, $A_2 \to A_1S$, $A_3 \to AC_1$ where A_2 and A_3 are two new variables are in G_1 and $V_1=\{S, A_1, A_2, A_3, B_1, C_1\}$.

So, all the production rules in G1 are of order 3 or lesser. Thus G is of order 3. One thing noticeable here that we have only one variable in left hand side of the production rule of order 4 in G. So, there is no need to execute second part of the case 2 in Lemma 12.1.

Lemma 11.2: Any context-sensitive grammar can be reduced to equivalent order 2 context-sensitive grammar.

Proof: Please see the Lemma 11.1 and corresponding reduction method can be applied more times to find out order 2 grammar. For order n ($n \geq 3$) context-sensitive grammar, there is need of applying (n-1) times the reduction method.

A context-sensitive grammar is **length-preserving** if for any rule $\alpha \to \beta$ it satisfies either of the following two conditions:

(1) α is the initial symbol

(2) β does not contain the initial symbol and lengths of α and β are equal

For example, $S \to aSBA$, $BA \to AB$, $A \to a$, $B \to b$ where S is the initial symbol. These production rules are length preserving.

A context-sensitive grammar G is **linear-bounded** if it satisfies following conditions:

(1) G is order 2

(2) Length preserving and

(3) Production rule $S \to EF$ shows E=S, where S is the initial symbol of G

Lemma 11.3: (**Kuroda Normal Form**) For any context-sensitive grammar G of order 2, there exists a linear-bounded grammar G_1 equivalent to G.

Proof: Let given grammar $G=(V_n, \Sigma, P, S)$ and equivalent linear-bounded grammar $G_1=(V_1, \Sigma, P_1, S_1)$. We defined the set of variables $V_1=V_n \cup \{S_1, Q\}$ where Q is new variable and S_1 is initial symbol. The production rules of G_1 are defined by rules R_1, R_2 and R_3:

Rule R_1: New production rules to derive initial symbol of G

$S_1 \to S_1Q$,

$S_1 \to S$ where S is the initial symbol of G

Rule R_2: New production rules for all symbols in $(V_n \cup \Sigma)$

$Q\alpha \to \alpha Q$,

$\alpha Q \to Q\alpha$ where $\alpha \in (V_n \cup \Sigma)$

Rule R_3: For given production rules of G

$A \to B$ if $A \to B$ is a rule in G,

AB→CD   if AB→CD is a rule in G,

AQ→BC   if A→BC is a rule in G

All the production rules of G_1 are linear-bounded.If G_1 derives string $w \in \Sigma^*$, it means $S_1 \overset{*}{\Rightarrow} w$. It follows $S \overset{*}{\Rightarrow} w$ from rule R_1. Therefore, $L(G_1) \subset L(G)$. If the string w is derived by G then it means $SQ^n \Rightarrow w$ is in G_1. So by applying R_1, we

Theorem 11.1: If G is a context-sensitive grammar then there is a linear bounded automaton (LBA) M such that L(M)=L(G).

Proof: Suppose the given context-sensitive grammar $G=(V_n, \Sigma, P, S)$. We will use four tracks tape for linear bounded automaton M. The length of the tape is in order of the input string. The first, second, third, and fourth tracks are used for input string, derivation using production rules of G, replacement, and replaceable sentence (RS) respectively.

Track No.	**Used For**
1	Input
2	Derivation
3	Replacement
4	Replaceable Sentence

Let us see the meaning and use of the terms derivation, replacement, and replaceable sentence (RS). Suppose P includes production rules {S→abc | aSAc, cA→Ac, bA→bb} where $S, A \in V_n$, and a, b, $c \in \Sigma$. The string w=aabbcc is produced by grammar G:

Production	Derivation	Replacement	Replaceable Sentence (RS)
S⇒a**S**Ac	aSAc	aSAc	S
⇒aab**cA**c	aabcAc	abc	S
⇒aa**bA**cc	aabAcc	Ac	cA
⇒aabbcc	aabbcc	bb	bA

It is clear from the above table illustration that the suitable right hand side of a production rule is considered as replacement and the left hand side of the that production rule is considered as replaceable sentence (RS).

Suppose $M=(Q, \Sigma_1, \delta, s, F)$ where $\Sigma_1=\Sigma \cup V_n \cup \{\#\}$. The LBA M is implemented based on the following algorithm.

Algorithm (Context-sensitive Grammar G, Linear Bounded Automaton M)

1. Input string is written on 1st track. The initial symbol S is written on 2nd track and 3rd and 4th tracks are blank.
2. Repeat
   (i) Read the 2nd track from the left end and find out replaceable sentence (RS) and write on the 4th track.
   (ii) Read the production rules of G and write right side of the RS on 3rd track.

(iii) Write content of 2nd track which is after RS on the 3rd track. If overflow occurs then EXIT with message "NOT ACCEPTED".

(iv) Copy the content of 3rd track on 2nd track replacing the RS and content after RS.

(v) Compare the contents of 1st and 2nd tracks. If contents are same then EXIT with message "ACCEPTED".

(vi) Make the 3rd and 4th tracks blank.

It is clear from the above algorithm that it tries to simulate the right derivation for the given input string on 2nd track. The 3rd track is used to hold the replacement for a RS. The 4th track is used to hold the current RS and find out the position of RS on the 2nd track. Without it the steps in 2(iii) and 2(iv) of the proposed algorithm will not function properly. Each time step 2(v) is executed, the contents of 1st and 2nd tracks are compared and if matched then LBA M accepts the input string. If overflow occurs in step 2(iii) then LBA terminates the process and string is not accepted.

The length of the derivation for a string w does not go beyond the length of the string w. So, the length of tape is in order of the length of input string. If the length of derivation on 2nd track goes beyond the length of the input string, it means either string w is not derived by G or LBA M does not follow the right replaceable sentence. If the LBA M does not select the right production rules of the grammar G then input string w might be rejected even it is derived by the G. So, we believe that LBA M exploits its nondeterminitic characteristic and select right production rules and RS. The space and time complexity of the LBA M are O(n) and O(n×m) respectively where n and m are length of input string and number of production rules in G respectively.

For example, consider the context-sensitive grammar G=({S, A}, {a, b, c}, {S→abc | aSAc, cA→Ac, bA→bb}, S). The LBA M=(Q, {a, b, c, S, A, #}, δ, s, F) be the automaton which accepts L(G). Suppose input string w=aabbcc is to be processed by M. The LBA M is implemented on above algorithm and executes the following. The tape contents in each step are:

1.

1st track	$aabbccψ
2nd track	$Sψ
3rd track	
4th track	

2(i)

1st track	$aabbccψ
2nd track	$Sψ
3rd track	
4th track	$Sψ

2(ii)

1st track	$aabbccψ
2nd track	$Sψ
3rd track	$aSAcψ
4th track	$Sψ

2(iii)

1st track	$aabbccψ
2nd track	$Sψ
3rd track	$aSAcψ
4th track	$Sψ

2(iv)

1st track	$aabbccψ
2nd track	$aSAcψ
3rd track	$aSAcψ
4th track	$Sψ

2(v)

1st track	$aabbccψ
2nd track	$aSAcψ
3rd track	$aSAcψ
4th track	$Sψ

	2(vi)	2(i)	2(ii)
1st track	$aabbccψ	$aabbccψ	$aabbccψ
2nd track	$aS**Ac**ψ	$a**S**Acψ	$a**S**Acψ
3rd track			$**abc**ψ
4th track		$Sψ	$Sψ

	2(iii)	2(iv)	2(v)
1st track	$aabbccψ	$aabbccψ	$aabbccψ
2nd track	$aSAcψ	$aabc**Ac**ψ	$aabcAcψ
3rd track	$abc**Ac**ψ	$abcAcψ	$abcAcψ
4th track	$Sψ	$Sψ	$Sψ

	2(vi)	2(i)	2(ii)
1st track	$aabbccψ	$aabbccψ	$aabbccψ
2nd track	$aabcAcψ	$aabc**Ac**ψ	$aabcAcψ
3rd track			$Acψ
4th track		$c**A**ψ	$cAψ

	2(iii)	2(iv)	2(v)
1st track	$aabbccψ	$aabbccψ	$aabbccψ
2nd track	$aabcAcψ	$aab**Acc**ψ	$aabAccψ
3rd track	$A**cc**ψ	$Accψ	$Accψ
4th track	$cAψ	$cAψ	$cAψ

	2(vi)	2(i)	2(ii)
1st track	$aabbccψ	$aabbccψ	$aabbccψ
2nd track	$aabAccψ	$aab**A**ccψ	$aabAccψ
3rd track			$**bb**ψ
4th track		$**bA**ψ	$bAψ

	2(iii)	2(iv)	2(v) **Accepted**
1st track	$aabbccψ	$aabbccψ	$aabbccψ
2nd track	$aabAccψ	$aa**bbcc**ψ	$aabbccψ
3rd track	$bb**cc**ψ	$bbccψ	$bbccψ
4th track	$bAψ	$bAψ	$bAψ

Lemma 11.4: If L is context-sensitive language then it is accepted by some linear bounded automaton (LBA).

(Please read the Theorem 11.1)

Lemma 11.5: If G is context-sensitive grammar then the language $L=L(G)-\{\varepsilon\}$ is accepted by some linear bounded automaton (LBA).

(Please read the Theorem 11.1)

Lemma 11.6: For any linear-bounded grammar G there exists a linear bounded automaton which accepts the language L(G) generated by G.

Proof: Suppose linear-bounded grammar $G=(V_n, \Sigma, P, S_1)$ and L(G) is accepted by linear bounded automaton $M=(Q, \Sigma_1, \delta, q_0, \{q_0\})$ where $\Sigma_1=V_n \cup \Sigma$. The set of states Q includes the states q_0, q_1, s_0, s_1, r_0, r_1, and s_A for each A such that $AB \rightarrow CD$ is in P. The state q_0 is the initial and final state. We suppose that input input is placed on the tape between two blank symbols (#w#). The transition function δ is defined as:

(1) $\delta(q_0, \#)=(q_1, \#, R)$

(2) $\delta(q_1, a)=(q_1, a, R)$ for all $a \in \Sigma$

(3) $\delta(q_1, \#)=(s_0, \#, L)$

(4) $\delta(s_0, \alpha)=(s_0, \alpha, R)$ and $\delta(s_0, \alpha)=(s_0, \alpha, L)$ for all $\alpha \in \Sigma_1$

(5) $\delta(s_0, B)=(s_0, A, S)$ for all production rules $A \rightarrow B$ in G

(6) $\delta(s_0, C)=(s_A, A, R)$ and $\delta(s_A, D)=(s_0, B, S)$ for all production rules $AB \rightarrow CD$ in G

(7) $\delta(s_0, S_1)=(r_0, S_1, L)$

(8) $\delta(r_0, \#)=(r_1, \#, R)$

(9) $\delta(r_1, S_1)=(s_1, \#, R)$ and $\delta(s_1, A)=(s_0, S_1, S)$ for all production rules $S \rightarrow SA$ in G

(10) $\delta(s_1, \#)=(q_0, \#, R)$

(11) $\delta(x, y)=(x, y, 0)$ for all other $\delta(x, y)$

The states q_0 and q_1 are used to verify the validity of the input. If input is placed between two blank symbol (#w#) then M enters states s_0. Otherwise input is rejected. Suppose w is the initial input on the tape then M finds x on the tape in states s_0, s_1, s_A after finite number of instructions. It means w is derived by x. In other words, if input w is derived by the grammar G then M finds $\#\#...\#S_1\#$ on the tape. When M reads S_1 in states s_0, it enters states r_0 and r_1. M moves back and forth in states r_1, s_1 and finally enters state q_0 (final) while reading # in state s_1. So, if $w \in L(G)$ then M accepts this string.

Theorem 11.2: If G is acontext-freegrammar then L(G) is accepted by some linear bounded automaton(LBA) M.

Proof: Let $G = (V_n, \Sigma, P, S_0)$ be the given context-free grammar (CFG). We construct a linear bounded automaton **M** such that the language accepted by M is **L(G).** We will discuss how M works based on the production rules of grammar G. We will use two tracks tape for M. The length of the tape is proportionate to length of input. On first track input is written and second track holds productions rules of G.

Step 1: Construction of LBA M:

Let LBA M=($\{q_o, q_1, q_2, h\}, \Sigma_1, \delta, q_o$), where $\Sigma_1=V_n\cup\Sigma$, the starting state is q_o. The starting symbol S_0 of G is written on second track. The transition function δ is defined by following three rules R_1, R_2, and R_3:

R_1: $\delta(q_o, \varepsilon, A)=\{(q_1, \varepsilon, \alpha_1, S), (q_1, \varepsilon, \alpha_2, S), \ldots, (q_1, \varepsilon, \alpha_n, S)\}$,

$\delta(q_1, \varepsilon, \beta)=(q_1, \varepsilon, \beta, L)$, $\delta(q_1, \varepsilon, \$)=(q_2, \varepsilon, \$, R)$ where $A\in V_n$, $\alpha_i\in((V_n\cup\Sigma)^+-\Sigma)$for i=1, 2, ..., n, and $\beta\in(V_n\cup\Sigma)$ such that $A\rightarrow\alpha_1|\alpha_2|\ldots|\alpha_n$, and S stands for static movement

R_2: $\delta(q_2, \varepsilon, A)=\{(q_0, \varepsilon, A, S)\}$, $\delta(q_2, a, a)=\{(q_2, \#, \#, R)\}$,

where, $a\in\Sigma$, $A\in V_n$, and R stands for right movement

R_3: $\delta(q_2, \psi, \#)=\{(h, \psi, \#, S)\}$,$\delta(q_2, \psi,\psi)=\{(h, \psi, \psi, S)\}$, where ψ is the right end marker of the tracks and # stands for blank cell.

Initially, LBA M puts right S-production rule on second track without reading the input symbol and remains static (R_1). For all other variables LBA M does the same thing; it keeps on reading ε on first track and places the right right-hand side of the variable on the second track and enters state q_2.In state q_2, M reads the content on second track and moves to left end the tape. Using rule R_2, M process the tape content in state q_2. If M reads a terminal symbol on second track then it compares with present input symbol on the first track and if it is matched, M moves to next input symbol. If M finds some variable, it moves to the state q_0 and use rule R_1 to copy the right hand side of the variable on second track. This process is going on for entire input symbols. Using rule R_3, M enters the final state h and string is accepted. If w is a string in the language L(G)then we have some leftmost derivation for w and that should be attempted by LBA M always. It means if M does not follow the right sequence which is in leftmost derivation of given string w then M will be failed.

If comparison is successful then M halts in final state and string on first track is accepted. If M does not guess the right transition then thecomparison fails and M halts without accepting.If w is in L(G)then there exists some sequence of moves in which the M constructs string w onsecond track. Likewise, for M to accept w, there must exist a sequence of moves such that w can be constructed on second track. Thus there must be a derivation of w from S_0 in G. It should be noticeable here that, the selection of production rules and intermediate forms in derivation are chosen randomly and it is believed that M chooses the right transition to accept the input string w.

Step 2: Proof for L(M)= L(G):

Let string w is in language L(G). Based on the construction method of LBA M, we have

Case1: Let $|w|=1$, it means w=a andrule $S_0\rightarrow a$ is in P, where $a\in\Sigma$.

$\delta(q_0, \varepsilon, S_0)=(q_1, \varepsilon, a, S)$, $\delta(q_1, \varepsilon, a)=(q_1, \varepsilon, a, L)$, $\delta(q_1, \varepsilon, \$)=(q_2, \varepsilon, \$, R)$, $\delta(q_2, a, a)=(q_2, \varepsilon, \varepsilon, R)$ and $\delta(q_2, \psi, \psi)=(h, \psi, \psi, S)$

Hence, string w=a, is accepted by LBA M.

Case 2: Let $|w|>1$, it means $w=a_1a_2\ldots a_n$, where $a_i\in\Sigma$ for i=1, 2 ... n and,

$S\overset{*}{\underset{L}{\Rightarrow}}w$ then $(q_0, \varepsilon, S_0)\overset{*}{\underset{M}{\vdash}}(q_2, \#, \#, R)$ (Using Rules R_1, R_2, and R_3)

And $\delta(q_2, \psi, \psi)=(h, \psi, \psi, S)$

Case 3: Let $|w|$=n+1 and w=$a_1a_2\ldots a_nb$

We have $S \overset{*}{\underset{L}{\Rightarrow}} w$ then $(q_0, \varepsilon, S_0) \overset{*}{\underset{M}{\vdash}} (q_2, b, b, R)$

And $\delta(q_2, b, b)=(q_2, \#, \#, R)$, $\delta(q_2, \psi, \psi)=(h, \psi, \psi, S)$ and string is accepted.

Therefore, all strings in L(G) are recognized by LBAM using rules R_1, R_2, and R_3if there is a leftmost derivation for w. Therefore, N(M)=L(G)

For **example**, consider a context-free grammar G=({A}, {a, b}, {A→aAb|ab}, A) and design a LBA and show the steps involved in processing of string w=ab.

Solution: Let LBA M=($\{q_o, q_1, q_2, h\}, \Sigma_1, \delta, \{q_o\}$), where $\Sigma_1=V_n\cup\Sigma$, the starting state is q_o. The transition function δ is defined as follows:

Using rule R_1:

$\delta(q_0, \varepsilon, A)=\{(q_1, \varepsilon, aAb, S), (q_1, \varepsilon, ab, S)\}$, $\delta(q_1, \varepsilon, A)=\{(q_1, \varepsilon, A, L)\}$, $\delta(q_1, \varepsilon, a)=\{(q_1, \varepsilon, a, L)\}$, $\delta(q_1, , b)=\{(q_1, \varepsilon, b, L)\}$, $\delta(q_1, \varepsilon, \$)=\{(q_2, \varepsilon, \$, R)\}$

Using rule R_2:

$\delta(q_2, \varepsilon, A)=\{(q_0, \varepsilon, A, S)\}$, $\delta(q_2, a, a)=\{(q_2, \#, \#, R)\}$, $\delta(q_2, b, b)=\{(q_2, b, b, R)\}$

Using rule R_3:

$\delta(q_2, \psi, \psi)=\{(h, \psi, \psi, S)\}$, $\delta(q_2, \psi, \#)=\{(h, \psi, \#, S)\}$

Processing of string w=ab:

$\delta(q_0, \$ab\psi, \$\underline{A}\psi) \underset{M}{\vdash} (q_1, \$ab\psi, \$a\underline{b}, S)$

$\delta(q_1, \$ab\psi, \$a\underline{b}\psi) \underset{M}{\vdash} (q_1, \$ab\psi, \$\underline{a}b\psi, L)$

$\delta(q_1, \$ab\psi, \$\underline{ab}\psi) \underset{M}{\vdash} (q_1, \$ab\psi, \underline{\$}ab\psi, L)$

$\delta(q_1, \$ab\psi, \underline{\$}ab\psi) \underset{M}{\vdash} (q_2, \$ab\psi, \$\underline{a}b\psi, R)$

$\delta(q_2, \$\underline{a}b\psi, \$\underline{a}b\psi) \underset{M}{\vdash} (q_2, \$\#\underline{b}\psi, \$\#\underline{b}\psi, R)$

$\delta(q_2, \$\#\underline{b}\psi, \$\#\underline{b}\psi) \underset{M}{\vdash} (q_2, \$\#\#\underline{\psi}, \$\#\#\underline{\psi}, R)$

$\delta(q_2, \$\#\#\underline{\psi}, \underline{\$\#\#\psi}) \underset{M}{\vdash} (h, \$\#\#\underline{\psi}, \$\#\#\underline{\psi}, S)$

Lemma 11.7: If G is context-free grammar then the language generated by G is accepted by some linear bounded automaton (LBA).

(Please read the Theorem 11.2)

Lemma 11.8: If G is context-free grammar then the language L=L(G)–{ε} is accepted by some linear bounded automaton (LBA).

(Please read the Theorem 11.2)

Theorem 11.3: If L is a language accepted by a linear bounded automaton M then L is context-sensitive.

Proof: We will discuss a construction method to build a context sensitive grammar from the given linear bounded automaton. Let M=(Q, Σ, δ, q_0, F) be the given linear bounded automaton (LBA) and the grammar G=(V_n, Σ, P, S_0) such that L(G)=L. The grammar G simulates the reverse of the operations of the LBA M.

Suppose Σ={a_1, a_2, a_3, ..., a_n} and Q={q_0, q_1, q_2, ..., q_m} are set of terminals and states respectively and q_0 is the initial state. We introduce variables (symbols) B_{ij} (i=1, 2, 3, ..., n; j=0, 1, 2, 3, ..., m) to represent terminal a_i and state q_j simultaneously. It is noticeable that |Σ|= n and |Q= m+1

The parameters of grammar G are defined as follows. V_n={b_{ij}}∪{S_0, A}, Σ is same for both G and M. The set of productions rules P is defined by three rules (R_1, R_2, R_3):

Rule R_1: S_0→B_{ij} and S_0→AB_{ij} are production rules in P. These rules are used to derive the variables B_{ij} from the starting symbol S_0. If LBA M reads symbol a_i in state q_j and enters a final state then A→a_i and A→Aa_i are in P for i=1, 2, 3, ..., n.

Rule R_2: To simulate the reverse operation of LBA M

(i) For δ(q_j, a_i)=(q_k, a_l, R), $a_l B_{rk}$→$B_{ij} a_r$ in P, where r=1, 2, 3, ..., n

(ii) For δ(q_j, a_i)=(q_k, a_l, L), $B_{rk} a_l$→$a_r B_{ij}$ in P, where r=1, 2, 3, ..., n

(iii) For δ(q_j, a_i)=(q_k, a_l, S), B_{lk}→B_{ij} in P

Rule R_3: B_{i0}→a_i for i=1, 2, 3, ..., n is in P.

It is very much clear from the production rules in P that all the rules are of type 1 and thus grammar G is type 1 grammar. Therefore, the language L accepted by LBA M is context-sensitive.

For example, consider a LBAM=({q_1, q_2, q_3, q_4, q_5}, {a, b, #}, δ, q_1, {q_5}) and transition function is defined as:

δ(q_1, a)=(q_2, #, R), δ(q_1, #)=(q_5, #, S), δ(q_2, a)=(q_2, a, R), δ(q_2, b)=(q_2, b, R), δ(q_2, ψ)=(q_3, ψ, L), δ(q_2, #)=(q_3, #, L), δ(q_3, b)=(q_4, #, L), δ(q_4, a)=(q_4, a, L), δ(q_4, b)=(q_4, b, L), δ(q_4, #)=(q_1, #, R)

Find the corresponding type 1 grammar.

Solution: Let grammar G=(V_n, Σ, P, S_0) be type 1 grammar corresponding to the given LBA M. The parameters of G are defined as:

Σ={a, b, #, ψ}, V_n={B_{ij}}∪{A, S_0} for i=1, 2, 3, 4 and j=1, 2, 3, 4, 5

P includes following production rules.

Using rules R_1:

S_0→B_{ij} and S_0→AB_{ij} are in P. When symbol # is read in state q_1, M enters the final state. So, rules A→# and A→A# are in P.

Using rule R_2:

For δ(q_1, a)=(q_2, #, R), rule #B_{r2}→$B_{11} a_r$ is in P where r=1, 2, 3, 4

For δ(q_1, #)=(q_5, #, S), rule B_{35}→B_{31} is in P

For δ(q_2, a)=(q_2, a, R), rule aB_{r2}→$B_{12} a_r$ is in P where r=1, 2, 3, 4

For δ(q_2, b)=(q_2, b, R), rule bB_{r2}→$B_{22} a_r$ is in P where r=1, 2, 3, 4

For $\delta(q_2, \psi)=(q_3, \psi, L)$, rule $B_{r3}\psi \rightarrow a_r B_{42}$ is in P where r=1, 2, 3, 4

For $\delta(q_2, \#)=(q_3, \#, L)$, rule $B_{r3}\# \rightarrow a_r B_{32}$ is in P where r=1, 2, 3, 4

For $\delta(q_3, b)=(q_4, \#, L)$, rule $B_{r4}\# \rightarrow a_r B_{23}$ is in P where r=1, 2, 3, 4

For $\delta(q_4, a)=(q_4, a, L)$, rule $B_{r4}a \rightarrow a_r B_{14}$ is in P where r=1, 2, 3, 4

For $\delta(q_4, b)=(q_4, b, L)$, rule $B_{r4}b \rightarrow a_r B_{24}$ is in P where r=1, 2, 3, 4

For $\delta(q_4, \#)=(q_1, \#, R)$, rule $\#B_{r1} \rightarrow B_{34}a_r$ is in P where r=1, 2, 3, 4

Using Rule R_3:

$B_{10}\rightarrow a$, $B_{20}\rightarrow b$, $B_{30}\rightarrow \#$, $B_{40}\rightarrow \psi$ are in P.

It is noticeable that all the variables induced by rules R_2 and R_3 are exactly the variable derived by S_0 using rule R_1. The terminals {a, b, #, ψ} are numbered as r = {1, 2, 3, 4} and states $\{q_1, q_2, q_3, q_4, q_5\}$ are numbered as j={1, 2, 3, 4, 5}.

Lemma 11.9: If w is a string generated by a context-sensitive grammar G, then it is accepted by some linear bounded automaton (LBA).

(Please read the Theorem 11.3)

Theorem 11.4: (Myhill-Landweber-Kuroda Theorem)

A language L is a context-sensitive language if and only if it is accepted by a linear bounded automaton (LBA).

(For proof, please read the Theorems 11.1 and 11.3)

Theorem 11.5: The halting problem of LBAis decidable.

Proof: We will focus on the argumentbased upon the number of possible configurations for alinear bounded automaton (LBA) M. Let us assume that we have aLBA with one track of length n, k instructions (number of states of M), an alphabet Σ forthe tape symbols. We will find the maximum number of possible configurations of M based on the number of states, number of input symbols, and length of the tape. Configuration of a linear bounded automaton consists of:

1. present state (an instruction) 2. the tape head's position, and 3. Content of the tape

Now, question ishow many different configurations can be there? We can easily find out the answer. With m symbols in Σ ($|\Sigma| = m$) and a tape having n cells, we can have only m^n different inputs. The head can read any of the n cells on the tape using any of the k instructions (k states). Therefore, there are only: $\mathbf{k \times n \times m^n}$ possible different configurations for the linear bounded automatonM which can executed by M. So, there is need of simulation and observationof M for $k \times n \times m^n$ steps. If it has not halted by then it must be in a loop and will never halt. So, the limited memory of the linear bounded automata solves the halting problem. If some LBA runs more than the possible configuration as discussed above then LBA is in loop and may never stop for the input. So, we can say that the halting problem for LBA is decidable.

Lemma 11.10: If L is a context-sensitive language and w∈L then a LBA M accepts w is decidable.

(Please see the Theorem 11.5)

Lemma 11.11: If L is a context-sensitive language and $w \in L$then whether a LBA M accepts w or not is decidable.

(Please see the Theorem 11.5)

11.2.2 Closure Properties of Context-Sensitive Languages

In this section, we will see different closure properties of context-sensitive languages. We will see that context-sensitive languages are closed under following properties:

1. Union
2. Concatenation
3. Complement
4. Intersection
5. Kleene Closure
6. Transpose

Theorem 11.6: If L_1 and L_2 are twocontext-sensitive languages then union of L_1 and L_2 is also a context-sensitive language (CSL).

Proof: Suppose language $L=L_1 \cup L_2$ where L_1 and L_2 are two given context-sensitive languages. We can prove L is a CSL by two ways; firstly using relevant grammars for L_1 and L_2 and finding the union of the two grammars and secondly by using the LBA.

(1) Using the Relevant Context-Sensitive Grammars

Let context-sensitive grammar $G_1=(V_{n1}, \Sigma_1, P_1, S_1)$ generates L_1, context-sensitive grammar $G_2= (V_{n2}, \Sigma_2, P_2, S_2)$ generates L_2 and grammar $G=(V_n, \Sigma, P, S)$ generates $L=L_1+L_2$. We construct the new grammar G as follows:

Step 1: Rename the variables of G_1:

Let $V_{n1}=\{S, A, B, \ldots, X\}$ then the renamed variables are $\{S_1, A_1, B_1, \ldots, X_1\}$. This modification should be reflected in production rules also.

Step 2: Rename the variables of G_2:

Let $V_{n2}=\{S, A, B, \ldots, X\}$ then the renamed variables are: $\{S_2, A_2, B_2, \ldots, X_2\}$. This modification should be reflected in production rules also.

Step 3: Union of the production rules of G_1 and G_2:

We introduce S-production as: $\mathbf{S \to S_1 \mid S_2}$, where S_1 and S_2 are starting symbols of grammars G_1 and G_2 respectively and S_1-productions and S_2-productions are remain unchanged.

Set of terminals $\Sigma=\Sigma_1 \cup \Sigma_2$, and set of variables $V_n=\{S_1, A_1, B_1, \ldots X_1\} \cup \{S_2, A_2, B_2, \ldots X_2\} \cup \{S\}$

Since, all production rules of G_1 and G_2 including $S \to S_1 \mid S_2$ are in context-sensitive form, so grammar G is a context-sensitive grammar (CSG).

Verification of Language generated by G:

L(G)=Language generated from S_1-productions **or** S_2-productions (Step 3)

$=L(G_1)$ or $L(G_2)$

$= L_1+ L_2$

Therefore, $L=L_1 \cup L_2$ is also a context-sensitive language.

(2) Using Linear Bounded Automata

Let L_1 and L_2 are accepted by two LBA M_1 and M_2 respectively as shown in Fig. 11.3(a) and

Fig.11.3 (b). We construct a third LBA M_3 which follows either M_1 or M_2 as shown in Fig. 11.3(c). LBA M_3 accepts a string if either M_1 accepts or M_2 accepts and rejects if either M_1 rejects or M_2 rejects. We can build LBA M_3 as a two tracks automaton. First and second tracks are used to simulate the behavior of M_1 and M_2 respectively. Obviously the language accepted by the M_3 is CSL. Therefore, union of two contest-sensitive languages is also contest-sensitive.

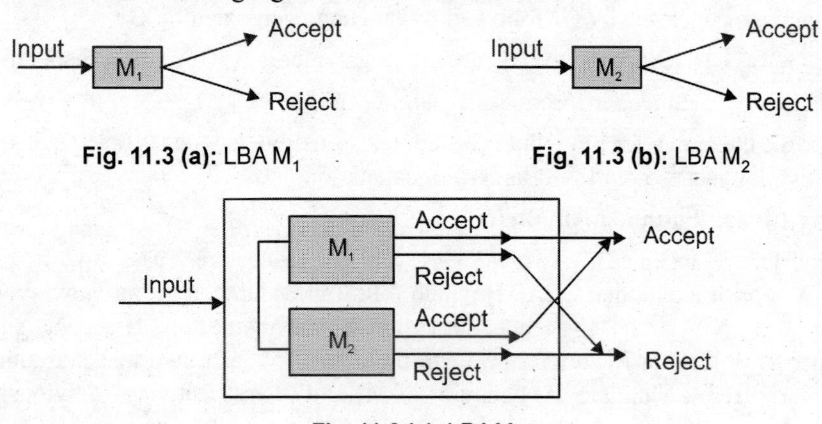

Fig. 11.3 (a): LBA M_1 **Fig. 11.3 (b):** LBA M_2

Fig. 11.3 (c): LBA M_3

Lemma 11.12: If G_1 and G_2 are two context-sensitive grammars (CSGs) then union of G_1 and G_2 is also a context-sensitive grammar.

(See the Theorem 11.6)

Theorem 11.7: If L_1 and L_2 are two context-sensitive languages then concatenation of L_1 and L_2 denoted by $\mathbf{L_1L_2}$ is also a context-sensitive language. In other words, context-sensitive languages are closed under concatenation operation.

Proof: Suppose language $L=L_1L_2$ where L_1 and L_2 are two given context-sensitive languages. We can prove L is a CSL by two ways; firstly using relevant grammars for L_1 and L_2 and finding the concatenation of the two grammars and secondly by using the LBA.

(1) Let context-sensitive grammar $G_1=(V_{n1}, \Sigma_1, P_1, S_1)$ generates language L_1 and context-sensitive grammar $G_2=(V_{n2}, \Sigma_2, P_2, S_2)$ generates language L_2. Let grammar $G=(V_n, \Sigma, P, S)$ generates $L=L_1L_2$. We construct grammar G as follows:

Step 1: Rename the variables of CSG G_1:

Let $V_{n1}=\{S, A, B, \ldots, P\}$ then the renamed variables are $\{S_1, A_1, B_1, \ldots, X_1\}$. This modification is reflected in production rules also.

Step 2: Rename the variables of CSG G_2:

Let $V_{n2}=\{S, A, B, \ldots, X\}$ then the renamed variables are: $\{S_2, A_2, B_2, \ldots, X_2\}$. This modification is reflected in production rules also.

Step 3: The productions of G_1 are followed by the productions of G_2 to get production rules of grammar G as follows:

$\mathbf{S \to S_1S_2}$, where S_1 and S_2 are starting symbols of grammars G_1 and G_2 respectively and S_1-productions and S_1-productions are remain unchanged.

$\Sigma=\Sigma_1\cup\Sigma_2$, $V_n=\{S_1, A_1, B_1, ..., X_1\} \cup \{S_2, A_2, B_2, ..., X_2\}\cup \{S\}$

Since, all production rules of G_1 and G_2 including $S\rightarrow S_1S_2$ are in context-sensitive form, so G is a context-sensitive grammar and thus L=L(G) is a CSL.

Verification of Language generated by G:

L(G)=Language generated by G_1 followed by language generated by G_2

$=L(G_1)L(G_2)$ (Since, S_1 and S_2 are starting symbols of G_1 and G_2 respectively.)

$= L_1L_2$ (Since, G_1 produces L_1 and G_2 produces L_2.)

We can prove the above for more than two context-sensitive languages using steps 1-3. Therefore, context-sensitive languages are closed under concatenation.

(2) Using Linear Bounded Automata

Let L_1 and L_2 are accepted by two LBA M_1 and M_2 respectively as shown in Fig. 11.3(a) and Fig.11.3 (b). We construct another LBA M_4 which follows $M_1$and then M_2 as shown in Fig. 11.4. LBA M_4 accepts a string $w=w_1w_2$if M_1 accepts substring w_1 and then after M_2 accepts substring w_2 and rejects if either M_1 rejects or M_2 rejects. We can build LBA M_4 as a two tracks automaton. First and second tracks are used to simulate the behavior of M_1 and M_2 respectively. Obviously the language accepted by the M_4 is CSL. We can prove it for more than two CFLs and therefore, concatenation of two contest-sensitive languages is also contest-sensitive.

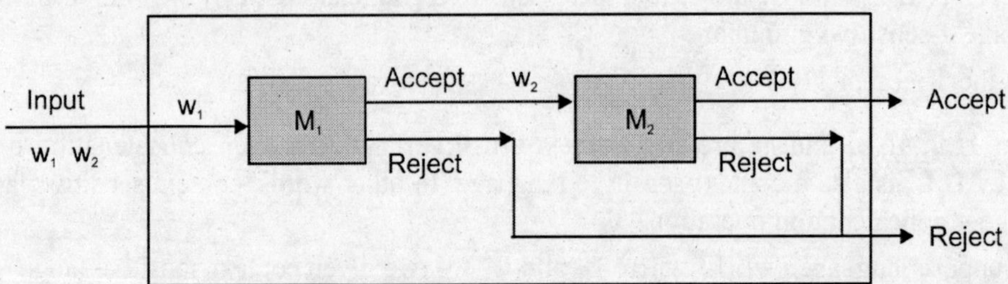

Fig. 11.4: LBA M_4

Lemma11.13: If G_1 and G_2 are two context-sensitive grammars (CSGs) then concatenation of G_1 and G_2 is also a context-sensitive grammar.

(See the Theorem 11.7)

Theorem 11.8: If L_1 and L_2 are two context-sensitive languages then intersection of L_1 and L_2 denoted by $\mathbf{L_1\cap L_2}$ is also a context-sensitive language. In other words, context-sensitive languages are closed under intersection operation.

Proof: Suppose language $L=L_1\cap L_2$ where L_1 and L_2 are two given context-sensitive languages. We can prove L is a CSL by building aLBA.

Let L_1 and L_2 are accepted by two LBA M_1 and M_2 respectively as shown in Fig. 11.3(a) and Fig.11.3 (b). We construct another LBA M_5 which follows M_1 and then M_2 as shown in Fig. 11.5. LBA M_5 accepts a string w if M_1 accepts and M_2 accepts and rejects if either M_1 rejects or M_2 rejects. We can build LBA M_5 as a two tracks automaton. First and second tracks are used to simulate the behavior of M_1 and M_2 respectively. Obviously the language accepted by the M_5 is a CSL. Therefore, intersection of two contest-sensitive languages is also contest-sensitive.

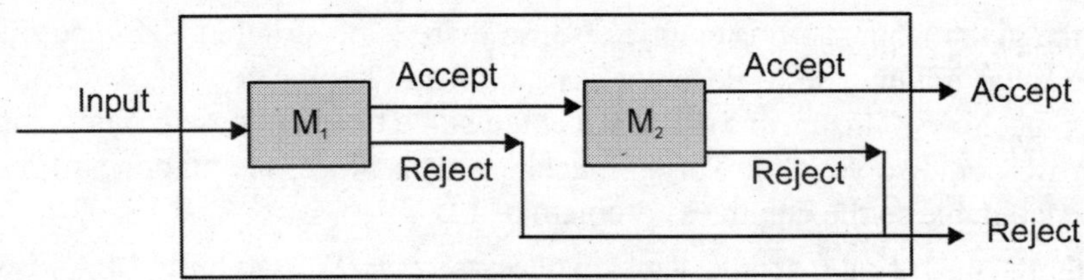

Fig. 11.5: LBA M_5

Theorem 11.9: If L is a context-sensitive language then complement of L is also a context-sensitive language (CSL).

Proof: Suppose language L is a context-sensitive over the alphabet Σ. The complement of L is language L_1. So, where L is the given context-sensitive language. We can prove L_1 is a CSL by using De Morgan's law.

Let R and S are two context-sensitive languages over Σ then as per De Morgan's law,

$$\Sigma^*\text{-}(\overline{\mathbf{R}}\,\text{È}\,\overline{\mathbf{S}})=\mathbf{R}\cap\mathbf{S}$$

Let $\quad P=\overline{R}\,\text{È}\,\overline{S}$

So, $\quad \Sigma^*\text{-}P=R\cap S$

or $\quad \overline{P}=R\cap S$

Since R and S are two context-sensitive languages so language R∩S is also a context-sensitive language (Theorem 11.8). So, the complement of language P. Since, P is union of two languages which are complement of R and S ($P=\overline{R}\,\text{È}\,\overline{S}$), so the complement of languages R and S are also context-sensitive. We know that intersection and complement are interchangeable using De Morgan's law, so whatever the truth about intersection is there, it is also applicable to complement. Therefore, we conclude that complement of a context-sensitive language is also context-sensitive.

Theorem 11.10: If L is a context-sensitive language generated by context-sensitive grammar $G=(V_n, \Sigma, P, S)$ then Kleene closure of L denoted by L* is also a context-sensitive language.

Proof: Let grammar $G'=(V_n, \Sigma, P', S')$ generates L*, where L is generated by context-sensitive grammar G. We define grammar G′ based on given grammar G.

L*={ε, L, LL, LLL, …}, since language L* includes null string, so G′ has production rule: **S′→ε** and from other production rules G′ has to generate multiple of language L like LL, LLL, etc. So, we have two recursive S′-productions: **S′→SS′ | S′S**, where S is the starting symbol of G.

So, P′={S′→ε | SS′ | S′S} ∪ {productions rules of grammar G}

Since, G is a context-sensitive grammar and all productions of G are in G′including production rules {S′→ε | SS′ | S′S}, so all production rules of G′are in context-sensitive form. Therefore, G′ is a context-sensitive grammar.

Verification of Language generated by G:

L(G′)={ε, L, LL, LLL, …}=L*

Theorem 11.11: If L is a context-sensitive language, whether L=ϕ or not is undecidable. In other words, the emptiness problem of CSLis undecidable for linear bounded automata.

Proof: Since the given language L is empty, L=ϕ, so there is no string in L. Suppose L is accepted by LBA M. Since L has nothing, so M does not have any valid halting configuration. LBA are restricted form of Turing machines. This means that if we could solve the emptiness problem for linear bounded automata then we could solve it for Turing machines also. Since, the emptiness problem for Turing machines is undecidable so the emptiness problem of LBA.

Suppose there is a Turing machine T which accepts w$\in$L. We can build LBA M which can verify the configurations of T for the string w. Let us represent the configurations of T for input string w as: $C_1, C_2, C_3, \ldots, C_n$ where C_n is halting configuration of T. These configurations are such that C_{i+1} comes after C_i. We will see how it happens.

Suppose C_i=(q_j, w_1, a, bw_2) and transition for T is $\delta(q_j, a)=(q_k, b, R)$ then C_{i+1}=(q_k, w_1a, b, w_2)

In general, we represent these configurations as

$$C_1 \vdash_T C_2 \vdash_T C_3 \vdash_T \ldots \vdash_T C_n$$

Let us see some constructive approach. The proposed LBA M verifies the configurations of T using the transition function of T as inbuilt instruction. M writes C_{i+1} on the first track and verifies it by the previous configuration C_i on the second track. At the start of the verification process, both tracks contain the first configuration C_1. M writes the next configuration C_2 on first track and verifies with the previous configuration C_1. After successful verification, M writes C_2 on second track and process the next configuration on first track. This process is on for the entire configurations. If $C_1, C_2, C_3, \ldots, C_n$ are accepting configurations sequence for T then M successfully verifies this trace. We can say that after verification of accepting configurations of T, M stops and always stops.

We have assumed nothing about the length of the input string w. Suppose the input string w=ε (null) then M should process the accepting configurations and stop. It means the halting problem of M is decidable and therefore halting problem of Turing machine T should be decidable also which is not. Let us extend our arguments further. What about the accepting configurations of T, there is nothing for M to process. So, M may or may not stop for w=ε. Therefore, the halting problem for LBA for empty string is not decidable.

Lemma 11.14: Halting problem of LBA for empty string is undecidable.

(Please see the Theorem 11.11)

Lemma 11.15: If a linear bounded automaton M accepts a string w over some alphabet Σ then there is another linear bounded automaton which can verifies the configurations of M for w.

(Please see the Theorem 11.11)

Lemma 11.16: If a linear bounded automaton M accepts a string w over some alphabet Σ then there is another linear bounded automaton which can accept w^R, where w^R is transpose (reverse) of w.

Please see the Theorem 11.11. We can build a linear bounded automaton which can process the configurations of M for w in reverse order. Hence if a LBA accepts w then there is another LBA which accepts w^R.

Theorem 11.12: The context-sensitive languages are closed under transpose operation.

(For proof, please see the Theorem 11.11 and Lemma 11.16.)

11.3 SOLVED EXAMPLES

Example 11.1. Construct context-sensitive grammar for language L={$a^nb^nc^n$: n ³ 1}.

Solution: Let context-sensitive grammar G=({S, A}, Σ, P, S) generates language L. The set of production rules P includes following rules:

S→aSAc | abc, cA→Ac, bA→bb

Example 11.2. Consider the context-sensitive grammar G=({S, A}, {a, b, c}, {S→abc | aSAc, cA→Ac, bA→bb}, S) of order 4. Find an equivalent grammar of order 2.

Solution: Suppose the equivalent grammar G_1=(V_1, {a, b, c}, P_1, S). There should not be any terminal in the production rules of G unless it is of the form A→a. So, we introduce following new production rules in G_1:

A_1→a, B_1→b, and C_1→c

Now, the production rules of G are

S→$A_1B_1C_1$ | A_1SAC_1, C_1A→AC_1, B_1A→B_1B_1

The given grammar is of order 4, so we first convert it into order 3 and then in order 2 grammar.

Order 3 Grammar:

Case 1: All production rules of order 3 or less are in G_1. So following rules are in G_1:

S→$A_1B_1C_1$, C_1A→AC_1, B_1A→B_1B_1, A_1→a, B_1b, and C_1→c

Case 2: Consider the production rules of G of higher order. There is only one production rule S→A_1SAC_1 of order 4.

So, production rules S→A_2A_3, A_2→A_1S, A_3→AC_1 where A_2 and A_3 are two new variables are in G_1.

Order 2 Grammar:

Case 1: All production rules of order 2 or less are in G_1. So following rules are in G_1:

S→A_2A_3, A_2→A_1S, A_3→AC_1, C_1A→AC_1, B_1A→B_1B_1, A_1→a, B_1→b, and C_1→c

Case 2: Consider the production rules of G of higher order. There is only one production rule S→$A_1B_1C_1$of order 3.

So, production rules S→A_4A_5, $A_4A_1B_1$, A_5→C_1 where A_4 and A_5 are two new variables are in G_1 and V_1={S, A_1, A_2, A_3, A_4, A_5, B_1, C_1}. Now all the production rules of G_1as given below are of order 2.

S→A_2A_3 | A_4A_5, A_2→A_1S, A_3→AC_1, C_1A→AC_1, B_1A→B_1B_1, $A_4A_1B_1$, A_5→C_1, A_1→a, B_1→b, and C_1→c where V_1={S, A_1, A_2, A_3, A_4, A_5, B_1, C_1}

Example 11.3. Consider the following context-sensitive grammar G=({S, A, B}, {a, b, c}, {S→abc | aAbc, Ab→bA, bB→Bb, aB→aa | aaA}, S). Find the order of the grammar and convert it into n-1 order grammar where n is the order of G.

Solution: The given grammar G is order 4 (S→aAbc). We have to convert the given grammar G into order 3 grammar. Suppose equivalent grammar G_1=(V_1, {a, b, c}, P_1, S) is of order 3. There should not be any terminal in the production rules of G unless it is of the form A→a. So, we introduce following new production rules in G_1:

A_1→a, B_1→b, and C_1→c

So the production rules of grammar G are

$S \rightarrow A_1B_1C_1 \mid A_1AB_1C_1, AB_1 \rightarrow B_1A, B_1B \rightarrow BB_1, A_1B \rightarrow A_1A_1 \mid A_1A_1A$

Case 1: All production rules of order 3 or less are in G_1. So following rules are in G_1:

$S \rightarrow A_1B_1C_1, AB_1 \rightarrow B_1A, B_1B \rightarrow BB_1, A_1B \rightarrow A_1A_1 \mid A_1A_1A, A_1 \rightarrow a, B_1 \rightarrow b$, and $C_1 \rightarrow c$

Case 2: Consider the production rules of G of higher order. There is only one production rule $S \rightarrow A_1AB_1C_1$ of order 4. We introduce two new variables A_2 and A_3 such that

$S \rightarrow A_2A_3, A_2 \rightarrow A_1A, A_3 \rightarrow B_1C_1$ are in G_1

Now, all the production rules of G_1 are order 3 or less. G_1 includes following production rules:

$S \rightarrow A_1B_1C_1 \mid A_2A_3, AB_1 \rightarrow B_1A, B_1B \rightarrow BB_1, A_1B \rightarrow A_1A_1 \mid A_1A_1A, A_2 \rightarrow A_1A, A_3 \rightarrow B_1C_1$ where $V_1 = \{S, A_1, A_2, A_3, B_1, C_1\}$

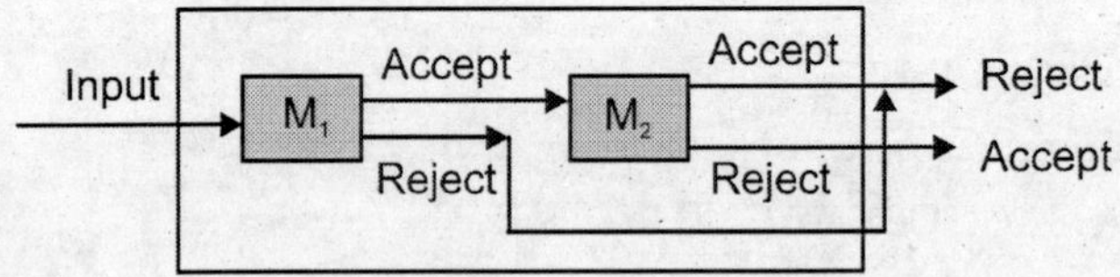

Fig. 11.6: LBA M_3

Example11.4. Suppose L_1 and L_2 are two context-sensitive languages. Prove that relative complement of L_2 over L_1 that is $L_1 - L_2$ is also context-sensitive.

Proof: Suppose language $L = L_1 - L_2$ where L_1 and L_2 are two given context-sensitive languages. We can prove L is a CSL by building a LBA.

Let L_1 and L_2 are accepted by two LBA M_1 and M_2 respectively as shown in Fig. 11.3(a) and Fig.11.3 (b). We construct another LBA M_3 which follows M_1 and then M_2 as shown in Fig. 11.6. LBA M_3 accepts a string w if M_1 accepts but M_2 rejects. M_3 rejectsif either M_1 rejects or M_2 accepts. We can build LBA M_3 as a two tracks automaton. First and second tracks are used to simulate the behavior of M_1 and M_2 respectively. Obviously the language accepted by the M_3 is a CSL.

Example 11.5. L_1 and L_2 are two context-sensitive languages over the alphabet Σ. Design linear bounded automata for the the languages

(a) $L_3 = L_1$ Ç $\overline{L_2}$ (b) $L_4 = \overline{L_1}$ Ç $\overline{L_2}$

Solution: Suppose the languages L_1 and L_2 are recognized by LBA M_1 and M_2 respectively as shown in Fig. 11.3(a) and Fig. 11.3(b).

(a) The language L_3 is recognized by LBA M_3 as shown in Fig. 11.7(a). If M_1 accepts the input w and it is rejected by M_2 then M_3 accepts w. If input w is rejected by M_3 if w is rejected by M_1 or w is accepted by both M_1 and M_2.

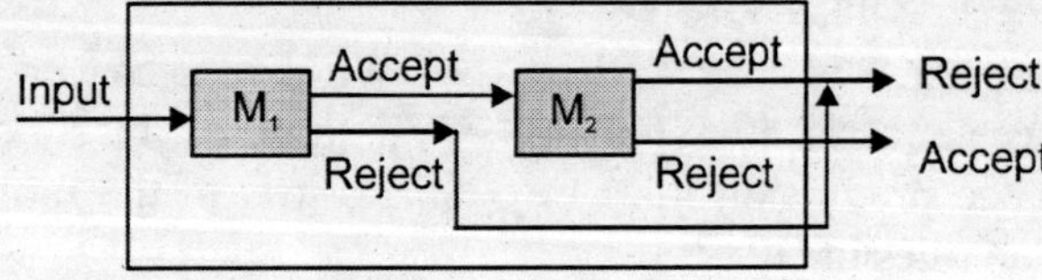

Fig. 11.7 (a): LBA M_3

(b) The language L_3 is recognized by LBAM$_4$ as shown in Fig. 11.7(b). The input w is accepted by M_4 if w is rejected by both M_1 and M_2. In other cases w is rejected by M_4.

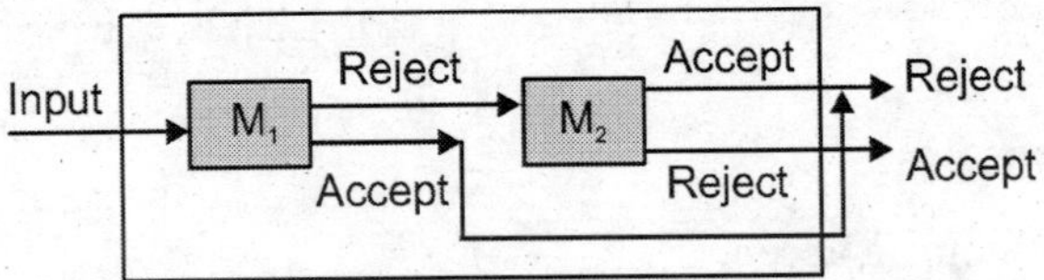

Fig. 11.7 (b): LBA M_4

TEST YOUR SKILLS

Supplementary Problems

11.1 Prove that every context-sensitive language is decidable.

11.2 What is Kuroda Normal Form? Find out Kuroda's normal form of the following grammar G=({S, A}, {a, b, c}, {S→abc | aSAc, cA→Ac, bA→bb}, S)

11.3 What is linear-bounded grammar? Explain with example.

11.4 Consider the following context-sensitive grammar G=({S, A, B}, {a, b, c}, {S→abc | aAbc, Ab→bA, bB→Bb, aB→aa | aaA}, S). Find the order 2 grammar equivalent to G.

11.5 Prove the following:

(a) Union of three context-sensitive languages is also context-sensitive.

(b) Union of context-sensitive and context-free languages is context-sensitive.

(c) Intersection of three context-sensitive languages is also context-sensitive.

(d) Union of Kleene closure of two context-sensitive languages is also context-sensitive.

(e) Union of context-sensitive and regular languages is context-sensitive.

(f) Union of complement of two context-sensitive languages is also context-sensitive.

(g) Concatenation of context-sensitive languages $L_1, L_2, L_3, \ldots, L_n$ for $n \geq 2$ is also context-sensitive.

(h) Union of context-sensitive languages $L_1, L_2, L_3, \ldots, L_n$ for $n \geq 2$ is also context-sensitive.

(i) Intersection of context-sensitive languages $L_1, L_2, L_3, \ldots, L_n$ for $n \geq 2$ is also context-sensitive.

(j) $L=((L_1-L_2)\cup L_3)L_4$ is context-sensitive language where L_1, L_2, L_3, and L_4 are context-sensitive languages.

11.6 Consider the context-sensitive grammar G=(V_n, Σ, P, S) whose production rules are S→0SBA | 01A, AB→BA, 1B→11, 1A→10, 0A→00 and V_n={S, A, B}. Find out equivalent order 2 and 3 grammars.

11.7 Design LBA for the languages $L=\{a^nb^nc^nd^n: n \geq 0\}$. Explain why this language is not accepted by any finite automaton or pushdown automaton.

11.8 Design linear bounded automata for the following languages:

(a) $L_1=\{a^nb^nc^na^mb^mc^m: m, n \geq 0\}$

(b) $L_2=\{a^nb^na^mb^mc^m: m, n \geq 0\}$

(c) $L_3=\{a^nb^nc^md^m: m, n \geq 0\}$

(d) $L_4=\{a^iba^j: i+j \geq 0\}$

11.9 If L_1 and L_2 are two context-sensitive languages over the alphabet Σ. Prove that following languages are also context-sensitive

(a) $L_3 = L_1$ Ç $\overline{L_2}$ (b) $L_4 = \overline{L_1}$ Ç $\overline{L_2}$

Multiple Choice Questions

11.10. Linear bounded automata accept

(a) Regular Languages (b) Context-free languages

(c) Context-sensitive Languages (d) All

11.11. Linear bounded automata are

(a) Restricted form of Turing machines (b) Generalized form of pushdown automata

(c) Generalized form of finite automata (d) None

11.12. Grammar G=({S, A, B}, {a, b}, {S→SA | B, BA→AB, A→a, B→b}, S) generates

(a) L={$a^n b$: n 3 0} (b) L={$a^n b$: n 3 1}

(c) L={$a^n b a^m$: n+m 3 0} (d) None

11.13. Grammar G=({S, A, B}, {a, b, c}, {S→abc | aAbc, Ab→bA, bB→Bb, aB→aa | aaA}, S) generates

(a) L={$a^n b^m c^n$: m, n 3 0} (b) L={$a^n b^n c^n$: n 3 0}

(c) L={$a^n b^m c^n$: m, n 3 1} (d) None

11.14. Length of tape used by a linear bounded automaton is

(a) Equal to length of input (b) Finite

(c) Proportionate to the length of input (d) Both (b) and (c)

11.15. Halting problem of linear bounded automata is

(a) Decidable (b) Undecidable

(c) Depends on input (d) Not known

11.16. The emptiness problem of a context-sensitive language for linear bounded automata is

(a) Undecidable (b) Decidable

(c) Depends on input (d) None

11.17. Contest-sensitive languages are closed under

(a) Union operation (b) Intersection operation

(c) Complement Operation (d) All

11.18. If $L=L_1 \cap L_2$ where L_1 and L_2 are regular and context-sensitive languages respectively then L is

(a) ϕ (b) Regular

(c) Context-sensitive (d) Both (b) and (c)

11.19. If $L=L_1 \cup L_2$ where L_1 and L_2 are regular and context-sensitive languages respectively then L is

(a) ϕ (b) Regular

(c) Context-sensitive (d) None

11.20. Which one of the following statements is true?

(a) The power of deterministic and non-deterministic linear bounded automata is equal

(b) The power of deterministic and non-deterministic pushdown automata is equal

(c) Context-free languages are closed under intersection operation

(d) Context-sensitive languages are closed under intersection operation

11.21. Which one of the following statements is not true

(a) The power of deterministic and non-deterministic Turing machines is equal

(b) Turing machine operation is simulated by linear bounded automata

(c) Turing machine operation cannot be simulated by linear bounded automata

(d) Context-sensitive languages are closed under intersection operation

11.22. The difference between finite automaton and linear bounded automaton is

(a) Length of the tape used (b) Reading capability

(c) Writing Capability (d) All

11.23. Which of the following languages is/are context-sensitive

(a) $L_1=\{a^n$:n is perfect square$\}$ (b) $L_2=\{a^nb^nc^n$: n ³ $0\}$

(c) $L_3=\{a^nba^m$: m+n ³ $0\}$ (d) All

11.24. Which grammar is in Kuroda normal form?

(a) $G_1=(\{S, A, B\}, \{a, b\}, \{S\rightarrow SA \mid B, BA\rightarrow AB, A\rightarrow a, B\rightarrow b\}, S)$

(b) $G_2=(\{S, A\}, \{a, b, c\}, \{S\rightarrow abc \mid aSAc, cA\rightarrow Ac, bA\rightarrow bb\}, S)$

(c) $G_3=(\{S\}, \{a, b\}, \{S\rightarrow ab \mid aSb\}, S)$

(d) None

11.25. The language $L=\{a^nb^mc^md^nabcd$: m, n ³ $0\}$ is

(a) Regular language (b) Context-free language

(c) Context-sensitive language (d) None

11.26. The language $L=\{a^nb^mc^md^n: m, n\leq 100\}$ is

(a) Regular language (b) Context-free language

(c) Context-sensitive language (d) All

11.27 If context-sensitive grammar G is order n ³ 3 and it is converted to equivalent order 2 grammar. In general how many phases are required for this conversion

(a) n (b) n-1

(c) n+1 (d) n+2

Answers

11.10 (d)	11.11 (a)	11.12 (c)	11.13 (d)	11.14 (d)
11.15 (a)	11.16 (a)	11.17 (d)	11.18 (d)	11.19 (c)
11.20 (d)	11.21 (c)	11.22 (c)	11.23 (d)	11.24 (a)
11.25 (c)	11.26 (d)	11.27 (b)		

CHAPTER 12

Introduction to Computational Complexity

We have been discussing about different kind of languages and their acceptors; finite automata (FA) for regular languages, pushdown automata (PDA) for context-free languages (CFLs), and Turing machines for type 0 languages in the previous chapters. But, still, we were not concerned about their relative performance. Performance of a machine can be measured based on different factors. Some major factors are given following:

1. How much time one machine takes to complete a task?
2. What is the output measured per unit time i.e., throughput?
3. When first response comes while processing a longer task?
4. How many resources (internal or external) are required to complete a task?
5. What is the structural complexity of that machine; whether machine is simple or complex?
6. How much storage required for processing a given task?

Considering a particular factor to select a machine is dependent on the kind of need. **For example,** consider two machines M_1 and M_2 doing the same job. The machine M_1 completes the job within 5 seconds and requires more resources as compared to M_2 and M_2 completes the job within 7 seconds and requires fewer resources as compared to M_1. Obviously, the choice between M_1 and M_2 depends on our need; whether we want the job to be completed at earliest basis or we want to use fewer resources but time is not a factor. So, for the first need we will select M_1 and for second M_2. Discussing the all factors of performance is out of scope of this book. We will concentrate on two major factors:

1. How much time a machine takes to complete a task?
2. How much storage required for processing a task?

12.1 COMPUTATIONAL COMPLEXITY OF TURING MACHINE

Computational complexity is also known as **Time-Space complexity**. Computational complexity of Turing machines is based on two factors:

1. Amount of time needed (**Time Complexity**), and
2. Amount of space or storage required in processing of a task (**Space Complexity**).

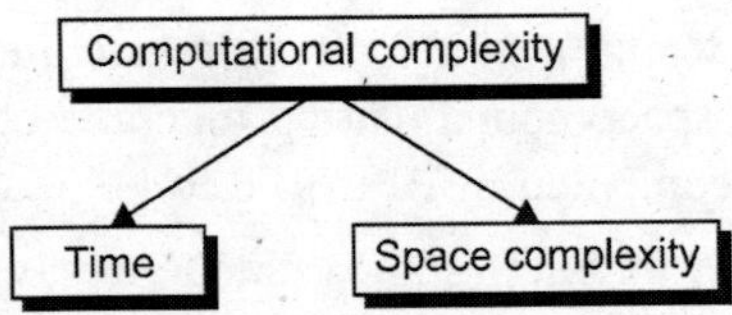

We have one question here. Which parameter will be considered to represent the Time-Space complexity? Whether it will be input's size, program size, or some thing else? No doubt, the size of the input will be the suitable option. We denote the time complexity by T and space complexity by S. Let $\boldsymbol{n}$ is the size of the input given to a Turing machine then $\boldsymbol{T(n)}$ is the time complexity and $\boldsymbol{S(n)}$ is the space complexity.

12.1.1 Time Complexity

Consider kTM (k-tape Turing machine) M shown in Fig. 12.1. M has k two-way infinite tapes, one of these tapes contains the input and all tapes including input tape can be written. Time complexity is defined as:

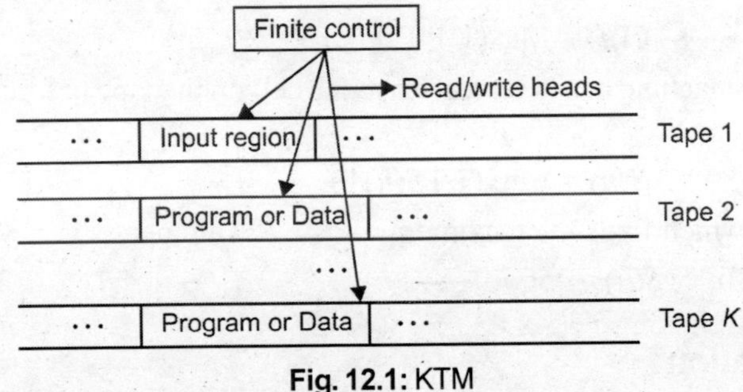

Fig. 12.1: KTM

"If for every input of length n ($n \geq 0$), M makes at most $T(n)$ moves before halting then M is said to be a $T(n)$ time bounded Turing machine (or of time complexity $T(n)$). The language recognized or function computed by M is said to be of time complexity $T(n)$."

12.1.2 Space Complexity

Consider an off-line Turing machine $\bar{M}$ of k tapes shown in Fig. 12.2. M has a read-only tape and k – 1 one-way infinite tapes. Space complexity is defined as:

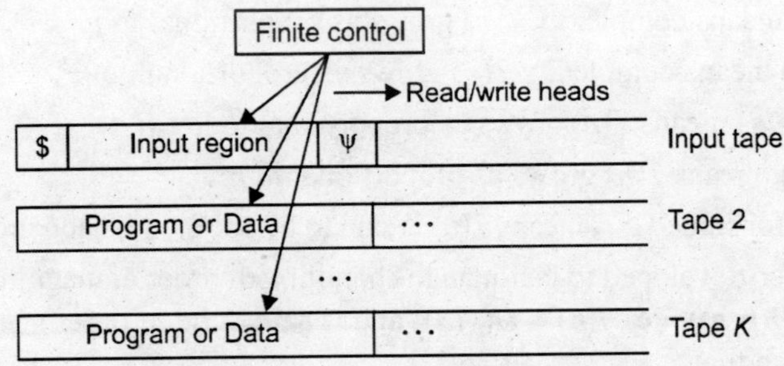

Fig. 12.2: Off-line turing machine

"If for every input stream of length n ($n \geq 0$), Turing machine M scans at most $S(n)$ cells on any tape then M is said to be a $S(n)$ space-bound Turing machine or space complexity of $S(n)$ and the language recognized or function computed by M is said to be of space complexity $S(n)$."

Generally, $S(n)$ is of linear growth, but in some case there may be the different growth rate. If head writes on the tape then the length of written is included in calculation of space complexity.

12.1.3 Special Assumption about Time-Space Complexity

The time complexity $T(n) = 0$ or space complexity $S(n) = 0$ is meaningless. So, we have to define these correctly in some situations where these seem to be zero (or incorrect).

As we know that if input length is n then a Turing machine has to read this input and then it may halt. So, a Turing machine moves at least $n + 1$ cells and then it may halt.

So, $$T(n) = \text{Max}(n + 1, \lceil T(n) \rceil),$$

Max is a function which finds the maximum of its two arguments

For example, suppose, $T(n) = \log_2 n$ and for $n = 1$,

$T(n) = \text{Max}(1 + 1, \log_2 n) = 2$

Similarly, a Turing machine has to read at least one cell on the tape before halt. So, we define space complexity as:

$$S(n) = \text{Max}(1, \lceil S(n) \rceil),$$

Max is a function which finds the maximum of its two arguments

Therefore, for $n = 0, 1$, $S(n) = \log_2 n = 1$

12.1.4 Big O Notation

Let us see how the growth rate of Time-Space complexity is represented. Generally, the growth is categorized as linear, quadratic, cubic, etc. We have seen earlier that importance of complexity is to study the relative performance of machines. We use big O notation to represent the Time-Space complexity. It is also known as order of complexity. **For examples,**

1. $T_1(n) = n + 2$, $T_2(n) = n - 1$, $T_3(n) = n$, then these all are of order n i.e., $T_1(n) = T_2(n) = T_3(n) = O(n)$
2. $T_1(n) = n^2 + 1$, $T_2(\text{n}) = n^2 + n + 1$, $T_3(n) = n^2 - 1$, then these all are of order n^2 i.e., $T_1(n) = T_2(n) = T_3(n) = O(n^2)$

Now, let us see what is the need of categorize the complexity as linear, quadratic, cubic, etc.:

(a) $T(n) = O(n)$ means complexity $T(n)$ grows as proportional to n.

(b) $T(n) = O(n^2)$ means complexity $T(n)$ grows as proportional to n^2.

(c) $T(n) = O(\log_2 n)$ means $T(n)$ grows as proportional to $\log_2 n$.

(d) $T(n) = \text{O}(n^3)$, means $T(n)$ grows as proportional to n^3.

(e) $T(n) = O(n^i)$ for some $i \geq 1$, means $T(n)$ is said to be polynomial and grows as proportional to n^i.

A notation has been developed to facilitate the handling of order of magnitude functions. A function $f(n)$ is defined to be $O(g(n))$, i.e., $f(n) = O(g(n))$ and is said to be of order $g(n)$, if there exists positive constants n_0 and c such that

$|f(n)| \leq c * |g(n)|$ **for all** $n > n_0$

For examples

- $400\ n^5$ is $O\ (n^5)$,
- $100n^3 + 50n^2 + 10n^1 + 30n^0$ is $O(n^3)$,
- $1 + 2 + 3 + \ldots + n = n(n + 1) / 2 = n^2 + O(n) = O(n^2)$, and
- 2402 is $O(1)$

Using the definition of a limit from calculus, the above definition can be shown to be equivalent to

$$\lim_{n \to \infty} \frac{|f(n)|}{|g(n)|} = c, \text{ where } c \text{ is a constant}$$

Using **L. Hospital's** rule is often useful for computing the limit. It states that if

$$\lim_{n \to \infty} f(n) = \infty \text{ and } \lim_{n \to \infty} g(n) = \infty$$

then $$\lim_{n \to \infty} \frac{|f(n)|}{|g(n)|} = \lim_{n \to \infty} \frac{|f'(n)|}{|g'(n)|}$$

where ***f'*** and ***g'*** are derivatives of ***f*** and **g**

For example,

$$\lim_{n \to \infty} \frac{\ln(n)}{n} = \frac{1/n}{n \to \infty 1} = \frac{1/n}{n \to \infty 1} = 0, \text{ so } ln(n) = 0(n)$$

Where ***ln(n)*** is the natural logarithm of ***n***. Using this notation we have:

$\boldsymbol{T_s(n) = O(n)}$ and $\boldsymbol{T_{MM} = O(n^3)}$, are the time analysis for summation of array and multiplication algorithm, respectively. Formally, $O(g(n))$ is the set of functions, f, such that for some $c > 0$,

$$f(n) < cg(n)$$

For all positive integers $n > n_0$, i.e., for all sufficiently large n_0, another way of writing the above is:

$$\lim_{n \to \infty} \frac{|f(n)|}{|g(n)|} = c$$

Informally, we say the $O(g)$ is the set of all functions, which grow no faster than g. The function g s an upper bound to functions in $O(g)$. We are interested in the set of functions defined by the O notation because we want to argue about the relative merits of algorithms; independent of their implementations. That is, we are not concerned with the language or machine used; we want a means of comparing algorithms, which is relevant to any implementation. We define two other functions: $\boldsymbol{\Omega(g)}$ and $\boldsymbol{\theta(g)}$. $\Omega(g)$ the set of functions $f(n)$ for which $\boldsymbol{f(n) \geq cg(n)}$ for all positive integers $n > n_0$ and

$$\theta(g) = \Omega(g) \cap O(g)$$

We can derive: $f \in \theta(g)$

If $$\lim_{n \to \infty} \frac{|f(n)|}{|g(n)|} = c$$

Thus, $\Omega(g)$ is a lower bound-functions in $\Omega(g)$ grow faster than g and $\theta(g)$ are functions that grow at the same rate as g. In these last two statements, as in most of the discussion on complexity theory – "within a constant factor" is understood. Different languages, compilers, machines, operating systems, etc. will produce different constant factors: it is the general behaviour of the running time as n increases to very large values that we're concerned with.

Properties of the big O notation

The following general properties of big O notation expressions may be derived:

1. Constant factors may be ignored:
   For all $k > 0$, kf is $O(f)$, e.g., an^2 and bn^2 are both $O(n^2)$.
2. Higher powers of $\boldsymbol{n}$ grow faster than lower powers:
   $$\boldsymbol{n^r \text{ is } O(n^s) \text{ if } 0 \leq r \leq s.}$$
3. The growth rate of a sum of terms is the growth rate of its fastest growing term:
   If f is $O(g)$, then $f + g$ is $O(g)$.
   e.g., $an^3 + bn^2$ is $O(n^3)$.
   The growth rate of a polynomial is given by the growth rate of its leading term (cf. (2), (3)):
4. If f is a polynomial of degree d, then f is $O(n^d)$.
5. If f grows faster than g, which grows faster than h, then f grows faster than h.
6. The product of upper bounds of functions gives an upper bound for the product of the functions:
7. If f is $O(g)$ and h is $O(r)$, then fh is $O(gr)$
   e.g., if f is $O(n^2)$ and g is O(log n), then fg is $O(n^2 \log n)$.
8. Exponential functions grow faster than powers:
   n^k is $O(b^n)$, for all $b > 1$; $k \geq 0$,
   e.g., n^4 is $O(2^n)$ and n^4 is $O(\exp(n))$.
9 Logarithms grow more slowly than powers:
   $\log_b n$ is $O(n^k)$ for all $b > 1$; $k > 0$
   e.g., $\log_2 n$ is $O(n^{0.5})$.
10. All logarithms grow at the same rate:
   $\log_b n$ is $\theta(\log_d n)$ for all b; $d > 1$.
11. The sum of the first n, r^{th} powers grows as the $(r + 1)^{th}$ power:
   $$\sum_{k=1}^{n} k^r \text{ is } q(n^{r+1}) \text{ e.g., } \sum_{k=1}^{n} k^r = (n+1)\, n/2 \text{ is } \theta(n^2)$$

12.2 DETERMINISTIC AND NON-DETERMINISTIC TIME-SPACE COMPLEXITY

The concept of Time-Space complexity is equally applicable to deterministic and nondeterministic machines.

For deterministic turing machine (DTM)

If for every input of length n ($n \geq 0$), DTM M makes at most $T(n)$ moves before halting then M is said to be a $T(n)$ time bounded Turing machine or of time complexity $T(n)$ and space complexity is $S(n)$ if it scans at most $S(n)$ cells.

For nondeterministic turing machine (NTM)

If for every input of length n ($n \geq 0$), NTM M makes at most $T(n)$ moves for at least one sequence of oves which leads to the halting then M is said to be a $T(n)$ time bounded TM or of time complexity $T(n)$ and space complexity is $S(n)$ if it scans at most $S(n)$ cells.

12.3 COMPLEXITY CLASSES

We have following complexity classes for deterministic Turing machines (DTMs) and nondeterministic Turing machines (NTMs):

DTIME($T(n)$): A language L is said to be of the class DTIME($T(n)$) if there exists a multi-tape deterministic Turing machine (DTM) that recognizes language L in time $T(n)$ unit.

DSPACE($S(n)$): A language L is said to be of the class DSPACE($S(n)$) if there exists a multi-tape deterministic Turing machine (DTM) that recognizes language L using storage size $S(n)$ unit.

We can have single tape deterministic Turing machine for defining the time-space complexity. So, it is not necessary for DTM to be multi-tape always.

NTIME($T(n)$): A language L is said to be of the class NTIME($T(n)$) if there exists a multi-tape nondeterministic Turing machine (NTM) that recognizes language L in time $T(n)$ unit.

NSPACE($S(n)$): A language L is said to be of the class NSPACE($S(n)$) if there exists a multi-tape nondeterministic Turing machine (NTM) that recognizes language L using storage size $S(n)$ unit.

We can have single tape Turing machine for defining the time-space complexity. So, it is not necessary for Turing machine to be multi-tape always. We have some relations among complexity classes:

1. Let a deterministic Turing machine (DTM) M_1 and a nondeterministic Turing machine (NTM) M_2 recognize the language L in time $T(n)$ unit then DTIME($T(n)$) $\subseteq$ NTIME($T(n)$)
2. If two Turing machines M_1 and M_2 recognize some language in time $T_1(n)$ unit and $T_2(n)$ unit respectively such that $T_1(n)$ is less than equal to $T_2(n)$ then

   $$T_1(n) = O(T_2(n))$$

   This implies that

   $$\text{DTIME}(T_1(n)) \subseteq \text{DTIME}(T_2(n)), \text{ and}$$

   $$\text{NTIME}(T_1(n)) \subseteq \text{NTIME}(T_2(n))$$

3. For an integer $m \geq 1$,

   $$\text{DTIME}(n^m) \subseteq \text{DTIME}(n^{m+1}), \text{ and}$$

   $$\text{NTIME}(n^m) \subseteq \text{NTIME}(n^{m+1})$$

Example 1: Consider the language $L = \{wcw^R: w \in (a + b)^*\}$ recognized by a deterministic Turing machine (DTM) M with two tapes. M does the following:

(a) M copies the w^R on the second tape,

(b) Now, M matches the w and w^R reading first tape from the beginning of the w and second tape from the end of w^R,

(c) When c is read on the first tape then M halts.

Show that $L \in$ DTIME(n).

Solution: Since, M moves $n + 1$ cells maximum for input string of length n, so

$$T(n) = O(n).$$

Thus, $L \in$ DTIME(n) i.e., language L belongs to time complexity class DTIME(n).

Example 2: Consider $L = \{a^nb^n: n \geq 1\}$ recognized by a single tape Turing machine M. Find the complexity class of the language L.

Solution: Let M does the following in order to accept the language L:

(a) M reads the first symbol a from the left and matches with the first symbol b from the right end,

(b) When M reads a symbol then it writes # and repeats until the end of the input.

Turing machine M is shown in Fig. 12.3.

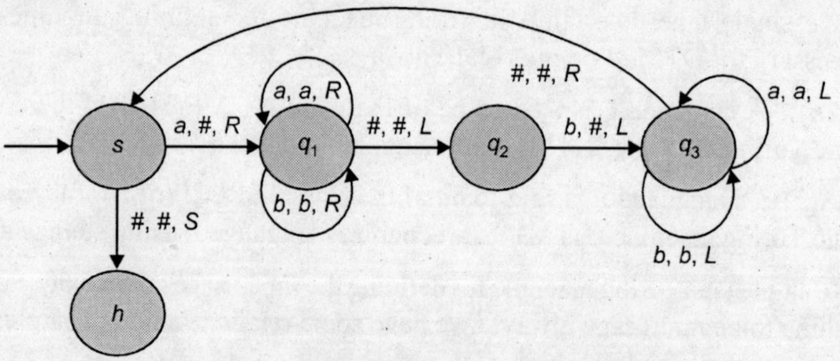

Fig. 12.3: Turing machine for $L = \{a^nb^n: n \geq 1\}$

Since, Turing machine M moves n cells right to find the first symbol b and comes to left moving n cells, so M moves $2n$ cells at most for each a.

Therefore, $T(n) = n*2n = 2n^2$ (approximately)

Thus, $T(n) = O(n^2)$

Hence, $L \in$ DTIME(n^2)

12.4 COMPLEXITY OF MEMBERSHIP ALGORITHM FOR CONTEXT-FREE LANGUAGES

By taking the reference of solved problem (14) of Chapter 7, we know that for a context-free grammar G, which has no null and unit productions, the exhausted parsing can take $2|w|$ rounds at most to decide whether $w \in L(G)$ or not. Now, consider a grammar G is in Greibach normal form (GNF) then the string w is derived in exactly $|w|$ steps if w is in $L(G)$.

Suppose P is the maximum number of productions for any variable in grammar G. So, in worst condition, each variable in derivation of w can have P choices to be replaced. Therefore, after $|w|$ steps, we have at most $P^{|w|}$ leftmost derivations. It means, the above algorithm to decide the membership of w can take exponential time ($P^{|w|}$) and hence has exponential time complexity, which is not desirable.

Complexity of CYK algorithm

As we know that CYK algorithm considers the context-free grammar in Chomsky normal form (CNF) and finds the list of variables for all substrings of a string and finally checks the list of variables for the parent string. If the final variables list contains the starting symbol then membership is there for the string otherwise not. Consider a string w of length n and a context-free grammar G in CNF. We know that the decidability of the question "$w \in L(G)$?" can be determined in exactly $2n - 1$ steps, that is, the membership of w can be determined in $2n - 1$ steps. As we know that the total number of substrings of w is $n(n - 1)/2$, where n is the length of w.

Now, the time complexity

$$T(w) = \Sigma \text{ Number of substrings} \times \text{Number of steps per substring}$$
$$= n \times 1 + (n-1) \times 3 + (n-2) \times 5 + \ldots + 1 \times (2n-1), \text{ where } n \text{ is the length of } w$$

Therefore, $\boldsymbol{T(w) = O(n^3)}$

The CYK algorithm has better performance as compare to the previous membership algorithm that has exponential time complexity.

12.5 TIME-SPACE COMPLEXITY OF NFA AND DFA

As we know that both nondeterministic finite automaton (NFA) and deterministic finite automaton (DFA) recognize regular languages. Suppose r is regular expression and NFA N recognizes this language. There is an equivalent DFA M equivalent to N, which also recognizes expression r. According to the construction of N, there can be at most $2|r|$ states in N and hence there are at most $2^{2|r|}$ states in M. So, the space complexity of N is order of $O(|r|)$ and for M is order of $O(2^{2|r|})$, that is

$$\textbf{Space}_N(w) = O(|r|), \text{ and}$$
$$\textbf{Space}_M(w) = O(2^{2|r|})$$

Now, consider the acceptability of string w by automaton N and M. As we know that the N is non-deterministic in nature and M is deterministic in nature and M takes exactly $|w|$. It means, the time complexity of DFA M is order of $\boldsymbol{O(|w|)}$, that is

$$\textbf{Time}_M(w) = O(|w|)$$

The NFA N can have at most $2|r|$ moves for one input symbol, so the time complexity of N is order of $\boldsymbol{O(|r| \times |w|)}$, that is

$$\textbf{Time}_N(w) = O(|r| \times |w|)$$

Suppose, there is deterministic Turing machine, which recognizes the language $L(r)$, it means,

$$\textbf{Time}_M(w) \subseteq \textbf{DTIME}(n), \text{ where } n \text{ is length of } w$$

In general, time complexity of recognization of regular languages is linear ordered and $\textbf{Time}(L_{\textbf{REG}}) = \textbf{DTIME}(n)$, where n is length of input string.

12.6 P AND NP COMPLEXITY CLASSES

In this section we will discuss two famous complexity classes *P* and *NP*. The *P* class includes those languages, which are recognized by some deterministic Turing machine (DTM) in polynomial time and the *NP* class includes those languages, which are recognized by some nondeterministic Turing machine (NTM) in polynomial time.

So,
$$P = \bigcup_{i \geq 1} \text{DTIME}(n^i), \text{ and}$$

$$NP = \bigcup_{i \geq 1} \text{NTIME}(n^i), \text{ where } n \text{ is the input length}$$

Class ***P*** consists of all those decision problems that can be solved by some deterministic Turing machine in an amount of time that is polynomial over the size of the input and the class ***NP*** consists of all those decision problems whose positive solutions can be found in polynomial time by some nondeterministic Turing machine. Some sets of problems in *NP* class have exponential time complexity. For example ***NP*-Complete** and ***NP*-Hard** problems. We will discuss these problems in coming sections.

Let us see the difference between *P* and *NP* classes. A language is said to be in class *NP* if some string w in L is recognized by some nondeterminsitic Turing machine in polynomial time over the length of w. Recognizing a string in L is not easier for nondeterministic Turing machines (NTM) due to nondeterminsm characteristic. So, language $L \in NP$ if $w \in L$ is recognized by some nondeterministic Turing machine (NTM) in polynomial complexity. There are harder problems in *NP* class that have exponential time complexity. One of the the biggest open question in Theory of Computer Science is:

Is $\boldsymbol{P = NP}$?

Most people think that the answer is probably "NO"; some people believe the question may be undecidable from the currently accepted axioms. We will consider this question later on in this chapter.

Now, we will see some practical things about complexity classes, which are very important. Let us consider some time complexities given below for input of length n:

1. $T_1(n) = 2^n$,
2. $T_2(n) = n^n$, and
3. $T_3(n) = n^{200}$

We see that T_1 and T_2 are still in approachable range for even for some higher values of n, but T_3 seems to be impractical even for smaller values of n. What we will expect from the machine having time complexity like T_3? Obviously, we have to wait more and more for result from the machine. So, we can conclude that any machine or algorithm whose complexity (time or space) growth is much higher when input size increases, cannot be very much useful in practice and definitely we would not like these types of machine or algorithm in our practical life. But how some machines have such impractical complexity? Is it due to problem's nature or due to inefficient algorithm design? Complexity of a machine depends on both factors: problem's nature and algorithm design. Let us focus on the problem's nature instead of algorithm design. We define tractable and intractable problems:

"When Time-Space complexity for a machine (or algorithm) is very much reasonable to solve certain problem then that problem is said to **tractable** or solvable in practice otherwise the problem is said to **intractable**."

Deciding the reasonable algorithm is based on the relative performance study of the different algorithms for same problem. Generally, when Time-Space complexity is expressed as polynomial of input size then problem is tractable. When Time-Space complexity is expressed as some exponential function over input size then the problem is intractable.

The first suggestion about tractable and intractable problems was introduced in **Cook-Karp Thesis**. According to Cook-Karp Thesis, a problem that is in P class is called tractable and that not in P class is called intractable. The Cook-Karp Thesis has also important in classifying the realistic and non-realistic problems. Obviously, an intractable problem has faster complexity growth as compared to tractable problem. The tractable problem problems solutions (algorithms), which are implementable in practice, have polynomial Time-Space complexity; whereas the intractable problems solutions have exponential Time-Space complexity over input size. As we discussed earlier that $P \subseteq NP$, but the fundamental question "Whether $P = NP$ or not?" is still unsolved. Computer scientists have introduced many related concepts and questions. Some of these concepts are *NP*-Complete and N*P*-Hard problems. C.A. Cook introduced the concept of *NP*-Completeness to solve "Whether $P = NP$ or not?" problem in his Thesis. Still, it is open for debate, "Is $P = NP$?".

12.7 POLYNOMIAL-TIME TRANSFORMATION

A language can be polynomial-time transformed or reduced to another language using a deterministic Turing machine. Let L_1 and L_2 are two languages over alphabets Σ_1 and Σ_2 respectively then L_1 can be polynomial-time transformed to L_2 if

1. There exists a function $\boldsymbol{F}: \boldsymbol{\Sigma_1 \to \Sigma_2}$ such that $w \in L_1$ if and only if $w \in L_2$, and
2. A deterministic Turing machine of polynomial time complexity can compute $\boldsymbol{F}$.

Language L_1 is also known as **polynomial-time reducible** to language L_2. If $L_2 \in P$ then $L_1 \in P$ and if $L_2 \in NP$ then $L_1 \in NP$.

12.8 *NP*-COMPLETE AND *NP*-HARD PROBLEM

A problem S is said to be ***NP*-Complete** if it satisfies following two conditions:

1. $S \in NP$, and
2. For every other problems $S_i \in NP$ for some $i = 1, 2, n$, there is polynomial-time transformation from S_i to S i.e., every problem in *NP* class polynomial-time reducible to S.

We conclude one thing here that if S_i is *NP*-Complete then S is also *NP*-Complete.

As a consequence, if we could find a polynomial time algorithm for P, then we can solve all *NP* problems in polynomial time, beacause all problems in *NP* class are polynomial-time reducible to each other.

"A problem P is said to be *NP*-Hard if it satifies the second condition given above, but not necessarily the first condition."

The notion of *NP*-hardness plays an important role in the discusson about the relationship between the complexity classes P and *NP*. It is also often used to define the complexity class *NP*-Complete which is the intersection of *NP* and *NP*-Hard. Consequently, the class *NP*-Hard can be understood as the class of problems that are *NP*-complete or harder. **For example,** an *NP*-Hard problem is the decision problem SUBSET-SUM which is:

"Given a set of integers, do any non empty subset of them add up to zero? That is a *yes/no* question, and happens to be *NP*-complete"

There are also decision problems that are *NP*-Hard but not *NP*-Complete, **for example**, the halting problem of Turing machine. It is easy to prove that the halting problem is *NP*-Hard but not *NP*-Complete. It is also easy to see that the halting problem is not in *NP* since all problems in *NP* are decidable but the halting problem is not (voilating the condition first given for *NP*-complete languages).

In complexity theory, the ***NP*-complete** problems are the hardest problems in *NP* class, in the sense that they are the ones most likely not to be in *P* class. The reason is that if we could find a way to solve any *NP*-complete problem quickly, then you could use that algorithm to solve all *NP* problems quickly. At present time, all known algorithms for *NP*-complete problems require time which is exponential in the input size. It is unknown whether there are any faster algorithms. C.A. Cook in 1971 proved that the Boolean satisfiability problem is *NP*-Complete. After Cook's original results, thousands of other problems have been shown to be *NP*-Complete by reductions from other problems previously shown to be *NP*-complete. **For example,**

Consider an interesting problem in graph theory known as "*Graph isomorphism*". Two graphs are isomorphic if one can be transformed into the other simply by renaming vertices. Consider these two problems given following:

Graph isomorphism: Is graph G_1 isomorphic to graph G_2?

Subgraph isomorphism: Is graph G_1 isomorphic to a subgraph of graph G_2?

The "Subgraph Isomorphism" problem is *NP*-complete, but the "Graph Isomorphism" problem is suspected to be neither in *P* nor *NP*-Complete, though it is obviously in *NP*. This is an example of a problem that is thought to be hard, but it is not thought to be *NP*-Complete.

Folllowing are some other *NP*-Complete and *NP*-Hard problems:

1. **The Boolean Satisfiability Problem (SAT):** In mathematics, a formula of propositional logic is said to be satisfiable if truth-values can be assigned to its free variables in such way that this assignment makes the formula true. The class of satisfiable propositional formulae is ***NP*-Complete problem**. Consider the logical operators defined following:

   AND: This is denoted by $\wedge$ and $0 \wedge 1 = 1 \wedge 0 = 0 \wedge 0 = 0$, $1 \wedge 1 = 1$,

   OR: This is denoted by $\vee$ and $0 \vee 1 = 1 \vee 0 = 1 \vee 1 = 1$, $0 \vee 0 = 0$, and

   NOT: This is denoted by $'$ and $0' = 1$, $1' = 0$.

   Now, consider the expressions

   (a) $E_1 = x' \vee y$, where x, y are variables; either 0 or 1

   So, $E_1 = 1$ if $x = 0$ or $y = 1$ or both

   Therefore, E_1 is satisfyable for $x = 0$ or $y = 1$ or both.

   (b) $E_2 = (x \vee y) \wedge x' \wedge y'$ is not satisfyable because every assignment for the variables x and y will make the value of E_2 0.

2. **The Travelling Salesman or Salesperson Problem:** The problem can be defined as: "Given a number of cities and the costs of travelling from one to the other, what is the cheapest roundtrip

route that visits each city and then returns to the starting city?" The most direct answer would be to try all the combinations and see which one is cheapest, but given that the number of combinations of cities is $N!$ (factorial n), this solution becomes impractical for larger n. *How fast are the best known deterministic algorithms?* This problem has been shown to be ***NP*-Hard**, and the decision version of it which is given below:

"Given the costs of routes between cities and a number N, decide whether there exists a tour programm for salesman to visit all the cities so that the total cost is less than or equal to N."

The above version of salesman problem is ***NP*-Complete** problem.

3. **The Hamiltonian Cycle or Hamiltonian Circuit Problem:** This problem is in graph theory to find a path through a given graph which starts and ends at the same vertex and includes each vertex exactly once. This is a special case of the travelling salesman problem obtained by setting the distance between two cities to unity if they are adjacent and infinity otherwise. The Hamiltonian cycle problem is ***NP*-Complete**.

4. **The Vertex Cover Problem:** This problem is stated as "Given a graph G and a natural number K, does there exist a vertex covering for G with K vertices." This is ***NP*-Complete** problem.

12.9 CONCLUSION ABOUT "WHETHER $P = NP$ OR NOT?"

We have considered many *NP*-Complete problems and we can find exonential time complexity algorithms for these, but none algorithm has found as polynomial time complexity. So, we conclude that

$$P \neq NP$$

This question is still open for future; let's hope that somebody could be able to prove $P = NP$. One thing is noticeable here that constructing an algorithm is totally dependent on human capability and skill. So, let's hope somebody could be able to find better algorithms for at least one *NP*-Complete problem whose time complexity will be polynomial rather than exponential and we could be able to say… $P = NP$.

12.10 SOLVED EXAMPLES

Example 12.1: Compute the time complexity of a Turing machine, which performs the addition of two positive integers.

Solution: Consider the Turing machine designed for addition in Chapter 8 shown in Fig. 8.12. Let m and n are two positive integers and $F(m, n) = m + n$, The designed Turing machine increments m by n i.e., $F(m, n) = m + 1 + 1 + \ldots n$ times. So, the time complexity $T(m + n) = m + n + 1$ (approximately), where input length $= m + n$

Example 12.2: Compute the time complexity of Turing machine designed for proper multiplication in Chapter 8 shown in Fig. 8.28.

Solution: Let $G(m, n) = mn$, where m, n are two positive integers.

The degigned TM cheks m and n first to find whether m or n is zero or not and then if $m, n \neq 0$ adds m to itself n times.

So, $T(m + n) = m + n + m*n + 1$ (Approximately)

Let $m = n = k$, then

$$T(2k) = k^2 + 2k + 1 = O(k^2)$$

Example 12.3: Find the complexity class of the language $L = \{a^n b^n c^n : n \geq 1\}$ using

(a) One-way infinite single tape Turing machine

(b) One-way infinite three tape Turing machine

Solution:

(a) The L can be accpeted by single tape TM as shown in Fig. 8.26. The TM copies all the a's after the right end of the input and then matches a's with b's and c's with a's.

Let number of a's = number of b's = number of c's = n, then

$$T(3n) = n*3n + 2n*n + 2n*n + 1 \quad \text{(Approximately)}$$
$$= 8n^2 + 1 = O(n^2)$$

So, $L \in \text{DTIME}(n^2)$

(b) The L is accepted by three tape Turing machine M. In order to accepts the language L, M does the following:

(i) M copies all a's on the second tape,

(ii) M copies all b's on the third tape, and

(iii) M matches c's, b's, and a's from the first tape, second tape, and third tape respectively. Let number of a's = number of b's = number of c's = n, then

$T(3n)$ = Moves for copying a's and b's + Moves for matching a's, b's and c's + 1

$T(3n) = 2n + n + 1 = 3n + 1$ (Approximately)

So, $T(3n) = O(n)$ and $L \in \text{DTIME}(n)$.

Example 12.4: Check following logical expressions are satifiable or not?

(a) $E_1 = X \oplus Y = X'Y \vee XY'$

(b) $E_2 = (X \oplus Y)'$

Where X and Y are logical variables.

Solution: Since, for being a satifiable logical expression, a expression should be TRUE (or 1).

(a) For $E_1 = X \oplus Y = X'Y \vee XY'$ following is the truth table:

X	Y	$X'Y$	XY'	$X \oplus Y = X'Y \vee XY'$
0	0	0	0	0
0	1	1	0	1
1	0	0	1	1
1	1	0	0	0

So, E_1 is satifiable if $X = 0$ and $Y = 1$ or $X = 1$ and $Y = 0$.

(**Note:** 1 stands for TRUE and 0 stands for FALSE.)

(b) For $E_2 = (X \oplus Y)' = X'Y' \vee XY$ following is the truth table:

X	Y	$X'Y'$	XY	$X \oplus Y = X'Y' \vee XY$
0	0	1	0	1
0	1	0	0	0
1	0	0	0	0
1	1	0	1	1

So, E_2 is satifiable if $X = 0$ and $Y = 0$ or $X = 1$ and $Y = 1$.

TEST YOUR SKILLS

Supplementary Problems

12.1 What do you think about $P = NP$?

(a) It is undecidable

(b) It is decidable

Explain your view.

12.2 Find the order of the following polynomial

$P(n) = a_1 n + a_2 n^2 + \ldots + a_n n^n$, where a_i is constant for $i = 1, 2, \ldots, n$.

12.3 Find the time complexity of TM (designed for proper division) shown in Fig. 8.30.

12.4 Show that $DTIME(2^n) \subset DTIME(2^{n+3})$

11.5 We know that time complexity of memebership (CYK) algorithm for CFGs is $O(n^3)$. Suggest, how we can improve the performance of membership algorithm?

If two CFGs G_1 and G_2 are given, G_1 is in CNF and G_2 is not in CNF. What do you think about the complexity of these two grammars? Are these same?

12.6 Suggest one solution to solve the Hamiltonian circle problem in graph theory.

12.7 Suggest some useful solutions to solve travelling salesman problem.

12.8 Discuss the time complexity of CYK algorithm for a context-free languages.

12.9 Discuss the Time-Space complexity of finite automaton.

Multiple Choice Questions

12.10 Which is true about complexity

(a) Performance measurement of machine or algorithm

(b) Rating of machines

(c) Rating of algorithms

(d) All the above statements

12.11 Which is true about about a good machine

(a) Time complexity is reasonable

(b) Space complexity dose not matter

(c) Resources requirement does not matter

(d) All the above statements

12.12 Choose the correct statement

(a) We use those machines whose time complexity is $O(n)$, where n is the input size

(b) We use those machines whose time complexity is $O(n^2)$, where n is input size

(c) We use less storage machines

(d) We select a machine (or algorithm) depending on the type of need.

12.13 Which one is correct about P class

(a) All the languages in P class accepted by some deterministic TM

(b) P stands for exponential time complexity

(c) P includes all the languages by some automaton

(d) None of the above statements

12.14 Which one is correct about NP class

(a) NP class contains all the languages accepted by some NTM

(b) NP contains all the languages accepted by some DTM

(c) The complexity growth of NP class is higher than the P class

(d) All the above statements

12.15 Which one is true about $P = NP$?

(a) Solved (b) Unsolved

(c) Undecidable (d) None

12.16 Choose the correct statement

(a) All tractable problems are in P class

(b) All tractable problems have reasonable time complexity

(c) All tractable problems are implementable in practice

(d) All the above statements

12.17 Choose the correct statement

(a) All tractable and intractable problems have reasonable time complexity

(b) All intractable problems have exponential time complexity

(c) All intractable problems are in NP class

(d) All the above statements

12.18 If $L = \{a^n b^n: n \geq 1\}$ is accepted by one-way infinite single tape DTM and n is the size of the input. Which one is true about L?

(a) $L \in$ DTIME(n^2) (b) $L \in$ DTIME(n)

(c) $L \in$ NTIME(n^2) (d) $L \in$ NTIME(n)

12.19 If $L = \{a^n b^n : n \geq 1\}$ is accepted by one-way infinite two tapes DTM and n is the size of the input. Which one is true about L?

(a) $L \in \text{DTIME}(n^2)$ (b) $L \in \text{DTIME}(n)$

(c) $L \in \text{NTIME}(n^2)$ (d) $L \in \text{NTIME}(n)$

12.20 Choose the correct statement

(a) All the *NP*-Hard problems are *NP*-Complete

(b) Not a single *NP*-Hard problem is *NP*-Complete

(c) It is not necessary for a *NP*-Hard problem to be *NP*-Complete

(d) None of the above statements

12.21 Choose the correct statement

(a) All *NP*-Hard problems have exponential time complexity

(b) If one *NP* problem could be solve in polynomial time, then $P = NP$

(c) The *HP* problem of TM is *NP*-Hard and undecidable

(d) All the above statements

12.22 If language L_1 is polynomial-time reducible to the language L_2, then

(a) If $L_2 \in P$, then $L_1 \in P$ (b) If $L_1 \in P$, then $L_2 \in P$

(c) If $L_1 \in NP$, then $L_2 \in NP$ (d) Both the statements (b) and (c)

Answers

12.10 (d)	12.11 (a)	12.12 (d)	12.13 (a)	12.14 (d)
12.15 (b)	12.16 (d)	12.17 (c)	12.18 (a)	12.19 (b)
12.20 (c)	12.21 (d)	12.22 (a)		

Appendix–A

COUNTABLE AND UNCOUNTABLE SETS

In Set Theory, a set is known as a finite set if there exists a one to one correspondence between its elements and the set of natural numbers $N = \{1, 2, 3, ..., n\}$ for some fixed natural number n. A set is called **countably infinite** if there exists correspondence between its elemets and the set of natural numbers N. A *countable set* is a set which is either *finite* or *countably infinite*. A set which is not countable set is known as *uncountable* set. One thing is noticeable here that *not all uncountable sets have the same size*.

The elements of a finite set can be enumerated one by one in corrsepondence with natural numbers. Let $A = \{a, b, c, \ldots, z\}$ be a finite set having 26 elements. Each element of the set A can be listed with an unique natural number as following:

$$a \leftrightarrow 1, b \leftrightarrow 2, c \leftrightarrow 3, \ldots, z \leftrightarrow 26$$

The above one-to-one correspondence betweeen the set A and the set $X = \{1, 2, 3, \ldots, 26\}$ is known as **bijection**. Now, we define the equal size set with the help of the bijection. Two sets are said to be of the same size if there is bijection between them. The above two sets A and X have same size and so these are equal size sets. *If we take any subset of the set A, then it will be finite set as its generator is finite.*

Now, consider one example of the countably infinite set. Let Y is the set of all the even numbers i.e. $Y = \{0, 2, 4, 6, \ldots\}$, then it has one-to-one correspeondence with the set of natural numbers N as following:

$$0 \leftrightarrow 1, 2 \leftrightarrow 2, 4 \leftrightarrow 3, 6 \leftrightarrow 4, \ldots$$

Therefore, the set $Y = \{0, 2, 4, 6, \ldots\}$ is countably infinite and so it is countable.

Before dicussing some theorems on the countable and uncountable sets, we will discuss the **Cantor's diagonal arguments** which is very useful in proving some theorems.

Theorem A.1: (Cantor's diagonal argument or principle): The set of real numbers is uncountable.

Proof: We know that the decimal part of a real number lies between 0 and 1. Suppose that the infinity of decimal numbers is the same as the infinity of counting numbers i.e. we have one-to-one correspondence between the decimal numbers and the set of the naturals numbers N and all the decimal numbers can be enumerated in a list as following:

$$1 \Rightarrow d_1 = 0.d_{11}d_{12}d_{13}d_{14} \cdots$$
$$2 \Rightarrow d_2 = 0.d_{21}d_{22}d_{23}d_{24} \cdots$$
$$3 \Rightarrow d_3 = 0.d_{31}d_{32}d_{33}d_{34} \cdots$$
$$\cdots$$
$$n \Rightarrow d_n = 0.d_{n1}d_{n2}d_{n3}d_{n4} \cdots$$

Now, consider a decimal number $\boldsymbol{x = 0.\, x_1 x_2 x_3 x_4 x_5 \ldots}$, where x_1 is any digit from {1, 2, 3, ..., 9} and is different from d_{11}, x_2 is different from d_{22}, x_3 is different from d_{33}, and so on. Now, x is a decimal number, and lies between 0 and 1, so it must be in the above list. But, where does x stand? The decimal number x can't be first in the list, because x's first digit differs from d_1's first digit d_{11}, x can't be second in the list, because x's second digit differs from d_{22} the second digit of d_2. In general, x is not equal to d_n, since their n^{th} digit are not equal.

In this way, x is nowhere to be found in the list. In other words, we have exhibited a decimal number that is assumed to be in the list but it not. No matter, how we try to list the decimal numbers, at least one will be left out. Therefore, listing or enumerating the decimal numbers is impossible, and therefore the real numbers are uncountable. In other words, the cardinality of the set of the real numbers is greater than the cardinality of those sets that have one-to-one correspondence with some countable set.

Note: Cantor's diagonal principle has a great impatance in the computer science. We will in the Turing machine chapter that how Allan Turing used this theorem to prove the hating problem as an undecidable problem. The same argument what Cantor used in his diagonal argument is used by Kurt Godel to prove the incompleteness theorem. For decimal numbers we assume that $1.25999 \equiv 1.26$ and $3.45600 \equiv 3.456$. We understand the Cantor's diagonal argument as following:

Suppose we have collection of n ($n \geq 1$) people, each people characterized by a unique characteristic as shown in Fig. A.1.

People ↓	Characteristic →					
	C_1	C_2	C_3	C_4	...	C_n
P_1	–	√	–	–	...	–
P_2	√	–	–	–	...	–
P_3	–	–	–	√	...	
...	...			–		–
P_n	–	–	–		...	√

Fig. A.1

Suppose, we have a person P_j which is not characterized by the characteristics C_1, C_2, ..., C_n, then P_j will not be in the list. If the number of people n tends toward the infinity then locating P_j will be impossible. This is the notion of the Cantor's diagonal argument.

Theorem A.2: (Cantor's Theorem for power set): For any set A, the power set of A denoted by 2^A is cardinally larger than A i.e. $|A| < |2^A|$.

Proof: Cantor proved that no matter how large a set we have, we can always consider a set that is yet larger. If we consider a finite set, then we can easily prove that the power set of the considered set is larger, but problem arise in the case of infinite sets.

We consider two infinite sets to be of the same size i.e. both the sets have the same cardinality, if and only if we can form a one-to-one correspondence (bijection) between the elements of the both the sets. If we show that bijection can't be established between two infinite sets, then we conclude that one of these sets must be cardinally greater than the other.

To prove this theorem, Cantor used his famous "**Diagonalization Argument**," which is a proof by contradiction. Initially, we assume that there is a largest infinite set and then prove that there must be one even larger set, which indicate the contradiction.

Suppose that the set A is represented as following:

$$A = \{a, b, c, d, e, ...\}$$

We have used the symbols $a, b, c, \ldots$ to indicate the elements of the set, and we are assuming that there are an infinite number of elements and A is the largest size infinite set i.e. no other set can be a bigger than A. Now, we know that we can always form the power set of A, denoted by 2^A. So, $2^A = \{\{a\}, \{b\}, \{c\}, \{d\}, \{e\}, \{a, b\}, \{a, c\}, ...\}$

We observe that 2^A is itself a set and according to our assumption it can't be bigger than A. Obviously, it can't be *smaller* than A, since it contains all of the elements of the set A, that is, it contains all the elements of the set A as $\{a\}, \{b\}, \{c\}, \{d\}, \{e\}, ...$ its elements. Consequently, these sets must be of the same size. In other words, there is one-to-one correspondence between the elements of A and 2^A with no element left over on either side. Suppose, this correspondence looks as following:

A		2^A
a	$\leftrightarrow$	$\{c, d\}$
b	$\leftrightarrow$	$\{a\}$
c	$\leftrightarrow$	$\{a, b, c, d\}$
d	$\leftrightarrow$	$\{b, e\}$
e	$\leftrightarrow$	$\{a, c, e\}$
...		...

One thing we notice that, some of the elements of the set A are matched with the elements of 2^A also known as subset of A that contain them. For example, here the element c is matched with the subset $\{a, b, c, d\}$ and other elements are matched with subsets that do not contain them. **For example,** the element a is matched with the subset $\{c, d\}$. Consider the set of all the elements of A that are not matched with subsets that contain them and name it B. It means, B is a subset of A, and it must appear somewhere in our correspondence listing above.

Now, if we establish another correspondence between the elements of the sets A and B, then what are the elements of A that match with elements B? There will be no element of B, because B is constructed such that it contains only those elements of A which do not match to sets containing them. On the other hand, B is the subset of the set A by definition of the set B and so all the elements of B should be in A. This is a contradiction and the existence of this contradiction shows that no element of A can be matched with B and thus our correspondence can't be completed.

Since, $B \subset A$, and therefore $B \subset 2^A$. Since, we can't establish one-to-one correspondence between A and B, therefore we can't establish one-to-one correspondence between A and 2^A. Further, we have already seen that 2^A can't be smaller than A, then there is only one possible conclusion that 2^A must be larger than A and hence $|A| < |2^A|$.

In other words, we think that all the elements of A are in the power set 2^A by the definition plus the subsets formed by the combination of the elements of A. So, clearly 2^A has more elements than A. It means, 2^A is bigger than A.

Note: The side effect of this Cantor's Theorem is the different degree of the infinity. For example if X is an infinite set, then its power set denoted by 2^X will be an infinite set and bigger than X. Two infinite sets may be different in size if they have not one-to-one correspondence between their elements.

Theorem A.3: A subset of an infinite countable set is countable.

Proof: Let A is a infinite countable set and has bijection with the set $N = \{1, 2, 3, 4, \ldots\}$ and B is a subset of A. Since, B is a subset of A, so B may be finite or infinite depending on the number of elements in B. If B is finite set, then its elements have one-to-one correspondence with N and hence B will be countable set. If B is an infinite set, then let $B = \{a_3, a_5, a_6, a_9, \ldots\}$, where $A = \{a_1, a_2, a_3, \ldots.\}$. Since, A has one-to-one correspondence with N as following. Now, B is a subset of A, so there is a correspondence between B and N.

A		**N**
a_1	$\leftrightarrow$	1
a_2	$\leftrightarrow$	2
a_3	$\leftrightarrow$	3
…	a_7	$\leftrightarrow$
a_n	$\leftrightarrow$	n
…		

B		**N**
a_3	$\leftrightarrow$	3
a_5	$\leftrightarrow$	5
a_6	$\leftrightarrow$	6
a_7	$\leftrightarrow$	7
a_9	$\leftrightarrow$	9
…		

Since, we have bijection between B and A, no matter what size B has, therefore a subset of an infinite countable set is countable.

Theorem A.4: The union of any finite number of infinite countable sets is an infinite countable set.

Proof: Suppose X is collection of $n \geq 2$ infinite countable sets $A_1, A_2, \ldots, A_n$. Since, $A_1, A_2, \ldots, A_n$ are infinite countable sets, so these sets have bijection with the set $N = \{1, 2, 3, \ldots.\}$. The set X is an infinite set because $A_1, A_2, A_3, \ldots, A_n$ are infinite sets. We establish one-to-one correspondence between X and N as following:

X						**N**
A_1	a_{11}	a_{12}	a_{13}	…	$\leftrightarrow$	1
A_2	a_{21}	a_{22}	a_{23}	…	$\leftrightarrow$	2
A_3	a_{31}	a_{32}	a_{33}	…	$\leftrightarrow$	3
…	…	…	…	…	…	
A_n	a_{n1}	a_{n2}	a_{n3}	…	$\leftrightarrow$	n

The element a_{ij} belongs to the set A_i and maps on the $i \in N$, where $i = 1, 2, 3, \ldots$. Since, we have one-to-one correspondence between the elements of X and N, so X is an infinite countable and hence the statement of the theorem is true.

Theorem A.5: The set of all pairs of natural numbers is countable.

Proof: Let S is the set of all pairs of natural numbers i.e. $S = \{(0, 0), (0, 1), \ldots, (1, 0), (1, 1), (1, 2), \ldots, (2, 0), (2, 1), (2, 2) \ldots\}$. Suppose S is union of the sets $S_0, S_1, S_2, \ldots$, where

$S_0 = \{(0, 0), (0, 1), (0, 2), \ldots\}$ (The set of all pairs having first element 0.)

$S_1 = \{(1, 0), (1, 1), (1, 2), \ldots\}$ (The set of all pairs having first element 1.)

$S_2 = \{(2, 0), (2, 1), (2, 2), \ldots\}$ (The set of all pairs having first element 2.)

...

and $$S = \bigcup_{i=0}^{\infty} Si$$

We follow the following to list the elements of S:

1. In the first round, we list the first element (0, 0) of S_0 and
   $(0, 0) \leftrightarrow 1$.
2. In the second round, we list the second element (0, 1) of S_0 and first element (1, 0) of the set S_1 and
   $(0, 1) \leftrightarrow 2$,
   $(1, 0) \leftrightarrow 3$
3. In the third round, we list the third element (0, 2) of S_0, second element (1, 1) of S_1, and first element (2, 0) of S_2 and
   $(0, 2) \leftrightarrow 4$,
   $(1, 1) \leftrightarrow 5$,
   $(2, 0) \leftrightarrow 6$
4. In general, in the nth round we list n^{th} element of S_0, $(n-1)^{st}$ element of S_1, ..., and first element of S_{n-1} and
   $\boldsymbol{(m, n-1) \leftrightarrow 0.5 * k * (k+1) + m + 1}$, where $k = m + n - 1$ and $(m, n-1) \in S_m$

We can easily understand the above process using the following diagram shown in Fig. A.2.

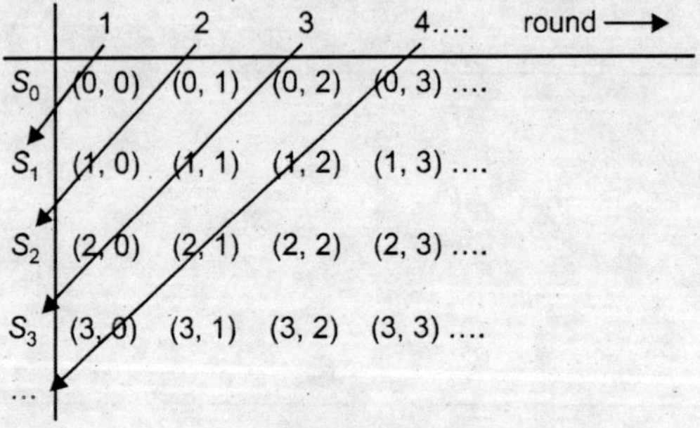

Fig. A.2

Hence, the set of pairs of all natural numbers is countable.

Theorem A.6: The Cartesian product of finite number of infinite countable sets is countable.

Proof: Let X denotes the Cartesian product of n infinite countable sets $S_1, S_2, S_3, \ldots, S_n$, where n is a fixed natural number. So, $X = S_1 \times S_2 \times S_3 \times \ldots \times S_n = \{(s_1, s_2, s_3, \ldots, s_n): s_1 S_1, s_2 \in S_2, s_3 \in S_3, \ldots, s_n \in S_n\}$

The number of elements in the X is infinite and each element is n^{th} ordered pair.

We use the same technique as discussed in Theorem 1.5 to map a pair of natural number to an unique element of the set $N = \{1, 2, 3, \ldots\}$. Here, we use multiple-mapping technique. Let the element $(s_1, s_2, s_3, \ldots, s_n)$ is to be mapped on some element of N. The first two members s_1, s_2 map on the $n_1 \in N$, where $n_1 = 0.5*k*(k+1) + s_1 + 1$ for $k = s_1 + s_2$, then the order of element reduces by one and now let it is $(n_1, s_3, s_4, \ldots, s_n)$. Now, we apply the same process until the reduction of the order to one i.e.,

$$(s_1, s_2, s_3, \ldots, s_n) \leftrightarrow (n_1, s_3, s_4, \ldots, s_n) \leftrightarrow (n_2, s_4, \ldots, s_n) \leftrightarrow \ldots. \leftrightarrow n_{n-1},$$
where n_i, and s_{i+2} map on the n_{i+1} for $1 \le i \le n-2$.

For example, the triple ordered element $(1, 2, 0)$ maps on 45, that is $(1, 2, 0) \leftrightarrow (8, 0) \leftrightarrow 45$. Since, we can list all the elements of the set X and X has bijection with N, so X is countable set.

Theorem A.7: The set of all rational numbers is countable.

Proof: Suppose Q is the set of all rational numbers. We know that $x = p/q$ is a rational number where $q \neq 0$. This number maps on tripled ordered (p, q, r), where $r \in \{1, 0\}$ and p, q are relatively prime number. When $p = 0$ or x is positive then $r = 0$ and when x is negative then $r = 1$. The triple ordered (p, q, r) maps on ordered pair (m, r), where $\boldsymbol{m = 0.5*k*(k+1) + p + 1}$, where $k = p + q$ and (m, r) maps on $0.5*a*(a+1) + m + 1$, where $a = m + r$.

For example,

$0 \leftrightarrow (0, 1, 0) \leftrightarrow (2, 0) \leftrightarrow 6$

$1 \leftrightarrow (1, 1, 0) \leftrightarrow (5, 0) \leftrightarrow 21$

$1/2 \leftrightarrow (1, 2, 0) \leftrightarrow (8, 0) \leftrightarrow 45$

$-1/2 \leftrightarrow (1, 2, 1) \leftrightarrow (8, 1) \leftrightarrow 54$

Since, each rational number maps on a unique natural number, it means we have one-to-one correspondence between Q and set of natural number N. Therefore, the set of all rational numbers is countable.

Theorem A.8: Prove that the power set of natural numbers N denoted by 2^N is uncountable.

Proof: We use Cantor's diagonal argument to prove the theorem. Since, N is the set of natural numbers, so $N = \{1, 2, 3, \ldots\}$. Assume that 2^N is countable set and all the subsets of 2^N are listed as following:

$2^N = \{A_1, A_2, A_3, \ldots\}$, where A_i maps on $i \in N$ for some $i = 1, 2, 3, \ldots$

Now, let us consider a subset of N defined as following:

$A = \{j : j \in N \text{ but } j \notin A_i\}$

Since, every subset of N should be an element of 2^N, i.e., $A = A_j$ for some $j \in N$. Now, consider the statement $j \in A_j$ for some $j \in N$, then $j \notin A$ (by definition) but $A = A_j$ which is a contradiction. Now, if $j \notin A_j$, then $j \in A$, but $A = A_j$ for some $j \in N$, which is a contradiction. It means, if $A = A_j$ for some $j \in N$, then

(a) If $j \in A_j$, then j should be in A, but $j \notin A$

(b) If $j \notin A_j$, then j should not be in A, but $j \in A$

Since, one these two statements $j \in A$ and $j \notin A$ must be true, but (a) and (b) indicate that neither $j \in A$ nor $j \notin A$. It means, our assumption that 2^N is countable is not correct. Therefore, 2^N where $N = \{1, 2, 3, \ldots\}$ is uncountable. We represent the above argument by matrix as following:

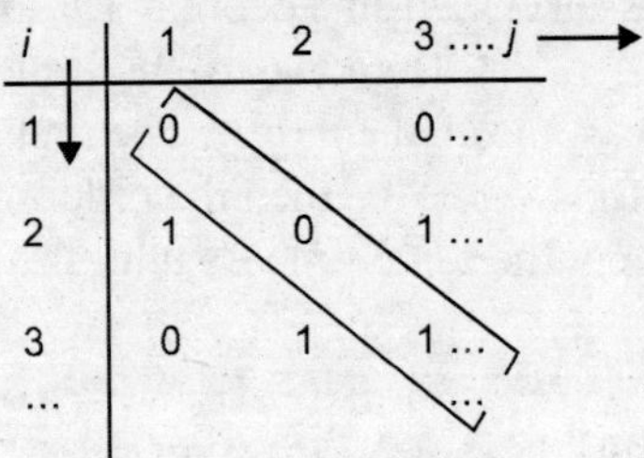

Fig. A.3: Hypothetical matrix

The subset A_i is in 2^N if and only if the matrix element $(i, j) = 1$ and diagonal elements of matrix are element of A. This is the reason why it is known as Cantor's diagonal argument.

Index

D

E

M

N

O

P

R

S

T

U

V

W

Z